Programming in Visual Basic 2010

This book is an introduction to programming using Microsoft's Visual Basic .NET 2010. It is intended for novice programmers with little or no programming experience or no experience with Visual Basic. The text emphasizes programming logic and good programming techniques with generous explanations of programming concepts written from a nontechnical point of view. It stresses input, processing, and output and sequence, selection, and repetition in code development. File input and output (I/O) and arrays are included. Later chapters introduce objects, event programming, and databases. By taking a slow and steady approach to programming ideas, this book builds new concepts from what the reader has already learned. VB tips and quips inject both humor and insight.

The book includes numerous programming examples and exercises, case studies, tutorials, and "Fixing a Program" sections for an in-depth look at programming problems and tools. Quizzes and review questions throughout each chapter get students to think about the materials and how to use them. Each chapter has a summary and glossary for extra review.

The accompanying web site has code downloads, I/O, and database files from small, simple files to large files with thousands of records, flowcharts, deskchecks, and audits to aid with program design, coding, and debugging, PowerPoint files for every chapter, and hundreds of ideas for programs and projects.

Dr. Jim McKeown has spent more than 20 years at Dakota State University, where he is an Assistant Professor. He currently teaches programming, computer hardware, software testing, and computer applications. He received a master's degree in computer education from Columbia University and holds a Ph.D. in instructional design from the University of Iowa. He has contributed several articles to the *Journal for Computing in Small Colleges* as well as various other publications.

Programming in Visual Basic 2010

The Very Beginner's Guide

Jim McKeown

Dakota State University

CAMBRIDGE
UNIVERSITY PRESS

CAMBRIDGE UNIVERSITY PRESS
Cambridge, New York, Melbourne, Madrid, Cape Town, Singapore,
São Paulo, Delhi, Dubai, Tokyo

Cambridge University Press
32 Avenue of the Americas, New York, NY 10013-2473, USA

www.cambridge.org
Information on this title: www.cambridge.org/9780521721110

First published 2010

Printed in the United States of America

A catalog record for this publication is available from the British Library.

Library of Congress Cataloging in Publication data

McKeown, James S.
Programming in Visual Basic 2010 : the very beginner's guide / James S. McKeown.
    p.   cm.
Includes bibliographical references and index.
ISBN 978-0-521-89653-5 – ISBN 978-0-521-72111-0 (pbk.)
1. Microsoft Visual BASIC.   2. BASIC (Computer program language)   3. Microsoft .NET.   I. Title.
QA76.73.B3M39723   2010
006.7'882–dc22   2010000054

ISBN   978-0-521-89653-5 Hardback
ISBN   978-0-521-72111-0 Paperback

Additional resources for this publication at
http://www.cambridge.org/us/catalogue/catalogue.asp?isbn=9780521721110

Quick, who won the Academy Award for Best Screenplay last year? Who won a Grammy last year? Who pitched the last game of the World Series? How often do the rich and famous make headlines for their good work, not their misdeeds? These people don't impact your life so why is society obsessed them? And you certainly don't want to emulate many of them. Look around and find the ones that do impact your life and pay attention to them.

Thank you to the reviewers. Without their hard and sometimes thankless work, this book wouldn't be nearly as good. I especially want to thank Rudy McDaniel for his keen eye and suggestions.

Thank you to Mrs. Heneghen, my first grade teacher, who taught me how to read and write and do arithmetic. She was a wonderful lady. Thank you to Mrs. Short. She instilled in me a love of learning I carry to this day. She's still my neighbor and I've never been able to turn her down when she's asked for a favor. Mrs. Pratt taught me multiplication and division, Mrs. Moulton taught me science, and Mrs. Stuefen first taught me geography. I still love doing math in my head, studying science, and poring over maps. Miss Haggerty – there wasn't a boy in the sixth grade that wasn't in love with her. I admired and respected Mr. Skovlund. Mr. Tordoff taught me typing. I still use it every day, but he taught his best lessons with a whistle in his hand. Mrs. Hefling was my English and speech teacher. I can make my living through writing and speaking because of her. Mr. Magnus taught me algebra and physics and always had time to answer questions. He was a good man. Mr. Vincent was my history teacher and coach. His quiet dignity touched students for nearly forty years. He made me a better person. Dr. Jerry Sweeney was my college advisor. He saw something in this skinny farm boy. Thank you to Anne Vollmer, Nancy Cunniff, and Howard Budin in grad school. Thank you to Dr. Jim Maxey. He was a vice president at ACT but still had time to help me with my dissertation. These teachers made a difference in my life and I'll never forget that.

To Delores. See? Being a computer geek finally paid off. Now, I can start working on the movie.

Jim McKeown
April 3, 2009

Brief Table of Contents

Appendices

Table of Contents

Preface

Who Should Use This Book?

This book is written for the newbie. It's not for those who already know programming. If you know the basics of the computer, like word processing, spreadsheets, email, and surfing, then you're ready to go.

What's Included?

This book covers the basics, like variable and assignment statements. It explains programming sequence, selection, and repetition structures – fundamentals to the design of any good program. It explains controls and their uses, the basic tools for designing your interface. Procedures and functions are covered, which are the basic building blocks of larger programs. File input and output (I/O) is introduced. Good programs run on data and I/O is how data get into and out of the computer. From there, arrays are introduced and used to implement more complicated programming logic including control breaks, sorting, and searching. Events make things happen in a program and one chapter is dedicated to events, including drag and drop. Objects are introduced and an understanding of them is crucial for successful developers. For a little fun, there's a chapter on graphics and sound, but you'll need a good foundation in programming sequence, logic, and repetition to get the most from it. The world runs on databases and the last two chapters cover the basics of databases, including an introduction to LINQ to SQL and Crystal Reports. LINQ connects programs to databases. SQL (Structured Query Language) is designed to find, update, and report data, and Crystal Reports is designed for data presentation.

Why Use Visual Basic?

Visual Basic is just one of dozens of programming languages, but it's one of the best and most successful. It's one of the most popular languages in the world. It's popular with business and in education. It's object-oriented and can do almost anything. Visual Basic is simple, the commands are straightforward, and the basics are easy to grasp. With it you can write and run a program on your first day. Once you have the fundamentals, you can write programs of your own design. It's powerful – powerful enough to take on almost any development project. Programs written in earlier versions of Visual Basic will almost always convert and run in the latest version.

What Do You Need?

Visual Basic comes in several flavors, from the free Express Edition available as a download from Microsoft to the Professional version that's a part of Visual Studio. It must be installed on your computer and you must know how to start it, navigate through the folders on your system, open and save files, and, in general, use a computer.

You'll also want a place to make backups. A Flash drive works well, but almost any storage drive will do. Take some time to organize your files and folders – I recommend saving them by chapter – and spend a little extra time when naming them. You'll be glad you did when you go looking for that program you wrote a couple of months ago – you know, the one that used loops to calculate and display interest earnings.

Any Advice?

You must write programs to get good at programming. You won't learn Visual Basic by reading the text and running the sample programs. You learn by doing. Write programs. Try things. Test things. Sometimes there's a best way or one right way to write your code, but usually there's more than one way to get things to work. Try things. Play "What if . . . ?" Nearly every chapter has a "Fixing a Program" section or two where a program has bugs that need fixing. These will help you understand the good and the bad in a program. "Potential Problems" sections outline common mistakes and ways to avoid them. "Open and Run" sections have sample programs and demonstrations to help with the code and controls. "On Your Own" provides ideas for programs to write on your own.

Each chapter has several "VB Quiz" questions. Most of them are designed to make you think or to stretch your understanding. The answers for these are at the end of every chapter. There are self-check questions at the end of every chapter, too. The answers are included in Appendix H.

What to Look For

Pay attention to the names used in the book. I grew up with cartoon characters and Bond movies and I'm always looking for a good name. The VB "Quips" and "Tips" inject a little humor and a little insight. A little fun never hurt.

Online Resources

Cambridge University Press has a website with student and instructor materials. Check it out at http://www.cambridge.org/us/catalogue/catalogue.asp?isbn=9780521721110.

Fundamentals of Design and Programming – Starting from Scratch

VB Quip   *Who cares how it works, just as long as it gives the right answer? –Jeff Scholnik*

That's a rather cavalier approach for anyone to take, especially when computers are involved. Knowledge is power and the more you know, the greater your power. One book isn't enough to give you all-consuming power, especially over a tool as powerful as a computer. It is, however, enough to get you started. One book won't turn you into a nerd that looks at his own shoes when talking, lives on caffeine and stale snack cakes, and would rather hack on a computer than go out on a date. That's just a stereotype perpetuated by teen movies. While it does fit a few people, almost all of the ones I know are smart, articulate, funny, and just all-around bright and inquisitive people. Above all, they're curious. And the best are curious about nearly everything, not just computers. How does it work? What happens when I try this? What if . . . ?

Programming is, above all else, about thinking and problem-solving. If for no other reason, it's useful because it makes you think about thinking and makes you describe how to solve a problem. For the computer to solve a problem, even simple tasks must be explained in great detail. For someone to explain the rules to a computer – in other words, to write a program – takes a great deal of thinking and understanding. Along the way it gives you an appreciation of just how marvelous the machine known as a computer really is, it gives you an understanding of how you think, it makes you think about thinking, it forces you to consider the steps and methods used in problem-solving, and it provides a process for expressing and explaining your thoughts.

The first part of this chapter deals with thinking and problem-solving, the basics of programming. The second part of the chapter familiarizes you with the Visual Basic interface – the nuts and bolts of how to create a program.

What Is Programming?

VB Quip   *A computer is essentially a trained squirrel: acting on reflex, thoughtlessly running back and forth and storing away nuts until some other stimulus makes it do something else. –Ted Nelson*

That's closer to the truth than you can imagine and it does an injustice to squirrels. The computer does exactly what you tell it to do, even when that's not what you want it to do. Forget about "computer error" and those million-dollar utility bills. That's not a computer error; it's probably a programmer's error. The person writing the directions for the computer is the one that made the mistake. It's called "human error," and at the heart of most computer problems is a person. Whether we like to admit it, most of the time computer error is merely human error in disguise.

Programming is simply giving the computer directions for completing a task. A *program* is a set of directions for the computer to complete a task. VB.NET takes the directions you write and turns it into a program. It translates your directions into a series of steps for the computer. If there is a mistake in the directions, the mistake gets translated by the computer. Just like a recipe or a set of driving directions, a computer program is only as good as its instructions. Therefore, programming should be about two things: teaching you how to write the directions in the first place, and teaching you how to write directions that won't cause problems. And, of course, the person writing the program is a *programmer*.

You can think of a program as a recipe. A recipe describes, in detail, the steps that need to be taken in order to, say, bake a cake. If the steps aren't correct or they aren't in the correct order, you won't get cake. You might end up with batter because you forgot the "turn the oven on" step. You might end up with a crusted pile of inedible goo because you forgot the "beat 200 times" step. To compound the problem, the directions must be written in a way the computer understands. As painful as it is, you have to learn how to write the directions so the computer can understand them. As yet, the computer cannot understand the directions in the way you want to write them. While VB.NET is much better at understanding your directions than many other languages, it still requires that the directions be written according to some very strict rules.

Basic Tasks

Most computer programs complete the same basic set of tasks and, lucky for you, complete them in the same order. Every program has input, processing, and output. *Input* puts data into the computer. It might be a number or some text. It might be data from a file. Depending on the system and the task, it could be input from a pen, mouse, or keyboard. If attached to sensors, the input could be almost anything, from a temperature sensor to a light meter. It's the stimulus for the computer. *Processing* is the task: In a business program it could be the payroll calculations; in a game, it may move the pieces on a board; in an air conditioning system, it may turn on the fan or turn off the heat. Processing is the work of a program. *Output* is the results, the answers. Often the results are displayed on the screen, but it could also be a printout or a file. Every program works with data. The data could be the numbers or text used by the program. They could be the hours and wages for the payroll or the temperature for the thermostat. They could be the number of spaceships for your "Alien Invaders" game. These data must be declared before you can use them. *Declarations* tell the computer what type of data you have for your program. Declarations almost always come at the beginning of a task.

In terms of your cake recipe, the declarations are the measuring cups, the measuring spoons, the mixing bowl, and the cake pan. You must make sure you have these before you start. The input is the ingredients, the cake mix, the eggs, the water, and such. The processing is the mixing and the baking – all the steps needed to turn your ingredients into a cake. The output is, well, the cake. The order for these tasks is usually declarations, input, processing, and output. So, in your cake program, you'd declare (or in this case make sure had on hand) the measuring cups and spoons, mixing bowl, and cake pan. Without them you couldn't handle the other tasks. The input would be adding the ingredients. Processing could be described as mixing the ingredients and baking the cake. Those are very general descriptions for a long series of steps, but the analogy fits. You take your input and, through a series of processes, turn it into output. The end result, your output, is a cake. If the steps are in the right order and the directions are clear, you get a cake. If not, well . . .

Almost any problem can be described in terms of declarations, input, processing, and output.

VB Quiz 01   *What are the four steps in programming?*
                  Which step comes first?
                  Describe how programming is like a recipe.
                  How is programming like a set of directions for a traveler?

Basic Procedures

Nearly every programming task falls into one of three categories: sequence, selection, or repetition. These tasks enable the computer to handle all processing procedures that come along. Each one has a particular utility that makes the computer function effectively. In many respects, these procedures turn the computer into the ideal employee. Think about it. The computer works long hours doing *exactly* what you tell it to do. Once given directions, it performs its task unerringly and with amazing speed and accuracy. It never tires; never asks for the weekend off; never asks for a raise; never takes a potty break; never goes on strike; doesn't need fringe benefits; and won't complain about the lighting, the room temperature, the mess in the break room, or the numbskull in the next cubicle. It is, in short, the perfect slave.

The *sequence* of commands is the order of commands in a program. Sometimes the order of the commands isn't critical, but usually, it is. If the steps aren't in the correct order, you probably won't be able to solve the problem. Sometimes the steps must be exactly in order. Sometimes the steps only need to be in a general order. Washing dishes is a good example. While washing the glasses is done before the plates, and the pots and pans are washed last, the exact order of the individual glasses or plates or pots usually isn't critical to the successful completion of the task.

Selection procedures enable the computer to make decisions. The computer is given two or more sets of directions and a criterion for selecting the correct set of directions. Based on its decision, it selects the appropriate path and follows those directions. Think about the laundry. The steps for washing whites are different from those for colors or delicates. A decision must be made at the start of every load. Depending on the type of load, you might use hot, warm, or cold water. You might add bleach or fabric softener. Depending on your decision, a different set of directions must be followed.

Repetition procedures allow the computer to repeat the same series of steps. Give the computer a set of directions to repeat, tell it when to start and when to end, and it will repeat the same process over and over. It might repeat the same process a specific number of times or it might repeat the process until certain requirements are met. Brushing your teeth is a good example of repetition. You might repeat the up and down process a specific number of times for each tooth. You might repeat the process for a specified amount of time or you simply might do it until you think you're done. The up-and-down brushing process is the repetition.

All programs make use of these procedures and all but the simplest programs are a combination of two or more of them. Your daily routine is filled with tasks that are a series of steps. Some of them are a sequence of steps. Some require decisions and some tasks are repeated. Within each of these tasks, there are probably more, even simpler, tasks. Go back to the sequence of steps for washing the dishes. Within that task is a repetition. You doubtlessly made a series of circular motions while washing a plate or pot. That motion was repeated a certain number of times or until the plate or pot was clean. Life is filled with sequence, selection, and repetition procedures if you stop to look at them.

For example, there are about ten steps to making a pot of coffee. If you skip a step, you get hot water instead of coffee. If you forget a different step, you end up with cold water instead of coffee. If you get the steps out of order, you run the risk of burns or electrocution. If you make a bad decision on how much coffee to add, you end up with a cup of sludge instead of a cup of joe. If you use the wrong number of repetitions when adding water, you won't get espresso. The real trick in a good cup of Java is to get the directions correct and then follow them.

Following Directions

Computers are great at following directions. Unlike teenagers and cats, they do exactly what you tell them to do. All you need to do is provide them with precise directions for the task and provide these directions in a language the computer will understand. That's the programming part. Of course, if the directions are wrong, then the computer makes "mistakes." That's the source of those million-dollar utility bills. Proper planning helps to avoid these problems, but even the best programs can still have mistakes in them. To minimize these mistakes, programmers need to learn the fundamentals for writing programs.

You need to have a plan for developing a set of directions for the computer: a program. This plan is commonly called an *algorithm*. An algorithm is a description of a program. Some algorithms are just a general description of the program. Some are very precise. It just depends on the amount of detail needed for the directions. For a vacation, you'd be perfectly happy with a set of directions that told you to drive to the airport, catch a flight to your destination, hop a cab to your hotel, and then enjoy yourself. That's a good general algorithm, but for each of these, you'd need a more specific algorithm. You'd need specific directions to the airport. You'd need to know the flight, its airline, the gate, and the departure time. Once you arrive, you'd need to be able to get to the hotel and, once you've checked-in, you'd want a list of sights and shows. All of these steps require more precise directions.

For the computer, the description of the steps to solve the problem becomes the algorithm. With it, a programmer decides the sequence of steps, the decisions that must be made, and the steps that need to be repeated. These directions are miniscule, incremental, and precise. On the computer, even the simplest task often takes considerable programming. Processes (thinking) that you have internalized – things that come almost automatically for you – have to be fully described for a program. If asked to give the largest number in a set of three numbers, you could solve that "without thinking." You'd have it completed within a split second of knowing the numbers. The real trick is to be able to describe the process you used to solve the problem and then translate that process into computer directions. You'll see more of this process in Chapter 5 on decisions. For now, it suffices to describe the process in general terms. First you'd declare the space that's needed for data. In this case, it's the numbers you're comparing. The second step is to get the numbers into the computer – the input step in the process. The processing step involves comparing the first number to the second number. Keep the higher of the two. To store it requires a storage space for the data. Then compare that number to the third and keep the higher of those two. Once completed, the computer would "know" the highest number in the list.

Although this description is detailed, it still isn't precise enough for a program. The details are even more exacting. It often takes several commands just for one task and each miniscule detail must be described. The steps in the process are incremental. Each one is spelled out in detail. The directions must be precise and spell out every detail exactly. In this example, you'd need to precisely describe the numbers to store, the numbers to compare, when to compare them, and where to store them. When that is completed, you'd provide precise directions for reporting the results. In short, the program must provide painstaking details. Each baby step is obvious and incremental; if you get the steps in the wrong order, you won't solve the problem. Forget a step and it's all over. And all this is to get the computer to do something you've been able to do "without thinking" since the second grade. Think about that the next time you're reading those "some assembly required" directions and it tells you to put tab A in slot B!

Let's go back to the cake-baking analogy. Your declarations are the utensils you need: the cups, spoons, bowls, and pans; your input is the ingredients; the processing is the mixing and baking; and the output is the finished cake. For us that might be a good enough description, but it wouldn't work for the computer. For the "add the ingredients" step, the computer needs far more direction. It follows the order specified, the sequence, and you must tell it the exact steps in the correct order. The specific amounts to be added and the order to add them must be described. Furthermore, "add an egg" to us means to take it out of its shell and add the inside parts, not the whole egg. That detail needs to be spelled out for the computer, even though we make assumptions for such things. Sometimes this order makes a difference and sometimes not. A good cook knows to put the liquid ingredients in first. That way the dry ingredients won't stick to the bottom of the mixing bowl. A good programmer learns such tricks as well. The mixing requires you to beat the mixture for a specified length of time. That's repetition. The directions call for changing the ingredients or the baking time if you're above a certain elevation. That's a decision and you'll follow one set of directions or another for that part of the process. Baking is one of the last steps in the process. For us, that's a close enough description. For the computer, you'd need to be more precise. If you get the steps out of order, you won't have dessert. And if you're good in the kitchen, you'll know enough to preheat the oven in advance rather than saving the "turn the oven on" step until you're ready to bake. It's safe to say you've never used a recipe or a set of directions quite as precise as those needed by the computer.

It's important to remember two things: (1) the computer does only what you tell it to do and (2) the computer has no intellect. Each command must be given to the computer and each must be in the correct order for the computer to successfully accomplish its task. You wouldn't have to give much thought to averaging four test scores. For the computer, each number needs its own storage location. These must be declared at the start. The program needs four inputs.

It then must add the inputs together to find the total. Once the total is known, it can calculate the average. The last step is to display the average. All of these must be in order and, if one is out of order or forgotten or done incorrectly, you won't find the answer. This simple, little program involves at least a dozen steps, nearly all must be in a specific order, and the correct calculations must be made in order to get an answer that you might be able to calculate in your head. Make just one mistake and it won't work properly. Most of us aren't accustomed to such detail.

The computer has no intellect, no imagination, and no insight. And worst of all, it doesn't have a sense of humor. It does exactly what you tell it to do and not what you want it to do. It makes no assumptions and doesn't correct your mistakes. If you incorrectly tried to find the average for your test scores before you knew the total, you'd back up, correct the mistake, and get it right. The computer can't do that. If your steps are out of order or wrong, the computer doesn't know it. It's only doing what it's told. In that respect, it's the ultimate passive-aggressive machine. The task of the programmer is to understand the program well enough to create a workable solution and then translate that into code the computer can handle.

VB Quiz 02

What three basic procedures are needed to write all computer programs? Describe these procedures.
What is an algorithm?
Explain why computer programs are miniscule, incremental, and precise.
Describe, in general terms, the process for balancing your checkbook.

Interface/Instructions – The Human/Computer Connections

Developer/User

You must assume two roles to write programs: the developer and the user. The *developer* is the person (or more likely a team) that develops the specifications, designs the program, creates the algorithm, writes the code, and tests the program. The *user* is the person that uses the finished program. Users also have a part in developing the specifications, designing the program, and testing it. At this stage, you're both the developer and the user. You'll design programs and use them, which offers some advantages and some disadvantages. You can see both sides of the program. You'll find out just how hard it is to design and code a program that the average person can use, how much work is involved in programming, and how difficult it is to anticipate the needs of the user. But, on the bright side, you can also design a program that exactly suits your needs.

You'll jump back and forth between programmer and user. When developing the program, you wear the programmer's hat. As a tester or user, you won't be interested in how a program works, only that it *does* work. You'll also run a program to do debugging. *Debugging* is the process of removing mistakes (*bugs*) from a program. While testing you'll act as a user, but you have a programmer's eye toward how the program runs, what works and what doesn't, and how to make the program work better for the user. Think of the developer as an inventor working on the design of a new widget. The user is the person testing the widget. In most cases, you're both the developer and the tester.

VB Quip   *There are only two industries that refer to their customers as "users." –Edward Tufte*

Design Time/Runtime

A developer works in design time and tests in runtime. *Design time* is when the program is developed, the interface is created, and the code is written. *Runtime* is when the program is running. In design time, a developer can add, delete, and modify code and make changes to the program settings. At runtime, the program is running, and changes to the program's design and code cannot be made. However, a programmer can write directions during design time that will change how a program looks and works in runtime. It is important to remember that at design time a developer decides everything that a program will be and can do. At runtime, the program executes the commands given to it at design time.

Form/Code

Most of your development in Visual Basic is done in two windows, the Form window and the Code window. The *Form window* is where the form is designed. That's where you put all the text, pictures, and controls for your program. This is often called the *interface* and is what the user sees when the program runs. The *Code window* is where the code is written. That's where you put the directions for the program. A user never sees the code window. A quick click on a tab switches you back and forth between them. As a developer, you must be familiar with both of these. You'll work with both of them to design and code a program.

Objects/Events

The controls on a form – the text, pictures, buttons, even the form itself – are *objects*. Visual Basic .NET is based on objects and it's far more than just the controls on a form. Objects are covered in much greater detail starting in Chapter 12. Without a knowledge of objects, it is difficult to move beyond the basics of programming. Think of an object as a building block for a program. There will be more on objects later, but for now simply consider them to be the form and all the controls on the form.

Events in a program include the ways a user interacts with the computer. These are things like clicking or double-clicking the mouse, typing in text, or pressing the Enter key. Events trigger a response from the computer. Events include far more than a click or a peck, but these are the most common. As a developer, you write code that runs in response to these events. If the user clicks on a button, the code for that event runs.

A popular term that's bantered about is *object-oriented, event-driven programming*. Throw that into your next conversation. It's a nice buzzword, but it simply means that a program was written with objects and is controlled by user events. Of course, if you don't understand objects and events, the term is meaningless. Suffice to say that most significant programming is done with objects and events.

Code Files/Program

Visual Basic .NET projects have a folder containing several files and other folders that contain files. These files are needed to create your finished program. All of them are used in development. Be very careful when moving or changing these files; one mistake can damage your project. It's best if you manage the project folder and leave the other files intact. Your finished program is an executable file with an .exe extension. This is a standalone program that you can run even if you don't have Visual Studio. To create or modify a program, you need the project folder and its files. These are used to create the executable file. There's more on this in an upcoming section.

What Is a Program?

In Visual Basic .NET, you create a program by developing a project. The project is stored in a folder and contains files and other folders. The finished program is in the bin folder and has an .exe extension. Within the project is at least one form file. A *form* is what the user sees when they run the program. For each form, there is at least one file containing the code for that form. These code files contain the directions for the program. Visual Basic controls the folders and files. As a developer, you are responsible for designing and creating the form and writing the code that makes that form work. The controls on the forms are linked to events. When an event is triggered, it runs the code behind that control. When writing the code, you need to be aware of the input needed from the user, the processing needed to solve the problem, and the expected output the user will get. You manage these resources during design time so the program can accomplish its tasks during runtime.

VB Quiz 03   *What two hats are worn when working with Visual Basic .NET?*
                               What is the difference between design time and runtime?

Who sees a form and who works with the code?

What is an object?

What is an event?

How many files make up a program? How many are in a project?

Your First Program – College Tuition

Define the Problem

The first step in any program is to define the problem. For this program, you must determine the cost of your tuition for the semester. To do the calculation by hand, you'd take the number of credits and multiply it by the tuition rate. The product is your tuition. The problem is simple and straightforward; you don't even give it much thought. For the computer, though, it involves numerous steps. You need to declare all the variables, get the user input, make the calculation, and display the output. All the basic steps for a program are incorporated: declarations, input, processing, and output. Nearly every program involves these steps in this order.

One of the hardest parts of programming is defining the problem. However, careful consideration in this step will save you time and effort in the long run. For every program, you must define the variables – the numbers or text needed to solve the problem. You must define the inputs – the data the user provides so you can solve the problem. You must determine the calculations needed to solve the problem. The order in this step is critical. And, finally, you must define the output – the results that solve the problem.

Once you have defined the problem, you can design the form. The form is the screen that the user sees at runtime. Although you may be tempted to do this step first, it's better to define and describe the other steps before you create your form. You can then develop the form and later code your program.

Define Inputs

The input for your program is the numbers or text entered by the user. For now, the input is handled with TextBoxes – more on that shortly. The input is the data for your program – what you need to know to solve the problem. Every program requires input of some kind. For this example, the input is the number of credits. This is a simple problem so we won't worry about undergraduate or graduate tuition rates, in-state or out-of-state tuition rates, or discounts for select groups. The only input the user needs to provide is the number of credits being taken.

Every program requires input. Input enables the user to distinguish one run of a program from every other. Without input from the user, the computer would return the same answer every time. For this program, the user enters the number of credits being taken and the program returns the tuition.

Determine Processing

The processing is the calculations. There's only one calculation for this program. The tuition is the product of the number of credits multiplied by the tuition rate. To keep this example simple, let's assume the tuition is $100 per credit. In more complicated programs the processing may involve numerous steps. It is critical that these steps be performed in the correct order. But for this program there's just one command. Later the programs become more complicated. As they do, the processing, and its code, becomes more complicated. Usually, the processing is the largest and most-complicated part of a program.

Define Outputs

The output is the answer. For this program, it's the cost of tuition, and there's just one calculation and one answer. For some programs, there may be many lines of calculations for one line of output. Often it's easiest to define the output first. Usually you know what you want for an answer before you know how to find it. From there, you can work your way backwards to determine the processing requirements and the inputs needed to do the calculations.

Determine Variables

This is often the hardest part for beginning programmers. In general, you need a *variable* for nearly every number in a calculation. Think of a variable as a storage location for numbers and text. This is where your data are stored during runtime. Decide on the variables you need before you start to code. Declare them before you write any other code. For your first program, you need three variables: one each for the number of credits, the tuition rate, and the cost of tuition.

Design Form

This is usually the most fun for beginning programmers. The form can be of almost any design as long as it accomplishes its task. There are guidelines for it and much of it is common sense. The developer has complete control over the size of the form, the color of the background and text, the font, its size, and its style. The objects on the form can be arranged in any manner the developer wants. For this program, you'll want to use a TextBox so you can enter the number of credits. You'll need a Label to display the output. You'll also want some other Labels to identify what's on the screen. You'll need Buttons, one to

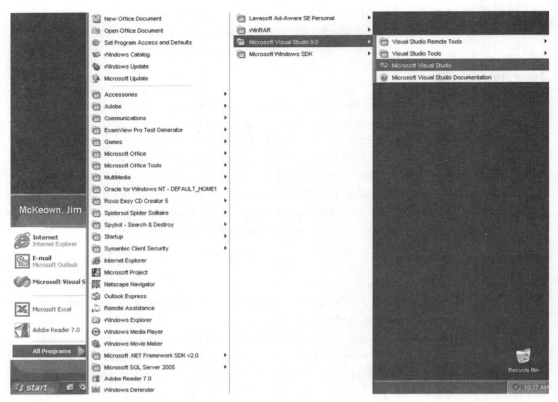

Figure 1.1   Starting Visual Basic

make the program do the calculation and another to end the program. After that, the design is up to you.

VB Basics

Starting/Ending

On the Start Button of the taskbar, select All Programs. From there, select Microsoft Visual Studio from the list. Where it is in the list depends on what is installed on your computer. The icon for it looks like the infinity sign – an "8" turned on its side. Visual Studio will take some time to load so be patient. If Microsoft Visual Studio is not available, it might not be installed on your computer. Check with your instructor about where it is or how to install it (see Figure 1.1).

Once Visual Studio has loaded, you'll probably see a screen similar to the one in Figure 1.2. This is the jumping off point for your VB programs. Recent projects show up in the upper left-hand corner. Right now you might not have any projects showing; however, once you start writing programs, the most-recent ones will show up there.

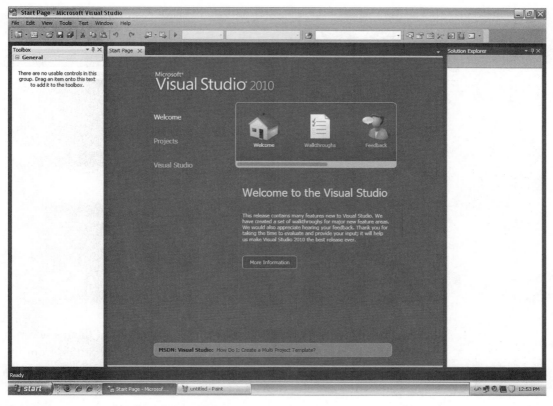

Figure 1.2   Visual Basic Start Page

To exit Visual Studio, simply select Exit from the File menu. If you have an unsaved project, you'll be asked if you want to save it before you quit.

VB Tour

Visual Studio is vastly different from most of the applications you're accustomed to running. It has multiple windows that can be rearranged to suit your needs. Your screen might look somewhat different, but all of the windows are available. Until you're comfortable with the windows and how to use them, don't get too reckless with moving or closing them. If needed, you can always reopen them by using the View menu. You can reset the windows to their original layout by going to the Windows menu and selecting Reset Windows Layout.

Start Page

The Start Page has a place for recent projects you've had open. From here, you could click on a recent project to open it or select a new project and start from scratch. The Start Page also has online help and some tutorials available just by

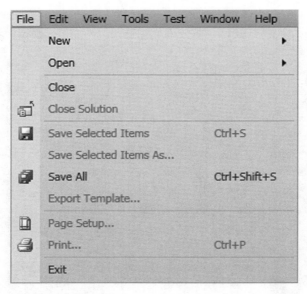

Figure 1.3   Visual Basic File Menu

clicking on the More Information button. Feel free to look at them when you have time. The Start Page opens every time you start Visual Studio from the Start Button. There's a tab at the top for activating the Start Page once you're in Visual Studio. You can also close this window by clicking on the Close Button. Be careful not to click on the Close Button on the Title bar of Visual Studio.

Creating a New Project

A new Visual Basic project can be created by selecting New Project from the File menu (Figure 1.3) or by selecting Projects on the Start Page and then clicking on the New Project icon (Figure 1.4). You can also create a new project by clicking on the New Project icon in the Toolbar.

Each of these opens up the New Project dialog box (Figure 1.5). This dialog is used to name the project and determine its type. You'll always create a Windows Forms Application and name it by entering a name near the bottom.

Naming a Project

The name of a project should reflect what the project will do. This program calculates tuition, so a good name is Tuition Calculator. The name used becomes the name of the project and the finished program. Be sure to use the Name blank and not the blank for the Solution Name. The Name is for the project and the Solution Name is for the folder. For now, just give them both the same name. You'll catch on to the difference once you've written a couple programs. When

Figure 1.4   New Project from Start Page

you create a project, the project's folder and all its files are saved in the Visual Studio folder in the My Documents folder on your computer. Do not move or rename the files in your project folder because it will cause problems with your project.

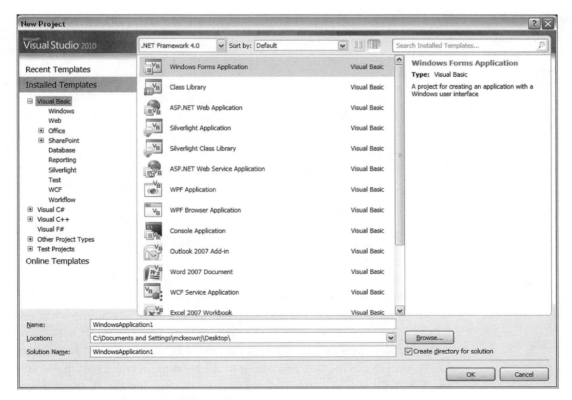

Figure 1.5   New Project Dialog Box

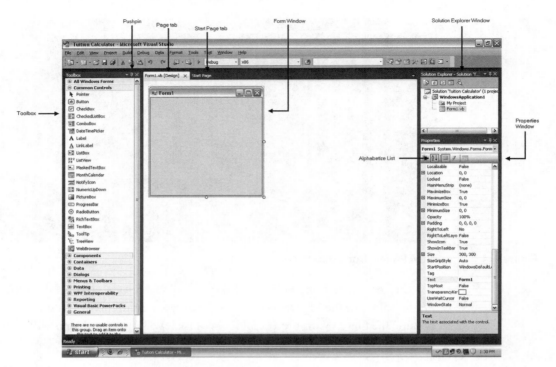

Figure 1.6   Visual Studio Designer Screen

Form Window

Once the project has been created, the form looks like Figure 1.6. For now the form window is called Form1. This form, once completed, is what the user sees when the program is run. You'll add *controls* to this form to create the user interface. A *user interface* is what the user uses to interact with the computer. Controls are the tools used to build the interface.

Toolbox

On the left is the Toolbox. The *Toolbox* contains the controls used to build the user interface. If the Toolbox isn't visible, go to the View menu and select Toolbox to display it. If the Toolbox shows up as a tab on the side of the screen, point to it to have it open. Then click on the pushpin on its title bar to "pin" it to the screen. That will keep it from automatically hiding when not in use.

The Toolbox contains the controls you need to design a form. You can click on a control in the Toolbox and drag it to the form to make it a part of the user interface. Each control in the Toolbox has a special use, just like the tools in real toolbox. You'll soon learn how to use some of the basic tools in the Toolbox.

Solution Explorer

On the right is the *Solution Explorer*. The Solution Explorer contains a list of files and forms in your project. If the Solution Explorer isn't visible, go the View menu and select Solution Explorer to display it. If the Solution Explorer shows up as a tab on the side of the screen, point to it to have it open. Then click on the pushpin on its title bar to pin it to the screen. That will keep it from automatically hiding when not in use.

Properties Window

The *Properties window* contains a list of properties for each control. When you select the form or any control on a form, the Properties window displays the properties for that control. The column on the left contains the names of the properties for that control. The column on the right contains the settings for the properties. You can change these settings, and thus change your program, by clicking on the name of the property and changing its setting on the right. Each control has its own unique set of properties. Most controls have similar properties so be careful to select the correct control on the form before you make changes to any properties.

Creating the Tuition Project

A form is created automatically when you create a new program. It is what the user sees when you run your program. It is the interface between the user and the computer. With it the user provides input and the computer provides output. A form is the yin and the yang.

Working with a Form

The form is how the user interacts with the computer when they run the program. As a developer, you decide which controls to use, the location of controls on the form, and the property settings for those controls. Click on the form in the Design window. A couple of things will happen. The form will get handles on the sides and corners. Use these to resize your form just like you'd use the handles in other Windows applications. The Properties window will display the properties for the form. It's an alphabetized list of the properties for that form. If the list isn't in alphabetical order, click on the A-Z button near the top of the window.

Adding Controls

There are two easy ways to add a control to your form. You can simply double-click on the control in the Toolbox and it will automatically be added to your form, or you can click on the control and drag it onto the form. Either way, once the control is on the form, you can click and drag it to where you want it on the form. You'll see *handles* on the control when it's selected. The handles let you resize it. Just click on one of the resize boxes, the pointer will change to the resize arrow, and you can drag the edges to change the size of the control. If you click on the inside of the control, you'll be able to move it to another location on the form. As you move it, Visual Studio will display blue alignment lines on the form to help you align the control with others on the form. Sometimes a pink line will appear as well. These horizontal lines help you align the text of the controls with each other.

Types of Controls and Their Uses

Each type of control has its own purpose. You'll learn a few of the basic ones now and more will be added later. Even though there are dozens of controls, most of the time you'll only need a handful of them for a project. Some controls are used to gather input from the user. A TextBox is a great example of this. RadioButtons and CheckBoxes are also used for input. Labels are used for output. They can either identify something on the form or they can be used to display results such as the answer to a calculation. Buttons are used for processing. You'll write code in them that will run when the user clicks on the Button. Code can be written in any control, but for now we'll put all our code into Buttons. An easy way to categorize controls is by their use for input, processing, or output.

For this example, we'll use a TextBox for input, two Buttons for processing, and several Labels for output. The TextBox will be used to get the number of credits from the user. One Button will be used to calculate the tuition and the other will be used to end the program. The Labels identify objects on the form and display the tuition calculation.

Naming Controls

Controls are identified by their names. You must use this name whenever you work with the control. Visual Studio has some specific rules for naming controls. We'll also add some naming rules to make it easier to keep track of the type of control and its use. Names must start with a letter. After that the name can contain any combination of letters, numbers, or underscores (_). Names cannot contain spaces. Some special characters can be used, but it's a good idea to avoid using any special characters. Names can be more than 1,000 characters long, but usually a good name will be less than twenty characters. In addition there are some informal rules that we'll use to make it easier to remember the type and purpose of a control. We'll start all controls with a three-character prefix that helps identify the type of control. If you know the type of control, then you're well on your way to understanding how it's used as well. Each name should also describe the control. For example, the TextBox used to get the number of credits being taken could be named txtCredits. The "txt" prefix describes the control as a TextBox. "Credits" helps identify it as the control containing the number of credits the student is taking. It's a good idea to capitalize the first letter of each word in a control name. It makes them easier to read.

Control	Prefix	Example	Purpose
Form	frm	frmTuitionCalculator	user interface
TextBox	txt	txtCredits	user input
Label	lbl	lblTuition	output or identification
Button	btn	btnExit	processing
PictureBox	pic	picLogo	displays graphics on the screen

Working with Properties

Properties describe an object. For example, a car is an object. Its properties include the color, style, accessories, and a long list of other things that describe it. The same is true for the properties of an object in VB. The form and the controls on it are all objects and each has its own set of properties. To change a property for one of the controls, simply click on the control and then change the appropriate property in the Properties window.

All the properties for a control have default settings. These settings can be changed to customize the control for your project. Once a property has been changed, it shows up in bold in the Properties list. To customize a car, you could change its color, put in leather, bucket seats, add a sunroof, and upgrade the media center. Certainly, customizing the properties of a control in VB is easier than customizing a car. It's more than just changing the font, the size, the style, or the color of a Label, but all of these are easy to accomplish.

The properties of a control can also be changed using code, but we'll hold off on that discussion for now.

Creating the Tuition Form

You'll want to name your form. Naming your controls makes it easier to identify and work with them. Find the Name property in the Properties window. It's near the top of the list and one of the few that's not in alphabetical order. Click on the word Name in the left column. You'll then be able to change the Name property. Type in frmTuitionCalculator and press Enter. That changes the name of the form. The process is similar for changing almost any property of any control (see Figure 1.7).

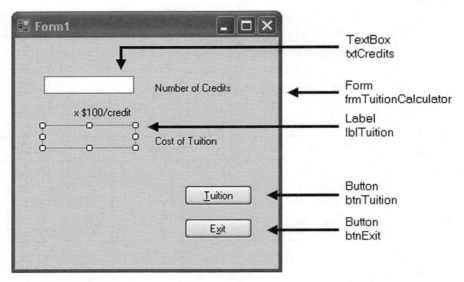

Figure 1.7   Tuition Calculator Form

The first control to add to your Tuition form is the TextBox. Controls can be added in any order, but we'll work our way from top to bottom in this example. Just double-click on the TextBox control in the Toolbox. It will add a TextBox to your form. Click and drag the TextBox to where you want it on the form. Once the TextBox is selected, the Properties window will display the properties for it. You'll want to change the Name property to txtCredits. Press Enter to complete the command. From now on when you want to work with this TextBox, you can refer to it by its name.

Next you'll want to add a Label to your form. Just double-click on the Label control in the Toolbox and it will automatically add a Label to your form. Drag the Label to the right of the TextBox. The name of this Label is automatically set to Label1. That's fine. This Label is only used to make the form easier to read. We won't be working with it, so the default name is just fine. You'll want to change the Text property of this Label, however. In the Properties window, click on the word Text in the left-hand column. Then enter Number of Credits in the space in the right-hand column. It should automatically replace Label1. Press Enter to complete the command.

VB Tip   *Always set the name of a control immediately. It should always be the first or second thing you do with a new control. It's a good habit and will prevent other problems later on.*

Next you'll want to add another Label to the form. Double-click on the Label in the Toolbox to automatically add another Label to the form. Click and drag it below the TextBox. This one doesn't need a name either, but the Text property must be changed. Click on Text in the Properties window and then type in and enter x $100/credit. That text will now be displayed in the Label.

Now you'll want to create a Label for your output. This Label will display the answer when the program runs. Double-click on the Label tool in the Toolbox to add the Label to your form. Click and drag it to the correct location. You must name this Label so click on it to select it. Then click on the Name property in the Properties window. Type in lblTuition and press Enter. This assigns the name to your Label. From now on when you work with this Label, lblTuition is its name. Next, find the AutoSize property. It's set to True so change the value of the property to False. That way the size of the Label won't change. Then click on the Text property and delete the text that's in there. Your Label is now named and ready for use.

Now add your last Label to the form. Double-click on the Label tool in the Toolbox to add another Label to your form. Click and drag it to the right of the lblTuition Label. Change the text property of this Label to Cost of Tuition.

Next, you'll add the Buttons to your form. Double-click on the Button tool in the Toolbox. This action adds a Button to your form. Click and drag it to the lower right of the form. Click on the Name property in the Properties window and change the name to btnTuition. This action names the control. You'll then want to change the Text property of the Button, which will change what gets displayed on the Button. Right now it says Button1. Change it to Tuition by clicking on the Text property, typing Tuition, and pressing Enter. btnTuition is how you and the computer keep track of the Button. Tuition is the text that displays on the Button.

Finally, you'll want to add an Exit Button to your form. Double-click on the Button tool in the Toolbox. That will add a Button to your form. Drag it below the Tuition Button. Change the name of it to btnExit. Change the text property to Exit. Your form is now complete.

VB Tip   *The name of a control is what you call the control when you work with it when writing code. The text property is what the user sees on the screen. You'll need to understand the difference between the two.*

Writing the Code

The code does the real work of a program. Although it's easy and fun to create a form, make it look nice, and dress it up, the code is what makes a program work. It's also what takes the most time and requires the most thinking.

Code Window

Your program code is written in the *Code Window*. An easy way to open the Code Window is to right-click on the form and select View Code from the popup. You can also just double-click on the form. Either way, a window opens up where you can edit your code. The Form window, the Code Window and the Start window all have tabs at the top. You can move between these windows by clicking on the appropriate tab.

Be careful where you write your code. You want some very specific things to happen when you run the program. For example, a click on the Tuition Button should calculate your tuition. A click on the Exit Button should end the program. For now, the best way to get the code in the right place is to double-click on the Button on your form. That will open the Code Window and place the cursor in the correct place for you.

Double-click on the Exit Button. That opens the Code Window and creates a *procedure*. A procedure is a block of code that completes a particular task. You should see a line that starts out `Private Sub` and another line that says `End Sub`. This is your procedure. Your code goes between these lines. Private, Sub, and End are all *keywords*. Keywords are special words in VB and have specific uses. All keywords show up in blue. There are other keywords on the form as well.

When you double-clicked on the Button, it created a click event for that Button. When you run the program, a click on the Button will now run the code for that Button. That's the event-driven part of programming. Type in the word End. End is a keyword and shows up in blue. It's a special command in VB. Now when you run the program and click on the Exit Button, it will end your program.

Now, click on the tab for your form. This takes you back to your form. Double-click on the Tuition Button. That opens up the Code Window and creates a click event for the Tuition Button. You'll see a line that starts out `Private Sub` and another line the reads `End Sub`, which marks the beginning and the end of the procedure for your Tuition Button. The code you write for this Button runs when you click on the Button.

IntelliSense

VB is one smart program. It keeps track of every Button, TextBox, and Label; in fact it keeps track of every control and more. IntelliSense keeps track of every variable, every control, and the properties for the controls. If you start typing the name of a variable, % IntelliSense brings up a list of the variables. When you type in the name of a control and then press the period, IntelliSense brings up a list of properties for that control. The basic form for this is control.property. Whenever you want to write code for the property of a control, you'll write it like that. For example, to work with the text property of the TextBox, you'd write txtCredits.Text. That tells VB that you want to work with or change the

Text property of the txtCredits TextBox. IntelliSense is a very handy feature and you'll soon rely on it for writing code.

Coding the Tuition Program

You'll need to write code for two Buttons for the program. The finished code will look like this:

```
Public Class frmTuitionCalculator
 Private Sub btnExit_Click(ByVal sender As System.Object,
    ByVal e As System.EventArgs) Handles btnExit.Click
 End
 End Sub

 Private Sub btnTuition_Click(ByVal sender As
    System.Object, ByVal e As System.EventArgs) Handles
    btnTuition.Click
 Dim shoCredits As Short
 Dim decTuition As Decimal
 shoCredits = txtCredits.Text
 decTuition = shoCredits * 100
 lblTuition.Text = decTuition.ToString
 End Sub
End Class
```

You'll recognize the click event for the Exit Button and the code that goes in it. You wrote End for that code and VB took care of the rest. However, the code for the Tuition Button is more complicated. You'll declare the variables you need, get the user input, do your calculation, and display your output.

Double-click on the Tuition Button on your form. This action opens the Code Window and places the cursor inside the click event for that Button. Now, duplicate the code *exactly* as it appears above. VB will automatically put the keywords in blue. You may notice IntelliSense at work as well. When you type in the name of a control and hit the period, it displays a popup with the properties of a control.

This code follows the general form you'll use for most of your programs. First, declare your variables. Then do your input, then the processing – that is, the calculations. And then do your output.

The following two Dim statements declare variables for storing your numbers:

```
Dim shoCredits As Short
Dim decTuition As Decimal
```

The first stores the number of credits and the second stores the cost of your tuition. That's how the computer keeps track of them.

The next line,

```
shoCredits = txtCredits.Text
```

is your input. It takes what's in the Text property of txtCredits and copies it into shoCredits. The computer now knows how many credits you're taking and that number is stored in a variable that can be used for calculation.

The next line does the calculation:

```
decTuition = shoCredits * 100
```

It's the real work of the program and what you want the computer to do for you. Input gets your data into the computer and output returns the results to you. The processing is where the computer does the work. This line takes the number of credits, multiplies it by 100, and places the answer in decTuition.

The last line is where the answer is displayed on the form:

```
lblTuition.Text = decTuition.ToString
```

It takes what's stored in decTuition and displays it in the Text property of lblTuition. The .ToString on the end of the statement tells the computer to change the number into characters of text. Don't worry about that for now.

What Can Go Wrong

At this point, there are so many things that can go wrong. A finished copy of the program is available so you can see how it should look and run. There are many reasons that a program, even a simple one like this, can go wrong. If you didn't get the names right, it won't work. Computers hate typos. If you got the code in the wrong order, it won't work. If you put the code in the wrong place, it won't work. In fact, consider yourself lucky if your program works; it means you're off to a good start. Practice will make the process of programming easier. As you learn more about Visual Basic, it will be easier. Remember how hard it was the first time you drove a car? There just seemed to be so much to remember. VB is the same way and it won't be long before you're good at it.

Saving Your Project

Save your project early and often. VB creates numerous files for a project and you'll want to save all of them in the same folder. You'll need all the files to reopen a project. There are several ways to save the files in your project. You can select Save All from the File menu, you can press Ctrl+Shift+S, or you can click on the Save All icon in the Toolbar (the one that looks like several floppy disks).

The name for the project is Tuition Calculator. You gave it that name when you created it. The folder name is also Tuition Calculator. All the files and folders for your project are in this folder. Don't move or rename them because it will cause problems! From now on you can save this project by simply clicking on the Save All Button, using the keyboard shortcut, or selecting Save All from the File menu. It will automatically save it with the same name and in the same location.

Running Your Program

Once your form is done and the code is written, be sure to save your project. You're then ready to run it. The first time you run the program, it will take several seconds for VB to create the finished program, save it, and run it. The first time it runs, it must *compile* the program; that is, it must convert the form and your code into computer language, create the executable program, and save it. Don't worry about those details for now. After that, it will start and run quickly.

Starting Your Program

There are several ways to start your program. You can click on the Start button in the Toolbar. It looks like an arrow pointing to the right, similar to the buttons you use to start a DVD player or an MP3 player. You can Press F5. You can select Start Debugging from the Debug menu. Any of these will work.

Stopping Your Program

You can stop a program by selecting Stop Debugging from the Debug menu. You can click on the Stop button on the Toolbar. It looks like a square, just like the Stop button on most electronic devices. You can press Ctrl+Alt+Break. You can also click on the Close Window button in the corner of your project window. Be careful to click on the window for your project and not on the one for Visual Studio. Any of these will stop the program and get you back to Visual Studio.

Running the Tuition Calculator Project

Start the Tuition Calculator project using one of the aforementioned methods. It will take several seconds for it to compile, save the files, and bring up your form. It should look just like the form you designed. Click on the TextBox on your form and type in the number of credits you're taking. When you click on the Tuition Button, it runs the code in that Button. That code creates your variables, takes the number from the TextBox, stores it in shoCredits, multiplies the number of credits by 100, and stores the answer in decTuition. Finally, it take that number and displays it in lblTuition.

Try the program with several different amounts. As the number of credits changes, so does the cost of tuition. When you're done, you can click on the Exit Button, which will run the code for that Button and end your program.

Opening a Project

There are several ways to open a project. You can start Visual Studio and open the project from there. Visual Studio remembers the last few projects you've worked on and you can click on a project in the Recent Projects. You can use the File menu to select Recent Projects and pick from the list. If it's been a while since you had that project open, you might use the Open Project option from the menu. That will present a dialog box and let you navigate through your folders to find your project.

You can use Windows Explorer to navigate through your folders to find a project. Visual Studio wants to save your projects in the Visual Studio 2010 folder and will start looking there. You can save your projects anywhere; just remember where you saved them. Open the Solution folder for your project and double-click on the file that ends with .sln. That's the Solution file and it will open your project in Visual Studio.

Project Files

Visual Studio creates many files and several folders when you write a program. It's best to leave the files and folders where they are. If you move them, save them in another location, delete them, or rename them, your project won't work. It's best to work with the folder for the solution when moving or making a backup of a project. Visual Studio expects the files to be in a specific location and any changes could destroy a project.

.exe file

In your Tuition Calculator folder is another folder called Tuition Calculator. It contains most of the files for your project. Inside that is a bin folder. It contains another folder called Debug. That folder contains several files.

You're interested in the file called Tuition Calculator.exe, which is your finished program. You can double-click on that and run it just like any other program. It's a standalone application that will work on other computers without the need of Visual Studio.

VB Quiz 04

What are the rules for naming variables?

What is stored in the Toolbox?

What are properties?

Why are naming conventions important?

How would you change the per-credit cost of tuition?

Why doesn't the computer display the cost of tuition until after you've clicked the Tuition Button button?

On Your Own

Change the Tuition Calculator program so that it calculates tuition for your school. You'll need to change the code so the tuition rate is the same as it is at your school.

Changing Properties Program

Properties control how a program looks and feels. When you change a property, it affects your program. There are two ways to change properties. The first is to change the settings at design time. You did that when you changed the text of your controls. The other way is to change them at runtime. You write code to do that.

Open the Changing Properties program and follow the directions here. It provides practice in setting and changing properties.

1. Open the form by double-clicking on the Form1.vb icon in the Solution Explorer.
2. Run the program and test all the Buttons to see how it works. You can run the program % by pressing F5. Stop the program before moving on.
3. Double-click on the Change Name Button. That will open the code window and take you to the code for that Button.
4. It says "Your Name" in red text. Replace it with your name. Be sure to leave the quotation marks.
5. Run the program. What happens when you click the Button?
6. Run the program. Click the Hide Name and Show Name. What happens? Exit the program. Double-click on the Button and look at the code. What property was changed?

7. Run the program. Click the Disable Button and Enable Button. What happens? Exit the program. Double-click on the Button and look at the code. What property was changed?

8. Run the program. Click the Label Color Blue Button. What happens? Exit the program. Double-click on the Button and look at the code. What property was changed?

9. Run the program. Click the Text Color Yellow Button. What happens? Exit the program. Double-click on the Button and look at the code. What property was changed?

10. Change Yellow to Green and run the program. What happens?

11. Run the program. Click on the Background Color Button. What happens? Exit the program. Double-click on the Button and look at the code. What property was changed?

Summary

This chapter is the start of programming. To write a program you must understand problem-solving. For a computer, that involves knowing the variables to declare, the input needed from the user, the processing required to solve the problem, and the output or the answer the user needs. All programming falls into three basic procedures: (1) sequence, (2) selection, and (3) repetition. Sequence is the correct order of steps for solving a problem. Selection is the ability of the computer to make a decision and act on it. Repetition is the ability of the computer to repeat a set of instructions. The Visual Basic interface was introduced along with the basics for working with it.

Review

Programming is the process of giving instructions to the computer.

A program is a set of directions to get the computer to complete a task.

A program can be likened to a recipe or a set of directions.

The order of steps in a program is usually declaration, input, processing, and output.

Programming tasks can be divided into three broad categories: (1) sequence, (2) selection, and (3) repetition.

The sequence of commands is essential to the completion of a programming task.

Selection procedures enable the computer to make decisions.

Repetition procedures allow the computer to repeat the same set of instructions.

Computers follow a set of directions called a program, and the description of a program is an algorithm.

Computer programs are miniscule, incremental, and precise.

Computers have no intellect and no insight. They blindly follow directions.

When writing programs, you assume the roles of developer and user, each with specific needs and requirements.

Design time is when a program is developed. Runtime is when the program is running.

Everything a program can do is determined at design time. At runtime, a program can only execute the commands given to it at design time.

The Form window is where the form is designed. The form is what the user sees while running a program.

The Code window is where the code for a program is written. The user never sees the code side of a program.

Objects include the form and the controls on the form. Advanced programming in VB.NET regularly involves objects.

Events can be user interaction with the computer. There are also many other events. Events trigger the execution of code in a program.

Most programming is done with object-oriented, event-driven code.

A Visual Basic .NET project is a folder that contains many files and other folders. Be cautious about making changes to these files. The finished program is an .exe file in the project folder.

Properties of a program can be changed at design time or runtime.

Terms

algorithm	a plan of action for solving a problem; usually it's an outline of steps or a formula for finding a solution
bugs	the mistakes and errors in a program
Code Window	the area where the developer writes and edits code for a program
compile	the process of converting a developer's forms and code into a standalone program
controls	the objects used to create a user interface; these include TextBoxes, Labels, Buttons , and more
debugging	the process of removing errors from a program
declarations	variables created at the start of a procedure; used to set aside memory for storing data
design time	the part of a programming project where the program is designed and coded
developer	the person who writes and develops a computer program
events	user-initiated activities; a click is an example of an event; a program can also initiate an event
form	a window; the user sees a form when running a program

Form window	the development window that contains the forms for a programming project
handle	the small squares on a selected control that allow the developer to resize a control; the handles indicate what control is currently selected
input	the data that go into a program so the computer can process them and produce output (results)
IntelliSense	a feature in Visual Basic that keeps track of every control and provides a list for the developer; it follows the notation control.property
interface	the connection between the user and the computer; what the user sees on the screen and works with while a program is running
keywords	also called reserved words; words in Visual Basic that have a special function and cannot be used as variables or control names
objects	sometimes called controls; the building blocks for a program
object-oriented, event-driven programming	the term used to describe programming techniques; older programming techniques were procedural
Output	the information that's produced by a program; usually it's displayed on the screen
procedure	a block of code that completes a specific task
processing	the calculations of a program; the work done by a program
program	a series of instructions for the computer to complete a task
programmer	the person who develops a computer program; often called a developer
programming	the "art" or writing computer programs
Properties window	a list of properties the developer sees for a selected control
repetition	repeating one or more steps in a program
runtime	the time when a program is running, either as a finished product or while it's being tested
selection	a decision structure in a program where the program follows one set of directions instead of another
sequence	a series of steps, executed in order
Solution Explorer	a window a developer sees showing the files for a programming project

Start page	the first page a developer sees when starting Visual Basic
Toolbox	a developer window that contains controls used for creating a program
user	the individuals who use a completed program
user interface	what the user sees when working with a program; it's what a developer creates when designing a program
variable	a "container" in memory for storing data

Keywords

Class	a pattern for creating an object
Decimal	a data type used to store larger numbers with decimals; used for currency
Dim	short for Dimension; used to create variables in a program
End	the command to stop a program
Private	a smaller class in Visual Basic
Public	a class in Visual Basic
Short	a data type used to store whole numbers
Sub	short for subroutine; a part of the code for a program

Self-check

1. Every computer error is, in reality, a human error.
2. Design time and runtime can never occur at the same time.
3. The interface of a program is the only thing a user sees.
4. A Visual Basic project consists of a single folder with three files in it.
5. In Visual Basic, all code is triggered by events.
6. Input comes from the developer and output goes to the user.
7. The Solution Explorer contains all the controls and properties for a program.
8. Every control name must be unique.
9. Control names cannot contain spaces or special characters.
10. Every control has a set of properties that describe it.
11. Which of the following is in the correct order?
    A. processing, output, input
    B. output, input, processing
    C. input, output, processing
    D. input, processing, output
12. "Some assembly required" is an example of:
    A. sequence
    B. selection

    C. repetition

    D. declarations

13. An algorithm is a:

    A. plan for solving a specific problem

    B. series of steps repeated a specified number of times

    C. decision-making process

    D. diagram showing the parts of a whole

14. Designing, writing, and testing a program is the job of a:

    A. consumer

    B. user

    C. developer

    D. investor

15. An example of an event includes:

    A. clicking the mouse

    B. entering text into a TextBox

    C. selecting an item from a menu

    D. all of the above

16. A variable:

    A. keeps track of a value while a program is running

    B. describes the settings for a control

    C. explains the steps in a process

    D. is a mistake in a program

17. The Solution Explorer is:

    A. a list of all the controls used in a project

    B. a list of the settings for a particular control

    C. the window where a developer writes their code

    D. a list of the files and forms in a project

18. Calculations are made using:

    A. controls

    B. variables

    C. properties

    D. declarations

19. Which of the following is an allowable control name?

    A. My Output Label

    B. LabelOutput

    C. lblOutput

    D. 1Output

20. IntelliSense:

    A. keeps track of every control and its properties

    B. keeps track of the value stored in every variable

    C. records every bug that's encountered

    D. all of the above

VB Quiz Answers

Quiz 01

The first step is to declare your variables, the second step is input, the third step is processing, and the last step is output.

The first step is to declare your variables.

A recipe is a set of directions; so is a program. Both have the steps needed to complete a task. And, usually, the steps must be completed in a particular order.

A good set of directions tells a traveler where to go and how to get there. A good program provides a set of directions as well. The declarations might be to watch for roads, miles, minutes, signs, or landmarks. The input might be the miles traveled, the minutes elapsed, or the number of lights passed. The processing would be the driving and the turns. The output would be the destination. Order is critical to a set of directions. The same is true for a program.

Quiz 02

The three basic procedures are sequence, selection, and repetition. All programs are written with combinations of one or more of these building blocks.

Sequence involves placing commands in the correct order for accomplishing a task. Selection involves giving the computer a choice and having it follow a particular set of directions. Repetition has the computer repeat the same tasks over and over again.

An algorithm is a plan – a series of steps for solving a problem. For a program, it's a description of the tasks to accomplish and the order to do them.

Each step in a program must be exactly clear. The computer can handle only one step at a time and that step must be precisely described. If any are wrong or out of order, the program won't work correctly.

To balance a checkbook, you'd need the previous balance. To that, add all deposits. To that add interest. To that add all corrections. From that, subtract all checks. From that, subtract automatic deductions. From that subtract charges and late fees. Usually, this is done on a daily basis.

Quiz 03

When working in Visual Basic .NET you act as either a developer or a user. The developer works to create the program. The user helps with the design and the specifications and tests the program.

Design time is when the program is under development. The developer works with the form and writes code. Runtime is when the programming is running.

Both the developer and the user see the form. The developer sees it during design time and the user sees it at runtime. The developer works with the code. The user never sees the code behind a program.

An object is a form or one of the controls on a form. An object is a building block for a program.

An event can be an action taken by the user, such as a click or pressing a key. There are other types of events as well. Events trigger code in a program.

A program is just one file. It has a .exe extension. A project contains all the files needed by Visual Basic .NET to create the program. The exact number varies, depending on the program.

Quiz 04

All variables must start with a letter. Names cannot contain spaces. Names can contain letters, numbers, and some special characters. Names can be up to about 1,000 characters long. Use meaningful names that describe the variable. Most names should be less than twenty characters for readability and ease of use. Avoid special characters because some of them won't work. Use a prefix that describes the data type.

The Toolbox stores controls. They are placed on a form when a program is being developed. These controls all have special uses.

Properties describe a control. Think of controls as nouns and properties as adjectives. Properties are the settings that describe a control.

Naming conventions make it easier to follow the code. If a control or variable has a prefix and a meaningful name, it is easy to determine what it is and how it's used.

In the code, you'd have to change the line of code that calculates the tuition. This is the line that needs to be changed:

```
decTuition = shoCredits * 100
```

Change 100 to the tuition rate for your school.

The code is in the Button and the code doesn't execute until the Button is clicked.

On Your Own Answers

5. Your name should appear in the Label near the top of the form.
6. The name disappeared when the Hide Name Button was clicked and it reappeared when the Show Name Button was clicked. The Visible property was changed.

7. The Change Name Button became gray when the Disable Button was clicked and it returned to normal when the Enable Button was clicked. The Enabled property was changed.

8. The background color of the Label with your name in it changed to blue. The BackColor property was changed.

9. The color of the text in the Label with your name in it changed to yellow. The ForeColor property was changed.

10. The color of the text changed to green.

11. The BackColor property was changed.

Variables and Constants – A Place for Everything and Everything in Its Place

VB Quip   *There are 10 types of people in the world: those that understand binary and those that don't.*

On a computer, memory is everything, or nearly so. Data are stored there and programs are loaded and run from memory. Memory is essential. Compared to what was available a few years ago, today's computers have a huge amount of memory. A few years ago that same comparison would have been true as well. Forty years ago we sent men to the moon with spaceships that had less memory than a good pocket calculator has today. All computers, old and new, have memory in common. Memory is where what the computer "knows" is stored. Much of programming comes down to allocating and managing memory. For the PCs of a generation ago, memory was a scarce and expensive commodity to be guarded closely and used judiciously. Programmers used it carefully and squeezed as much as they could from it. At the time, conserving memory gave you a leg up on development and helped make your programs faster and more efficient. And, today, while the *amount* of memory isn't as much of an issue, the *management* of memory is. When you work on your computer, you work with its "desktop." These days, it's the size of a table. In the early days of programming, that "desktop" was the size of a postage stamp. Variables and constants are two important components of a computer program. Both are created in memory and are assigned values. Control of these is essential to getting good input from the user, processing their data, and returning usable information to the user. Most of this chapter focuses on how programmers assign, use, abuse, and conserve memory. You'll get your first opportunity to write programs that require you to manage memory. You'll also be introduced to flowcharts and deskchecks, two tools for designing and testing programs.

Computer Memory: Location, Location, Location

Binary Storage

All computers use binary, 0s and 1s, for everything. Data are stored in binary. Calculations are made in binary. Files get transferred in binary. Everything is

Table 2.1   Finger (and Thumb) Counting

Decimal	1	2	3	4	5	6	7	8	9	10
Binary	1	10	11	100	101	110	111	1000	1001	1010

binary. You probably worked with binary math in junior high and most likely hated it. While this won't be as tedious, there are a few principles to learn, and they will make understanding computer memory and programming easier.

All computer math is done in binary. If you were to count the digits on your hand, you'd probably count 1, 2, 3, 4, 5. Computer geeks usually start at zero, so they'd count 0, 1, 2, 3, 4. In binary the only digits you get are 0 and 1. So, starting at 0 like any self-respecting propeller-head, you'd count 0, 1, 10, 11, 100. If humans had more fingers or fewer fingers, or if we counted our toes as well, base 10 math would seem odd. So, while binary seems odd for us, it's standard for a computer. In a technical sense, it's the tiny electrical charge on a circuit or a hard drive that determines if a digit is a 0 or a 1. Counting to 10 in binary would be easy: 1, 10. Counting our fingers and thumbs in binary would go 1, 10, 11, 100, 101, 110, 111, 1000, 1001, 1010 (see Table 2.1).

Luckily, computers and programming have advanced enough over the years so that we don't have to work in binary. The computers take care of that for us. We only have to be aware of how it affects the way computers work.

If you use a series of eight binary digits, which is standard on a computer, you can use numbers from 0000 0000 to 1111 1111. You'll have to put in a 0 or 1 for all eight spaces because the computer is checking for that electrical charge. We'd see this series as 0 to 255 (see Table 2.2).

You can take those eight binary digits, each of which is called a *bit*, and put them together to form a *byte*. So, if you reserve a byte of memory in the computer, you can store any integer from 0 to 255. To store larger numbers, numbers with decimals or negative numbers, you'd need more than one byte. In that case, you'd reserve more space in the computer's memory. For example, two bytes give you the ability to store integers from −32,768 to 32,767. If you use more bytes, you can work with a wider range of numbers and numbers with decimals. Years ago, this was a big issue in programming, but now it's more just a matter of managing memory and less a matter of conserving it.

VB Tip   *Multiples: Computers work in multiples of two. If you start at 2 and keep doubling, you get 2, 4, 8, 16, 32, 64, 128, 256, 512, 1024, 2048, 4096, 8192, 16384, 32768 . . . You'll recognize some of these numbers. One is probably the number of megabytes of memory in your system. Don't worry; these won't have to be memorized.*

That's fine for numbers, but what if you want to use letters? The same principles are used to represent letters on the computer. Take a series of 0s and 1s, a byte, and use each to represent a particular letter or character. 0100 0001 represents

Table 2.2   Binary and Decimal Comparison

Binary	Decimal
0000 0000	0
0000 0001	1
0000 0010	2
0000 0011	3
0000 0100	4
0000 0101	5
0000 0110	6
0000 0111	7
0000 1000	8
. . .	
1111 0111	247
1111 1000	248
1111 1001	249
1111 1010	250
1111 1011	251
1111 1100	252
1111 1101	253
1111 1110	254
1111 1111	255

A; 0100 0010 is B; and 0111 1010 is z. With this convention you can represent most of the letters and characters you'd use on a daily basis. Check Appendix A for the ASCII chart, which is a full listing of the binary representations for letters, numbers, and special characters. ASCII is the American Standard Code for Information Interchange. It is the standard binary representation for the letters, numbers, and symbols we commonly use in writing.

VB Tip   *Unicode: Unicode is a much larger standard and contains a much larger set of symbols, including many foreign characters. It uses two bytes per character.*

If 0100 0001 in binary is A and it's also 65, how can the computer tell it apart? It can't. The computer has no intellect. It doesn't know the difference. It only follows the rules it's given, which is done in programming. When a programmer reserves memory, the computer is told what type of data is represented by all of those 0s and 1s. If that grouping of bits is a letter, it's reserved as a storage space for letters. If it's a number, it's reserved as a storage space for numbers. When a larger chunk of memory is needed – for storing large numbers like the national debt – a programmer reserves more space and tells the computer what type of number to store.

We can think of these storage locations as containers. If you like, they could be plastic storage containers from the kitchen, disposable plastic cups you would use at a picnic, or even the glass jars used for home canning and running moonshine. Just think of them as containers of various sizes that are capable

Figure 2.1   Storage Containers

of storing items. Each one has a name, and each stores only one item. We can see what's in each container – maybe a number or some text. The programs we write will create the containers, put values in them, and change what's stored in each container. They could look like Figure 2.1.

VB Quiz 01   *Larry Wall once said, "Don't tell me there isn't one bit of difference between null and space because that's exactly how much difference there is." Use the ASCII chart to explain why he's right.*

Computer memory has been compared to cups and jars. What else could be used in an analogy for computer memory?

Creating Variables: Storage Containers for Your Data

Data Types

To work with data on your computer – anything from the text that is your name or your address, to numbers like your age or a test score, and to dates like your birthday or graduation date – you must use a *variable*. A variable is a storage container for your data. Many types of variables exist, each with a specific use, or what programmers call a *data type*. That is, each type is designed to store a particular type of data. Some store whole numbers, integers. Some store numbers with decimals. Some are for dates; some store text, in what programmers call *strings*. There are a few other types as well, but, for now, we'll stick with a few basic data types.

To make use of these containers, you first have to create them. In programming this is called *declaration*. You write a statement that creates a variable. To change the value in a variable, use an *assignment*. This is where the rules of programming take over, in what's called *syntax*. Nearly every statement you write in your code has to follow very strict rules. Often the hardest part of programming is getting your commands written in a way the computer understands. For the most part, we'll try very hard to keep it simple. First, let's look at declarations.

shoTest

Figure 2.2   Initialized Storage Container

To create a variable, let's say, one to store your last test score, use a statement something like this:

```
Dim shoTest as Short
```

There are other ways to do it, but this is about as simple as it gets. You write a statement that creates a variable, gives the variable a name, and tells the computer what type of data can be stored in it. In this statement, "Dim," short for dimension, tells the computer to set aside some memory. shoTest is the name of the variable. You'll use this name every time you work with it. Think of it in the same way you think of *n* in a math equation. As Short tells the computer what type of data will be stored in the variable, in this case a Short (see Table 2.3 for more on this). When you run the program, this line creates a container called shoTest. It will store Short variables, which simply means it will store whole numbers from –32,768 to 32,767. Any whole number in that range can be stored there. Try to put anything else in there and you'll run into trouble. This line also does one other thing. It automatically assigns 0 to it. All numeric variables get assigned 0 when they're created. That is, they are *initialized* to 0. So, once this line of code in your program has run, you could see something like Figure 2.2.

Technically, the statement is formed like this:

```
Dim varName As Type
```

where varName is the name of the variable and Type is the data type. While experienced programmers enjoy seeing definitions like this, it often doesn't provide much help for the novice. For your use, substitute your variable name for varName and change Type to the data type you want that variable to be.

The variable name must follow several rules. It

- can only use letters, numbers, and underscores (_);
- must start with a letter or underscore;
- cannot have spaces;
- cannot use special characters; and
- cannot be a keyword (more on keywords later).

Table 2.3   Data Types, Ranges, and Prefixes

Data Type	Prefix	Range	Bytes
Byte	byt	0 to 255	1
Short	sho	−32,768 to 32,767	2
Integer	int	−2,147,483,648 to 2,147,483,647	4
Long	lng	−9,223,372,036,854,775,808 to 9,223,372,036,854,775,807	8
String	str	0 to ~2 billion	1 per character
Decimal	dec	1.0e−28 to 7.9E+28	16
Single	sng	1.5E45 to 3.4E+38	4
Double	dbl	5.0E324 to 1.7E+308	8
Date	dat	January 1, 0001 to December 31, 9999 0:00:00 to 23:59:59	8
Boolean	bln	True or False	2
Char	chr	one Unicode character	2
Object	obj	data of any type	−

We'll also add some other naming conventions, which will make it easier to recognize variables, their type, and what they contain. Variables should

- have a meaningful name,
- start with a lowercase letter,
- include a prefix that describes the data type, and
- include a name in which the first letter of each word is capitalized.

It's not as hard as it sounds. This variable was declared as a Short. To help you remember its type, the prefix "sho" was used. "Test" describes what is stored in the variable. It could have just as easily been called shoTestScore, shoTest_Score, shoFirstTest, shoTest1, or shoTest1Score. All of these names are valid and all describe the type of variable and what's stored in it. The names make sense, they all start with a lowercase letter, the prefix describes the data type, and the first letter of each word of the name is capitalized to make it easier to read. "shoTestOneScoreForComputerProgrammingClass" would work as well, but you wouldn't want to type a name that long. Of course, you could also use t for a variable name, but it would be tough to keep track of more than just a few variables if their names were this short.

   The data type must be one of a handful, as shown in Table 2.3. Each has a specific purpose and takes up a certain amount of space in memory. The data type of the variable determines how the data are stored in the variable. For example, you could store the number 42 in a numeric variable or you could store "42" in a string variable. As a numeric variable, you could use it as a number and do calculations with it. As a string, you couldn't do math with it, but it would be a good way to represent, say, your locker number.

You can see from Table 2.3 that some data types take up more space than others. A good rule when creating variables it to pick a data type large enough to hold what you might store in it, but not so large that it wastes space. The storage container analogy works well for this. If you had some leftovers to store in the refrigerator, you would pick a storage container large enough to hold all the leftover casserole but not so large that it wastes the limited space of your refrigerator. The storage container analogy also works for the data type. When you're selecting the type of container to use, you have to make sure it fits the data. For leftover spaghetti sauce, you would want a container with a good lid so it wouldn't leak. Data types for numbers need a particular type of variable, too. Those with decimals would need a Decimal, Single, or Double type. A Short data type wouldn't work for numbers with decimals, because it isn't the right type of container.

VB Tip   *Zip codes: You cannot store zip codes as a number. Although most of them would work as a number, you never do math with them, so there's no need to store them as numbers. Besides, the zip codes for the New England states all start with zero, and numeric variables cannot display leading zeroes.*

Declaring Variables

Many of the variables you'll work with, especially early on, fall into a few data types. These data types are highlighted in bold in Table 2.3. Most of them are numeric so you can handle numbers. One other important data type is a string. It's used for storing a series of characters. Use a string to store your name, an address, or anything that contains text. It's also used for numbers that aren't treated as numbers. Your Social Security number, a zip code, a part number, or your student ID are all good examples of numbers that aren't really "numbers." Declaring a string variable is very similar to declaring numeric variables. The one exception is that string variables are initialized to null. A string will be empty until you put something in it. To declare a string you would write something like this:

```
Dim strLastName As String
```

This statement creates a variable called strLastName. Its initial value is "". The prefix is str, which tells you the variable contains a string of characters. The first letter of each word of the name is capitalized to make it easier to read.

You could initialize a variable at the same time you declare it. It's very handy sometimes and always easy to do. For example,

```
Dim shoCaseSize As Short = 24
```

could be used to create a variable for storing the number of items in a case – say, the number of bottles of ketchup in a case. This creates the variable as a Short with the name shoCaseSize and puts the value 24 in the variable instead of 0.

For a string:

```
Dim strLastName As String = "Jefferson"
```

This statement creates the variable strLastName as a String and stores "Jefferson" in it. Quotation marks around a string are essential. They tell the computer where the string starts and ends. Literally, this will put the last name of the third President into the strLastName variable. Without the quotation marks, the computer wouldn't know where to start or end the string. Any character that shows up between the quotation marks ends up in that variable. Spaces within the string are just fine, so you could have easily assigned "Thomas Jefferson" to the string.

VB Tip   *A string cannot contain quotation marks. The quotation marks are used to show where the string starts and ends. When you put a quotation mark in the middle of a string, the computer thinks that's the end of the string. If you really need quotes around something in a string – a title, for example – you should use single quotes (').*

VB Quiz 02   *Why wouldn't your phone number be a number?*
Why would an address need to be a string?
How would you write a line of code that would create a string variable and assign a movie title to it? Indicate that it's a title by putting single quotes around it.

Assignment Statements: Filling a Storage Container

A programmer must have a way to get data into a variable For us, it's a way to put something into that storage container. This is done with an assignment statement. Use an assignment statement to place a value in a variable. There are several ways to assign a value to a variable. It can be done by literally assigning a value to a variable,

```
shoTestScore = 88
```

by assigning the value of one variable to another,

```
strNewAddress = strOldAddress
```

or by using a mathematical equation,

```
shoTotal = shoNum1 + shoNum2
```

or

```
shoTotal = shoNum1 + 10
```

The variable is always on the left and the value being placed in the variable is always on the right. Use the equals sign to assign the value. An easy way to remember this is to tell the computer where to store the answer before you tell the computer how to find the answer.

In math, we were taught that the equals sign meant that whatever was on one side was equal to what was on the other side. That's not true in an assignment statement in programming. Instead of reading that as "equals," think of it as "gets the value of" or simply "gets." So, the last statement might be read as "shoTotal gets shoNum1 plus shoNum2." The computer takes the values in shoNum1 and shoNum2, adds them together, and puts the answer into shoTotal.

If you want, visualize a slip of paper in the container. The assignment statement "writes" on that slip of paper and you can check the container to see what's in it.

You Do the Math – Getting the Computer to Calculate

The whole idea behind computers was to get them to do the math, and computers are very good at math. The first functional computer, started during World War II, was designed to do trajectory calculations for the Navy. It was designed to quickly and accurately find the firing solutions for the big naval guns. It was a government project so, of course, it had problems, went over budget, and wasn't completed until after the war was over. Still, it was a marvel. It greatly reduced the time needed to perform the complex calculations. It was also very accurate. Furthermore, it reduced the drudgery of solving long mathematical equations by hand. Even today, speed, accuracy, and release from drudgery are a few of the biggest advantages of computers.

VB Tip *Computers take their name from the people they replaced. The first "computers" were all women.*

Mathematical Operations

Computers can easily do addition, subtraction, multiplication, division, and exponentiation. The rules for writing assignments statements are fairly easy as well. Of course, the more complicated the formula, the harder it is to write. The best practice is to write down the formula, keep it easy to understand, and test it to make sure it's right.

To get the computer to add, use the plus (+) sign. Subtraction is done with the minus sign (−). For multiplication, use the asterisk (*). The "x" won't work. If you've used a spreadsheet, you already know this. Division can be done several ways. Use the slash (/) for division. The result might have a decimal. For example, $17/5 = 3.4$. Use the backslash (\) for integer division. The result will be

Table 2.4   Mathematical Operators in Visual Basic

Operation	Mathematical Sign	VB Equivalent
Addition	$+$	$+$
	$A + B$	shoNum1 + shoNum2
Subtraction	$-$	$-$
	$X - Y$	decSubtotal − decDiscountAmount
Multiplication	$\times$	*
	$R * S$	decSubtotal * decDiscountRate
Division	$\div$	/, \, Mod
	$H \div K$	shoTotal / shoNumScores
		shoNumCases \ shoCaseSize
		shoTotalBottles Mod shoCases
Exponentiation	$(\ )^n$	^
	T^2	shoSide^3

an integer. For example, $17 \backslash 5 = 3$. Use Mod to find the remainder. For example, 17 Mod 5 = 2. Mod is short for *modulus*. Use the circumflex (^), sometimes called the caret or hat, for exponentiation. Table 2.4 shows the mathematical operators.

Rules of Precedence

One other major difference is how multiplication is done when parentheses are involved. In math, you might have written $2(L + W)$ when you wanted to add L and W and then multiply by 2. The computer will not automatically multiply by 2. You literally have to put in the multiplication (*) sign. So, if you were writing a formula to find the perimeter of a rectangle, the formula would be

Perimeter = 2(length + width)

but the assignment statement in the computer might look like this:

```
sngPerimeter = 2*(sngLength + sngWidth)
```

It's almost the same, but it's just different enough to be maddening and confusing.

The computer doesn't respond well to errors. You cannot try to do math with strings; the computer won't like it. You cannot divide by zero either – it will cause your program to crash. There are ways to avoid this, and you'll have to, to write good programs. But don't lose sleep over it just yet.

When you assign a value to a variable, you must make sure it can store the answer. For example, if you were trying to find your test average, you would add up the scores on your tests. We'll say there are four scores. You'd then divide that total by 4 to find the average. The mathematical formula would look like this:

Average = (Test1 + Test2 + Test3 + Test4)/4

On the computer, you must follow its rules, so it might look like this:

```
sngAverage = (shoTest1 + shoTest2 + shoTest3 + shoTest4)/4
```

First, add all four test scores. That's why those variables are in the parentheses. Then divide by 4. The answer gets assigned to sngAverage. It should be declared as a Single data type. Single can store numbers with decimals and it's possible, in fact very likely, that the answer will have a decimal.

If you were adding the total points scored by an NBA player in his career, a Short variable wouldn't work, because it can only store numbers up to 32,767. Several NBA players have career totals greater than that. The program would crash and you would have a mess, much like the mess you would have if you tried to squeeze all the leftovers into a container that was too small. This error in your code is called a *bug*.

Again, think of these variables as containers. Each container has a slip of paper in it. That slip of paper has the value for that container written on it. Look in the container and you can see what value it stores.

VB Tip –
Zero, not O

The computer "knows" the difference between zero and oh. That is, it treats 0 (the number) differently than it treats O (the letter). Pay close attention to this and you won't have a problem. Often programmers use Ø for zero to make the intent clearer.

The preceding calculation has a set of parentheses in it. The computer follows several rules of precedence. There are just a few given here as reminders. They are nearly the same as the rules for math. In VB, do

- what's in parentheses first and work your way out,
- exponentiation before other mathematical calculations,
- multiplication and division from left to right, and then
- addition and subtraction from left to right.

Creating Constants – Storage Containers with Lids on Them

VB Quip

One man's constant is another man's variable. – A. Perlis

Constants are like variables except their values cannot be changed while the program is running. The idea is to create the storage location, assign a value to it, and make sure the program won't change that value while the program is running. Constants are very useful, extremely helpful, and, thankfully, very easy to write. Constants are created, named, and assigned a value all in one statement.

To create a constant, let's say one to store the current sales tax rate, use a statement something like this:

```
Const sngSalesTaxRate As Single = 0.05
```

There isn't much more to it than this. Const is used to create the constant. sngSalesTaxRate is the container. From the name, you can surmise its use for storing the sales tax rate. AS Single reserves enough memory to store a number with decimals. The end of the statement assigns 0.05 to it.

The same can be done with strings. For example:

```
Const strTitle As String = "A Tale of Two Cities"
```

Const is used to create the constant. strTitle is the container. It's created as a string. The assignment part of the statement puts "A Tale of Two Cities" into the container. The quotes will not show up inside the constant. They are used to indicate the start and the end of the string.

A constant is set when it's declared and it cannot be accidentally changed in the rest of the code. It's good practice to use constants whenever you have values that won't change during a program run. In general, use variables or constants on the right-hand side of an assignment statement. Use constants whenever there is a value that won't change. You'll see many good uses for this throughout the next chapters.

VB Tip   *Put all of your constants at the top. That way they're easy to find and easy to change.*

VB Quiz 03   *What is wrong with each of the following?*

```
shoNum + shoNum2 = shoTotal
shoNum = 10 * 4
Dim decPrice As Decimal = "$4.99"
shoCube = (shoSide)3
```

Declarations, Input, Processing, Output – No Program Should Be Without Them

It is difficult to write a program that can accomplish any significant task without declaring variables, getting input from the user, processing the data, and turning it into information and then providing the user with the output. In general, one of the first things to do in a program is to declare all the variables and constants that are needed. There are arguments about when and how to do this, but that's something that can be discussed at a later time. For now, all variables and constants are declared first, which makes it easier on you. Declarations are the first part of your code.

Once the variables and constants have been created, you'll need to take the user *input* – for now that's what they've typed into a TextBox – and move it to a variable. Later, you'll learn other ways to do input. At this point, let's keep it simple. As a general rule, you won't do any calculations or manipulations of data unless it's in a variable. There are shortcuts, but shortcuts are for those that know their way around. Input is the second part of your code.

With all of the user input safely moved into variables, the next step is to process the data. This is where the calculations take place. Calculations are the real work of a program, where the raw data from the user gets changed into information. In other words, that's where the facts and figures become information that can be used to make a decision. *Processing* is done with assignment statements. For some programs, this might be as little as one line. For other programs, it might involve pages of code. For now, your programs will only need a few lines of code. Processing is the third part of your code.

Once you have the answers, the last task is to take the answers and move them to *output*. Usually the output is to the screen. There are other places to send output, but the screen is easy and immediate. Later, you'll learn other ways and places to do output. At this stage, we'll just send the output to Labels on the screen. Output is the fourth part of your code.

All of this could be done in just a couple lines of code, but that makes it very complicated and very hard to understand the process. We'll break the process into simpler steps and use these small steps to create a program. These small steps are an *algorithm* – a planned series of steps to solve a problem. It's your recipe for solving a problem.

The Perimeter Program – Getting Around Variables

This program is a simple, little program to find a perimeter. It might be the perimeter of a room, so you could find how many feet of molding you need for it or how many feet of border for the wallpaper. It could be edging for the flower garden or it might be for a fence for a lot. In any case, we need to know how far it is around the outside of a rectangular area so you'll know how much material you'll need. Back in grade school you learned that the perimeter is the distance around an area. The formula for the perimeter of a rectangle is generally stated as perimeter = 2(length + width), which is the formula you'll use in the processing part of the program. You want to find the perimeter; that's the answer, or in computer parlance, the output. To find the answer, you need two numbers: the length and the width. Those are your inputs. In programming, you're always looking at the problem in terms of inputs and outputs. Ask yourself, "What am I after?" And, "What do I need to get there?" The answer is your output. The input is what you need to find the answer. The processing is the formula(s) you need to find the answer.

Once you know the input(s) and the output(s) for a program, you'll need to create variables for them. Each input needs a variable and each output needs a variable. For this program, there are two inputs and one output. These variables need names and you need to determine the type of data stored in them. Let's say we were going to fence the backyard. We'd need to know the length and width, probably in feet, and the answer would also be given in feet. With a typical backyard, these numbers probably aren't very big. We'll keep it simple and expect the input in whole numbers. Short data types should do nicely. That gives us a range from 0 (we won't have negative numbers for this) to 32,767; 32,767 feet is about 6 miles so that should be more than large enough. We could use a Byte for this. That would give a range from 0 to 255. That would probably work for most backyards, but not all of them, and it probably wouldn't be large enough for a playground. The output will be larger than the input. You'll be multiplying the inputs so you have to make sure you leave plenty of room. If you used a Byte, the largest yard would be only a little more than 60 feet by 60 feet, or 240 = 2(60 + 60). That's not a very big yard and you want to make sure the variable is large enough to handle any possible problem. Again, it looks like a Short variable should work nicely. With that you could fence in an area about 1 mile wide and 2 miles long.

The names for the variables should be descriptive. The length and width could be just that. Remember the prefix for the data type and you'll get shoLength and shoWidth. Spaces aren't allowed and the capitalization makes them easier to read. The perimeter will be much the same. shoPerimeter is a good name. These will be added to the code at the right time.

The processing line is just about written once you know the variables. You know the formula so it's just a matter of plugging variables into the assignment statement and remembering the rules. Always tell the computer where to put the answer before you tell it how to find the answer. Equals means "gets" for an assignment statement. You have to include the multiplication (*) sign. It should look like this:

```
shoPerimeter = 2*(shoLength + shoWidth)
```

Of course, if you used a different data type or a different name for any of the variables, your names would be slightly different.

With the inputs and outputs defined and a good handle on the variables and the processing, the next step is to create a form. Start VB and create a new solution. You can name it Perimeter and save it on your hard drive. If needed, refer to Chapter 1 for how to create a program.

The form needs two inputs, one for length and the other for width. Use a TextBox for each of them. It will need one output, the perimeter. A Label works for that. The Text property of the TextBoxes and Labels is used to send and receive data with the variables. We'll need a Button to do the work. That's where we'll write the code. It should have an Exit Button so the user can end the program. There will be code in that as well. There should also be several Labels to, well, label things. A good program is designed to make it easier for the user. This is a simple program, so we'll keep the interface simple as well.

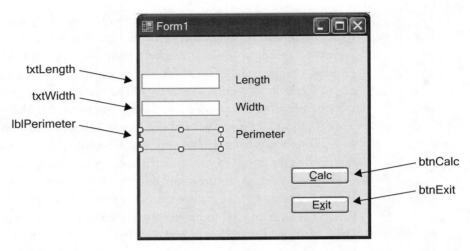

Figure 2.3   Perimeter Form

What the form could look like is shown in Figure 2.3.

Chapter 1 gave you the basics for adding controls to the form. Each control on the form needs a name. Add the controls and arrange them as needed. It is good practice to add the control to a form and then name it right away. Naming a control should always be one of the first things you do when you place it on a form. Name the controls as shown. Remember that each control should have a name that describes it and it should have a prefix that tells you what type of control it is. Spaces aren't allowed. Then change the text property of the controls as needed. For some you'll enter text to describe the control.

Now is a good time to save your program.

Let's do the easy part first. Double-click on the Exit utton. The code window opens. Enter End where the cursor is flashing. Don't change anything else. It should look like this once you've typed it in:

```
Private Sub btnExit_Click(ByVal ...
    End
End Sub
```

Switch back to your form. If you run your program at this point, the Exit Button should work, but not the Calc Button. That's because there's no code in the Calc Button. The Exit Button runs just fine when you click on it, though. Let's get the Calc Button working.

Double-click on the Calc Button on your form. If you click on this Button while your program is running, it will execute the code you're about to write. That's the idea. Put your code in the click event of the Calc Button. Here's how it works.

The declarations come first. These are the Dim statements where you declare your variables and reserve memory to store your data. Type in the following:

```
Dim shoLength As Short
Dim shoWidth As Short
Dim shoPerimeter As Short
```

That's all you need for the declarations section. Next comes the input section, which is where you'll get the user's input from the TextBoxes and store it in variables for processing. It looks like this:

```
shoLength = txtLength.Text
shoWidth = txtWidth.Text
```

This is the input section of your code. The first line takes what's in the Text property of the txtLength TextBox and puts it into shoLength. The second line takes what's in the Text property of the txtWidth TextBox and puts it into shoWidth. As long as the user types in a number, you'll be fine. If they type in something else, there'll be problems; but let's proceed one step at a time. Later, you'll learn how to handle the problem of a user providing bad input.

Next comes processing. It's where you do the calculation for the program. Type in

```
shoPerimeter = 2*(shoLength + shoWidth)
```

This will take what was just stored in shoLength and shoWidth, add the values together, multiply it by 2, and put the answer in shoPerimeter. It's as if the computer found the answer and wrote it on a slip of paper and put it into the shoPerimeter container.

The last section is output. You need to get the answer out of the variable and onto the form so the user can see it. The answer is stored in shoPerimeter. Figuratively, you need to look at the slip of paper in the shoPerimeter container to see what's on it. You then need to take that number and put it on the form. Use a Label on the form to display it. The one created for that purpose is called lblPerimeter and the answer needs to go into the Text property so it can be seen. The .ToString that comes at the end converts the number into a string so it can be displayed properly. You'll learn more about the ToString method later so don't worry about it now. The line of code looks like this:

```
lblPerimeter.Text = shoPerimeter.ToString
```

That should do it. If there aren't any squiggly blue lines, you probably have it. If there are, you'll need to check for mistakes. The squiggly blue lines indicate something the computer doesn't understand. It's a bug and bugs are the enemy. That's your program in short, simple lines of code. There's more that can be

Table 2.5   Perimeter Program Deskcheck

Code	shoLength	shoWidth	shoPerimeter
Declarations	0	0	0
shoLength = txtLength.Text	100	0	0
shoWidth = txtWidth.Text	100	50	0
shoPerimeter = 2*(shoLength + shoWidth)	100	50	300

done with it, but, at this point, you need to walk before you run. And speaking of run, you should be able to run your program at this time.

Manually Testing Your Code – The Deskcheck

VB Quip   *To understand a program, you must become both the machine and the program. – A. Perlis*

Once you've written your code, it's a good idea to walk through the program one line at a time to make sure what you've written will work. This is called a *deskcheck*. It's also a good idea to do this so you can see just how the computer handles code. What the computer does and what the programmer thinks the computer should do might be two very different things. At this stage of programming, the odds are pretty good that you'll see things differently than the computer. Try your best, but the computer will win on this. You have to play by the computer's rules and write all of your code so the computer understands it. It's something akin to ordering a meal in a fancy French restaurant. The waiter, the snobby type, insists that you order in French. Being the snobby type, he probably understands English, but he will insist you use French, nonetheless. You need to know enough of the language to be able to order a meal. Mess up and you'll get raw snails instead of escargot – that's just how it works. Programming is the same way. You need to know enough to get the computer to do your bidding. If it's not done correctly, or in the right order, you'll go hungry.

A deskcheck is a line-by-line check of your code. When the computer expects input, you supply it. You take it a line at a time and write down all the changes to your variables. The deskcheck is an excellent way to learn exactly what the computer is doing with any line of your code. Create a column for each variable and constant and keep track of the current values for each. As each line of code is executed, update the values. A deskcheck for the Perimeter program is shown in Table 2.5.

We expect the user to enter two numbers; for this example we'll use 100 in the length TextBox and 50 in the width TextBox, and then click on the Calc Button. At this point, the code in the Calc Button takes over. The variables are declared and automatically assigned 0. That's the first line of the deskcheck. The variable columns have been updated to reflect the values now stored in them. The next line takes 100 from the Text property of the txtLength TextBox and assigns it to the shoLength variable. The next line takes 50 from the Text property of the txtWidth TextBox and assigns it to the shoWidth variable. The numbers in the TextBoxes haven't changed or been removed; the code merely takes those values and copies them to the variables. The last line takes what is stored in shoLength and shoWidth, inserts those values in the formula, and calculates the answer for shoPerimeter. You can see how the value in the last column has changed from 0 to 300.

From a deskcheck you should be able to tell the value of any variable at any time during the program run. A deskcheck is invaluable for gaining an understanding of how a program runs and for seeing the results from each line of code.

Go With the Flow – A Graphic View of Your Code

VB Quip   *Weeks of programming can save you hours of planning. – Anonymous*

Ideally, a *flowchart* would be developed before you ever write a single line of code. It's part of the planning process and no self-respecting programmer would declare a variable without first designing a flowchart. However, this is just the start of programming and we can take some liberties with the process. Besides, it seems a little odd that you would have to learn how to design a flowchart before you can start learning how to program. In this case, we'll take the finished program and show you what the flowchart looks like. Later, you can develop flowcharts to see how a program should "flow" and that should make it easier to design and, later, write your programs.

Some of the common symbols used for flowcharts are shown in Figure 2.4. They provide a graphical roadmap for a program. The complete list is given in Appendix B.

The flowchart for the Perimeter program is shown in Figure 2.5.

The first symbol shows where the program starts. It's pretty obvious for this program, but longer, more complicated programs have more complicated flowcharts and need a clear starting point. No symbol indicates the declarations. The flowchart indicates what variables are needed for the program. The next two symbols indicate user input for the program. They could be combined into one, but this makes the process just a little clearer. The rectangle represents processing. This is where the calculation is done. In this case, the inputs (length and width) are transformed into the output (perimeter). The next step is output. The same symbol as input is used, but this one indicates that the perimeter should be displayed. The last symbol indicates the end of the program. All programs must have a way to end cleanly.

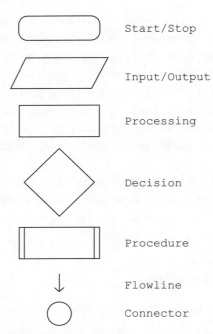

Symbol	Label
	Start/Stop
	Input/Output
	Processing
	Decision
	Procedure
	Flowline
	Connector

Figure 2.4   Flowchart Symbols

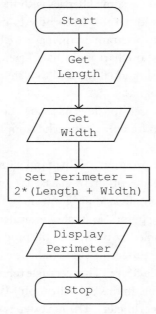

Figure 2.5   Perimeter Flowchart

Notice how the flowchart follows the process of input, processing, and output. Few programs stray from this basic path. Some flowcharts are precise and detailed and give a clear indication of program flow. Others are more general and only indicate the general steps to be taken. Programmers typically use flowcharts as a way to communicate their intent and the relationships within a program. Flowcharts are a roadmap. Some have great detail and others are short on specifics. The amount of detail depends, in part, on the level of understanding needed at the time, the concepts being conveyed, and the detail required to convey them. It is likely that you could write most of the programs in this book without needing a flowchart. It is also likely that you couldn't undertake a business programming project without one.

Potential Problems – A Few Things That Can Go (Horribly) Wrong

VB Quip   *Judgment comes from experience. Experience comes from poor judgment.*
– Robert E. Lee

So far you've been led along the primrose path. As long as you've followed directions (exactly), everything has worked. However, as anyone who has followed driving directions knows, if you're only following directions, you're just one wrong turn from being lost. So, what can go wrong? Just about everything. And some of the best programming lessons are only learned from making mistakes.

Names

Your names must match exactly. The names used for controls on your form must be exactly the same as the names in your code. If you want to get input from a TextBox, the name in the code must be the name you used on the form. The same is true for Labels. If you want to put output on the screen, the name you use in your code must be an exact match of the name you gave the Label on the form. The variable names must be consistent throughout your code. Humans are great at inferring what was meant. Computers cannot do that; it has to be exactly right. Close only counts in horseshoes, hand grenades, and your best girlfriend. It doesn't count in programming.

Declarations

You need a variable for every input and output. At times you might need others as well; that depends on the program. You must make sure the variables are capable of storing any possible value you could put into them. Take a look at the potential values that need to be stored in the variable and make sure you have a data type that fits.

Input

The adage is "Garbage in, garbage out." If you provide bad or no input, you won't get any output. At runtime, the user must provide good inputs for the program. For this program, if you leave a TextBox blank or put in something other than a whole number, the program will crash. Try it and you'll see. That's part of the learning experience.

Processing

The largest part of a program is usually the processing. You'll spend more time writing this part of the code than any other part. It's where most of the mistakes happen, too. In this program, you may have written the wrong formula, in which case you might get an answer, but it wouldn't be the right answer. As a programmer, don't trust the computer. Check your answers. The order of your code is crucial. If you tried to do the processing before the input, your program wouldn't have worked. It wouldn't work if you tried to do the processing after the output. While it's natural for us to put the steps in the right order when we solve a problem on our own, it's much tougher to write the directions for the computer to do it. Most of the time we don't give much thought to the process. However, on the computer, the correct order and the right process are indispensable. As your programs get longer, you'll see how the order of the commands becomes crucial to their successful execution. Move the calculation above your input and see what happens. Try it with the processing written after the output. Change the formula and see what happens. You'll still get output, but it won't be correct.

Output

You might do everything correctly up to this point and still not get output. If you don't use the right variable name or if you put the answer in the wrong Label, you won't have output. If you try to do your output before you finished your calculations, it won't work. If your output is 0, odds are that there are problems with your calculation. If you don't get the answer you're expecting, check your math and check your formula.

VB Quiz 04   *Variables used for input are associated with what controls on a form?*
Variables used for output are associated with what controls on a form?
Why might a variable used for output have to be of a different type than a variable used for input?
What declarations, inputs, processing, and outputs are needed to calculate the area of a rectangle?

Second Verse – Same as the First

The BugSpray Program

The next program is very similar to the first program. For this one, you want a program that will let you enter the number of cans of bug spray you want to buy. A good programmer can never have enough bug spray. Bug spray is $2.95 a can. For now, we won't worry about getting the answer to display in dollars and cents.

First you need to determine the inputs and outputs for the program. Often it's easier to see the end result – the output – and then use that to determine what needs to go into the program. The output for this program is the cost of the bug spray. The input is the number of cans. This program will have one output and one input.

Next is the processing. If you were doing this by hand, almost without thinking, you'd know that the number of cans multiplied by the price would give you the cost. You know the user is going to enter the number of cans and the output will be the cost. The price could be an input, but the user would have to enter that. The description of the program says the price is 2.95. That's a perfect place to use a constant.

You need to determine the numbers of variables and constants for your program and determine their data types. You know there's one output, which requires a variable. There's one input; that's another variable. And the price is a constant. How many cans of bug spray are needed? It will be a positive number and it will be a whole number. You wouldn't buy a negative number of items and you couldn't buy half a can. So, how many are enough? For this program a Byte variable works for the number of cans. With that, you could buy up to 255 cans. A Short will work as well. With that, you could get thousands of cans at one time. The output will be in dollars and cents. For this you should use Decimal. Decimal is almost always used when currency is involved. For the price, use a constant. It, too, can be a Decimal.

BugSpray Flowchart

Now is a good time to develop the flowchart. It should provide a basic roadmap for developing your program (see Figure 2.6).

Remember, the flowchart should follow the standard form: declarations, input, processing, and output. The first symbol is the start; the last one is the end. In between, you want your declarations. In your delarations, you want to make sure you declare your variables and constant. Next comes input. You need one input/output symbol to get the number of cans into your program. Next is the processing rectangle, where you take the number of cans multiplied by the price to get the cost. There's just one output, the cost, for this program.

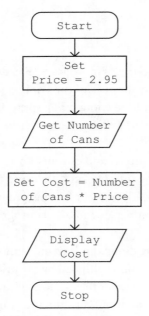

Figure 2.6   BugSpray Flowchart

You need one input/output symbol to show the cost being displayed in a Label on your form. That's it.

BugSpray Form

Next, determine what your form should look like. It needs one input for the number of cans of bug spray. Use a TextBox. You need one Label for the output. In that you'll put your output – the cost of the bug spray. You'll need one Button to end the program. You'll need another to calculate the cost of the bug spray. There should also be Labels to identify the controls on the form. Your form could be similar to the one shown in Figure 2.7.

Armed with your flowchart and a design for your form, you should now be able to create your program, design your form, write your code, and test your work.

Start VB and create a new solution. Name it BugSpray. You should get a blank form. Create and name the controls as shown in Figure 2.7. Be sure to change the text property of the Buttons to Exit and Cost. Save your form.

Once the form looks the way you want it, you're ready to write your code. Double-click on the Exit Button. Type in End. Don't change any of the other code. If you do, there could be problems.

BugSpray Code

Go back to the form and double-click on the Cost Button. This takes you to the code window and you'll be ready to type in your code. Do the declarations first,

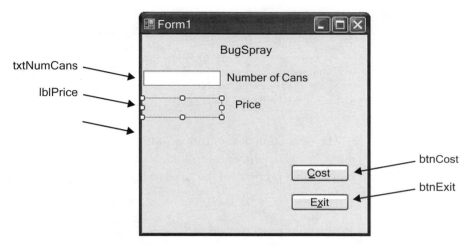

Figure 2.7   Names for the BugSpray Form

then your input, processing, and output. The flowchart should be your guide. If you want to try it on your own first, don't look ahead. Of course, if you're afraid of bugs, then by all means, follow along.

First, write your declarations. You want a variable for the number of cans, a variable for the cost, and a constant for the price. Follow the naming conventions. The following will work, but they aren't the only possible names that can be used.

```
Dim bytNumCans As Byte
Dim decCost As Decimal
Const decPrice As Decimal = 2.95
```

Don't use the dollar sign when you enter the price. If you get a squiggly blue line, check to see what's wrong.

Next is the input section. There's just one line of code for this, which will take what the user enters in the TextBox on the form and put it into the variable.

```
bytNumCans = txtNumCans.Text
```

Processing is next. There's just one line for this as well. Don't forget to tell it where to put the answer on the left side and how to find the answer on the right side.

```
decCost = bytNumCans * decPrice
```

You could have written this without the constant and simply put the 2.95 into the formula. It would work, but it's poor practice. It makes your code harder to change and harder to debug. Writing it correctly takes a little longer right now, but it's a good investment.

Table 2.6   BugSpray Program Deskcheck

Code	bytNumCans	decPrice	decCost
Declarations	0	2.95	0
bytNumCans = txtNumCans.Text	2	2.95	0
decCost = bytNumCans * decPrice	2	2.95	5.9

The last section of your code is output. You just need to take your answer and put it in a Label on your form. Here's the line of code. Notice how it must go into the Text property of the Label so it will show up on the form.

```
lblPrice.Text = decCost.ToString
```

Save your program and run it. See if the program works as it should. Enter the number of cans you want and click the Cost Button. If the answer is what you were expecting, then congratulations! Click the Exit Button to make sure it works. Try the program again with several other numbers to see if the results are right. Then try to crash it. See what happens with negative numbers, numbers with decimals, text, and a blank TextBox.

BugSpray Deskcheck

Now do a deskcheck of your code. Walk through the code line by line to see how it works. If you enter 2 for the number of cans of spray, it should look something like Table 2.6.

VB Quiz 05
> *Give other examples of where a flowchart is used.*
> *How is a major purchase similar to a program? Describe it in terms of declarations, input, processing, and output.*
> *A deskcheck is a dry run or a rehearsal. Where else are these used?*
> *How could you indicate the price of a can of bug spray to the user?*

On Your Own

Try writing a program on your own that determines miles per gallon. The user enters the number of miles driven and the number of gallons of gas used. From that, use the formula MPG = miles / gallons to determine the mileage. Before you start, you should be able to answer these questions:

How many inputs are needed?
How many outputs are needed?
How many lines of processing will you need?
How many variables are needed? How many constants?
What data types are needed for the variables?

How will division affect the data types needed for the program?

Which type of division will you do: /, \, or Mod?

What type of control is needed for input?

What type of control is needed for output?

Summary

This chapter introduced you to basics of binary, the fundamental method of handling data on a computer. It introduced variables and constants and showed you the basics of using them to write programs. It introduced flowcharts as an aid to design and deskchecks as an aid to understanding code.

Review

All computer operations are performed in binary, 0s and 1s.

Today's computers have huge memory capacities compared to that of older computers.

A single 0 or 1 on the computer is a bit. A series of eight bits is called a byte.

A storage container is a good analogy for the variables used in computer memory.

There are numerous data types, each with a specific use.

All variables must be declared before they can be used. Declarations are used to name and type a variable.

Variables and constants must all conform to VB naming conventions. Only letters, numbers, and underscores (_) can be used; the name must start with a letter; it cannot have spaces or use special characters; and it cannot be a keyword.

Programmers typically use additional naming conventions to make it easier to identify variables by using meaningful names, starting with a lower-case letter, capitalizing the first letter of each word, and using a prefix that describes the data type.

An assignment statement is used to change the value stored in a variable.

All numeric variables are automatically initialized to zero. All string variables are initialized to null.

All assignment statements assign to the variable on the left and calculate on the right.

The math symbols in VB are +, −, *, /, \, Mod, and ^. The asterisk is for multiplication, the slash does division, the backslash does division and returns only the integer part of the answer, Mod does division and returns only the remainder, and the circumflex is used for exponentiation.

Computer calculations must follow specific rules of precedence: do what's in parentheses first and work your way out; exponentiation is done before other operations; multiplication and division are next and are done from left to right; and addition and subtraction are next and are done from left to right.

Constants are used to store data that do not change while the program is running.

Programs follow the same general order: declarations, input, processing, and output.

Declarations are used to declare variables and constants. Input is used to get data from the user. Processing manipulates the data to find results. Output returns the results to the user.

Input comes from TextBoxes. Output goes to a Label.

A deskcheck is used to manually step through a program. As a value in a variable changes, it is noted in the deskcheck. From this process, the programmer gets a clear picture of how a program runs.

A flowchart is a graphical depiction of a program. It is used as an aid to develop programs and as a means to discuss a program with other programmers.

There are many potential problems with any program. The best way to understand a program is to run it and test it.

Terms

algorithm	a plan, roadmap, or structure for solving a problem; in programming, the structure used to plan the solution to a programming problem
ASCII	American Standard Code for Information Interchange – the standard representation for letters, numbers, and special characters on the computer; see Appendix A; see Unicode
assignment	a statement used to place a value into a variable; the drudgery teachers place on students in the hopes that they'll learn
bit	a *binary* dig*it* – a single 0 or 1 for the computer, a building block for a byte
bug	an error in computer code that prevents a program from working correctly; a logical or syntactic error that prevents a program from working correctly; bugs are nasty and evil and should be squashed
byte	a series of eight bits that can represent a single character of text or small numbers; when combined with other bytes it can represent larger numbers
constant	a storage location that is assigned a value when it is created; that value cannot be changed while the program is running
data	the facts and figures that are used in decision making, generally considered raw information

data type	a set of specific methods for storing data in a variable; each data type is designed to hold data of a particular structure; e.g., strings hold text, shorts hold small numbers, singles hold numbers with decimals
declaration	the process of creating a variable and determining the type of data it will store; variables are declared using a declaration
deskcheck	the manual process of checking each line of code and updating the values of the variables to determine if the program functions as it should; the manual processing of checking for and finding errors in a program
flowchart	a graphical depiction of a program, which shows input, processing, decisions, loops, and output for a program
initialize	the process of placing the first value into a variable or constant; numeric variables it automatically places a 0 in the variable; string variables are automatically initialized to null; other data types are initialized to other values
input	the process of getting data into the computer for processing; any data that are sent to the computer for processing; data added by the user to a program
modulus	number by which two given numbers can be divided and produce the same remainder
null	an empty set; string variables are initialized to null
output	the process of getting information from the computer to the user; the information sent by the computer to the user
processing	the method by which data are converted to information; the calculations and manipulations by which the computer finds answers
syntax	the required structure of a line of code
Unicode	a two-byte representation of characters on the computer; a much larger standard than ASCII
variable	a memory location for storing data; variables can be one of many different data types, each designed to store a specific type of data; programmers change the value of variables with assignment statements; a variable is declared with a Dim statement

Keywords

+	the operator for addition
−	the operator for subtraction; the symbol for a negative number
*	the operator for multiplication
/	the operator for division; the result returns a value that could include a decimal

\	the operator for integer division; the result returns a whole number
Const	short for constant; used to declare constants
Dim	short for Dimension; used to declare variables
Mod	modulus; the result returns an integer remainder of a division
String	a data type for storing characters of text
.ToString	a method that converts a numeric value to a string so it can be formatted and displayed or stored as text

Self-Check

1. A bit is smaller than a byte.
2. The letter "M" in binary is stored as 01001101 and so is the number 1001101. The only difference is how the computer handles these values.
3. All variables contain 0 until it's replaced with another value.
4. The value of a variable is assigned by the user.
5. The value of a constant is set by the developer.
6. A Short variable can store numbers with decimals, but not negative numbers, while a Decimal variable can store numbers with decimals but not negative numbers.
7. There's no difference between division using / and division using \.
8. A constant cannot be used to store the answer to a calculation.
9. A control and a variable cannot share the same name.
10. A flowchart is a graphical depiction of an algorithm.
11. A single 0 or 1 is a _____ while eight of them is a _____
    A. byte, bit
    B. byte, nibble
    C. bit, byte
    D. nibble, byte
12. The data type for a variable is determined when the variable is:
    A. first used
    B. declared
    C. assigned a value
    D. none of the above
13. Syntax is:
    A. the order of statements in a program
    B. the rules for writing a programming statement
    C. the plan for solving a programming problem
    D. a method for checking the accuracy of code
14. Which of the following would properly create a variable to store a company name?

     A. Dim strCompany As String

     B. Dim str Company Name As String

     C. Dim companyname As String

     D. Dim As String strCompanyName

15. Which of the following is not a valid variable name?

     A. strLocation

     B. numTotal

     C. decSalary

     D. shoWeight

16. A part number is 293459DSI049. What type of variable should be used to store it?

     A. Short

     B. Byte

     C. Decimal

     D. String

17. What factors should be considered when creating a variable to store your average for this class?

     A. The variable must be capable of storing numbers.

     B. The variable must be capable of storing numbers with decimals.

     C. The variable must be capable of storing negative numbers.

     D. More than one of the above.

18. What is the correct order for solving a mathematical problem in Visual Basic?

     A. parentheses, what's on the left, addition and subtraction, multiplication and division

     B. what's on the left, parentheses, multiplication and division, addition and subtraction

     C. parentheses, exponentiation, multiplication and division, addition and subtraction

     D. parentheses, exponentiation, addition and subtraction, multiplication and division

19. On a flowchart, processing is shown as:

     A. rectangle

     B. oval

     C. parallelogram

     D. circle

20. On a flowchart, a calculation is represented by:

     A. a circle

     B. an oval

     C. a rectangle

     D. an arrow

VB Quiz Answers

Quiz 01

Null is ASCII character 0. The space is ASCII character 32. Convert ASCII 0 to binary and you get 0000 0000. Convert ASCII 32 to binary and you get 0100 0000. The only difference between them is the second bit.

Boxes, baskets, or cans could be used. There are other possibilities as well as long as the containers are easy to visualize and can be of different sizes.

Quiz 02

A phone number isn't used for math so there's no real reason to store it as a number. It has a hyphen it in. Numbers don't have hyphens in the middle of them and numeric variables can't handle them. It might have parentheses around the area code. Those won't work in numeric variables. Sometimes, a phone number is listed with letters instead of the numbers. For example 888 TOO MUCH. Some have started listing their number with a period instead of a hyphen, 555.1212. A variable needs to be able to handle any of these and a string is the only one that will work.

An address probably has text in it so a numeric variable won't work. A string is the only answer.

```
Dim strMovie as String = "'It's a Wonderful Life'"
```

Quiz 03

The assignment is on the wrong side. It should read

```
shoTotal = shoNum + shoNum2
```

There's no reason to have a mathematical equation for this. You could simply assign 40 to shoNum.

You cannot use quotes for this. Either make the variable a string or simply assign 4.99 to decPrice.

This should probably be written as shoSide + shoSide. This would find the volume of a cube.

Quiz 04

Variables that are used to store input from the user must get their input from a handful of controls on the form. So far, you've seen this process used with the TextBox. There are numerous others that will be used later.

Labels are used to display information from output variables. There are others that can be used and they will be introduced later.

Sometimes the result will be much larger than the input. A larger data type might be needed. Many times the result will have a decimal, but the input is an integer. The BugSpray program is a good example because the price of a can is a decimal while the input is a whole number. The result is a decimal. A test average is another example: the scores could be integers, but the average, because of division, would likely be a single.

You would need to declare variables to store the input and output. The input would be the length and width. The output would be the area. The processing would be area = length * width.

Quiz 05

There are many instances where a set of procedures is used. Many are in the form of a flowchart and many aren't. CPR has an established set of procedures. Changing a tire has a procedure and your owner's manual has pretty pictures showing how to do it. NASA has a set of procedures for launching a shuttle. There are many office procedures that are typically followed. College admissions are usually handled through an established process. In government class, you probably learned the procedures for how a bill becomes law – yet another procedure. If there was a diagram for the process, it was in the form of a flowchart.

Let's say you were going to buy a car. You would know how much money you have and the price of the car; both would be variables. You'd need to find out what the monthly payments would be. That would mean more declarations. The input would be price of the car, the length of the car loan, and the interest rate for a car loan. The processing would be the calculations, the amount owed after the down payment, and the monthly payments. The output would be the purchase price minus the down payment and the monthly payment.

A home loan would be very similar.

A dry run could be for almost any process. You simply walk through the steps to see if it works or if you've made a mistake in the process. Any rehearsal is similar to a deskcheck. You go through the process step by step to see if it works. A wedding rehearsal is a good example and rehearsals for a play are another. Almost any formal occasion requires such practice and testing. Graduation is a good example.

It should be indicated on the form. It should be in a Label and clearly indicate it is the price.

3

Writing Programs – First You Walk, Then You Run

I really hate this darn machine;
I wish that they would sell it.
It won't do what I want it to,
but only what I tell it. – Programmer's Lament

Think of a program as a play and you're the director. The actors are the controls and the code is your script. It's up to you to bring all of them together to make it work. Most actors can get the words right and learn to hit their marks, but there's far more to it than just memorizing lines and taking cues. As a developer you have to make your program – your play – flow and get all the parts to work together.

Most programs follow the same general path: declarations, input, processing, and output. That helps, but the hard part is getting a human to understand how the computer works. Usually, this understanding comes only from practice. To become a good programmer, you must write programs. To write good programs, you often must write lots of code. And the more code you write, the more mistakes you'll make. Mistakes are a good thing, though. Often, especially in programming, mistakes are a great way to learn. Just like a good director needs to rehearse lots of scenes and try them in many ways, a programmer has to learn what works and what doesn't. In programming, mistakes can be your ally. "OK, this worked, but what if I try this?" "What happens if . . . ?"

This chapter focuses on writing programs. You'll gain a greater understanding of how the parts fit together to make a whole. And, you'll get lots of practice. Some of it will be to make things work. Some of it will be to see how things don't work. You'll learn more about the programming environment and how to dress up your programs. When you complete the chapter, you should be able to write simple programs on your own.

Following IPO

IPO, declarations, input, processing, and output is the general sequence of a computer program. The programs in this chapter all follow this general structure.

For every program, you need the right controls – the actors for your melodrama. You must declare variables; that is, you'll have to cast the right data type for the right role. Every program needs input – something from the user. It then takes that input and processes it, often in a mathematical calculation. The results are the answers or what a developer calls output. Following the play analogy, every control is an actor and every actor is acted upon by events. In a play, these events are often a crisis or a predicament, but nothing so dramatic for the computer. In a program, these events are the click of a mouse or the press of a key. In a play, they change the actor, making them better or worse and changing the audience by changing their outlook. In a program they change the properties of a control or change the value of a variable and produce output in the end. Just like a play sets up a situation, introduces change, and brings about results, so will your programs. You determine the controls, their settings and what changes (calculations) will be made. Your output is the resolution. Just like a play, a program has a beginning, middle, and end.

Getting Things to Work Together

The key to a program is to understand what controls and variables can do and then to make them do it. Each has a particular strength and specific part to play. Each fills a particular role.

Controls

Controls are stored in the Toolbox. Each control has a specific purpose. Some are used for input, some for output. Some are containers that make your work easier. So far, you've seen TextBoxes; these are used for input. There are many others that can do input as well. You've used Labels for output and there are others that are even more useful. Buttons are used for your code, but any control can contain code.

Each control has properties. By changing these properties you can control them. The user also has limited control over some of the properties of a control. At runtime, for example, the user can change the text property of a TextBox.

Think of controls as nouns. They are the persons, places, and things for your program.

Properties

Properties describe a control. They determine what it looks like and how it behaves. The properties of a control can be changed at design time by changing a setting in the Properties window. They can also be changed at runtime when a line of code changes a property.

Think of properties as adjectives. Adjectives describe a noun. So the properties of a control help to describe the control. Change a property on a control, and you change the way it looks or works.

Events

An *event* is something that happens while a program is running. You've seen a click event, but there are literally hundreds of events in a program. Luckily, you'll only need to learn a few now, and a few more as you go. Most of them are pretty easy to understand and all of them have utility. An event can trigger some code. In your first programs, a click event on a Button triggered the code in that Button. For now, almost all of your code will be triggered by a click event.

Think of events as verbs. These are actions. Verbs make things happen to nouns so events act on the nouns – the controls – in your program.

Variables

Variables are created by the developer. As you saw in Chapter 2, there are many types. While they cannot create variable types, developers can create variables from any existing type. Variables are different from controls in that most controls can be seen on a form and the user can interact with them. Variables cannot be seen on the form and the user cannot interact with them. Controls have properties that can be changed at design time or during runtime. Variables have values that can only be changed at runtime. As a developer, you're free to assign values at design time, but the variables are created in memory at runtime and their values change only while a program is running. We'll see more on that later.

Code

Code is everything. Without it, nothing happens in your program. User input goes unnoticed, there are no calculations, and there's no output. Your code makes all of that happen. As a developer, you must make sure the code you write is positioned in the right place in your program. When your design calls for the code to run when a Button is clicked, then that code must be placed in the click event for that Button. At runtime, a user's click on the Button runs that code. As a developer, you must know what you want to happen and when it should happen.

VB Quiz 01

If a program is like a play, who are the actors and what is the script?
Describe the Perimeter program from Chapter 2 in terms of nouns, verbs, and adjectives.

Commenting Your Code

VB Quip   *All programmers are playwrights and all computers are lousy actors. – Anonymous*

Developers often write comments into their code. Comments explain and describe the code. They might explain a particular line or describe what happens in a long procedure. During development, they might be notes or reminders. Comments are essential to a good program. A fair amount of programming involves debugging and adding features to an existing program. Comments are extremely helpful, especially when it's been six months since you last looked at that piece of code. Furthermore, good comments are really helpful for the next developer. Odds are that you won't be fixing and updating the same code forever. You'll move on to other projects and a new developer will be stuck fixing your mistakes. Or think of it another way: you'll move on to write and maintain code that was originally developed by someone else and you'll really appreciate the comments they left behind!

To set a comment in your code, simply start the line with an apostrophe ('). Everything that comes after that apostrophe becomes a comment for your code. It doesn't affect your program. It won't slow it down and it won't make your finished program larger. Comments show up as green text in your code.

Comments should be used to explain or describe your code. They can also be the internal documentation for it. Some developers are happy with little or no commenting. Some write extensive comments to help explain their code.

Prologue

A prologue is a set of comments at the beginning of a program that describe that program. It should include the developer, the company, the name of the project, the development dates, the version, the files used, and a general description of what the program does. A prologue can have more or less than that and it varies depending on company policy. For your work, it might include the class, section, date and time, instructor, and other descriptions.

A sample prologue might look like this:

```
'Your Name
'Class
'Class day and time
'Instructor
'Description of the program
```

Formatting Your Output

So far your output has been plain. When an answer needed to be displayed, it just showed up in the Label in whatever form the computer generated. There

Table 3.1   Format Specifiers for Displaying Output

Format Specifier	Name	Description
c	currency	Displays the number with a dollar sign Includes commas as needed Negative numbers are in parentheses Defaults to two decimal places
e	scientific	Displays one digit to the left and six digits to the right followed
	notation	By e and a three-digit integer expressing the exponent of a Power of 10 Negative numbers have a minus sign
f	fixed-point	Indicates the number of decimal places to include Negative numbers start with a minus sign
n	number	Displays numbers with commas and fixed decimals Negative numbers start with a minus sign
p	percent	Displays the number with a trailing percent sign Multiplies the number by 100 before displaying it Negative numbers start with a minus sign

hasn't been a format for it. Usually a number requires formatting, dollar signs, percent signs, commas, and decimal places to make it look right and easy to read. Formatting a number is easy and makes use of the .ToString method. Simply add the formatting instructions at the end of it. For example, if you wanted your output formatted to currency, simply add ("c") to the end of the .ToString, e.g. decPrice.ToString("c"). The ("c") tells the computer to format the number with a dollar sign at the beginning, cents at the end, and commas where needed. If you wanted to display a percentage you could use ("p") to put the percent sign at the end. You can prescribe the number of decimal places by adding a number inside the quotes like this: sngGrade.ToString("p2"). The number will be formatted with two decimal places and a percent sign. The letter is not case-sensitive so you could use either c or C. The content in the parentheses is called an argument. That means it contains some code in one of several possible values. You'll see more arguments as you learn how to code (see Tables 3.1 and 3.2).

VB Tip   *Run Prog03.01 FormattingOutput to see how to format numbers.*

Errors in Your Program

VB Quip   *Computers are good at following instructions, but not at reading your mind. – D. Knuth*

Even the best programs have errors in them. Every program you've written so far is just one mistake away from crashing. At this level, errors are expected. As a developer and a user, you can control most of the problems just by being careful.

Table 3.2   Formatted Output Examples

1234.56	decPrice.ToString("c")	$1,234.56
−876543.21	decDeficit.ToString("c0")	($876,543)
123.456	sngSize.ToString("e")	1.234560e+002
−9876.543	sngDepth.ToString("e")	−9.876543e+003
3.14159	dblDistance.ToString("f3")	3.142
−345.6789	sngDiff.ToString("f2")	−345.68
54321.098	sngAverage.ToString("n")	54,321.10
12345.6789	sngRemainder.ToString("n3")	12,345.679
0.406	sngBattingAvg.ToString("p3")	40.600 %
0.845	sngGrade.ToString("p")	84.50 %

Users in the real world won't be so forgiving. For now, we don't worry too much about some types of errors. We'll simply make sure that we run the program in controlled circumstances. Later, you'll see several ways to bug-proof your code.

Programming errors fall into three general categories: syntax, logical, and runtime. *Syntax errors* are spelling or usage errors in your code. The computer doesn't understand what you've written. *Logical errors* are errors in your thinking. The computer understands the commands, but the "what to do" or "how to do them" is different than what you were expecting. *Runtime errors* are problems that crash a program. A mistake in the code or its execution causes the program to fail.

Syntax

Syntax errors are spelling or grammatical errors in your code. The computer doesn't understand what you've written. Maybe you wrote Dum instead of Dim – that's a syntax error. Maybe the statement was written incorrectly with the contents out of order or a quotation mark, comma, or parenthesis missing or out of order. When that happens, VB underlines the offending text with a squiggly, blue line. It's often called the "blue line of death." A program will not run if it has a syntax error.

VB catches syntax errors. You'll see the blue lines under the code and VB expects you to correct the problem. It will provide a message, but that might only provide a little help. Sometimes the mistake is obvious, sometimes it's not, and sometimes the mistake is even in a different place. Some errors are easy enough to catch and some are more difficult. With practice, it becomes easier to spot them. Sometimes the best help is to have someone else look at your code.

Logical

Logical errors are errors in your thinking. The syntax of the code is correct, but what the program does or how it does it is incorrect. Earlier you learned that programs do input, processing, and output, in that order. A logical error would be writing code that did output before the input or processing. Another logical error would be a mistake in a mathematical calculation, for example, adding instead of subtracting.

VB will not catch logical errors. It won't know if you really wanted to add those numbers instead of subtracting them. It won't know that you did your output before your processing. You might figure it out when your total comes out to zero, though. Logical errors are harder to correct. Fortunately, there are techniques that will help you avoid them and methods to help you correct them.

Runtime

Runtime errors are problems that cause the program to crash. Right now you can crash your programs just by leaving a TextBox empty. The program expects the user to enter a number in the TextBox and, when it's empty, the program can't handle it, gives up, and crashes. There are ways to avoid runtime errors as well. Later you'll learn some of them, but for now, we'll just expect you to be careful.

Debugging Practice

Let's try some debugging practice. The idea is to find the errors in the code, fix them, and get the program to work.

Syntax Errors

Open Prog03.02 Syntax Errors to practice finding and fixing syntax errors in a program. The program calculates and displays the cost, sales tax, and total for umbrellas. You must find and fix the syntax errors in the code. Be careful. The blue line of death indicates a syntax error in the code, but the error isn't always in the code that's underlined. Point to the underlined word. A little tool tip window will appear with a description of the error. Sometimes that is very helpful in fixing the problem.

```
'Declarations
Constant sngSalesTaxRate As Single = 0.05
Const decPrice As Decimal = 4.95
Dim shoNumItems As Short
Dim decSubtotal As Decimal
Dimm decSalesTax As Decimal
Dim decTotal As Decimal

'Input
shoNumItems = txtNum
```

```
'Processing
shoNumItems * decPrice = decSubtotal
decSalesTax = decSubtotal * sngSalesTaxRate
decTotal = decSubtotal + decSalesTax

'Output
lblSubtotal.Text = decSubtotal.ToString("c")
lblSalesTax.Text = decSalesTax.ToString("c")
decTotal.ToString("c") = lblTotal.Text
```

Point to the word Constant. The tip says "Name 'Constant' is not declared." For this you want Const instead of Constant. The second line of code has the correct spelling. Wonder of wonders, it also fixes the other two "errors" in that line. It's a good example of how VB handles syntax errors. It didn't understand the first part of the code and assumed there were other problems in the line as well. Take heart, though. It did recognize the error.

The next blue squiggly is in the word Dimm. That should be an easy fix. Change it to Dim. Again, that swats two bugs with one fix.

The next error is tougher. The tip provides a long, cryptic message about being unable to convert to Short. That's no help. Take a look at the line of code and decide what the code is supposed to do. It's input, so it's probably set up to get input from the user and store it as a variable. It looks like it should be taking txtNum and assigning it to shoNumItems. But what part of txtNum? There's the problem and it's a common mistake. You want to take the Text property of txtNum and put it in the variable. So, it should read txtNum.Text. Make the change and the error disappears. Tuck that nugget away for future use.

The next error is in the processing section. Point to shoNumItems and the tip says "Expression is not a method." That sounds more like a fortune cookie than an error message. Point to the asterisk and it says "Expression expected." Neither is much help and they seem to contradict each other. Consider the purpose of the line. It's an assignment statement so it should multiply the number of items by the price. The problem is that the expression is backward. You always have to tell it where to store the answer before you calculate the answer. This line tries to do the math and then store the answer. The syntax error is that the expression is backward. Rewrite it so it says decSubtotal = shoNumItems * decPrice

That fixes the error. Tuck that nugget away as well. Always tell it where to store the answer before you do the calculation.

The output section also has a syntax error. Point to it and you'll see another cryptic message. This is output, so it should display the answer on the screen. There's the problem: it's trying to take what's in the Label and put it in the variable. It should be written the other way around. Remember what's on the right always gets assigned to what's on the left. For this one, the Label should be on the left and the variable should be on the right. It's a common mistake.

Change this line so it looks like the other lines of output, with the variable on the right being assigned to the Text property of the Label on the left.

There's just one more error but you won't find it until you run the program. When you click on the Exit Button, it doesn't work. Click on the X in the title bar to end the program and then check the code in the Exit Button. There's the problem. There's a comment in front of the End command. Remove the apostrophe and the Button now works. There's a completed version of the program in case you had trouble finding the errors.

Logical Errors

Logical errors are tougher to find and fix. You have to understand what the program is supposed to do in addition to what it's doing wrong. Open the program called Account Balance to practice finding and fixing logical errors in a program. The program takes the beginning account balance, adds deposits, subtracts withdrawals, and displays the ending balance for an account. The syntax for the code is correct, but the logic of the program is wrong.

```
Private Sub btnExit_Click(ByVal sender As System.Object,
ByVal e As System.EventArgs) Handles btnExit.Click

    'Declarations
    Dim decBeginningBalance As Decimal
    Dim decEndingBalance As Decimal
    Dim decDeposits As Decimal
    Dim decWithdrawals As Decimal

    'Input
    decBeginningBalance = txtDeposits.Text
    decDeposits = txtBeginningBalance.Text
    decWithdrawals = txtWithdrawals.Text

    'Output
    lblEndingBalance.Text = decEndingBalance.ToString("c")

    'Processing
    decBeginningBalance = decEndingBalance - decDeposits +
        decWithdrawals
End Sub
Private Sub btnBalance_Click(ByVal sender As System.Object,
    ByVal e As System.EventArgs) Handles btnBalance.Click
    End
End Sub
```

Run the program and enter numbers for the beginning balance, deposits, and withdrawals. Click on the Balance Button. The program quits. Check the code for that Button. It says End – that's the first logical error. The code for the Balance Button is in the wrong place. Cut the code from the Exit Button and put it in the Balance Button. Be careful to get the just the code and not the Private Sub line or the End Sub line. Then put End in the procedure for the Exit Button. That should fix the first bug.

Run the program again and enter numbers into the TextBoxes. Click the Balance Button. It displays an ending balance. Odds are you weren't expecting an ending balance of $0.00. When you get 0 for an answer that usually means there's a calculation error. Many times it means that the answer was never calculated. Let's go to the code. Checking the comments you see that IPO wasn't followed. The declarations are there, but the input, processing, and output are in the wrong order. Change the output and the processing lines so that the output is below the processing. Run the program again and you'll probably get a balance other than zero. There are still errors, but at least you now have input, processing, and output in the correct order.

This might be a good time for a deskcheck. Go through the code line by line to see what the program does. This is a good way to compare what the program actually does compared to what you think it should do. It might help you spot the next error. Look at the input section. The number assigned to the beginning balance actually comes out of the TextBox for deposits. That must be changed. The number assigned to the deposits comes from the beginning balance TextBox. These two were written incorrectly and should be exchanged. Do that. It leads to an important point. You must be careful when naming your controls and variables. This error was easy to spot because the names were descriptive. A good trick is use the same name to name the TextBox and the variable associated with it. The only difference between the names is the prefix. That way you can match them up. Output can be handled the same way. Use the same description for the output variable and the Label. They'll differ by the prefix, but it will be easier to remember the names and to keep them straight.

Run the program again. It still comes up with $0.00 for the output. You know you fixed a bug before, but it didn't seem to help. Check the names of the TextBoxes. Sometimes the developer gets careless and puts the TextBoxes in the wrong place. That's not the case here, but it can happen.

Now it's time to do an *audit*. An audit is when you work backward through the code. The last line says to take decEndingBalance and display it in the Label. How did decEndingBalance get its value? Look backward in the code until you see decEndingBalance on the left side of an assignment statement. That's when its value was assigned. There's the error! It was never assigned a value. If you check backward you'll get all the way to the declarations without seeing a value assigned to it. And, remember, when it was declared, it was automatically assigned 0.

So, you must find where decEndingBalance should have been assigned a value. That should have happened in processing. When you check your processing code, you find the problem. Instead of assigning the balance to decEndingBalance, the formula put it in decBeginningBalance. Change that line so that the answer is assigned to decEndingBalance and try it again.

The answer still doesn't work out to what you were expecting. Now check the formula itself. To find the ending balance, you should take the beginning balance, add the deposit, and subtract the withdrawals. The formula says to take the ending balance, subtract the deposits, and add the withdrawals. Change the formula so that it's correct. On the right side of the assignment statement, you'll need to change decEndingBalance to decBeginningBalance. Change the minus sign to a plus sign and change the plus sign to a minus sign. It should look like this:

```
decEndingBalance = decBeginningBalance + decDeposits -
decWithdrawals
```

Try it again to see if it works. Check it a couple of times to make sure. When debugging a program, it's a good idea to make a change and then test it. That way you'll know if you're making the problem better or worse.

VB Quiz 02   *When and how should you use comments?*

Why should your output be formatted?

How could a logical error cause a runtime error?

How could a user error cause a runtime error?

Why can't the computer catch a logical error?

Controlling Your Controls

Controls are the visual part of a program. They're what the user sees while the program is running. In Chapter 2 you were introduced to a few of the properties for controls such as the Visible and Enabled properties. These "dress up" the way a program looks and makes the computing experience better for the user. Additionally, they make a program look more professional. Later you'll be introduced to controls that the user can't see, but for now we'll work with a few that directly affect the user's computing experience. The properties for a control can be changed at design time and they can be modified at runtime. Either way, the goal is to make the computing experience better for the user, even if it means more work for a developer. Remember, the interface is how the user interacts with the computer. The easier the interface is to work with, the better their computing experience. The extra development time invested by a developer is recouped by saving time and effort for hundreds, thousands, or even millions of users.

Controlling Forms

VBTip   *Use the Controlling Your Controls program to work through this next section. Controlling Your Controls Finished is the finished version. Use that as a reference if needed.*

There are a number of properties to control a form. Open the Controlling Your Controls program to work through this next section.

The Text property of a form controls the text that appears in the title bar of the form. Change the Text property to Controlling Your Controls.

The StartPosition determines where the form appears on the screen at runtime. The default is WindowsDefaultLocation, but change it to CenterScreen so it's in the center of the screen at runtime.

Next change the Minimize and Maximize Buttons to False. The default is True. When False, they disappear and the user cannot minimize or maximize the form.

The Size property controls the size of the form. The default is 300 pixels by 300 pixels and it's shown as 300, 300. The first number controls the width and the second number controls the height. The plus sign next to the property name lets you expand that property. When it's expanded, you can see the Width and Height settings. Change the Width to 500 and the Height to 400.

The Icon property lets the developer place an icon in the title bar. When the program is minimized, the icon will show up in the Taskbar as well. To place an icon in the title bar, click on the Icon property. That will display an ellipsis icon, that little . . . in Windows that indicates there's a dialog box available. Click on the icon and the dialog appears. Navigate through the folders to find the .ico file you want. For this example find the lighton.ico file in the project folder. That places the icon in the title bar. You can also open and edit icon files in Visual Studio. This is a handy little feature for creating your own icons. The ShowIcon property can be set to True or False to hide or show the icon. The default is True, but check it to make sure your icon will be displayed.

The BackColor controls the background color of the form. Control is the default color, a light gray. Feel free to select other colors. Be careful! Some colors aren't meant to be mixed. And while you might find certain colors pleasing, the color of your controls will probably be decided by company policy or the end user. It's your job to satisfy their needs, not to create your own eye candy (see Fig. 3.1).

The FormBorderStyle determines the appearance and border style of the form. The default is Sizable, which lets the user resize the form and move it around

Figure 3.1   Icon Editor

the screen. Set it to Fixed3D to lock the size of the window. Other settings will work as well; feel free to test them.

Controlling TextBoxes

TextBoxes provide a way for the user to enter data into the computer, but they can also be used for output. Simply change the ReadOnly property to True and the text in the TextBox is locked.

You can change the TextAlign property from the default setting of Left to either Center or Right. Changing it to Right is a handy feature when you're expecting numbers in a TextBox. That way the numbers appear on the right-hand side of the TextBox. Change the TextAlign property of the txtStudyGuide to right.

You can customize TextBoxes to help control user input. This makes it faster and easier for the user and easier for a developer. The AutoCompleteCustom-Source property can contain a collection of items. This collection can be set by the developer and will pop up when the user starts entering data into the TextBox. The txtTime TextBox has this. It contains a list of class times. The AutoCompleteMode is set to Suggest. When the user starts typing, it suggests items for the TextBox. The AutoCompleteSource property is set to Custom-Source. Together these help control user input and suggest faster and easier ways for entering data. Modify the txtClass TextBox to accept several different class names. Be sure change all three properties.

Most controls have a TabIndex. The TabIndex is a number that controls the tab order for controls. The user can then use the Tab key to move from one control to another. The TabIndex is set automatically as you add new controls to a form. The first item has an index of 0 and the rest are numbered in order from there as they're added. You can always change the order to suit your needs.

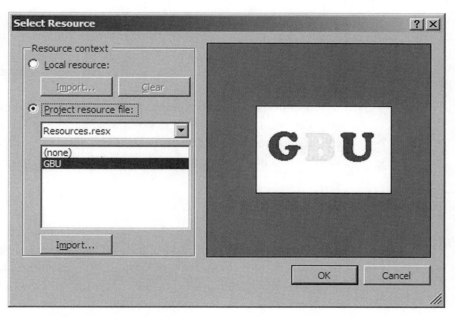

Figure 3.2   Image Selector

For this example change the TabIndex of the TextBoxes to 0, 1, and 2 so that the user can tab through them easily. The TabIndex of other items will automatically adjust as needed.

You can view the tab order by selecting Tab Order from the View menu. A small number indicating the tab order pops up over each control. To increase the tab order, simply click on that control. Select View, then Tab Order, to hide the numbers when you're finished.

You can clear the text from a TextBox by using the Clear() method for it. When used, it removes all the text from the TextBox. So, to clear the text from a TextBox called txtName, you'd write txtName.Clear().

VB Tip   *Geek Counting. TabIndex is just another example of VB starting a numbered list with 0. Get used to it.*

There are many more examples of numbered lists starting with zero. By rights, the first chapter of this text should have been Chapter00!

Controlling Pictures

Use the PictureBox control to display pictures on a form. The image property controls the image that can be displayed. Click on it and then click on the ellipsis button to select a picture. Choose Import and then choose a picture for the control. There are several pictures in the solution folder. Select one of them (see Figure 3.2).

The graphic displays in the PictureBox, however, only part of it shows up. Change the SizeMode property from Normal to AutoSize. This automatically sets the size of the PictureBox to the size of the graphic.

PictureBoxes have a Visible property just like Labels. You can control them in the same way.

You can create your own graphics files by using any painting program. The graphics in this example are 150 pixels wide and 100 pixels tall. Feel create to create your own and add them to the form. Graphics files are automatically saved as part of the form.

Controlling Labels

You've already worked with the Enabled and Visible properties for Labels. Labels have a BackColor property just like forms. They also share a ForeColor property that controls the color the the text. Select the Class, Section, and Time Labels and change the ForeColor property. You can change the BackColor for the Labels and the form as well. Try your school colors to see how they look.

You'll want to set the AutoSize property to False. When True, it resizes the Label to fit the text in it. In development, a Label is often empty and waiting to be filled with output at runtime. With AutoSize set to True, the Label is small and difficult to locate and adjust. Simply get into the habit of setting AutoSize to True and manually adjusting the size of the Label.

The TextAlign property for a Label determines the relative placement of text in a Label. Click on it and you get a popup with nine options ranging from TopLeft to BottomRight. Text can be left-aligned, but numbers should be right-aligned when possible. Headings should be centered. Set the TextAlign property for the lblCostStudyGuides to TopRight.

There's no Clear method for Labels like there is for TextBoxes. Instead use the ResetText() method. To remove the text from a Label called txtAnswer, you'd use txtAnswer.ResetText().

Controlling Buttons

You can set a shortcut key for a Button by adding the ampersand (&) to the Text property of the Button. Place it in front of the character that you want as the shortcut. In this example, add the & in front of the C in the Text property. It should read &Calc. Set the Text property of btnExit to E&xit. That will make the x key the shortcut. At runtime, Alt-C will calculate, just like a click on the Button. Alt-x becomes the shortcut for btnExit.

VB Tip   *If you wanted the ampersand in the Text property of a Button, then use two of them,*
&&. So Save & Print would be written in the Text property as Save && Print.

Common Properties

Many controls share properties, so when you learn a property for one control, you're ready to use it on other types of controls. You can select several controls at once using click and drag. Just click and drag across them to select them. When selected, they'll all have handles. You can shift-click to select and deselect multiple items. You can use Select All in the Edit menu to select all the items on a form. That makes it easy to make the same change to several controls all at once.

You can nudge controls one pixel at a time by using the arrow keys. That helps to align them. As you drag items, Visual Studio helps to automatically align them. They drop in order if you get close to aligning them. The blue *proximity lines* that appear help to vertically and horizontally align items. The purple line will help to horizontally align text on your controls.

You can also use the Format menu to align items. The Align option has several options to let you align items. Select the TextBoxes and then use the Align option of the Format menu to align the left sizes of the TextBoxes.

You can also use the Format menu to control the size and spacing of items. Try it with Labels until you get them to align correctly.

Controls have a Locked property that can be used to lock them into position on a form. Once you have settled on a design for your form, simply choose Select All from the Edit menu and then set the Locked property to True. A small padlock will appear on the controls, indicating they're locked.

The Font property controls the font, size, and style of the font. It's a dialog similar to the dialog in other Windows programs so you should already be familiar with it. Use it to change the font, size, and style of your controls. Again, be careful with them. Your preferences may not appeal to everyone. Your best bet is to get feedback from the user during development and then stick with choices they like.

VB Quiz 03

What controls have a Text property?

Why is it important to create an interface that the user likes?

Why is consistency important when designing an interface? Use your knowledge of the properties of VB controls as an example.

Data Type Conversion

You've already been introduced to data type conversion. Whenever you use the .ToString method, you're converting a number to a String. Remember, text and numbers are stored differently in memory. Different types of numbers are also stored differently. Different data types come in different sizes and some data types can store decimals while others cannot. Recall, too, that some programs

Table 3.3   Data Type Conversions

Type	Syntax	Description
Byte	bytNum = Convert.ToByte(txtNum.Text)	Converts the String into a Byte
Short	shoNum = Convert.ToInt16(txtNum.Text)	Converts the String into a Short
Integer	intNum = Convert.ToInt32(txtNum.Text)	Converts the String into an Integer
Long	lngNum = Convert.ToInt64(txtNum.Text)	Converts the String into a Long
Single	sngNum = Convert.ToSingle(txtNum.Text)	Converts the String into a Single
Double	dblNum = Convert.ToDouble(txtNum.Text)	Converts the String into a Double
Decimal	decNum = Convert.ToDecimal(txtNum.Text)	Converts the String into a Decimal

have TextBoxes that expect the user to enter a number and, if the user doesn't, it crashes the program.

To make matters worse, you simply cannot drop one type of data into the variable for another type without the risk of a runtime error. Fortunately, there are type-conversion functions built into VB. These do the hard work of converting one type to another. You still must be cautious to avoid trying to squeeze a Double into a Single or a Long into a Short. Some will fit and others won't.

So far, you've used TextBoxes for input. That input has included text and numbers. The Text property of a TextBox stores these characters as a string. Sometimes you must convert these strings into numbers. We've safely ignored this so far, but it's time to take another step forward. When you want your input to be treated as a number you should convert it and store it as a number. It's a little more work, but it will improve the quality of your programs. Of course, if the characters cannot be converted to a number, then it won't work, but we'll deal with that problem later.

VB Tip   *Think of the Convert class as the opposite of .ToString. Instead of turning a number into a String, it turns a String into a number.*

To change a string of characters into a number, use the *Convert* class. Think of a *class* as a definition. For this the Convert class defines our numbers. There are numerous ways to convert a String into a number, one for each numeric data type (see Table 3.3).

Each one converts a number into a specific data type. To convert to a Short, you'd use the ToInt16 method. It might seem strange, but it's really saying to convert it to a number that's stored in 16 bits. Recall that 16 bits is 2 bytes and that Shorts take up two bytes of memory. The conversion to Integer and Long are similar and now they're much less confusing.

You should use these to convert your input into a number before using it. In controlled circumstances this can be ignored and you'll write and run many programs that don't follow this standard. Bear in mind that, in the real world,

Table 3.4   Jim Soxx Pricing Structure

Footballs	$44.95
Basketballs	$49.95
Volleyballs	$39.95

this conversion is an expectation and you wouldn't dare turn a program loose in the wild without such bulletproofing.

VB Tip   *Run the Data Type Conversion program to see how data types are converted.*

VB Quiz 04   *Why should a developer spend so much time creating an enjoyable and satisfying user experience when it would be faster and easier to create a simpler interface?*

Why can some data types be converted to another while the opposite isn't true?

Jim Soxx Sports Sales Program

Jim Soxx sells footballs, basketballs, and volleyballs. OK, it's not much of a business and he does it out of the back of his van, but he pays sales tax and the IRS is OK with it. His pricing structure is shown in Table 3.4.

The sales tax on all items is 5%.

You must develop an application that Jim can use to enter the number of each type of ball for a customer, find the total number of balls, calculate the cost of each item, the subtotal, the sales tax and the total. It must display these and the total number of items. The finished design should look like Figure 3.3.

The form should be centered on the screen, and the Minimize and Maximize buttons should be removed. The user should be able to tab from one item to the next. Lock the controls. The output should be formatted and the program should use good design and programming techniques.

Your first step is to define the problem. Then create a flowchart. The third step is to design the form. You can then code and test the program.

VB Tip   *Run the Jim Soxx Sports Sales Program to see what it looks like and how it works.*

Define the Problem

This program needs to get the number of footballs, basketballs, and volleyballs from the user. TextBoxes are fine for this process. It needs to calculate the cost of all the footballs and display it. It needs to do the same for the basketballs and volleyballs. These three costs then must be totaled. This becomes the subtotal used to calculate the sales tax. The sales tax rate is 5%. The subtotal and the sales tax are added together to calculate the total. In addition, the program must calculate the total number of items. It must display the cost for each type of ball, the subtotal, the sales tax, the total cost, and the number of items. Use a

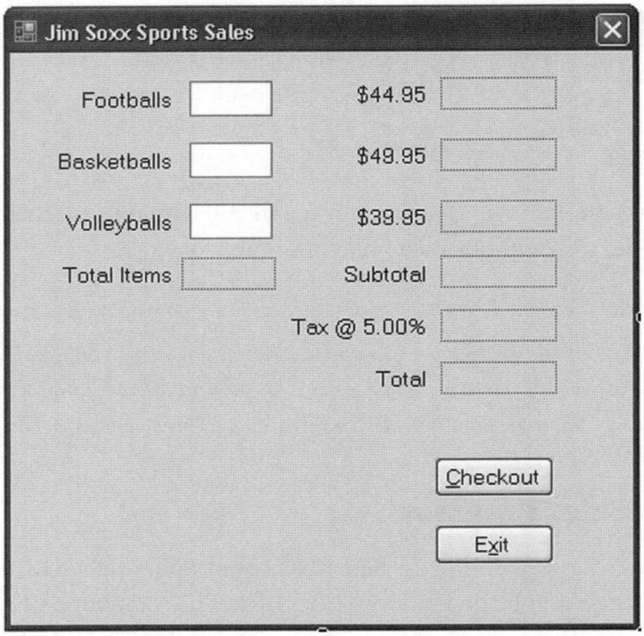

Figure 3.3   Jim Soxx Form

Button for the calculation and Labels for the output. Another Button should end the program. From the definition, most of the code will be written for just one Button.

There are several constants for this program. The prices for the items can be a constant, as can the sales tax rate.

You'll need a variable for each input. Because there are three types of balls, you'll need a variable for each. These can be Integers, because you can't sell half a ball. Any integer data type will work for this. Remember, he sells them from the back of his van so customers probably won't buy very many at a time.

You'll need a variable for each output. One is for the total number of items. This will be a whole number so use a data type that stores only whole numbers. Any integer data type will work. The ones containing dollar amounts should be declared as Decimal. There are six of these: one each for the subtotal for footballs, basketballs, and volleyballs; one for the subtotal of all the balls; one for the sales tax; and the other for the total cost.

Calculate the cost of the footballs by multiplying the number of footballs by their price. Calculate the cost of the basketballs by multiplying the number of basketballs by their price. Calculate the cost of the volleyballs by multiplying the number of volleyballs by their price. The subtotal is the sum of these three numbers. The sales tax is 5% of the subtotal. The total is the subtotal plus the sales tax. Be careful not to confuse the sales tax rate (5%) with the amount of sales tax, which is a dollar amount added to the cost of their purchase. Calculate the total number of items be adding the number of items together.

If you're keeping track, and you should be, there are three inputs, seven calculations, and seven outputs for this program. You'll need four constants and ten variables.

Create the Flowchart

The next step in your design is to create a flowchart to graphically show your understanding of the program. It may seem like a waste of time, but it's good practice and it does provide you with a framework for programming tasks. Even the best developers use a flowchart to show program flow. Display your input first and your output last. The calculations must be ordered so be careful with them. Calculate the cost of each ball first. Then add these to get the subtotal. You cannot calculate the sales tax until you know the subtotal. Once you have the sales tax, you can add the subtotal and the sales tax to find the total. The total number of items can be calculated anywhere in processing.

Your completed flowchart could look like Figure 3.4.

Design the Form

There are three inputs, seven outputs, and two Buttons for this program. Generally, the form should be clean and neat with the components neatly arranged and aligned. For this program, the three inputs should be TextBoxes arranged near the top of the form. Each should have a Label near it to identify it. The outputs should be arranged in a way that makes sense. For this program, they can be arranged like an invoice. Each output should be labeled to make it easy to identify. The Buttons should be aligned and the names should indicate their functions.

The names for the controls are partly a matter of taste and mainly a matter of practicality. Follow the naming conventions. It might seem like a hassle, but it will save you confusion in the long run. The Labels used to identify the controls don't need a name. As a general rule, if a control is only used for cosmetic reasons, it doesn't need a name. Although it isn't required, it certainly helps if the control names are similar to the variable names. For example, the TextBox for the number of footballs could be named txtNumFootballs. The variable used with it could be shoNumFootballs. That way it's easy to see that the two belong together, it's easier to remember their names, and the names indicate what they are and how they're used. Of course, you'd follow the same guidelines for the basketball and volleyball TextBoxes.

The Labels should indicate their purpose. For example, the Label that displays the subtotal for the footballs could be lblSubtotalFootballs. The lbl prefix

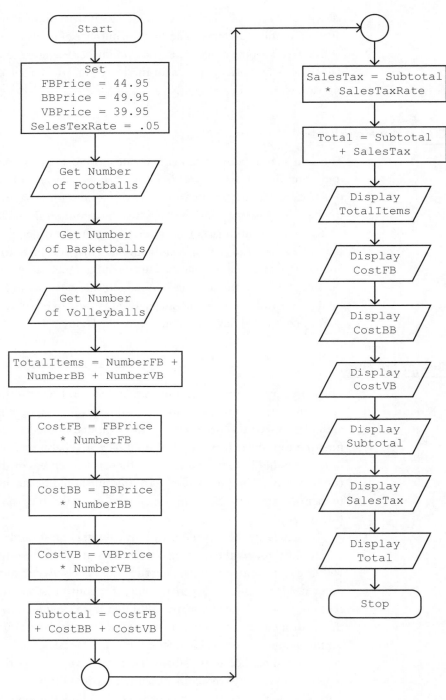

Figure 3.4   Jim Soxx Flowchart

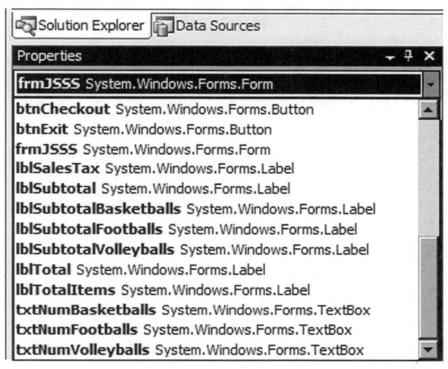

Figure 3.5   Jim Soxx Control Names

indicates it's a Label and Labels are for output. SubtotalFootballs indicates it's for the cost of the footballs. The name of the variable that goes with it could be decSubtotalFootballs. The dec prefix indicates it's a decimal variable and it's easy to see that the two belong together. Similar names could be used for the basketball and volleyball subtotals.

The subtotal should indicate that it's the subtotal for the items. lblSubtotal works well, lblSalesTax works for the sales tax, and lblTotal is fine for the total.

The Buttons could be named btnCheckout and btnExit.

Don't worry if the names are somewhat different from the ones you'd use. They don't have to match exactly and part of it is personal preference. Just keep in mind that a little planning can save you programming time later (see Figure 3.5).

Code the Program

The code falls into four general categories: declarations, input, processing, and output. The code doesn't have to be written from the top down. Sometimes that works; sometimes it's easier to skip around. The flowchart should be your guide for coding. The first box in the flowchart indicates that constants must be set for the prices of the balls and the sales tax rate. Here is the code for it:

```
'Declarations
Const decPriceFootballs As Decimal = 44.95
Const decPriceBasketballs As Decimal = 49.95
Const decPriceVolleyballs As Decimal = 39.9
Const sngSalesTaxRate As Single = 0.05
```

The declarations for the input variables are next. Input variables are used for input. They store user input from TextBoxes. Typically, variable declarations aren't displayed in a flowchart.

```
Dim shoNumFootballs As Short
Dim shoNumBasketballs As Short
Dim shoNumVolleyballs As Short
```

The total number of items is declared next.

```
Dim shoTotalItems As Short
```

The output variables are next. They are used to store the values used in the output part of the program. These are declared as decimals because the output needs to be in currency. The names are similar to the Labels on the form.

```
Dim decSubtotalFootballs As Decimal
Dim decSubtotalBasketballs As Decimal
Dim decSubtotalVolleyballs As Decimal
Dim decSubtotal As Decimal
Dim decSalesTax As Decimal
Dim decTotal As Decimal
```

The next three symbols indicate the input for the program. The input/output symbols and the word Get indicates that user input is gathered. The code for these gets the values entered by the user at runtime and stores them in a variable for processing. The values are converted from text into Short variables at this time.

```
'Input
shoNumFootballs = Convert.ToInt16(txtNumFootballs.Text)
shoNumBasketballs = Convert.ToInt16(txtNumBasketballs.Text)
shoNumVolleyballs = Convert.ToInt16(txtNumVolleyballs.Text)
```

The next seven symbols are for processing. There's no input or output for these. The rectangles indicate that values are being assigned with assignment statements. The first line indicates the number of balls purchased. This could have been done at any time during processing because it doesn't depend on other calculations. If the flowchart is accurate, then the coding for the processing should go smoothly. Part of the design process is to understand the requirements of the program. When a developer understands the requirements, the flowchart becomes the roadmap for solving the problem.

```
'Processing
'Find total number of items
shoTotalItems = shoNumFootballs + shoNumBasketballs +
   shoNumVolleyballs
```

The rest of the processing is dependent on the flow of the program. The subtotal for each type of ball must be determined before the subtotal can be calculated. If you were writing this invoice by hand, you'd do that automatically. The same is true for your program.

```
'Calculate cost of each item
decSubtotalFootballs = shoNumFootballs * decPriceFootballs
decSubtotalBasketballs = shoNumBasketballs * decPrice-
Basketballs
decSubtotalVolleyballs = shoNumVolleyballs *
decPriceVolleyballs
```

Once these subtotals are known, the next step is to calculate the subtotal of all the balls.

```
'Calculate subtotal
decSubtotal = decSubtotalFootballs + decSubtotalBasketballs +
   decSubtotalVolleyballs
```

Once you have the subtotal, you can calculate the sales tax. Sales tax is the subtotal multiplied by the sales tax rate.

```
'Calculate Sales Tax
decSalesTax = decSubtotal * sngSalesTaxRate
```

Once the amount of the sales tax has been determined, the total for the purchase can be calculated. The total is the subtotal plus the sales tax.

```
'Calculate Total
decTotal = decSubtotal + decSalesTax
```

The rest of the flowchart is for output. The exact order doesn't matter, but programmers typically keep these in a logical order to improve readability and debugging. Each is assigned to the text property of a Label and is formatted as needed to provide an attractive display.

```
'Output
lblTotalItems.Text = shoTotalItems.ToString("n0")
lblSubtotalFootballs.Text = decSubtotalFootballs
   .ToString("c2")
```

```
lblSubtotalBasketballs.Text = decSubtotalBasketballs
  .ToString("c2")
lblSubtotalVolleyballs.Text = decSubtotalVolleyballs
  .ToString("c2")
lblSubtotal.Text = decSubtotal.ToString("c2")
lblSalesTax.Text = decSalesTax.ToString("c2")
lblTotal.Text = decTotal.ToString("c2")
```

Deskcheck

Once the code is written, you should do a deskcheck and walk through the code. Put in a value for each input, do the processing, and track the changes in the variables. Check to make sure your output is what you expected. A spreadsheet works well for deskchecking. The deskcheck should help the developer visualize what the code is doing and it provides a quick check on the flow of the program.

VB Tip   *Open and inspect the JSSS.xls spreadsheet to see a deskcheck for the program.*

Test the Program

An essential part of programming is testing and the bigger the project, the more extensive the testing. In fact, testing might take almost as much time as any other part of the development process. For this program, the testing should be relatively easy. There aren't many calculations and the processing is straightforward.

Run the program to test it. Enter a 1 in each TextBox and click the Checkout Button. The total number of items should be 3. If it's not, there's a bug. The subtotal for each ball should be the same as the price. If it's not, there's a bug. Part of the reason to use 1 for each input is to make it easy to see if there's a bug. Check the subtotal to see if it's reasonable. If it is, then check the sales tax to see if it's 5% of the subtotal. The total should be the subtotal and tax added together.

Even if all of these are correct, don't assume that the program works. There are still many potential problems. Try the program again, this time putting in 1 for the number of footballs and 0 for the others. Check the output. Try it again with a 1 for basketballs and 0 for the others. Try it again with 1 volleyball and 0 for the others. If there are mistakes, this will help you find them. Now try it with larger numbers. The purpose of starting with 1 is to make it easy to check the math. Using 0 will flush out some mistakes associated with 0. Testing with larger numbers should help determine if it works properly and if the output will display properly. Of course, you should check the math for all of them.

Testing is essential. In 1999, NASA lost the Mars Climate Orbiter. The $125 million spacecraft crashed because one team of engineers used English units and another used metric units. Better testing might have found the error and prevented the crash of the spacecraft.

Potential Problems

The larger the project is, the greater the potential for problems. Misusing a variable or a control is a potential problem. For example, you could have used the same variable name twice. If you used shoNumFootballs twice in this line

```
shoTotalItems = shoNumFootballs + shoNumBasketballs +
    shoNumVolleyballs
```

it would have made it hard to find the error during your first run. However, it should have shown up when you tested the program by purchasing just one ball. You could have put the output in the wrong Label. The totals would have been correct, but the Labels would have been wrong. That might have gone unnoticed with 1 of each type of ball, but you should have picked up on it when buying just one ball. The calculations could be off. The only way to know is to test the program and check the math. For example, you might have confused the sales tax with the sales tax rate. It's a very common mistake. Care in the definition of the program and thoughtful selection of variable names would help. However, there's still the chance that you have named them correctly and then simply misused them in the code. Deskchecks and audits are a great way to catch problems with your code and your logic.

VB Quiz 05

What would it take to change the price of the balls?
What must be done if the sales tax rate is increased to 6%?
What must be done so Jim could sell soccer balls at $34.95?
What would it take to add a Clear Button to the program?

Open and Run

Open and run the following programs to make sure you understand how they work. The first finds the test average for a student. There are four tests in the class, including the final. The final counts double in the average.

The second program calculates the cost of clothing. Tom sells t-shirts, polos, and sweatshirts. The program should calculate the cost of each, the shipping, and the total for the order.

Average Program

Figure 3.6 shows the interface of the Average program.

```
'Declarations
Dim sngTest1 As Single
Dim sngTest2 As Single
```

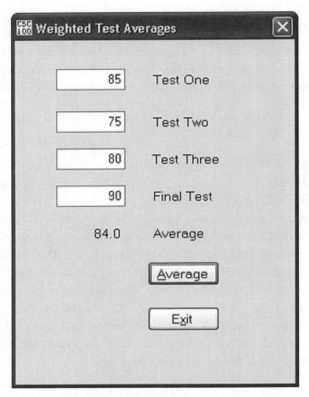

Figure 3.6   Weighted Test Average Form

```
Dim sngTest3 As Single
Dim sngFinalTest As Single
Dim sngTotal As Single
Dim sngAverage As Single

'Input
sngTest1 = Convert.ToSingle(txtTest1.Text)
sngTest2 = Convert.ToSingle(txtTest2.Text)
sngTest3 = Convert.ToSingle(txtTest3.Text)
sngFinalTest = Convert.ToSingle(txtFinalTest.Text)

'Processing
'Calculate Average
'Final Test is weighted double
sngTotal = sngTest1 + sngTest2 + sngTest3 + (sngFinalTest * 2)
sngAverage = sngTotal / 5

'Output
lblAverage.Text = sngAverage.ToString("n1")
```

The program has four inputs – the scores from the four tests. Six variables were declared. Four of them are used for test scores, one for the total of the scores, and the other for the average. The scores are converted from Strings in the TextBoxes to Singles for storage in the variables. Singles were chosen because the scores might have a decimal. There are two calculations in the processing section of the code. The first adds the scores from the four tests and counts the final twice. A Single data type was used for the variable because all the test scores are Singles. This could have been written a couple of different ways depending on how you wanted to do the math. The other calculation finds the average. The answer is stored as a Single because there's division in the formula. The answer might have a decimal, so the data type for the variable has to be able to handle it. These two statements could have been combined into something like this:

```
sngAverage = (sngTest1 + sngTest2 + sngTest3 +
    (sngFinalTest * 2))/5
```

That's an easy way to do it, it involves one less variable, and it saves a little processing time. It's a little more complicated to look at, but it's still a very workable solution.

VB Tip

Most of the time, the text will take the long route for making such calculations. It makes the math a little easier to understand, is a little closer to how most people think of the solutions, and makes for greater clarity. For those that have a good understanding of the math involved in a solution, by all means combine statements and save some of those electrons!

There's just one output for the program – the average. It's formatted to one decimal place. You can see how the program follows the declarations, input, processing, and output sequence. Most of the code must be in this order. Some of the input statements could be rearranged. It would still work, but it would make it a little harder to read and understand. Of course, the input must be done before the processing and the processing must precede the output.

T-Shirts Program

Figure 3.7 shows the T-shirts program interface.

The code for the btnBuy Button is as follows:

```
Const decTShirtPrice As Decimal = 10
Const decSweatshirtPrice As Decimal = 20
Const decPoloPrice As Decimal = 22
Const decShipping As Decimal = 1.25
Dim shoTShirt As Short
Dim shoSweatshirt As Short
Dim shoPolo As Short
```

Figure 3.7   Tom's T-Shirts Order Form

```
Dim decTShirtCost As Decimal
Dim decSweatshirtCost As Decimal
Dim decPoloCost As Decimal
Dim decSubtotal As Decimal
Dim decShippingCost As Decimal
Dim decTotal As Decimal

'Input
shoTShirt = txtTShirt.Text
shoSweatshirt = txtSweatshirt.Text
shoPolo = txtPolo.Text

'Processing
decTShirtCost = shoTShirt * decTShirtPrice
decSweatshirtCost = shoSweatshirt * decSweatshirtPrice
decPoloCost = shoPolo * decPoloPrice
decSubtotal = decTShirtCost + decSweatshirtCost +
  decPoloCost
decShippingCost = (shoTShirt + shoSweatshirt + shoPolo) *
  decShipping
decTotal = decSubtotal + decShippingCost
```

```
'Output
lblTShirtCost.Text = decTShirtCost.ToString("c")
lblSweatshirtCost.Text = decSweatshirtCost.ToString("c")
lblPoloCost.Text = decPoloCost.ToString("c")
lblSubtotal.Text = decSubtotal.ToString("c")
lblShipping.Text = decShippingCost.ToString("c")
lblTotal.Text = decTotal.ToString("c")
```

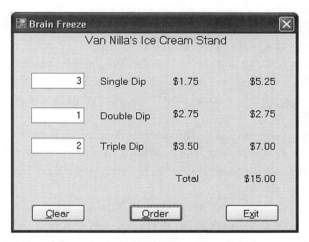

Figure 3.8   Van Nilla's Ice Cream Stand Form

The code for the btnClear Buttonis as follows:

```
txtTShirt.Clear()
txtSweatshirt.Clear()
txtPolo.Clear()
lblTShirtCost.ResetText()
lblSweatshirtCost.ResetText()
lblPoloCost.ResetText()
lblSubtotal.ResetText()
lblShipping.ResetText()
lblTotal.ResetText()
```

Fixing a Program – Van Nilla's Ice Cream Stand

Van Nilla runs a little ice cream stand that sells single, double, and triple cones for $1.75, $2.75, and $3.50, respectively. Van tried to write a little program to help calculate the cost of cones (see Figure 3.8). Unfortunately, he's better at scooping ice cream than he is at hacking code. He wants you to fix the bugs in his program.

Run the program and enter some numbers. Click the Order Button and it clears the Labels and TextBoxes – not a good sign. Try it again and the same thing happens. On the third try, click the Clear Button instead. Now it seems to work. However, you notice the numbers don't seem correct and the total displays 0 as a percentage. Mental note: check that in the code.

Now check the names of the controls. You'll see that the names are all OK, but txtDouble and txtTriple are in the wrong order. Rename them to fix that problem. The rest of the form looks OK.

Check the code. Sure enough it looks like the code for the Order and Clear Buttons was put in the wrong place. Cut and paste the code to put them in the correct place. Test the program. The Buttons now work better. The math still doesn't work and that percent sign is annoying.

Check the input and there's trouble. The input from the TextBoxes is wrong. It works, but the input goes to the wrong variables. Make the changes so the input goes to the correct variables. Mental note: meaningful names really pay off.

Test the program again. The numbers look good, but the total is 0. You check and the code seems right. The total is the sum of the costs of the single, double, and triple cones. Change the "p" to "c" in the last output line. Still no good, but at least it's now $0.00.

Work your way through the code. decTotal should contain the total cost of all cones. The code is correct, but it's in the wrong place. It adds them before the cost is calculated! You move that line of code to the end of processing, and the logical error fixed. High five! Fist bump!

You run it again and expect it to work. The total now works, but the numbers still aren't correct. Single and triple cones return the right answers, but double cones are wrong. Go back to the code for more bug hunting. Work your way backward through the code. The output is correct, the processing is correct, and so is the input. None of the names are wrong and everything looks right. Still, it comes up with the single price for a double cone. That's when you find it, the constant was set at 1.75 instead of 2.75. Test it again and it works. Moral dilemma: Either tell Van it was tough work so he'll give you free ice cream for a month or tell him it was just a couple of little things so he'll feel better and you'll still look like a programming wiz.

Mental note: Ask Van to barter ice cream for free VB tutoring.

VB Tip   *Open the corrected version of this program to see how it should look.*

On Your Own

Create a four-function calculator. Input should come from two TextBoxes. Output should go to a Label. The form should have separate Buttons for addition, subtraction, multiplication, and division, and an Exit Button. Each function Button should do input, processing, and output.

Create a program that calculates interest. The formula is $P(1 + r)^y$, where P is the principal, r is the interest rate, and y is the years. Principal, interest rate, and years are the input. The interest is the output.

Create a program to calculate the area of a triangle. Input should be the base and height. The output is the area. The formula is (base * height)/2.

Create a program to perform temperature conversion from Fahrenheit to Celsius. The formula is C = (F - 32)/1.8.

Create a program to calculate ticket sales for a theater. Childrens tickets are $5, adults are $8, and seniors are $6. Enter the number of tickets for each group. Find the total number of tickets, the total for each group, and the total sales.

Summary

This chapter tied together some programming techniques. You got a better picture of how the parts work together to create a program. Controls and properties were explained in greater detail. You were shown data conversion and formatting. You got your first, but not your last, look at programming errors and how to deal with them.

Review

Most programs do declarations, input, processing, and output, in that order.

Controls and variables each have specific uses in a program and both must work together to solve a problem.

Controls can be thought of as nouns.

Properties can be thought of as adjectives.

Events can be considered verbs.

Comments are used to explain and describe code.

Use an apostrophe at the beginning of a line to create a comment.

A prologue is a set of comments at the beginning of a program that describes the program.

Output can be formatted to make it easier to read and understand. To format output to currency use ("c") at the end of the .ToString method. e, f, n, and p can also be used for formatting.

The number of decimal places can be specified when formatting. Add a number to the argument to specify the number decimals to display.

An argument is one of several possible values used to write a section of code.

Programming errors fall into three categories: syntax errors, logical errors, and runtime errors.

Syntax errors are spelling or usage errors in your code.

Syntax errors are underlined with a squiggly, blue line.

Logical errors are differences in the way a developer understands the code and how the computer executes it.

Runtime errors are when a program crashes.

An audit is a backward trace through the code to locate and fix errors.

Developers are expected to create a program that is easy and enjoyable for the user.

Properties are used to control the appearance and function of controls.

Controls on a form can be aligned using proximity lines and the Format menu.

Type conversion converts one data type to another type. Data type conversion is typically used to convert Strings into a numeric format.

The Convert class is used to automatically convert between compatible data types.

Testing is an essential part of programming.

Terms

audit	in programming, the process of working backward through the code to find programming errors
class	a definition for an object
data type conversion	the conversion of data from one type to another; for example, the conversion of a String of text into a number
event	an action in a program; a click is an event for a Button. Events trigger code that makes changes to a program
logical errors	errors in the developer's thinking that make a program work differently than expected
proximity lines	blue and sometimes purple lines used to help align controls on a form
syntax	the correct structure of a line of code; syntax defines the rules of a programming language

Keywords

Convert	used to convert a value from one data type to another

Self-check

1. In general, the correct order for code in a program is input, processing, and then output.
2. Variables have properties but controls do not.

3. Comments should be used sparingly because they slow down a program.

4. Formatting determines the appearance of your output at runtime.

5. A program will run with syntax errors, but it cannot run with logical errors.

6. 18 stored as a String is equal to 18 stored as a Short.

7. The size of controls such as the Form, TextBoxes, Labels, and Buttons is measured in pixels.

8. Shortcut keys are set using the ampersand (&).

9. The ForeColor property controls the color of text in a Label.

10. Numbers that might contain decimals must always be declared as Strings.

11. The Toolbox contains all of the following except:
    A. Labels
    B. TextBoxes
    C. Properties
    D. Buttons

12. Which of the following is not an event?
    A. clicking the mouse on a Button
    B. entering text in a TextBox
    C. double-clicking the mouse
    D. calculating a value

13. Respectively, events, properties, and controls can be considered:
    A. verbs, adjectives, and nouns
    B. nouns, verbs, and adjectives
    C. adjectives, nouns, and verbs
    D. verbs, nouns, and adjectives

14. _____ text is a comment and _____ text is a keyword.
    A. Black, blue
    B. Red, green
    C. Green, blue
    D. Blue, green

15. A syntax error is similar to a:
    A. spelling error
    B. mathematical error
    C. organizational error
    D. judgment error

16. A line-by-line trace of the code to check the values assigned to variables is called a(n):
    A. deskcheck
    B. audit
    C. inspection
    D. flowchart

17. Data type conversion:
    A. changes the value in a variable from one data type to another

B. prevents a user from clicking in the wrong place

C. prevents the user from entering text when a number is needed

D. all of the above

18. The TabIndex property:

A. determines if the control has a tab stop

B. determines the tab order of controls on a form

C. determines if a control is visible

D. is determined solely by the order that controls are added to a form

19. Which of the following would convert a String to a Short?

A. Convert.ToShort(txtUnits.Text)

B. Convert.ToString(txtUnits.Text)

C. Convert.ToInt16(txtUnits.Text)

D. Convert(txtUnits.Text).ToShort

20. Which of the following is in order from smallest to largest?

A. Byte, Short, Long, Integer

B. Short, Long, Byte, Integer

C. Byte, Short, Integer, Long

D. Integer, Short, Long, Byte

VB Quiz Answers

Quiz 01

The actors are the controls for your program and the script is your code. In a play, the script determines what happens, just like the code determines what happens in a program.

The nouns in the program are the controls. In the Perimeter program they are the two TextBoxes used to input the width and height, the two Buttons to do the calculation and end the program, and the Labels used for output. The adjectives are the property settings for the controls. These settings determine the location, size, and contents of the controls. When the text property is changed, it changes the contents of these controls. The verbs are the click events for the Buttons. When a Button is clicked, it runs code and makes changes in the program. The click event acts on a Button just like a verb acts upon a noun.

Quiz 02

Comments should be used to explain major parts of a program, such as declarations, input, processing, and output. They should be used to explain complicated code. They can be used as reminders and notes. The prologue for a program is a series of comments that explains what the program does and serves as documentation for it. Not every line needs to be commented, but if something is confusing or obscure, then it should be commented.

Output is for the user and formatting helps explain your output. The purpose of a program is to make work (or play) easier for the user.

For example, forgetting to assign a value to a variable is a logical error. If that variable is then used as the dividend in a division program, it would cause a runtime error – division by zero – and crash the program.

If the user does something unexpected, it could crash the program. For example, let's say the user neglected to enter a number in a TextBox. That could cause the program to crash. It could also crash if the developer anticipated that the user would enter a number and the user entered text.

The computer has no intellect and doesn't recognize the illogical order of commands. If the syntax of the commands is correct, the computer assumes the logic of the commands is correct also. It's up to the user to put the commands in the correct order.

Quiz 03

Most controls have a Text property, including the form, TextBox, Button, and Label.

The user must work with the interface. If they find it cumbersome, it lessens the likelihood they'll use it, cause more errors and decrease productivity. The interface should enhance the user experience instead of being an obstacle.

Consistency makes it easier for the user to learn and use other controls. By knowing how to use the Font property of one control, it is easy to transfer that knowledge to other controls in VB. The Locked property was easy to learn and use because it was consistently applied for all controls. You should strive for the same consistency and ease of use in your programs.

Quiz 04

Developers spend more time creating an interface so it can actually save the user time and trouble. The extra time spent in development leads to a better program, a more satisfied user, and cost savings in the long run.

Some data types can store all the possible numbers from another data type, but the reverse isn't true. For example, Bytes are Integers from 0 to 255. Shorts have a range from −32,768 to 32,767. So, any number that's a Byte can also be stored as a Short. The opposite isn't true, though. All the negative numbers and numbers greater than 255 will not fit into a Byte. Think of them as different-sized containers. The contents of Byte easily fits into Short, but there's not enough room in Byte for everything from Short. Yes, that really bites. Pardon the pun.

Quiz 05

The prices are declared as constants in the code. To change a price, a developer must find that line of code and then change the price.

To change the sales tax rate, simply find that constant and change the rate. If all the constants are created at the top of your code, they'll be easy to find and easy to change.

The form would need to be redesigned to handle soccer balls. Some of the controls would need to be moved to make room for new controls for soccer balls. The code would need to be changed. A constant would be needed to hold the price. You would need a variable for the number of soccer balls and the subtotal for them. You would need to change the line of code that determined the total number of balls. You'd need to change the line of code that determined the subtotal for all the balls. Also, he may need a bigger van.

First, you would need to determine what to clear on the form. For this program, the TextBoxes and output Labels would need to be cleared. Add a Button and name it, btnClear. Change the Text property to &Clear. In the code for the Button, adds lines that would clear the text property for the TextBoxes and the Labels used in output.

4

Writing Programs II – More Controls and New Logic

VB Quip

All programmers are optimists. Perhaps this modern sorcery especially attracts those who believe in happy endings and fairy godmothers. Perhaps the hundreds of nitty frustrations drive away all but those who habitually focus on the end goal.

Perhaps it is merely that computers are young, programmers are younger, and the young are always optimists. But however the selection process works, the result is indisputable: "This time it will surely run" or "I just found the last bug."   —*Fred Brooks*

Programming is all about making the user happy. As a developer, your mission is to produce a product that fulfills a need for the user and makes them want to use your program. The easier you can make their computing experience, the better. That's a double-edged sword. Often, it's easier to make a program work than it is to keep the user happy. And, the more you try to please the ubiquitous end user, the harder it is for you as a developer. It's often said, "This whole software development thing would be a whole lot easier if it wasn't for all those end users." While that may seem true, the computer industry wouldn't be where it is today without end users. They buy programs to make their work faster and easier and their fun more enjoyable. They're demanding, fussy, stubborn, and every year they spend billions on what works.

This chapter expands your knowledge of variables and their use. You'll get a taste of methods. The ones you'll see right now are similar to functions in Excel. You'll learn a few new controls that will make your programs more user-friendly. And you'll learn how to do string manipulation. Think of it as math for text.

Variable Scope

So far all the variables you've used have been created, used, and discarded all within a procedure. That's great and often that's enough. But, there are times when you want a variable to store a value for longer than that. There are times when you want a variable that will work in more than one procedure. That's where the *scope* of the variable becomes important.

The scope of a variable is controlled by where it's declared and how it's declared. When a variable is declared in a procedure, such as what you've done so far in the click events for your Buttons, the variable is *local* in scope. It can only be used in that Button. When a variable is declared at the *module* level, it can be used in any procedure on the form.

VB Tip   *The scope of a constant can be managed as well. Its visibility depends on where it is declared.*

Local Variables

All the variables you have used up to this point have been local variables. They are only used in the place where they are declared. So far, that's worked well, but it has its limits. Local variables are used for values that are only needed for a short time. That saves memory and simplifies some of the processing. With local variables, the Dim statement creates the variable and initializes it. It is then assigned a value and used somewhere in your click event. The variable is discarded as soon as the event is over. Every time you click on the Button, the variable is declared again. Although it might seem like a waste, it really isn't. The computer hangs on to it only as long as it's needed. People do the same thing all the time. They'll look up a phone number and remember it only long enough to dial it or find a page number in the index and remember it just long enough to turn to that page. How much was your last utility bill? Odds are you remembered the amount only long enough to pay the bill. What was the score of the game last week? What movie got the Oscar for best picture last year? What was the name of your second grade teacher? Each of these is similar to the scope of a variable. Depending on your need to remember them, you'd create a variable that's capable of storing them for as long as needed.

Module Variables

Module-level variables store values as long as the form is being used. They're created when the form is created and persist until the form is closed. For right now, that means a module-level variable is created when your program loads and it sticks around until you close the program.

Module-level variables are created in the Declarations of your code. They'll work in any procedure on your form. You can use them in any Button on the form and their values are retained as long as you are running the program. That opens up some interesting possibilities.

To create a module-level variable simply move to the top of the code window and click on the line below Public Class. There are two drop-down boxes near

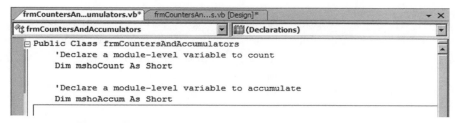

Figure 4.1   Module-Level Declarations

the top of the window. The one on the left has the class names in it. The one on the right has the method names. You can always select the form name on the class drop-down and Declarations on the method drop-down.

Declaring a module-level variable is similar to creating a local variable. Use the keyword Dim to create a variable. Start module-level variables with 'm' to indicate their scope, give the variable a meaningful name, and follow the naming conventions. Then give them a data type and initialize them if needed (see Figure 4.1).

VB Tip   *Constants can be declared at the module level as well.*

Module-level variables have the advantage of being visible anywhere on your form. The downside is that they're assigned memory as soon as the form is created and they hang around until the form is closed.

VB Tip   *Avoid using the same name for local variables and module-level variables. VB can handle it, but it's confusing. A safe practice is to always use 'm' at the start of a module-level variable.*

Counters and Accumulators

Counters and accumulators are two of the best uses for module-level numeric variables. They're the Swiss Army knives of variables – practical, easy to understand, and eminently useful. Counters keep count. You can use them to count the number of clicks, count the number of records processed, or to do a countdown. Generally, they count up (or down) by 1. *Accumulators* keep a running total. Use them to keep track of total points accumulated by a student throughout the semester or the total wages earned by employees. Generally, accumulators add a variable amount to a total.

Declare counters and accumulators at the module level. Do this in the declarations for your form. They can then be accessed by any procedure on the form.

VB Tip   *Run the CountersAndAccumulators program.*

Counters

Generally, counters add 1 to a total. You'll see them used throughout the rest of the text. Use an assignment statement to add to (or subtract from) a counter. In general, a counter looks like this:

```
count = count + 1
```

where count is a numeric variable.

That looks strange, and it is. In grade school you learned that you cannot add 1 to any value and still have that value. But this is programming, so the surreal is often the rule, not the exception. Don't look at that statement as an equality. count does not equal count + 1. This is an assignment statement where the value on the right is *assigned* to the variable on the left. The statement literally says, "Takes what's on the right and assign it to the variable on the left." It takes the value in count, adds 1 to it, and then puts it back into count. You've done that since you've been able to count. Put this statement in a Button and it will add 1 to the variable every time the Button is clicked.

Counters add by a set value so you could use them to add by 2s or 3s or 10s. They are also used to count backward. So, instead of +1 in the code, you'd use +2, or +3 or +10 or even −1. Every time the counter line executes, it changes the value of the variable by that amount.

Accumulators

Accumulators add a variable to a running total. You'll see these throughout the rest of the text. Use an assignment statement to add to a total. While a counter adds by a set amount, an accumulator adds the value from a variable. In general, an accumulator looks like this:

```
accum = accum + var
```

where accum is the accumulator and var is a numeric variable.

This looks just as strange and runs counter to what you learned in math class, but remember, it's an assignment statement. It says, "Take the value in accum, add to it the value in var, and then store it in accum." An accumulator statement does the math on the right side of the equals sign and then assigns the result to the variable on the left.

Counters and accumulators go together with module-level variables like chocolate and peanut butter. To work properly, the values in a counter or an accumulator must be persistent. That is, the values in them have to stick around in between uses. That's easily accomplished by declaring them in the Declarations section of your form. That way, they're created when the form is created and they won't be disposed of until the form is disposed. That's nearly perfect

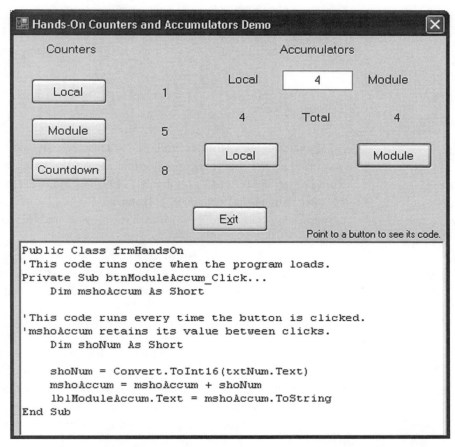

Figure 4.2   Counters and Accumulators Demo

for what we need right now. Variables Dimmed in a click event don't work as well for counters and accumulators. Their values don't persist between clicks.

Run the Hands-on Counters and Accumulators program to see how local and module-level variables work with counter and accumulators (see Figure 4.2).

VB Quiz 01   *When should local variables be used? When should module-level variables be used?*
When are local variables created and when are they destroyed?
When are module-level variables created and when are they destroyed?
How do counters and accumulators differ? How are they similar?
Explain how counters and accumulators work.

More Data Types

So far you've used several different data types. One type has been used for storing strings and the others have been used to store various sizes and types of numbers. That's great, but sometimes you need to store something other than strings and numbers. VB can store dates and times in a Date variable and can store logical data, a Boolean, as well. Both of them are handy, as you'll soon see.

Date

A *Date* variable stores the date and time as a number. The date is the integer part of a number and the time is the decimal part of the number. The date ranges from January 1, 0001, to December 31, 9999. The number 1, when converted to a Date, is January 1, 1900; 36892 is January 1, 2001. This makes it relatively easy to manipulate dates. Simply work with the number and then display the output as a date.

The time is the decimal part of the number. So, 36892.5 is noon on January 1, 2001; 36892.25 is 6:00 a.m. on New Years Day; and 36892.75 is 6:00 p.m. on that day. Any time, down to the fraction of a second, can be stored this way.

VB Tip

Run the DateTimeDemo program to see how it works.

The system clock on your computer has the current date and time. You can obtain the date and time from there and store them in variables. Then it's easy to manipulate them as needed for a program. Dates and times are formatted in any of several ways depending on your needs. You can display the entire date or time in one of several formats or extract a part of a date or time and use it as needed.

VB Quip

A man with a watch knows what time it is. A man with two watches is never sure. –Segal's Law

To declare a variable to store the date or time,

```
Dim datToday As Date
Dim datTime As Date
```

To get the current date and time from the system,

```
datToday = Now
datTime = Now
```

These are formatted to display as needed (see Table 4.1).

```
lblToday.Text = datToday.ToLongDateString
lblToday.Text = datToday.ToShortDateString
```

Table 4.1   Date and Time Formattings

Variable	Formatting	Displays
datToday	datToday.ToLongDateString	Friday, June 11, 2010
datToday	datToday.ToShortDateString	6/11/2010
datToday	datToday.Month.ToString	6
datToday	datToday.Day.ToString	11
datToday	datToday.Year.ToString	2010
datToday	datToday.DayOfWeek.ToString	Friday
datToday	datToday.ToLongTimeString	9:42:34 AM
datTime	datTime.ToShortTimeString	9:42 AM
datTime	datTime.Hour	9
datTime	datTime.Minute	42

You can assign a specific date to a variable, just like you can assign text to a string. The syntax is slightly different, but it still works. Use the crosshatch to enclose the date and use slashes to separate the units:

```
datToday = #09/26/1948#
```

The time can be assigned in much the same manner:

```
datTime = #9:42:34 AM#
```

And both can be assigned:

```
datRightNow = #09/26/2010 9:42:34 AM#
```

VB Tip   *Run the DateDiffDemo program to see how it works.*

Date and time are stored as numbers in a program. As such, dates and times can be compared. With a start date and an end date, you can calculate the time between dates. You can take a start date, add a fixed amount of time, and determine the maturity date for an investment. With a start time and an end time you can calculate the elapsed time. Use the *DateDiff* function for this. DateDiff can find the number of days between two dates. It can also determine the number of months, quarters, weeks, years, hours, minutes, or seconds. For the following example,

```
lngDaysPast = DateDiff(DateInterval.Day, datStart, datEnd)
```

the DateDiff function requires three *arguments*: the interval, the starting date, and the ending date. DateInterval.Day finds the number of days between datStart and datEnd. By changing the DateInterval to another unit, you can determine the difference in that unit. Using this you could calculate how old you are in days, hours, or minutes. You could determine payment dates for a loan or how many days until graduation. datStart is the starting date for the comparison and datEnd is the ending date.

Later in this chapter, you'll learn ways to enter dates and times into a program.

VB Tip   *Microsoft Excel uses the same scheme to store and manipulate dates and times.*

Boolean Data Type

The *Boolean* data type stores True or False. It's named for George Boole, a famous mathematician. He developed an algebraic system of logic in the mid-nineteenth century but hasn't done much since. A Boolean only stores True or False. It's black or white, on or off, yes or no; there's no gray area. Declare a Boolean data type like this:

```
Dim blnSwitchOn as Boolean
```

Boolean variables are assigned values like this:

```
blnSwitchOn = True
```

Booleans store and assign a true or false value. They'll come in handy in the next chapter.

VB Quip   *The opposite of a correct statement is a false statement. But the opposite of a profound truth may well be another profound truth. – Niels Bohr*

Methods

A *method* is a procedure contained in a class. A method may return a value. That's not much help is it? Methods simplify a process. For instance, they can take a complicated calculation and reduce it to a couple of inputs. You just used the DateDiff method. It took the complicated process of calculating the number of days between two dates and turned it into a manageable function. The list of methods is similar to the built-in functions in Excel.

Mathematical methods are contained in the System.Math class. You can use these with either System.Math or just Math. IntelliSense recognizes the Math class and brings up a list of available methods. Each method has a different list of arguments that must be completed. The arguments are placed in parentheses following the method and are separated by commas. The general form of a method is:

```
var = Math.Method(arg1,arg2 ...)
```

where var is the variable that stores the answer, Method is the method being used, and arg are the values needed to complete the calculation.

VB Tip   *Run the MethodsDemo program to see how methods work.*

What follows is a list of some of the more useful methods.

SqRt

SqRt finds the square root of a number. There's one argument for it – that is, it takes one number as its input.

var = Math.SqRt(num)

where var is the variable that stores the answer, Math.SqRt calls the square root method, and num is the number for which you want to find the square root.

Int

Int gets the integer part of a number. There's one argument for it, the number that you want to convert to an integer.

var = Int(num)

where var is the variable that stores the answer, Int is the method that gets the integer part of a number, and num is the number to be converted.

Rnd

Rnd is short for random. It's used to generate a random number. Random numbers are great. They can be used to randomly generate drone fighters for the latest version of "Alien Invaders" or to determine how much life force you get when you pick up a gamma pod. Random numbers are used to determine the cards that are dealt in any computer game or the number rolled for a die for any board game.

Rnd generates a random number greater or equal to 0 and less than 1. The range is 0 to .999999. That doesn't sound like much, but with a little math you can turn that into a random number for any range you want. It works like this:

var = Rnd()

where var is the variable that stores the answer and Rnd is the method that generates a random number greater than or equal to 0 and less than 1.

From there you can add to it to pick a range of numbers. Here's what to do if you want to get a random number from 1 to 10:

var = Rnd() * 10

This returns a number from 0 to 9.99999. Now, if you add 1 to this,

$$var = Rnd() * 10 + 1$$

the result is a number from 1 to 10.99999. And, if you find the integer portion of this number,

$$var = Int(Rnd() * 10 + 1)$$

the result is an integer from 1 to 10!

If you want a different range, then use different numbers. For example, a guessing game from 1 to 100 would use 100 instead of 10. If you wanted to randomly pick a card from a deck, use 52. For a die, use 6. If you wanted 0 in the range, then don't add 1. It's about the neatest thing since sliced bread.

Pow

The Pow method raises a value to a specified power. There are two arguments for it: the number and the power it's raised to:

$$var = Math.Pow(num, power)$$

where var is the variable that stores the answer, Math.Pow calls the power method, num is the number, and power is the power to raise it to. If num is 2 and power is 4, then var equals 2^4 or 16.

Abs

Abs finds the absolute value of a number. Think of the absolute value of a number as its distance from zero on a number line. It's handy when working with some business and financial functions. It takes one argument, the number for which you want to find the absolute value:

$$var = Math.Abs(num)$$

where var is the variable that stores the answer, Math.Abs calls the absolute value method, and num is the number for which you want to find the absolute value.

Max

Max finds the larger of two numbers. There are two arguments for it, the numbers you're comparing:

$$var = Math.Max(num1, num2)$$

where var is the variable that stores the answer, Math.Max calls the maximum method, num1 is the first number, and num2 is the second number being compared. var gets the larger of num1 and num2.

Min

Min finds the smaller of two numbers. There are two arguments for it, the numbers you're comparing:

var = Math.Min(num1, num2)

where var is the variable that stores the answer, Math.Min calls the minimum method, num1 is the first number, and num2 is the second number being compared. var gets the smaller of num1 and num2.

Pmt

Pmt is the payment method. It calculates the payment on a loan. There are three arguments for it: the interest rate, the length of the loan in years, and the amount financed. The answer is a negative number because it is considered a debt owed by the borrower.

var = Pmt(rate, periods, principal)

where var is the answer, Pmt calls the payment method, rate is the interest rate in decimal form, periods is the term in years, and principal is the amount financed. The answer is an annual payment, but there are easy ways to modify this to calculate monthly payments that are typical for car loans and mortgages.

FV

FV is the future value method. It calculates the future value of an investment. There are three arguments for it: the interest rate, the length of the investment, and the amount that's regularly invested. The answer is a negative number.

var = FV(rate, periods, payment)

where var is the answer, FV calls the future value method, rate is the interest rate in decimal form, periods is the number of years the money is invested, and payment is the amount invested each period. The answer is the value that includes the money invested each year and the interest earned on it. FV is used to calculate a regular savings account, an IRA, or a 401(k).

The Load Event

Until now you've used the click event to trigger your code. At runtime, the user clicked on a Button that triggered code you had written for that Button. Now it's time to extend that to another event. Just before your form is displayed, a *Load* event is triggered. You can create an *event handler* for this. An event handler simply stores and runs the code for an event. Click events all have event handlers for them. An event handler is a procedure with a *Handles* command on it. The handler knows when to trigger the code.

In a Load event, the code is triggered when the form loads. It looks like this:

```
Private Sub frmDemo_Load(ByVal sender As Object, ByVal e
    As_System.EventArgs) Handles Me.Load
    Randomize
End Sub
```

The procedure is frmDemo_Load, the form is named frmDemo, and the handler is at the end of the line. It says to trigger the code in the procedure when it loads. There are numerous uses for the Load event and you'll see them throughout the rest of the text. There's one line of code in this example and it contains the Randomize command. You'll learn about that next.

Randomize

On the computer, random numbers really aren't random. Without a little help your random numbers are predictable. The Rnd command generates random numbers in the same order every time. Without help a list of "random" numbers is the same every time. The *Randomize* command makes the process random. Insert the keyword Randomize into the Load event for your form and random numbers become truly random.

VB Tip   *Run the RandomNumberDemo program to get a better feel for how to generate and use random numbers.*

VB Quiz 02   *How are numbers used to store and manipulate dates and times in VB?*
                  Give several examples of the True/False value for a Boolean.
                  How do methods make complicated mathematical calculations easier?
                  In your own words, explain the Load event and event handlers.
                  Explain how the Randomize command makes computer games interesting.

More Controls

So far input has been with a TextBox and output has been with a Label. But, a glance at the Toolbox reveals there are so many more controls. Each control has its own uses and advantages just like the tools in any toolbox. We'll add a few more tools now to make input easier for the user and improve the look of our output.

VB Tip   *Run the Chap04NewControls program.*

NumericUpDown

The *NumericUpDown* control is used for numeric input. There are advantages to this. The developer can control what input the user provides. It's less confusing for users and there's no chance for a runtime error like there is with numeric input from a TextBox. It is scrollable with a minimum and maximum value defined by the developer. It can also be set so the user can manually enter a value. The prefix for a NumericUpDown is nud. Set the Minimum property to the lowest value the user can enter. Set the Maximum property to the highest value the user can enter. The Increment property controls how much a value can change when scrolling. The ReadOnly property determines if the user can type in an acceptable value. When set to True, they can type in any value in the range. When set to False, they must enter a value by scrolling through the list.

Use a NumericUpDown to control the numbers a user can enter. For example, a nud could be used to enter a person's age. Use it to enter the number of items in an online order, the score on a test, or the amount of a loan. A nud works for almost any place where numeric input is required.

Use the Value property for input and the Text property for a default value. The ValueChanged event is triggered every time the Value property changes. The Value property can be changed by scrolling, typing a value, or by setting the Value property programmatically (see Figure 4.3).

RichTextBox

The *RichTextBox* displays multiple lines of text on a form. A Label works well, but it's usually used for just a word or two of output. The RichTextBox handles multiple lines of output and can be used to create a report. A line of output to a RichTextBox is often called a *detail line*. A detail line displays formatted output and is usually one of many similar lines of output. The prefix for a RichTextBox is rtb. Use the AppendText method to add text to a RichTextBox. For example:

```
rtbOutput.AppendText("Your age is:")
```

will add the text in quotation marks to the rtbOutput RichTextBox. To display a variable in a RichTextBox, use

```
rtbOutput.AppendText(shoAge.ToString)
```

The two are joined together using the ampersand (&). For example:

```
rtbOutput.AppendText("Your age is:  "& shoAge.ToString)
```

The Clear method clears the text from a RichTextBox. For example:

```
rtbOutput.Clear()
```

clears all the text from a RichTextBox.

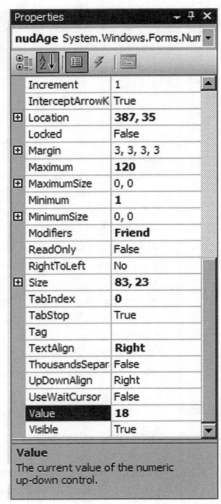

Figure 4.3   NumericUpDown Properties

AppendText adds text at the spot of the cursor. Text wraps in a RichTextBox. To end a line of text, use vbNewLine. For example:

```
rtbOutput.AppendText("This is one line of text."
    & vbNewLine)
```

Recall that strings are contained inside quotation marks. About the only thing that cannot be part of a string is a quotation mark. So, to display a quotation mark inside a RichTextBox takes a little effort and something called *ControlChars* (see Figure 4.4). It's a set of special characters used for controlling text:

ControlChars.Quote

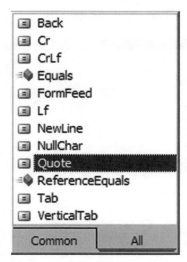

Figure 4.4   Control Characters

Another handy control character is the Tab. It looks like this:

ControlChars.Tab

Although it's useful, later you'll learn even better ways to control text.

VB Tip   *Use Courier New font to get the text to align properly in a RichTextBox.*

ToolTip

The *ToolTip* provides a helpful hint for the user in the form of a popup message when pointing to a control. The ToolTip control is added to the *component tray* and is invisible on the form. The component tray sits below a form and stores a variety of controls. When a ToolTip is added to a form, the ToolTip property for a control becomes active. Simply add a message to the property and it will display when pointing to a control (see Figure 4.5).

MessageBox

A MessageBox is a *dialog box* that displays a message to the user. When executed, a Windows dialog box pops up. A MessageBox can be use to inform or warn a user. It can also be used to gather input from the user. There are several formats for a MessageBox. The general form for a MessageBox is

MessageBox.Show(message, title, button, icon)

where MessageBox.Show opens a new MessageBox, message is the message displayed, title is the text for the title bar, button is the button or buttons

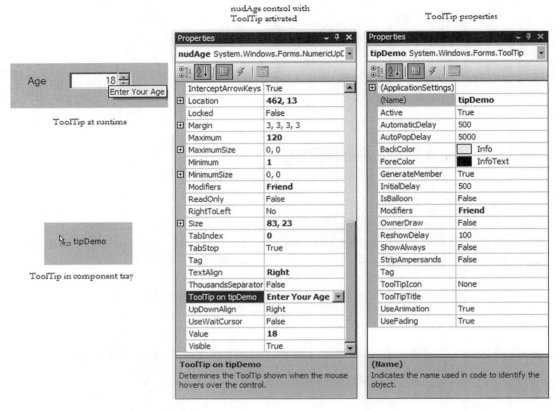

Figure 4.5   ToolTip Control

displayed, and icon is the type of icon displayed. The message argument is required, but the others are optional.

A simple message is displayed with

```
MessageBox.Show("This is a MessageBox.")
```

A caption can be added to the title bar of the dialog box:

```
MessageBox.Show("This MessageBox has a title.",
    "Your Title Goes Here")
```

A MessageBox can have buttons. Code can be written to handle the user's response. There are several types of buttons that can be used depending on the developer's needs.

```
MessageBox.Show("This MessageBox has Buttons.",
    "Your Title Goes Here", MessageBoxButtons.OKCancel)
```

In addition to the OKCancel buttons, MessageBoxes can have several other button combinations (see Figure 4.6).

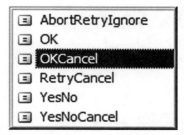

Figure 4.6   MessageBox Button Options

A MessageBox can also have an icon. There are several types of icons that can be used, depending on the developer's needs.

```
MessageBox.Show("This MessageBox has an icon.",
   "Your Title Goes Here", MessageBoxButtons.OKCancel,
   MessageBoxIcon.Information)
```

In addition to the Information icon, MessageBoxes can have several other icons (see Figure 4.7).

InputBox

An InputBox is another way to get user input. The general form for an InputBox is

```
InputBox(prompt, title, default)
```

where InputBox displays an InputBox, prompt displays a message for the user, title is the text for the title bar, and default is the initial value displayed in the InputBox. The text entered by the user is stored in a string.

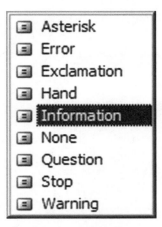

Figure 4.7   MessageBox Button Icons

Figure 4.8   InputBox Example

A simple InputBox looks like this.

```
strAge = InputBox("Enter your age.", "Your Title
  Goes Here")
```

The InputBox displays on the screen. The user enters their age in the InputBox and the value is stored as a string in strAge (see Figure 4.8).

A default value can be added to an InputBox. The prompt is a string and is displayed on the input line when the InputBox is displayed.

An InputBox with a prompt looks like this:

```
strAge = InputBox("Enter your age.", "Your Title Goes
  Here", "18")
```

The InputBox displays on the screen; 18 is already in the input line. The user can accept this value or enter their own. The advantage of a prompt is that it saves the user some effort (see Figure 4.9).

VB Tip   *The InputBox has its uses, but most developers use it sparingly.*

VB Quiz 03   *What advantages do NumericUpDowns have for a user?*
                        When should a RichTextBox be used?
                        Describe how to use a ToolTip.
                        What are the similarities and differences between a MessageBox and an InputBox?

Figure 4.9   InputBox with Prompt Example

Controlling Strings

So far most of your programming has involved mathematical calculations. Visual Basic also has built-in commands for manipulating strings of text. With them, you can work with a single character, words, or even multiple lines of text. These methods are powerful tools for a developer and make the computing experience easier for a user. Internet searches rely on string manipulation. They are used for comparisons for testing and databases rely on string comparisons. Just like ToString, these methods are added to the end of the string. Use IntelliSense to display a list of these methods (see Figure 4.10).

VB Tip

Run the ControllingStrings program to see examples of how to manipulate strings.

ToUpper

ToUpper converts a string into capital letters. It looks like this:

```
result = string.ToUpper
```

where string is the string, ToUpper is the method and the answer is stored in result. Use ToUpper to change lowercase letters into capital letters.

ToLower

ToLower does just the opposite; it converts letters to lowercase. It looks like this:

```
result = string.ToLower
```

where string is the string, ToLower is the method, and the answer is stored in result.

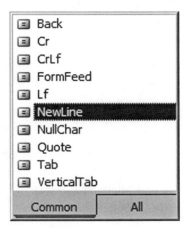

Figure 4.10   String Methods

Concatenation

Strings are joined together using an ampersand (&). These can be a string or a string contained in quotation marks. For example:

```
result = string1 & string2
```

where string1 and string2 are combined and stored in result. So if string1 contains "Visual" and string2 contains "Basic", result is assigned "VisualBasic". There's no space between the words. To put a space between them, you have two choices. You can either put a space inside the quotes or add another string containing a space. Or,

```
result = "Micro" & string
```

where string = "soft" results in "Microsoft". You can even take numeric variables, use the ToString method, and concatenate them into a string. For example, if bytNum = 1 and bytSum = 2, then:

```
strresult = bytNum.ToString & " + " & bytNum.ToString
    & " = " & bytSum.ToString
```

creates

$$1 + 1 = 2$$

Length

The Length method returns the number of characters in a string. Spaces are included in a string. So,

```
result = string.Length
```

where string is a string and result is a number. If there are no characters in the string, then the answer is 0.

Proper

The Proper method converts a string into proper case. It's useful for capitalizing names or capitalizing titles. The syntax is a little different:

```
result = StrConv(string, VbStrConv.ProperCase)
```

where result is the string in proper case and string is the original case. Although it's not perfect, it does allow the conversion of most names to proper case. For example, mcmahon converts to Mcmahon, instead of the correct form, McMahon.

VB Quiz 04   *What is the difference between the ToUpper and ToLower methods?*
              How is the ampersand used to concatenate strings?

How can spaces be added to a string?
What is the length of a null string?
What is the limitation of the Proper case method?

Tying It All Together

It's now time to tie all of this together. You're armed with new controls for input and output and new functions for calculations. We'll put all of them to use.

Car Loan Program

Lem Uhn runs a used car lot and provides financing on the some of the vehicles sold. He needs an application to calculate monthly payments on the vehicles he finances. He provides financing from $5,000 to $10,000 in $100 increments for 1 to 5 years with an interest rate from 5% to 8% in .25% increments. The application needs to be user friendly so customers can use it to calculate and compare payment options. You suggest a form like Figure 4.11.

The form uses NumericUpDowns for input – one for the principal, one for the interest rate, and one for the time. Output goes to a RichTextBox. Each line is a payment option. There are three Buttons on the form. The Clear Button clears

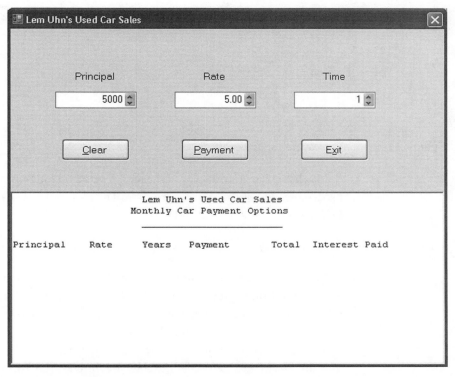

Figure 4.11   Car Payments Form

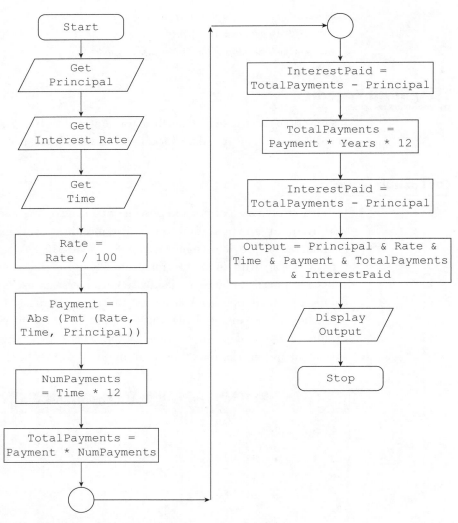

Figure 4.12   Car Payments Flowchart

the RichTextBox and displays a header. The Payment Button does the input, processing, and output for the program. The Exit Button ends the program (see Figure 4.12 and Tables 4.2 and 4.3).

VB Tip   *Open and run the CarPayments program.*

Input comes from the value property of NumericUpDown. The interest rate is a percent. Convert it to a decimal for use in the Pmt function. People generally refer to interest rates as percentages, but the calculations are always a decimal. Convert it by dividing the input by 100.

The Payment function calculates an annual payment. For this application, monthly payments are needed. Change the interest rate from a yearly rate to a monthly rate by dividing by 12. The number of periods is multiplied by 12 to

Table 4.2   Car Payments Control and Property Settings

Name	Function	Property	Settings
frmCarPayments	Main program form	Text	Lem Uhn's Used Car Sales
		MinimizeBox	False
		MaximizeBox	False
		StartPosition	CenterScreen
		Size	600, 500
nudPrincipal	Loan amount	Minimum	5000
		Maximum	10000
		Increment	100
		TextAlign	Right
nudRate	Interest Rate	Minimum	5
		Maximum	8
		Increment	0.25
		TextAlign	Right
nudTime	Years	Minimum	1
		Maximum	5
		TextAlign	Right
btnClear	Clears rtb	Text	&Clear
btnPayment	Calculates payment	Text	&Payment
btnExit	Ends the program	Text	E&xit
rtbOutput	Displays output	Font	Courier New
		Size	10
		Dock	Bottom

*   Three unnamed Labels.

get monthly payments. Recall that Pmt returns a negative number. Users are accustomed to positive payment numbers so use the Abs to make it a positive number. The total amount paid is the number of payments multiplied by the number of years and then multiplied by 12. The interest paid is the total amount paid minus the principal.

Output is a detail line in the RichTextBox. The detail is built by concatenating the formatted variables and storing the result in string variable. The string is then appended to the RichTextBox.

Table 4.3   Car Payments Variable Names, Type, and Use

Name	Type	Use
decPrincipal	Decimal	loan principal from input
sngRate	Single	interest rate from input
bytTime	Byte	length of loan from input
bytNumPayments	Byte	number of monthly payments
decPayment	Decimal	monthly payment from calculation
decTotal	Decimal	total of all payments from calculation
decInterestPaid	Decimal	interest paid from calculation
strOut	String	detail line for output

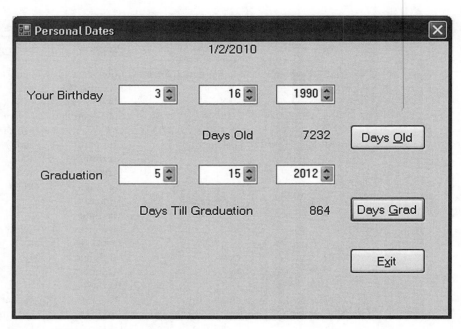

Figure 4.13   Personal Dates Program

The Clear Button clears the RichTextBox. It also displays the header lines so the user knows the contents of each column of output. Every time the user clicks the Clear Button, the RichTextBox is cleared and then the header lines are appended. These header lines appear in the RichTextBox when the program runs. Add these lines to the Load event for the form and they'll appear at runtime.

Be sure to include a prologue and comments in your code.

VB Tip   *Check your answers using the Pmt function in Excel.*

Personal Dates Program

June Bugg wants to know how many days old she is and how many days it is until graduation. No reason; she just wants to know. The application needs to get today's date, her birthday, and the graduation day. You suggest a form like that in Figure 4.13.

The form uses NumericUpDown for input. To determine her birthday, there is one for the month, one for the date, and one for the year. There are NumericUpDown controls for the graduation day as well: one for the month, one for the date, and one for the year. Output goes to Labels. The Days Old Button determines the number of days since she was born. The Days Grad Button determines how many days until graduation. The current date is determined in the Load event. The Exit Button ends the program (see Figure 4.14 and Tables 4.4 and 4.5).

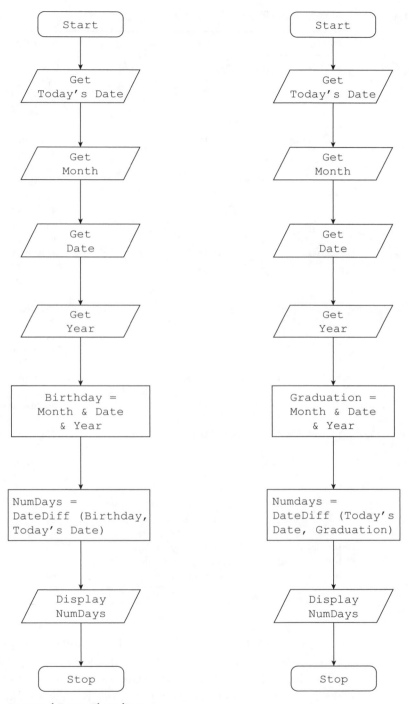

Figure 4.14   **Personal Dates Flowchart**

Table 4.4   Personal Dates Control and Property Settings

Name	Function	Property	Settings
frmPersonalDates	Main program form	Text	Personal Dates
		MinimizeBox	False
		MaximizeBox	False
		StartPosition	CenterScreen
		Size	500, 350
nudMonth	Birth month	Minimum	1
		Maximum	12
		Increment	1
		TextAlign	Right
nudDate	Birth date	Minimum	1
		Maximum	31
		Increment	1
		TextAlign	Right
nudYear	Birth year	Minimum	1900
		Maximum	2010
		Increment	1
		Value	2010
		TextAlign	Right
nudGradMonth	Graduation month	Minimum	1
		Maximum	12
		Increment	1
		TextAlign	Right
nudGradDate	Graduation date	Minimum	1
		Maximum	31
		Increment	1
		TextAlign	Right
nudGradYear	Graduation year	Minimum	2009
		Maximum	2020
		Increment	1
		Value	2009
		TextAlign	Right
lblDaysOld	Displays age in days	TextAlign	TopRight
lblTillGrad	Displays days until graduation	TextAlign	TopRight
lblToday	Displays today's date	TextAlign	TopCenter
btnDaysOld	Calculates age in days	Text	Days &Old
btnDaysGrad	Calculates days until graduation	Text	Days &Grad
btnExit	Ends the program	Text	E&xit

* Four unnamed Labels.

There are four inputs needed to find the number of days old, today's date, plus the month, date, and year of birth. The month, date, and year are combined in a string and then converted to a Date. Remember that dates can be strings in the format #mm/dd/yyyy#. The string must be in this format to be converted to a Date. Concatenate the crosshatches (#), slashes (/), and numbers and then convert this string to a Date. Use this date and today's date in the DateDiff function to find how old she is in days. Display the output in a Label.

Table 4.5   Personal Dates Variable Names, Type, and Use

Name	Type	Use
mdatToday	Date	current date
bytMonth	Byte	birth month
bytDay	Byte	birth date
shoYear	Short	birth year
strBirthday	String	birthday as a String
datBirthday	Date	birthday as a Date
lngDaysOld	Long	number of days old
bytGradMonth	Byte	graduation month
bytGradDay	Byte	graduation date
shoGradYear	Short	graduation year
strGraduation	String	graduation day as a String
lngTillGrad	Long	graduation day as a Date
datTillGrad	Date	number of days until graduation

Calculating the days until graduation is similar. There are four inputs: today's date, plus the month, date, and year of graduation. Combine the month, date, and year into a Date and use the DateDiff function to find the number of days until graduation.

Find today's date in the Load event. Use a module-level variable to store it so you'll be able use it in in all the procedures on the form.

Be sure to include a prologue and comments in your code.

VB Tip   *Open and run the PersonalDates program to see how it works.*

Sentence Builder Program

The object of this program is to string together words to make sentences. The program has a series of TextBoxes for input. The output is the completed sentence with capitalization and punctuation. The processing builds the sentence and tracks the number of words and sentences. The form should look like Figure 4.15.

The controls are set as shown in Figure 4.16 and Tables 4.6 and 4.7.

VB Tip   *Open and run the SentenceBuilder program.*

Fixing a Program

Dusty Lenzkapp runs a small camera store in the mall. He sells digital cameras and equipment. Employees are paid a commission based on their daily sales. He wants a simple program to list employee sales, their commissions, and the total for the day. The commission rate varies between 3% and 8%. Right now,

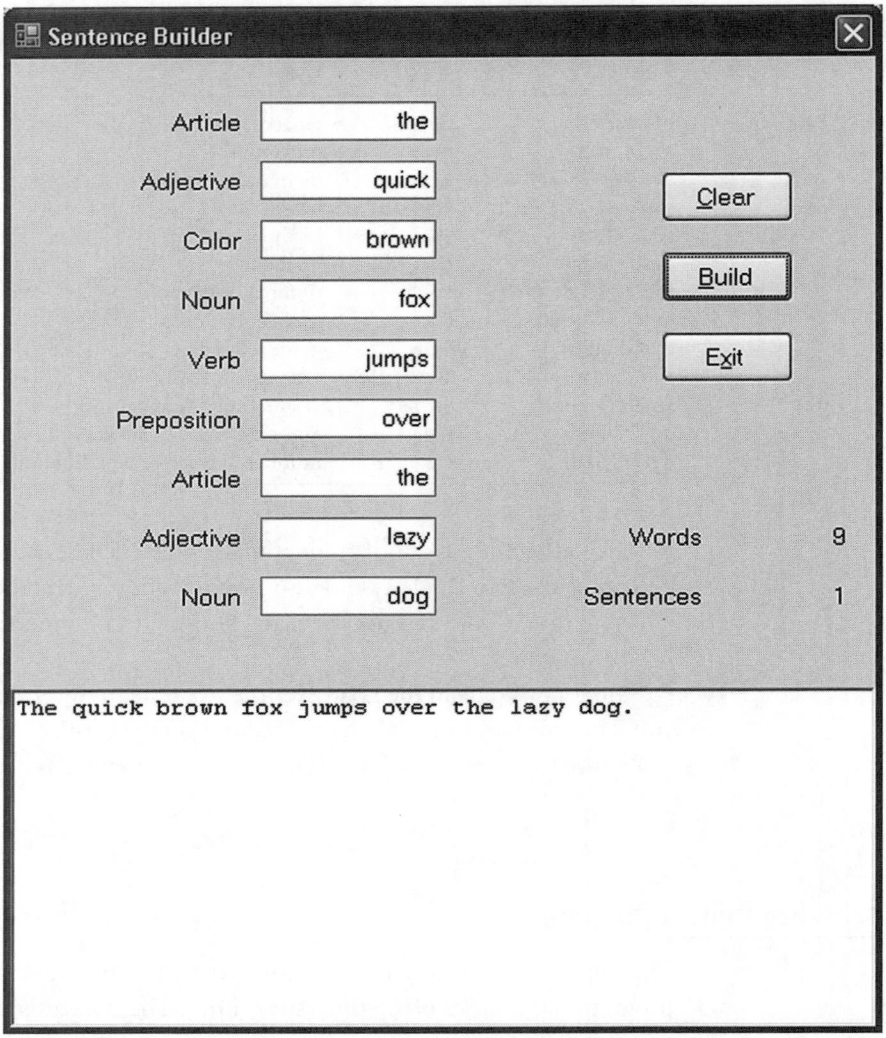

Figure 4.15   Sentence Builder Program

the program doesn't work and it's your job to fix it. You start by running the program (see Figure 4.17).

When compared to the completed form, you notice the date doesn't display at the top. You check to code to see why. There's no code in the Load event. Scanning through the rest of the code, you find it in the Add Button. Cut and paste it into the Load event and test it. One problem fixed.

Run the program again and notice the NumericUpDown for the commission rate displays from 1 to 100. You change it to display from 3 to 8.

Run the program again, enter some sample data, and click the Add Button. The output doesn't look quite right. Sales shows up as a percentage and the rate is the same as the sales amount and is displayed in currency. The math for the

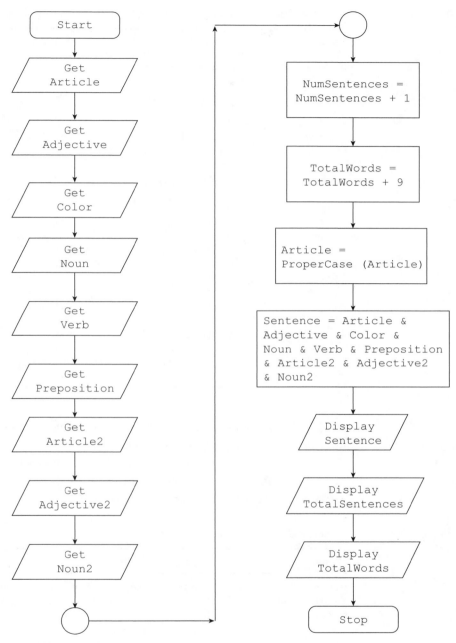

Figure 4.16   Sentence Builder Flowchart

commission is wrong and the total line shows up as well. It looks like there are several problems right now.

It's time to break it into smaller problems and solve them one at a time. The commission is way off, so you tackle that one first. Check the code and you'll

Table 4.6   Sentence Builder Control and Property Settings

Name	Function	Property	Settings
frmSentenceBuilder	Main program form	Text	Sentence Builder
		MinimizeBox	False
		MaximizeBox	False
		StartPosition	CenterScreen
		Size	500, 600
btnClear	Clears rtb	Text	&Clear
btnBuild	Add sentence to rtb	Text	&Build
btnExit	Ends the program	Text	E&xit
rtbOut	Displays output	Font	Courier New
		Dock	Bottom
txtArt	Input	TextAlign	Right
txtAdj	Input	TextAlign	Right
txtColor	Input	TextAlign	Right
txtNoun	Input	TextAlign	Right
txtVerb	Input	TextAlign	Right
txtPrep	Input	TextAlign	Right
txtArt2	Input	TextAlign	Right
txtAdj2	Input	TextAlign	Right
txtNoun2	Input	TextAlign	Right
lblTotalWords	Displays total words	TextAlign	TopRight
		AutoSize	False
lblNumSentences	Displays number of sentences	TextAlign	TopRight
		AutoSize	False

* Eleven unnamed Labels.

see that the calculation is correct. The problem must be above it in the code. Recall that the NumericUpDown is a whole number and the commission rate is a percentage. That's the problem. The variable contains a whole number instead of a decimal. You must add a line of code to ensure the calculation is made with a decimal instead of with a whole number.

Table 4.7   Sentence Builder Variable Names, Type, and Use

Name	Type	Use
mshoNumSentences	Short	counter for number of sentences
mshoTotalWords	Short	accumulator for number of words
strArt	String	stores first word
strAdj	String	stores an adjective
strColor	String	stores a color
strNoun	String	stores a noun
strVerb	String	stores a verb
strPrep	String	stores a preposition
strArt2	String	stores second article
strAdj2	String	stores second adjective
strNoun2	String	stores second noun
strSentence	String	stores the completed sentence for rtb

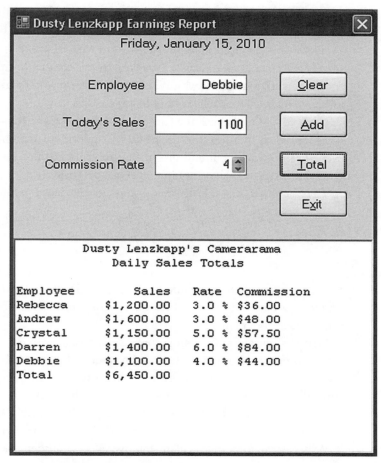

Figure 4.17   Dusty Lenzkapp Program

Run the program again and check the output. The commission looks OK, but it looks like the sales and commission rate are transposed. Check the code again and turn these two items around in the assignment statement. That fixes the detail line.

The Total line is out of place and should only appear once at the end. You move that code from the Add Button to the Total Button, thinking it will solve the problem. It doesn't. Oops! Instead of fixing the problem, it produces an error when you try to run the program. It says decTotalSales is not declared. Of course it's not declared! If you declare it in the Total Button, the output will be zero because there's no assignment statement in it. And, if you move the declaration out of the Add Button, it produces an error in that procedure. The answer is to make it a module-level variable. Rename it mdecTotalSales and declare it at the module level. Be sure to change the name in all the places it's used.

Run the program again and it's better, but it's still not fixed. It runs as it should, but the output is incorrect. Test it until you think you have it solved. The problem is in the accumulator line. Instead of adding the sales to the total, it merely increments the total by 1. Change it from a counter to an accumulator and try it again. This time it works. Whew! At this point, you realize that sometimes a change makes it worse instead of fixing a problem.

Next, you should check the Clear Button. It clears the RichTextBox, but you want it to clear it and put in the header. Copy the correct lines from the Load event to the Clear event and test it. Be sure to reset the accumulator to 0 and clear the TextBoxes. That should fix the last problem.

That's another lesson learned and some more tricks for your VB toolbag.

VB Tip   *Open the corrected version of this program to see how it should look.*

On Your Own

Write a program to find the number of days until Christmas. In the Load event, find today's date, determine the numbers of days until December 25, and display the number of days in a Label.

Write a program to find the future value of an investment. Use NumericUp-Down to input the amount, the interest rate, and the time. Use a RichTextBox for output and include the investment, interest rate, time, and ending value on a detail line. Include a Clear Button to clear the RichTextBox.

Write a program to determine the longest side of a right triangle. Use Pow and SqRt methods in your calculations. Display the answer in a Label.

Write a program to calculate the average for student test scores. Use an InputBox to get the student's name. Use InputBoxes for three test scores, and calculate and display the average. Send all the output to a RichTextBox. For an added challenge, weight the high score twice in your calculation. Use the Max method to find the highest score and count it twice in your calculation.

Summary

This chapter introduced new tools for input and output and new methods for calculations. New ways to create and use variables were introduced. You learned two new data types and were introduced to the Load event.

Review

User satisfaction is important in software development.
Variable scope determines where a variable can be used.
Local variables are declared, used, and discarded, all in the same procedure.
Module-level variables are declared in the Declarations of a form and can be used in any procedure on that form.

Counters are variables that keep count. Usually they count up by 1, but they can be used to count by any fixed number, either up or down.

Accumulators add a variable to a running total.

Date variables can store date and time.

Boolean variables store True/False data.

The integer part of a Date variable stores the date.

The decimal part of a Date variable stores the time.

Date variables contain the individual parts of a date and time.

DateDiff is used to compare dates and times.

Methods are a procedure contained in a class.

Methods can be used to complete complicated calculations.

The Load event contains code that runs when a form is loaded and just before it is displayed on the screen.

Randomize is used to randomize the number generation process.

A NumericUpDown is used to control numeric input.

A RichTextBox is used to display multiple lines of output.

ControlChars contains several methods for controlling text.

The ToolTip provides a popup message when the mouse hovers over a control.

A MessageBox is a dialog that displays a message to the user.

An InputBox is used to gather input from the user. It takes control of the program until the user acts upon it.

There are several methods for controlling and manipulating strings.

Terms

accumulator	a variable that increments by a varying amount; used to keep a running total; typically, an accumulator increases by the value of another variable
AppendText	a method used to add text to a RichTextBox
arguments	values used to complete a method or procedure
Boolean	a data type used to store True or False values
Clear	a method used to remove the text from a RichTextBox
component tray	an area below a form that's used to store controls that are a part of a form, but are not displayed on the form
Concatenation	to join; used to combine two strings into one
ControlChars	a method containing special characters used for output to a RichTextBox
counter	a variable that increments (or decrements) by a set amount; typically, they add one to a variable, but any amount can be used

Date	a data type used to store dates and times
DateDiff	a method for calculating the difference between two dates or times
detail line	a formatted line of output; Usually, one line of a multiple lines of similar output
event handler	a method that responds to actions by the user
Handles	a keyword that directs a program to trigger an event
InputBox	a control used to gather input from the user
Length	a method used to determine the number of characters in a string; spaces are counted also
Load	an event that is triggered when a program is loaded into memory
local variable	a variable that is declared in a procedure; it is only visible in that procedure and can only be used there
MessageBox	a control used to display information to a user or to gather input from the user
method	a procedure contained in a class; it performs an operation on data stored in the class
module-level variable	a variable that is declared at the top of a module; it is visible in all the procedures for that module
NumericUpDown	a control that allows numeric input within a predetermined range
Randomize	a command that randomizes the random number generation process
RichTextBox	a control used to display multiple lines of text
scope	the visibility of a variable in a program; where a variable can be used in a program
Show	a method used to display a control
ToLower	a method used to convert letters to lower case
ToolTip	a popup message provided for controls; a property for controls
ToUpper	a method used to convert letters into upper case
vbNewLine	a method used to end a line of output in a RichTextBox and begin a new line

Keywords

Abs	a method that returns the absolute value of a number
AppendText	a method that adds text to the end of a RichTextBox

Boolean	a data type that stores a True or False value; named for George Boole, a nineteenthth-century mathematician
Clear	a method that clears the text from a control
ControlChars	a method containing special characters used to format output
Date	a data type containing a date and time
DateDiff	a method that calculates the difference between two increments of time
FV	a method that calculates the future value of an investment
Handles	a command that knows when to trigger an event
InputBox	a control used to gather a single user input at a specified time
Int	a method that returns the integer part of a value
Length	a method that determines the number of characters in a string
Load	an event that occurs whenever a form is loaded
Max	a method that finds the largest of two numbers
MessageBox	a control used to display messages or control the flow of a program
Min	a method that finds the smallest of two numbers
Pmt	a method that calculates the payment on a loan
Pow	a method that raises a value to a specified power
Quote	a method used to display a quotation mark ("); quotations marks cannot be displayed in a string
Randomize	a command the randomizes the first number in the random number generator
Rnd	a method that generates a random number greater than or equal to zero and less than one
Show	a method used to display a control on the screen
SqRt	a method that returns the square root of a value
Tab	a method the moves the cursor to a predefined column in a RichTextBox
ToLower	a method that converts a string to all lower case letters
ToUpper	a method that converts a string to all upper case letters
vbNewLine	a command that ends a line in a RichTextBox and starts a new line
VbStrConv.ProperCase	a method that converts a string into mixed proper case

Self-check

1. Module-level variables must be created using the Public statement.
2. A counter always adds 1 to the value it's counting.
3. The integer part of a Date variable stores the date while the decimal part of a Date variable stores the time.
4. A Boolean stores one of two potential values.
5. Rnd generates a random number greater than or equal to zero and less than one.
6. Every form has a Load event that's triggered when the form is activated.
7. Use the Append method to add text to a RichTextBox.
8. User interaction with a MessageBox is limited to clicking on a Button.
9. An InputBox can handle only one input.
10. A String can contain a quotation mark.
11. Accumulators:
    A. are designed to keep track of the number of clicks a user makes
    B. increment by an established value every time
    C. keep a running total
    D. all of the above
12. Which of the following is not a counter?
    A. shoCount = shoCount + 1
    B. shoItemsLeft = shoItemsLeft − 1
    C. intDouble = intDouble * 2
    D. intValue = intValue + 3
13. Now:
    A. sets the date and time
    B. gets the current date and time from the system
    C. compares the current time to the last time the date and time were checked
    D. calculates the difference between two dates
14. In Excel, they're called functions, but in Visual Basic they're called:
    A. classes
    B. calculations
    C. methods
    D. formulas
15. Use the _____ method to find the larger of two numbers and the _____ method to find the smaller of two numbers.
    A. Max, Min
    B. Lar, Sml
    C. Big, Lit
    D. >, <

16. Storing specific code to run when triggered by a particular event is managed by a(n):
    A. method
    B. event log
    C. property manager
    D. event handler

17. A ValueChanged event is associated with:
    A. a TextBox
    B. a Button
    C. a NumericUpDown
    D. the Load event for a form

18. A detail line is:
    A. one line of multiple lines of similar output in a report
    B. a specific calculation used repeatedly to determine a specific value
    C. a calculation that uses a built-in method
    D. the term used for any line of output in a report

19. The ampersand is used to:
    A. concatenate two strings
    B. add a number and a string
    C. reset the value of a constant
    D. none of the above

20. The Length method:
    A. determines how many lines of code there are to run
    B. determines the number of characters in a string
    C. can be used on numbers and strings
    D. determines the amount of time between two dates

VB Quiz Answers

Quiz 01

Local variables should be used when a variable is needed only for that procedure. If the variable is only used inside a click event, then it should be declared locally. Module-level variables are needed when a variable is needed in more than one procedure or click event or when the value in it must be stored and used multiple times by an event.

Local variables are created at the top of a procedure. They're used only in that procedure and are destroyed and their memory released as soon as the event is finished.

Module-level variables are declared when a form is created. They can be used anywhere on the form and are destroyed when the form is destroyed.

Counters typically count by 1. They can count up or down by other values, but that value is always fixed. Accumulators change by a variable amount. Both use a variable in the assignment statement, change it and place the new value back in the same variable. Both use module-level variables.

Counters take the value in a variable and add (or subtract) a fixed amount to it. That value is then stored in the same variable. Accumulators take the value in a variable and add the value of a second variable to it. The result is then stored in the original variable.

Quiz 02

Dates are stored as numbers. Time is the decimal part of the number. Dates and times are handled the same way in Excel. Dates and times can be manipulated using Date variables.

A Boolean must be one value or another. A lightswitch is an example of a Boolean. It is either on or off. AM and PM are an example. X and O from tic-tac-toe are Booleans. Pregnant or not pregnant is a Boolean.

A method eliminates an often-complicated formula. Instead, a list of arguments is used and VB uses a built-in formula to perform the calculation.

The Load event is a procedure that runs when a form loads. The event handler is a method that triggers the Load event. When called, it runs the code in that procedure.

The Randomize command seeds the computer so that the random numbers are more "random." This randomization makes games less predictable. Without randomness, cards games would always play the same way, games of chance would have very little chance, and arcade games would always be the same.

Quiz 03

A NumericUpDown makes it clear that the program expects a numeric input. The parameters for a NumericUpDown can be set to the expected range of the input. Input from a NumericUpDown is a value while input from a TextBox is a string and must be converted to a number. Improper input from a TextBox can crash a program, but that won't happen with a NumericUpDown.

Typically, a RichTextBox is used when multiple lines of output are needed. Use a RichTextBox to display detail lines where the output is similar for each line.

A ToolTip control must be added to the component tray. That enables the ToolTip property for the controls on the form. Enter the tip in the Property window and change the other settings as needed. The tip appears when the user points to the control at runtime.

Both are windows that open when used. The InputBox requires input from the user while the MessageBox requires a response. Both have Buttons, but the Buttons on the MessageBox are the only user input for them. The MessageBox can have an icon.

Quiz 04

ToUpper converts text to upper case and ToLower converts text to lower case.

The ampersand (&) is used between variables, literal strings, and methods. An ampersand concatenates these strings into one string.

A space can be added to a string by literally adding the space. For example, " " can be concatenated to a string. " " can be assigned to a string and then the string can be concatenated where needed.

A null string, "", has a length of zero.

The Proper case method does not properly capitalize some names and words that contain capitalization in the middle of a word.

Using If and Case – Decisions, Decisions, Decisions

VB Quip   *The best thing about a Boolean is even if you are wrong, you are only off by a bit.*

– Anonymous

What Are Decision Structures?

Decision structures give the computer a brain. Sort of. So far, every program has followed a sequence of commands. Every command has executed, in order, when needed. That's great if you're riding the kiddie cars at the carnival, but you want some real power and the ability to make your own decisions. Think open road, the wind in your face, and the power to take whatever road suits your fancy. That's where If and Case statements come in. Quite literally you'll be able to pick one path or the other with an If statement. With a Case statement, you'll be able to choose one path from many. Are you hungry? Do you need gas? Then stop. It's your decision. Without them, you're merely a passenger on the bus and someone else makes all the decisions. With them, you turn the computer from a calculator that can only solve one problem into a thinking machine that can make decisions for various outcomes based on the input provided and the directions given to it by the developer. In short, you're on your way to teaching the computer how to think.

If . . . Then . . . Else Structures

Decision structures give the computer multiple *blocks* of code and the ability to select the block of code to execute. Every *If* structure has a statement that must be either true or false and two alternatives. One alternative is for true outcomes and the other is for false outcomes. Just as in real life, sometimes one of the options is to do nothing.

The general form of an If structure looks like this:

```
If condition Then
    statement(s)
Else
    statement(s)
End If
```

Table 5.1   Relational Operators

VB Symbol	Mathematical Symbol	Meaning
=	=	equals
<	<	less than
>	>	greater than
<=	$\leq$	less than or equal to
>=	$\geq$	greater than or equal to
<>	$\neq$	does not equal

Think of this as a block of statements that must stay together. When you see an If statement always look for the *End If* statement. All the lines in between belong to the If. In the middle there might be an *Else* statement. The Else separates one set of statements from the other. If you like, it separates one path from the other. When there's no Else, it means that the option is to do the statements after the *Then* or do nothing at all.

The condition must be a statement that is either true or false (a Boolean). When the condition is True, the computer does the statement(s) between the Then and the Else. When the condition is False, the computer does the statement(s) between the Else and the End If.

It will always do one or the other. Sometimes the condition is true, so it runs the top part (the True part) and sometimes the condition is false, so it runs the bottom part (the False part). Just like that fork in the road, you choose one path or the other. Sometimes you'll take one, at other times, you'll take the other, but you can never do both on the same trip.

Relational Operators

The condition always contains a *relational operator*. A relational operator compares the values on either side of it. You first learned these in grade school, although the symbols on the computer are slightly different. Relational operators work for numbers and strings. String comparisons are evaluated using ASCII values (see Table 5.1).

Flowchart Update

New logic requires an update to the flowchart symbols. The diamond shape indicates a decision structure. Follow the path on the right when the decision is true. Follow the left path when the condition is false. On any trip through the flowchart, the decision will be either true or false and that will determine the path and the code for that trip. The rectangles in the decision path indicate one or more lines of code to execute. The circle at the bottom is a *connector*

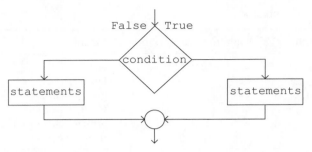

Figure 5.1   If Flowchart

that merely indicates the two paths have merged into a single path again (see Figure 5.1).

Largest Program

Now it's time to put some of this new knowledge to work. Let's find the largest of three numbers. The three numbers are the input, and the output is the largest of the three numbers. This is a problem you've been able to solve "without thinking" since grade school. It's a little trickier for the computer, though, but we'll follow the same logic (see Figure 5.2).

Once you have the input, the key is to compare the first two numbers. This code makes the comparison:

```
'Processing
If shoNum1 > shoNum2 Then
```

Based on whether shoNum1 or shoNum2 is larger, you'll follow one of the two paths. When the statement is true, you'll run this code:

```
shoLargest = shoNum1
```

When it's false, you'll run this code:

```
shoLargest = shoNum2
```

Either way, once you get to the End If statement, the larger of the two numbers is in shoLargest.

Think of the If statement as the diamond and the End If statement as the circle. The right side is the True part. That's the code that comes between the Then and the Else. The False code is between the Else and the End If. It can run only one of these.

The other If statement in the flowchart has a True part, but no False. The comparison says:

```
If shoNum3 > shoLargest Then
```

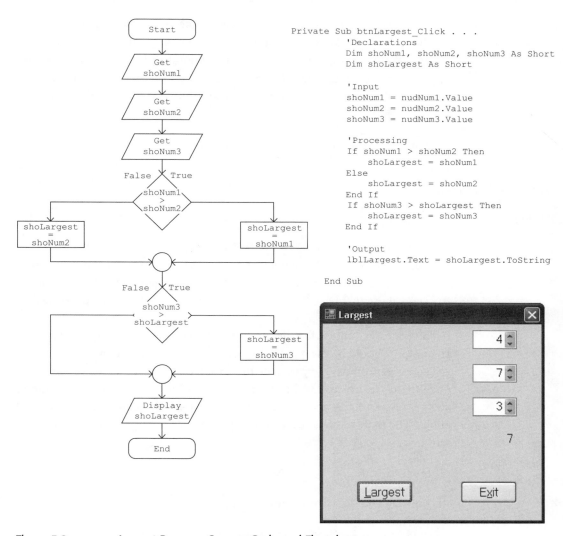

```
Private Sub btnLargest_Click . . .
        'Declarations
        Dim shoNum1, shoNum2, shoNum3 As Short
        Dim shoLargest As Short

        'Input
        shoNum1 = nudNum1.Value
        shoNum2 = nudNum2.Value
        shoNum3 = nudNum3.Value

        'Processing
        If shoNum1 > shoNum2 Then
            shoLargest = shoNum1
        Else
            shoLargest = shoNum2
        End If
        If shoNum3 > shoLargest Then
            shoLargest = shoNum3
        End If

        'Output
        lblLargest.Text = shoLargest.ToString

End Sub
```

Figure 5.2   Largest Program Screen, Code and Flowchart

So, if the third number is greater than shoLargest, then it will run the code that comes after the Then:

```
shoLargest = shoNum3
```

There's no Else section, so it won't do anything if the condition is false. That makes sense. If shoLargest is greater than shoNum3, then shoLargest is the largest. Either way, shoLargest now contains the largest of the three numbers and can be displayed using the following:

```
'Output
lblLargest.Text = shoLargest.ToString
```

Odds are that you probably used the same logic to find the largest of the three numbers. Once you knew the first two, you remembered the value of the larger of them. You then compared that to the third number. If the third number was larger, you remembered that. If it wasn't, then you held on to the other number.

We'll revisit this simple program later and introduce a little different logic for it.

VB Tip   *Open and run the Largest program to see how it works.*

Overtime Program

VB Quip   *First, solve the problem. Then, write the code. – John Johnson*

The typical workweek is 40 hours. Generally, when a wage earner exceeds 40 hours in a week, they're eligible for overtime. Overtime is usually one-and-a-half times the hourly wage. Most hourly workers are familiar with the concept, especially those that have done the math when they've stayed late or worked an extra shift.

There are two inputs for this problem: the hours worked and the pay rate. The output should be the regular pay, overtime pay, and total pay.

There are two possible paths for this problem. One path involves the values when there's no overtime. The other determines the values for overtime. Either way, you have to take the two inputs provided and calculate the three output values. The path taken is determined by whether there was any overtime. The condition is

hours worked > 40

Of course, it could also be expressed as

hours worked <=40

and either will work. It just depends on how you look at the problem. The If for this problem looks like this (see Table 5.2):

```
If sngHours > 40 Then
    'OT
    sngRegHours = 40
    sngOTHours = sngHours - 40
Else
    'No OT
    sngRegHours = sngHours
    sngOTHours = 0
End If
```

Table 5.2   Overtime Program Variables

Variable	Use	Contains	Formula
decPayRate	Input	hourly wage	none
sngHours	Input	hours worked	none
sngRegHours	Processing	hours worked up to and including 40 hours per week	40 or sngHours
sngOTHours	Processing	hours greater than 40 in a week	sngHours −40
decRegPay	Output	wages earned up to and including 40 hours per week	sngRegHours * decPayRate
decOTPay	Output	wages for any hours over 40 in a week	sngOTHours * decPayRate * 1.5
decTotalPay	Output	total pay for the week	decRegPay + decOTPay

A general rule in programming is to never write the same code twice if you can avoid it. So, we'll do as little as possible in the If structure and do the calculations below it. The If must determine the number of regular hours and the number of overtime hours. If there are more than 40 hours, then the regular hours are 40 and the overtime hours are the hours over 40. When there's no overtime, the overtime hours are 0 and the regular hours are the hours worked. Either way, when the If is completed, we'll know both of these values and can use them in the calculations.

The calculations are straightforward. Calculate regular pay, overtime pay, and total pay (see Figure 5.3):

```
decRegPay = sngRegHours * decPayRate
decOTPay = sngOTHours * decPayRate * 1.5
decPay = decRegPay + decOTPay
```

VB Tip   *Open and run the Overtime program to see how it works.*

Using Strings in If Statements

Strings can be used in the conditions for an If statement. String variables can be compared to other string variables and string variables can be compared to string literals. The same six comparison operators used for numeric comparison are also used for strings. If

```
strRightAnswer = "T"
strStudentAnswer = "F"
```

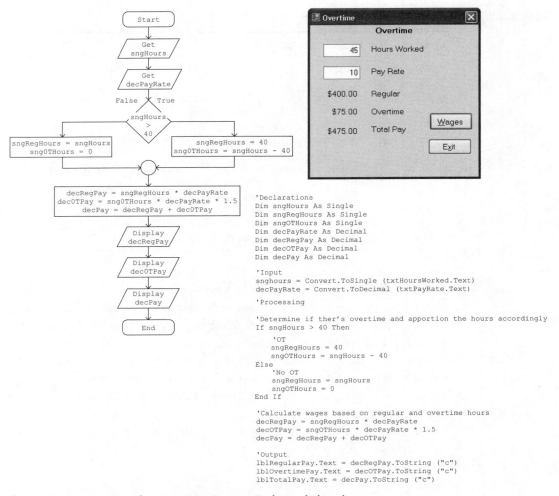

Figure 5.3   **Overtime Program Screen, Code, and Flowchart**

an If that uses strings could look like this:

```
If strStudentAnswer = strRightAnswer Then
    MessageBox("You are correct!",
    MessageBoxButtons.OK, "Quiz")
Else
    MessageBox("Sorry.", MessageBoxButtons.OK, "Quiz")
End If
```

"T" does not equal "F" so the Else block of code is executed. The user sees the MessageBox for a wrong answer.

String comparison could also look like this:

```
strSize = "XL"
```

Table 5.3   String Comparisons

String Comparisons		
Comparison	**Result**	**Reason**
If "A" = "a" Then	False	"A" and "a" are different
If "B" < "C" Then	True	"B" comes before "C" in ASCII
If "SHOUT" = "shout" Then	False	upper case and lower case are different
If "Cat" > "cat" Then	False	"C" comes before "c" in ASCII
If "sun" <> "moon"	True	"sun" and "moon" are different

```
If strSize = "XL" Then
    MessageBox("$2 additional charge for larger sizes.",
    MessageBoxButtons.OK, "Alert")
End If
```

This example compares a string variable to a literal, literally "XL". There's an additional problem if the user entered "xl" or "Xl" or "xL". If the program expects "XL", the two won't match (see Table 5.3). This can be avoided by using the ToUpper method. This makes it easier for the developer and more forgiving for the user.

```
If strSize.ToUpper = "XL" Then
    MessageBox("$2 additional charge for larger sizes.",
    "Alert", MessageBoxButtons.OK)
End If
```

VB Tip   *Check Appendix A for the ASCII table to see the order of characters.*

VB Tip   *Computers often have trouble putting lists with upper- and lower-case items in the correct order because all the upper case letters come before any of the lower case letters.*

IsNumeric

IsNumeric is a built-in function that examines a string of characters and determines if it is a number. Until now, input from a TextBox was risky because the user might not enter a number when needed. The solution is the IsNumeric function. It returns True when the string is a number and False when it's not. The form is

IsNumeric(string)

In this case, the string is what's contained in the text property of a TextBox and the result is True or False. When it's part of an If statement, a True result means the Then part of the If executes. When the result is False, the Else part of the If runs.

Here's how it was used in the Overtime program.

```
If IsNumeric(txtHoursWorked.Text) Then
    sngHours = Convert.ToSingle(txtHoursWorked.Text)
Else
    MsgBox("Please enter the hours worked.",
    MsgBoxStyle.OkOnly, "Data Entry Error")
End If
```

The If uses IsNumeric to see if the user input is a number. If it is, then processing can proceed. If not, a MessageBox appears asking the user to enter a number. The variable sngHours was initialized to 0 when declared. If the IsNumeric is True, the hours worked gets assigned to sngHours. If it's False, the program doesn't run the line assigning the text from the TextBox to sngHours. That's great, because that line won't work and crashes the program. Instead, the MessageBox appears warning the user, sngHours remains 0, and that value is used in the calculation.

The code for entering the pay rate is similar:

```
If IsNumeric(txtPayRate.Text) Then
    decPayRate = Convert.ToDecimal(txtPayRate.Text)
Else
    MsgBox("Please enter the pay rate.",
    MsgBoxStyle.OkOnly, "Data Entry Error")
End If
```

IsNullOrEmpty

Another handy little method for checking user input is *IsNullOrEmpty*. It checks a string to see if there is a value in it. When there isn't anything in the string, the result is True. If the string has something in it, the result if False. Use it to check the user's input. Sometimes a user might leave a TextBox blank or click the Button before completing their input. That could lead to an error or crash and frustration on the part of the user.

```
'Input
strAnswer = txtAnswer.Text
If String.IsNullOrEmpty(strAnswer) = True Then
    MsgBox("Please enter your answer first.",
    MsgBoxStyle.OkOnly, "Input Problem")
Else
    'Continue processing
End If
```

In this example, the user enters their answer in txtAnswer. The input is stored in strAnswer. It's then used as a parameter in the String.IsNullOrEmpty method in the If condition to see if the user typed anything into the TextBox. If they didn't, the If is True and the MessageBox pops up. Of course, if it's not empty, the condition is False and it can be processed.

VB Quiz 01

Why is an If statement always a Boolean?

Why must the multiple lines of an If structure be considered a single block of code?

How are decision structures depicted on a flowchart?

What's wrong with writing the same code twice?

How are strings compared in an If statement?

What are the only possible outcomes of an IsNumeric function?

Logical Operators – And, Or, Not, XOr

VB Quip

How do you know when someone is a computer scientist?

She recites as she plucks the flower petals: "He loves me, XOr, he loves me not . . . " – David Lowenstein

Sometimes matching one criterion isn't enough. Think about your little trip. If you're hungry or you need a bathroom break, then you'll stop. It means you'll make a comfort call if you're hungry or you need a restroom. Then again, you might stop only if you were hungry and thirsty. So, you'd push on until you needed both. Of course, if you need gas, you'll stop even if you don't need to pay attention to personal matters. What if you're running late? Would you make a pit stop if it meant being late for an appointment? And, what if the place is a dive? Should you just keep going? In programming, these decisions are handled with *logical operators.*

The And operator joins two conditions, each of which must be true for the entire condition to be true. If only one is true, then the condition is false. The Or operator requires one of the conditions to be true. When both are true, the condition is still true. It's only false when both are false. The Not operator reverses the conditions. It may seem strange, but it has its uses. The XOr operator works when one or the other is true. It won't work if both are true or both are false (see Table 5.4).

Logical operators combine conditions in an If statement. Many times the satisfaction of one condition isn't enough to determine the path of a computer operation. Sometimes, you might need to have a number within a certain range to complete a calculation. For example, a large or medium investor might earn more interest on a deposit than a small investor. In the following example, investments under $10,000 earn 4%, those $50,000 and over earn 6%, and those

Table 5.4   Logical Operators

Operator	Meaning	First Condition	Second Condition	Result
And	Both conditions must be true	Hungry?	Thirsty?	
		True	True	Stop
		True	False	Keep going
		False	True	Keep going
		False	False	Keep going
Or	One or the other condition must be true or both can be true	Need gas?	Tired?	
		True	False	Stop
		True	True	Stop
		False	True	Stop
		False	False	Keep going
Not	Reverses the value; true becomes false and false becomes true	Not a Dive?		
		True		Stop
		False		Keep going
XOr	One or the other must be true, but both cannot be true	Quaint?	Quirky?	
		True	True	Keep going
		True	False	Stop
		False	True	Stop
		False	False	Keep going

in between earn 5%. The code can be set up as follows:

```
If decAmt < 10000 Then
    sngIntRate = .04
End If
If decAmt >= 10000 And decAmt < 50000 Then
    sngIntRate = .05
End If
If decAmt >= 50000 Then
    sngIntRate = .06
End If
```

The first and last If statements are straightforward, but the middle one needs a little explanation. It must be written as two complete conditions. In conversation we might say, "if the amount is greater and/or equal to $10,000 and less than $50,000," where it's understood that the statement says the amount is $>= 10000$ and < 50000. The statement must be explicit for the computer, however. The first condition is $>= 10000$ and the second condition is < 50000. The And in the statement requires both be true for the condition to be true. That limits the range to deposits between $10,000 and $50,000. It covers all the numbers in that range.

It's sometimes easier to see these conditions as a number line. That makes it easier to see the relationships and the boundaries. In this example, the number line looks like Figure 5.4.

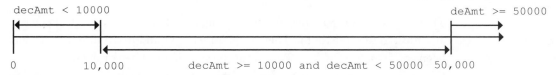

Figure 5.4   Investment Number Line

Deskcheck

Sharon Sharalike manages an online music service that lets users download MP3 files for $1 each. However, if they download 10 to 20 files in a month, the price is 89 cents each. If they download more than 20 in a month, the price drops to 79 cents each. The service counts the number of downloads in a month and bills the user's credit card. Here's the If structure that determines the monthly charge:

```
If shoNumDownloads < 10 Then
    decPrice = 1
End If
If shoNumDownloads >= 10 And shoNumDownloads < 20 Then
    decPrice = .89
End If
If shoNumDownloads >= 20 Then
    decPrice = .79
End If
decCharge = shoNumDownloads * decPrice
```

From the sample number of downloads, determine the price for each download and then calculate the charge for that month (see Table 5.5).

VB Tip   *Simple If statements can be written on one line without the End If. For example,*
                  If shoNumDownloads < 10 Then decPrice = 1

Table 5.5   Download Charges

shoNumDownloads	decPrice	decCharge
5	1	5
8	1	8
10	89	8.90
15	89	13.35
20	79	15.80
30	79	23.70

Potential Problems

There's always the potential for misplacing the statements in an If. Pay close attention to the code in the Then and Else sections and make sure they haven't been accidentally switched. There must be code in the Then or the Else sections. Of course, you can put code in both of them if needed. Make sure the condition covers exactly what's needed. Pay close attention to whether the condition needs a < or <=. Of course, the same goes for > or >= conditions. Strings cannot be compared to numbers, so always compare numbers to numbers and strings to strings. Compound conditions are tricky. Writing out the requirements, drawing a flowchart, completing a number line, and doing a deskcheck will all help to clarify your code. Be careful with And and Or. And conditions are usually more exclusive and Or conditions are more inclusive. And, be sure to write out both conditions when compound statements are used.

Data Validation

Data validation ensures that the user's input can be processed. NumericUp-Downs limit numeric input to an acceptable range. That makes programming for their input much easier, but sometimes the range or the number of possibilities makes them unwieldy. And, they won't work for text input. Take a home mortgage, for example. The principal could range from a few thousand dollars to several hundred thousand dollars and the amount is seldom a round number. In this case, the easiest input might be a TextBox where the user could simply type in the amount. The code could then make sure the amount is a number (using IsNumeric!) and that it's within the acceptable range. From there, it can be processed. With string input, the data can be validated as well. Just use If statements and only allow the input you want.

Data Validation Example

An online store needs to verify the jacket size when it takes an order. The customer enters the size of the jacket they're ordering, S for small, M for medium, L for large, or XL for extra large. Based on the size, the store can determine the price for a jacket. In this example, the input is from a TextBox. If the user doesn't enter a valid size, a MessageBox appears to warn them. If the input is valid, then processing can continue.

```
Private Sub btnPrice_Click...
    'Declarations
    Dim strSize As String
    Dim decPrice As Decimal
```

```
'Input
strSize = txtSize.Text
strSize = strSize.ToUpper

If strSize = "S" Or strSize = "M" Or strSize = "L"
      Or strSize = "XL" Then
    'Processing
    If strSize = "S" Then
        decPrice = 29.95
    End If
    If strSize = "M" Then
        decPrice = 34.95
    End If
    If strSize = "L" Then
        decPrice = 39.95
    End If
    If strSize = "XL" Then
        decPrice = 44.95
    End If
    'Output
    lblPrice.Text = decPrice.ToString("c")
Else
    MsgBox("Please enter S, M, L or XL for the size.",
    MsgBoxStyle.OkOnly, "Jacket Size")
End If
End Sub
```

Input for the program is with the txtSize TextBox. The next line converts the input to upper case. That makes it easier to validate. If the customer entered "s", it would convert it to "S". That makes it much easier to validate. The If statement has four possibilities" "S", "M", "L", or "XL". If strSize is any of these, then processing can continue. If it's not, the MessageBox appears, asking the customer to reenter their size. Note the line for the MessageBox is in the Else part of the If statement.

The If statement uses the Or logical operator. It can be read as follows: "If the size is small, or the size is medium, or the size is large, or the size is extra large, then do this processing." It wouldn't work if And had been used because strSize would have to be small and medium and large and extra large all at once. Using Or means the statement is true when any one of the comparisons is true. And, that's exactly what you want.

The Then part of the code determines the price based on the size. There are four If statements for this. Each one sets the price for the proper size. The output section displays the price.

VB Tip	*Open and run the JacketSize program.*
VB Quiz 02	*Explain the differences between the logical operators And, Or, Not, and XOr.*
	How can a number line be helpful when creating the If statements for a range of numbers?
	What is the value of data validation?

Nested If Structures

Nested statements are statements that are part of a larger block of code. With nested If structures, it means one block of If statements is completely inside another If statement. There were two examples of nested statements in the LargestDemos program. Take a look at examples three and four in that program to see the code and flowcharts for them. And, the JacketSize program you just saw used a nested If. With nested Ifs, a developer can check for a condition and then branch and check for other conditions. Pretty much the same thing can be done with logical operators, but nested If statements are more flexible and, usually, much easier to follow.

A nested If structure could look like this:

```
If condition Then
    If condition Then
    Else
    End If
Else
    If condition Then
    Else
    End If
End If
```

The True part of the first If statement has a block of code containing a second If structure. The False part of the first If also contains another If structure. When the first If is True, it will evaluate the second If. That's the only way for it to get to that code. When the first If is false, it jumps down to the Else part and evaluates the last If structure. The only way for it to get to this code is for the first If to be false.

Let's look at an example. Jack Carr runs a pre-owned auto (which sounds much better than a used car) dealership. His sales force works on a commission that's based on their weekly sales and their years of service. When sales are $100,000 or more and the salesperson has more than 5 years of experience, the rate is 6%. Less-experienced staff has a rate of 4%. When sales are under $100,000 the commission is 5% for those with more than 5 years of experience and 3% for the others. Table 5.6 makes it easier to understand.

Table 5.6   Car Sales Commission Rates

Weekly Sales	Experience	Commission Rate %
>= $100,000	> 5	6
>= $100,000	<=5	4
< $100,000	> 5	5
< $100,000	<=5	3

The program has two inputs: the weekly sales and the years of experience. The first If checks the total sales. When True (that is, the sales were >= $100,000), it then checks the years of experience, and, based on that, assigns the commission rate. When the first If is False (that is, the sales were < $100,000), it then checks the years of experience, and, based on that, assigns the commission rate. Once the commission rate is known, the program calculates the commission and displays the output (see Figure 5.5).

Test the flowchart with sample data and follow the traces (see Table 5.7). Then follow the code through the same path to make sure you understand how the code works.

VB Tip   *Open and run the SalesCommission program.*

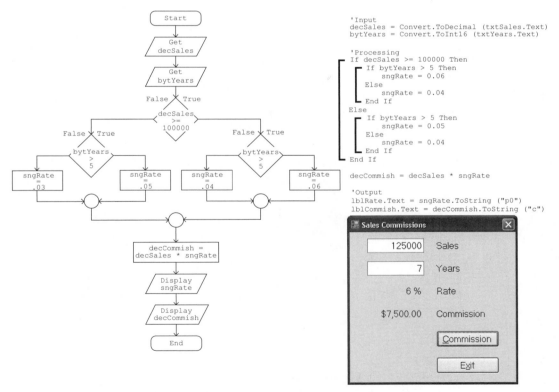

Figure 5.5   Jack Carr Commission Program Screen, Code, and Flowchart

Table 5.7   Car Sales and Experience

Sales	Years
$50,000	7
$125,000	7
$140,000	3
$75,000	2

If statements can be nested in many ways. Of course, there doesn't have to be code in both the Then and the Else sections. It's enough to have code in either one of them. Multiple Ifs can be nested inside each other as well as shown in this grading example.

Draw a line connecting the If with its End If. That helps to separate the statements and makes it easy to see where each one belongs. If done correctly, the lines will not cross. In fact, you'll see how one If block fits nicely inside another.

VB Tip   *The End If will always be directly below the If statement that belongs with it. VB does that with the autoindent feature.*

```
'Input
bytPercent = nudPercent.Value

'Processing
If bytPercent >= 90 Then
    strGrade = "A"
Else
    If bytPercent >= 80 Then
        strGrade = "B"
    Else
        If bytPercent >= 70 Then
            strGrade = "C"
        Else
            If bytPercent >= 60 Then
                strGrade = "D"
            Else
                strGrade = "F"
            End If
        End If
    End If
End If

'Output
lblGrade.Text = strGrade
```

VB Tip   *Open and run the IfGrades program.*

Stacked If Structures

If structures can also be written one on top of another. Instead of nesting them one inside the other, they can be stacked. *Stacked Ifs* execute one after another. None are dependent on the others. Here is the code for finding grades written as stacked If statements. The If statements are more complicated. Furthermore, the program must look at each of them, regardless of the percentage. It works, but there are better ways to write this code. And soon you'll see Case structures which will simplify this even more.

```
'Input
bytPercent = nudPercent.Value

'Processing
If bytPercent >= 90 Then
    strGrade = "A"
End If
If bytPercent >= 80 And bytPercent < 90 Then
    strGrade = "B"
End If
If bytPercent >= 70 And bytPercent < 80 Then
    strGrade = "C"
End If
If bytPercent >= 60 And bytPercent < 70 Then
    strGrade = "D"
End If
If bytPercent < 60 Then
    strGrade = "F"
End If

'Output
lblGrade.Text = strGrade
```

VB Tip   The data validation example that found the price based on jacket size uses a stacked If structure.

ElseIf

Another way to write this same code is to use *ElseIf*. It's like combining separate If structures into a compact block of code. The computer tests the first If. When it's true, it runs the Then code. If it's False, it looks at the ElseIf statement and evaluates that. The last ElseIf can have an Else statement as kind of a catch-all. When the If and all the ElseIf statements are False, the Else is True. An Else is not required with ElseIf.

```
'Input
bytPercent = nudPercent.Value

'Processing
If bytPercent >= 90 Then
    strGrade = "A"
ElseIf bytPercent >= 80 Then
    strGrade = "B"
ElseIf bytPercent >= 70 Then
    strGrade = "C"
ElseIf bytPercent >= 60 Then
    strGrade = "D"
Else
    strGrade = "F"
End If

'Output
lblGrade.Text = strGrade
```

VB Tip   *Open and run the IfGrades program.*

Potential Problems

As your code becomes more complicated, so do the problems. Nested If structures are tricky because every End If is at the bottom. It's hard at first to match the If with its End If. Remember, they automatically line up vertically. Stacked If structures are a little simpler to write, but they aren't very efficient. The program must go through each If even when it's not needed. That slows down your program. ElseIf works well, but it's easy to start mixing and matching the comparisons. Be sure to have a good grasp of the logic when using them. As always, flowcharts, number lines, pseudocode, and deskchecks are all helpful.

GPA Program

A student's grade point average (GPA) is very important. It's tied to honors and scholarships and it's used for determining financial aid and official status in school. In this example, a student's GPA is used to determine standing. A NumericUpDown is used to enter the GPA and a Button determines the student's standing. The output is the student's standing (see Table 5.8).

There are four possible outcomes for this program, so there must be four possible paths for the flow of the program. A number line for this starts at zero and runs to 4.0 with divisions at 2.0, 3.0, and 3.5. The If statements can

Table 5.8   GPA Requirements

GPA Range	Standing
< 2.0	Probation
2.0 to <3.0	Good Standing
3.0 to <3.5	Scholarship
>=3.5	Dean's List

be written in any of several ways as long as they force the flow into the proper outcome.

VB Tip   *Open and run the GPA program to see how it works.*

Discount Program

Horace Pharm runs a petting zoo. Single admission is $5.00. Groups of 5 to 9 people are $4.00 each. Groups of 10 to 20 are $3.50 each, and groups of more than 20 are $3.00 each (see Table 5.9). Use a NumericUpDown for the number of visitors in each group, a Label for the total, and a Button to hold the code.

This program has four possible outcomes. Again, there must be four paths for the program flow.

Table 5.9   Horace Pharm Petting
                             Zoo Admission Rates

Visitors	Rate
1 to 4	$5.00
5 to 9	$4.00
10 to 20	$3.50
>20	$3.00

VB Tip   *Run the HoracePharmAdmissionRates program to see how it works.*

VB Quiz 03   *How could the commission code be written using And in the If statements?*
                           What would the flowchart for a stacked If structure look like?
                           How many possibilities are there for an If Then Else structure? How many are there for two of them stacked on top of each other?
                           Is the ElseIf the True part or the False part of a statement?

Guessing Game Case Study

Claire Voient enjoys playing the little game of guessing a number from 1 to 100. This version of the game has the computer generate a random number and has the user guess the number. With each guess, the program compares the guess to the correct answer. It then tells the user if their guess was too high or too low.

Of course, if they guess the right number, they win. To add to the excitement of the game, we'll add a little code to count the number of guesses it takes to find the right number.

The first step is to create the flowchart. From that blueprint you can design the interface and write the code. The Start and Guess Buttons both have code. And, both of them must work together.

The Start Button generates a random number and resets the number of guesses to zero. It disables the Start Button and enables the Guess Button.

The Guess Button gets the user's guess, checks to see if it's too high, too low, or just right. When it's too low or too high, it responds to the user accordingly. When the guess is right, it tells the user they have the correct guess, enables the Start Button so they can play again, and disables the Guess Button so they can't guess again until a new random number is generated. Right or wrong, it adds one to the counter and displays the current number of guesses.

Pseudocode is often used to describe a programming problem. Pseudocode is a cross between programming code and description of a program. Developers use it to describe a program. It works because developers can use it to think through the logic for a program without worrying about the syntax of the code. The pseudocode for the program looks like the following.

Guess Button

Get Guess

If guess = right answer
    Response = "Correct"
    Enable Start Button
    Disable Guess Button
Else
    If guess > right answer
        Response = "Too high"
    Else
        Response = "Too low"
Add 1 to number of guesses
Display response
Display number of guesses

Start Button

Get random number between 1 and 100

Disable Start Button
Enable Guess Button
Set number of guesses to 0
Display number of guesses

Table 5.10   Guessing Game Variable Names and Uses

Variable Name	Scope	Type	Use
mbytNum	Modular	Byte	Random number from program
mshoNumGuesses	Modular	Short	Number of guesses taken
bytGuess	Local	Byte	User's guess
strResponse	Local	String	Response to user

The pseudocode describes what has to happen in both Buttons. From it, a developer can write the code. Developers use it to explain the logic without getting bogged down in the syntax. It forces them to think through the logic *before* they start writing code. It is easy to write because there are no strict rules for it. It's easy to modify and update or throw away. Most developers have a hard time discarding code once they've written it. A little time thinking through the problem before trying to write the code is a good investment (see Figure 5.6 and Tables 5.10 and 5.11).

Guessing Game Code

The following is the code for the Guessing Game program.

```
Public Class frmGuessingGame
    Dim mbytNum As Byte
    Dim mshoNumGuesses As Short
    Private Sub btnStart_Click(ByVal sender As
      System.Object, ByVal e As System.EventArgs)
      Handles btnStart.Click
      'Generate a random number
      mbytNum = Int(Rnd() * 100 + 1)
      'Enable Guess Button
      btnGuess.Enabled = True
      'Disable Start Button
      btnStart.Enabled = False
      'Reset and display number of guesses
      mshoNumGuesses = 0
      lblNumGuesses.Text = mshoNumGuesses.ToString
    End Sub
    Private Sub btnExit_Click(ByVal sender As
        System.Object, ByVal e As System.EventArgs)
        Handles btnExit.Click
        End
    End Sub
    Private Sub btnGuess_Click(ByVal sender As
```

```
        System.Object, ByVal e As System.EventArgs)
        Handles btnGuess.Click
    Dim bytGuess As Byte
    Dim strResponse As String
    'Input
    bytGuess = nudGuess.Value
    'Processing
    If bytGuess = mbytNum Then
        'Tells the user they've guessed the right number
        strResponse = "Correct"
        'Resets the Buttons so you can start a new game
        btnGuess.Enabled = False
        btnStart.Enabled = True
    Else
        If bytGuess > mbytNum Then
            'Guess is too high
            strResponse = "Too High"
        Else
            'Guess is too low
            strResponse = "Too Low"
        End If
    End If
    'Add one to the number of guesses
    mshoNumGuesses = mshoNumGuesses + 1
    'Output
    lblResponse.Text = strResponse
    lblNumGuesses.Text = mshoNumGuesses.ToString
End Sub
Private Sub frmGuessingGame_Load(ByVal sender As
    System.Object, ByVal e As System.EventArgs)
    Handles MyBase.Load
    'Randomizes the number generation process
    Randomize()
End Sub
End Class
```

VB Tip   *Open and run the Guessing Game program.*

Potential Problems

Without the Randomize command, the same numbers come up, in the same order, every time. The wrong Random command will generate a random number in the wrong range. The numbers could end up having decimals where

Table 5.11   Guessing Game Control Names and Uses

Control Name	Type	Use
nudGuess	NumericUpDown	Gets the user's guess
btnStart	Button	Generates random number and resets game
btnGuess	Button	Checks guess and responds to the user
btnExit	Button	Ends the game
lblResponse	Label	Displays the response to the user
lblNumGuesses	Label	Displays the number of guesses taken
One unnamed Label		Displays "Guesses"

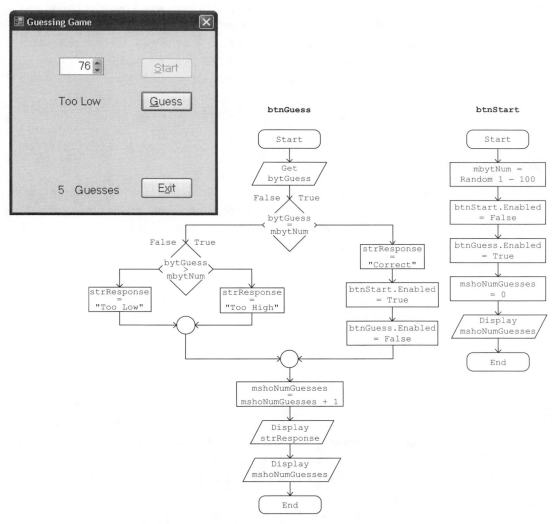

Figure 5.6   Guessing Game Program Screen and Flowchart

they wouldn't match the guesses. They might extend outside the range of guesses or they might fall within a small range instead of the entire range of 1 to 100. The variable for the random number must be a module-level variable. If not, the program won't retain a value from one guess to another. The counter must also be a module-level variable. Otherwise, it won't retain its value from one guess to another. If the responses are transposed, the user will be given the wrong feedback with each guess. The Buttons might not be enabled when needed. This may be tricky until you realize that you turn one on and turn the other off and vice versa.

VB Quiz 04

What would it take to make a guessing game for the numbers 1 to 10 or 1 to 1,000?
Can you create a flowchart for this program?
What are the potential problems for the user if the Start and Guess Buttons aren't disabled when not needed?
What would it take to display the lowest guess that's too high and the highest guess that's too low?
Does the pseudocode fit the flowchart and the finished code?

Case Structures

If statements are great, but they have their limits. As more programming options are needed, If statements become more cumbersome. So far the programming options have been limited to a handful of options and If statements have worked well. Now, it's time for a more powerful structure, the Case.

```
Select Case var
    Case value
        statement(s)
    Case value
        statement(s)
    Case Else
        statement(s)
End Select
```

Case structures are controlled by a single variable or expression. Case works with numbers or strings. It selects the first Case that matches and ignores all the rest. There is an optional Case Else at the end the only works when none of the Case statements match.

Let's consider the IfGrades program again. It generates a letter grade based on the student's percentage and requires numerous If statements to write. The Case structure simplifies this, both for the developer and anyone debugging or updating the code at a later date.

```
'Input
bytPercent = nudPercent.Value
'Processing
Select Case bytPercent
    Case Is <= 90
        strGrade = "A"
    Case Is >= 80
        strGrade = "B"
    Case Is >= 70
        strGrade = "C"
    Case Is >= 60
        strGrade = "D"
    Case Is < 60
        strGrade = "F"
End Select
'Output
lblGrade.Text = strGrade
```

The code compares the percent to a series of conditions. It starts at the top and works through the conditions until it finds a match and then runs the code in that part of the structure. It only runs the code for the first match and ignores the remaining comparisons. Case structures are clean and easy to interpret. This example compares bytPercent to the conditions in the Case statements. When it finds a match, it assigns a letter grade to strGrade.

Another way to write the structures is shown below. This code specifies the range for each condition. It's easier to read and follow because none of the Cases is dependent on the ones above it:

```
Select Case bytPercent
    Case 90 To 100
        strGrade = "A"
    Case 80 To 89
        strGrade = "B"
    Case 70 To 79
        strGrade = "C"
    Case 60 To 69
        strGrade = "D"
    Case 0 To 59
        strGrade = "F"
End Select
```

The flowchart for a Case structure has one entrance and one exit but multiple paths through it. Start on the left and evaluate each path based on the decision value. Follow the path of the first match (see Figure 5.7).

VB Tip   *Open and run the CaseGrades program.*

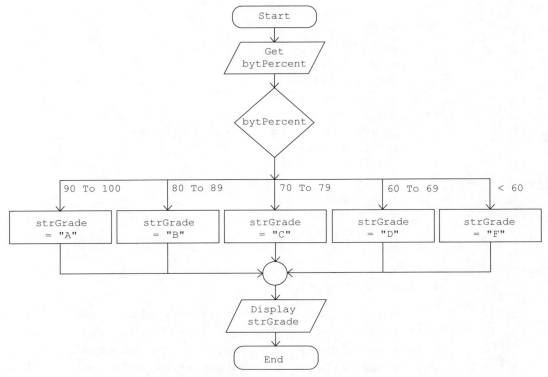

Figure 5.7   Select Case Grades Flowchart

Strings can be used to control Cases as well. Let's find the jacket price using Case instead of If statements:

```
'Input
strSize = txtSize.Text

'Processing
Select Case strSize
    Case = "S"
        decPrice = 29.95
    Case = "M"
        decPrice = 34.95
    Case = "L"
        decPrice = 39.95
    Case = "XL"
        decPrice = 44.95
End Select

'Output
lblPrice.Text = decPrice.ToString("c")
```

Case can be used for specific instances as well. A comma separates them in the Case statement. The example below also uses the Case Else statement. The first Case assigns "Vowel" when the letter is a vowel. For the other letters, the Case Else is triggered and "Consonant" is assigned.

```
'Input
strLetter = txtLetter.Text

'Processing
Select Case strLetter
    Case Is "A", "E", "I", "O", "U", "Y"
        strOutput = "Vowel"
    Case Else
        strOutput = "Consonant"
End Select

'Output
lblType.Text = strOutput
```

VB Tip   *The word "To" can be used for strings as well. For example, Case "A" To "D" would select A, B, C, or D.*

Potential Problems

Sometimes the Case statements are written in the wrong order. Be careful with the order when one Case statement is dependent on the ones above it. It is usually cleaner and clearer to write the Case with a range and the To keyword. Include a Case Else statement at the bottom whenever there's the chance that the Case statements won't cover every possible outcome. String comparisons must include quotation marks and strings cannot be compared to numbers.

VB Quiz 05   *When are Case structures easier to use than If structures?*
Explain how a Case structure works.
Why can't strings be compared to numbers?

A Roll of the Dice Case Study

Dice are used for many games, from the board games you played as a child to games of chance at a casino. The computer can simulate the roll of a die by generating a random number from 1 to 6, then using that number to display the appropriate graphic. Sometimes, two or more dice are needed. For that, simply generate two random numbers.

For this simple demonstration, we'll generate two random numbers, find their total, display the appropriate graphic for each, and display the total for the roll. This demo can then be the basis for future programs you develop.

Table 5.12   Dice Roll Variable Names and Uses

Variable Name	Scope	Type	Use
bytDie1	Local	Byte	Number rolled for first die
bytDie2	Local	Byte	Number rolled for second die
bytTotal	Local	Byte	Total of two dice

VB Tip

While it's possible to use one random number to simulate the roll of two dice, it's not recommended. Two dice will always total between 2 and 12, but the odds are not the same for every total. The odds of 2 or 12 are much smaller than the odds for 7, so always use multiple random numbers for multiple dice.

Each random number controls the display of one die. It will take a little work to simulate the six faces of each die, though. To do that, we'll need six different graphics, one of each face, and a PictureBox for each. Load a different graphic into each and set the Visible property to False. That way they won't be visible when the program starts.

The Roll Button does all the work. It generates two random numbers, each of which ranges from 1 to 6, just like a die. Find the total of these two numbers. Hide all the PictureBoxes. You don't know what PictureBoxes were displayed with the last roll so it's easiest just to set the Visible property of all the PictureBoxes to False and then display the ones that are needed. Display the total in a Label. Then use a Case to display to correct PictureBox for the first die. Use another Case to display the correct PictureBox for the other die (see Figure 5.8 and Tables 5.12 and 5.13).

Table 5.13   Dice Roll Control Names and Uses

Control Name	Type	Use
picDie11	PictureBox	Displays 1 for first die
picDie12	PictureBox	Displays 2 for first die
picDie13	PictureBox	Displays 3 for first die
picDie14	PictureBox	Displays 4 for first die
picDie15	PictureBox	Displays 5 for first die
picDie16	PictureBox	Displays 6 for first die
picDie21	PictureBox	Displays 1 for second die
picDie22	PictureBox	Displays 2 for second die
picDie23	PictureBox	Displays 3 for second die
picDie24	PictureBox	Displays 4 for second die
picDie25	PictureBox	Displays 5 for second die
picDie26	PictureBox	Displays 6 for second die
btnRoll	Button	Rolls the dice and displays output
btnExit	Button	Ends the program
lblTotal	Label	Displays the total for that roll
One unnamed Label		Displays "Total"

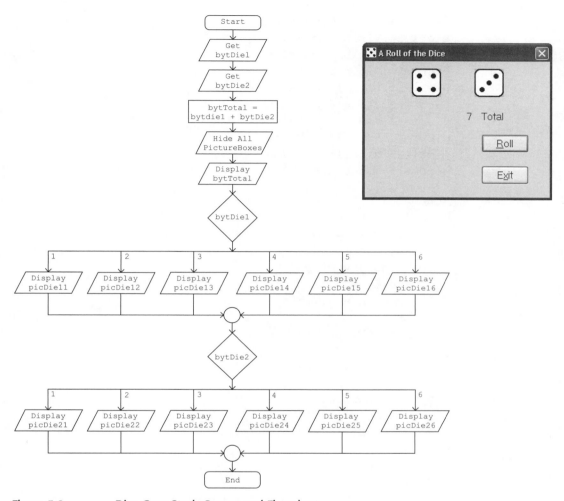

Figure 5.8   Dice Case Study Screen and Flowchart

```
'Declarations
Dim bytDie1 As Byte
Dim bytDie2 As Byte
Dim bytTotal As Byte

'Input
'Generate random numbers
bytDie1 = Int(Rnd() * 6 + 1)
bytDie2 = Int(Rnd() * 6 + 1)
'Processing
bytTotal = bytDie1 + bytDie2
'Hide all dice
picDie11.Visible = False
picDie12.Visible = False
```

```
picDie13.Visible = False
picDie14.Visible = False
picDie15.Visible = False
picDie16.Visible = False
picDie21.Visible = False
picDie22.Visible = False
picDie23.Visible = False
picDie24.Visible = False
picDie25.Visible = False
picDie26.Visible = False

'Output
'Display total
lblTotal.Text = bytTotal.ToString
'Display Die 1
Select Case bytDie1
    Case 1
        picDie11.Visible = True
    Case 2
        picDie12.Visible = True
    Case 3
        picDie13.Visible = True
    Case 4
        picDie14.Visible = True
    Case 5
        picDie15.Visible = True
    Case 6
        picDie16.Visible = True
End Select
'Display Die 2
Select Case bytDie2
    Case 1
        picDie21.Visible = True
    Case 2
        picDie22.Visible = True
    Case 3
        picDie23.Visible = True
    Case 4
        picDie24.Visible = True
    Case 5
        picDie25.Visible = True
    Case 6
        picDie26.Visible = True
End Select
```

VB Tip   *Open and run the DiceCaseStudy program.*

Potential Problems

Be sure to put the Randomize command in the Load event. Without it, the numbers won't be random. Create the PictureBoxes, name them, and place the graphics in them as needed. Once the program is working correctly, arrange them one on top of the other for the first die. Do the same for the PictureBoxes for the second die. With them scattered, it's easier to run and test your program. With them arranged on top of each other, it looks like just one graphic. You could use just one PictureBox for each die and load the appropriate graphic with each roll, but that hasn't been covered and it's a little slower. Change the visible property of the PictureBoxes to False so they don't appear until called. Be sure to generate numbers from 1 to 6. If they're out of range, the graphic won't display. Check the Case structures to make sure the right PictureBox will display. The names make it easier to keep track of the controls, but it also makes it easier to confuse them.

Tying It All Together

The key to writing programs with decision structures is to understand how data flow through the program from input, through processing, to output. That's the beauty of a flowchart. It's a visual roadmap for data traveling through your program. In the overtime program, there were two possible paths for your data. You had to transform the hours and the payrate from input to output on one of two possible paths. The If statement determined which path the data took. As a developer, you must understand what the data must do regardless of the path they take. Each path must be written to handle the data on it. The decision structure merely determines the path to take. The decision structure gives your program flexibility and lessens the work for the user. Without the If statement, the user would need to make the decision. They'd need to enter their hours and then click the Regular Pay Button or the Overtime Pay Button to get their output, and that's harder for them. And, as always, development is about making it easier for the user.

Fixing a Program

Russ Pupie runs a copy store near campus. He charges various rates for copies depending on the number of copies and the color and weight of the paper. Business and personal copies are subject to 7% sales tax, but clubs and nonprofit organizations aren't. Table 5.14 lists the rates. The program has bugs and needs debugging (see Figure 5.9).

Start by running the CopyStore program.

You run the program and enter good data for the inputs. It pops up a MessageBox saying you didn't enter the number of copies. In disbelief you try again.

Table 5.14   Copy Store Pricing

Copies	1–9	10–25	25–99	100+
50# white	10¢	8¢	6¢	5¢
100#white	15¢	14¢	13¢	12¢
50#colored	15¢	13¢	12¢	10¢
100#colored	20¢	18¢	16¢	15¢

Same result. You check the code. Sure enough, the If statement has the code turned around. As written, the MessageBox appears when there is a number entered and it tries to process it when there isn't a number. Oops. You change the code and try again. This time the MessageBox doesn't show up.

However, there's no tax even though you enter "B" for the business type. Check the last If in the processing. It has an And in it. That means the business type must be "B" and "P" before it sets the tax rate to 7%. Since it can't be both at once, you change the And to Or. That's better. You run the program again and try it with a lower-case "b" and it doesn't work. The If is set up for only upper-case letters. There are two choices: you could add more comparisons to the If statement so it would check for upper- and lower-case letters or you could convert the input to upper case. You decide to convert the input to upper case. That fixes that.

Next you test the program with 20 copies, a nice round number that makes the math easy. The totals come up goose eggs. The program worked with other numbers, but not 20. Logically, the 20 could be the problem. You check the Case structure and it's set for 10 to 15. The boundaries were set incorrectly and skipped a range of numbers. You check the table and the range should

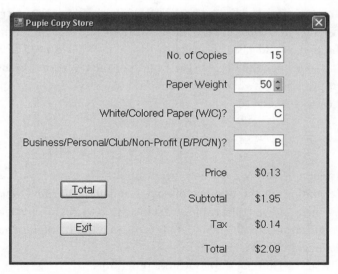

Figure 5.9   Copy Store Program Screen

be 10 to 25. You run the program again with the same input and this time it works. Ta da!

Pricing and customer satisfaction are important, so you check the prices to make sure they're correct. Compare each one to the table and you'll see that the prices for 25 to 99 copies are set incorrectly. That can happen, so always check and then test them by running the program. Remember, the devil is in the details.

VB Tip   *Open the corrected version of this program to see how it should look.*

On Your Own

Write a program that gets a number from the user and determines if the number is positive, negative, or zero. Add IsNumeric to your code to make sure that the input is a number and to display a MessageBox if it isn't.

Write a program to calculate a student's grade based on four test scores. Throw out the lowest of the four scores. Calculate the average and determine the student's grade based on the 90–80–70–60 scale. Display the average and the grade.

Write a multiple choice question with four possible answers. The user should enter an answer and receive feedback based on the answer. Incorrect answers should provide a hint and the correct answer should congratulate the user.

Write a program to determine the user's credit rating. Have the user enter their credit score and, based on that, return the user's rating and the interest rate for a home mortgage. Credit scores are from 300 to 850.

Summary

Decision structures give the computer the power to think. A developer provides the criteria and the program does its processing based on those criteria. Any data type can be used for a decision structure. If structures have two possible outcomes: one when the condition is True and the other when it's False. A number of choices can be created by stacking If structures on top of each other. If structures can be nested inside one another to provide choices based on multiple criteria. The Case structure provides a clear choice between multiple options from the same variable. Flowcharts and number lines provide visual guides for creating and understanding decision structures.

Review

Decision structures allow the computer to execute alternate blocks of code based on the outcome of a decision.

A block of code is a series of statements that belong together in the code and cannot be separated.

An If structure is based on a condition. When the condition is True, it runs the Then part of the code. When it's False, it runs the Else part of the code.

All conditions will be either True or False and only one block of code will run on any given pass.

There are six relational operators: <, <=, >, >=, =, and <>.

Relational comparisons are based on the ASCII code.

A diamond represents a decision structure in a flowchart. A circle is a connector.

Strings and numbers cannot be compared to each other in a decision structure.

Strings must match exactly in a comparison.

IsNumeric has one parameter. If that parameter can be a number, the IsNumeric is True.

And, Or, Not, and XOr are logical operators.

Both comparisons must be True for an And to be True.

Either condition can be True for an Or to be True.

Not reverses the outcome of a condition.

XOr can only be True if one of the conditions is True. It is False if both of them are False or if both of them are True.

Data validation checks the user's input to make sure it's within an established range before processing. This prevents processing problems.

Nested If structures are Ifs that are completely inside other Ifs.

Stacked If structures are Ifs that are stacked one on top of another in the code.

ElseIf is a command that lets a developer combine an If and an Else in the same command.

Pseudocode is human language that's used to explain a programming problem.

Case structures are based on one variable and have multiple options, depending on the outcome.

Case structures can be based on any data type.

Case Else is used at the bottom of a Case structure as a "catch-all."

The key to writing decision structures is to understand how data flow through a program.

Developers strive to make the computing experience easier for the user.

Terms

block	a series of related statements in a program
condition	a statement that evaluates to either True or False
connector	a flowchart symbol represented by a circle that connects two parts of the flowchart

data validation	testing to ensure that user input falls within an acceptable range or meets a specified set of conditions so it can be processed without errors
logical operators	And, Or, Not and XOr. These are used to create compound statements to handle complex logical operations
nested Ifs	If structures that are completely contained inside other structures
nested statement	a statement that is part of a larger block of code
pseudocode	cross between program code and a description; English-like statements that describe what a program should do
relational operator	a comparison sign: =, >, <, >=, <= or <>. These symbols are used to compare the values on either side
stacked Ifs	If statements that are stacked one on top of another

Keywords

And	an operator that combines two expressions; both must be True for the statement to be True
Case	a command that selects one set of statements from a list by matching a value with items in a list
Case Else	the last option in a Select Case structure; it's only used when none of the other options match the comparison value
Else	a command that marks the beginning of the False part of an If statement
ElseIf	the False part of an If statement when one more conditions follow the first If
End If	a command that marks the end of an If statement
End Select	the command that ends a Select Case structure
If	a statement that evaluates a condition and determines which lines of code to execute
Is	an operator used to compare two values
IsNullOrEmpty	a method that determines if a variable contains a value
IsNumeric	a method that determines if a value is a number
Not	an operator that reverses the value of a condition; True becomes False and False becomes True
Or	an operator that combines two expressions; one must be True for the statement to be True

Select Case	a statement that evaluates a variable, selects the first item in the list that matches it, and runs the code associated with it
Then	a command that marks the beginning of the True part of an If statement
To	an operator used to set the range of values in a comparison
XOr	an operator that combines two expressions; one and only one must be True for the condition to be True

Self-check

1. The outcome of an If statement is always True or False.
2. The Then part of an If structure cannot be empty.
3. All If statements must compare numeric values.
4. "TextBox" = "textbox".
5. An If statement that uses an Or has three possible True outcomes.
6. In a flowchart, an If structure is represented by an inverted Y.
7. One End If statement controls all the If statements in a nested If.
8. Pseudocode is a written description of the logic of a program.
9. The options in a Case structure are all based on the same variable.
10. Data validation is useful in preventing crashes.
11. An If statement:
    A. can have anywhere from one to three possible outcomes
    B. will always evaluate to True or False
    C. can be based on a variable or a constant
    D. all of the above
12. A nested If structure is:
    A. an If structure inside another If structure
    B. two or more If structures in a row in the code
    C. two comparisons with the same outcome
    D. two If statements combined by an And or an Or
13. IsNumeric:
    A. compares a string to a number to see if they're identical
    B. checks to see if a string is a numeric value
    C. converts a string to a number
    D. returns a number when given an ASCII value
14. When presented with multiple outcomes for a given value, a developer should use a(n):
    A. If structure
    B. stacked If structure
    C. nested If structure
    D. Case structure

15. For an either-or but not both comparison, the best option is:
    A. Or
    B. And
    C. XOr
    D. Not

16. Data validation involves:
    A. checking an input to see if it is of the right data type and within an acceptable range
    B. determining if the user needs help
    C. correctly formatting output before it's displayed
    D. none of the above

17. Which of the following is in ASCII order?
    A. A, a, 1
    B. p, T, 9
    C. 9, c, S
    D. 4, R, c

18. Which of the following is a logical operator?
    A. +
    B. &
    C. Or
    D. >=

19. If shoMyNum = 4 and strMyNum = "4" Then:
    A. If shoMyNum <= 10 And shoMyNum > 20 is True
    B. If Not shoMyNum = 4 is True
    C. If shoMyNum = strMyNum is True
    D. If shoMyNum > 0 And shoMyNum <= 8 is True

20. Aids to programming include:
    A. comments in the code
    B. flowcharts
    C. pseudocode
    D. all of the above

VB Quiz Answers

Quiz 01

The answer to an If will always be True or False. Depending on the input, the condition will always be one or the other. When True, the Then part of the If runs. When False, the Else part runs.

An If always has a Then that goes with it. Sometimes there's an Else and usually there's an End If. All of them work together and must be considered together in the code.

Diamonds are used to depict an If structure. The Then (True) path is on the right and the Else (False) path is on the left. One path or the other is followed based on the result of the condition.

It's wasteful to write the same code twice and it can be confusing. If there's a bug, it must be corrected in both places. If it's only fixed in one place, the problem is made that much worse.

Strings are compared using the ASCII table. Capital letters come alphabetically before any lower case letters. For strings to be equal, they must match exactly.

IsNumeric will be either True or False. Either the string is a number or it's not.

Quiz 02

And is used when all conditions must be true for the If statement to be true. If one condition is false, the entire condition is false. Or is used when one or more of the conditions must be true for the statement to be true. It can only be false when all of them are false. Not reverses the condition. XOr is used when one of the two conditions is true. It's false when both are true or both are false.

A number line is useful for creating a picture of the range of numbers in an If statement. It can show areas of overlap and areas that are missed.

Data validation helps prevent crashes. It can provide feedback for the user and it simplifies some of the programming statements.

Quiz 03

The code could be written with the following statements:

```
If decSales >= 100000 And bytYears > 5 Then
If decSales < 100000 And bytYears <= 5 Then
If decSales >= 100000 And bytYears <= 5 Then
If decSales < 100000 And bytYears > 5 Then
```

The flowchart for a stacked If structure has two or more Ifs on top of one another. Each If executes in turn and follows either the True or the False path.

There are two possible outcomes for an If Then Else. It will either be True or False. There are four possible outcomes for two stacked If Then Else structures.

The ElseIf is the False part of an If statement. It will only execute that code when the condition in the If statement is False.

Quiz 04

Change the range in the Random command. Use 10 or 1,000 instead of 100. That will change the range for the game.

Yes, a flowchart can be created for this program. The input is the random number in the Load event. Compare it to the guess the user makes and respond accordingly.

With both Buttons enabled, the user could click on the wrong one. A click on the Start Button in the middle of the game would generate a new number and it would probably throw off the user. There's no reason to click on Guess once the correct number has been found. By controlling when the Buttons are available, the user won't become frustrated by clicking on the wrong Button.

Two variables are needed: one to store the lowest guess that's too high and the other to store the highest guess that's too low. An If is needed for each of these and it needs to go in the correct place in the code. When a guess is too low, check to see if there's already been a higher guess that's too low. If there hasn't, make the guess the highest too-low number and display it. When a guess is too high, check to see if there's already been a lower guess that's too high. If there hasn't, make the guess the lowest too-high number and display it. A user mentally tracks this when guessing. Your code merely converts the algorithm into code.

All three should fit together and describe the program. The pseudocode is textual and the flowchart is graphical. Both are aids to writing the code.

Quiz 05

For a range, the Case is often easier to write and generally easier to examine in the code. When there are numerous possible alternatives, the Case is usually a cleaner option.

A Case is based on one variable. Each Case statement in the structure can contain code that handles that part of the decision. Each alternative is examined and the structure follows the first path that matches. Only one Case runs and the rest are ignored. If none of them match it follows the Case Else statement at the end.

Strings and numbers are represented differently by the computer and cannot be compared directly. To compare them one must be converted to the type of the other and then compared.

6

Loops – Once Is Not Enough

VB Quip

I have always wished that my computer would be as easy to use as my telephone. My wish has come true. I no longer know how to use my telephone. –Bjarne Stroustrup

Life is filled with repetition. And every once in a while it throws you for a loop. Every day and every week has a routine. For example, chores are a series of often mundane tasks that get repeated time and again. Make your bed, take out the garbage, walk the dog, do the dishes. That's why they're chores. You've probably reduced these tasks to a series of steps and then repeated them as needed. Business is much the same. The steps to calculate the weekly pay are pretty much the same for every employee. So is the process for calculating a bill or determining a student's grade. Once you know the proper steps for a process, it's easy to repeat them. However, if you can get the computer to do these tasks, it will be much faster and cheaper. And, it would free you to do more pleasant and important tasks.

Until now, the only way for the computer to repeat these tasks was by clicking on a Button over and over. That's slow and hard and boring. This chapter covers repetition structures – in programming parlance, loops. With them, a series of commands can be repeated. Some loops run a specified number of times. Others run while a condition is true while others run until a condition becomes true. One line of code marks the beginning of a loop and another marks the end of the loop. What's in between gets repeated. With loops, you'll have the last piece of a programmer's basic toolkit. By combining sequence, selection, and repetition, you'll be able to write almost anything. And with them, the possibilities are endless.

What Are Loops?

A *loop* is a series of commands that gets repeated. Just like If and Case structures, a loop is a block of code and must be treated as a series of related steps instead of individual lines of code. Every loop has a line that starts the loop and another that ends the loop. The lines of code in between get repeated. Every loop has a condition that determines when it runs and when it stops. Some loops run a specific number of times while others run until a condition is met.

The pseudocode for a simple grading program looks like this:

Get first test score
Get second test score
Get third test score
Get final test score
Add test scores
Average = total / 4
Display Average

These steps could be repeated by enclosing them in a loop. The loop can run a specific number of times, once for each student, or it could run until all the students have been processed. Without a loop, you'd be forced to write this code once for each student or you'd have to run the program repeatedly until all the students had been processed. Either way, it's time-consuming and clumsy. That's what makes loops so useful.

Here's the pseudocode to process the tests for 20 students:

Do index = 1 to 20
    Get first test score
    Get second test score
    Get third test score
    Get final test score
    Add test scores
    Average = total / 4
    Display Average
Loop

The same steps get repeated 20 times, once for each student. And, with a little practice, you'll be able to set up the loop so that each trip through it does exactly the processing you need for that record.

For . . . Next Loops

For . . . Next loops are usually used when you know the number of times you want to repeat a loop. The top of the loop is marked with a *For* statement and *Next* marks the end of the loop. For loops use a counter to keep track of times it runs.

Code	Output

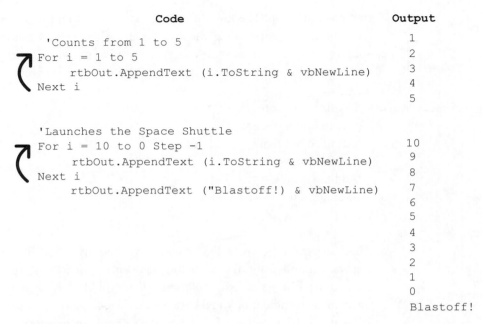

```
'Counts from 1 to 5
For i = 1 to 5
    rtbOut.AppendText (i.ToString & vbNewLine)
Next i
```

```
'Launches the Space Shuttle
For i = 10 to 0 Step -1
    rtbOut.AppendText (i.ToString & vbNewLine)
Next i
    rtbOut.AppendText ("Blastoff!) & vbNewLine)
```

Output:
```
1
2
3
4
5

10
9
8
7
6
5
4
3
2
1
0
Blastoff!
```

Figure 6.1   For...Next Loop Examples

Counting Loops

The general format for a For loop looks like this:

```
For counter = StartValue To EndValue [Step increment]
    statement(s)
Next [counter]
```

That looks intimidating, but it's easily deciphered. Always start the loop with For and end it with Next. The lines in between get repeated. StartValue is where you start counting. Usually that's 0 or 1, but it can be any number. EndValue is where the loop stops. counter keeps track of the number of times you've been through the loop and must be a declared numeric variable. It is considered good form to include it after the Next statement. Although that's not required, it does make it easier to read the code. To is required between the StartValue and EndValue. The syntax in brackets is optional. You must use the Step command when you want the loop to count backward or to count by something other than 1. And, when counting backward, the StartValue must be greater than the EndValue. Think of it as a countdown (see Figure 6.1).

VB Tip

Loops automatically indent to make it easier to see and read them. The start line and end line for a loop always align vertically.

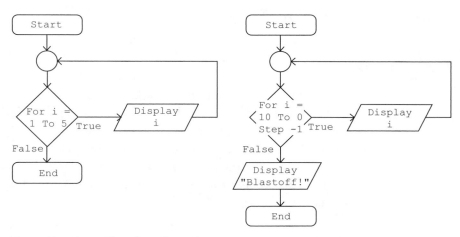

Figure 6.2   For...Next Loop Flowchart Examples

Loops are often used for counting. The first example above simply counts from 1 to 5. The second example counts backward from 10 to 0. And then, for good measure, it launches the Space Shuttle.

The variable i is the counter that controls this loop. Declare it as an integer variable in your declarations. The standard practice in programming is to use i, j, and k as loop control variables. The For statement says to start the loop at 1 and stop when it reaches 5. It's exactly like counting from 1 to 5. In fact, the output is just that. The first time through the loop, i equals 1. That value gets displayed in the output. The next time through the loop, i is 2 and it gets displayed. Every time control of the program gets back to the For statement, it increments i. Each trip through the loop is called an *iteration*.

The second loop is controlled by i. This time it starts at 10 and counts backward to 0. Every time through the loop, i decrements by 1. The StartValue for this loop is 10 and the EndValue is 0. The Step command forces the loop to count by −1 each time. The last line of code displays "Blastoff!" And, that is pretty much all it takes to be a rocket scientist!

VB Tip   *Do not alter the value of i inside your loop. It will cause problems for you and your program!*

Loop Flowchart

Flowcharts are used to display loops. Follow the arrow and you'll see it loops back in the code. A decision symbol indicates where the decision to repeat the loop is made. It follows this loop until the loop has been repeated the specified number of times. It then continues with the sequence of commands. In the second example, the program loops until i gets to 0. It then exits the loop and displays "Blastoff!" (see Figure 6.2).

VB Tip   *Do a deskcheck on both loops to verify how they work.*

Step Parameter

The Step parameter determines how fast you move through a loop. Think of it as counting by twos or threes or tens. Without the Step parameter in the For statement, a loop increments by 1 each time. To get your loop to increment by some other value, you must include the Step command. And, to count backward, *decrement*, the starting value must be larger than the ending value.

For loops can use positive and negative numbers, and they can also change by decimal values.

Loop Control Variables

The numeric variable that controls a For . . . Next loop increments until it's larger than its limit. (If it steps backward, it decrements until it's smaller than its limit.) So, if i controls a loop that's set up to run from 1 to 5, the final value of i is 6. Developers often start a loop at 0 so its final value ends up being the same as the number of iterations. For example, if i controls a loop that runs from 0 to 4, i ends up at 5. That way i ends up with the same value as the number of trips through the loop. Developers find that it comes in handy. And, while that may be a bane for new developers, it comes in handy for those that know how to use it.

VB Tip   *Run the ForNextDemos program to see how For . . . Next loops work.*

VB Quiz 01   *What are some routine activities that involve loops?*

What are some business activities that could be accomplished with loops?

Give examples of when a loop could be used for a countdown.

Write a program to prove that the final value of a loop control variable is 6 for a loop that runs from 1 to 5.

Do While Loops

The Do . . . While is the second type of loop. There are several ways to set up a *While* loop. It can be set up to run a specified number of times, just like a For . . . Next loop. But, while a For . . . Next loop is controlled by a numeric variable, a While loop can be controlled with a string, a Boolean, or a numeric variable. While loops are set up with a condition and run while that condition is true. There must a line of code inside the loop that can change that condition. The general form for a While loop looks like this:

```
Do While condition
   statement(s)
Loop
```

Counting Loops

A While loop can mimic a For...Next loop. It can be initialized to any value, increment or decrement as needed, and end when a specified value is reached. Here is an example:

```
i = 1
Do While i <= 5
    rtbOut.AppendText(i.ToString & vbNewLine)
    i = i + 1
Loop
```

The output is:

```
1
2
3
4
5
```

In the preceding code, i is initialized to 1 above the loop. Inside the loop the value of i is displayed in the RichTextBox and 1 is added to i. Every time the *Do* line of code executes, it checks to see if the condition is True. The loop continues as long as i is less than or equal to 5. Once the condition in the Do line becomes False, control skips to the code below the Loop line.

Notice how i is initialized to 1 and <= 5 is part of the condition. That's an easy way to see and remember the limits on this loop. It starts at 1 and ends at 5.

Do Loop While

There's a variation on the While loop. Instead of putting the condition in the Do line, the While condition is placed in the Loop line. For example:

```
i = 1
Do
    rtbOut.AppendText(i.ToString & vbNewLine)
    i = i + 1
Loop While i <= 5
```

The output is:

```
1
2
3
4
5
```

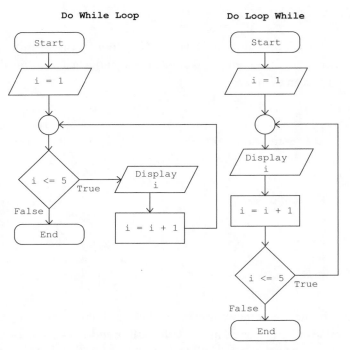

Figure 6.3   Do While Loop and Do Loop While Flowchart Examples

where i is initialized to 1 above the loop. Inside the loop the value of i is displayed in the RichTextBox and 1 is added to i. Every time the Loop line of code executes, it checks to see if the condition is True. The loop continues as long as i is less than or equal to 5. Once the condition in the Loop line becomes False, control skips to the code below the Loop line (see Figure 6.3).

Sentinel Values

For ... Next loops are controlled by numeric variables. While loops are controlled by a condition. As long as the condition is True, the loop runs. In addition to numeric variables, Boolean and string variables can be used to control a loop. These are *sentinel values*. Sentinel values are set with each trip through the loop. As soon as that value makes the condition False, the loop ends. Following are two examples. One uses a string variable and the other uses a Boolean.

```
Do While strFavFoods <> "zzz"
    strFavFoods = InputBox("Enter zzz to end", "Favorite
      Foods")
    If strFavFoods <> "zzz" Then
        rtbOut.AppendText(strFavFoods & vbNewLine)
    End If
Loop
```

The loop seeks the favorite foods from the user. They are then listed in the RichTextBox. When the user enters zzz, the loop ends. This is handy when you don't know how many times you'll need the loop.

Investment Program

Your goals are to work hard, give back, and retire with a million dollars. You're not sure how much you'll need to save every year or how many years you'll need to work to save a million dollars, so you create a program to do the work for you.

Your inputs are the yearly contributions to your retirement account and the annual interest rate. Your output is the final total and the number of years it will take.

Use NumericUpDowns for the input: one for the annual contribution and one for the interest rate. Users typically see the interest rate as a whole number, but the calculation must be a decimal. The output should be to Labels.

The loop is set up to run while the investment is less than $1,000,000. Each year the contribution is added to the total and the interest for that year is calculated. Add the annual contribution and the accrued interest to the total. Add 1 to the counter that's tracking the years.

The flowchart for the program is given in Figure 6.4.

Here's the code from the flowchart:

```
'Input
decYearly = nudYearly.Value
sngIntRate = nudIntRate.Value
sngIntRate = sngIntRate / 100

'Processing
Do While decTotal < 1000000
    decIntEarned = (decTotal + decYearly) * sngIntRate
    decTotal = decTotal + decYearly + decIntEarned
    shoYears = shoYears + 1
Loop

'Output
lblYears.Text = shoYears.ToString
lblTotal.Text = decTotal.ToString("c")
```

VB Tip   *Open and run the RetirementSavings program.*

VB Quiz 02   *What would happen if you got into a loop and couldn't get out of it?*

Could you set up a Do While Loop that never runs?

Explain why a Do Loop While must run at least once.

What is a sentinel value?

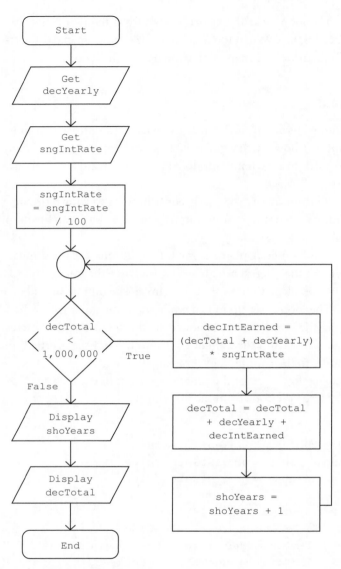

Figure 6.4   Investment Program Flowchart

Do Until Loops

Do While loops run while their condition is True. Do *Until* Loops, as the name implies, run until the condition becomes True. In other words, Until loops run as long as their condition is False. Until loops, just like While loops, must have a line of code inside the loop that can change that condition. The general form for an Until loop looks like this:

```
Do Until condition
   statement(s)
Loop
```

Counting Loops

This loop is set up to run from 1 to 5:

```
i = 1
Do Until i > 5
     rtbOut.AppendText(i.ToString & vbNewLine)
     i = i + 1
Loop
```

The output is

1
2
3
4
5

where i is initialized to 1 above the loop. Inside the loop the value of i is displayed in the RichTextBox and 1 is added to i. Every time the Do line of the code executes, it checks to see if the condition is False. The loop continues until i is greater than 5. Once the condition in the Do line becomes True, control skips to the code below the Loop line.

Notice how i is initialized to 1 and > 5 is part of the condition. That's an easy way to see and remember the limits on this loop. It starts at 1 and ends at 5.

VB Quip

Theory is when you know something, but it doesn't work. Practice is when something works, but you don't know why. Programmers combine theory and practice: Nothing works and they don't know why. –Anonymous

Factorial Program

A factorial is a nonnegative integer represented by "n!". It is the product of all positive integers less than or equal to it. So 5! = 1 * 2 * 3 * 4 * 5, or 120. It's easy enough to calculate a factorial for small numbers, but it gets increasingly difficult with each new integer. Wouldn't it be nice if the computer could do the work? You bet your slide rule! See Figure 6.5.

```
i = 1
shoTotal = 1
Do Until i > 5
     shoTotal = shoTotal * i
     i = i + 1
Loop
lblOut.Text = shoTotal.ToString
```

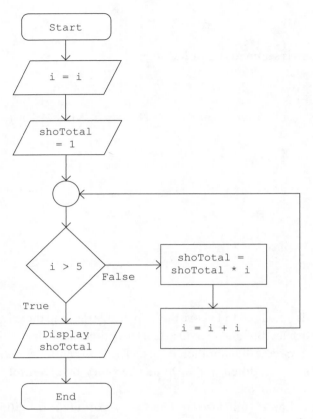

Figure 6.5   Factorial Program Flowchart

In this example, i is initialized to 1 above the loop. The loop checks to see if i is greater than 5. When it's False, the loop runs. Inside the loop, the value of shoTotal is multiplied by i and stored in shoTotal. This is a little different than the accumulators you've worked with before, but it works in the about the same way. The next line adds 1 to i. This line controls the value of i and the value of i controls the loop. Without this line, you'd never get out of the loop. The loop stops when i is greater than 5. The last line displays the total.

Do Loop Until

There are two flavors of the Until loop. Just like the Do Loop While, the Do Loop Until has the condition in the Loop line at the bottom of the loop. For example:

```
i = 1
Do
      rtbOut.AppendText(i.ToString & vbNewLine)
```

```
    i = i + 1
Loop Until i > 5
```

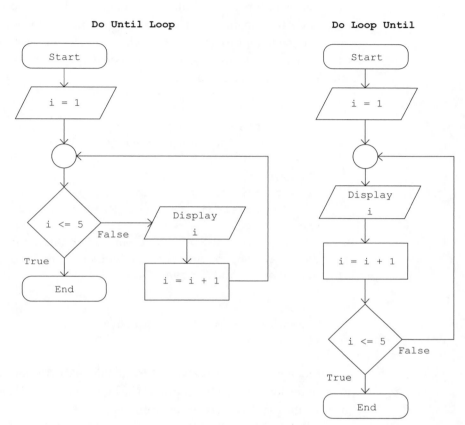

Figure 6.6   Do Until Loop and Do Loop Until Flowchart Examples

The output is

1
2
3
4
5

In this case, i is initialized to 1 above the loop. Inside the loop, the value of i is displayed in the RichTextBox and 1 is added to i. Every time the Loop line of code executes, it checks to see if the condition is False. The loop continues until i is greater than 5. Once the condition in the Loop line becomes True, control skips to the code below the Loop line (see Figure 6.6).

Login Program

The user login for the computer is a good example of a Do Loop Until. The user enters their login to gain access to a computer, network, or site. It takes at least one attempt to gain access and, if you make a mistake, it might take two or three tries. However, every good system has security, and repeated failed attempts must be prevented.

```
Do
    shoAttempts = shoAttempts + 1
    strLogin = InputBox("Enter your login", "System
      Access")
    strLogin = strLogin.ToUpper
    If strLogin <> strAccess Then
        MsgBox("Login failed", MsgBoxStyle.OkOnly)
    End If
Loop Until strLogin = strAccess Or shoAttempts >= 3
'If login isn't correct, then end the program
If strLogin <> strAccess Then
    End
Else
    MsgBox("Welcome!", MsgBoxStyle.OkOnly)
End If
```

The loop must run once. It goes through the code in the loop and then checks to see if the loop should be repeated. The loop repeats until the correct login is given or the user has exceeded their number of attempts. The If below the loop either allows access or ends the program (see Figure 6.7).

VB Tip   *Open and run the Login program.*

VB Quiz 03   *How could you change the factorial program so it would display the factorial for every number in the list?*
How would you redesign the factorial program so the user could decide the value of n!?
Why have five different types of loops?

Loop Questions

There are several questions to ask yourself whenever you see a loop in the code. The answers are vitally important to understanding what the program does. Developers have internalized these questions and automatically use them when they see new code. As a greenhorn, you'll have to settle for a more mechanical

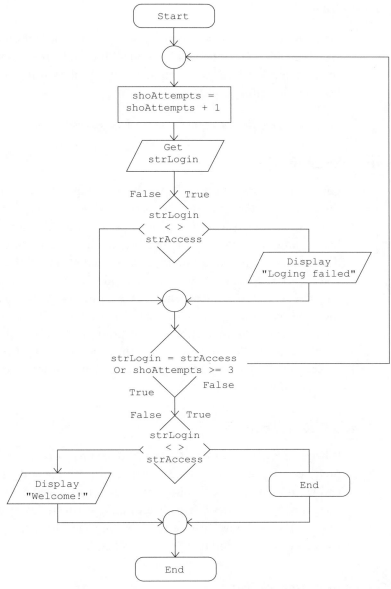

Figure 6.7   Login Program Flowchart

approach, but rest assured, even the most grizzled veteran still looks at loops and asks these questions.

Where Does It Start?

Find the top of a loop. It always starts with For or Do, which marks the top of the loop, and the code that follows is part of the loop.

Where Does It End?

Once you've found the top of a loop, find the last line of the loop. The line starts with Next for a For loop and Loop for While and Until loops. In Visual Basic, the first and last lines of a loop are vertically aligned in the code. Everything between these lines is part of the loop.

VB Tip   *If you need to, draw a line to connect them. It's a good way to create a block of code.*

What Controls the Loop?

Once you've blocked off the loop, the next step is to determine what controls the loop. In a For loop, it's the first variable after the For and it's always a numeric variable. While and Until loops are a little trickier. They're controlled by a condition that's either in the Do line or the Loop line. Check these and determine what the condition is. Changes in that condition determine when to end the loop. Normally, the first line inside the loop or the last line inside the loop contain an assignment statement that can change the variable that controls the condition. It might be an assignment statement that controls a counter or an input statement that gathers input from the user. It could be a calculation, but there must a line that can change the condition and get you out of the loop. Once you've determined that, you know when and where the loop starts and ends and how it ends.

How Many Times Does It Loop?

It helps to know how many times the loop runs. For . . . Next loops are usually pretty easy to determine because there's a start value and an end value. While and Until loops are a little different. They might repeat a set number of times, such as when a counter is used. They might be controlled by user input. In that case, you won't know the exact number of times they'll loop, but you'll know what ends the loop and that's extremely helpful.

Is It Top-Driven or Bottom-Driven?

In computerese, these conditions are known as *pretest* and *posttest*. It's simply an indication of where the condition is placed in the loop. Pretest loops have them at the top and posttest loops have them at the bottom. *Top-driven loops* check the condition at the top of the loop. *Bottom-driven loops* check them at the bottom. A top-driven loop might not run; it depends on the way it's written. A bottom-driven loop must run once. It goes through the code of the loop once before it checks to see if the loop should repeat. Both types have their uses and it's important to understand when and why to use them.

Is It a True or False Loop?

It may be better to ask whether the loop runs while it's true or if it runs until it becomes true. While loops run while their condition is true. Until loops run until the condition becomes true. In other words, once the condition in a While loop becomes false, the loop stops. An Until loop runs as long as its condition is false. Any more explanation and it would become confusing.

Ask yourself these same questions when you devise code. What type of loop should I use? Should it be top- or bottom-driven? What variable should control this loop? How many times should it run? Do I need it to run while it's true or should it run until it's true?

When you can answer these questions, then you're ready to start coding.

VB Quip

It's not at all important to get it right the first time. It's vitally important to get it right the last time. –Andrew Hunt and David Thomas

Infinite Loops

An *infinite loop* is a loop that starts and never ends. It's a bad thing. If your program has an infinite loop, all the cool programs will make fun of it. An infinite loop runs, but it has a logical error in it. The loop starts but there's no gracious way out of it. The user either ends the program manually or the program eventually crashes on its own. Either way is messy.

Infinite loops have several causes. It may be missing the line of code that changes the value of the loop control variable. It may have a logical error that resets the value of the loop control variable. It may be impossible to set the value of the loop control variable to a valid value.

VB Tip

To end an infinite loop, you need to click on the Stop Debugging button or press Ctrl-Alt-Break on the keyboard. That will end the program and take you back to the Visual Basic interface.

```
'Infinite loop
Do While i < 5
    i = i + 1
    rtbOut.AppendText(i.ToString & vbNewLine)
    i = 0
Loop
```

This is just one example of an infinite loop. The variable i controls the loop and the loop runs while i < 5. The second line adds 1 to the value of i. That's fine. The value of i is then displayed. Still good. The next line sets the value of i to 0. Bad news. The Do line checks the value of i, finds that it's less than 5, and repeats the loop.

VB Quip   *A developer wanders through the forest and stumbles upon a wise, old man. "How do I write error-free code," he asked. "The secret is in this tome," said the old man, who handed him a piece of paper and disappeared in a puff of smoke. One side of the parchment read, "The secret to good code is on the other side." The developer flipped it over and read the other side. It read, "The secret to good code is on the other side."*

Nested Loops

Just about any code can be inside a loop. That includes other loops. These are called *nested loops*. A loop is a series of repeated steps. A nested loop is a series of repeated steps inside another set of repeated steps. A semester is a nested loop. Each week in a semester has the same schedule of classes. That's the inside loop. Each semester has the same pattern of classes, midterms, classes, and finals. That's the outer loop.

Each loop must be controlled by a different variable. The inner loop must be completely inside the outer loop. The total number of iterations can be found by multiplying the repetitions for each loop. Any combination of loops can be used, but the following example uses For loops.

VB Tip   *Developers often use i, j, and k for the loop control variables for nested loops. It makes it easier to following the nesting.*

```
rtbOut.Clear()
rtbOut.AppendText("i j" & vbNewLine)
For i = 1 To 3
    For j = 1 to 4
        rtbOut.AppendText(i.ToString & " " & j.ToString
            & vbNewLine)
    Next j
Next i
```

The output for this code looks like this:

```
i j
1 1
1 2
1 3
1 4
2 1
2 2
2 3
2 4
3 1
3 2
3 3
3 4
```

The outer loop is controlled by i. It loops three times. The inner loop is controlled by j and loops four times. The variables i and j are displayed each time it passes the output line. The j loop completes its work before it gets to the Next i line. i gets incremented and the j loop starts all over. Between the two loops, there are 12 lines of output. You can see how i stays at 1 while the j loop completes its work. The i loop then repeats, forcing the j loop to start all over. Once the j loop is done for the second time, control goes back to the i loop and it starts the j loop over again.

VB Tip   *Open and run the NestedLoops program to see how it works.*

Let's change the code just a little to see what happens:

```
rtbOut.Clear()
rtbOut.AppendText("i j Count" & vbNewLine)
For i = 1 To 3
    For j = 1 to 4
        bytCount = bytCount + 1
        rtbOut.AppendText(i.ToString & " " & j.ToString & " " &
            bytCount.ToString & vbNewLine)
    Next j
Next i
```

The output for this code looks like this:

```
i j Count
1 1 1
1 2 2
1 3 3
1 4 4
2 1 5
2 2 6
2 3 7
2 4 8
3 1 9
3 2 10
3 3 11
3 4 12
```

1 gets added to bytCount each time it hits this line of code. Between the two loops, it hits this line of code 12 times (see Figure 6.8).

Draw lines on the flowchart in Figure 6.8 to indicate the flow of the program. There should be twelve lines that go through the output.

VB Tip   *bytCount = bytCount + 1 could have been written as*

bytCount += 1

It's shorthand for a counter and works with any value and any calculation.

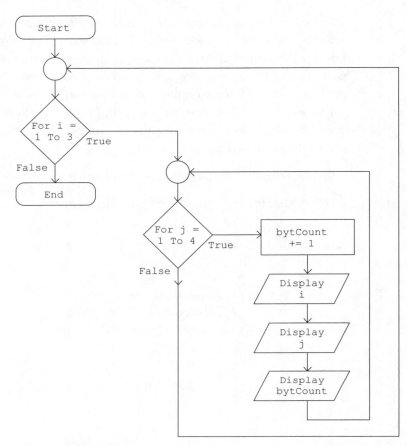

Figure 6.8   Nested Loops Flowchart

Exit

Exit For is used to short-circuit a For . . . Next loop. *Exit Do* is used to short-circuit Do loops. Sometimes a loop doesn't need to be completed. That's where the Exit command is used. It's used to get you out of a loop early (see Figure 6.9).

VB Quiz 04   *How do the loop questions help you to understand how loops work?*
                       What steps can be taken to avoid an infinite loop?
                       Explain how knitting is like nested loops.
                       In the nested-loop example, what are the final values for i, j, and bytCount?

Chr and Asc Commands

VB Tip   *Check the ASCII chart in Appendix A.*

Chr is short for character. Computer characters all have a standard representation using bits – those little 0s and 1s that do everything on the computer. Chr

Code	Output
```Do Until i >= 5```	
``` rtbOut.AppendText (i & vbNewLine)```	
	0
``` If i = 3 Then```	1
``` Exit Do```	2
``` End If```	3
``` i += 1```	
```Loop```	

```
Do While i <= 5
   rtbOut.AppendText (i & vbNewLine)
```
```
   If i = 3 Then
       Exit Do
   End If
```
```
   i += 1
Loop
```
Output:
```
0
1
2
3
```

```
For i = 0 To 4
   rtbOut.AppendText (i & vbNewLine)
```
```
   If i = 3 Then
       Exit For
   End If
```
```
Next i
```
Output:
```
0
1
2
3
```

Figure 6.9   **Exit Loop Early Examples**

is the numeric equivalent for the ASCII characters. For example, Chr(65) is capital A and Chr(66) is capital B. The common characters on the keyboard, as well as special characters, can all be represented using Chr. Characters can also be manipulated using Chr. Asc is the other side of the coin. Use Asc and the character to get the numeric value for a character. Chr(34) is the quotation mark ("). Remember that a quotation mark is about the only thing that can't be contained in a string. So it's impossible to put a quotation mark inside a string and it's hard to display a quotation mark. Chr(34) is the numeric value for a quotation mark and that can be used when a quotation mark is needed.

Chr(86) & Chr(66) converts to "VB".
Asc("V") & Asc("B") translate to 86 and 66.

VB Tip   *Run the ChrAscDemo to see how it works.*

A Little Fun With Graphics

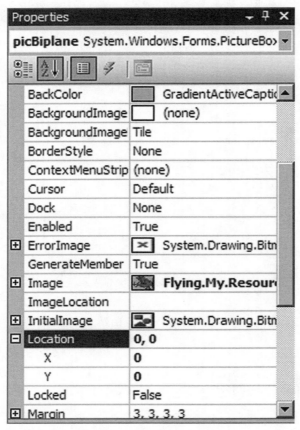

Figure 6.10   picBiplane Properties

Most of what you've seen with loops so far has been pretty mundane. This section won't have much of a business use, but it will be good practice with loops and should be a little more fun.

First, we need a little background. Controls – a Button, TextBox, Label, or PictureBox – are positioned on the screen using X,Y coordinates. The top left of the form is location 0,0. The distance from the left side of the form is X and the distance from the top is Y. These are usually measured in *pixels* and are controlled with the *Left* and *Top* properties. The Top and Left properties are part of the Location Property. These two numbers determine the position for any control. When you change the position of a control, the Top and Left properties change. It also works the other way. Change the Top and Left properties and the control changes its position on the screen. Let's use loops to control the Top and Left properties of a PictureBox (see Figures 6.10 and 6.11).

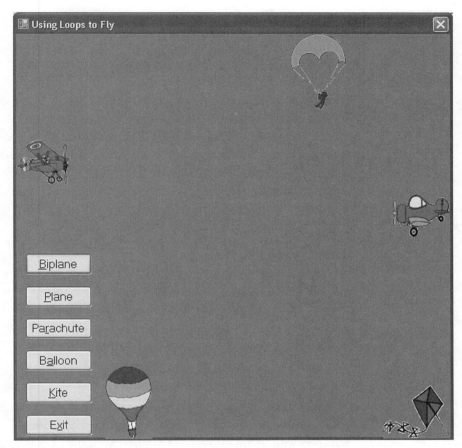

Figure 6.11   Airshow Program Screen

Create a new solution called AirShow. Change the BackColor property of the form to GradientActiveCaption. Create a PictureBox called picBiplane and position it in the top left corner of the form. Check the X,Y coordinates to make sure they're 0,150. You can set them manually if you like. Place the biplane.bmp image in the PictureBox and set the SizeMode property to AutoSize.

Create a Button called btnBiplane. This Button will control the biplane and you'll get it to fly across the form from left to right. Do that by changing the Left property of picBiplane. Set it to 1 and it creeps ever so slightly to the right. Change it to 2 and it jumps a little more. You could accomplish that with the following code:

```
picBiplane.Left = 1
picBiplane.Left = 2
```

But, to move it all the way across the screen this way would take hundreds of lines of code. There's an easier way, a loop!

```
Dim i As Double
For i = 0 To 700
    picBiplane.Left = i
Next i
```

Declare i as a Double and use it to control a For...Next loop. More on why it's a double in a minute. Then set up a loop to run from 0 to 700. Inside the loop is just one line. That line sets the Left property of the PictureBox to i. The first time through the loop, i is 0. The next time, it's 1, the next time, it's 2, and so on until it gets to 700.

Just below the loop, add

```
btnBiplane.Enabled = False
```

to turn off the Button.

Run the program. It runs correctly, but the plane scoots across the screen too quickly. That's because the loop runs so fast. Now, there's no way to slow down the loop. The computer executes the lines of code as fast as it can, and most of the time, you're happy that it runs so fast. The best way to slow down the plane is to get the loop to take smaller steps. Change the For line to read:

```
For i = 0 To 700 Step 0.00001
```

Now, it takes 100,000 little steps for each pixel. Instead of flashing across the screen, it now glides. That's why i was declared as a double, so it could store numbers with decimals. Feel free to tinker with the loop and the numbers until you understand exactly how it works.

Next, let's get another plane to fly the other way. Create a PictureBox called picPlaneII. Set the SizeMode to AutoSize and add the planeII.bmp image to it. Position the PictureBox on the right side of the form and note the Left property of it. You'll need to know that for your loop. Create a Button called btnPlaneII. Inside it, write a loop that runs from that number backward to −100. That way the plane will disappear off the left side of the form. The Step value must be a negative number so the loop decrements. Be sure to turn off the Button when the loop is finished. It might look like this:

```
Dim i As Double
For i = 513 To -100 Step -0.00001
    picPlaneII.Left = i
Next i
btnPlaneII.Enabled = False
```

The loop starts at 513 because that's where the PictureBox is positioned. (Your value may be different). The value of i decreases slightly with every pass through the loop, which changes the Left property of the PictureBox and moves the image to the left. Eventually, it disappears off the left side of the form and disables the Button. The planes flies!

Next, create a PictureBox called picParachute. Place it at the top of the form and add the parachute.bmp image to it. Create a Button called btnParachute and code it. This time the Top property must change for the skydiver to land. Set the loop so i starts at 0 and increases. Change the Top property of picParachute inside the loop. The loop should increment so the value of i increases. Disable the Button once the loop is finished. It might look like this:

```
Dim i As Double
For i = 0 To 700 Step 0.00001
    picParachute.Top = i
Next i
```

Your skydiver should now float gently to the ground. Geronimo!

Next, create a PictureBox called picBalloon, set the SizeMode to AutoSize, and add the balloon.bmp to it. The balloon should ascend into the sky. The Top property has to decrease for this to happen. Note the Top property of picBalloon. Create a Button called btnBalloon and write the code for it. Start the loop with this value and end it at −150, which makes the balloon float off the form. Disable the Button once the loop is finished. This code is similar to the following:

```
Dim i As Double
For i = 471 To -150 Step -0.00001
    picBalloon.Top = i
Next i
btnBalloon.Enabled = False
```

Tinker with the Step value for this one. A larger number makes the balloon rise faster. A smaller number slows it down.

The last one is a little trickier. Create a PictureBox called picKite, set the SizeMode to AutoSize, and add the kite.bmp graphic. Position picKite at 500, 500. The plan is to have the kite move up and left. Create a Button called btnKite and write the code for it. The loop must start at 500 and end at −100. Be sure to set the Step value to a negative number. There are two lines of code inside the loop. One line changes the Top property of picKite and the other changes the Left property of picKite. Disable the Button once the loop is finished.

Be sure to save your work. Good job.

```
Dim i As Double
For i = 500 To -100 Step -0.00001
    picKite.Left = i
    picKite.Top = i
Next i
btnKite.Enabled = False
```

VB Tip   *Open and run the Flying program to see how it works.*

VB Quiz 05   *Write your name using Chr values.*
                          Translate the following Chr values to come up with a name. Who is it?
                          77, 120, 121, 122, 112, 116, 108, 107
                          Change the loops in the Airshow program from For loops to While or Until loops.
                          How would you get a plane to dive from the top left to the lower right?
                          How would you get a plane to dive from the top right to the lower left?

Tying It All Together

It's time to try some examples using loops.

Depreciation Program

Business assets depreciate over time. Buy a piece of equipment – a computer, for example – and its value decreases as long as you own it. At some point, its value is nearly gone, and it's left with what is called the salvage value. Take the value of the equipment, its expected life, and its salvage value, and you can calculate the depreciation of the item over time. The formula for depreciation is

depreciation = (value – salvage value) / life

Depreciation is the amount of value an item loses each year. You can calculate the value for an item using

value = value – depreciation

There are three inputs for this program: the value of the item, its salvage value, and its expected life. Let's assume the initial value of a computer is $1,000 and its salvage value is $100. You anticipate a life expectancy of 5 years. Use NumericUpDown for the input. Use a RichTextBox for the output and display the year and the remaining value of the computer. Determine the annual depreciation for the computer and then use a Do While loop to calculate the value and display the year and the remaining value for the computer (see Figure 6.12).

```
decDeprec = (decValue - decSalvage) / bytLife
Do While decValue > decSalvage
    bytYear += 1
    decValue = decValue - decDeprec
    'Output
    rtbOut.AppendText(bytYear.ToString & " " &
        decValue.ToString("c") & vbNewLine)
Loop
```

Each pass through the loop increases the year by 1 and subtracts another year's depreciation from the value of the computer. The loop runs as long as the value

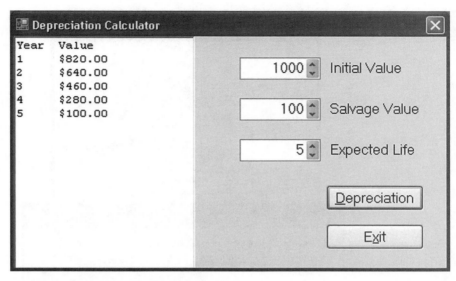

Figure 6.12   Depreciation Calculator Program Screen

of the computer is greater than its salvage value. This method of depreciation is called straight-line depreciation.

VB Tip   *Open and run the Depreciation program.*

Multiple Choice Program

Drill and practice programs often ask multiple choice questions. These questions can repeat until the learner gets the correct answer. It takes, of course, at least one attempt to get the correct answer. This is a good time to use a bottom-driven loop.

Set up a program that uses an InputBox to display a question and get the learner's answer. Put this inside a loop that repeats until the learner enters the correct answer. Then display a message indicating that their answer is correct. Use a Do Loop While. The loop repeats while their answer is incorrect (see Figure 6.13).

```
strRightAnswer = 5
Do
    strAnswer = InputBox("How many different types of
        loops are there?", "Multiple Choice")
Loop While strAnswer <> strRightAnswer
MsgBox("That's right! For loops, Do While, Do Until,
    Do Loop While and Do Loop Until", MsgBoxStyle.OkOnly,
        "Correct Answer")
```

VB Tip   *Open and run the MultipleChoice program.*

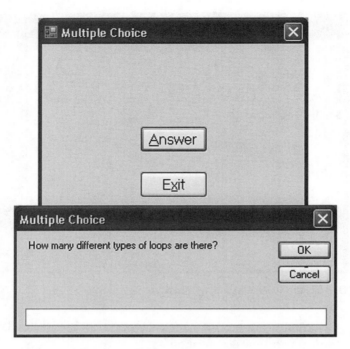

Figure 6.13   Multiple Choice Program Screen

Business Growth Program

Whether it's the neighborhood kid's lawn-mowing service or the next Internet startup, most businesses expect to grow. They plan to grow and establish goals with that in mind. For input, take the initial value of a company, the growth goal, and the annual growth rate. The growth rate should be converted from a percentage to a decimal. The output is the number of years it will take to accomplish that goal. The formula for growth is

value = value + (value * growth rate)

Create a loop that repeats while the value of the business is less than the goal. Use a Do Until loop. Calculate the yearly growth and keep track of the number of years. The output is the number of years it takes to reach the goal and is reported below the loop (see Figure 6.14).

```
sngRate = sngRate / 100
Do Until decValue > decGoal
    decValue = decValue + (decValue * sngRate)
    shoYears += 1
Loop
'Output
lblYears.Text = shoYears.ToString
```

VB Tip   *Open and run the BusinessGrowth program.*

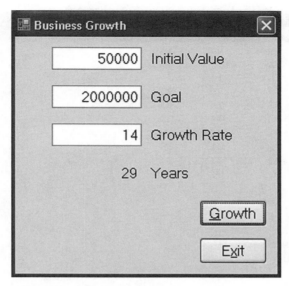

Figure 6.14   Business Growth Program Screen

Computerized Guesses Program

We've all played the little guessing game where you pick a number from 1 to 100, and a program was written for it in Chapter 5. But, is the computer smart enough to play a guessing game on its own? Get the computer to generate a random number from 1 to 100. Then set up a loop to have the computer "guess" the number. The computer guesses by generating another random number. Compare the two and if they are equal, the computer guessed correctly.

The computer can also be given intelligence. When a guess is too low, have the computer remember that guess, and when it's too high, have it remember that guess as well. Use these numbers to set the range for the next guess. Repeat the loop until the correct number is guessed. It will take at least one guess so make it a bottom-driven Do Until loop.

The If structures to find the range look like this:

```
If bytGuess > bytNum Then
    bytHigh = bytGuess
End If
If bytGuess < bytNum Then
    bytLow = bytGuess
End If
```

Use bytHigh and bytLow for the limits on the next guess. It should look like this:

```
bytGuess = Int(Rnd() * (bytHigh - bytLow) + bytLow)
```

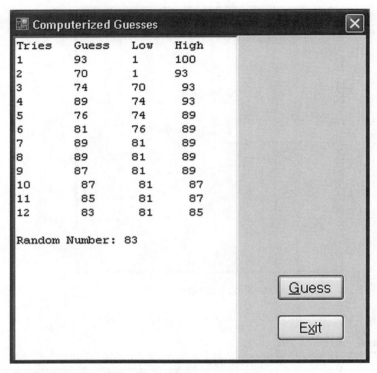

Figure 6.15   Computerized Guesses Program Screen

The code gets a random integer. bytHigh – bytLow determines the distance between the highest and lowest possible numbers. Add bytLow to the number to get a random number in the correct range.

The loop repeats until the two guesses match. Each iteration adds 1 to the number of guesses. Each time it displays the number of tries, the current guess, and the range of remaining numbers in the RichTextBox. Once there's a match, it displays the correct number (see Figure 6.15).

```
bytLow = 1
bytHigh = 100
bytNum = Int(Rnd() * 100 + 1)

rtbOut.Clear()
rtbOut.AppendText("Tries Guess Low High" & vbNewLine)
Do
    bytTries += 1
    bytGuess = Int(Rnd() * (bytHigh - bytLow) + byt-
Low + 1)
    rtbOut.AppendText(bytTries.ToString &   " " &
      bytGuess.ToString & " " & bytLow.ToString & " " &
      bytHigh.ToString & vbNewLine)
```

```
        If bytGuess > bytNum Then
            bytHigh = bytGuess
        End If
        If bytGuess < bytNum Then
            bytLow = bytGuess
        End If
Loop Until bytNum = bytGuess
rtbOut.AppendText(vbNewLine & "Random Number: " &
    bytNum.ToString)
```

VB Tip   *Open and run the ComputerizedGuesses program.*

Simple Graphics Program

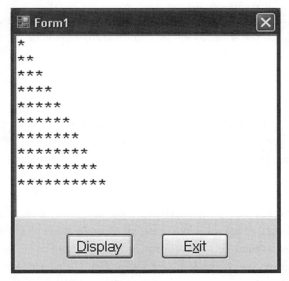

Figure 6.16   Simple Graphics Program Screen

Simple graphics can be created in a RichTextBox by using loops. The one shown in Figure 6.16 shows a triangle that was created with nested loops. Here's the code:

```
For i = 1 To 10
    For j = 1 To i
        rtbOut.AppendText("*")
    Next j
        rtbOut.AppendText(vbNewLine)
Next i
```

Change the font of the RichTextBox to Courier New. It will be easier to align the graphics if you do. The outer loop (i) runs ten times. Each iteration results in one line of output. The inner loop (j) runs i times. The first time it runs, it runs just once because i is 1. Then next time i is 2 so the loop runs twice. The next time i is 3 so the loop runs three times. The inner loop (j) adds an asterisk with every pass. Once the j loop is done, a new line is started. Notice how the line

```
rtbOut.AppendText(vbNewLine)
```

is below the j loop.

Change the number of times i repeats to see what happens. Create your own shapes using loops and combine them to make more complicated graphics.

VB Tip   *Open and run the SimpleGraphics program.*

VB Quiz 06   *How could you set up the loop for the multiple choice program so the learner would get up to three tries to get the correct answer?*
In the Computerized Guesses program, does the computer get smarter with each guess?
How could you get the nested loop to display ten asterisks on the first line and decrease until there was just 1 on the last line?

Potential Problems

Loops are fraught with peril. Most problems can be solved with any type of loop, but some types work better than others. It just depends on the task. Take care to know the starting and end values for a loop. Problems can often be traced to these. While and Until loops must have an assignment statement that changes the value of the variable that controls the loop. That line should be either the first line inside the loop or the last line. Be sure to increment the counter.

Set the initial value for a loop control variable above the loop. If a loop starts at 1, be sure to include a line above the loop that assigns 1 to the variable. It is critical to initialize the variable for loops that decrement. If you plan to count down the final 8 seconds of a scoreclock, be sure to initialize the variable to 8.

Each trip through a loop repeats one or more actions. Be sure to reset values and reinitialize variables as needed for each loop. That might include resetting variables, clearing variables, or clearing the values from a Label or TextBox.

The ending value for the loop control variable in a For loop is one more than the highest value inside the loop. A loop that runs from 1 to 5 has an ending value of 6.

Some loops may not run. This is usually an initialization error or an error when writing the condition for a loop. Infinite loops occur when a loop starts but cannot exit. These are usually initialization errors or a failure to increment a loop control variable.

Output can be above the loop, inside the loop, or below it. Output above a loop happens once and any other output comes after it. Use it for a header.

Output below a loop happens once after all the processing has completed. Use it for displaying totals, averages, and such. Output inside a loop gets repeated and almost always results in multiple lines of output.

Fixing a Program

Anne Nuitty has just been hired for her first job and wants to calculate her lifetime earnings. The input should be the starting salary, the annual percentage raise, the year she starts working, and the number of years she intends to work. It's supposed to calculate the annual raise, the salary for the year, and the accumulated earnings and then display the salary, total earnings, and raise for each year.

However, the program doesn't work correctly. Run it once and it only shows the total for the first year and it doesn't display a lifetime total. After checking the code, you realize there's no output inside the loop. The only output comes after the loop is finished. You move the output line of code up and inside the loop, expecting to get output for every year of work. It doesn't display any output. Hmm.

You then check the code that controls the loop. It says to go through the loop while the current year is the same as the end year. It looks like it never runs the loop and you want the loop to run until the retirement year. The easy way to see if the program gets to the code inside the loop is to put in a simple test line. Inside the loop you add:

```
rtbOut.AppendText("Test" & vbNewLine)
```

The output from this line should show up every time the loop runs. Nothing shows up when you run the program so your suspicion is confirmed. You change the equals sign in the Do While line to a < sign and run the program.

This time there's output, but it's for the same year every time. Even worse, the program crashes. Panic time. The same year comes up on every line so you suspect that's where the problem lies. shoYear is the variable for the current year. It also controls the While loop, so somewhere inside the loop this value must change. It doesn't! Aha! shoYear and shoEndYear never change so you never get out of the loop.

You add a counter for shoYear and try again. Yes, it works! We do the dance of joy. There's now output for every year and it looks like a tidy sum of money for a lifetime's work. However, there's still one problem. There's no income for your first year. You're a stickler for accuracy, so you copy the output line of code and paste it above the loop. That gives you output for your first year. Remove the test line of output you used for debugging and you're done (see Figure 6.17).

VB Tip   *Open and run the LifetimeEarnings program.*

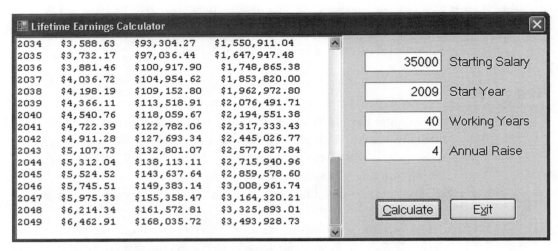

Figure 6.17　　Lifetime Earnings Program Screen

On Your Own

Write a program to calculate the average daily sales for a business. Use an InputBox inside a loop to gather the input. Calculate the total sales and the daily average. Display them both.

Write a program to find the square root of each number from 1 to 30. Display the number and its square root.

Write a program to display the upper and lower case letters of the alphabet. Use one loop and Chr and display the upper and lower case of each letter on a line.

Write a program that asks the user for a number. If that number is even, multiply it by 5 and subtract 1. If it's odd, add 1 and divide by 2. Repeat the loop until the number is greater than 100. Display each answer and the total number of calculations.

Your new boss, Royal Payne, offers you a $5,000 per month salary or a penny that doubles every day of the month. Write a program to determine which offer is better.

Summary

Loops allow the computer to repeat instructions. Repetition is one of the most powerful features of a programming language. There are five different types of loops. A developer must know where a loop starts and ends, the variable that controls the loop, the exit criteria for the loop, and the number of times the loop will repeat. Loops can be nested, where one loop is completely contained inside another. Infinite loops indicate a logical error in the code. They repeat indefinitely.

Review

A loop is a series of commands that repeat.

A loop is a block of code and is treated as a series of related steps.

Use a For . . . Next loop when the number of iterations is known in advance.

Loops can be used to count upward or downward.

The last line of a loop automatically aligns with the first line of a loop.

Use a flowchart to indicate the flow of a program through a loop.

The Step parameter controls For loops that increment by something other than 1.

Programmers typically use i, j, and k to control For . . . Next loops.

Do While loops can be controlled by any type of variable.

Do While loops run while the loop condition is True.

Do Loop While loops have their decision at the bottom of the loop.

Do loops can be controlled by a sentinel value. Sentinel values are set with each trip through a loop.

Do Until loops run as long as their condition is False.

Do Loop Until loops have their decision at the bottom of the loop.

A developer should be able to answer several questions for every loop in a program: Where does the loop start? Where does the loop end? What controls the loop? How many times does it loop? Is it top-driven or bottom-driven? Is it a true loop or a false loop?

An infinite loop runs but never gets out of the loop. An infinite loop contains a logical error.

A nested loop is a loop that's inside another loop.

Exit For and Exit Do are used to short-circuit a loop and leave it early.

Chr is the numeric equivalent for an ASCII character.

Asc is used to get the numeric equivalent for a character.

The Top and Left properties control the location of controls on a form.

The top left of a control or a form is 0, 0.

Terms

bottom-driven loop	a loop where the decision to go through the loop is made at the bottom of the loop; a posttest loop
decrement	to decrease the value of a loop control variable with each iteration of a loop
infinite loop	a loop that start and never ends; an infinite loop will either run forever or run until the program crashes
iteration	a single trip through a loop
loop	a series of commands that gets repeated
nested loops	one loop inside another loop

pixel	picture element; one dot on the screen
posttest	a loop where the condition that controls the loop is placed at the bottom of the loop
pretest	a loop where the condition that controls the loop is placed at the top of the loop
sentinel values	values used to control While and Until loops
top-driven loop	a loop where the decision to go through the loop is made at the top of the loop; a pretest loop

Keywords

Asc	the command that accepts a character value and returns the corresponding ACSII numeric value for that character
Chr	the command that accepts a numeric value and returns the corresponding ASCII character for that value
Do	the statement that marks the beginning of a While or Until loop
Exit	the command to leave a loop early
For	a statement that creates a loop with a specified beginning and end, which increments by a specified value
Left	the property that sets the left location for a control
Loop	the statement that marks the end of a While or Until loop
Next	the statement that marks the end of a For . . . Next loop
Step	a command that establishes the size of the increment (or decrement) in a loop
To	an operator used to set the range of values in a For . . . Next loop
Top	the property that sets the top location for a control
Until	the statement that creates a loop condition that executes until the condition becomes True
While	the statement that creates a loop condition that executes while the condition is True

Self-check

1. A loop is a set of instructions that can be repeated.
2. All loops are controlled by a condition and the loop runs as long as that condition is True.
3. All loops run a predetermined number of times.
4. All loops are controlled by a numeric value.
5. While loops and Until loops must have a way to change the loop control variable somewhere inside the loop.

6. A sentinel value can be a string, a numeric variable, or a Boolean.

7. Each loop in a nested loop must have its own loop control variable.

8. Each trip through a loop is called an orbit.

9. An infinite loop is the result of a syntax error.

10. The Top and Left properties of a control determine its location on a form.

11. When the number of iterations is known, the correct loop to use is:
    A. For ... Next
    B. Do While
    C. Do Until
    D. Do Loop While

12. The Step command:
    A. must be used when a For ... Next loop increments by a value other than 1
    B. works with integer values and decimals
    C. is not required by For ... Next loops that increment by 1
    D. all of the above

13. An iteration is:
    A. the variable that controls a loop
    B. a single trip through a loop
    C. the processing that takes place outside of a loop
    D. the name for the flowchart symbol for a loop

14. Which of the following will not set up a loop that runs 10 times?
    A. For i = 1 To 10
    B. For i = 0 To 9
    C. For k = 10 To 0 Step −1
    D. For j = .9 To 0 Step −.1

15. What is the final value of i for this loop?
    For i = 0 to 7
    Next i
    A. 0
    B. 1
    C. 7
    D. 8

16. One loop completely inside another loop is known as a:
    A. stacked loop
    B. nested loop
    C. sentinel loop
    D. bottom-driven loop

17. Which of the following Do Until loops will repeat five times?
    A. `Do Until i = 5`
       `    i = i +1`
       `Loop`

```
     B. Do Until i > 5
            i = i + 1
        Loop
     C. i = 1
        Do Until i >= 5
            i = i + 1
        Loop
     D. i = 1
        Do Until i >= 5
        Loop
```

18. A Do Loop Until is useful for a:
    A. user login
    B. nested loop
    C. infinite loop
    D. all of the above
19. The Exit For command:
    A. is used to indicate the end of a For . . . Next loop
    B. is used to exit a For . . . Next loop early
    C. lists conditions for exiting a For . . . Next loop early
    D. none of the above
20. The best place to place a detail line is:
    A. above the loop
    B. inside the loop
    C. below the loop
    D. none of the above

VB Quiz Answers

Quiz 01

The actors are the controls for your program and the script is your code. In a play, the script determines what happens, just like the code determines what happens in a program.

Payroll can be done using loop as can accounts payable. Billings are done with loops. Almost any repetitive process can be accomplished with loops.

Scoreclocks and shot clocks count down to zero. Many timers count down to zero. They can be used to track the number of items left to process.

Write a program with a loop that runs from one to five. Use i to control the loop and display it every time it goes through the loop. Display i again below the loop. It will display 6 proving that the final value of a loop that runs from 1 to 5 ends up at 6.

Quiz 02

It's possible to set up a loop that starts but never exits. The computer, being the obedient servant, continues to run the loop. Eventually, it might crash, but that might take months or years. Just be careful when writing loops.

It's easy to set up a loop that never runs. This one never runs because i starts out at 10. The loop only runs while i is less than or equal to 5. It skips right over it!

```
i = 10
Do While i <= 5
    rtbOut.AppendText(i.ToString & vbNewLine)
    i = i + 1
Loop
```

Do marks the top of the loop. The code for the loop follows and the test for the loop is at the bottom. It must go through the loop once before it checks to see if it should repeat the loop. Do Loop While loops are handy for a task that must run at least once.

A sentinel value controls a loop. When the user enters a value that matches the sentinel value, the loop ends.

Quiz 03

Use a RichTextBox to display the output. Add a line of code inside the loop to display the value of shoTotal. With each iteration of the loop the factorial for i is displayed.

Create a NumericUpDown or other input control. Get the value of the user's input. Then use that value as the upper value for the loop.

Each type of loop works slightly differently and is best for a particular task. Just like there are many types of hammers, each with its own best use, each type of loop has a best use. Of course, most problems could be solved with one of several types of loops, just like any hammer will work for most jobs. Still, it is best to select the right tool for the job.

Quiz 04

The best way to understand how a block of looping code works is to answer these questions. The answers provide you with the limits of the loop, its iterations, and termination. Flowcharts and deskchecks are other ways to wrap yourself around the code to understand it. The real trick to understanding the code is to turn the mechanical understanding of the code into an intuitive understanding of its workings. When you see a loop, you want to be able to say to yourself, "That's a loop. It starts here, ends here, and is controlled by this value. It runs this many times and every time it runs, this happens."

Take care to write and test your statements. Infinite loops are always logical errors and logical errors are almost always an incomplete understanding of the problem or an incomplete solution to the problem. A good technique is to write the code that controls the loop before you write the content for the loop. Write the first and last lines of the loop and, for While and Until loops, the control statement, before you write the contents of the loop.

Knitting follows a series of stitches to produce a pattern. Repeating the pattern produces a row and repeating the row eventually produces the basics for a sweater or booties.

After both loops are done, i is 4, j is 5, and bytTotal is 12. Remember that For loops increment past their last value. That's why developers often start their loops at zero. That way the final value is the number of iterations of the loop. In later chapters, this logic will become obvious and useful even though it's a burden now.

Quiz 05

Answers will vary, but the answer should include the Chr value for the capitalized first letter of the student's name and then the Chr value for the lower case letters in the student's name.

The values translate to the letters Mxyzptlk. Mxyzptlk was a villainous imp from the fifth dimension in the Superman comics. Superman had to trick him into saying or spelling his name backward to get him to return to the fifth dimension. Superman is a copyright of DC Comics.

Answers will vary, but the loops should have the same sequence as the For loops.

The Top and Left properties of the graphic must increase as the plane moves. Use a loop that increases in value.

A plane that moves from top right to bottom left must have its Top value increase while its Left value decreases. For example, create a loop that runs from 0 to 500. The Top property can use i and work correctly. However, the Left property must use 500 − i. That way, as i increases, a greater value is subtracted from 500 and the plane moves to the left.

Quiz 06

The condition for the loop could be written so it would stop with the correct answer or once there had been three tries, whichever came first. It could also be set up so it loops three times but can exit early with a correct response.

The computer seems to get smarter with each guess – at least it narrows the range with every guess. However, that's not true intelligence. The algorithm is set up to narrow the range with each attempt. Children learn this ploy early. Besides, the computer has to relearn this every time it runs.

Run the i loop so it starts at 10 and goes to 1. Each iteration decrements i, so each succeeding line has fewer asterisks.

Procedures and Functions – Divide and Conquer

VB Quip

Specialists learn more and more about less and less until they know everything about nothing. Generalists learn less and less about more and more until they know nothing about everything. – Anonymous

We live in a world of specialization. Want a cup of coffee? There's a store that specializes in coffee, any way you like it. Need a doughnut to go with it? There's a company that makes and sells the best doughnuts. Need something to read while you're enjoying a bite? Pick from thousands of magazines or millions of books on any and all topics imaginable. Gone are the days of the local handyman – the resident "Mr. Fixit" – who could fix anything and get anything to work. Today's world has specialists. A mechanic specializes in car repair. The cable guy handles your TV problems. When the office copier is on the fritz, call the copier guy. Everyone's an expert.

Programming is the same way. Blocks of code are written for a particular purpose. Some do simple tasks, but do them often. It's easier to write a procedure once for a task and then call it multiple times as needed. Other blocks of code might do a complicated calculation or solve a particular problem. These provide a specific function. It's easier to write and store these functions and then use them when needed than it is to create them from scratch. That's the basis for procedures and functions. Procedures are used to separate and perform simple tasks as needed. Functions supply answers to complex or often-used problems. Both of them make programming better. Trust me, I'm an expert!

Why Use Procedures?

Procedures turn a complicated process into a series of simpler steps. A procedure is called with a simple command. Control is transferred to that section of code where the statements in the procedure are executed. When completed, control returns to the line that called the procedure.

Use procedures to break a complicated problem into simpler steps or to avoid redundant code. You've already broken a program into input, processing, and output sections. That's called *modularization* and it simplifies a program.

In a business setting, one developer might be assigned the input part of the code, another might get the processing, and a third might work on the output. Programs are too large and complicated to be completed by one person. And, it's faster to break a program into components and assign a component to one or more developers. Of course, these parts might be further subdivided and parceled out to developers. Use procedures to avoid redundant code. Instead of writing the same lines of code several times in several places, use a procedure. Write the code once and call the procedure when and where it's needed.

Creating Procedures

Every click event is a procedure. The computer creates these and, so far, all you've had to do is add code to them. However, you can write your own procedures just as easily. A procedure cannot be inside another procedure so just find some clear space between existing procedures in the code window. The general form is

```
Private/Public Sub ProcedureName(arguments)
  statement(s)
End Sub
```

Every procedure is a series of statements tucked between the start and end lines of the procedure. End Sub ends a procedure. The top line identifies a procedure by name, defines its scope, and provides an optional list of values for it. Let's break it down. Every procedure has a scope, just like variables. Public procedures can be used anywhere in a program. Private procedures can only be used on that form. The distinction won't matter much for now so just use Private. Every procedure needs the word Sub to identify it as a procedure. ProcedureName is the name you provide for the procedure. It should describe what the procedure does – PrintHeading, for example. Capitalize the first letter of each word and follow the naming conventions for variables. The arguments in parentheses is for optional values that you might want to send along to the procedure. A simple procedure might look like this:

```
Private Sub PrintHeading()
    rtbOut.Clear()
    rtbOutput.AppendText("  Dusty Lenzkapp's
      Camerarama" & vbNewLine)
    rtbOutput.AppendText("  Daily Sales Totals" &
      vbNewLine & vbNewLine)
    rtbOutput.AppendText("Employee  Sales Rate
      Commission" & vbNewLine)
End Sub
```

Use this code in the Load event and it will display in the RichTextBox when the program starts. Use it in the Clear Button and it will display the header again after the RichTextBox clears. It's handy because the code must only be written once. That's great if there's a bug in it or if you want to make a change.

VB Tip   *Use verb–noun combinations for naming procedures such as PrintHeading. It describes what the procedure does.*

Calling a Procedure

Call a procedure with a Call statement. It looks like this:

```
Call PrintHeading(arguments)
```

The keyword Call isn't required. You could simply use the name of the procedure and it would work just fine. arguments is for an optional list of values to send to the procedure. More on that shortly.

Divide and Conquer

Typically, programs are based on input, processing, and output. That's a good way to learn procedures. Each part of the program is broken into small, manageable parts and a procedure handles each part. Each procedure is called, in order, as needed. Procedures are written separately and one procedure can call another.

```
Public Class frmDivideAndConquer
    'Declarations
    Dim msngDivisor As Single
    Dim msngDividend As Single
    Dim msngQuotient As Single
    Private Sub btnExit_Click(ByVal sender As
        System.Object, ByVal e As System.EventArgs)
        Handles btnExit.Click
            End
    End Sub

    Private Sub btnDivide_Click(ByVal sender As
        System.Object, ByVal e As System.EventArgs)
        Handles btnDivide.Click
            'Call Procedures
            Call Input()
            Call Processing()
            Call Output()
    End Sub
```

```
Private Sub Input()
      msngDivisor = txtDivisor.Text
      msngDividend = txtDividend.Text
End Sub

Private Sub Processing()
      msngQuotient = msngDivisor / msngDividend
End Sub

Private Sub Output()
      lblQuotient.Text = msngQuotient.ToString("n1")
End Sub
End Class
```

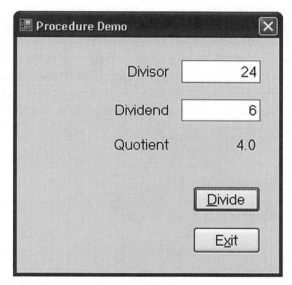

Figure 7.1   Divide and Conquer Program

The variables were declared at the module level to simplify the preceding example. btnDivide calls the Input, Processing, and Output procedures. Control passes to the Input procedure, which handles the input for the program. Control returns to btnDivide, which calls the Processing procedure. The code in the Processing procedure does the calculation for the program and, when finished, passes control back to btnDivide. The next line of btnDivide calls the Output procedure, which displays the output for the program. Control returns to btnDivide and the click event is over.

Of course, the program would be simpler and easier without procedures. However, it is a good example of how procedures and procedure calls work (see Figure 7.1).

VB Tip   *Open and run the DivideAndConquer program.*

Passing Arguments

The set of parentheses following the procedure name supplies an optional list of arguments for the procedure. The Call statement and the first line of the procedure each need a matching list of arguments for the statements to work. A procedure doesn't need an argument list to work, but when they're used, both the procedure and its call statement must agree. There are two ways to pass arguments to a procedure: one is *ByVal* and the other is *ByRef.*

You can also pass multiple arguments. Just make sure that the data type and the order of the arguments between them match exactly.

ByVal

The purpose of arguments is to customize a procedure. Here's a simple example. A company might generate reports three times a day: the morning report, the midday report, and the final report. The only difference in the heading would be the type of report. Instead of three report headers that are all essentially the same, the procedure could accept an argument that customizes the report. Its Call statement might look like this:

```
strType = "Morning"
PrintHeading(strType)
```

And, the procedure could look like this:

```
Private Sub PrintHeading(ByVal strTime as String)
    rtbOut.Clear()
    rtbOutput.AppendText("  Dusty Lenzkapp's Camerarama"
      & vbNewLine)
    rtbOutput.AppendText("  " & strTime & " Sales Totals"
      & vbNewLine & vbNewLine)
    rtbOutput.AppendText("Employee  Sales Rate
      Commission" & vbNewLine)
End Sub
```

The Call statement passes a value (in this case, the word "Morning") to the procedure. The procedure is set up to accept that value and plugs it in where needed. Then, later in the day, the other reports are generated, with their customized heading, by using

```
strType = "Midday"
PrintHeading(strType)
```

and

```
strType = "Final"
PrintHeading(strType)
```

Each one calls the PrintHeading procedure and customizes it as needed. The argument list in the first line of the PrintHeading procedure accepts the value and uses it in the procedure. Note that the value was passed as a string and the procedure accepted a string. Any data type can be passed, but the Call statement and procedure must match.

This example passed the argument ByVal, which means that data are passed by value. VB makes a copy of the data and sends the copy along when the procedure is called. The original variable remains unchanged. However, you're free to change the value of strTime inside the procedure. strType won't be affected by it. Think of the data as one-way. It's sent to the procedure, but the value won't get sent back.

The procedure needs a variable to accept this value. That's handled by this part of the statement:

```
ByVal strTime as String
```

which declares a string variable called strTime. ByVal tells it to accept the value that's passed and store it in strTime. So, in this example, strTime contains "Morning". Of course, if the other procedure calls were used, it could contain "Midday" or "Final".

ByRef

The other way to pass an argument is ByRef. That's short for "by reference." It's a two-way street. Not only can values be passed to a procedure, the procedure can modify them and assign the value to the original variable. Here's an example:

```
Private Sub btnByRef_Click(ByVal sender As System.Object,
   ByVal e As System.EventArgs) Handles btnByRef.Click
    Dim strPassed As String = "Passed"
    'Display the value passed
    lblStart.Text = strPassed

    'Pass the value
    Call PassByRef(strPassed)

    'Display the value returned
    lblReturned.Text = strPassed
End Sub
```

```
Private Sub PassByRef(ByRef strReceived As String)
    'Display the value received
    lblPassed.Text = strReceived

    'Change the value
    strReceived = "Returned"
End Sub
```

The variable strPassed is assigned the word "Passed". It's then displayed in a Label as proof. The PassByRef procedure is called and strPassed forwards the value to the procedure. The PassByRef procedure receives it and stores the word "Passed" in its own variable called strReceived. As proof, it displays it in a Label. The last line of the procedure changes the value of strReceived to the word "Returned". The procedure is finished so control returns to the line that called the procedure. As proof that strPassed was updated by the procedure, the last line of the click event displays strPassed. Sure enough, it displays the word "Returned".

Technically, when ByRef is used, it passes the location of the variable in memory, not the value. So, if that value gets changed, it's changing the original value in its original location.

VB Tip   *Run the PassingArgumentsToProcedures program to see how arguments are passed ByVal and ByRef.*

99 Bottles Program

You're familiar with the classic drinking song "99 Bottles of Beer on the Wall," even if you've never sung all 99 verses. Let's try it using procedures.

First, you need a loop that runs from 99 to 1. That's not too hard. Inside the loop, you need a line to call the procedure and pass the number of bottles of beer. The procedure accepts the number of bottles when control is passed to it. Inside the procedure, the lyrics for that verse are displayed. The number of bottles must decrease by 1 in the middle of the verse so the lyrics are correct. You could pass the number of bottles ByVal and have the loop keep track of it. Or you could pass the number of bottles ByRef and let the procedure update the number of bottles as needed. That way the procedure always has the correct number of bottles.

Of course, there are several ways to write this, but this is a cute and handy way to demonstrate procedures and arguments (see Figure 7.2):

```
Private Sub btnSing_Click(ByVal sender As System.Object,
    ByVal e As System.EventArgs) Handles btnSing.Click
    Dim i As Byte
```

```
        rtbLyrics.Clear()
        'Loop starts at 99 and goes to zero
        i = 99
        Do While i > 0
            Verse(i)
        Loop
    End Sub

    Public Sub Verse(ByRef bytVerse As Byte)
        'Display first two line
        rtbLyrics.AppendText(bytVerse & " bottles of beer on
            the wall, " & bytVerse & " bottles of beer." &
            vbNewLine)
        rtbLyrics.AppendText("You take one down and pass it
            around, " & vbNewLine)
        'Update number of bottles
        bytVerse = bytVerse - 1
        'Display last line
        rtbLyrics.AppendText(bytVerse & " bottles of beer on
            the wall!" & vbNewLine)
        rtbLyrics.AppendText(vbNewLine)
    End Sub
```

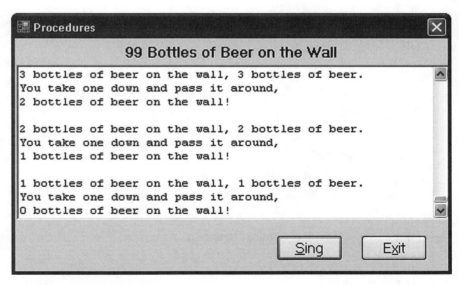

Figure 7.2   99 Bottles of Beer Program

VB Tip   *Open and run the 99Bottles program.*

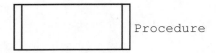

Figure 7.3   Procedure Symbol

Flowcharting Procedures

The flowchart symbol is shown in Figure 7.3.

Simply insert this symbol into the flowchart and create another flowchart with the code from the procedure. The flowchart for the procedure is similar to a regular flowchart except that it indicates the start and end of the procedure. Procedures shorten a flowchart and let the developer see the "big picture" of a program without worrying about the details. Each procedure has a specific function and can be analyzed for the details on that portion of the program (see Figure 7.4).

VB Quiz 1   *What are the advantages of using procedures?*

What is the difference between passing ByVal and passing ByRef?

Apply procedures and loops to the following punishment. Number and write, "I will behave myself in study hall from now on." 500 times.

How are flowcharts with procedures similar to those fan-fold roadmaps used by travelers?

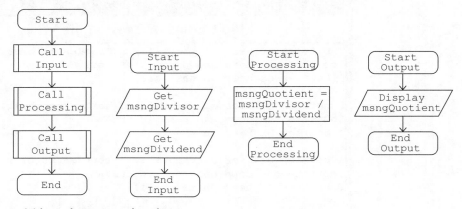

Figure 7.4   Divide and Conquer Flowchart

Potential Problems

Procedures add another level of complication to a program. Once you're used to them, they're great, but there are potential problems to their use. Be careful when naming procedures. Generally, the procedure name should be something that describes the procedure – use action words. Be careful when dividing a program into procedures. Usually, the best way to create a procedure is to segment a particular function, such as input, calculations, or output. Another use for a procedure is for common code that's called in more than one place.

Passing arguments is tricky. Pass ByVal when you don't want the value to change. Pass ByRef when you want the procedure to update a variable. Be careful with values. A common mistake is to ignore the data that need to be passed to a procedure. Without data, most procedures won't work. The order of arguments must be exactly the same between the call and the procedure. The data types must match as well. A good way to write procedures is to create the procedure first and then write the call line. IntelliSense picks up on the procedure and provides references for writing the call.

Functions

VB Quip

These machines have no common sense; they have not yet learned to "think," and they do exactly as they are told, no more and no less. This fact is the hardest concept to grasp when one first tries to use a computer. –Donald Knuth

A *function* supplies an answer in a program. Sometimes a function is a simple calculation that's used over and over. Sometimes, it's a complicated formula or one that changes frequently. In the first instance, it's easier to write it once and use it many times. In the other, it's better to write it once, use it when needed, and only have one calculation to worry about.

For example, the formula to calculate the area of a rectangle is simple. It's just length multiplied by width. In programming, it's easier to write this as a function and use it where needed. Some formulas, however, are long and complicated and they might change from time to time. Take the calculation for the Dow Jones Industrial Average® (DJIA). It is long and complicated. It started out as the total price for a handful of stocks, but today, because of mergers, changes, and stock splits, the formula for the DJIA is a monster. It's better to write the function just once and then call it as needed in an application. That way, when it changes – and it will – only one formula needs to change.

You're familiar with functions in Excel. These functions are available as methods in Visual Basic. Functions in Visual Basic are written by a developer to solve a problem. The function receives one or more arguments, does its work, and returns the answer.

Creating a Function

A function takes its own space in the code, just like procedures. The format for a function is

```
Private/Public Function FunctionName(arguments) As
  Datatype
  statement(s)
End Function
```

The function can be Private or Public, depending on where it's shared. Function declares it as a function. FunctionName is the name of the function. It should follow the naming conventions for variables and should be an action word or phrase that describes what the function does. The arguments is a list of values passed to the function. It might be one value or several, depending on what the function does. The data type is a variable and the type of answer generated by the function. Often this is a numeric data type, but others can also be used. A function has one or more statements that perform a calculation. When the calculation is complete, the function returns a value, that is, it sends an answer back to the line that called the function. For example:

```
Private Function CalcArea(ByVal sngWidth as Single,
  ByVal sngLength As Single) As Single
    CalcArea = sngWidth * sngLength
End Function
```

The function is named CalcArea because it calculates the area of a rectangle. Two values – arguments – are passed to it, the length and the width. The first is stored in sngWidth and the other is stored in sngLength. Both are declared as singles and accept the argument ByVal. The answer is stored in a variable declared as a single and named CalcArea. The function calculates the area, stores it in CalcArea, and returns that value.

That line could also be written like this:

```
Return sngWidth * sngLength
```

Calling a Function

Functions are called with a single statement. The function call must include all the values needed by the function and they must be in order. The general form for a function call is

```
var = FunctionName(arguments)
```

Here's an example:

```
sngArea = CalcArea(sngRoomWidth, sngRoomLength)
```

CalcArea is the function being called. It needs two arguments. sngRoomWidth and sngRoomLength are passed to the function. When the function returns the answer, it's assigned to sngArea.

The number and type of the arguments passed must match exactly with the function. It won't work without them (see Figure 7.5).

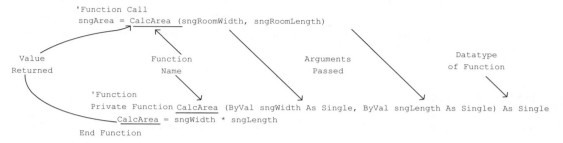

Figure 7.5   Function Diagram

VB Tip   *If you write the function first or use an existing one, VB picks up on the arguments and lists them as you write the function call.*

Arguments

Functions have at least one argument, that is, they have at least one value that's passed to them. When you think about it, the values passed to a function are really what make the function useful. The number and type of the arguments must agree between the function and the statement that calls it. The arguments must also be in order. That is, you can pass a single and then a decimal to a function, just as long as the function is set up to accept a single and then a decimal. Just like procedures, the variable names between them can be different as long as the data types match.

Return

Functions return one value. That's a major difference between functions and procedures. There are two ways to return a value:

```
CalcArea = sngWidth * sngLength
Return sngWidth * sngLength
```

Both return the answer. You can either assign the answer to a variable named for the function (in this example, CalcArea) or you can use the keyword Return.

Passing Arguments

Values can be passed to a function in two ways, ByVal and BeRef. The rules and results are the same for functions as they are for procedures. Passing ByVal is a one-way pass. The statement that calls the function sends along the value, and the function accepts the value but cannot modify the original value. When passed ByRef, it's a two-way street. The original value gets passed to the function and the function can modify it and update the original value. The function determines the order of the arguments and whether they're passed ByVal or ByRef. The statement that calls the function must abide by these settings.

Sales Tax Program

```
Private Sub btnTotal_Click(ByVal sender As System.Object, ByVal e As System.EventArgs) Handles btnTotal.Click
    'Declarations
    Dim decSale As Decimal
    Dim decSalesTax As Decimal
    Dim decTotal As Decimal

    'Input
    decSale = txtSale.Text

    'Processing
    'Call CalcSalesTax function and pass it the amount of the sale
    'Function returns the sales tax at 5%
    decSalesTax = CalcSalesTax(decSale)

    decTotal = decSale + decSalesTax

    'Output
    lblSalesTax.Text = decSalesTax.ToString("c")
    lblTotal.Text = decTotal.ToString("c")

End Sub

Private Function CalcSalesTax(ByVal decAmtSale As Decimal) As Decimal
    'Function determines the amount of the sales tax
    'Tax rate is 5% of the sale

    Const sngTaxRate As Single = 0.05

    Return decAmtSale * sngTaxRate

End Function
```

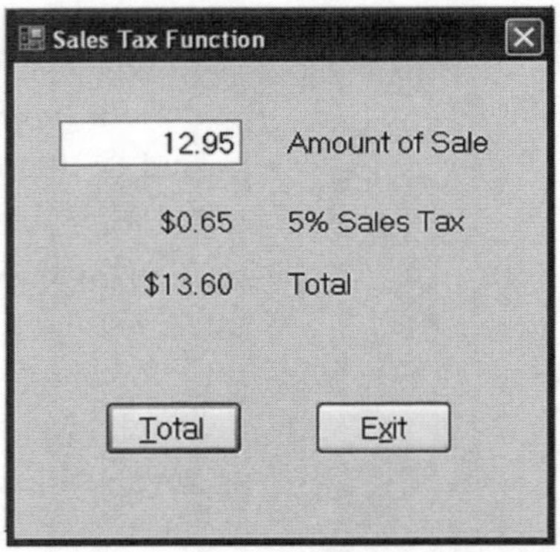

Figure 7.6   Sales Tax Function Program and Code

Most purchases are subject to sales tax. Use a function to determine the amount of the sales tax. When passed the amount of the sale, the function determines the tax. The function then returns the sales tax (see Figure 7.6).

The function requires one argument, the amount of the sale. Inside the function is the sales tax rate. It's a constant set at 5%. Once the function gets the amount of the sale, it determines how much to charge for sales tax and returns that value.

The statement that calls the function passes along the amount of the sale. The function returns the amount of the sales tax, which it stores in decSalesTax. The procedure then calculates the total of the sale and displays the sales tax and the total.

VB Tip   *Open and run the SalesTaxFunction program to see how it works.*

Last, first program

```
Private Sub btnLastFirst_Click(ByVal sender As System.Object, ByVal e As System.EventArgs) Handles btnLastFirst.Click
    'Declarations
    Dim strFirst As String
    Dim strLast As String
    Dim strLastFirst As String

    'Input
    strFirst = txtFirst.Text
    strLast = txtLast.Text

    'Processing
    'Call LastFirst function and pass it the first name and last name
    'Function returns a string Last, First
    strLastFirst = LastFirst(strFirst, strLast)

    'Output
    lblLastFirst.Text = strLastFirst

End Sub

Private Function LastFirst(ByVal strFName As String, ByVal strLName As String) As String
    'Gets first and last name and returns them in Last, First format
    Return strLName & ", " & strFName

End Function
```

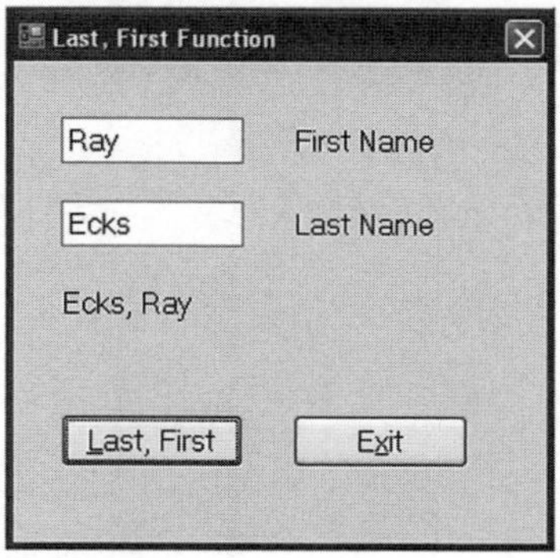

Figure 7.7   Last, First Function Program and Code

Sometimes the first and last name of a person must be displayed as last, first. This is handy when displaying a list of names arranged in alphabetical order and it's a good excuse to use a function with strings (see Figure 7.7).

The function is called with the following statement:

```
strLastFirst = LastFirst(strFirst, strLast)
```

The first name and last name are passed to a function called LastFirst. The function looks like this:

```
Private Function LastFirst(ByVal strFName As String,
    ByVal strLName As String) As String
    'Gets first and last name and returns them in Last,
    'First format
    Return strLName & ", " & strFName
End Function
```

It accepts two values passed ByVal As string. It creates a new string with the format Last, First and returns the string. The statement that called the function places the result in strLastFirst. It's then displayed.

VB Tip   *Open and run the LastFirstFunction program to see how it works.*

Credit Card Minimum Payment

A credit card company needs to calculate the minimum monthly payment for their credit cards. This is a great place for a function. Here are their rules. When

Figure 7.8   Minimum Payment Program

there's no balance, there's no payment. When the balance is $25 or less, the amount must be paid in full. Otherwise, the cardholder must pay 10% of the balance or $25, whichever is greater. The input is the balance on the card as entered in a TextBox. Check the balance. If it's 0, then simply post the minimum payment as 0. If there's a balance, then call the function, get the result, and post it (see Figure 7.8).

```
Private Sub btnPayment_Click(ByVal sender As
   System.Object, ByVal e As System.EventArgs) Handles
   btnPayment.Click
     'Declarations
     Dim decBalance As Decimal
     Dim decMinimum As Decimal

     'Input
     decBalance = txtBalance.Text

     'Processing
     'Calls function when there's a balance
     'CalcMinPayment returns minimum payment
     If decBalance > 0 Then
         decMinimum = CalcMinPayment(decBalance)
     Else
         decMinimum = 0
     End If
     'Output
     lblMinimum.Text = decMinimum.ToString("c")
End Sub
```

```
Private Function CalcMinPayment(ByVal decBal As Decimal)
   As Decimal
      'Balance must be paid in full when <= $25
      'Balances over $25 are the greater of 10% of the
      'balance or $25
      'Function returns minimum payment
      Const sngMinPercent As Single = 0.1
      Const decPayInFull As Decimal = 25
      Const decMinPayOnBalance As Decimal = 25
      Dim decMinPayment As Decimal

      If decBal <= decPayInFull Then
          decMinPayment = decBal
      Else
          decMinPayment = decBal * sngMinPercent
          If decMinPayment < decMinPayOnBalance Then
              decMinPayment = decMinPayOnBalance
          End If
      End If

      Return decMinPayment

End Function
```

The btnPayment Button gets the current balance. If the balance is 0, then there's no minimum payment and the function isn't called. If there is a balance, the CalcMinPayment function is called and the card balance is passed to it.

CalcMinPayment takes the balance and determines the minimum payment. First, it checks to see if the balance is less than or equal to $25. If so, that's the minimum payment. If not, it calculates 10% of the balance. It then checks to see which is greater, the balance or 10% of the balance. It keeps the larger of the two. The function returns the minimum payment to the line that called it. Once control is back in the btnPayment procedure, the payment is displayed.

VB Tip   *Open and run the MinimumPaymentFunction program to see how it works.*

Flowcharting Functions

Flowcharting a function is similar to flowcharting a procedure. It breaks away from the main line of the flowchart to run code on a separate line. However, a function returns a value and that value must be assigned upon return. Figure 7.9 shows the flowchart for the sales tax function from earlier. Note how it handles the function call and the value returned.

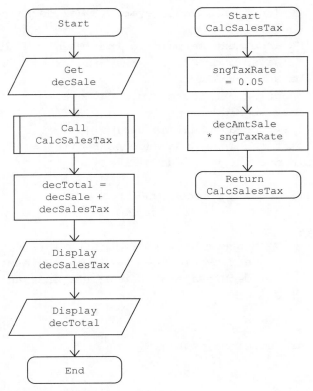

Figure 7.9   Sales Tax Function Flowchart

Potential Problems

Functions return a value, so the line that calls the function must be set up to accept a value in return. Every function call must pass the correct arguments, in the correct order, to the function. The data types passed must also match the function. The function declaration must include a data type. The type used is the type of data returned by the function. The variable names between a function and the procedure that calls it don't have to be the same. For example, shoNumPassed might be passed to the function. However, the function could accept it as shoNumReceived. As long as they are both short variables, there's no problem.

Use a function when you need an answer. Use a procedure when you want to combine a series of steps into their own block of code or when there are some commands that can be used in more than one place.

VB Quiz 02   *How are functions similar to procedures?*
How are they different?
How would you change the CalcMinPayment function to handle changes in the rules for calculating a minimum payment?

New Controls – Menus and Timers

Menus

Nearly every program uses menus. They neatly store features and options in a program and they can be tucked away, freeing up room on the screen. What's more, they're easy to create and use. The ToolBox has an item called a *MenuStrip*. Double-click on it or drag it to a form to create a menu. The control appears near the bottom of the screen in an area called the *component tray*. It also creates a menu strip at the top of the form.

Microsoft has guidelines for naming and using menus. The leftmost menu should be the File menu and should contain items relating to files. You're familiar with the typical options in the File menu: New, Open, Save, Exit, and some others. Next to it should be the Edit menu. It generally contains Undo, Cut, Copy, Paste, and other editing options. The rightmost menu should be the Help menu, containing Help and About options. The menus in between will vary depending on what the program does.

Name a menu with mnu as the prefix. The MenuStrip can be named mnuMain. Name each option in the menu with the menu title and the option title in the name. That way, developers can easily determine where an option is in the menu hierarchy. For example, the Exit menu should be named mnuFileExit and the Copy menu should be mnuEditCopy.

Menus are similar to Buttons in that they both have Name and Text properties. Use the Text property to display the name the user sees at runtime. Don't forget that the ampersand (&) can be used to designate a shortcut for the menu, just like it's used in Buttons. And, remember to name the menus before you code them. A double-click on the menu item opens a click event for it in the code window. Set the Shortcut property to add a keyboard shortcut to a menu item. The Shortcut property has a dropdown list with dozens of shortcut options. A menu can be deleted by a right-click and selecting Delete from the popup menu (see Figure 7.10).

Let's put it to use. The following table contains shows the menu hierarchy for the MenuExample program:

	MenuExample Hierarchy
File (*mnuFile*)	Shape (*mnuShape*)
Exit (*mnuFileExit*)	Rectangle (*mnuShapeRectangle*)
	Perimeter (*mnuShapeRectanglePerimeter*)
	Area (*mnuShapeRectangleArea*)
	Triangle (*mnuShapeTriangle*)
	Perimeter (*mnuShapeTrianglePerimeter*)
	Area (*mnuShapeTriangleArea*)
	Circle (*mnuShapeCircle*)
	Circumference (*mnuShapeCircleCircumference*)
	Area (*mnuShapeCircleArea*)

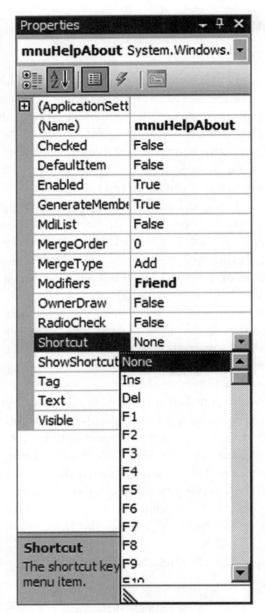

Figure 7.10   Menu Shortcuts Menu

Add a MenuStrip to the component tray and name it. Then click on the menu and name it mnuFile. Set the Text property to &File. Add the Exit menu below the File menu, name it mnuFileExit, and change the Text property to E&xit. Then move to the menu next to the File menu and click on it. Change the Text property to &Shape and name the menu mnuShape. Underneath it, create and name the other menus as needed to complete the structure.

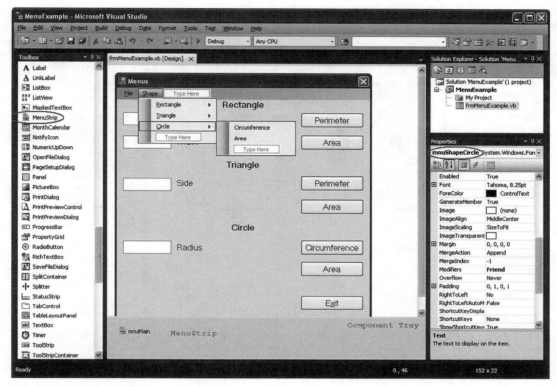

Figure 7.11   Menu Creation Screen

Double-click on the menu item to open a click event in the code (see Figure 7.11).

The program determines the perimeter and area for rectangles, equilateral triangles, and circles. It has procedures and functions and contains Buttons and menus for each calculation. Rather than write the code twice for each calculation, place it in procedures. The appropriate menu and Button then call the procedure. There are advantages to this approach: the user has two ways to find the answer, either a Button or the menu. However, the code is written just once, which takes less space and makes it easier to debug.

Inside each procedure is a function call. The function does the math and returns the answer. These functions can be shared when needed for other calculations.

VB Tip   *Open and run the MenuExample program. Finish the program by adding procedures and functions for the remaining items.*

Timers

A *Timer* is another handy control. When added to a program, it shows up in the component tray. Think of the Timer as an alarm clock. It can be turned on and

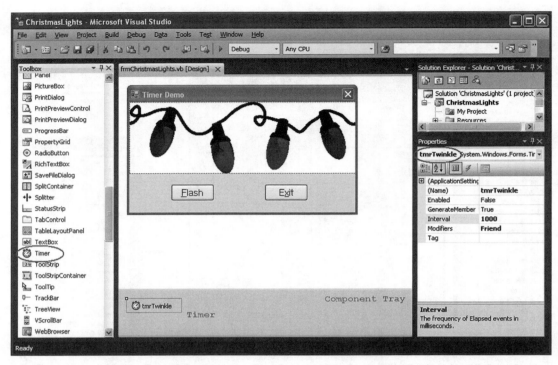

Figure 7.12   Timer Creation Screen

off, and it can be set to go off at a set interval. Set the Enabled property to True to activate the Timer. Set it to False to stop the Timer. A *Tick* event controls the Timer. A tick is one thousandth of a second. Any code in the Timer's Tick event runs whenever the Timer goes off. Change the *Interval* property to change the frequency of the Timer event. Change the Enabled property to False to turn the Timer off.

Here's a little example with holiday lights (see Figure 7.12). The form has two PictureBoxes, one with the lights on and the other with the lights off. By switching between them, it gives the illusion of flashing lights. Pretty festive, huh?

```
Private Sub btnFlash_Click(ByVal sender As System.Object,
    ByVal e As System.EventArgs) Handles btnFlash.Click
    'Turn the lights on
    tmrTwinkle.Enabled = True
End Sub

Private Sub tmrTwinkle_Tick(ByVal sender As
    System.Object, ByVal e As System.EventArgs) Handles
    tmrTwinkle.Tick
    'Makes the lights flash
    If picOn.Visible = True Then
```

```
        picOff.Visible = True
        picOn.Visible = False
    Else
        picOn.Visible = True
        picOff.Visible = False
    End If
```

The Flash Button turns on the Timer. The Interval for the tmrTwinkle control is set to 1,000 – that's one second. The code checks to see if the picOn picture is visible. It's visible when the Visible property is set to True. It switches the PictureBoxes by alternating the Visible properties of them. A Tick event is triggered once per second.

VB Tip   *Open and run the ChristmasLights program. Add a Button to turn the lights off.*

VB Quiz 03   *What advantages do Buttons have? When are menus more useful?*
What property activates and disables a Timer and how often does it run?
List the events that have been covered so far.

Tying It All Together

Use a procedure when the same task must be used in more than one place or when there are similar tasks that can be easily customized. Build a function when a calculation is needed. Not every calculation needs a function, but look to use them for complicated or repetitive calculations. Menus are as easy to create and use as Buttons. Buttons are handier for young users and those with accessibility issues. Menus take up less space and provide a sense of organization. Timers are used to trigger events automatically.

"Wheels on the Bus" Program

You probably sang this song in your younger years. The words in each verse are similar, with just three differences in each verse. So, set up the program with a procedure to display a verse. Pass the unique words for that verse when the procedure is called and have the procedure plug them in and display the lyrics. Clear the screen and display the song title at the top. This is a great place for another procedure. The song has many verses and each one fits well in a menu item. Add a Help menu to display the credits for the copyright holders (see Figure 7.13).

```
Private Sub Title()
    'Clears the rich text box and displays the title
    rtbLyrics.Clear()
```

```
        rtbLyrics.AppendText("    The Wheels on the Bus" &
        vbNewLine & vbNewLine)
End Sub

Private Sub Verse(ByVal strThing As String, ByVal strVerb
    As String, ByVal strSound As String)
        'Displays a verse of the song
        'The object making the noise is passed along with the
        'noise and the verb
        'Parameters are mixed with the lyrics to make the verse
        rtbLyrics.AppendText("The " & strThing & " on the bus" &
        strVerb & strSound & "," & vbNewLine)
        rtbLyrics.AppendText(strSound & ", " & strSound & "."
        &vbNewLine)
        rtbLyrics.AppendText("The " & strThing & " on the bus" &
        strVerb & strSound & "," & vbNewLine)
        rtbLyrics.AppendText("all through the town!")
End Sub

Private Sub mnuSongWheels_Click(ByVal sender As
    System.Object, ByVal e As System.EventArgs) Handles
    mnuSongWheels.Click
        'Variables declared for necessary words in the verse
        'Title is called to clear the screen and display
        'the title
        'These values are passed to Verse procedure to
        'produce a verse
        Dim strThings As String = "wheels"
        Dim strVerb As String = "go "
        Dim strSound As String = "round and round"
```

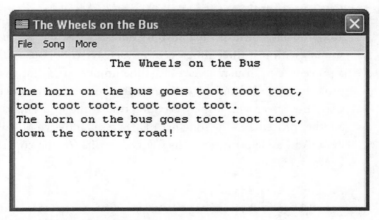

Figure 7.13   Wheels on the Bus Program

```
      Call Title()
      Call Verse(strThings, strVerb, strSound)
   End Sub

   Private Sub mnuHelpAbout_Click(ByVal sender As
      System.Object, ByVal e As System.EventArgs) Handles
      mnuHelpAbout.Click
        'Displays writers and programmer
        Call Title()
        rtbLyrics.AppendText("  by Judy and David Gershon" &
        vbNewLine)
        rtbLyrics.AppendText("  (c)1992" & vbNewLine &
        vbNewLine)
        rtbLyrics.AppendText("  adapted by Your Name" &
        vbNewLine)
   End Sub
```

VB Tip   *Open and run the WheelsOnTheBus program.*

Countdown Program

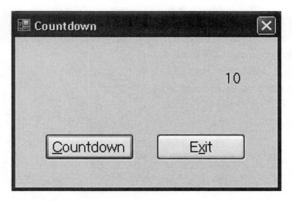

Figure 7.14   Countdown Program

Let's put the Timer to work to do a countdown (see Figure 7.14). Create a Timer
called tmrCountdown and set the Interval to 1000. Create a Button that turns
the Timer on and sets mshoCountdown to 10. The Timer displays the value of
mshoCountdown and then decreases it by 1. You want the countdown to stop
at 0, so put in an If statement to check mshoCountdown. When it's less than 0,
turn off the Timer and, for a little flair, display "Blastoff!"

Remember, the Timer runs until the Enabled property is turned off. Be sure
to turn it off when its work is done.

```
Public Class frmCountdown
    Dim mshoCountdown As Short

    Private Sub tmrCountdown_Tick(ByVal sender As
        System.Object, ByVal e As System.EventArgs) Handles
        tmrCountdown.Tick
          'Display count
          lblCountdown.Text = mshoCountdown.ToString
          'Take one from count
          mshoCountdown -= 1
          'Check to see if count is 0
          If mshoCountdown < 0 Then
              lblCountdown.Text = "Blastoff!"
              tmrCountdown.Enabled = False
          End If
    End Sub

    Private Sub btnExit_Click(ByVal sender As
        System.Object, ByVal e As System.EventArgs) Handles
        btnExit.Click
          End
    End Sub

    Private Sub btnCountdown_Click(ByVal sender As
        System.Object, ByVal e As System.EventArgs) Handles
        btnCountdown.Click
          'Turn timer on and set count to 10
          tmrCountdown.Enabled = True
          mshoCountdown = 10
    End Sub
```

VB Tip *Open and run the Countdown program.*

Markup Program

Markup is the percentage added to the wholesale price of an item to get the retail price. This program gets the name of an item and its wholesale price. It calculates the markup and then displays the item, its wholesale price, the markup percentage, and the retail price. The input, processing, and output are procedures. The markup is calculated with a function. The program also uses a procedure to create the heading of the output (see Figure 7.15).

```
Public Class frmMarkup
    Dim mstrItem As String
    Dim mdecWholesale As Decimal
    Dim mdecRetail As Decimal
```

```
Private Sub frmMarkup_Load(ByVal sender As
  System.Object, ByVal e As System.EventArgs) Handles
  MyBase.Load
    Call ClearForm()
End Sub

Private Sub btnClear_Click(ByVal sender As
  System.Object, ByVal e As System.EventArgs) Handles
  btnClear.Click
    Call ClearForm()
End Sub

Private Sub btnExit_Click(ByVal sender As
  System.Object, ByVal e As System.EventArgs) Handles
  btnExit.Click
    End
End Sub

Private Sub btnMarkup_Click(ByVal sender As
  System.Object, ByVal e As System.EventArgs) Handles
  btnMarkup.Click
    Call GetInput()
    Call DoProcessing()
    Call DisplayOutput()
End Sub

Private Sub GetInput()
    'Handles Input
    mstrItem = txtItem.Text
    mdecWholesale = txtWholesale.Text
End Sub

Private Sub DoProcessing()
    'Call CalcMarkup
    mdecRetail = CalcMarkup(mdecWholesale)
End Sub

Private Sub DisplayOutput()
    'Handles Output
    Dim strOut As String
    strOut = mstrItem & "     " & mdecWholesale
    .ToString("c") & "        50%      " & mdecRetail
    .ToString("c") & vbNewLine
    rtbOut.AppendText(strOut)
End Sub
```

```
Private Sub ClearForm()
    'Clear form
    rtbOut.Clear()
    rtbOut.AppendText("Item  Wholesale  Markup
        Retail" & vbNewLine)
    txtItem.Clear()
    txtWholesale.Clear()
End Sub

Private Function CalcMarkup(ByVal decPrice As Decimal)
  As Decimal
    'Calculates 50% markup and returns retail price
    Const sngMarkup As Single = 0.5
    CalcMarkup = decPrice + (decPrice * sngMarkup)
End Function

End Class
```

VB Tip   *Open and run the Markup program to see how it works.*

A procedure called ClearForm clears the form and adds a heading. It's called in the Load event and the Clear Button. One block of code gets used in two

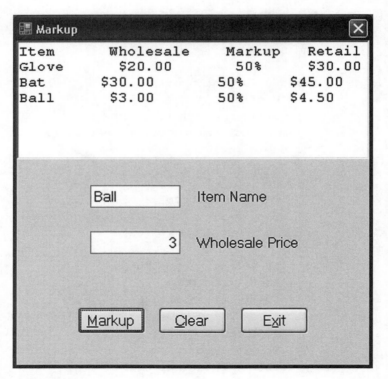

Figure 7.15   Markup Program

places. That's modularization. If the code from the GetInput, DoProcessing, and DisplayOutput procedures was placed in the Click event for the btnMarkup Button, the code would be pretty much the same. Note the CalcMarkup function in the last block of code. It's called from the DoProcessing procedure. The markup could have been calculated in the procedure. However, when it's made into a function, it can be used elsewhere. In the long run, that's a great way to code, even though it makes this program more complicated.

There's nothing in this program that hasn't been used before. It's just arranged differently to modularize the code. It's a big step in the direction of writing large, useable programs.

VB Tip   *A good way to learn how to write procedures and functions is to write the code without them and then modify the code to use them.*

Fixing a Program

Every paycheck has deductions. Part of it is Federal Insurance Contributions Act (FICA) tax – what is usually referred to as Social Security. It's 7.65% and it's divided between Social Security and Medicare. You need to debug the program so it works. Right now the wages are entered into the program, which should calculate and return the FICA amount.

You run the program and enter $100. It displays $0.00 for FICA. Hmm? Often a 0 for output means that a variable wasn't assigned a value. That's a good place to start.

You check the code and that's not the problem this time. It gets the wages and passes that value. The calculation looks like it will work. However, there's never a value assigned for output. decFICA is initialized to 0 when declared in the click event for btnFICA and it's never updated.

Closer inspection reveals that a procedure was used instead of a function. Procedures don't return a value and, in this case, you need a function that does the work and gives you an answer. You rewrite the procedure so it's a function. It should look like this:

```
Private Function CalcFICA(ByVal decPay As Decimal)
    As Decimal Const sngFICA As Single = 0.0765

    Return decPay * sngFICA
End Function
```

Instead of Private Sub, it should be Private Function. Functions require a data type when declared so you tack As Decimal onto the end of the line. The FICA rate is correct, 7.65%, which shows up as 0.0765 when displayed as a decimal. The value passed is decFICA and it ends up in decPay in the function. You think about that for a minute, but then remember that it's OK to have different names for these as long as the data types match. There was also something about being

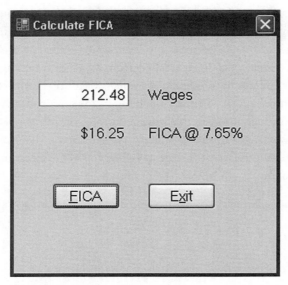

Figure 7.16   FICA Function Program

able to call functions from many places and still getting them to work as long as the values can be passed back and forth. You think you understand it, but make a mental note to pay close attention to this concept until it's completely understood.

Another problem is the calculation. FICA is the pay times the rate. That part's fine, but it turns around and puts the answer into decPay. The answer should be sent back to the line that called the function instead of sitting in a variable in the function. You change that line and you're happy with how the function looks.

You now turn your attention to the line that calls the function. It's still set up to call a procedure. You rewrite the line to call the CalcFICA function and accept the value it returns. The line looks like this:

```
decFICA = CalcFICA(decWages)
```

It calls the function and sends it the wages. CalcFICA returns the amount, which is stored in decFICA. The last line correctly displays the amount withheld (see Figure 7.16). Yahtzee!

VB Tip   *Open and run the FICAFunction program and fix it. The FICAFunctionFixed program runs correctly.*

On Your Own

Write a program using procedures that displays the lyrics to the children's song "Old McDonald's Farm." Pass the name of the farm animal and the sounds it makes to a procedure that displays the verse.

Write a program to calculate the hours and minutes worked. Input is the start time and end time. The output is the hours and minutes worked. Use procedures and functions as needed.

Write a program that determines the letter grade for a student. Use a function that accepts their average and returns the grade. Use 90–80–70–60 for the grading scale.

Write a program that times a three-minute egg. Use a Timer and have it display the remaining time as it counts down.

Write a program using menus that offers diners choices from a food stand. Put three choices in the Sandwich menu, three choices in the Beverage menu, and three choices in the Dessert menu. Display each choice and its price in a RichTextBox. Include a Total option in the File menu that totals and displays the order. Use procedures and functions as needed.

Summary

Procedures and functions make modular programming possible. They complicate the code, but result in programs that are more powerful and flexible. Procedures combine commands into a block that can be called when and where it's needed. Functions perform a calculation and return an answer. Menus provide an easy, intuitive way to group commands in a program. Most programs use menus, making them familiar to the user. The Timer control is used to activate code at a set interval.

Review

Procedures break a complicated process into a series of simpler steps.

Procedures are used when the same set of commands is used more than once, especially when they're used in different places.

Procedures are written into their own section in the code. They cannot be part of another block of code.

Arguments (values) can be passed to a procedure. They can be passed ByVal or ByRef.

Arguments passed ByVal cannot change the value of the original variable.

Arguments passed ByRef can change the value of the original variable.

Control of a program passes to a procedure, which runs and then returns control back to the line that called it.

The flowchart symbol for a procedure or function is a rectangle with an extra set of lines on the side.

Functions receive one or more arguments (values) and return an answer.

Arguments can be passed to a function ByVal or ByRef.

Every function must be declared with a data type.

Use functions for complicated calculations or for calculations that are used often.

The component tray sits below a form and stores controls that don't display on the form.

Menu guidelines create a familiar interface for a user and should be followed when possible.

A click event triggers the code in a menu.

A Timer stores code that is triggered by a Tick event.

Once activated, a Timer runs its code at a set interval.

The timing of a Timer is controlled by a Tick, one thousandth of second.

Terms

arguments	optional values passed to procedures and functions
component tray	an area near the bottom of the screen that contains controls that normally won't show up on the form
function	a procedure that supplies an answer
MenuStrip	the ToolBox control that contains the components to create a menu
modularization	separating a program into smaller, related components
procedure	a set of statements in a program
Return	the command that returns a value from a function to the statement that called the function
Tick	one thousandth of a second
Timer	a component with an alarm that automatically triggers the code through a Tick event

Keywords

ByRef	the keyword that indicates values are being passed by reference
ByVal	the keyword that indicates values are being passed by value
Call	the optional keyword that calls a subprocedure
Function	a programming routine that determines a value and returns that value
Interval	a property of a Timer control that determines the length in milliseconds between Tick events
Private	a level of exposure for a component or procedure in a program; Private declarations make them available only in the procedure where they're declared
Public	a level of exposure for a component or procedure in a program; Public declarations make them available anywhere on a form
Return	a command that instructs a function to return the stated value
Sub	a keyword that defines a subprocedure; short for subprocedure

Self-check

1. A procedure can be called from almost any place in a program.
2. Values sent to a procedure are called arguments.
3. A procedure cannot call another procedure.
4. The flowchart symbol for a procedure is a triangle.
5. Arguments must be passed to a procedure in the order specified by the procedure.
6. A value passed to a procedure ByRef can be modified by the procedure.
7. A function can return multiple values.
8. A function can accept arguments of any data type, but all the arguments passed to a function must be of the same data type.
9. A function must be declared with a data type.
10. The code in a Timer is triggered by a Tick event.
11. The process of breaking a complicated process into simpler steps is:
    A. prioritization
    B. modularization
    C. accommodation
    D. polarization
12. Values passed to a procedure or a function are called:
    A. arguments
    B. methods
    C. transfers
    D. tickets
13. When passing ByRef, the named variable:
    A. can be modified in the procedure
    B. automatically gets returned by the procedure
    C. is treated like a constant
    D. must be at the module level
14. A function call:
    A. must contain the same number of arguments as the function
    B. must pass arguments of the same data type to the function
    C. must pass arguments in the correct order to the function
    D. more than one of the above
15. Functions return a value. Procedures don't return a value. A function can have up to three arguments. A procedure can have only one argument.
    A. The first statement is true and the others are false.
    B. The first two statements are true and the last two are false.
    C. The first and last statements are true and the other two are false.
    D. The first and third statements are true and the other two are false.
16. Menus:
    A. must be in alphabetical order
    B. should start with File and end with Help

     C. must have a shortcut

     D. more than one of the above

17. Regarding ByVal and ByRef,:

     A. both cannot be used in the same Call statement

     B. ByVal is for numeric variables while ByRef is for all other data types

     C. ByVal passes the value of the named variable while ByRef passes the memory address

     D. more than one of the above

18. Functions are useful when a:

     A. program calls for a complicated formula

     B. formula is needed more than once

     C. formula may change and need to be updated

     D. all of the above

19. A tick is:

     A. one second

     B. one thousandth of a second

     C. one millionth of a second

     D. determined by the developer when creating a Timer

20. Controls in a program that don't appear on the form:

     A. are stored in the gutter

     B. cannot be activated until they're added to the form

     C. are stored in the component tray

     D. are automatically deleted once they've been used

VB Quiz Answers

Quiz 01

Procedures break a program into manageable parts. Developers can work on their own sections of the code without interfering with the work of other developers. Procedures allow the reuse of code.

Both pass values called arguments to a procedure. Values passed ByVal cannot be changed by the procedure. Values passed ByRef can be modified by the procedure. The original value in a variable passed ByVal stays the same. When passed ByRef, the value in the variable that's passed can be modified by the procedure.

```
For i = 1 To 500
    rtbOut.AppendText("I will behave myself in study hall
        from now on." & vbNewLine)
Next i
```

Roadmaps often provide a guide from one city to another. Once you've arrived, the general detail of the roadmap isn't enough and you must resort to the smaller city maps that are included. The large map provides general information on the trip while the detail map provides the details for some parts of the trip.

Quiz 02

Each function has its own section of code, just like procedures. Both can be passed arguments, either ByVal or ByRef. Both modularize a program.

Functions return a value, while procedures do not. Procedures don't need an argument, while functions should have one. A procedure can be called with the Call command. The line that calls a function must accept the value returned by the function.

Rather than code the values for a minimum payment, the function should use constants. That way, changes to the rules could be easily implemented.

Quiz 03

Buttons provide easy access for those that aren't comfortable or capable of using menus. Children are a good example of those that often benefit more from Buttons than menus. With Buttons, the controls are visible on the screen. However, they do take up some screen space, limiting what is available at any time. Menus take less screen space than Buttons. They are easy to arrange in a hierarchy. For most, they are easy to navigate. Some users have trouble navigating through menus and the commands are hidden until the menu is accessed.

The Enabled property controls a Timer. When True, the code in the Timer runs. When False, the code won't run. Timers run at set times determined by the Interval property. The Interval property is set in Ticks, or one thousandth of a second.

The Click, Load, ValueChanged, and Tick events have been covered. More events will be covered in later chapters.

Writing Programs III – Tying It All Together, So Far

It claims to be fully automatic, but actually you have to push this little button here.

–Gentleman John Killian

The more work you put into your programs, the less work they'll be for the user. A developer might not like that, but a good program might be used hundreds or thousands of times by millions of users. If you make it just a little easier for every one of them every time they use it – well, you get the idea. Your programs aren't quite there yet, but the basic principles are the same. Just develop an interface with the user in mind and spend a little more time getting the details right. The interface takes care of input and output and the developer worries about the details to handle the processing that comes in between. Good programs are fun and easy to use. They allow the user to concentrate on solving a problem rather than forcing them to figure out how to use the computer.

This chapter introduces new tools. Most of them make it easier for the user and more complicated for the developer. There are also a few other odds and ends to clean up your output.

RadioButtons

RadioButtons are used to select one option from a list of several options. Click on a RadioButton to select it. A black dot appears inside the circle to indicate it's selected. Click on another RadioButton to select it and deselect the original. One and only one RadioButton is selected at any time. Use them when you must have one option from a list of several options.

RadioButtons are grouped in something called, with great originality, a *GroupBox*. A GroupBox puts other controls in a group and allows them to act together. A GroupBox sets them apart from other controls and forces them to work together. This is especially helpful when there are two or more sets of RadioButtons on a form (see Figure 8.1).

A pizza order is a good example of when to use RadioButtons. When you order a pizza, you must specify the size. That's a great use for RadioButtons. Use another set to specify the type of crust.

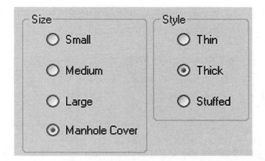

Figure 8.1   Owt Pizza GroupBoxes and RadioButton Example

Use grp as the prefix for a GroupBox and rad as the prefix for RadioButtons. Use the handles on the sides to resize a GroupBox and the tab on the top to move them. Drop RadioButtons into a GroupBox, name them, add a description to the Text property, and arrange them as needed.

The *Format menu* is handy for aligning and spacing RadioButtons. Select the RadioButtons and use the options in the Format menu to align them, make the spacing between them even, and make them the same size.

When the program runs, a user can select one size and one crust style for the pizza. Set the Checked property of a RadioButton to True to have that option automatically selected at runtime. The Checked property of a RadioButton can be set in code by setting the Checked property as in this example:

```
radMedium.Checked = True
```

A developer can use an If statement to test if a RadioButton is checked. For example:

```
If radMedium.Checked = True Then
    strSize = "Medium"
    decPrice = 10.95
End If
```

This code fits nicely into a Button or menu and by checking each RadioButton in this manner, a developer determines which one is selected.

VB Tip

If radMedium.Checked Then
says the same thing, but it's shorter to write.

Another way to use RadioButtons is to work with the CheckedChanged event. This event is triggered every time the user changes their selection. For example:

```
Private Sub radMedium_CheckedChanged( ...
    mstrSize = "Medium"
    mdecPrice = 10.95
End Sub
```

which sets the size and the price every time the user selects the size of their pizza. The RadioButtons for the crust style are similar.

VB Tip   *Open and run the OwtPizza program to see how it works. The program is incomplete at this point.*

T-shirts Program

Figure 8.2   VB Masters T-Shirt Order Form Program

The class decides to order VB t-shirts. A student selects the size of t-shirt and then clicks on the Order Button. It displays the size and the price of the t-shirt (see Figure 8.2).

```
Public Class frmVBMasterTShirts
    Dim mstrSize As String
    Dim mdecPrice As Decimal
    Private Sub radSmall_CheckedChanged(...
        mstrSize = "Small"
        mdecPrice = 8
    End Sub
    Private Sub radMedium_CheckedChanged(...
        mstrSize = "Medium"
        mdecPrice = 8
```

```
        End Sub
        Private Sub radLarge_CheckedChanged(...
            mstrSize = "Large"
            mdecPrice = 10
        End Sub
        Private Sub radExtraLarge_CheckedChanged(...
            mstrSize = "Extra Large"
            mdecPrice = 10
        End Sub
        Private Sub radXXL_CheckedChanged(...
            mstrSize = "XXL"
            mdecPrice = 12
        End Sub
        Private Sub btnOrder_Click(...
            lblSize.Text = mstrSize
            lblPrice.Text = mdecPrice.ToString("c")
        End Sub
        Private Sub btnExit_Click(...
            End
        End Sub
End Class
```

Each RadioButton has a CheckedChanged event that sets the size and price of the t-shirt. The size is stored in mstrSize and the price goes into mdecPrice. The Order Button displays the size and price in a Label (Figure 8.3).

```
Public Class frmVBMasterTShirts
        Private Sub radSmall_CheckedChanged(...
            PlaceOrder("Small")
        End Sub
        Private Sub radMedium_CheckedChanged(...
            PlaceOrder("Medium")
        End Sub
        Private Sub radLarge_CheckedChanged(...
            PlaceOrder("Large")
        End Sub
        Private Sub radExtraLarge_CheckedChanged(...
            PlaceOrder("Extra Large")
        End Sub
        Private Sub radXXL_CheckedChanged(...
            PlaceOrder("XXL")
        End Sub
        Private Sub btnExit_Click(...
            End
        End Sub
```

```
Private Sub PlaceOrder(ByVal strSize As String)
    Dim decPrice As Decimal
    Select Case strSize
        Case Is = "Small"
            decPrice = 8
        Case Is = "Medium"
            decPrice = 8
        Case Is = "Large"
            decPrice = 10
        Case Is = "Extra Large"
            decPrice = 10
        Case Is = "XXL"
            decPrice = 12
    End Select
    lblSize.Text = strSize
    lblPrice.Text = decPrice.ToString("c")
End Sub
End Class
```

Figure 8.3   VB Masters Alternative T-Shirt Order Form Program

In this example, each CheckedChanged event calls the PlaceOrder procedure and passes the size of the t-shirt. PlaceOrder accepts the t-shirt size and uses it to determine the price. The size and price are then displayed. The advantage of this approach is that it eliminates the Button.

VB Tip   *Open and run the VBMasterTShirtsAlternative to see how it works. Compare it to the VBMasterTShirtsprogram program.*

VB Quiz 01   *Why are RadioButtons considered input?*
                      What advantages do RadioButtons have over other types of input?
                      Describe how a group of RadioButtons is like a Case structure.

CheckBoxes

CheckBoxes are similar to RadioButtons, but different. Where a group of RadioButtons allows only one choice from the group, CheckBoxes allow any combination. A user is free to select all items, none of them, or any combination in between. CheckBoxes are used when more than one option in a list can be used. CheckBoxes belong in their own group. It's not that they work in concert like RadioButtons, but more as a way to indicate they all belong together.

The prefix for a CheckBox is chk. The Text property controls the title next to the CheckBox. Use the Format menu to align and evenly space them.

Sticking with the pizza analogy, CheckBoxes work well for selecting the toppings. Some people may want just cheese, others may prefer their pizza loaded, and everyone has their favorite topping or combination of toppings.

Set the Checked property to True to have it automatically checked at runtime. The Checked property of a CheckBox can be set in code by setting the Checked property as in this example:

```
chkPepperoni.Checked = True
```

A developer can use an If statement to test if a CheckBox is checked. For example:

```
If chkPepperoni.Checked = True Then
    strToppings += "Pepperoni "
End If
```

This code fits nicely into a Button or menu and by checking each CheckBox in this manner, a developer determines which ones are selected.

VB Tip   *If chkPepperoni.Checked Then*
                      says the same thing, but it's shorter to write.

Figure 8.4   Owt Pizza GroupBox and CheckBoxes Example

Another way to use CheckBoxes is to work with a CheckedChanged event. This event is triggered every time the user clicks on the CheckBox. A click on an unchecked CheckBox places a check in it. A click on one that's already checked removes the check. The code can check to see if the CheckBox is checked (see Figure 8.4).

```
If chkPepperoni.Checked = True Then
    blnPepperoni = "True"
Else
    blnPepperoni = "False"
End If
```

Here is the code that handles the pizza toppings:

```
Private Sub btnOrder_Click( ...
    Dim strToppings As String
    Dim strReservations As String = "none"
    mdecTotal += mdecPrice

    If chkPepperoni.Checked Then
        strToppings += "Pepperoni "
    End If
```

```
        If chkSausage.Checked Then
            strToppings += "Sausage "
        End If

        If chkCandianBacon.Checked Then
            strToppings += "Canadian Bacon "
        End If

        If chkBeef.Checked Then
            strToppings += "Beef "
        End If

        If chkGreenPeppers.Checked Then
            strToppings += "Green Peppers "
        End If

        If chkOnions.Checked Then
            strToppings += "Onions "
        End If

        If chkOlives.Checked Then
            strToppings += "Olives "
        End If

        If chkMushrooms.Checked Then
            strToppings += "Mushrooms "
        End If

        If chkAnchovies.Checked Then
            strToppings += "Anchovies "
        End If

        rtbOut.AppendText("1" & ControlChars.Tab & mstrStyle
          & ControlChars.Tab & mstrSize &
          ControlChars.Tab & ControlChars.Tab &
          ControlChars.Tab & mdecPrice.ToString("c") &
          vbNewLine)
        rtbOut.AppendText(strToppings & vbNewLine)
        rtbOut.AppendText("Reservations: " &
          strReservations & vbNewLine)

    End Sub
```

VB Tip   *Open and run the OwtPizzaUpdate program to see how it works. The program is incomplete at this point.*

Gift Wrapping Program

Figure 8.5   Karen Foryou Gift Wrapping Program

Karen Foryou runs a little gift-wrapping kiosk in the mall. She charges by the size of the package: $2.50 for small packages, $3.50 for medium packages, and $5.00 for large packages. In addition, she offers ribbons, bows, and cards for an added charge of $.50 each. Use RadioButtons to determine the price based on the size of the package and a CheckBox for each amenity. The CheckChanged events for the RadioButtons and CheckBoxes call a procedure that determines which ones are selected, then calculates and displays the price (see Figure 8.5).

```
Public Class frmKarenForyouGiftWrapping
    Private Sub CalcTotal()
    Const decAmenities As Decimal = 0.5
    Dim decTotal As Decimal
    'Calc charge for package size
    If radSmall.Checked Then
        decTotal = 2.5
    ElseIf radMedium.Checked Then
        decTotal = 3.5
    Else
        decTotal = 5
    End If
```

```
'Calc charges for amenities
If chkBow.Checked Then
    decTotal += decAmenities
End If

If chkRibbon.Checked Then
    decTotal += decAmenities
End If

If chkCard.Checked Then
    decTotal += decAmenities
End If

'Display total
lblTotal.Text = decTotal.ToString("c")

End Sub

Private Sub btnExit_Click( ...
    End
End Sub

Private Sub radSmall_CheckedChanged( ...
    CalcTotal()
End Sub

Private Sub radMedium_CheckedChanged( ...
CalcTotal()
End Sub

Private Sub radLarge_CheckedChanged( ...
    CalcTotal()
End Sub

Private Sub chkBow_CheckedChanged( ...
    CalcTotal()
End Sub

Private Sub chkRibbon_CheckedChanged( ...
    CalcTotal()
End Sub

Private Sub chkCard_CheckedChanged( ...
    CalcTotal()
End Sub

End Class
```

Figure 8.6　　　　Owt Pizza Reservations ListBox Example

VB Tip　　　　*Open and run the KarenForyouGiftWrapping program to see how it works.*

Potential Problems

Every RadioButton and CheckBox must be coded. If one is skipped, it won't work. VB will automatically select a RadioButton at runtime if one isn't selected. Change the Checked property to True at design time to have it automatically selected at runtime. One of them can be coded as Checked by setting its Checked property to True. Only one at a time is selected so don't even try to code more than one as Checked.

CheckBoxes can be check or unchecked, depending on the need. A good developer knows which option is the best and codes accordingly.

The test to see which RadioButton in a set is checked can be done with nested If statements or by using ElseIf. Only one of them will be checked, making them mutually exclusive. CheckBoxes must be tested individually because more than one of them might be selected. Only a series of stacked If statements will work for this.

VB Quiz 02　　　　*How are CheckBoxes the same as and different from RadioButtons?*

What advantages are there to writing a procedure and calling it from the CheckChanged event?

With four sizes of pizza, three types of crust, and nine different toppings, how many possibilities are there?

ListBoxes

VB Tip　　　　*"A bus station is where a bus stops. A train station is where a train stops. On my desk I have a workstation . . . " – Anonymous*

ListBoxes are used to select an item from a list of several options. They're handy when space is limited or there's a large selection from which to choose. Click on an item in the list to select it. If the list is too long for the ListBox, scrollbars automatically appear so the user can scroll through the list (see Figure 8.6).

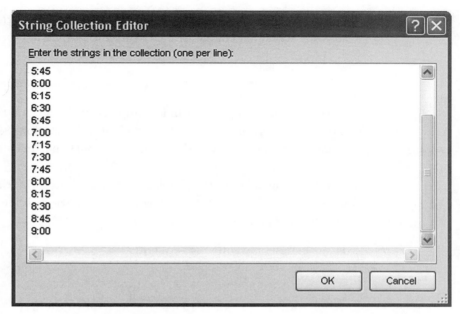

Figure 8.7   Reservations Collection Editor Screen

Use lst for the prefix for a ListBox. Each option in a ListBox is part of a collection of items. The list of items in a ListBox is stored in the Items property. Add *items* to a ListBox in one of two ways. Place them in a *collection* at design time or add them to the Items list at runtime. Select the Items property and double-click on the ellipses to open the *Collection Editor*. Place one item per line in the list and click OK when finished. These Items will appear at runtime. Use the Add method for the Items property to add items to the list at runtime. For example:

```
lstReservations.Items.Add(strNewTime)
```

where strNewTime is the time of the reservation (see Figure 8.7).

The *Items* property contains a list (one per line) of the items in a ListBox. Each item has its own index number. The first index number is always 0. One way to distinguish items in a list is with this Index number.

The user selects an item from the list by clicking on it. A developer writes code to determine which item was selected and then processes that selection as needed. There are a couple ways to accomplish this. One way is to use the *SelectedItem* property. It contains the item the user has selected, and it can then be assigned to a variable and used in processing:

```
strReservations = lstReservations.SelectedItem
```

In this example, a patron selects a reservation time. The *SelectedIndex* property contains the number of the selected item which is used in processing:

```
strReservations =
    lstReservations.Items(lstReservations.SelectedIndex)
```

This line uses the SelectedIndex property of the ListBox to find the index number of the item that's selected. Think of lstReservations.SelectedIndex as a number. That number is used to get the text from that item in the list and assign it to strReservations.

When no item in a ListBox is selected, then the SelectedIndex is -1. That helps to explain the If statement that follows. When the SelectedIndex is -1, there's no item to select and an error could result:

```
If lstReservations.SelectedIndex > 0 Then
    strReservations =
        lstReservations.Items(lstReservations.SelectedIndex)
End If
```

The number of items in a ListBox is determined using the Count method of the Items property, like this:

```
shoCount = lstReservations.Items.Count
```

The first item in a ListBox is 0. The last item in a ListBox is always one less than the total number of items in the ListBox. That is, it's always one less than Count. When the SelectedIndex is −1, there's no item selected.

VB Tip

To deselect an item in a ListBox, use:
lstReservations.SelectedIndex = −1

Normally, items are added to a ListBox by placing them at the end of the Items list. However, items can be added in a specific position by using the *Insert* method of the Items property. For example:

```
lstReservations.Items.Insert(shoIndex, strItem)
```

where shoIndex is the index number where the item will be inserted and strItem is the item to be added. Any item(s) in the ListBox from that index on are moved down the list.

Items can be removed from a ListBox in two ways. One is to specify the item to be removed and the other is to *remove* an item by its index number. For example:

```
lstReservations.Items.Remove("9:00")
```

removes the 9:00 reservation time from the list.

```
lstReservations.Items.RemoveAt(0)
```

removes the first item from the list.

Use the Clear method to remove all items from a list. For example:

```
lstReservations.Items.Clear()
```

removes all the reservations times from the list.

Adding and removing items from a ListBox can cause problems for the user. An easy way to keep a ListBox organized is to set the Sorted property to True. It's set to False by default, but when it's True, it keeps the list in alphabetical order. That makes it a little easier for a user to find items on the list. Change the Sorted property to True at design time to create and maintain a sorted list. At runtime, the list can be sorted by changing the Sorted property to True. For example:

```
lstReservations.Sorted = True
```

VB Tip   *Open and run the OwtPizzaMore program to see how it works. The program is incomplete at this point.*

To Do List Program

Penny Loafer has put off all of her errands until Saturday, and now, with a bundle of them to do, she needs a list to get organized. What she really needs is a handy little program to help her get organized. The main feature is a ListBox where she can put all of her errands. Errands can be added to the list using a TextBox. As they're completed, they can be removed from the list and her current errand can be displayed in a Label. In addition, some features and bulletproofing should be added to the program.

A good way to create programs is to get the basics working and then add the doodads once the nuts and bolts are in place. So, do the easy stuff first.

Use a TextBox for input and add an item to the ListBox with an Add Button. The Remove Button should remove the selected item from the list. The Display Button should display the current errand just as a reminder. Of course, the Exit Button ends the program (see Figure 8.8).

The Add Button is easy enough; just take what's in the TextBox and add it to the ListBox:

```
strFavorite = txtFavorite.Text
lstToDo.Items.Add(strFavorite)
```

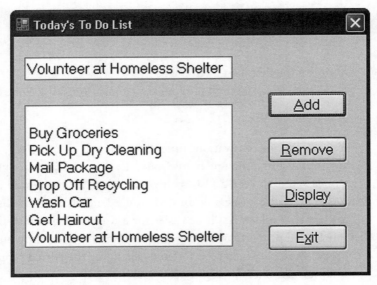

Figure 8.8   To Do List Program

The Remove Button is just one line. It removes the selected item from the list:

```
lstToDo.Items.Remove(lstToDo.SelectedItem)
```

The Display Button is just as easy. It displays the selected item from the ListBox in a Label:

```
strDisplay = lstToDo.SelectedItem
```

And, if you can't code the Exit Button by yourself, you're a couple of hundred pages too far into this book!

That's the nuts and bolts of the program. However, using it could be tricky and there are ways to crash the program. A good developer always tries to protect the user from himself. It's time to go back and add some safeguards.

The Add Button should check to see if the user has entered something into the TextBox before adding it to the list. If the TextBox is empty, then there's no reason to add an item to the ListBox.

```
strFavorite = txtFavorite.Text
If strFavorite = "" Then
    MsgBox("Please enter your item in the TextBox.",
    MsgBoxStyle.OkOnly, "Oops!")
Else
    lstToDo.Items.Add(strFavorite)
    btnRemove.Enabled = True
End If
```

This code checks to see if anything was entered. If not, a MessageBox displays the oversight. Otherwise, it enters the errand into the ListBox. In addition, the Remove Button is enabled. The Remove Button is designed to remove items from the list once they're completed. Of course, the program starts with an empty ListBox so there's no reason to have the Remove Button enabled at the start. Once the list has an item, then the Remove Button becomes useful. Set the Enabled property of the Remove Button to False.

Next is the Remove Button. It's already set up to remove the selected item from the list. However, it's possible that there aren't any items left on the list and it's possible that an item wasn't selected before the Button was clicked. A developer codes for such contingencies:

```
shoItemNum = lstToDo.SelectedIndex
If shoItemNum = -1 Then
    MsgBox("Please select an item from the list.",
        MsgBoxStyle.OkOnly, "Oops!")
Else
    If shoItemNum > 0 Then
        lstToDo.Items.Remove(lstToDo.SelectedItem)
    End If

End If

If lstToDo.Items.Count <= 0 Then
    btnRemove.Enabled = False
End If
```

The first line finds the index number of the selected item. Remember, when an item isn't selected, the SelectedIndex is -1. The first If statement handles that part. When there isn't a selected item, it displays a MessageBox.

The first item in a ListBox has an index of 0. In this one, the first item was left blank. That's handy sometimes, especially when a choice isn't required. The Reservations ListBox is a good example of this. The second If checks this and only removes an item from the list when the index is greater than zero.

The last If checks to see how many items are on the list. When the list is empty, it disables the Remove Button. Again, a developer protects the user whenever possible.

The last block of code handles the Display Button. Its purpose is to display an item the user has selected on the list. A couple of potential problems exist for this Button. The user might not select an item or might select the blank item at the top of the list. You must code around these pitfalls:

```
shoItemNum = lstToDo.SelectedIndex
If shoItemNum = -1 Then
    MsgBox("Please select an item from the list.",
      MsgBoxStyle.OkOnly, "Oops!")
Else
    If shoItemNum = 0 Then
        MsgBox("Please select another item on the list.",
          MsgBoxStyle.OkOnly, "Oops!")
    Else
        strDisplay = lstToDo.SelectedItem
        lblDisplay.Text = strDisplay
    End If
End If
```

The first If checks to see if an item was selected. If one wasn't selected, it displays a MessageBox. If not, it checks to see if the first item, the blank one, was selected. Its index is 0 and, when selected, a MessageBox is displayed.

When both If statements are False, it means a valid item was selected and it gets displayed in the Label.

Although it's not perfect, the program now performs its purpose and offers the user some protection:

```
Private Sub btnRemove_Click(ByVal sender As
    System.Object, ByVal e As System.EventArgs)
    Handles btnRemove.Click
Dim shoItemNum As Short
shoItemNum = lstToDo.SelectedIndex

If shoItemNum = -1 Then
    MsgBox("Please select an item from the list.",
      MsgBoxStyle.OkOnly, "Oops!")
Else
    If shoItemNum >= 0 Then
        lstToDo.Items.Remove(lstToDo.SelectedItem)
    End If
End If

If lstToDo.Items.Count <= 0 Then
    btnRemove.Enabled = False
End If

End Sub
```

```
Private Sub btnDisplay_Click(ByVal sender As
   System.Object, ByVal e As System.EventArgs)
   Handles btnDisplay.Click
Dim strDisplay As String
Dim shoItemNum As Short
shoItemNum = lstToDo.SelectedIndex

If shoItemNum = -1 Then
    MsgBox("Please select an item from the list.",
      MsgBoxStyle.OkOnly, "Oops!")
Else
    strDisplay = lstToDo.SelectedItem
    lblDisplay.Text = strDisplay
End If

End Sub


Private Sub btnExit_Click(ByVal sender As System.Object,
   ByVal e As System.EventArgs) Handles btnExit.Click
      End

End Sub
```

VB Quiz 03

What advantages does a ListBox offer?

Why does a developer plan for the unexpected when coding?

What other protection and features should the ToDoList program offer?

ComboBoxes

A *ComboBox* is similar to a ListBox, but with some variations and some cool features. Most of the properties, methods, and events for a ListBox also apply to a ComboBox. A Collection stores items in the list that can be changed at runtime using the Add and Remove methods.

ComboBoxes come in three styles: *Simple, DropDown,* and *DropDownList.* The style is set at design time with the DropDownStyle property. The default style is DropDown. It takes up just one line of space on a form and the options appear in a DropDown box when the down arrow is clicked. Items can be added to the list by placing them in the collection during design time or through code at runtime. The Simple style displays the list of items below the text line. It takes up more space, but it combines a TextBox and a ListBox into one control. The developer controls the size of a Simple ComboBox. The DropDownList looks like the DropDown, but a user cannot add items to the list. Use a DropDownList to save space and control the items the user can select from a list. Use a DropDown

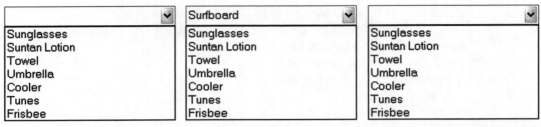

| Simple ComboBox | DropDown ComboBox | DropDownList ComboBox |

Figure 8.9   ComboBox Options

when you have a list, but want to allow the user to add their own items to the list. Use Simple when space is limited (see Figure 8.9).

Beach Supplies Program

Lou Ow is planning a day at the beach and wants a program to build a list of supplies for the trip. He always takes these supplies: sunglasses, suntan lotion, towel, umbrella, cooler, tunes, and a frisbee, so you include these in the Collection for a ComboBox. He wants to be able to include other items and modify the list to suit his needs. You include Add, Remove, Sort, and Exit Buttons. The Sort Button puts the list in alphabetical order to make the items easier to find. You set it up so that he can't add duplicate items to the list. In addition, you add some code to control when the Add Button is enabled (see Figure 8.10). Here goes!

```
Dim strFavorite As String
Dim i As Integer
Dim shoCount As Short
Dim blnFound As Boolean

strFavorite = cboBeachSupplies.Text
shoCount = cboBeachSupplies.Items.Count
shoCount = shoCount - 1

For i = 0 To shoCount
    If strFavorite.ToUpper =
        cboBeachSupplies.Items.Item(i).ToUpper Then
        blnFound = True
    End If
Next i

If Not blnFound Then
    cboBeachSupplies.Items.Add(strFavorite)
End If
```

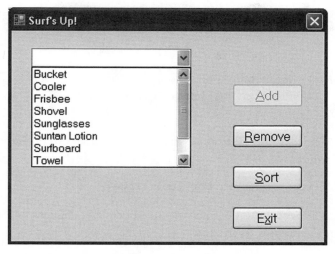

Figure 8.10   A Day at the Beach Program

The Add Button gets the contents of the Text property of the ComboBox. It contains the item to be added to the ComboBox. The next two lines get the number of items currently in the list and subtract 1 from it. Remember, the first item in the list has an index of 0, so the last item has an index that is one less than the Count.

VB Tip

The two lines can be combined into one like this:

```
shoCount = cboBeachSupplies.Items.Count - 1
```

The items in the list are numbered from 0 to shoCount, so use a loop to run through the list. Each time through the list, check to see if the new item matches any of the existing items. Use the ToUpper method to make comparisons easier. If there's a match, set the blnFound variable to True. It's a Boolean variable that always stores either True or False. It is only set to True if it finds a match. Then below the loop add an If statement. The item gets added to the list only when blnFound is False.

VB Tip

Boolean variables must be True or False. And, remember, Not switches the result. In this example Not blnFound is True when there's no match.

```
Dim shoItemNum As Short

shoItemNum = cboBeachSupplies.SelectedIndex

If shoItemNum = -1 Then
    MsgBox("Please select an item from the list.",
    MsgBoxStyle.OkOnly, "Oops!")
Else
```

```
cboBeachSupplies.Items.Remove(cboBeachSupplies.
  Items.Item(shoItemNum))
End If

If cboBeachSupplies.Items.Count = -1 Then
    btnRemove.Enabled = False
End If
```

The Remove Button is virtually the same except for the name of the ComboBox:

```
cboBeachSupplies.Sorted = True
```

The Sort Button has just one line of code. It changes the Sorted property of the ComboBox to True.

```
Private Sub cboBeachSupplies_TextChanged(ByVal sender As
    Object, ByVal e As System.EventArgs) Handles
    cboBeachSupplies.TextChanged
    If cboBeachSupplies.Text <> "" Then
        btnAdd.Enabled = True
    Else
        btnAdd.Enabled = False
    End If
End Sub
```

The Add Button starts out with its Enabled property set to False. There's nothing in the Text property of the ComboBox, so there's nothing to add and no reason to have the Button enabled. As soon as something is entered into the ComboBox, the Enabled property is set to True. You can accomplish this with the TextChanged property of the ComboBox. The code checks to see if there's anything in the Text property. The comparison is

```
cboBeachSupplies.Text <> ""
```

and when it's True – that's is, when there's something in it – the Add Button is enabled. If it's empty – that is, when it's equal to " " – it sets the Enabled property of the Add Button to False.

VB Tip   *Remember, you can use the DropDown lists in the code window to select a control and the events for that control.*

VB Tip   *Open and run the ADayAtTheBeach program.*

VB Quiz 04   *Why have a Collection with a list of items already in it?*
                         When would you use a DropDownList ComboBox?
                         How does a TextChanged event work?

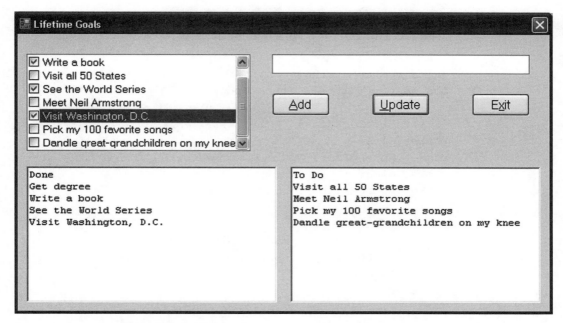

Figure 8.11   Lifetime Goals Program

CheckedListBoxes

A *CheckedListBox* is a combination of a ListBox and CheckBoxes. The prefix for it is clb. Each item in a CheckedListBox has a CheckBox. Items are added, removed, and selected, just like other ListBoxes, but the advantage is that each item has a CheckBox associated with it that can be selected with a double click. The checked and unchecked items can be evaluated and used in your code.

Everyone needs goals. They focus our attention and it's great to check one off once it's met. Sage Advice is looking for a program that will list her current goals and the ones she has yet to accomplish. A program with a CheckedListBox is useful for listing those goals and checking off the ones that are met (see Figure 8.11).

The Add Button adds items to the list. It's similar to the previous ones you've seen:

```
Dim strAdd As String
strAdd = txtAdd.Text
clbGoals.Items.Add(strAdd)
```

It takes the string from the TextBox, stores it in a variable, and then adds it to the CheckedListBox.

The Update Button goes through the list one by one. When an item is Checked, it adds it to the Done list. When it's not checked, it adds it to the Yet list.

```
'Find number of items and highest item number
shoCount = clbGoals.Items.Count - 1

'Clear RichTextBoxes
rtbMet.Clear()
rtbMet.AppendText("Done" & vbNewLine)
rtbYet.Clear()
rtbYet.AppendText("To Do" & vbNewLine)

For i = 0 To shoCount
    If clbGoals.GetItemChecked(i) Then
        rtbMet.AppendText(clbGoals.Items.Item(i) &
        vbNewLine)
    Else
        rtbYet.AppendText(clbGoals.Items.Item(i) &
        vbNewLine)
    End If
Next i
```

The number of items in the list is contained in Count, just as it is in other ListBoxes. Subtract one from it to find the index for the last item in the list.

The Met and Yet RichTextBoxes display the goals that have been met and the ones that aren't done yet. Clear these and add a short heading. Each item will either be checked or not, so, regardless of their status, they'll go on one of the lists.

The loop goes through each item in the list. For each item in the CheckedList-Box, it checks the *GetItemChecked* property. GetItemChecked is True when the item is checked and False when it's not. Depending on whether it's True or False, the If statement inside the loop will add the item to the appropriate list.

VB Tip   *Open and run the LifetimeGoals program to see how it works.*

VB Quiz 05   *What would it take to modify the LifetimeGoals program to place the "Met" and "Not Yet" lists into ListBoxes?*
What practical use is a ListBox if the items must be programmed by a developer or added manually by a user?

Tab Controls, ScrollBars, and TrackBars

VB Quip

What is this talk of "release"? We do not make software "releases." Our software "escapes," leaving a bloody trail of designers and quality assurance people in its wake! –attributed to a Klingon software engineer

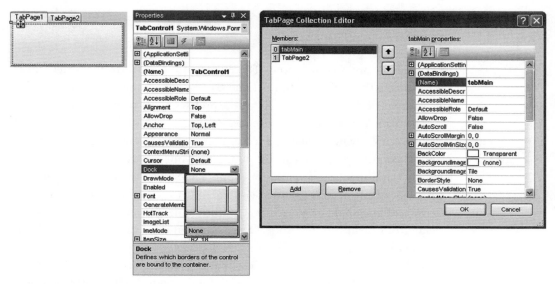

Figure 8.12   TabControl Screens

The *Tab* control is an easy way to increase the screen space for a program. A Tab control contains multiple pages and each page can contain multiple controls. A page can be brought to the front by clicking on its tab at the top of the control. Add pages to a Tab control by using the Collection Editor, just like adding items to a collection in a ListBox. Pages can be added or removed by clicking on the Add Tab or Remove Tab links in the Property window. Be careful when naming controls on Tab pages. The controls must all have unique names even though they are on separate pages of a Tab control. Use tab for the prefix for Tab controls and be sure to name each page in the Tab collection. Resize a Tab control by using the handles just like you'd resize other controls. The top left corner has an arrow that points in all four directions. Use that to move the Tab control and position it on the form. The Dock property controls the borders that are bound to the Tab control. When docked to the top of a form, it always stays docked to the top of the form. When docked to all four sides, it remains the same size as the form regardless of any changes to the size or shape of a form. Use a Tab control when screen space is at a premium or when there are several related items that can be separated on their own Tab page (see Figure 8.12).

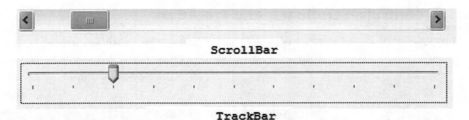

ScrollBar

TrackBar

Figure 8.13   ScrollBar and TrackBar Examples

ScrollBars are used for input. There are two types, *HorizontalScrollBars* and *VerticalScrollBars*. They both work the same way, but one is horizontal and the other is vertical. Use hsb and vsb for the prefixes when naming them.

The *Scroll* event triggers their code. When the user moves the ScrollBar, the code executes, which makes them handy and easy for a user. Set the Minimum and Maximum properties to the limits for your controls. These control the smallest and the largest values for input. The SmallChange and LargeChange properties control how far the ScrollBar moves when the user clicks on the arrows or the shaft, respectively. Use the Value property to get the current value from them for your code. Make sure that your variable can handle any number in the range of values for a ScrollBar.

TrackBars are very similar to ScrollBars. Their look is a little different, but they can be used in the same way. Use trb for the prefix for TrackBars. The Value property has the current value. Just like ScrollBars, the Scroll event is triggered when the value of the TrackBar changes. The Minimum and Maximum values control the limits for a TrackBar. The small lines at the bottom of a TrackBar are set with the TickFrequency property. The default for a TrackBar is horizontal, but it can be changed to vertical by changing the Orientation property (see Figure 8.13).

Conversions Program

It's time to put these three controls to work. Cora Laited needs a program to show the conversions between various measurements. You create a quick demo as a proof of concept. If she likes it, you're confident that you can add other measures quickly and easily (see Figure 8.14).

```
Private Sub hsbGallons_Scroll ...
    Dim sngCups As Single
    Dim sngPints As Single
    Dim sngQuarts As Single
    Dim sngGallons As Single

    'Input
    sngGallons = hsbGallons.Value
```

```
'Processing
sngCups = sngGallons * 16
sngPints = sngGallons * 8
sngQuarts = sngGallons * 4

'Output
lblCups.Text = sngCups.ToString("n0")
lblPints.Text = sngPints.ToString("n0")
lblQuarts.Text = sngQuarts.ToString("n0")
lblGallons.Text = sngGallons.ToString("n0")
End Sub
```

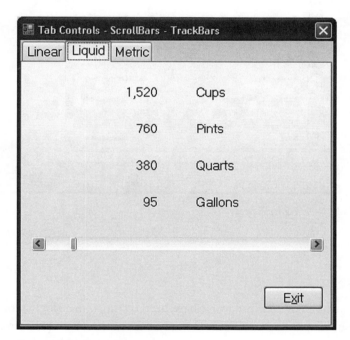

Figure 8.14   Conversions Program

The program displays linear, liquid, and metric measures. Each Tab has a different conversion and it's easy to switch between them by clicking on the appropriate Tab. By moving the ScrollBar or TrackBar, a Scroll event is triggered. The code calculates and changes the values in the Labels. The preceding code is for liquid conversion. Cora seems pleased and wants you to add other measures and conversions. Geeks rule!

VB Tip   *Open and run the ConversionsProgram to see how it works.*

VB Quiz 06   *Why is a Tab control useful for organizing content?*
        Why are ScrollBars and TrackBars considered input controls?
        Why use the Scroll event instead of a Button and a Click event?

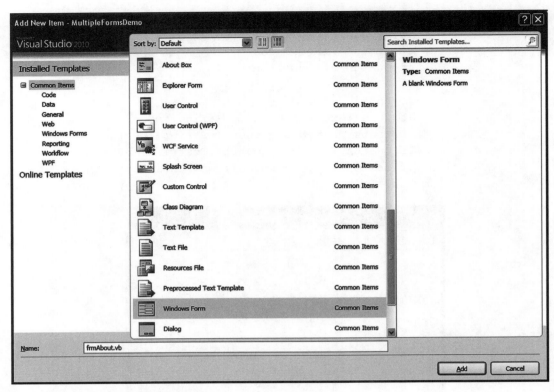

Figure 8.15   Add New Form Screen

Multiple Forms

So far all of your programs have been confined to a single *form*. However, it's a simple process to create and use multiple forms for a program. An easy way to demonstrate multiple forms is with About and Help screens. So much more is possible, but this is a good place to start.

Use the Add Windows Form option under the Project menu to create a new window. It brings up the Add New Item dialog box. Be sure to select Windows Form and name your form before adding it. As always, the prefix for a form is frm. The form gets created and added to the Solution Explorer. At this point, you're ready to use the form.

A new solution automatically comes with a form. That's the *startup form* for your program and is the form that opens first when the program runs. Be sure to leave it as the main form for your program (see Figure 8.15).

VB Tip   *Later, you'll learn how to use predefined forms to create and customize Startup and About forms for a program.*

Your main form must have some code to open the new form. Depending on your needs, you might also want to hide the main form. Of course, your new form must have some code that takes you back to the main form and removes the new form.

The About menu on the main form contains the following code:

```
'Display About form
Dim frmAbout As New frmAbout
Me.Hide()
frmAbout.Show()
```

The first line creates a new form called frmAbout that looks just like the frmAbout form file. The next line hides the main form. *Me* refers to the current form, in this case frmMain. The *Hide* method hides the form but leaves it in memory. The last line uses the *Show* method to display frmAbout. These three lines create the About form, hide the main form, and display the About form.

The Back Button on the About form sends the user back to the main form. The code in the Back Button looks like this:

```
Me.Close()
Me.Dispose()
```

Me refers to the current form, in this case the About form because the code is on that form. The first line closes the form, which removes it from view but leaves it memory. The next line has the *Dispose* method, which actually removes the form from memory. You still must show the main form, however. That's done with this line:

```
frmMain.Show()
```

The *Show* method takes a form that's already in memory and displays it. This line displays the main form for the program. This line belongs in the *FormClosing* event for the About form. Use the Class Name DropDown ListBox at the top of the code window to select the Events for the form. Then use the Method Name DropDown ListBox right next to it to select the FormClosing event. Add the code and it runs when the form closes.

The Show method displays a form, while the Hide method hides it but leaves it in memory, making it quick and easy to display it again when it's needed. If a form is no longer needed, then use the Dispose method to remove it from memory. But always keep at least one form visible on the screen at all times. Without it, the user won't be able to see your program (see Figure 8.16).

VB Tip   *Open and run the MultipleFormsDemo program to see how it works.*

VB Quiz 07   *Why have more than one form for a program?*

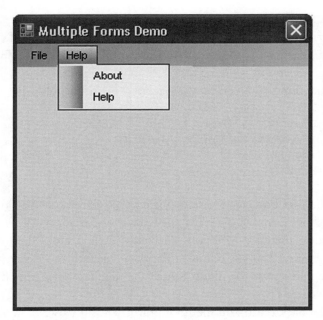

Figure 8.16   Multiple Forms Program

Controlling Strings

So far, output has been pretty simple. Most has been displayed either in a Label or in a RichTextBox. Most of the formatting has been limited to formatting numeric output and inserting line breaks. And you may have noticed that the output wasn't always very neat. Fortunately, VB has a full set of commands to format and manipulate strings of characters. You've already seen a few of them. You have control over the number of decimal places and can convert text to upper case and lower case at will. Now it's time to do more with strings and clean up your output.

PadRight

The *PadRight* method adds spaces to the right of a string. Simply specify the width of your string. When a string is shorter than the length you need, PadRight adds spaces to the end. If your string is longer than that width, it still displays the whole string. Examples for this are much better than explanations:

```
strName = "Washington"
lblName.Text = strName.PadRight(12)
```

The output is "Washington ". Note there are two spaces at the end of the string.

```
strName = "Washington"
lblName.Text = strName.PadRight(8)
```

The output is "Washington". When the string is longer than the padding, it ignores it and displays the entire output.

Use this output to create columns of output with the characters left-aligned and extra spaces on the right.

PadLeft

PadLeft adds spaces to the left of the string. This is handy for numeric output because the padding keeps the number properly aligned on the right. For example:

```
decSalary = 3418.59
lblSalary.Text = decSalary.ToString("c").PadLeft(12)
```

The output is " $3,418.59". Note there are three spaces at the beginning of the string. Another example is

```
decSalary = 3418.59
lblSalary.Text = decSalary.ToString("c").PadLeft(8)
```

where the output is "$3,418.59". Even though the formatting wasn't wide enough for the entire string, it still displayed the entire string. Otherwise, you might get a very small paycheck!

A space is the default character for padding; however, other characters can be used. For example:

```
decSalary = 3418.59
lblSalary.Text = decSalary.ToString("c").PadLeft(12, "*")
```

The output is "***$3,418.59". Note there are three asterisks at the beginning of the string. They're inserted to make the output 12 characters wide. Some checks are written this way to prevent the unscrupulous from adding a little extra to the amount.

Use the PadLeft method to right-align the output in a column. This is particularly handy for aligning numeric output with a decimal point.

Methods can also be combined to make the output more flexible. For example:

```
strName = "Washington"
lblName.Text = strName.ToUpper.PadRight(12)
```

The output is "WASHINGTON " in all caps and with two spaces at the end.

VB Tip   *The output in a RichTextBox will align vertically when you use Courier New font.*

Length

The *Length* method is used to determine the length of a string of characters. For example:

```
strNumChars = "Washington"
bytLength = strNumChars.Length
lblLength.Text = bytLength.ToString
```

The output is 10 because there are ten characters in the string. Each character has an index starting with 0. So "W" has an index of 0, "a" has an index of 1, and the last "n" has an index of 9. The length of the string will always be one more than the index of the last character.

Substring

The *Substring* method is used to extract characters from a string. It has two arguments: the first character to retrieve and the number of characters to retrieve. The first character in a string has an index of 0, just like the items in a ListBox. With that in mind, determine the first character needed and the number of characters needed when selecting a Substring. Here's an example:

```
strName = "Washington"
strResult = strName.Substring(0, 4)
```

The result is "Wash". The Substring method starts with the 0th character, in this case, "W", and gets 4 characters.

```
strName = "Washington"
strResult = strName.Substring(2, 4)
```

The result for this is "shin". The Substring method starts with "s" and gets 4 characters. It's a little confusing to start counting at 0, but it's a well-thought-out strategy and it does have its advantages.

StartsWith and EndsWith

The *StartsWith* method determines if a string starts with a particular pattern. It returns True when there's a match and False when there isn't a match. Here's an example:

```
strName = "Mr. Smith"
If strName.StartsWith("Mr. ") Then
    strGender = "Male"
End If
```

The comparison finds a match and assigns "Male" to strGender.

EndsWith looks at the end of a string. For example:

```
strName = "Martin Luther King, Jr."
If strName.EndsWith("Jr.") Then
    strRelation = "son"
End If
```

The EndsWith method compares the end of the string and returns either True or False. In this example, strName ends with "Jr.", so there's a match.

IndexOf

IndexOf looks at a string and returns a numeric value. When there's a match, it returns the index of the first character of the match. If there's no match, it returns -1; so you'll know your search turned up empty. With a larger number, you'll know where in the string to find your match. For example:

```
strThing = "shoestrings"
bytIndex = strThing.IndexOf("string")
lblIndex.Text = bytIndex.ToString
```

where IndexOf finds a match starting with character 4. Remember, it started counting at 0. The match must be exact and it's case sensitive. Think of it as the Find option in word processing.

```
strThing = "shoestrings"
intIndex = strThing.IndexOf("shine")
lblIndex.Text = intIndex.ToString
```

The preceding example doesn't find a match, so it returns -1.

Replace, Remove, and Insert

The *Replace* method works much like the Replace option in word processing. It takes one string and replaces it with another. For example:

```
strDate = "10.14.2009"
strUpdated = strDate.Replace(".", "-")
lblUpdated.Text = strUpdated
```

where the Replace method replaces periods with hyphens. Techniques like this are often used to make data consistent. Of course, if there's no match, there's no change.

The *Remove* method removes characters from a string. It has two arguments, the index to start and the number of characters to remove. For example:

```
strSpelling = "missspelled"
strCorrected = strSpelling.Remove(2, 1)
lblCorrected.Text = strCorrected
```

In this example, it starts with the first "s" because it has an index of 2 and it removes 1 character. The result is "misspelled", which is the correct spelling.

The *Insert* method adds characters to a string. There are two arguments, the starting index and the character(s) to be added to the string. For example:

```
strPresident = "Harry Truman"
strInserted = strPresident.Insert(6, "S. ")
lblInserted.Text = strInserted
```

It starts where the "T" is because that character has an index of 6 and inserts "S. ". The result is "Harry S. Truman".

Trim, TrimStart, and TrimEnd

The *Trim* method removes spaces from the beginning and end of a string. *TrimStart* removes leading spaces and *TrimEnd* removes trailing spaces. The default character is a space, but other characters, when specified, can be trimmed as well:

```
strExtra = "   SPACE   "
strTrimmed = strExtra.Trim
lblOutput.Text = strTrimmed
strExtra = "   SPACE   "
strTrimmed = strExtra.TrimStart
lblTrimmed.Text = strTrimmed
strExtra = "   SPACE   "
strTrimmed = strExtra.TrimEnd
lblTrimmed.Text = strTrimmed
```

The first example trims extra spaces from the beginning and end. The result is "SPACE". The second example removes the spaces at the start of the string. The result is "SPACE ". The leading spaces are gone, but the trailing spaces remain. The last example removes the trailing spaces, resulting in " SPACE".

Trim is particularly useful when working with user input. A user may accidentally add extra spaces at the beginning or end of their input. The Trim methods remove them.

Like

The *Like* method is used for matching patterns of characters. *Wildcard characters* are used to match one or more characters in the string. Wildcard characters include those listed in the following table.

?	any character	"b?ll" matches "ball", "bell", "bill", "boll", and "bull"
*	zero or more characters	"a*" matches "a", "ask", "at", and anything starting with "a"
#	any digit	"A#" matches "A1", "A4", but not "AOK"
[]	any list of characters	"b[aeiou]ll" matches "ball", "bell", "bill", "boll", and "bull"

Combinations of wildcard characters are used to find matches. Consider part numbers, which often have a series of letters and numbers. These usually have meaning for the manufacturer and can be used to find out when and where a part was produced. It comes in handy when there's a recall.

```
strPartNum = "CQD04141912"
If strPartNum.Substring(0, 1) Like "[A-Z]" Then
    lstRecalledNumbers.Items.Add(strPartNum)
End If
```

The preceeding If statement looks at the first character and returns True if it's a letter. The string is then added to the list of recalled part numbers.

Strings methods become very useful when combined. Use IndexOf to search through a string to find a match. You can then remove or replace characters as needed. Use Like to determine if a string matches a pattern. From there, you can use other methods to manipulate and massage the string to your liking. You've already seen how ToUpper and ToLower make string comparison easier.

MaskedTextBox

A *MaskedTextBox* is similar to a regular TextBox, however, it already has validation built into it. There are several built-in input masks, and a developer can create custom ones as well. A *mask* is simply the required format for any input. A mask forces a user to enter data in a particular way. It's a handy way to make the user enter a date in way that can be processed or to make them enter all the digits for a Social Security Number. Developers can create custom formats to handle things like a Student ID number or a part number (see Figure 8.17).

VB Tip   *Open and run the ControllingStringsDemo program to see how it works.*

VB Quiz 8   *How do PadRight and PadLeft help the user?*

Of what practical use are the Substring methods?

How are the Like method and a MaskedTextBox similar?

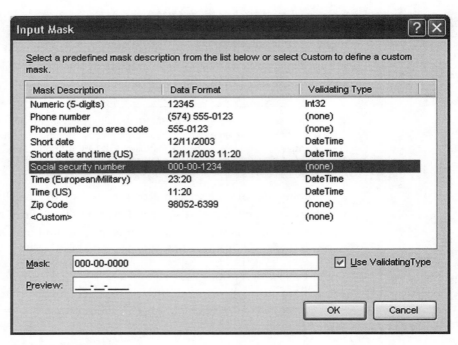

Figure 8.17   Input Mask Screen

Pizza Program Finished

VB Quip   *What do you call the pizza boxes that Owt Pizza uses for delivery? Owt Boxes!*

VB Tip   *Use the underscore (_) at the end of a line of code to extend the line of code to the next*
                       physical line. It separates a logical line of code into multiple physical lines. It makes
                       them easier to read and work with than one long line of code.

The finishing touches for Owt Pizza should make the program more user-friendly. Although it's by no means ready for release, it does provide a taste of what's needed to create a functional program that will meet the needs of a user.

It's time to add a ListBox to select the location, dine-in, carryout, or delivery. Been there, done that – so that should be easy enough to do. However, there will be some code for it as well. In addition, the delivery charge of $1.50 per pizza must be added. This code belongs in the Order Button.

There's an 8% sales tax added to the total. These charges must be displayed and all the output must be formatted so it looks nice. This code belongs in the Total button.

The Clear Button needs completion as well.

```
If lstLocation.SelectedIndex >= 0 Then
    strLocation = lstLocation.Items(lstLocation.
    SelectedIndex)
End If
```

Place the preceeding code in the Order Button to determine whether the order is for dine-in, carryout, or delivery. Display the location in the output also. That line could look like this (note that the reservation is padded to add some spacing):

```
rtbOut.AppendText("Reservations: " & _
strReservations.PadRight(10) & strLocation & vbNewLine)
```

The following code goes below it:

```
If strLocation = "Delivery" Then
    mdecTotal += decDelivery
    rtbOut.AppendText("Delivery:   " & _
    decDelivery.ToString("c") & vbNewLine)
End If
```

It adds the delivery charge to the total and displays the change in the output.

```
Const sngSalesTaxRate As Single = 0.08
Dim decSalesTax As Decimal
Dim decGrandTotal As Decimal
```

The code for the Total Button needs some changes as well. Here is the finished code:

```
decSalesTax = mdecTotal * sngSalesTaxRate
decGrandTotal = mdecTotal + decSalesTax
rtbOut.AppendText("Subtotal: " & _
  mdecTotal.ToString("c").PadLeft(32) & vbNewLine)
rtbOut.AppendText("Sales Tax: " & _
  decSalesTax.ToString("c").PadLeft(31) & vbNewLine)
rtbOut.AppendText("Your Total: " & _
  decGrandTotal.ToString("c").PadLeft(30) & vbNewLine)
```

The sales tax rate, sales tax amount, and grand total were declared. The sales tax and grand total were calculated. The last three lines are output. Formatting was added to get the totals to align. Take note of the PadLeft formatting after each variable. PadLeft adds spaces to the string until the output is the width specified in the parentheses. Often it requires trial and error to get the output to look right.

The Clear Button does more than just remove the text from the RichTextBox. It also resets the variables and controls. The general premise of the Clear Button is to return the settings to their original condition so the user can start fresh.

```
mdecTotal = 0
PrintHeading()
lstReservations.SelectedIndex = -1
radMedium.Checked = True
radThick.Checked = True
chkPepperoni.Checked = False
```

```
chkSausage.Checked = False
chkCanadianBacon.Checked = False
chkBeef.Checked = False
chkGreenPeppers.Checked = False
chkOnions.Checked = False
chkOlives.Checked = False
chkMushrooms.Checked = False
chkAnchovies.Checked = False
```

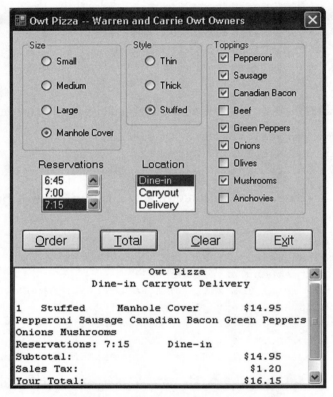

Figure 8.18   Owt Pizza Program

The total resets to 0, making it ready for a new order. The PrintHeading procedure gets called, which clears the RichTextBox and places a header at the top. Any selection in the reservations ListBox is removed. The RadioButtons are set back to their defaults. Any checks in the CheckBoxes are removed. You have no way of knowing which ones, if any, were checked on the last order, so you must make sure all of them are unchecked. That prevents confusion and mistakes and makes it easier for the user (see Figure 8.18).

VB Tip   *Open and run the OwtPizzaFinished program to see how it works.*

VB Quiz 09   *What else could be included in the Owt Pizza order form?*
What design changes might be needed to make the form easier to use?

Tying It All Together

There are several new controls available, ways to manipulate strings and new commands for formatting output, and it's time to put some of them to work. The Mortgage program shows payment comparisons for a home mortgage. The ID generator generates IDs, logins, and passwords for a new employee. The ice cream stand offers several choices for a sweet tooth.

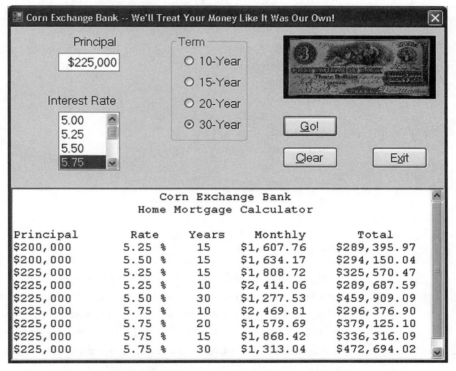

| Figure 8.19 | Mortgage Payments Program |

Mortgage Payments Program

The Corn Exchange Bank (a real bank that helped finance the first transcontinental railroad) offers home mortgages. Potential homebuyers can run a small program to calculate their monthly mortgage payment. The program inputs are finance amount, the length of the mortgage, and the interest rate. The output is the monthly payment and the total of the loan (see Figure 8.19).

Enter the principal using a MaskedTextBox. The format for it is $###,###. Trim the dollar sign and the comma and convert the input to a number. Use the ListBox to determine the interest rate. The rate is displayed in a format familiar to a user, but it must be converted to a decimal, which means dividing it by 100.

Use RadioButtons for the term of the loan. That involves writing some code to determine which RadioButton was checked.

```
'Input
'Remove $ and comma from input and put in numeric
  variable
strPrincipal = mtbPrincipal.Text
strPrincipal = strPrincipal.TrimStart("$")
strPrincipal = strPrincipal.Remove(3, 1)
decPrincipal = Convert.ToDecimal(strPrincipal)

sngRate = lstRate.Items.Item(lstRate.SelectedIndex)
sngRate = sngRate / 100

'Determine which RadioButton is checked
If rad10Year.Checked Then
    bytYears = 10
ElseIf rad15Year.Checked Then
    bytYears = 15
ElseIf rad20Year.Checked Then
    bytYears = 20
Else
    bytYears = 30
End If
```

The Payment (Pmt) function determines the monthly payment, and it requires three parameters – the interest rate, the term of the loan, and the principal. Pmt calculates an annual payment. To determine a monthly payment, the interest rate must be divided by 12 and the number of payments must be multiplied by 12. Pmt returns a negative number, so the Abs method is used to find the absolute value, a positive number.

The total amount of the loan is the monthly payment multiplied by the number of payments. The number of payments is the length of the loan times 12.

```
'Processing
'Calculate monthly payment and total amount
decMonthly = Math.Abs(Pmt(sngRate / 12, bytYears * 12,
  decPrincipal))
decTotal = decMonthly * bytYears * 12
```

The output is a single line displayed in a RichTextBox. It displays the Principal, Rate, Monthly Payment, and Total amount of the loan. Note the use of formatting and padding, which align the output in columns, making it neat and orderly.

```
'Output
rtbOut.AppendText(decPrincipal.ToString("c0").PadRight(14) & _
sngRate.ToString("p2").PadLeft(7) & _
bytYears.ToString.PadLeft(6) & _
decMonthly.ToString("c").PadLeft(13) & _
decTotal.ToString("c").PadLeft(15) & vbNewLine)
```

A procedure named Clear clears the RichTextBox and displays the header:

```
Private Sub Clear()
    rtbOut.Clear()
    rtbOut.AppendText(" Corn Exchange Bank"
      & vbNewLine)
    rtbOut.AppendText(" Home Mortgage Calculator"
      & vbNewLine & vbNewLine)
    rtbOut.AppendText("Principal Rate Years Monthly Total" & _
      vbNewLine)
End Sub
```

The procedure is called from two places, the Clear Button and in Form_Load. That way, the header information always appears in the RichTextBox. Form_Load has two other lines of code, which automatically check the 15-year mortgage option and the 5.75% interest rate.

```
Call Clear()
rad15Year.Checked = True
lstRate.SelectedIndex = 3
```

Still, the program isn't crash-proof. Without a number for the principal, it won't work. As a developer, how could you fix this?

VB Tip   *Open and run the MortgagePayments program to see how it works.*

ID Generator

Van Dullism runs Shue Strings, Inc., a security firm that outsources network security software. He offers a program that generates user IDs, network logins, and passwords (see Figure 8.20).

The program generates an employee ID, the network login, and an initial password for the network. These are generated from their first, middle, and last names, the department, the current date, random characters, and random numbers.

The user enters his or her name and selects the department from the ComboBox. The current date comes from the computer during the Load event. From there, each string is generated and displayed.

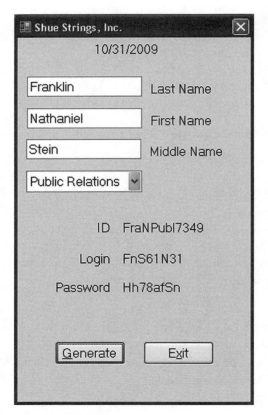

Figure 8.20   ID Generator Program

The ID has the format LllFDeptnnnn, where L is the first letter of their last name in upper case, ll is the next two letters of their last name in lower case, and F is the first letter of their first name in upper case. Dept is the first four letters of the department and nnnn is a four-digit random number.

The login format is LfMnnCdd, where L is the first letter of their last name in upper case, f is the first letter of their first name in lower case, M is the first letter of their middle name in upper case, nn is a two-digit random number, C is a random upper case letter, and dd is the date. The date is padded to two characters where needed.

The password is cCnnclMf, where c is a random lower case letter, C is a random upper case letter, nn is a two-digit number, c is a random lower case letter, l is the first letter of the last name in lower case, M is the first letter of the middle name in upper case, and f is the first letter of the first name in lower case.

Here is the code:

```
'Find and Display today's date
mdatToday = Now
lblToday.Text = mdatToday.ToShortDateString
```

```
'Input
strLast = txtLast.Text
strFirst = txtFirst.Text
strMiddle = txtMiddle.Text
strDept = cboDept.SelectedItem
strDate = mdatToday.Day.ToString

If strDate.Length < 2 Then
    strDate = "0" & strDate
End If

intNum = Int(Rnd() * 8999 + 1000)
bytChar = Int(Rnd() * 26 + 65)

'Processing
'Get ID: LllFDeptnnnn
'Where L is last name, F is first name Dept is Dept.
'and nnnn is a random number
'Gather characters as needed in strTemp and append to strID
strID = strLast.Substring(0, 1).ToUpper
strTemp = strLast.Substring(1, 2).ToLower
strID = strID & strTemp
strTemp = strFirst.Substring(0, 1).ToUpper
strID = strID & strTemp
strTemp = strDept.Substring(0, 4)
strID = strID & strTemp
strTemp = intNum.ToString
strID = strID & strTemp

'Get Login: LfMnncdd
'Where L is last name, f is first name, M is middle name,
' nn is number, C is a character and dd is the date
strLogin = strLast.Substring(0, 1).ToUpper
strTemp = strFirst.Substring(0, 1).ToLower
strLogin = strLogin & strTemp
strTemp = strMiddle.Substring(0, 1).ToUpper
strLogin = strLogin & strTemp
intNum = Int(Rnd() * 89 + 10)
strTemp = intNum.ToString
strLogin = strLogin & strTemp
bytChar = Int(Rnd() * 26 + 65)
strTemp = Chr(bytChar)
strLogin = strLogin & strTemp
strLogin = strLogin & strDate
```

```
'Get Password: cCnnclMf
'Where c is a character, nn is a number, l is last name,
'M is middle name and f is first name
bytChar = Int(Rnd() * 26 + 65)
strPassword = Chr(bytChar)
bytChar = Int(Rnd() * 26 + 97)
strTemp = Chr(bytChar)
strPassword = strPassword & strTemp
intNum = Int(Rnd() * 89 + 10)
strTemp = intNum.ToString
strPassword = strPassword & strTemp
bytChar = Int(Rnd() * 26 + 97)
strTemp = Chr(bytChar)
strPassword = strPassword & strTemp
strTemp = strLast.Substring(0, 1).ToLower
strPassword = strPassword & strTemp
strTemp = strMiddle.Substring(0, 1).ToUpper
strPassword = strPassword & strTemp
strTemp = strFirst.Substring(0, 1).ToLower
strPassword = strPassword & strTemp

'Output
lblID.Text = strID
lblLogin.Text = strLogin
lblPassword.Text = strPassword
```

Break the code into smaller segments. The first segment is from the Load event and finds the current date.

The next segment gets the user's input. The If statement checks the length of the date to see if it's less than two characters long. Days from the first through the ninth have only one character. A zero is added to the left of these to make the string two characters long. intNum is a random, four-digit number. The function generates a number from 1000 to 9999, the range of four-digit numbers. The last line for this input section uses another random number to get an ASCII character. The range of the random number is from 65 to 91 – the range in the ASCII code for upper case letters.

The variable strID stores the ID and it's built one segment at a time. strTemp is used to extract the next segment of the ID, which is then added to strID. For example:

```
strID = strLast.Substring(0, 1).ToUpper
strTemp = strLast.Substring(1, 2).ToLower
strID = strID & strTemp
```

where strID gets the upper case version of the first letter of the last name, and strTemp gets the second and third letters of the last name and stores them in lower case. The next line concatenates these two strings. The process continues for the rest of the characters in the last name. The variable strTemp is used to get the next segment of the ID, which is then added to strID.

The login is built in the same manner. The variable strTemp is used to get each new segment, which is then added to strLogin. A two-digit random number from 10 to 99 is generated and added to the string, as is a random upper case letter. As each segment is generated, it's added to strLogin.

The password is stored in strPassword. Its format is cCnnclMf, where c is a random lower case letter, C is a random upper case letter, nn is a random two-digit number, c is a random lower case letter, l is the first letter of the last name in lower case, M is the first letter of the middle name in upper case, and f is the first letter of the first name in lower case.

The last three lines display the output.

The program may seem complicated, but it's a series of simple steps that make the whole. Given a person's name and the current date, with a few random numbers and letters, you could create the same values. Just like a long trip is a series of simple segments, this program is a series of simple segments put together in the correct order to make an intricate result.

At this point, the program may still crash. If any part of the user's name doesn't have enough characters in it, the program won't know what to do and will give up. How could you prevent this?

VB Tip   *Open and run the IDGenerator program to see how it works.*

Ice Cream Stand

Rocky Road runs a little ice cream stand that offers a variety of frozen treats and a choice of flavors in various sizes. The customer may select a cone, dish, or cup and top it off with one or more toppings (see Figure 8.21).

```
Const mdecSmall As Decimal = 1.95
Const mdecMedium As Decimal = 2.95
Const mdecLarge As Decimal = 3.95
Const mdecBrainFreeze As Decimal = 5.95
Const mdecCone As Decimal = 0.25
Const mdecToppings As Decimal = 0.15
```

The price depends on the size, whether they select a cone, and the toppings that are chosen.

```
'Get flavor
strFlavor = cboFlavor.Items(cboFlavor.SelectedIndex)
'Get cone price and size
```

```
If radSmall.Checked Then
    decTotal = mdecSmall
    strSize = "Small"
ElseIf radMedium.Checked Then
    decTotal = mdecMedium
    strSize = "Medium"
ElseIf radLarge.Checked Then
    decTotal = mdecLarge
    strSize = "Large"
Else
    decTotal = mdecBrainFreeze
    strSize = "Brain Freeze"
End If

'Check to see if they want a cone
If radSugarcone.Checked Then
    decTotal += mdecCone
    strContainer = "Sugar Cone"
ElseIf radWaffleCone.Checked Then
    decTotal += mdecCone
    strContainer = "Waffle Cone"
ElseIf radDish.Checked Then
    strContainer = "Dish"
ElseIf radCup.Checked Then
    strContainer = "Cup"
End If

'Check for toppings
If chkSprinkles.Checked Then
    decTotal += mdecToppings
    strToppings += "Sprinkles "
End If

If chkChocolate.Checked Then
    decTotal += mdecToppings
    strToppings += "Chocolate "
End If

If chkNuts.Checked Then
    decTotal += mdecToppings
    strToppings += "Nuts "
End If

If chkWhippedCream.Checked Then
    decTotal += mdecToppings
    strToppings += "Whipped Cream"
End If
```

```
'Output
rtbOut.Clear()
rtbOut.AppendText("Size Flavor Price" & vbNewLine) _
rtbOut.AppendText(strSize.PadRight(14) & _
strFlavor.PadRight(12) & _
decTotal.ToString("c").PadLeft(10) & vbNewLine)
rtbOut.AppendText("Container: " & strContainer & _
vbNewLine)
rtbOut.AppendText(strToppings)
```

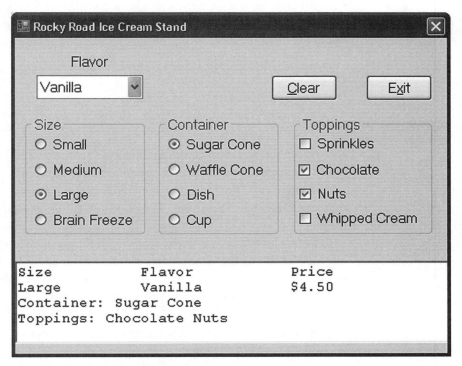

Figure 8.21   Rocky Road Ice Cream Program

The flavor is selected in the ComboBox and stored in strFlavor. The code checks for the size and assigns the price to decTotal and the size to strSize. It then checks for the type of container. When a sugar cone or waffle cone is selected, $0.25 is added to the price. Separate If statements are needed for the toppings. The customer could select any combination of toppings, so each must be checked separately. When checked, $0.15 is added to the price and the topping is added to strToppings.

The output is to a RichTextBox. It's cleared every time and then displays the size, flavor, price, container, and toppings. The formatting aligns the output and makes it neat and orderly.

Most of the work is done in the CalcTotal procedure. It's called from the CheckedChanged event for every RadioButton and CheckBox. The output updates every time the customer makes a change to their order.

Each control has a ToolTip that provides the price of the item.

```
cboFlavor.SelectedIndex = 1
```

The Load event automatically selects a flavor. That way there's always a value for this input.

The Clear Button clears the RichTextBox and resets the other controls. It automatically selects a medium-size vanilla sugar cone with no toppings. Because items are automatically selected each time, the program won't crash because of null input.

VB Tip   *Open and run the RockyRoadIceCreamStand program to see how it works.*

Potential Problems

Remember, the first character in a string has an index of 0 and the last character has an index that's one less than the number of characters in the string. ListBoxes are the same way. The first item has an index of 0 and the last item has an index that's one less than the Count. The reason for such logic is covered in later chapters.

Only one form can be active at a time even though there might be more than one form visible on the screen. Be careful not to hide all the forms at once. There must always be at least one form visible. If not, a program might still be running and have the forms using memory, but the user won't have anything to see or work with!

Even though controls might be on separate tabs, they are all on the same form and must have unique names.

Output is sometimes hard to align correctly. Sometimes trial and error is the easiest way to get the output to look good. Simply make one or two small changes at a time and test them until you're satisfied. A non-proportional font such as Courier New makes it easier to align columns of output.

On Your Own

Write a program with RadioButtons where the user, an incoming freshman, selects a dorm room. Choices include Patton Hall, Sherman Hall, Pershing Hall, and Scott Hall. They may also select a floor with quiet hours, quiet mornings, or regular hours, as well as male, female, or co-ed floors. Display the user's choices in Labels.

Anne Immal runs a veterinary clinic and provides basic services for dogs. She charges $23 for worming, $45 for rabies shots, $18 for teeth-cleaning, $95 to spay or neuter, and $32 for a shampoo and trim. Write a program with CheckBoxes where the user selects the services they want and the items and total are displayed.

Les Klew needs a program to determine supplies for his new dorm room. Write a program that includes a list of essential items for a dorm as well the ability to add other items to the list. Let Les select and display the items he needs for his room.

Write a program with Tabs to organize a class schedule. Use a separate Tab for each class and include such information as class day and time, instructor, text (including picture), building and room, and so on.

Write a program with multiple forms. Have the user select a form from a menu. Each form should have an example of one type of control from this chapter.

Write a program with a TrackBar to manage the exchange rate between U.S. and Canadian dollars. As the TrackBar moves, it should display both values. Use USD 1.00 = Can 0.75 for the exchange rate.

Write a program to get the first, middle, and last name from a user and display the user's initials.

Write a program to find the future value of investments. Use the FV function and format the output into columns.

Summary

This chapter introduced many new controls and introduced the code to control them. New ways to manipulate strings were explained and formatting techniques were provided to improve the look of your output. All of these were designed to make the computing experience better for the user.

Review

User satisfaction is important in software development.

RadioButtons are used to select one option from a group of many options.

Only one RadioButton in a group can be selected at a time and one RadioButton in a group is always selected.

Use a GroupBox to get RadioButtons to act together.

Use If statements to examine the Checked property to determine which RadioButton is selected.

The Format menu contains several options for arranging and aligning controls.

The CheckedChanged event is triggered when the user clicks on a RadioButton.

CheckBoxes allow a user to select any combination from a group.

None, some, or all the CheckBoxes in a group may be selected at a time.

The Checked property is True when a CheckBox is selected and False when it's not.

Use If statements to examine the Checked property to determine when a CheckBox is checked.

A CheckedChanged event is triggered every time the user clicks on a CheckBox.

ListBoxes contain a list of items and the user can selected any item in the list, one at a time.

Items can be added, inserted, or removed from a ListBox.

A Collection Editor is used to code items for a ListBox.

Each item in a ListBox has an index number.

The first item in a ListBox has an index of 0.

The SelectedItem property contains the item the user has selected in a ListBox.

The Count method contains the total number of items in a ListBox.

The SelectedIndex contains the number of the selected item in a ListBox.

When no item in a ListBox is selected, the SelectedIndex is -1.

The items in a ListBox can be ordered using the Sorted property.

ComboBoxes are similar to ListBoxes and come in different styles.

A Simple ComboBox combines a TextBox and a ListBox.

A DropDown ComboBox is the default style for a ComboBox. It combines a TextBox with a ListBox.

A DropDownList ComboBox has items that are set by the developer. A user cannot add items to it.

A CheckedListBox combines a ListBox with a CheckBox for every item.

Use the GetItemChecked property in a CheckedListBox to determine if the item is checked.

A Tab control contains multiple pages, each accessed by clicking on its tab.

The Dock property controls how a control is pinned to the form.

ScollBars come in two types: HorizontalScrollBars and VerticalScrollBars. They're used for numeric input within a specified range.

Moving a ScrollBar triggers a Scroll event.

TrackBars are similar to ScrollBars

The range for ScrollBars and TrackBars is set with the Minimum and Maximum properties.

Additional forms can be added to a program by using the Solution Explorer.

Multiple forms can be visible on the screen, but only one screen can be active at any time.

Me refers to the current form in a program.

Closing a form leaves it in memory. Dispose it to remove it from memory.

Show displays a form, and Hide hides it.

Always have at least one form displayed on the screen.

The first character in a string has an index of 0.

PadRight adds additional spaces to the right of a string.

PadLeft adds additional spaces to the left of a string.

The Length method determines the number of characters in a string. The Length of a string is always one more than its highest index.

The Substring method is used to extract characters from a string.

StartsWith and EndsWith determine if the beginning or ending of a string matches a particular pattern.

IndexOf returns the index of the first character of a string that matches a search.

Characters can be replaced, removed, or inserted in a string.

Trim, TrimStart, and TrimEnd are used to remove spaces in a string.

The Like method is used to match patterns of characters in a string.

A MaskedTextBox employs a mask to force the user to enter input matching a particular pattern.

String manipulation and formatting improve the appearance of output in a program.

A developer should strive to make a program that is intuitive and easy to use.

Terms

CheckBox	a control that allows a user to select an option; usually used with other CheckBoxes
CheckedListBox	a combination of ListBox and CheckBoxes; provides a list of items, each with a CheckBox next to it
Collection	the ListBox property used to store items
Collection Editor	the property used to place items in a ListBox at design time
ComboBox	a variation of a ListBox with additional features; comes in three styles: Simple, DropDown, and DropDownList
DropDown ComboBox	a ListBox that's only one line high; options appear on it when clicked
DropDownList ComboBox	a ListBox with preset items; the user cannot add items to this type of ComboBox
Format menu	a menu filled with options for aligning and positioning controls on a form

GroupBox	a control used to organize other controls, usually RadioButtons and CheckBoxes
HorizontalScrollBar	a control aligned horizontally, used to input numbers within a specified range
Items	a property in a ListBox that contains individual entries
items	individual entries in a ListBox; each item is given its own line in the collection
ListBox	a control containing several choices from which the user can select one
mask	the required character or characters for input
MaskedTextBox	an input control with text validation; the mask is the required format of the input
Me	references the current form
RadioButton	a control, when used with others, that allows a user to select one option from the group
ScrollBars	a control, either horizontal or vertical, used to input numbers within a specified range
Simple ComboBox	a ListBox that combines a TextBox with a ListBox; the first line is used to add items which are displayed below it
Startup Form	the first form that automatically loads and displays when a program runs
Tab control	a control with multiple tabbed pages, each capable of containing other controls
TrackBar	a control used to input numbers within a specified range by dragging the pointer on it
VerticalScrollBar	a control aligned vertically, used to input numbers within a specified range
wildcard characters	special characters used in a search to represent a range of characters; * represents zero or more characters and ? represents a single character

Keywords

Add	the method used to add an item at the end of a ListBox
Checked	a property of RadioButtons and CheckBoxes that determines if the control is selected
CheckedChanged	an event that runs when the value of the Checked property of a RadioButton or CheckBox is changed
Clear	the method used to clear a control

Count	the method that determines the number of items in a ListBox
Dispose	the method used to remove a form from memory
Dock	the property of a control that attaches it to a side of another contol and automatically resizes as the size of the control changes
EndsWith	a method used to determine if a string ends with a specified character or string of characters
Form	a control used to contain other controls; the window on the screen
FormClosing	an event that's triggered when a form is closed
GetItemChecked	the property in a CheckedListBox that knows if an item is checked
Hide	the method used to hide a form
IndexOf	a method that searches a string for a specified character or characters
Insert	a method that inserts a specified string into a specific location in a string; the method used to add an item at a specified location in a ListBox
LargeChange	the property of a ScrollBar that determines how much the slider moves when the shaft is clicked
Length	the number of characters in a string
Like	a method that determines if a string of characters matches a predefined pattern of characters
Maximum	the property the contains the largest allowable value for a control
Me	the active form
Minimum	the property that contains the smallest allowable value for a control
Orientation	the property of a TrackBar that determines whether its orientation is horizontal or vertical
PadLeft	the method that adds spaces (or other characters) to the left of a string until it reaches a specified length
PadRight	the method that adds spaces (or other characters) to the right of a string until it reaches a specified length
Remove	the method used to remove an item from a ListBox; a method that removes a specified character or characters from a string
RemoveAt	the method used to remove the item at the specified index in a ListBox

Replace	a method that replaces a specified substring in a string with another string of characters
Scroll	an event in a ScrollBar or a TrackBar that's triggered when the user moves the slider
SelectedIndex	the numeric value of the selected item in a ListBox
SelectedItem	the property that holds the value of the currently selected item in a ListBox
Show	the method to display a form
SmallChange	the property of ScrollBar that determines how much the slider moves when the arrows are clicked
Sorted	the property that places items in a ListBox in alphabetical order
StartsWith	a method used to determine if a string starts with a specified character or string of characters
Substring	a part of a string; a method that returns a specified portion of a string
TickFrequency	the property that determines the spacing of ticks on a TrackBar
Trim	a method that removes leading and trailing spaces from a string
TrimEnd	a method that removes trailing spaces from a string
TrimStart	a method that removes leading spaces from a string
Value	the property of a control that contains its numeric value

Self-check

1. Only one RadioButton in a group can be selected at any time.
2. A CheckedChanged event is generated when a RadioButton is selected.
3. At least one CheckBox in a group must be selected at all times.
4. Each item in a ListBox is numbered starting with 1.
5. Items cannot be added or removed from a ListBox at runtime.
6. The default event for a TrackBar is a ValueChanged event.
7. A project can have multiple forms but only one form can be active at any time.
8. PadLeft adds characters to the beginning of a string.
9. IndexOf returns an integer.
10. A MaskedTextBox displays only dots or asterisks.
11. When several related RadioButtons or CheckBoxes are on a form:
    A. use a GroupBox to organize them
    B. make sure all of them have the same name
    C. separate them using a Tab control
    D. make sure none of them are selected when the program runs

12. You can select a CheckBox or a RadioButton in code by setting the:
    A. Selected property to True
    B. Checked property to True
    C. Button property to Enabled
    D. Visible property to True

13. RadioButtons, CheckBoxes, and ListBoxes are all considered:
    A. input
    B. processing
    C. output
    D. all of the above

14. Respectively, use a ____ to determine which RadioButton is selected in a group of RadioButtons and a ____ to determine which CheckBoxes are selected in a group of CheckBoxes.
    A. Case structure, nested If
    B. nested If, stacked If
    C. stacked If, nested If
    D. nested If, Case structure

15. A collection:
    A. organizes related RadioButtons and CheckBoxes
    B. stores controls that aren't displayed on a form
    C. stores items in a ListBox
    D. is an individual page in a Tab control

16. Respectively, the default events for a RadioButton, ListBox, and TrackBar are:
    A. CheckedChanged, SelectedIndexChanged, Scroll
    B. CheckedChanged, Selected, IndexChanged
    C. Checked, Selected, Scroll
    D. Selected, SelectedIndexChanged, Drag

17. When a Form is opened it generates a ____ and when it's closed it generates a ____.
    A. Load, Dropped
    B. Open, Closed
    C. Load, FormClosing
    D. Activated, Deactivated

18. When using PadLeft and PadRight:
    A. the default character is a space
    B. the minimum length of the output is set by the developer
    C. the output string is not truncated if it's longer than the set length
    D. all of the above

19. The Trim method:
    A. removes all digits from a string
    B. removes all spaces from a string

    C. removes the formatting from a numeric value

    D. removes any special characters from a string

20. Which of the following matches the pattern "b?bb*"

    A. babble

    B. bubble

    C. bobble

    D. all of the above

VB Quiz Answers

Quiz 1

The user selects one RadioButton from a group and this selection is used in processing.

RadioButtons provide the options for a user. They're faster and easier for the user and the developer to use instead of TextBoxes. It's easier to control the input and all of the alternatives are visible on the screen. There's little chance for input error.

A group of RadioButtons allows only one choice. The same is true for a Case structure. Only one alternative in a Case structure is selected to the exclusion of the others.

Quiz 02

Both are grouped in GroupBoxes. Both have a CheckedChanged event. Both are used for input. However, RadioButtons allow only one selection in a group while CheckBoxes allow none, any, or all to be selected.

Most of the code is repetitive so it makes good sense to write the code once in a procedure and then call the procedure as needed. By using the CheckedChanged event, a user doesn't have to make a selection and then click on another Button to see the results.

There are over four million possible combinations of size, crust, and toppings – and that without getting the pizza half-and-half. Think about that the next time you tip your server!

Quiz 03

A ListBox offers space-saving on a form. A ListBox can contain a long list of items. It's easy to add or remove items from the list, which can't be done with RadioButtons or CheckBoxes.

Users don't always act as you'd expect. They don't follow the rules and what they want or expect may be different from was developed. A developer must be prepared for the unexpected and develop a program to handle the unexpected.

The program should have Help and directions. There should be Labels to describe what's on the screen. A Button to sort or organize the list may be helpful. There's no way to prevent the user from entering junk, but the ability to check for duplicate errands would be helpful.

Quiz 04

It's helpful to provide the user with a list of items from which to choose. That way the user doesn't have to type in the selection. It's also easier to code because the developer doesn't have to code for every possible correct entry. It's usually faster for the user to select an item than to enter it. And, it gives the developer more control over a list.

Use a DropDownList when the exact items for the list are known in advance. The user has a choice, but only from the items provided, which prevents the user from entering incorrect data and it makes it easier for the developer to code the input.

A TextChanged event is triggered every time the Text property changes. When the user types a character into a TextBox or a ComboBox, a TextChanged event is triggered. The same is true if they delete a character because the text in the control has changed.

Quiz 05

Two changes are needed to the statements in the If structure inside the loop. Instead of appending lines to RichTextBoxes, add items to ListBoxes, one for goals that have been met and the other for those yet to meet.

As such, these programs have little practical value. As yet, their worth is educational. Later, you'll learn how to read and write data to a file. At that point, users will be able to store their data from one run to another. At that point, the programs will become exponentially more useful.

Quiz 6

The Tab control displays the content a user needs at that moment while keeping other content out of the way yet accessible. A click on a tab brings the content forward and it's ready to use.

ScrollBars and TrackBars are designed to allow the user to select a numeric value within a specified range. The user selectes a value by moving the control or clicking on the control to move it in the desired direction.

The Scroll event is triggered whenever there's a change in the Value property. So, whenever the user moves one of them, it changes the Value property and triggers the event. This is easier than selecting a value in a ScrollBar or TrackBar and then processing it through a Click event.

Quiz 07

Multiple forms allow a developer to separate content. For example, an About form or a Help form is seldom needed. By placing them on separate forms, their content isn't loaded or used until it's needed, and, once the user it done with it, it can be removed. It also simplifies development. In large, complicated programs, each developer can work on their own form and its content without interfering with other developers.

Quiz 08

Formatting such as PadRight and PadLeft improves the look of the output, making it easier for the user to look at and understand the results. Text and numbers that align correctly are easier to view and interpret.

Substring methods make it easier to manipulate strings of data. A developer can look at any character and work with it any way they want.

Both the Like method and a MaskedTextBox examine characters. A MaskedTextBox limits input to a specified pattern. The Like method examines a string to see if it fits a particular pattern.

Quiz 09

Right now the form only does pizzas. There's no way to order beverages, salads, desserts, or any other items. The form should include the server's name or the deliverer's name, the date and time of the order, the table number, and the store location. These all show up on the form. Orders might come in person, over the phone, or even from the Internet. In addition, the program could track back-end operations for things like total sales and inventory. From these there could be business analysis, such as what sizes or toppings are most popular, what time of day is busiest or slowest, or what days are busy or slow. There are many other possibilities.

The order of items might need an overhaul. Right now, the prices don't show up on the form. The daily specials could be displayed. The size of the form may need changing to make it easier to use. All of these are up to the user.

File I/O – Files and Records and Fields, Oh My!

VB Quip

On two occasions I have been asked (by members of Parliament), "Pray, Mr. Babbage, if you put into the machine wrong figures, will the right answers come out?" I am not able rightly to apprehend the kind of confusion of ideas that could provoke such a question.
–Charles Babbage

By now you've come to realize that the real bottlenecks of your programs are input and output. Some of that is because users can only type and click so much and some of it is because input is repetitive. You've created useful output but have been unable to hang on to it. So far, every program run has meant starting from scratch with your data, entering it as needed, calculating the results, and then losing all of that work with a click of the Exit Button. No more. File input and output gives you the ability to store data and retrieve it as needed. File input takes data stored in a file and puts it into your program. File output stores the results in a file so you can use the data at a later date. This chapter covers the details of opening a data file, reading the data, processing the data, displaying the output, and writing the results to a file.

The Basics of File Input and Output

A *data file*, for our purposes, is a text file. Each line in the file is a *record*. A record consists for one or more *fields*. A bank might have a data file with a record for each savings account, where each record contains several fields, notably last name, first name, account number, and balance. It probably has dozens of other fields as well, but that's not a concern for us. Each line is a record containing related data for that account. A comma usually separates the fields in a record.

Successful *file input and output (I/O)* relies on getting the right file open, reading the data a record at a time, processing each record, and displaying the output. Once all the records are processed, the file is closed. *Data processing* – an industry term – involves taking records, sometimes millions of them, and performing a series of tasks on them. Sometimes the results are merely posted for viewing. Sometimes the information is written to a file for later processing.

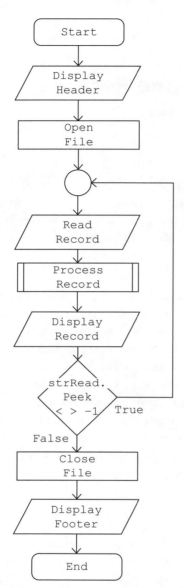

Figure 9.1   File Input/Output Flowchart Example

Following is the general algorithm for *batch processing, which* is merely the process for handling a file of related records. All of them are processed at the same time and all the records are handled by the same routine (see Figure 9.1).

Display Header
Open file

```
Do
    read record
    process data
    post results
Until all records are read
Close file
```

These steps can be broken into preprocessing, processing, and postprocessing. *Processing* is the easiest to understand, just read a record, process it, and display the answers. Of course, it's more complicated than that, but not much. Repeat this process once for each record in the file. You've been doing this with most of your programs already. File I/O merely automates the input for you. *Preprocessing* happens before the data are processed. Usually, it involves the steps for opening a file, writing the header for your output, and doing the setup tasks for processing. These happen before the processing loop and happen only once. *Postprocessing* happens after the processing loop and occurs only once. The data files are closed and final results are displayed.

Sequential File Access

Records are accessed in sequential order in our data files. Random file access is not covered here. *Sequential file access* simply means that records are read from the file, in order, from start to finish. This input is called a *data stream* and your code controls the stream.

Four lines of code control file access. The first,

```
Dim srdFile as System.IO.StreamReader
```

declares an object named srdFile that's set up as a StreamReader class. System. IO.StreamReader is a namespace and different ones have been used before. (Recall that Convert was used for data types and Math was used for built-in functions.) srd is the prefix for StreamReader objects. Use these to control data read from a file.

The next line,

```
srdFile = New System.IO.StreamReader("GPA.dat")
```

sets up a new instance of srdFile, associates the GPA.dat file with it, and opens the file for input. Any reference to srdFile now applies to the GPA.dat file. The data file must be in the bin\Debug folder of your project. If it's not, your program won't be able to find it and the program will crash. You can add the drive and path to the filename to get the program to look in a specific location for the file. That makes it a little easier to locate the file and it doesn't have to be buried in a folder. For now, it works. Soon you'll learn an easier way to open and close files.

We'll leave them as separate lines, but they can be combined into one line like this:

```
Dim srdFile as New System.IO.StreamReader("GPA.dat")
```

The line

```
strLine = srdFile.ReadLine()
```

reads one line from the file. One line in a data file is a record, so this line reads a record. srdFile references GPA.dat, keeps track of what records have been read, and applies the ReadLine method to it. For those who aren't fluent in Geekspeak, it reads the next unread line from the file. Repeat this line as long as there are records in the file. You're done with the file when it reads a blank line from the file.

The last line,

```
srdFile.Close()
```

closes the file. Just like you learned in kindergarten, "If you open it, close it." Once you're done with a file, close it. That prevents problems for your program and your data file.

VB Tip   *Place your data file in the bin\Debug folder of your project folder so your program can find it.*

Although most of the records in the middle were removed, the GPA.dat file looks like this:

```
2.97
3.45
2.23
...
2.01
2.52
```

Each line contains the GPA of a student. We need a loop to process each record (see Figure 9.2). It looks like this:

```
Do Until srdFile.Peek = -1
    'Read
    strLine = srdFile.ReadLine()
    rtbOut.AppendText(strLine & vbNewLine)
Loop
```

The loop reads a record from the file and displays it in the RichTextBox. It repeats the process until an empty line is read from the file. At that point, the loop ends and you've processed a batch of records. The Do Until statement

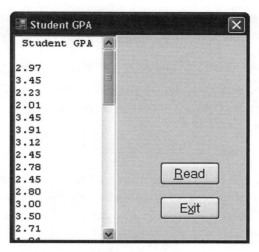

Figure 9.2   Student GPA Program

repeats the loop until it finds a blank line. The *Peek* method looks at the line before reading it. If the line has data, the loop continues. If the line is empty, it ends the loop. You've encountered -1 before. It was used for null references with ListBoxes and strings. Therefore, Peek = −1 means there's no record to read.

Here's the complete code:

```
Private Sub btnRead_Click ...
    Dim srdFile As System.IO.StreamReader
    Dim strLine As String
    rtbOut.Clear()
    rtbOut.AppendText(" Student GPA" &_
      ControlChars.NewLine &_ ControlChars.NewLine)
  srdFile = New System.IO.StreamReader("GPA.dat")
    Do Until srdFile.Peek = -1
        'Read
        strLine = srdFile.ReadLine()
        rtbOut.AppendText(strLine & vbNewLine)
    Loop
    srdFile.Close()
End Sub
```

The RichTextBox is cleared, a header is added to it, and the GPA.dat file is opened. The loop repeats until there's nothing in strLine. Every time it goes through the loop, it reads another line from the file, places it in strLine, and then displays it in the RichTextBox. The file is closed as soon as the loop ends.

The program has no processing per se. Certainly, there could be some processing with it such as counting the GPAs of Probation, Good Standing, Scholarship, and Dean's List students. In fact, you can place any processing you want between the input line and the output line.

VB Tip	*Open and run the StudentGPA program to see how it works.*
VB Quiz 01	*Find the preprocessing, processing. and postprocessing for the GPA code.*
	Is there a limit to the number of records that can be processed in this manner?

Finance Charge Program

Data files are opened and read with just a few lines of code. However, processing a record is more complicated. A record almost always contains multiple fields and these fields are usually separated by a comma. Here's an example:

```
Anderson, Andy, 39495, 2127.43
```

The record contains the last name, first name, account number, and loan balance for a customer. Other records in the file must share this same format. Each field is separated by a *delimiter*, in this case a comma. Any character can be a delimiter, but usually commas or tabs are used. The data cannot contain the delimiter because that would contaminate the data. That's why the large numbers in the balance field don't have commas in them. There's no real limit to the number of fields a record can contain as long as they are separated by a delimiter.

The data stream is a string and records are read a line at a time so each record gets stored in memory as a string. The next trick is to separate the fields so the data can be handled. The term for this is *parse*, or to break into component parts. It takes several lines of code, all working together, to do this.

```
Dim strRecord() As String
strLine = srdFinanceCharges.ReadLine
strRecord = strLine.Split(",")
strLast = strRecord(0)
strFirst = strRecord(1)
strAcctNo = strRecord(2)
decBalance = Convert.ToDecimal(strRecord(3))
```

The Dim statement belongs in the Declarations along with the other Dim statements. There's one difference in it. Notice the parentheses after the variable name. It creates an array (more on arrays in Chapter 10). The parentheses are used to store the field number. Fields are numbered starting with 0. You've already seen this concept with ListBoxes and strings.

The second line reads a record from the file. There was a similar line in the GPA program.

The third line takes the record and splits it into the proper fields using the *Split* method. The comma inside the parentheses is the delimiter. When it finds a comma in the line, it splits it and stores the data in the strRecord array. In essence, this is what the Split method does for the first record:

```
strRecord(0) = "Anderson"
strRecord(1) = "Andy"
strRecord(2) = "39495"
strRecord(3) = "2127.43"
```

All of them are strings at this point. The next four lines move the data from the array into more-familiar variables. Notice that the last line converts the string into a decimal value. At this point, the record has been read, parsed, and assigned to variables. It's as if the user had entered these data manually.

The next step is to process the data. For this example, we'll calculate 1.5% interest on the balance for each account and accumulate the total charges. The code that handles it looks like this:

```
Const sngFinanceRate As Single = 0.015
Dim decFinanceCharge As Decimal
Dim decTotal As Decimal

'Processing
decFinanceCharge = decBalance * sngFinanceRate
decTotal += decFinanceCharge

'Postprocessing
rtbOut.AppendText("Total Charges:" & _
   decTotal.ToString("c").PadLeft(41) & vbNewLine)
```

There is a constant for the finance rate and two variables: one for the amount of the finance charge for each account and one for the total for all accounts.

There are two line of processing. One line calculates the finance charge and the other adds that amount to the accumulator.

The total finance charge is displayed by the last line of code. This line is after the loop, so it displays after the records have been processed.

Here is the finished code:

```
Private Sub btnCharges_Click...
Const sngFinanceRate As Single = 0.015
Dim srdFinanceCharges As System.IO.StreamReader
Dim strLine As String
Dim strRecord() As String
Dim strLast As String
Dim strFirst As String
Dim strAcctNo As String
Dim decBalance As Decimal
```

```
Dim decFinanceCharge As Decimal
Dim decTotal As Decimal

'Display header
rtbOut.Clear()
rtbOut.AppendText("    Monthly Finance Charges" &
vbNewLine & vbNewLine)
rtbOut.AppendText("Last Name    First Name   Acct. No.
Balance   Charges" & vbNewLine)

'Open file
srdFinanceCharges = New
System.IO.StreamReader("FinanceCharges.dat")
Do Until srdFinanceCharges.Peek = -1
    'Input
    'Reads record
    strLine = srdFinanceCharges.ReadLine
    'Splits record
    strRecord = strLine.Split(",")
    strLast = strRecord(0)
    strFirst = strRecord(1)
    strAcctNo = strRecord(2)
    decBalance = Convert.ToDecimal(strRecord(3))

    'Processing
    decFinanceCharge = decBalance * sngFinanceRate
    decTotal += decFinanceCharge

    'Output
    rtbOut.AppendText(strLast.PadRight(12) & _
      strFirst.PadRight(12) & strAcctNo.PadRight(10) & _
      decBalance.ToString("c").PadLeft(11) & _
      decFinanceCharge.ToString("c").PadLeft(10) &
      vbNewLine)
Loop

'Postprocessing
'Close file
srdFinanceCharges.Close()

'Display total
rtbOut.AppendText("Total Charges:" & _
   decTotal.ToString("c").PadLeft(41) & vbNewLine)
End Sub
```

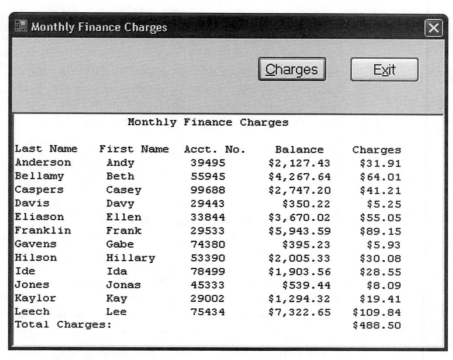

Figure 9.3   Monthly Finance Charges Program

The program follows the same general format of input, processing, and output as nearly every program you've written. The major difference is that the data come from a file instead of from user input (see Figure 9.3).

VB Tip   *Open and run the FinanceCharges program to see how it works.*

VB Tip   *Any word processor can open a data file. Just be careful not to change the file. And never save them in a word processing format. Save them as a text file instead.*

VB Quiz 02   *Find the preprocessing, processing, and postprocessing code for the FinanceCharges program.*
Find the input, processing, and output code for the FinanceCharges program.
Find the header and footer code for the FinanceCharges program.
How would the program change if there were more fields for each record?
How would the program change if there were more records in the file?

File Output

VB Quip   *Garbage In, Garbage Out.*

How did the data get to a file in the first place? There are two ways to create data files. The first is to use a word processor or spreadsheet. Another way is to write a program that writes data to a file. That's the output part of file I/O.

Output to a file takes only a few lines of code. However, there are two ways to write to a data file. The first is to use *CreateText*. This method creates a new data file. If there's already a file by that name, it automatically replaces it. This method could destroy existing data, so be careful! The other method is *AppendText*. If there's no file by that name, it creates it and writes the data to the file. If the file exists, it appends the data to the end of the file. This method leaves the existing data intact and writes data at the end of the file.

```
Dim swrFile As System.IO.StreamWriter
swrFile = System.IO.File.CreateText("filename.dat")
```

or

```
swrFile = System.IO.File.AppendText("filename.dat")
swrFile.WriteLine(strDetail)
swrFile.Close()
```

The first line creates a StreamWriter object. The next line assigns a filename to the StreamWriter object and opens the file. If it's opened as CreateText, the file is empty. If the file already exists, it's replaced. If the file is opened as AppendText, it adds text to the end of the file. If the file doesn't exist, it creates the file.

The next line writes the data to a file. It writes a string – in this example, strDetail. strDetail must contain the data, with commas, that make up a record. This line executes once for each line written to a file. The last line closes the file.

Write is an alternative to the WriteLine method. It looks like this:

```
swrFile.Write(strDetail)
```

It writes the data from strDetail, but it doesn't end the line. You might use this method when writing one field at a time to a record. To end a record and start a new line in a file, you'd need to use WriteLine or use vbNewLine in the detail line.

Save Bowling Scores Program

Lucky Strikes Bowling League wants to keep track of the scores for their bowlers. Each bowler rolls three games a night. The program must get the bowlers' names and scores for three games and store them in a file. The interface is shown in Figure 9.4.

The bowlers enter their names, use the TrackBars to select their scores, and then click the Save Button to add them to the file. A Scroll event automatically displays a game score when the bowler moves a ScrollBar.

Here's the code:

```
Private Sub btnSave_Click...
    'Declarations
```

```
        Dim swrBowlingScores As System.IO.StreamWriter
        Dim strFirst As String
        Dim strLast As String
        Dim shoGame1 As Short
        Dim shoGame2 As Short
        Dim shoGame3 As Short
        Dim strDetail As String

        'Preprocessing
        swrBowlingScores = IO.File.AppendText("BowlingScores.dat")

        'Input
        strFirst = txtFirst.Text
        strLast = txtLast.Text
        shoGame1 = tbrGame1.Value
        shoGame2 = tbrGame2.Value
        shoGame3 = tbrGame3.Value

        'Processing
        strDetail = strFirst & "," & strLast & "," & _
        shoGame1.ToString & "," & shoGame2.ToString & _
        "," & shoGame3.ToString

        'Output
        swrBowlingScores.WriteLine(strDetail)

        'Postprocessing
        swrBowlingScores.Close()
End Sub
```

The variables are declared in the Declarations; swrBowlingScores is the object to handle the data file. (Objects are covered in detail in Chapter 12.) The file is opened to AppendText in preprocessing and is named "BowlingScores. dat".

The input section gets the first and last names from TextBoxes and the scores from the Value property in the TrackBars.

The processing builds a string called strDetail. The bowler's first name is added to the string, followed by a comma. The last name is added to the string followed by a comma. The score from the first game is turned into a string and added to strDetail. The other scores are handled in the same manner and the fields are separated by commas.

The output is a WriteLine to the file that appends strDetail to the file.

The file is closed in postprocessing.

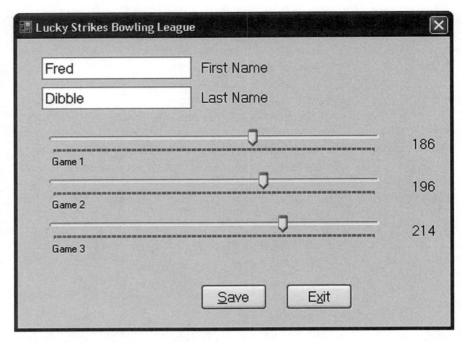

Figure 9.4   Lucky Strikes Bowling League Program

Here's what the data in the file look like:

```
Fred,Dibble,186,196,214
```

Other records have the same format.

VB Tip   *Run the FileIODemo program to see how input and output work.*

VB Quiz 03   *What's needed to read the data from the file?*
        Does the order of the fields in a record matter?
        What would happen if the file had been opened as CreateText instead of AppendText?
        Why not save the total scores and the averages as well?

Dialog Boxes

You've used dialog boxes with other programs. Certainly, you've used them to open or save files and you've probably used them for printing or formatting. A *dialog box* is a window that opens to let a user determine a set of conditions before fulfilling an action. For example, when you save a file, the Save File dialog opens and lets you set the filename, file location, and file type. Visual Basic has a full set of dialog boxes in the Toolbox. Place them in a project by adding them to the component tray.

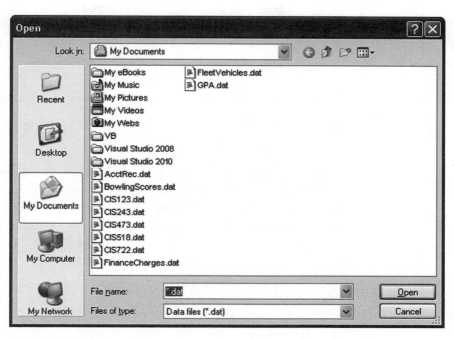

Figure 9.5   Open File Dialog Screen

OpenFileDialog Control

Use the *OpenFileDialog* to open a file for use. Double-click on the OpenFileDialog control to add it to the component tray. Use ofd as the prefix for this control. Activate the control at runtime with this line of code:

```
ofdOpenFile.ShowDialog
```

The command opens the OpenFileDialog window as a dialog. From there, the user selects the options and navigates through the drives and folders to find the file to be opened (see Figure 9.5).

Control of the program stays with this dialog until the user clicks OK or Cancel. With this dialog, the user selects the drive, folder, and file that must be opened. That file is stored in the *FileName* property of the OpenFileDialog control. Slip that into the command that assigns the filename to the StreamReader control like this:

```
srdFile = New System.IO.StreamReader(ofdOpenFile.FileName)
```

There are some other nice properties of the OpenFileDialog that are easy to put to use and helpful for the user. The *InitialDirectory* property can be set to any drive and folder at design time or in code like this:

```
srdFile.InitialDirectory = "C:\DataFiles"
```

The *FileName* property can be set to a specific file at design time or in code like this:

```
srdFile.FileName = "*.dat"
```

The *Filter* property can be set either way as well. The code is

```
srdFile.Filter = "Data files (*.dat)|*.dat |All
    Files (*.*)|*.*"
```

The filter looks for specific types of files, which reduces the clutter and minimizes the likelihood that they'll open the wrong file type. The filter property is a little convoluted. A developer can designate the type of files to look for by how the filter is written. The filetype and the filename are paired and are separated by a vertical bar (|). Each set is also separated by a vertical bar.

Files of type	File name
Descripton	Filter
Data files (*.dat)	*.dat
All Files (*.*)	*.*

If the user selects Data files (*.dat) in the Files of type dropdown, it displays all files with a .dat extension in the dialog. If All Files is selected from the dropdown, then all the files are shown in the dialog. Other filters can also be added as needed.

But what happens if the user decides to click Cancel? As a developer you need to plan for both possibilities. Do that with an If. When the user clicks OK, open the file and process it normally. If the user cancels, then display a MessageBox instead. It could look something like this:

```
If ofdOpenFile.ShowDialog = _
    Windows.Forms.DialogResult.OK Then
      'Open file
      Do Until srdFile.Peek = -1
          'Read records
          'Process records
          'Display output
      Loop
      'Close file
Else
    MessageBox.Show("Operation cancelled.")
End If
```

The If statement looks at the DialogResult for the OpenFileDialog. If it's OK, then the user has clicked OK and processing can continue. If not, it skips down to the Else and displays a MessageBox. Score one for user friendliness.

SaveFileDialog Control

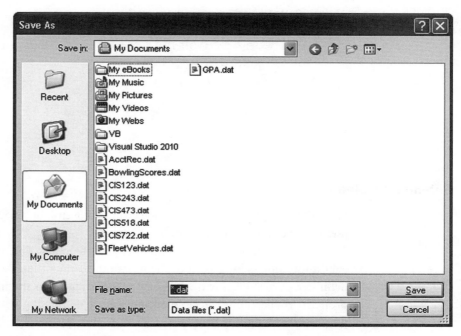

Figure 9.6   Save File Dialog Screen

The *SaveFileDialog* control manages the file-saving process. With it the user gets the Save As dialog, where the user can enter the name of the file and select the drive and folder where the file gets saved. Add a SaveFileDialog to the component tray by double-clicking on the SaveFileDialog icon in the Toolbox. The icon appears in the component tray. Use sfd as the prefix for the control when naming it (see Figure 9.6).

The SaveFileDialog has several properties to assist a user. The InitialDirectory can be set in code or at design time. With it, a developer selects a default drive and folder for the user. The user is still free to navigate elsewhere. The Filter property is controlled in the same way as the OpenFileDialog. The Filter property is controlled in the same way as the OpenFileDialog.

The command to display a SaveFileDialog is

```
sfdSavefile.ShowDialog()
```

It opens the Save As dialog so the user can name the file and select the drive and folder where it will be stored.

There are two Buttons for the SaveFileDialog, the Cancel Button and the Save Button. When the user clicks the Save Button, the data should be written to the file. Of course, if the Cancel Button is clicked, the save should be cancelled and control of the program returned to the user. The code is handled in much the same way as the OpenFileDialog:

```
If sfdSaveFile.ShowDialog = _
   Windows.Forms.DialogResult.OK Then
      swrFile=System.IO.File.AppendText(sfdSaveFile.FileName)
      'Write record(s) to file
      swrFile.Close()
Else
      MessageBox.Show("Operation cancelled.")
End If
```

Potential Problems

File I/O is fraught with peril. It's powerful and useful, but reading and writing files presents a whole new series of problems.

All the records in a file must have the same structure. The order of the fields isn't important as long as all of them have the same order. Be careful with the delimiter. If there's an extra one or one's missing, then the file won't process properly. A file cannot have blank lines in it or missing data. It won't read properly if it does.

The file must be in the correct location. If dialog boxes are used, the user can navigate to the file. Be careful if they're not used. Be sure to open a file before using it and to close it when you're finished. A good tip is to open the file just before it's used and to close it as soon as you're done with it.

All files are read from the beginning. You cannot skip records or skip fields. They must be read even if they're not used. You cannot retrace your steps in a file. Once it's read, you cannot go back to it without starting over.

There's a big difference between creating and appending a file. Appending a file adds records to the end of the file. Be careful of record duplication when using this method. Creating a file might destroy existing records. Either create a new file with a separate name or be sure the existing records aren't needed.

There are additional hazards with files, but many of these concerns will be relieved in the upcoming section on Try-Catch blocks.

VB Quiz 04

How do dialog boxes give power and flexibility to a user?

How does the use of standardized controls like dialog boxes benefit a developer and a user?

Try-Catch Blocks

VB Quip

If the automobile had followed the same development cycle as the computer, a Rolls-Royce would today cost $100, get a million miles per gallon, and explode once a year, killing everyone inside. –Robert X. Cringely

One goal for a developer is to write bulletproof software. A crash is the worst outcome for a program. It annoys the user, slows them down, risks the loss of data, and makes a developer look incompetent. None of these outcomes are good. Some random problems, such as a power cord or a hardware failure, cannot be avoided. However, most errors fall into a handful of categories and can be avoided. These errors are managed with *exception handling*. That's the fancy term for it, anyway. It simply means that the program encountered something that the developer hadn't anticipated or coded around and, instead of giving up, the program handles it. You've seen exceptions every time you've left a TextBox empty or tried to divide by zero. Your program probably crashed and you were left to figure out what happened.

Some exceptions are very specific and should be anticipated by a developer. An empty TextBox might cause problems and should be *trapped*, that is, there should be a Try-Catch block to manage a possible exception. Data conversion is another potential problem. Some numbers are too large to fit into certain data types and some strings cannot be converted to numeric values. Developers anticipate these potential problems. File I/O has many potential problems, from missing or misnamed files, to incorrect drive locations or missing drives on a network, to bad data in a file, to empty files. Any of these could spell disaster and must be managed. In fact, most code eventually ends up inside a Try-Catch block.

VB Tip

Exception handling is covered here, but will largely be ignored in subsequent chapters. As a developer, you're expected to use it, but as a student, it merely complicates the learning of other material.

Exceptions are handled with a Try-Catch block. The general form looks like this:

```
Try
    'Programming statement(s)
Catch ex As Exception
    'How to handle specific exceptions
Finally
    'Other programming statements
End Try
```

The Try starts with the *Try* statement. What follows is one or more lines of code that could, potentially, have problems. The *Catch* statement starts a list of exceptions and the code for handling them. Catches start with specific errors and how to handle them and proceed to general errors. When an exception occurs, the program grabs the first Catch statement that can handle the error and ignores the rest. In that respect, it's similar to a Case structure. The *Finally* statement can include other statements to try inside your Try block of code. *End Try* is the end of the Try block of code.

```
Try
    'Input
    shoFTAttempts = Convert.ToInt16(txtFTAttempts.Text)
    shoFTMade = Convert.ToInt16(txtFTMade.Text)
    'Processing
    sngFTPercent = shoFTMade / shoFTAttempts
Catch ex As Exception
    MessageBox.Show("Sorry, there was an error.",
      "Exception Handled", MessageBoxButtons.OK,
      MessageBoxIcon.Exclamation)
Finally
    'Output
    lblFTPercent.Text = sngFTPercent.ToString("p1")
End Try
```

The Try section contains the input and processing sections of the code. These are usually more susceptible to errors. In this example, Catch looks for an exception. When there's a problem with the code in the Try section, the Catch section runs, and this example displays a MessageBox. Usually, you want to check for specific errors and report them. That provides the user with a better indication of the problem. There can be more than one Catch in a Try, so start with specific errors and use the Catch ex As Exception as the last one to catch any unspecified errors. The Finally block runs regardless of whether there was an exception. This example displays the free throw percentage. As written, it's fine. The variable sngFtPercent was declared and initialized to 0. If the code runs without an exception, its value will be the free throw percentage. If there is an exception, the value would still be 0 and would display as 0%.

Try-Catch blocks can also be nested. That way, specific exceptions can be handled within other general exceptions. In fact, most code should be inside a Try-Catch block of some kind.

VB Tip   *Open and run the TryCatchExamples program to see how it works.*

Intro to Namespaces

In Visual Basic, everything is an *object*. Your form, all of your controls, almost everything, are objects. And, they'll do wonderful things. *Namespaces* are organized into a hierarchy. There are literally thousands of namespaces, enough

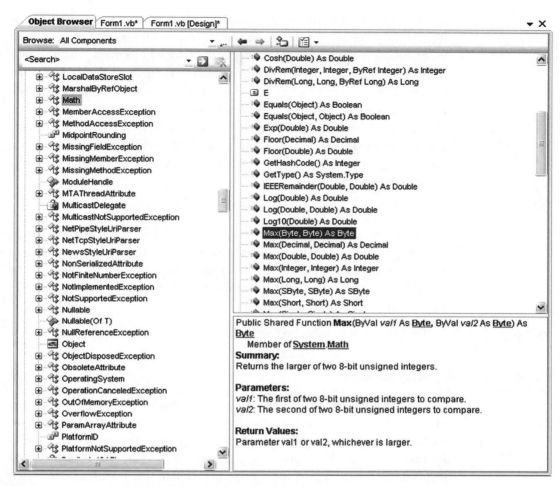

Figure 9.7   Namespaces from the Object Browser

to cover a wall. You'd never understand them or even come close to understanding them without that hierarchy. One of the main branches of this organization is the System namespace. Inside it are many other namespaces and inside many of them are more. Recall the Math namespace. Inside it are dozens of methods for making complex calculations and converting numbers. Earlier in the chapter you were introduced to the System.IO namespace, which controls the I/O functions. In later chapters you'll learn more about the Drawing namespace and how to create your own blueprint – something called a class.

The *Object Browser* has a list of the namespaces (see Figure 9.7). F2 opens the Object Browser. It's also available under the View menu. The left window shows the hierarchy. Navigate through the list to find the namespace you want. Use the plus and minus signs to expand or shorten the list as needed. Click on a namespace to display its members on the right side of the window. Click on a function to display a summary.

Your controls show up in the namespaces under Namespace. That's how IntelliSense picks up on your controls when you start typing their names. With thousands of namespaces, a hierarchy is the only way to manage and display them. Each one has its own specific function – a little code that it uses when needed. This code isn't loaded into Visual Basic or included in your program unless it's needed. That's the only way to make your programs manageable. Without such a system, you'd either have to write it all yourself or find and copy it into your programs. Namespaces save space in your programs because that code is only loaded when you need it. For example, you created an instance of a StreamReader with this line:

```
Dim srdFinanceCharges As System.IO.StreamReader
```

It used namespaces to find the System namespace that contains the IO namespace. Inside that is the StreamReader namespace with the code needed to open and read a file. It does most of the heavy lifting for your code. Without it, you might have to write dozens or hundreds of lines of code to handle a complex task. Whew!

VB Tip   *Objects are covered in detail in Chapter 12.*

Control Break Programming

Control break programming is a tried-and-true method for processing a batch of records from a file. It involves *business logic*, that is, a programming algorithm with a specific business purpose. Control breaks produce a report that's useful for making business decisions. It takes an ordered file, reads it, processes it, and displays the results in a report. The report contains the total for each related group of records and the total for all records. It ties together many of the programming techniques you've learned so far.

File Requirements

All the records in a control break data file must have the same structure. The records must be in order by a *key field*. The key field is generally an employee, a department, a category, or another similar field. The records do not have to be alphabetized, but all related records must be together, that is, all the records with the same key field must be together.

Here are the records from the sample control break data file. The records all have the following fields: Emp. Num., Last Name, First Name, Sales, and Shift:

```
1654,Book,Rita,1215.46,M
1654,Book,Rita,1186.25,M
1654,Book,Rita,1145.98,A
1654,Book,Rita,2064.56,A
```

```
1654,Book,Rita,1199.03,E
1654,Book,Rita,1245.63,E
2187,Coddle,Molly,1325.65,M
2187,Coddle,Molly,1316.78,M
2187,Coddle,Molly,1368.98,A
2187,Coddle,Molly,1374.02,A
2187,Coddle,Molly,1354.91,A
2187,Coddle,Molly,2073.55,E
2187,Coddle,Molly,2012.45,E
3504,Hisgun,Drew,1654.25,M
3504,Hisgun,Drew,1796.65,A
3504,Hisgun,Drew,1453.66,A
3504,Hisgun,Drew,1157.31,A
3504,Hisgun,Drew,1207.60,E
3504,Hisgun,Drew,1490.36,E
4037,Okie,Kerry,1152.45,M
4037,Okie,Kerry,1611.39,M
4037,Okie,Kerry,2074.61,A
4037,Okie,Kerry,1548.24,A
4037,Okie,Kerry,1490.34,E
4037,Okie,Kerry,1367.25,E
4037,Okie,Kerry,1340.28,E
5646,Iffice,Ed,1204.73,M
5646,Iffice,Ed,1248.31,M
5646,Iffice,Ed,1494.61,A
5646,Iffice,Ed,1682.94,E
5646,Iffice,Ed,1766.34,E
```

The records are organized by the employee number. They don't need to be alphabetized, but all the records with the same employee number must be together. This is the key field for the control break. Depending on the data, almost any field can be used for a control break as long as all the records are organized by that field.

Priming the Pump

Control break processing requires a technique called "*priming the pump*." The term originated with the hand pumps used in the days before electricity. Water was pumped from a well by hand and sometimes a bit of water had to be poured into the pump to get it to work, that is, to prime it. In a program, the first record is read above the processing loop so that control break variables can be set before the processing begins. This changes the basic input, processing, output logic (IPO) inside the processing loop, but it is a great little exercise for understanding and applying programming logic.

Control Break Logic

In a control break program, the first record is read above the processing loop so a variable called a *key* can be set before entering the processing loop. The values for this variable come from the ordered field of a file and determine when the control break is called. It checks this variable each time a record is processed and, when its value differs from the previous record, it's time to call a control break.

The control break is an If statement inside the processing loop. The If is controlled by the key variable. If the key changes from one record to the next, it means a new group of records has started. The control break displays the total for that group of records, updates the grand total, sets the total accumulator to zero, and updates the key variable. Record processing then continues until the next control break is encountered.

After all the records have been read, the file is closed, the last record is processed, the total for the last set of records is displayed, and the grand total for all records is displayed (see Figure 9.8).

In previous I/O programs, the algorithm for the processing loop was input, processing, and output (IPO). In a control break program, the algorithm for the processing loop is processing, output, and input (POI). As a whole, the program still follows the tried-and-true IPO algorithm. The first input is in preprocessing and its processing and output are inside the processing loop. The next record is read at the bottom of the loop with its processing and output on the next iteration of the loop. The processing loop continues the POI sequence until all the records have been read. The last input stops the processing loop. If you do a deskcheck, you'll see it follows IPO for each record.

VB Tip

Open and run the CBDemo program to see how it works.

```
'Preprocessing
'Display header
rtbOut.Clear()
rtbOut.AppendText(" Tabb Lett Computer Sales, Inc." &
    vbNewLine)
rtbOut.AppendText(" Daily Sales Report" & vbNewLine &
    vbNewLine)
rtbOut.AppendText("Emp. No.  Employee Name Sale  Shift" &
    vbNewLine)
'Open file
srdCBDemo = New System.IO.StreamReader("CBDemo.dat")
'Read the first line of the file
'Prime the pump
strLine = srdCBDemo.ReadLine()
```

```
'Set Control Break for first break
strRecord = strLine.Split(",")
strKey = strRecord(0)
Do Until srdCBDemo.Peek = -1
    'Processing
    'Split
    strRecord = strLine.Split(",")
    strEmpNum = strRecord(0)
    strLast = strRecord(1)
    strFirst = strRecord(2)
    decSale = System.Convert.ToDecimal(strRecord(3))
    strShift = strRecord(4)

    If strKey <> strEmpNum Then
        'Process Control Break
        'Display employee total
        rtbOut.AppendText("Total for Employee No. " & _
          strKey.PadRight(6) & _
          decTotal.ToString("c").PadLeft(13) & vbNewLine) _
          rtbOut.AppendText(vbNewLine)

        'Reset variables
        decGrandTotal += decTotal
        decTotal = 0
        strKey = strEmpNum

    End If

    decTotal += decSale

    'Display record
    strDetail = strEmpNum.PadRight(10) & _
    strFirst.PadRight(10) & strLast.PadRight(8) & _
    decSale.ToString("c").PadLeft(14).PadRight(18) & _
      strShift.PadRight(4)
    rtbOut.AppendText(strDetail & vbNewLine)
    'Read record
    strLine = srdCBDemo.ReadLine()

Loop

'Postprocessing
'Close file
srdCBDemo.Close()
```

```
'Split
strRecord = strLine.Split(",")
strEmpNum = strRecord(0)
strLast = strRecord(1)
strFirst = strRecord(2)
decSale = System.Convert.ToDecimal(strRecord(3))
strShift = strRecord(4)

decTotal += decSale

'Display record
strDetail = strEmpNum.PadRight(10) & _
strFirst.PadRight(10) & _ strLast.PadRight(8) & _
decSale.ToString("c").PadLeft(14).PadRight(18) & _
strShift.PadRight(4)
rtbOut.AppendText(strDetail & vbNewLine)

'Process Control Break for last employee
'Display Employee Total
rtbOut.AppendText("Total for Employee No. " & _
strKey.PadRight(6) & _
decTotal.ToString("c").PadLeft(13) & vbNewLine)
rtbOut.AppendText(vbNewLine)

'Add last employee to total
decGrandTotal += decTotal

'Display grand total
rtbOut.AppendText("Total for All Employees " & _
decGrandTotal.ToString("c").PadLeft(18) & vbNewLine)
```

This is the pseudocode for the control break code:

Preprocesing
  Display header
  Open file
  Read record
  Split record
  Assign Employee Num. to strKey
Processing
  Split record
  Assign strEmpNum, strLast, strFirst, decSale and strShift
  If strKey <> strEmpNum Then
    Display decTotal
    Add decTotal to decGrandTotal
    reset decTotal to 0
    set strKey to strEmpNum

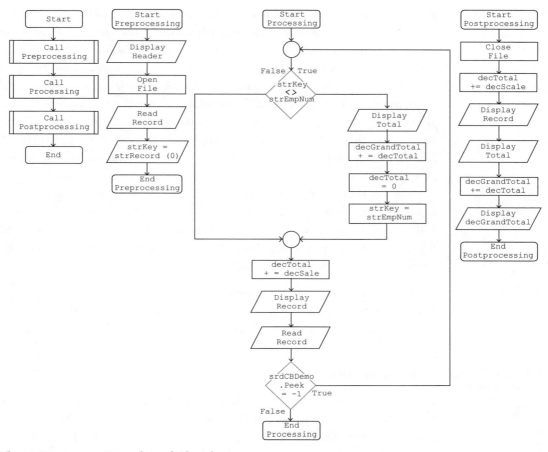

Figure 9.8   Control Break Flowchart

       End If
       Add decSale to decTotal
       Display record
       Read record
    Loop
    Postprocessing
       Close file
       Split Record
       Display last record
       Display decTotal for last employee
       Add decTotal to decGrandTotal
       Display decGrandTotal

The first record is read above the processing loop and is processed in the loop. The first record is split twice. While this appears redundant, the split in preprocessing allows the key variable to be set. The split at the top of the processing loop assigns all the fields to their appropriate variables and is needed for all the rest of the records in the file. Each record is processed and displayed in the order read. The next record is read at the bottom of the loop and the process continues. When strKey differs from strEmpNum, it means a new group of records has started and it's time to display the total for the last group. The control break handles this. It updates decGrandTotal, the variable that accumulates the grand total for all employees. It resets decTotal to zero. That's the variable that accumulates the total sales for each employee. The last step in the control break is to set the key field, strKey, to strEmpNum. That resets the key field to the new group of records.

Postprocessing takes place after all the records have been processed. The file is closed. The last record gets processed, total for the last employee gets displayed and the grand total is accumulated. Note that this is the same code that displayed the employee total and accumulated the grand total in the control break. The last step is to display the grand total. Ta da!

VB Quiz 05   *What would happen if the records weren't organized by a key field?*

Why is the first record split twice? How is it assigned differently to variables?

What is the practical use of control break processing?

Minor Control Break Processing

A *minor control break* is an additional set of breaks within another set of control breaks. Minor control breaks produce subtotals for a subset of records within a group. The key for a minor control break is based on another field in the record and that field must be ordered within that group of records. They provide additional information for a report and can be helpful when working with a report that contains a large number of records.

Additional File Requirements

All the records must have the same structure. The records must be in order by a key field, which is used for the control break. Additionally, within a group of records, the records must be ordered by a second field – the minor key. Look at the data from the previous program again:

```
1654,Book,Rita,1215.46,M
1654,Book,Rita,1186.25,M
1654,Book,Rita,1145.98,A
1654,Book,Rita,2064.56,A
1654,Book,Rita,1199.03,E
1654,Book,Rita,1245.63,E
```

The records are grouped by employee number, but within each employee the records are grouped by shift. The records for employee number 1654, Rita Book, have all the records for morning sales grouped together, the sales for the afternoon shift grouped together, and her sales for the evening shift grouped together. A minor control break based on the shift would provide further information on her sales for each part of the day.

Additional Break Logic

A minor control break requires much of the same logic as a control break. The pump must be primed in preprocessing, there must be a control break inside the processing loop, and the total for the last minor break must be called in postprocessing. There must be a separate key variable based on another key field. This variable must be set in preprocessing and reset with the minor control break in processing. There must be an accumulator for the total within a minor control break. It must be reset at the end of the minor control break (see Figure 9.9).

The algorithm for a minor control break is quite similar to that for a control break, but there is an additional If statement that invokes the minor control break. This If statement must be above the major control break. That's because, when there's a break between employees, the total for the last shift must be displayed, then the total for the last employee gets displayed, and then the first record for the new employee gets displayed.

There are two new variables for a minor control break. The first is strMinorKey. It controls the minor control break. The second is decMinorTotal. It's an accumulator for the total sales for any shift.

The variable strMinorKey is primed in preprocessing. Its value gets reset within the minor control break. The variable decMinorTotal finds the total sales for each shift for each employee, and decSale is added to it in processing. The total is displayed in the minor control break and then the accumulator is reset to zero at the end of the minor control break.

The last detail line and the total for the last shift for the last employee are displayed in postprocessing. Then the total for the employee is displayed. Finally, the grand total for all employees is displayed. This order is crucial to the orderly display of information from the file.

VB Tip　　　　　*Open and run the MinorCBDemo program to see how it works.*

```
'Preprocessing
'Display header
rtbOut.Clear()
rtbOut.AppendText(" Tabb Lett Computer Sales, Inc." & _
    vbNewLine)
rtbOut.AppendText(" Daily Sales Report" & vbNewLine & _
    vbNewLine)
```

```vb
rtbOut.AppendText("Emp. No. Employee Name Sale Shift " & _
  vbNewLine)

'Open file
srdCBDemo = New System.IO.StreamReader("CBDemo.dat")

'Read the first line of the file
'Prime the pump
strLine = srdCBDemo.ReadLine()

'Set Control Break for first break
strRecord = strLine.Split(",")
strKey = strRecord(0)

'Set Minor Control Break
strMinorKey = strRecord(4)

Do Until srdCBDemo.Peek = -1
    'Processing
    'Split
    strRecord = strLine.Split(",")
    strEmpNum = strRecord(0)
    strLast = strRecord(1)
    strFirst = strRecord(2)
    decSale = System.Convert.ToDecimal(strRecord(3))
    strShift = strRecord(4)

    If strMinorKey <> strShift Then
        'Process Minor Control Break
        rtbOut.AppendText("Total for Shift " & _
        strMinorKey.PadRight(6) &
        decMinorTotal.ToString("c").PadLeft(20) & _
        vbNewLine)
        rtbOut.AppendText(vbNewLine)

        'Reset variables
        decMinorTotal = 0
        strMinorKey = strShift
    End If

    If strKey <> strEmpNum Then
        'Process Control Break
        'Display employee total
        rtbOut.AppendText("Total for Employee No. " & _
        strKey.PadRight(6) & _
        decTotal.ToString("c").PadLeft(13) & vbNewLine)
        rtbOut.AppendText(vbNewLine)
```

```
            'Reset variables
            decGrandTotal += decTotal
            decTotal = 0
            strKey = strEmpNum
        End If

        decTotal += decSale
        decMinorTotal += decSale

        'Display record
        strDetail = strEmpNum.PadRight(10) & _
        strFirst.PadRight(10) & _
        strLast.PadRight(8) & _
        decSale.ToString("c").PadLeft(14).PadRight(18) & _
        strShift.PadRight(4)
        rtbOut.AppendText(strDetail & vbNewLine)

        'Read record
        strLine = srdCBDemo.ReadLine()

Loop

'Postprocessing
'Close file
srdCBDemo.Close()

'Split
strRecord = strLine.Split(",")
strEmpNum = strRecord(0)
strLast = strRecord(1)
strFirst = strRecord(2)
decSale = System.Convert.ToDecimal(strRecord(3))
strShift = strRecord(4)

decTotal += decSale
decMinorTotal += decSale

'Display record
strDetail = strEmpNum.PadRight(10) &
strFirst.PadRight(10) & strLast.PadRight(8) & _
decSale.ToString("c").PadLeft(14).PadRight(18) & _
strShift.PadRight(4)
rtbOut.AppendText(strDetail & vbNewLine)
```

```
'Process Minor Control Break for last employee
'Display Shift Total
rtbOut.AppendText("Total for Shift " & _
strMinorKey.PadRight(6) & _
decMinorTotal.ToString("c").PadLeft(20) & vbNewLine)
rtbOut.AppendText(vbNewLine)

'Process Control Break for last employee
'Display Employee Total
rtbOut.AppendText("Total for Employee No. " & _
strKey. PadRight(6) & _
decTotal.ToString("c").PadLeft(13) & vbNewLine)
rtbOut.AppendText(vbNewLine)

'Add last employee to total
decGrandTotal += decTotal

'Display grand total
rtbOut.AppendText("Total for All Employees " & _
decGrandTotal.ToString("c").PadLeft(18) & vbNewLine)
```

The following is the pseudocode for the minor control break code:

Preprocesing
  Display header
  Open file
  Read record
  Split record
  Assign Employee Num. to strKey
  Assign Shift to strMinorKey
Processing
  Split record
  Assign strEmpNum, strLast, strFirst, decSale and strShift
  If strMinorKey <> strShift Then
    Display decShiftTotal
    reset decShiftTotal to 0
    set strMinorKey to strShift
  End If
  If strKey <> strEmpNum Then
    Display decTotal
    Add decTotal to decGrandTotal
    reset decTotal to 0
    set strKey to strEmpNum
  End If
    Add decSale to decTotal

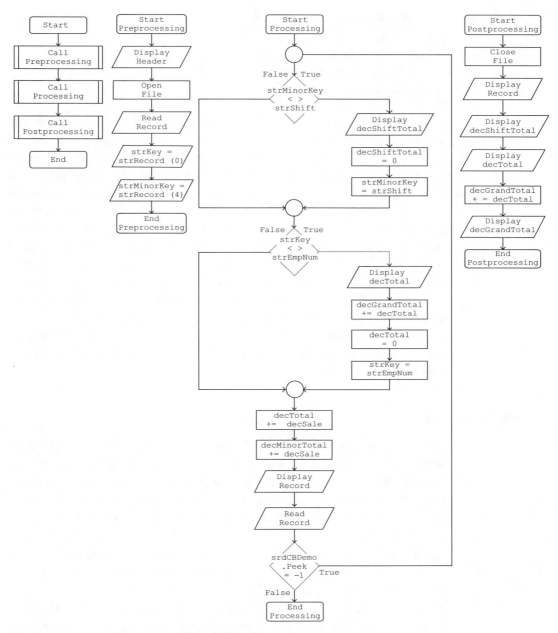

Figure 9.9   Minor Control Break Flowchart

       Display record
       Read record
   Loop
   Postprocessing
      Close file
      Split Record

Display last record
Display decShiftTotal for last employee
Display decTotal for last employee
Add decTotal to decGrandTotal
Display decGrandTotal

The first record is read before the processing loop and processed in the loop. The first record is split twice. Again, this is redundant, but this little glitch in the algorithm actually makes for better processing for a batch of records. Only the first record gets split twice – a small price to pay for the efficiency of processing a file full of records. Two keys are set in preprocessing. One checks for changes in the employee number and the other watches for changes in the shift. When the shift changes, a minor control break gets called. It displays the total for all records for that shift for that employee. It resets the shift total to zero and updates strShiftKey, the variable that keeps track of the shift. The strKey variable checks for changes in the employee number and calls a control break when needed.

Postprocessing has just one addition. The shift total for the last employee must be totaled and displayed before the total for the last employee.

A control break gets called for every new employee. A minor control break gets called for every shift for every employee. That means there are more calls to a minor control break than for a regular break.

Potential Problems

Control break programming includes file I/O, so include most I/O problems in the list of potential control break problems. The file must be ordered to do control break processing and the ordered field must be used for the control break. If not, there may be a control break for each record. The key field must be initialized in preprocessing. If not, a control break gets called on the first record. If initialized to the wrong field, a control break may be called for each record, or it may not get called at all. The key field must be updated at the end of the control break call. If it isn't, the control break won't work properly. The totals must be reset to zero in the control break. If not, the total for the control break will be too large. Display the totals in the control break. If a total displays for each record, then the output is probably in the processing loop and not the control break. If the totals display in the wrong place, then the output code is in the wrong place. The processing loop must be set up to do processing, output, and input. The input must be at the bottom of the loop. If not, the records won't process correctly. The totals for the last control break must be displayed in postprocessing. If there's no total for the last control break, then the output was left out. The grand total might be zero or contain the wrong total. This might happen if the accumulator isn't updated or updated in the wrong place. There are two ways to calculate the grand total. One method is to add the control break total to the grand total when a control break is called. The other method is to add to the grand total every time a record is processed.

VB Quiz 06   *What is needed to have a third-level control break?*

Could more than one field be totaled within a control break?

Why base a control break on an employee number (or other ID number) instead of the employee name?

Updating Files

Updates are a constant chore in any business. If a customer or employee changes an address or a phone number, the data require an update. Every billing cycle means an update for customer records. Every payroll means changes for the employee records. You get the idea.

Problem Description

Bedford Savings and Loan maintains a record of the account balances for their savings accounts. Each month these records are updated with the new account balance. The bank pays 3.6% annually on savings. You must open the AprSavingsBal.dat account, calculate the new balance, and write the data to the MaySavingsBal.dat file. The program has both files open at the same time. It reads data from the first file, calculates the new account balance, and writes the data to the second file. Records are read, processed, and written one at a time. The program handles only one record at a time and must release one record before reading the next record. The program is small and requires little memory to run because it handles only one record at a time. The disadvantage is that all the processing for a record must be completed before the next record is read. The program cannot hang onto a record for later processing or go back to a previous record (see Figure 9.10).

Code and Flowchart

Following is the code for the Savings Account Balance program and its flowchart (see Figure 9.11).

```
'Preprocessing
'Header
rtbOut.Clear()
rtbOut.AppendText("  Bedford Savings and Loan" & _
  vbNewLine)
rtbOut.AppendText("  Savings Account Balances —
  May 2010" & vbNewLine & vbNewLine)
rtbOut.AppendText("Acct Num.  April Balance  Interest
  May Balance" & vbNewLine)
```

```
Do Until srdApr.Peek = -1
    'Input
    strLine = srdApr.ReadLine
    strRecord = strLine.Split(",")
    strAcctNum = strRecord(0)
    decAprBalance = Convert.ToDecimal(strRecord(1))

    'Processing
    decInterest = decAprBalance * sngRate
    decMayBalance = decAprBalance + decInterest

    'Output
    'Screen
    rtbOut.AppendText(strAcctNum.PadRight(12) & _
      decAprBalance.ToString("c").PadLeft(15) & _
      decInterest.ToString("c").PadLeft(10) & _
      decMayBalance.ToString("c").PadLeft(15) & _
      vbNewLine)

    'File
    swrMay.WriteLine(strAcctNum & "," & _
      decMayBalance.ToString("f2"))
Loop

'Postprocessing
srdApr.Close()
swrMay.Close()
```

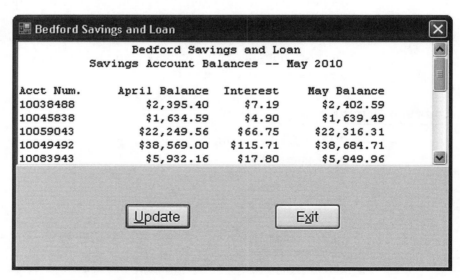

Figure 9.10   Savings Account Balance Program

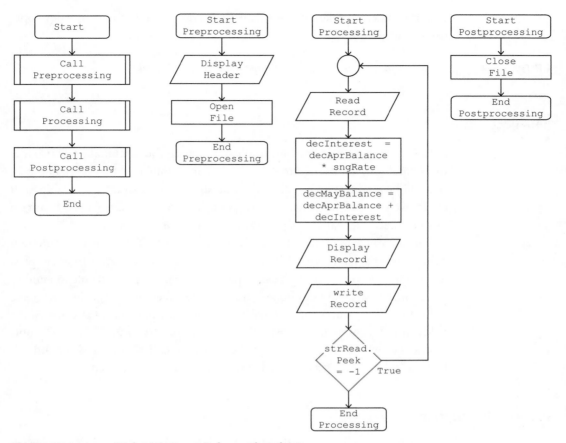

Figure 9.11   Savings Account Balance Flowchart

VB Tip   *Do a deskcheck on some of the figures to make sure the calculations are correct.*

Two files, one for input and one for ouput, are opened in preprocessing and a header is displayed on the screen. The processing loop reads a record from the input file. The account balance is used to calculate the interest earned for the month. The balance and the interest earned are added to get the new account balance. This amount and the account number are written to the new file. The account number, balance, interest earned, and new balance are also displayed on the screen. Both files are closed in postprocessing.

Test several records to make sure the results are correct. It is generally impractical to test all the records from a file, but a developer must test some of them. A spreadsheet works well for this task. Use several records at the beginning and others from the end of the file. Then select other representative values and some extreme values to make sure the calculations are correct. From these, a developer can be fairly confident that the code works.

VB Tip   *Open and run the SavingsUpdate program to see how it works.*

Merging Files

Merging files has a valuable business use. A *merge* is the combination of two files that contain similar data. It might be a client or customer list that gets combined. It could be accounts receivable files or an inventory lists that are combined. It could even be two book lists or two guest lists for a wedding. It's a common business need that calls for a programming solution.

For dissimilar lists, it could be a complicated task. If the lists have different fields or one list has more fields than the other, it could get messy. In its simplest form, a merge could simply mean appending the data from one file to another file. More likely is that a developer would take two files and merge them to create a third file. That leaves the original data intact, just in case. If the order of the fields in the original files varies, it might require extra work. Here's a simple example of where the order of one file is lastname, firstname and the other is firstname, lastname. It's not much, but it's still a factor to consider.

Problem Description

Ray Diator, a salesperson on the staff of an auto dealership has taken another job and you're in charge of merging his contact list with that of another salesperson. We'll simply ignore the real-world likelihood that there are probably dozens of fields for the contacts and concentrate on a few fields: last name, first name, phone, prospect, and vehicle type. Both files have these fields and the files are small because this is an example.

You must open three files to complete the merge: the two existing files to read the data and the third file that will contain the merged data. Each record is held only long enough to handle the data. Once a record is read, it's written to the merge file before another record is processed. The order of the data in the records of all three files is last name, first name, phone, prospect, and type, which makes the merge easiser.

The program opens all three files. It then processes the records from one file. A processing loop reads each record, displays it on the screen, and writes to the merge file. The second file is processed in the same manner. Close the files once all the data have been merged. The key is to remember that a record is held only long enough to process it. Once a new record is read, the data from the previous record disappear.

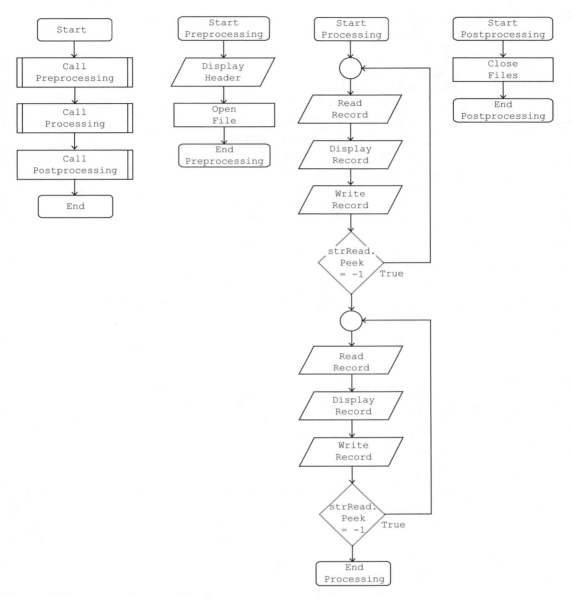

Figure 9.12   File Merge Flowchart

Code and Flowchart

Following is the code for the File Merge program and its flowchart (see Figure 9.12).

```
'Preprocessing
'Header
rtbMerge.Clear()
```

```
rtbMerge.AppendText("Last name   First name   Phone
   Prospect   Vehicle" & vbNewLine & vbNewLine)

'Processing
Do Until srdFirst.Peek = -1
    'Input
    strLine = srdFirst.ReadLine
    strRecord = strLine.Split(",")
    strLast = strRecord(0)
    strFirst = strRecord(1)
    strPhone = strRecord(2)
    strProspect = strRecord(3)
    strType = strRecord(4)

    'Output
    'Screen
    strDetail = strLast.PadRight(12) & _
    strFirst.PadRight(12) & strPhone.PadRight(10) & _
    strProspect.PadRight(12) & strType.PadRight(10)
    rtbMerge.AppendText(strDetail & vbNewLine)

    'File
    strDetail = strLast & "," & strFirst & _
      "," & strPhone & "," & _
      strProspect & "," & strType
    swrMerge.WriteLine(strDetail)

Loop

Do Until srdSecond.Peek = -1
    'Input
    strLine = srdSecond.ReadLine
    strRecord = strLine.Split(",")
    strLast = strRecord(0)
    strFirst = strRecord(1)
    strPhone = strRecord(2)
    strProspect = strRecord(3)
    strType = strRecord(4)

    'Output
    'Screen
    strDetail = strLast.PadRight(12) & _
      strFirst.PadRight(12) & strPhone.PadRight(10) & _
      strProspect.PadRight(12) & strType.PadRight(10)
    rtbMerge.AppendText(strDetail & vbNewLine)
```

```
'File
strDetail = strLast & "," & strFirst & "," & _
strPhone & "," & _ strProspect & "," & strType
swrMerge.WriteLine(strDetail)

Loop

'Postprocessing
srdFirst.Close()
srdSecond.Close()
swrMerge.Close()
```

VB Tip   *Open and run the MergeExample program to see how it works.*

Potential Problems

One way to treat a record from a file is to envision it as user input typed in
TextBoxes. Input from TextBoxes is easy to process, but it can only be used until
there's new input. Once the user enters new data, the previous input is discarded
and new the data replace it. Batch processing is the same way. As soon as a new
record is read, there's no way to recover the old data. A developer must make
sure that any processing on a record is done before the next record is read.

There's always a risk with input from one file and output to another. Be careful
not to confuse the two and make sure they have different names. Keep backups
of the data files. Check the file once the data are written. Make sure that the fields
are in the desired order, that the delimiters are in place, and that all records are
written.

Test data to make sure the calculations are correct. Remember, garbage in,
garbage out!

VB Quiz 07   *Why is planning and testing so critical with file I/O?*
         Why is it impossible to run a modern business with data processing?
         How could errors creep into a data file?
         Why merge data from two files into a separate file?

Fixing a Program

Dewey, Swindel, and Howe Real Estate has several holdings including homes,
farms, and industrial and commercial real estate. Each year it runs a program that updates the estimated values of its holdings. The program,
UpdateRealEstateValues, is not working correctly and you must fix it (see

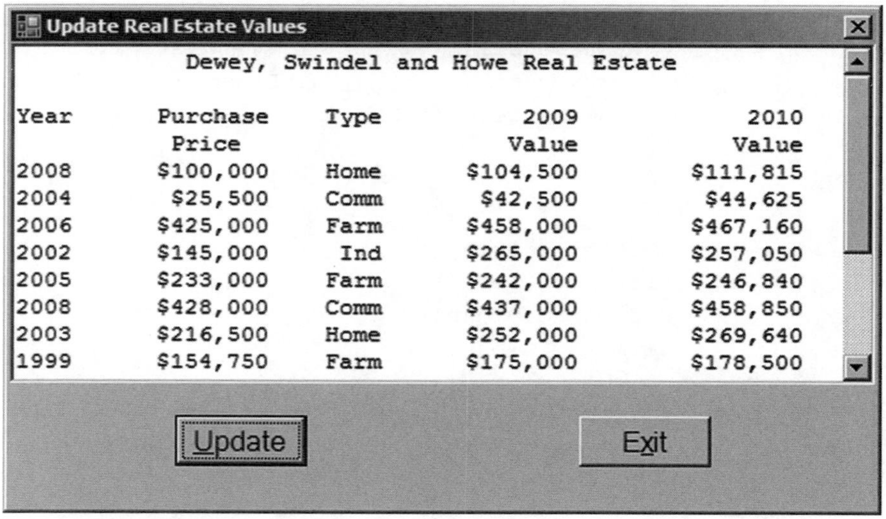

Figure 9.13   Update Real Estate Values Program

Figure 9.13). It has a data file named 2009RealEstateValues.dat containing basic data on these holdings and looks like this:

```
2008,100000,Home,104500
2004,25500,Comm,42500
2006,425000,Farm,458000
2002,145000,Ind,265000
2005,233000,Farm,242000
2008,428000,Comm,437000
2003,216500,Home,252000
1999,154750,Farm,175000
2001,395000,Ind,546500
2001,279000,Comm,483000
2002,199900,Home,225000
2007,382000,Ind,402000
2007,485000,Farm,508500
2005,315000,Home,347500
```

The first field is the year of the purchase, the second field is the purchase price, the third field is the type of holding, and the last field is its 2009 value. The program should read the data from this file, calculate new values based on real estate trends, and write the data to a new file named 2010RealEstateValues.dat. The fields for the new file should be year, purchase price, type, and 2010 value and they must be in that order. By their estimates, home values increased 7%, commericial real estate increased 5%, industrial real estate decreased 3%, and farm real estate increased 2%.

First, you run the program, UpdateRealEstateValues, and it crashes. It gets to this line:

```
strRecord = strLine.Split(",")
```

and it says the variable was used before it was assigned a value. So, strLine is empty. You backtrack in the code and realize strLine was never assigned the input from the file. This line

```
strLine = srd2009Values.ReadLine
```

must be above the Split command. The two lines are in the wrong order! You switch them and try again. Curses, it crashes again, this time on this line:

```
Do Until srd2009Values.Peek = -1
```

It says you can't read from a closed file. First, you check to make sure the file was opened. Sure enough, there's a line in preprocessing that opens the file. You check to make sure the document is in the correct folder and that there's data in it. Yep. So now what? You know the file was opened, so when, where, and how did it get closed? Time to check the code. There it is – this line,

```
srd2009Values.Close()
```

closes the file. It was in the wrong place. With it inside the loop, it gets closed before all the records are read. You move it into postprocessing where it belongs and try again.

This time it runs. You think life is good, but then, just to be safe, you check the output file, 2010RealEstateValues.dat, just to be safe. You're glad you did. The first record looks like this:

```
Home,100000,2008,$111,815.00
```

That's not good. The order should be year, purchase price, type ,and 2010 value. You quickly realize the year and type are mixed up. The line

```
strDetail = strType & "," & decPurchase.ToString & ","  &
    strYear & "," & dec2010Value.ToString("c")
```

should look like this:

```
strDetail = strYear & "," & decPurchase.ToString & "," &
    strType & "," & dec2010Value.ToString("c")
```

with strYear and strType in the correct locations. Easy enough. Remembering the adage "garbage in, garbage out," you try the program again, just to be sure. This time the first record from the file looks like this:

```
2008,100000,Home,$111,815.00
```

However, there's still trouble. The last field should have the 2010 value in it, but it contains a dollar sign, commas, and decimals. You know that the comma is the delimiter for this file and that it will throw off everything. You go back to the code and change the detail line to

```
strDetail = strYear & "," & decPurchase.ToString & "," &
    strType & "," & dec2010Value.ToString
```

to remove the currency from that field. You feel better, but you've made a change to the code so you run it again, just to be sure. You take one last look at the data file and you're glad you did. The records are in the correct order and the fields are set up correctly, but the file has too many records. The program was set up to AppendText instead of CreateText. So make that change and check it again. Yippee!

VB Tip   *Open and run the UpdateRealEstateValuesFixed program to see how it works.*

On Your Own

Write a program to display the states and capitals in ListBoxes. Use the StatesCapitals.dat file to populate a ListBox for states and another for capitals. When you select an item in one ListBox it should also select the appropriate item in the other ListBox. The delimiter for the data file is a tab.

Write a program to display and total the wages for a list of workers. Use the Wages.dat file for input. The fields for each record are last name, first name, department, rate, and hours. Calculate overtime and display regular pay, overtime pay, and total pay. Total and display the columns as well.

Write a program to store information on your family history. The records should have fields for the first name, middle name, last name, date of birth, mother, and father. The program should open, display the records in a Rich-TextBox, and close the file. It should have controls so the user can enter data for new family members and add the data to the file. Name the data file Family.dat.

Write a program to display the data in the StatePop.dat file. The fields are state, current population, 2000 population, and rank. Display the data in a RichTextBox. Add exception handling to your code.

Write a program to do control break processing for SoftHardware.dat. The fields are last name, first name, employee number, sales, and department. Base the control break on employee number and find totals for each employee. Display the results in a RichTextBox. For an added challenge, do a minor control break based on department. If you have a masochistic streak, write the report to a file. Each line of output in the RichTextBox becomes a line of output to a file. The file becomes a report file that can be opened in a word processor and printed.

Summary

This chapter introduced file input and output. File input takes records from a file and reads them into your program. File output writes your data as records in a file. Open and Save dialog boxes were introduced to manage file naming and location. Exception handling was introduced. The technique helps a program recover from an error and prevents crashes. Namespaces contain specific controls and methods. They simplify code management and make for smaller and faster programs. Record updating and control break processing was introduced.

Review

A data file is a text file.

Every line of a data file contains a record.

Records consist of one or more fields.

Fields are separated by a delimiter, usually a comma.

Data processing involves reading data from a file and turning that data into information.

Batch processing takes records from a file and processes all of them in the same manner.

Data processing usually includes preprocessing, processing, and post-processing.

Preprocessing happens before the records are read.

Processing reads and processes the records.

Processing occurs in a loop with one iteration for each record in a file.

Postprocessing happens after all the records are processed.

Data files are accessed in sequential order. Once a record has been read, it cannot be accessed again without starting over.

Data files are usually in the bin\Debug folder of a project.

File input is controlled by a StreamReader object.

Files must be opened before they can be used.

Records are read one at a time using the ReadLine method.

Close a data file as soon as you're done using it.

A processing loop is controlled by the Peek method. When Peek $= -1$, the end of the file has been reached.

Most records contain multiple fields separated by a delimiter. Use the split method to separate fields in a record.

Each record is a string when read. Convert the strings to the appropriate data type when splitting the record into its component fields.

File output involves writing data to a text file.

CreateText creates a new data file. If a file with that name already exists, it is replaced with the new file. Any data in the original file are lost.

AppendText adds new records to the end of an existing file. If the file doesn't exist, it is created.

File output is handled with a StreamWriter object. Records are written to a file one line at a time.

A dialog box opens a window that allows the user to select settings. The dialog must be handled before control returns to your program.

The OpenFileDialog controls the location and name of files that are opened for input.

The SaveFileDialog controls the location and name of files that are opened for output.

Use a filter to screen the list of files in an open or save dialog.

Exception handling manages errors that occur while a program runs.

Use a Try-Catch block to manage exceptions. Exceptions are trapped by the Try part of the block and handled in the Catch.

A Namespace is an object. Namespaces are organized by category and arranged in a hierarchy. Use the Object Browser to view Namespaces.

Control break programming involves using business logic to process a batch of records. Records must be organized by a key field and processed by that field. All records must have the same structure. Each group of related records is totaled or summarized.

Priming the pump is used in control break processing to read the first record and set key fields from it before processing the records in the file.

The processing loop in a control break reads the records at the bottom of the processing loop. Its processing algorithm is processing, output, input.

A minor control break processes related records within a group of related records. Totals are found and displayed for each group of related records within a larger group of related records.

Data files are typically updated on a regular basis. This often means opening one or more files for input and, at the same time, opening other files for output.

Merging files involves taking two or more files and combining their records into a single file. Often the data must be manipulated when the two files are merged.

Terms

batch processing	the technique of processing a set of data records as a group; each record is read and processed individually and in sequential order
business logic	a programming algorithm with a specific business purpose

control break	a programming method for processing a batch of records; ordered records are processed as a group with totals for select fields of data
data file	a text file that contains one or more records
data processing	the computerized processing of business transactions
data stream	the stream of text to or from a data file
delimiter	the character, usually a comma, that separates fields in a data file
dialog box	a specialized window used to gather specific input from the user before processing
exception handling	the process of handling runtime errors in a program
field	a single part of a record; one or more fields comprise a record
file I/O	the process of reading data into the computer (input) or writing data to a file (output)
key	the variable used to control a control break; the ordered data from a field that's used for calling a control break procedure
key field	a field in a data file; records in the file are ordered by a key field for control break processing
merge	the process of combining two separate entities; in file I/O it's the process of combining two separate files into one
minor control break	a control break within a control break; an ordered field in a group used to process control breaks within that group
object	a self-contained programming element used as a building block
Object Browser	a window that lists all the classes and components available to a project
OpenFileDialog	a window used to gather information on the location and name of a file about to be opened
parse	the process of splitting fields in a record so they can be processed
postprocessing	tasks handled by the computer after the processing of a batch of records
preprocessing	tasks handled by the computer prior to processing a batch of records
"priming the pump"	the process of reading a record in preprocessing for the purpose of setting key fields
processing	the manipulation of records or data by a computer

record	one line in a text file, usually composed of one or more fields
SaveFileDialog	a window used to gather information on the location and name of a file about to be saved
sequential file access	the technique used to access records, in sequential order, from a data file
trap	catching and handling runtime errors in a program; errors are trapped with a Try-Catch block

Keywords

AppendText	a method used to add text to the end of a file; automatically creates a file if one doesn't exist
Catch	the keyword used to start a list of methods to handle exceptions in a Try-Catch block
CreateText	a method used to create a new file for output; automatically overwrites an existing file with the same name
End Try	the keyword used to end a Try-Catch block
FileName	a property in I/O objects that controls name of a file
Filter	a property in OpenFileDialog and SaveFileDiaog objects that controls the types of files that are displayed in the folder
Finally	the keyword used to start a block of code that runs at the end of a Try-Catch block
InitialDirectory	a property in OpenFileDialog and SaveFileDialog objects that controls the initial directory that opens
Namespace	a hierarchical organization of classes, controls, properties, and methods in VB
Peek	a method used by a StreamReader object to determine the next character in a file; when it's -1, the end of the file has been reached
ReadLine	a StreamReader method used to read a line from a data file
Split	a string method used to split a string by a delimiter; generally used to split a record into fields
StreamReader	an object used to read data from a file
StreamWriter	an object used to write data to a file
Try	the keyword used to start a Try-Catch block
Write	a StreamWriter method used to write data to a file; writes only the data and does not end the line in the file
WriteLine	a StreamWriter method used to write a line to a file

Self-check

1. Each item in a record is separated by a comma.
2. You cannot move backward through a data file.
3. Data files must be stored in the bin\Debug folder.
4. All records in a file are read from a file at once with a single Read command.
5. If it exists, the CreateText method automatically replaces an existing data file.
6. Files can only be opened with an OpenFileDialog control.
7. All data files are read starting at the beginning of the file.
8. Exception handling helps to prevent logical errors.
9. A developer must know the number and order of fields in a record when doing file I/O.
10. Records must be sorted in ascending order when doing control break processing.
11. A data file:
    A. is a text file
    B. has one record per line
    C. is read one record at a time from beginning to end
    D. all of the above
12. Which character is the best for a delimiter?
    A. hyphen
    B. comma
    C. space
    D. quotation mark
13. The StreamReader class handles file:
    A. input
    B. output
    C. updates
    D. creation
14. Parse means to:
    A. read a record from a file
    B. check to see if there's an unread record still to be read
    C. separate a record into its component fields
    D. see if the data file is open
15. To add records to an existing file, use:
    A. UpdateText
    B. CreateText
    C. AppendText
    D. AddText
16. A data file:
    A. must be in the bin\Debug folder

B. must have its name written into the code by the developer

C. can be used for input or output, but never both

D. none of the above

17. Exception handling catches:

A. syntax errors

B. logical errors

C. runtime errors

D. all of the above

18. Respectively, a Try block and a Catch block is the code:

A. attempting to run and the code that runs when an error occurs

B. attempting to run and the alternate code that accomplishes the same thing

C. that runs when the condition is true and the code that runs when the condition is false

D. that runs first and the code that runs when the first code is finished

19. Use the Object Browser to:

A. view the code for each control and event

B. view and select the controls to add to a form

C. view a list of namespaces

D. all of the above

20. A control break is called based on:

A. a set number of records

B. a change in the key field from one record to another

C. a total reached by accumulating values in the key field

D. none of the above

VB Quiz Answers

Quiz 01

The preprocessing, processing, and postprocessing are shown as comments in the following code:

```
'Preprocessing
rtbOut.Clear()
rtbOut.AppendText(" Student GPA" & ControlChars.NewLine &
  ControlChars.NewLine)
srdFile = New System.IO.StreamReader("GPA.dat")

Do Until srdFile.Peek = -1
  'Processing
  'Read
  strLine = srdFile.ReadLine()
  rtbOut.AppendText(strLine & vbNewLine)
```

```
Loop
'Postprocessing
srdFile.Close()
```

Yes and no, but the limits are more the size of the file and the amount of data that can be displayed. Very little memory is needed to process records from a file. That's one of the biggest advantages of record processing. Other methods require more memory as the number of records increases, so, from a practical standpoint, record processing is very efficient.

Quiz 02

The sections of code are shown as comments in the code:

```
'Preprocessing
'Display header
  rtbOut.Clear()
  rtbOut.AppendText("  Monthly Finance Charges" &
    vbNewLine & vbNewLine)
  rtbOut.AppendText("Last Name  First Name  Acct. No.
     Balance Charges" & vbNewLine)
  'Open file
  srdFinanceCharges = New
    System.IO.StreamReader ("FinanceCharges.dat")
  Do Until srdFinanceCharges.Peek = -1
    'Input
    'Reads record
    strLine = srdFinanceCharges.ReadLine

    'Splits record
    strRecord = strLine.Split(",")
    strLast = strRecord(0)
    strFirst = strRecord(1)
    strAcctNo = strRecord(2)
    decBalance = Convert.ToDecimal(strRecord(3))

    'Processing
    decFinanceCharge = decBalance * sngFinanceRate
    decTotal += decFinanceCharge

    'Output
    rtbOut.AppendText(strLast.PadRight(12) &
      strFirst.PadRight(12) & _ strAcctNo.PadRight(10) &
      decBalance.ToString("c").PadLeft(11) & _
```

```
                decFinanceCharge.ToString("c").PadLeft(10) &
                vbNewLine)

        Loop

        'Postprocessing

        'Close file
        srdFinanceCharges.Close()

        'Display footer
        rtbOut.AppendText("Total Charges:" &
            decTotal.ToString("c").PadLeft(41) & vbNewLine)
```

With more fields, a program requires more variables, one for each field. Each field would have to be assigned to a variable after the record is split. That would mean more lines of code for that process. More processing and output may be required to handle and display the extra data.

Little would change with more records in the file. The code is set up to handle almost any number of records in the file. That's one of the beauties of batch processing.

Quiz 03

The code needs a StreamReader object set up to handle the file. Open the file in preprocessing and close it in postprocessing. A processing loop is needed to handle the records. The loop needs a line to read the data, a record at a time, from the file. Each record must be split and the resulting fields must be converted to their appropriate data type and stored in varibles. From there, each record can be processed.

The order of the fields is of little importance. The order doesn't make a difference to the data, the file, or the program. However, from an aesthetic viewpoint, the fields are usually arranged to make it easier for a developer to manage them.

When opened as CreateText, the existing file is overwritten. Any data in that file are lost. As AppendText, the existing data are maintained and new records are added at the end of the file.

Calculated values are seldom stored in a file. They take up additional space in the file and may not be needed. Besides, if needed, the total and average can be easily calculated from the data.

Quiz 04

A dialog box lets the user select the file and its location. Without them, the file, folder and drive have to be selected and hardcoded by the develoer.

Standard dialogs are much faster and easier for a developer to add and use. Users are generally familiar with them, usually because they've seen and used them in other programs. There's little learning curve for them which makes them more attractive than non-standard forms.

Quiz 05

Without an ordered key field, the control break would be called at random. Report totals for such a program would be worthless.

The first record is split in preprocessing and again at the top of the processing loop. It's used to set the key field in preprocessing and as part of record processing inside the loop. The code is redundant, but only for the first record. Although it seems wasteful, it's actually the best method for the application. Other algorithms have been tried, but none work as well as this method.

Control breaks are useful for looking at totals and for breaking down parts of a report. They allow a deeper look at the numbers so a manager can see trends and look at the individual components of a report. In the example, the control break allows a manager to see which employees have the best sales.

Quiz 06

The file must be ordered properly. That means records within the minor control break must be ordered by another field. A third key must be set up and checked with every record. The third control break must be checked above the minor control break in the processing loop. The total must be accumulated, and output displays and variables must be updated within the third control break. In postprocessing, the third control break total must be displayed before the minor control break and the major control break.

Certainly. Sales were totaled in the example, but if another field with the number of customers was in the file, it could be totaled as well.

An ID number is almost always used because it's unique. Generally, an employee name takes up two fields, last name and first name. That makes it more complicated for a key in a control break. In addition, there's the potential, especially in large files, that there will be duplicates. Always use an ID number.

Quiz 07

Planning and testing are critical because most records won't be checked. The results are simply taken at face value. With hundreds, thousands, or even millions of records, the accuracy of one record is assumed from the planning and testing of a few test records. If there's an error or a problem, it may not show up immediately and it will probably be a significant problem when it does surface.

Good planning and testing is key to eliminating errors and preventing those million-dollar utility bills!

Without computers and data processing, the work of a business would have to be completed by hand, but that process is too time-consuming, labor-intensive, cumbersome, and expensive. Data processing is faster, more accurate, and cheaper than manual processes. From a bottom-line perspective, it is the only way to manage a modern business.

Data entry is a likely first source of errors. If a name or number gets entered inaccurately, it gets stored in the file that way. A processing error or a miscalculation is another way for errors to creep into data. Sometimes the wrong fields or data find their way into a file.

By creating a separate file, the original data are maintained in the original file. That way, if there's a problem, the original data are still available.

Arrays and Structures – Organizing Data

VB Quip

[By the end of the 20th Century there will be a generation] to whom it will not be injurious to read a dozen quire of newspapers daily, to be constantly called to the telephone [and] to live half their time in a railway carriage or in a flying machine. – Max Nordau in 1895

So far you have seen how a sequence of steps lets you build a program that will do your bidding. You've seen how decision structures give the computer the ability to make decisions. You've learned how to get the computer to repeat instructions, giving it the ability to do the same task over and over. And, you've taught it how to read and write. Well, it can't read and write, but it can access and store data in a file. All of these give the computer the ability to access and process data at remarkable speed. But, you've been limited to only a handful of names and numbers – only what you could hold in your hand and keep track of in your head. You've been forced to discard one thing in order to grab the next. It's as if the world was a full-screen movie and you're stuck looking at stills in the family photo album. Enter arrays. With an array you can grab an armful of data and process it as you wish. Instead of stills on Grandma's porch, you've got a DVD on HD and control of the remote. You can run it forward, backward, and rewind and pause. With your data in arrays, you can manipulate it as you like. You can sort your data and search through it, find what you want, and pull it out to look at it. You'll learn new controls to display your data on the screen. And you'll learn how to create structures – think of them as boxes – to store your containers. Data runs the world and you're in control of the data.

Arrays – Order by the Numbers

An *array* is a series of related variables. All have the same name and all share the same data type. The only difference is their *index*, an integer that is unique to each item in the array. That's not much help, though. Think of an array as a shelf. The shelf has a name and each item on the shelf is numbered. Visualize

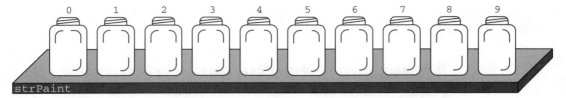

Figure 10.1   Paint Array

a shelf called Paint and each item is a can of paint, and each can is a different color. The shelf is in a hardware store that only employs gnomes: colorblind, illiterate gnomes. It wouldn't do any good to put the color or the name of the color on the paint cans. The only way to get the color you want is to go to the Paint shelf and get the number of the color of paint you want. The computer is much like that. It's illiterate and colorblind, but it can find the shelf and it does a great job with numbers. Just give the computer the name and its number and it will handle the rest (see Figure 10.1).

VB Tip   *Notice that the first item in the array is 0. Arrays are zero-based. They start at zero.*

An array is remarkably useful. It lets you use one name to control a long list of items. Each item in the list has a different number. That's great because computers are better at handling numbers than names. You can create an array with just one statement instead of using one statement for each individual item. Instead of a long list of items, each with a different name (like what you faced with individual variables for test scores), you have just one name and each item has its own number. All items in an array are the same, except for their number. Items in the array are stored in the computer's memory. It's much faster and easier to use them when they're sitting in memory than when they're stored in a file. With batch processing you only had control of one item in a list at a time. To get the next item, you had to discard the one you had. In an array it, and all similar items, are available all the time. Arrays and loops work well together. A loop lets you move through an array. You can get to any item just by moving through the loop.

The downside of an array is that all the items are stored in memory. The more items you have, the greater the burden. With batch processing, a million invoices can be processed with ease. You couldn't use an array to load that many items at once. There simply isn't enough memory to do that.

Creating an Array

An array must be declared, just like other storage locations. The data type for all items in an array must be the same. You can declare an array with a specific number of items or no items. You can populate the array when it's declared. Let's start simple. Here's an array for the cans of paint:

```
Dim strPaint(9) As String
```

This creates an array that can store 10 string items. Each item in the array is a string. For this example, they're the colors of paint. Right now there's nothing in any of the array items. The number in the parentheses must be an integer. That number is called a *subscript*. It's what differentiates each item in the array. By the way, these items are called *elements*. To put something into an array element, you need to assign it, just like any other variable. It could look something like this:

```
strPaint(0) = "Royal Blue"
```

Use an element in an array just like any other variable. For instance:

```
lblPaintColor.Text = strPaint(0)
```

puts Royal Blue into the lblPaintColor Label.

Here's the syntax for declaring an array:

```
Dim varName( ) As Type = {List}
```

Dim creates the array, varName is the name of the array, and Type is the data type. There is no integer placed in the parentheses. List is a comma-separated list of items for the array that lets you initialize the array when it's declared. Following are some examples.

```
Dim strQuartet(3) As String
```

declares an array of four items.

```
Dim strCheese( ) As String = {"Swiss", "Cheddar",
   "Mozzarella", "American", Parmesan"}
```

declares an array with five items and initializes each item in the array. They look like this:

```
Dim decChair( ) As Decimal = {29.95, 39.95, 89.95, 129.95}
```

The preceding code declares an array with an undetermined number of items. The number of items is then defined by the number of items initialized by the list. It's a little strange, but it works (see Figure 10.2).

```
Dim bytSize( ) As Byte
```

The preceding statement declares an array but doesn't determine the size. Later you'll find you need another statement to determine the size of the array. This is actually quite handy and you'll use it in several programs later in the chapter.

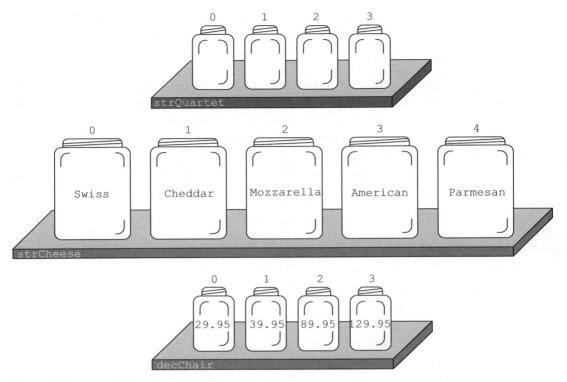

Figure 10.2   **String Array Examples**

VB Tip

The number of items in an array is one more than the number used when declaring the array. The first item has a subscript of 0; that's where the "extra" item comes from. Some simply ignore the first item in the array. It wastes space, but it does make it easier to keep track of the size and number of items in an array.

VB Quiz 01

How would you declare an array to store:
the names of the fifty states?
four test scores?
the balance due for customers of your website design business?
the points scored in a game for every player on the basketball team?

Using an Array

Let's declare a simple array and put it to use. The array will store the number of homes each realtor at a real estate agency has listed. Let's call the array shoPlace and set it up with space for five entries. From there each item in the array can be populated with an InputBox. Once all the data are entered, you can calculate the average and then display the numbers and the average. The best way to accomplish this is by using loops (see Figure 10.3).

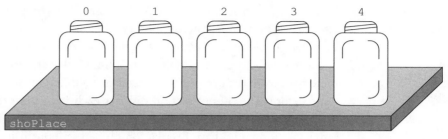

Figure 10.3   shoPlace Array Example

```
'Declarations
Dim shoPlace(4) As Short
Dim i As Short
Dim shoTotal As Short
Dim sngAverage As Single
'Input
For i = 0 To 4
    shoPlace(i) = InputBox("How many homes do you have
        listed?")
Next i

'Processing
For i = 0 To 4
    shoTotal = shoTotal + shoPlace(i)
Next i

sngAverage = shoTotal / i

'Output
rtbOut.Clear()
For i = 0 To 4
    rtbOut.AppendText(shoPlace(i).ToString & vbNewLine)
Next i

rtbOut.AppendText("Total: " & shoTotal.ToString & _
  vbNewLine)
rtbOut.AppendText("Average: " & sngAverage.ToString & _
  vbNewLine)
```

The first declaration sets up the array. It has 5 variables in it, numbered 0 to 4.
The other variables are used to control the loop and to store the total and the
average. The input section has a loop with an InputBox in it. You've seen this
before. The real difference this time is the array in this statement. Instead of
assigning it to a variable that would be reused with each iteration, it assigns each

input to its own place in the array. At this point, this is only a little twist on things you have already done. There's another loop for processing, which simply takes each item in the array and adds it to find the total. You've done accumulators inside a loop before. The difference this time is that the accumulator gets each increment from the array. Again, this is just a different way to do what you've done before. The output section displays each item from the array, then the total, and then the average. The array items are displayed using a loop. The same solution could have been accomplished without using an array, but, as presented, it gives a very simple introduction to arrays.

The same results could have been obtained without separate loops. It looks like this:

```
'Declarations
Dim shoPlace(4) As Short
Dim i As Short
Dim shoTotal As Short
Dim sngAverage As Single

rtbOut.Clear()

For i = 0 To 4
    'Input
    shoPlace(i) = InputBox("How many homes do you have
      listed?")

    'Processing
    shoTotal = shoTotal + shoPlace(i)

    'Output
    rtbOut.AppendText(shoPlace(i).ToString & vbNewLine)
Next i

'Output
sngAverage = shoTotal / i

rtbOut.AppendText("Total: " & shoTotal.ToString &
  vbNewLine)
rtbOut.AppendText("Average: " & sngAverage.ToString &
  vbNewLine)
```

This version eliminates two of the loops, although the processing does become a little harder to visualize. But even this version doesn't really need the array. To this point, the purpose has just been to show how an array could be used.

So, let's add a requirement to the program – something that makes an array useful. In addition to finding the average number of homes listed, let's find the input that's closest to the average. To do that all the entries must be retained and then compared to the average. The one closest to the average is the one we're looking for. The input stays the same, as does the processing code to find the average. At that point, the array must be processed in a loop so each item in the array can be compared to the average. The one closest to the average is the one to keep. It looks something like this:

```
'Declarations
Dim shoPlace(4) As Short
Dim i As Short
Dim shoTotal As Short
Dim sngAverage As Single
Dim sngDifference As Single = 1000000
Dim shoItem As Short

For i = 0 To 4
    'Input
    shoPlace(i) = InputBox("How many homes do you have
        listed?")

    'Processing
    shoTotal = shoTotal + shoPlace(i)
Next i

'Processing
sngAverage = shoTotal / i

For i = 0 To 4
    If sngDifference > Math.Abs(sngAverage - shoPlace(i)) Then
        sngDifference = Math.Abs(sngAverage - shoPlace(i))
        shoItem = i
    End If
Next i

'Output
rtbOut.Clear()

For i = 0 To 4
    rtbOut.AppendText(shoPlace(i).ToString & vbNewLine)
Next i

rtbOut.AppendText("Total: " & shoTotal.ToString & vbNewLine)
rtbOut.AppendText("Average: " & sngAverage.ToString("N2") &
    vbNewLine)
rtbOut.AppendText("Difference: " & _
    sngDifference.ToString("N2") & vbNewLine)
```

```
rtbOut.AppendText("Closest: " & _
    shoPlace(shoItem).ToString &  vbNewLine)
```

The only way to find this is to hang on to all the items so they can be compared to the average. With only five items, it could have been done without an array. It would have meant a little more code, but it's still possible. But as the number of items increases, the value of an array becomes apparent. Without an array, as the number of items increases, the list becomes increasingly difficult to process.

The first loop gets the input and adds to the total. Once this loop is completed, the average of all the items is found. Once the average is known, it is compared to each item in the array. That's what the second loop does. The If inside the loop compares the average to the absolute value of the average minus that item in the loop. When the stored difference is greater than the difference for that item, two things happen: the stored difference is replaced with the new difference and the number of the item is stored. That's because the new difference is smaller than the stored one, and, hence, all previous ones. It also stores the index of the array in shoItem. In the output, shoItem is used to display the number that was entered by the user. This illustrates a good point; the subscript of an array item is an integer and can be used to reference that item in the array.

Also notice that sngDifference was declared and initialized to a large number. If it hadn't been initialized to a large number, you wouldn't have been able to find the smallest difference. The same process was used in a Chapter 7 to find the smallest number in a group of numbers.

VB Quiz 02

Do a deskcheck for this code and then answer these questions. Use 12, 10, 7, 11, and 9 for your input.
What value is stored in shoPlace(i)?
What is the final value assigned to sngAverage?
What is the last value assigned to sngDifference?
What value is stored in shoItem?
What value gets displayed in the last line of the program?

Arrays and Loops – Hand in Hand

Arrays and loops go together like peas and carrots. Loops are great for getting the computer to repeat a process. Given the speed and accuracy of a computer and its ability to unflaggingly perform the same task, it only makes sense to take advantage of it. Arrays can store similar data in a way that takes advantage of a program's ability to loop. The index of an array is used by the loop to process data. That way, the number-handling power of the computer can be turned to its advantage. In addition, there are methods built into an array structure that makes it even easier for them to be processed by loops.

An array has several methods that make it easier to use them with loops. The *GetLowerBound* method contains the lowest index number of the array, usually zero. The *GetUpperBound* method contains the highest index number of the array, usually one less than the total number of items in the array. The *Length* method contains the number of items in the array, usually one more than GetUpperBound. Take a look at the following code to see how these methods work. It has an array of quiz scores stored in an array called bytScore. The loop displays the items, but, rather than using literals to start and end the loop, the upper and lower bounds of the array control the loop:

```
'Display quiz scores
Dim bytScore() As Byte = {12, 10, 16, 14, 8, 6, 9}
Dim i As Short
rtbOut.Clear()
For i = bytScore.GetLowerBound(0) To
    bytScore.GetUpperBound(0)
    rtbOut.AppendText(bytScore(i).ToString & vbNewLine)
Next i
rtbOut.AppendText("Total items: " & _
  bytScore.Length.ToString)
```

The array, bytScore, is declared without an array size in parentheses because the number of items in the array is determined by the number of items in the list at the end of the declaration. The list goes inside braces and each item is separated by a comma. The loop is controlled by i. It starts at the lower bound of the array (0) and continues to the upper bound (6) of the array. The last line of code displays the total number of items in the array by using the Length method. You'll need to put (0) at the end of the GetLowerBound and GetUpperBound methods. Visual Basic expects an argument for a parameter and won't work without it. However, you don't need that argument when using the Length method. The best part about using these methods is for when the array size becomes dynamic. If the size of the array changes, you won't have to modify the loop part of the code to keep the program working. As you'll soon see, this gives your programs power and flexibility.

VB Tip   *Open and run the QuizScores program to see how it works.*

Loading an Array From a File

As you learned in Chapter 9, data entry is cumbersome, and a good way to ease that burden is with file input. So, it makes sense that you should know how to populate an array with data from a file. There are several things that have to happen for this to work. You must have a file with the data you need. You must open the file, set up a loop to read the file, and close the file when you're done reading it. That much you've done before. To populate an array from a file, you must read the data from the file into the array and you must be able to resize the array as you go. If you're thinking ahead, you might consider substituting array variables for regular variables in the loop. That will work, but it's an incomplete solution. You must know how many items are in the file so you can create an array large enough to hold them, create the largest array possible to hold all the items regardless of how many items there are, or resize the array as you read in the data.

If you know exactly how many items are in the file, you could create an array that's the right size for storing them. That would work, but it wouldn't be flexible. If the size of the file changed, you'd need to rewrite your program. That's not a very good solution. You could create an array that would always be big enough to hold all the data from the file with room to spare, but that's a waste of memory and would be slow and inefficient. The third alternative is to create an array and resize it every time you need to add a record from the file. There are technical issues with this as well, but we won't worry about them. For now, it's the best way to go. You'll just need to know a little more about arrays to get this to work.

There are two commands to know if you need to resize an array. The first is the *ReDim* statement. It lets you resize an array. The command takes an existing array and resizes it. You can make it larger or smaller depending on your needs:

```
ReDim shoPlace(20)
```

The preceeding line takes the shoPlace array that you just worked on and resizes it to store 21 items. The general form for this is

```
ReDim varArray(n)
```

ReDim resizes an existing array. The existing array is named varArray, and (n) is the new size of the array.

The drawback of the ReDim command is that any data already stored in the array are lost. However, there is a way to resize the array and retain the data already in the array. It's the *Preserve* command. Any data already in an array when it is resized is preserved. So resize your array and keep what's already in it in use:

```
ReDim Preserve shoPlace(20)
```

This line takes the shoPlace array that you just worked on and resizes it to store 21 items. The data already in the array are retained and new array items are created. The general form for this is

```
ReDim Preserve varArray(n)
```

ReDim resizes an existing array, Preserve retains the data that are already in the array, varArray is the name of the existing array, and (n) is the new size of the array.

With these commands, you can now create an array to store data from a file. When it's time to read another item from the file into the array, you ReDim to hold one more item than you already have and Preserve the array so what's already in it isn't lost. When written properly, the array will always be large enough to hold the data from the file, yet it won't ever waste memory.

Let's take a data file and load it into arrays. The file contains a number of records. Each record has the first name, last name, and the number of cases of cookies they've sold for a fundraiser. The data are stored in Cookies.dat and look like this:

```
First     Last     Number
Matt      Innay    45
Harry     Kerry    25
Bill      Board    37
Cal       Orry     61
Al        Erggy    84
Jim       Naseum   54
Ella      Vator    156
```

Following is the code to create a simple program that would open the file, read the data into arrays, and then display the output. All of this could be done without using arrays. Later, real functionality can be added.

```
'Declarations
Dim strLast() As String
Dim strFirst() As String
Dim shoCase() As Short
Dim shoCount As Short
Dim strRead As String
Dim strField() As String
Dim srdReader As System.IO.StreamReader

'Clear RichTextBox
rtbOut.Clear()

'Open file
srdReader = IO.File.OpenText("Cookies.dat")

Do
    'Resize array and keep existing data
    ReDim Preserve strLast(shoCount)
    ReDim Preserve strFirst(shoCount)
    ReDim Preserve shoCase(shoCount)

    'Read record and parse it
    strRead = srdReader.ReadLine()
```

```
        strField = strRead.Split(",")
        strFirst(shoCount) = strField(0)
        strLast(shoCount) = strField(1)
        shoCase(shoCount) = strField(2)

        'Display output
        rtbOut.AppendText(strFirst(shoCount).ToString
            .PadRight(8) & _
          strLast(shoCount).ToString.PadRight(8) & _
          shoCase(shoCount).ToString.PadLeft(4) & vbNewLine)
        shoCount = shoCount + 1
Loop Until srdReader.Peek = -1

'Close file
srdReader.Close()
```

The file is opened in preprocessing. The processing loop resizes the arrays and preserves the data already in them. The next line is read from the file, parsed, and added to the arrays. It's then displayed in the RichTextBox. The value of using arrays is that the data are still in memory and more processing could be done with them.

VB Tip   *Open and run the Cookies program to see how it works.*

Test Scores Program

VB Quip   *A computer program does what you tell it to do, not what you want it to do. – Greer's Third Law*

Read File and Load Array

Now it's time to get some practical use out of arrays. Let's load data from a file into an array for processing. The file contains test scores for a class and is called Scores.dat. Each record is for one student and stores that student's scores for four tests during the semester. The structure of a record in this file looks like this:

```
ID, Test1, Test2, Test3, Test4
```

The first record looks like this:

```
5076,82,85,90,81
```

An example of what the form should look like is shown in Figure 10.4. It has a RichTextBox for the output, a Button to load the data from a file, a Button for each of the processes, and an Exit Button. The input comes from the file.

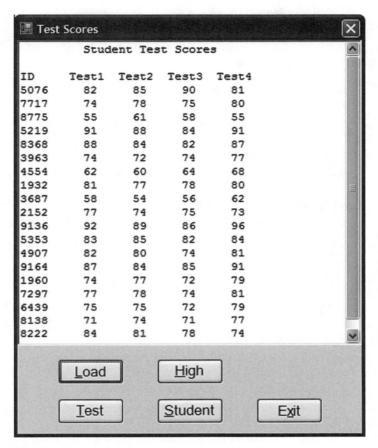

Figure 10.4   Test Scores Program

You want to load the data into arrays. From there, use the arrays to find the average score for each test, the high scorer for each test, and the average score for each student.

Use an array for each field from the file, one for the student ID, and one for each test. Those are the inputs for this program. Make them module-level variables so they can be used in any of the Buttons of the program. Use a counter to keep track of the number of records. It's needed to populate the arrays. It must be module-level as well. The total number of students doesn't matter because you'll simply read the file until all the students have been read. Once the data are loaded into the arrays, you'll be able to process them as you see fit.

The following is the code to declare the module-level variables:

```
Public Class frmTestScores
Dim mintCount As Integer
Dim mstrID() As String
Dim mshoTest1() As Short
Dim mshoTest2() As Short
```

```
Dim mshoTest3() As Short
Dim mshoTest4() As Short
```

And here's the code to load the arrays:

```
Private Sub btnLoad_Click( ...
'Declarations
Dim srdFile As System.IO.StreamReader
Dim strFields() As String
Dim strLine As String
Dim strDetail As String
'Input
ofdTestScores.ShowDialog()
srdFile = New System.IO.StreamReader(ofdTestScores
  .FileName)

rtbOut.Clear()
rtbOut.AppendText("    Student Test Scores" & _
  vbNewLine & vbNewLine)
rtbOut.AppendText("ID  Test1   Test2   Test3   Test4" & _
  vbNewLine)

Do While srdFile.Peek <> -1
    ReDim Preserve mstrID(mintCount)
    ReDim Preserve mshoTest1(mintCount)
    ReDim Preserve mshoTest2(mintCount)
    ReDim Preserve mshoTest3(mintCount)
    ReDim Preserve mshoTest4(mintCount)

    'Read
    strLine = srdFile.ReadLine()

    'Parse
    strFields = strLine.Split(",")
    mstrID(mintCount) = strFields(0)
    mshoTest1(mintCount) = (1)
    mshoTest2(mintCount) = (2)
    mshoTest3(mintCount) = (3)
    mshoTest4(mintCount) = (4)
    strDetail = mstrID(mintCount).PadRight(2) & _
    mshoTest1(mintCount).ToString("n0").PadLeft(7) & _
    mshoTest2(mintCount).ToString("n0").PadLeft(7) & _
    mshoTest3(mintCount).ToString("n0").PadLeft(7) & _
    mshoTest4(mintCount).ToString("n0").PadLeft(7) & _
        vbNewLine
    rtbOut.AppendText(strDetail)
    mintCount = mintCount + 1
```

```
Loop

'Close
srdFile.Close()
```

Find Test Averages

With the data loaded, the next step is to add code in the processing section to determine the average for each test, the high score for each test, and the average score for each student. Let's separate each of these three processes and solve them, one at a time. First, let's get the average score for each test.

More variables are needed for this solution. They belong in the Declarations section of the code for that Button. It takes one variable for the total scores and another for the average to do the calculations for a test. There are four tests, so you'll need these variables for each test. A loop is needed to process all of the items in the arrays. Inside the loop, add the score from each test to find the total of the scores for that test. Then, below the loop, divide that total by the number of students to find the average score for the test.

Here's the code to create the variables and to calculate the average score for the tests:

```
Dim i As Integer
Dim strDetail As String
Dim intTotalTest1 As Integer
Dim intTotalTest2 As Integer
Dim intTotalTest3 As Integer
Dim intTotalTest4 As Integer
Dim sngAverageTest1 As Single
Dim sngAverageTest2 As Single
Dim sngAverageTest3 As Single
Dim sngAverageTest4 As Single

'Process Records
For i = 0 To mintCount - 1
    intTotalTest1 = intTotalTest1 + mshoTest1(i)
    intTotalTest2 = intTotalTest2 + mshoTest2(i)
    intTotalTest3 = intTotalTest3 + mshoTest3(i)
    intTotalTest4 = intTotalTest4 + mshoTest4(i)
Next i

'Average
sngAverageTest1 = intTotalTest1 / mintCount
sngAverageTest2 = intTotalTest2 / mintCount
sngAverageTest3 = intTotalTest3 / mintCount
```

```
sngAverageTest4 = intTotalTest4 / mintCount
'Output
rtbOut.Clear()
rtbOut.AppendText("  Test1   Test2   Test3   Test4" & _
    vbNewLine)
strDetail = "Avg."    & sngAverageTest1.ToString("n1")
    .PadLeft(7) & _
sngAverageTest2.ToString("n1").PadLeft(7) & _
sngAverageTest3.ToString("n1").PadLeft(7) & _
sngAverageTest4.ToString("n1").PadLeft(7) & vbNewLine
rtbOut.AppendText(strDetail)
```

If the data were displayed in a spreadsheet or printed, it would be easy to look through the list of scores for the first test and add them to find the total. Simply divide this total by the number of scores to find the average. The process is almost automatic when the data are readily visible. With an array you must think of the data set as a list. In this case, it's a list of numbers and you need to add the numbers. Now think of where those numbers are stored. They're in an array and the score for each test is an element of that array. You must add each element of the array to the total. The first time through the loop it adds the 0th item of the array to the total. The next time through, it adds the 1th item. The next time it adds the 2th item, and so on, until the entire array is processed. It's very similar to the accumulators you've used previously. Here's the code that does the actual work:

```
'Process Records
For i = 0 To mintCount - 1
    intTotalTest1 = intTotalTest1 + mshoTest1(i)
Next i
```

If you substitute the values for each, it becomes even easier. The first time through the loop, i is 0, so substitute 0 for the subscript, as in Figure 10.5.

$$\text{intTotalTest1} = \text{intTotalTest1} + \text{mbytTest1}(\overset{0}{X})$$

Figure 10.5   **Index Variable Substitution on First Pass**

If you look at what's in that array variable, you'd see 82 and add that to the total. On the next trip through the loop, i is 1. So substitute that, as in Figure 10.6.

$$\text{intTotalTest1} = \text{intTotalTest1} + \text{mbytTest1}(\overset{1}{X})$$

Figure 10.6   **Index Variable Substitution on Second Pass**

If you look at what's in that array variable, you'd see 74, so add 74 to the total. The same process continues for the rest of the items in the array.

The next step is to do the same thing for the other three tests. If you're stumped about this, there are two routes to take. You could add more loops to your code.

They would be very similar to the loop for the first test, but each would find the total for a different test. That works, but it wastes resources. A better way to do this is to add the necessary code inside the existing loop. It's faster and more efficient to do this and, when you're done, it's elegant. Here are the declarations and the updated code showing the total scores and averages for each of the four tests. The total for each of the four tests is added as the loop is processed. Once the loop has completed, the average is calculated.

```
Dim i As Integer
Dim strDetail As String
Dim intTotalTest1 As Integer
Dim intTotalTest2 As Integer
Dim intTotalTest3 As Integer
Dim intTotalTest4 As Integer
Dim sngAverageTest1 As Single
Dim sngAverageTest2 As Single
Dim sngAverageTest3 As Single
Dim sngAverageTest4 As Single

'Process Records
For i = 0 To mintCount - 1
    intTotalTest1 = intTotalTest1 + mshoTest1(i)
    intTotalTest2 = intTotalTest2 + mshoTest2(i)
    intTotalTest3 = intTotalTest3 + mshoTest3(i)
    intTotalTest4 = intTotalTest4 + mshoTest4(i)
Next i

'Average
sngAverageTest1 = intTotalTest1 / mintCount
sngAverageTest2 = intTotalTest2 / mintCount
sngAverageTest3 = intTotalTest3 / mintCount
sngAverageTest4 = intTotalTest4 / mintCount
```

The next step would be to display the average for each test. Add this code to the output section of your code:

```
'Output
rtbOut.Clear()
rtbOut.AppendText("        Test1   Test2   Test3   Test4" & _
    vbNewLine)
strDetail = "Avg." &
  sngAverageTest1.ToString("n1").PadLeft(7) & _
  sngAverageTest2.ToString("n1").PadLeft(7) & _
  sngAverageTest3.ToString("n1").PadLeft(7) & _
  sngAverageTest4.ToString("n1").PadLeft(7) & vbNewLine
rtbOut.AppendText(strDetail)
```

Find High Scores

To find the high scorer for each test, look through the array and keep track of the ID of the person who had the high score and of the score itself. For that, variables are needed for ID and for high score. There must be a loop to go through the array, an If inside the loop to compare each score with the high score, and some lines of code for the output:

```
Dim strDetail As String
Dim i As Integer
Dim strHighScoreID As String
Dim bytHighScore As Byte
'Find High Score for First Test
For i = 0 To mintCount - 1
    If mshoTest1(i) > bytHighScore  Then
        bytHighScore  = mshoTest1(i)
        strHighScoreID  = mstrID(i)
    End If
Next i

'High Score Output
rtbOut.Clear()
strDetail = "Test 1 High Score: " & _
  strHighScoreID.PadRight(6) & _
  bytHighScore.ToString("n0").PadLeft(4) & vbNewLine
rtbOut.AppendText(strDetail)rtbOut.AppendText(strDetail)
```

Run through the logic and the code to find the high score for the first test. The loop looks at the test score for every student. If it's higher than any of the previous scores on that test, that score becomes the high score and updates the ID so you'll know who the student is. For now, don't worry about two students sharing the high-score honors. A similar process with nested If statements was used earlier to find the high score.

Do a deskcheck for the loop. When the score is greater than bytHighScore, you'll need to update the high score and the ID. The If inside the loop does the update. As the loop runs, it compares each item in the array to the high score. When needed, it updates the high score and student ID. Once the loop has been completed, you'll have the student ID and the score for the first test. From there, just display that output.

Now make a couple of changes to find the high score for each of the tests. The first step might be to create arrays to hold the ID and high score for all four tests:

```
Dim strHighScoreID(3) As String
Dim bytHighScore(3) As Byte
```

The current loop works just fine for finding all the high scores. It's capable of going through all the arrays at once so we can use that loop and some new If statements to find the other high scores:

```
For i = 0 To mintCount - 1
    If mshoTest1(i) > bytHighScore(0) Then
        bytHighScore(0) = mshoTest1(i)
        strHighScoreID(0) = mstrID(i)
    End If
    If mshoTest2(i) > bytHighScore(1) Then
        bytHighScore(1) = mshoTest2(i)
        strHighScoreID(1) = mstrID(i)
    End If
    If mshoTest3(i) > bytHighScore(2) Then
        bytHighScore(2) = mshoTest3(i)
        strHighScoreID(2) = mstrID(i)
    End If
    If mshoTest4(i) > bytHighScore(3) Then
        bytHighScore(3) = mshoTest4(i)
        strHighScoreID(3) = mstrID(i)
    End If
Next i
```

Each If in the loop searches one of the test score arrays and keeps track of the high score and the student's ID.

What's needed next are more output lines for the results:

```
'High Score Output
rtbOut.Clear()
strDetail = "Test 1 High Score: " & _
    strHighScoreID(0).PadRight(6) & _
bytHighScore(0).ToString("n0").PadLeft(4) & vbNewLine
rtbOut.AppendText(strDetail)
strDetail = "Test 2 High Score: " & _
    strHighScoreID(1).PadRight(6) & _
bytHighScore(1).ToString("n0").PadLeft(4) & vbNewLine
rtbOut.AppendText(strDetail)
strDetail = "Test 3 High Score: " & _
    strHighScoreID(2).PadRight(6) & _
bytHighScore(2).ToString("n0").PadLeft(4) & vbNewLine
rtbOut.AppendText(strDetail)
strDetail = "Test 4 High Score: " & _
    strHighScoreID(3).PadRight(6) & _
bytHighScore(3).ToString("n0").PadLeft(4) & vbNewLine
rtbOut.AppendText(strDetail)
```

This code clears the RichTextBox and then builds and displays a detail line for each test.

With time, it becomes easier to see the data and work with the code. With guidance, it's easier to see better ways to program. With practice, it's easier to see ways to make your code work harder for you. There are other ways to manipulate the scores, but that will come later.

Find Student Averages

The last task is to find the test average for each student. Although it may not be the case, let's assume every student took every test. What you need to do is to add up all the test scores for a student and then divide the total by four. Again, if you were looking at a table with the students and scores for each test, it would be easy to determine the total and calculate the average for each student. Think about where those data are stored and the names and subscripts for the arrays where they're stored. That's a big step toward understanding how to get to those data for processing. Once you know where to look, it will be much easier to program it. The trick is to get the computer to do the work for you.

Here are the data from the file:

```
5076,82,85,90,81
7717,74,78,75,80
8775,55,61,58,55
5219,91,88,84,91
8368,88,84,82,87
3963,74,72,74,77
4554,62,60,64,68
1932,81,77,78,80
3687,58,54,56,62
2152,77,74,75,73
9136,92,89,86,96
5353,83,85,82,84
4907,82,80,74,81
9164,87,84,85,91
1960,74,77,72,79
7297,77,78,74,81
6439,75,75,72,79
8138,71,74,71,77
8222,84,81,78,74
9508,68,64,62,67
```

When you look at the problem you'll see that you're adding the elements from four different arrays: Test 1, Test 2, Test 3, and Test 4. The data for the first student are stored in the array variables with subscripts of 0. For the second student, all of the subscripts are 1. For the third student, the subscript is 2, and so on for the rest of the students. To add the scores for the first student, the code would contain something like this:

```
shoStudTotal = mshoTest1(0) + mshoTest2(0) +
    mshoTest3(0) + mshoTest4(0)
```

For the second student, the code would be something like this:

```
shoStudTotal = mshoTest1(1) + mshoTest2(1) +
    mshoTest3(1) + mshoTest4(1)
```

You can see that the subscript increments for each student. That means a loop will work well for this, if it's set up properly.

Now, where should the totals and average for each of students be stored? You could create an array for total and store the totals in the appropriate element of the array. An array for the average would work as well. These would be useful if you needed to get to the totals and averages again. For this program, the totals and averages are only needed for a short time, so an array really isn't necessary. Instead, just use a single variable over and over again. If those numbers were needed to do more processing later, then an array might be more appropriate.

To determine the average, a line of code is needed to divide the total by the number of tests. In this case, there are four tests, so the code would look like this:

```
sngStudAverage = shoStudTotal / 4
```

The average, like the total, can be one variable that's used over and over. The only limitation on using one variable each for the total and the average is that you must do your output before you start processing the next student. That's just a matter of putting the output lines of code inside the loop and is similar to the batch processing from Chapter 9.

Once again, use a loop to go through all the elements of the arrays. For each student, add the scores for their four tests, calculate the average, and display the output. Here's the code for it:

```
Dim strDetail As String
Dim i As Integer
Dim shoStudTotal As Short
Dim sngStudAverage As Single
rtbOut.Clear()
rtbOut.AppendText("Student  Average" & vbNewLine)
For i = 0 To mintCount - 1
    shoStudTotal = mshoTest1(i) + mshoTest2(i) +
        mshoTest3(i) + mshoTest4(i)
```

```
      sngStudAverage = shoStudTotal / 4
      strDetail = mstrID(i).PadRight(10) & _
        sngStudAverage.ToString("n1").PadLeft(6) & vbNewLine
      rtbOut.AppendText(strDetail)
Next i
```

Each trip through the loop processes another student. One line of code adds their scores, the next line calculates the average, and the last two display the results.

VB Tip   *Open and run the TestScores program to see how it works.*

Recap

If the data hadn't been in arrays, you would have had to open the file multiple times to pull out the data you needed. That would have been very slow. You would have had to write more code and the code would have been more complicated. The use of arrays in this instance made your calculations easier and faster.

Potential Problems

There are many potential problems. One of the keys is to get your data into your arrays. Your best bet is to write the code to read the file and then display it. Even if your specifications don't call for displaying it, it's still a good idea to load the data and test it. Read the data from the file into your arrays. Write some code that will display the data in a RichTextBox and then check it. That way you're sure to have the data in the arrays. If not, you might spend considerable time later on trying to solve a problem that was caused by misloaded data.

Make sure you understand the structure of your data. There are times you might confuse the records and fields of your data. If that happens, you won't be able to get your program to work properly.

When working with arrays, there's always the potential for losing data. Odds are that you'll probably drop the data at the end of the array. It's also possible to overwrite the values in your array. Or you might end up with empty variables, which means you probably didn't get any data added to the arrays. You might end up with all the elements containing the same data, which means you probably miscoded the assignment statements. You might have forgotten to ReDim your arrays, in which case the arrays won't be large enough. You might have forgotten to Preserve your data, in which case the elements will have 0 (or null for strings) in them and only the last element will have valid data.

That's why it's always a good idea to test your program to make sure your arrays are loaded. Once you know you have the correct data in your arrays, you can delete the testing part of the code.

VB Quiz 03

Why were module-level variables used for the arrays?

How many students are there?

How many total variables were needed to hold the data from the file?

How would you calculate the average score for all students on all tests?

Searching an Array

Searches are a useful and very powerful advantage of computers. Searches let you find information with a search engine like Yahoo® or Google®, find classes when it's time to register for the upcoming semester, find items at your favorite online store, look up a phone number or email address, and even check the spelling in a word processing document. After all, what good is all that data if you can't find what you want?

That's where searches come in. In its simplest form, a search starts with the first item in a list and compares it with the search item. If there's no match, it moves on to the next item. If there's no match, it moves on to the next, and the next, and the next, until it finds a match or it gets to the end of the list. Once you find a match, you display the data associated with it. For example, people seldom "look up" a phone number. Instead they look up a name and then get the phone number associated with the name. That's what we're out to do with a search, use the data we have to locate the information we want.

Linear Search

A *linear search* starts with the first item in the list and continues, one at a time, through the entire list. It's like starting at the beginning of the phone book and looking through each item one at a time. OK, that sounds boring, but remember, computers never get bored.

In this example, there are two arrays. One contains the names of the states. The other has the corresponding state capital. The objective is to look through the state names to find a match and then return the state and the capital for that state. Here are the declarations for the arrays:

```
Dim strState() As String = {"Alabama", "Alaska",
"Arizona", "Arkansas", "California", "Colorado",
"Connecticut", "Delaware", "Florida", "Georgia",
"Hawaii", "Idaho", "Illinois", "Indiana", "Iowa",
"Kansas", "Kentucky", "Louisiana", "Maine", "Maryland",
"Massachusetts", "Michigan", "Minnesota", "Mississippi",
"Missouri", "Montana", "Nebraska", "Nevada",
```

```
"New Hampshire", "New Jersey", "New Mexico", "New York",
"North Carolina", "North Dakota", "Ohio", "Oklahoma",
"Oregon", "Pennsylvania", "Rhode Island",
"South Carolina", "South Dakota", "Tennessee", "Texas",
"Utah", "Vermont", "Virginia", "Washington",
"West Virginia", "Wisconsin", "Wyoming"}

Dim strCapital() As String = {"Montgomery", "Juneau",
"Phoenix", "Little Rock", "Sacramento", "Denver",
"Hartford", "Dover", "Tallahassee", "Atlanta",
"Honolulu", "Boise", "Springfield", "Indianapolis",
"Des Moines", "Topeka", "Frankfort", "Baton Rouge",
"Augusta", "Annapolis", "Boston", "Lansing",
"St. Paul", "Jackson", "Jefferson City", "Helena",
"Lincoln", "Carson City", "Concord", "Trenton",
"Santa Fe", "Albany", "Raleigh", "Bismarck",
"Columbus", "Oklahoma City", "Salem", "Harrisburg",
"Providence", "Columbia", "Pierre", "Nashville", "Austin",
"Salt Lake City", "Montpellier", "Richmond", "Olympia",
"Charleston", "Madison", "Cheyenne"}
```

Depending on how the interface is designed, there are many ways the user could do a search. For this example, it will be simple, the user just types the name of the state into a TextBox and then clicks on the Search Button(see Figure 10.7). The algorithm searches through the elements of the first array and, on a match,

Figure 10.7   States and Capitals Program

returns the corresponding element from the other array and displays both in a RichTextBox. The following is the code for it. Do a deskcheck on it. Try it with matching items and with an item that doesn't match.

```
'Declarations
Dim strState() As String = {"Alabama", ...
Dim strCapital() As String = {"Montgomery", ...
Dim strSearch As String
Dim i As Integer

'Input
strSearch = txtSearch.Text

'Processing
rtbOut.Clear()
rtbOut.AppendText("State".PadRight(15) & "Capital" & _
   vbNewLine)

For i = strState.GetLowerBound(0) To
   strState.GetUpperBound(0)
     If strSearch = strState(i) Then
         'Output
         rtbOut.AppendText(strState(i).PadRight(15) & _
           strCapital(i).PadRight(15) & vbNewLine)
     End If

Next i
```

The code isn't very efficient. There must be a perfect match before it returns a *hit*. Although the items in the list are in alphabetical order, the code isn't written to take advantage of that. We can make it a little easier by converting the search string and the comparisons to upper case and then comparing them. Simply substitute the following code for the corresponding line in the previous example:

```
If strSearch.ToUpper = strState(i).ToUpper Then
```

The code starts at the beginning and checks each record in order. It keeps searching, even after a match is found. It's like looking for your car keys even after you found them. We can help it a little by adding:

```
Exit For
```

at the end of the If statement inside the loop. Once a match is found and displayed, it ends the loop. At least that stops the loop once there's a hit. However, the loop is still inefficient because it's a linear search. It's like looking up phone numbers by always starting with the first name in the phonebook!

VB Tip   *Open and run the SearchStatesAndCapitals program to see how it works.*

Binary Search

A better way to search an ordered list is to use a *binary search*. A binary search is similar to how you might guess a number from 1 to 100. You wrote a program for that in Chapter 5. The idea is to eliminate half of the remaining numbers with every search. Each search gets you closer to the number you want by eliminating half of the unsearched numbers. In a small list, this isn't very efficient, but in a larger list, it's extremely powerful and a great way to quickly narrow the search to find the item you want. For example, let's say the number to guess is 22. Your first guess would be 50. That eliminates half of the numbers. The computer tells you to guess a number that's higher or lower. In this case the number should be lower. You'd then guess 25 because it's the midpoint of the numbers that haven't been guessed. Again, the computer compares and tells you to guess lower. Your new midpoint would be 12, halfway between 1 and 25. This time the computer makes the comparison and tells you to guess higher. You'd then know the number is between 12 and 25. Again you cut the remaining list in half, this time with a guess of 18. The computer compares that and tells you to guess higher. So you cut out half again by guessing the midpoint, this time by guessing 21. The computer compares and tells you to guess higher. The correct number is now between 21 and 25. You cut the difference in half with a guess of 23. The computer tells you to guess lower. The only thing left is 22, the correct answer.

In just seven guesses, you got the correct number. If you had tried a linear search, it would have taken 22 comparisons to find it, and it would have taken many more if the number was higher. As long as you have a list that's in order by your search field, a binary search is going to work better. It might not be better for every search, but in the long run, it will be faster for most searches. And in a large list with thousands or millions of records, the advantages are obvious. Of course, if your list isn't in order by the field you're searching, a binary search won't work.

When you use a binary search to play the guessing game, you know how many items are in the search. You quickly did the math in your head to eliminate half of the list with every guess. For a binary search algorithm, make the computer do that math. It must keep track of the low end and the high end of the list. From there, find the middle and guess. If it's a hit, you're done. If not, determine whether the next guess should be above or below that mark. Reset the lower and upper limits accordingly and guess again.

VB Tip

Open and run the Binary Search program to see how it works.

Here's the code to do a binary search of the states to find the corresponding capital:

```
'Declarations
Dim strState() As String = {"Alabama", "Alaska", ...
```

```
Dim strCapital() As String = {"Montgomery", "Juneau, ...
Dim strDetail As String = "Not Found"
Dim strSearch As String
Dim intLow As Integer
Dim intMiddle As Integer
Dim intHigh As Integer = strState.GetUpperBound(0)
Dim blnDone As Boolean

'Input
strSearch = txtSearch.Text

'Processing
rtbOut.Clear()

rtbOut.AppendText("State".PadRight(15) & "Capital" & _
   vbNewLine)

Do While intLow <= intHigh And Not blnDone
    intMiddle = (intLow + intHigh) \ 2
    If strSearch.ToUpper = strState(intMiddle).ToUpper Then
        strDetail = strState(intMiddle).PadRight(15) & _
          strCapital(intMiddle).PadRight(15) & vbNewLine
        blnDone = True
    Else
        If strSearch.ToUpper < strState(intMiddle).ToUpper
          Then
            intHigh = intMiddle - 1
        Else
            intLow = intMiddle + 1
        End If
End If
Loop
'Output
rtbOut.AppendText(strDetail)
```

The variables intLow and intHigh are set to the extremes for the array. You
enter the loop and set the middle by adding intLow and intHigh together and
dividing by 2. It takes the integer part of the quotient. It then compares the
search string to the item in that element of the array. If the item stored there is
not equal to the search item, it then checks to see if the item is greater than or
smaller than the search item. If it's greater than the search item, then intLow is
assigned intMiddle + 1, which is now the lowest possible match that's left. If it is
less than the search item, then intHigh is assigned intMiddle − 1, which is now
the upper end of the search. The loop continues as long as intLow <= intHigh

or blnDone is False. Of course, if the search string matches intMiddle, blnDone is set to True and a match is reported.

The variable strDetail is assigned "Not Found" at design time. If the entire array is searched without success, that's what is reported. If there is a match, then the matching state and its capital are displayed.

Sometimes a partial match is close enough – it's easier than trying to get an exact match. Your search might return multiple items, and that's often a plus, especially if you're not sure what you're searching for. In this example, we'll search the whole list so that all partial matches can be found. Let's modify the states and capitals search to handle partial matches. Change the code so that it finds all matches for partial names. Set it up so that when the user types in a letter or a few letters, it searches with those letters and returns all the matches. If the user typed in Mi, it would find Michigan, Minnesota, Mississippi, Missouri, and their respective capitals. All this takes is a couple of minor changes. Determine the number of characters in the user's search and compare that many characters. In the example, the user typed in "Mi", so the comparison would be made to the first two characters of the state name. Any match that's found is added to the list. Here's what it looks like:

```
'Declarations
Dim strState() As String = {"Alabama", "Alaska",...
Dim strCapital() As String = {"Montgomery", "Juneau",...
Dim strSearch As String
Dim strPartial As String
Dim i As Integer

'Input
strSearch = txtSearch.Text

'Processing
rtbOut.Clear()
rtbOut.AppendText("State".PadRight(15) & "Capital" & _
  vbNewLine)

For i = strState.GetLowerBound(0) To
    strState.GetUpperBound(0) strPartial =
    strState(i).Substring(0, strSearch.Length)
    If strSearch.ToUpper = strState(i).ToUpper Then
        'Output
        rtbOut.AppendText(strState(i).PadRight(15) & _
        strCapital(i).PadRight(15) & vbNewLine)
    End If
Next i
```

The code searches through the loop and compares the items in the array. strSearch.Length determines the number of letters the user has typed, which is how many letters are pulled out and stored in strPartial. The next line then compares the strSearch to strPartial. When there's a match, that state and capital are displayed.

VB Tip   *Most search routines are much more complicated than these examples. They can search with wildcards, they are optimized to be as fast as possible, and they can return a specified number of hits, all of which is designed to put information at your fingertips.*

Sorting an Array

An array can be used to put your data in order. There are many different algorithms for sorting data. Some are relatively easy to write and use, but they aren't very efficient. Others are harder to write, but are much faster. Some sort routines work well with unsorted data while others are better with partially sorted data. The first sort routine that most developers learn is a *bubble sort*. It gets its name from the way data "bubbles" into sorted order. The bubble sort combines arrays, loops, file I/O, and If statements, most of what you've studied so far. Conceptually, it's the most complicated bit of programming you've tackled so far, but, it's also some of the most fun.

Bubble Sort

Let's say you had a group of items to sort – your CDs in a rack, for example. You probably wouldn't have a pattern for sorting them. You could have a couple in your hands and rearrange the ones in the rack as needed to get them sorted. You might pull several out and put them on the floor until they're needed and you might drop some of them near their correct location (like putting your ZZ Top near the bottom) so they'd be handy when you were ready to put them in order. You'd get them sorted, but it might not be the most efficient method and it's very likely you wouldn't have an algorithm for it. That's very different on the computer. You need a plan for sorting them. The plan must work, in other words, when it's finished, it must have all the CDs in the correct order. And, although not required, it certainly would be nice if the plan was efficient.

For the bubble sort algorithm, you'll go through the entire list and compare one item to the next item in the list. When these two items aren't in order, you'll swap them. You'll move on to the second and third in the list, compare them and swap if needed. From there, you'd compare the third and fourth items, swapping them if needed. Continue this pattern until you get to the last two items in the list. That will get the last item in the right place, in this case, your ZZ Top CD.

The next step is to repeat this process. Compare the first two and swap them if needed. Move on to the next item in the list, compare and swap if needed. Continue until you get to the end of the list. The next item will now be in order. This process continues until the entire list is sorted.

How many comparisons are needed and how many times do you need to go through the list? The number of comparisons is one less than the number of items in the array. The number of times you'll need to go through the array to ensure all the items are sorted is one less than the number of items in the array.

VB Tip   *The number of comparisons is always one less than the number of items in your list.*

Let's take a simple array and put it in order:

```
Dim strColor() As String = {"Violet","Indigo","Blue"
    "Green","Yellow","Orange","Red"}
```

The goal is to put the items in this array in alphabetical order. The first step is to get one item in order. To do that you'll need to compare the first item in the list to the next item in the list. If these two aren't in order, you'll switch them. You'll then compare the second item to the third item and switch them if needed. Continue comparing one item to the next in the list until you get to the second-to-the-last item in the array. That one is compared to the last item in the list. In the strColor array you have seven items. You'll compare the first to the second, the second to the third, the third to the fourth, the fourth to the fifth, the fifth to the sixth, and the sixth to the last. That's six comparisons, one less than the total number of items in the array, which is an important point to remember.

Use a loop. Compare the nth item to the nth + 1 item. strColor(0) is compared to strColor(1). If needed, the two items are switched. That is, the data stored in the array variables are switched. You cannot switch the array variables themselves, just the data that are in them. You'll then compare strColor(1) to strColor(2). Switch them if needed. It continues until the last two items in the array are compared. The code looks like this:

```
For j = strColor.GetLowerBound(0) To
    strColor.GetUpperBound(0) - 1
    If strColor(j) > strColor(j + 1) Then
        strSwap = strColor(j)
        strColor(j) = strColor(j + 1)
        strColor(j + 1) = strSwap
    End If
Next j
```

To swap the two array items, you must have a third variable to temporarily hold the data during the swap. To swap strings it can be called strSwap. Take the first array item and put it in strSwap. Take the second array item and put it the first. Take the strSwap item and put it in the second array item (see Figure 10.8).

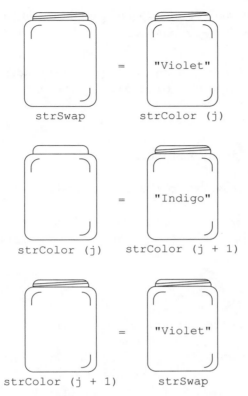

strSwap   strColor (j)

strColor (j)   strColor (j + 1)

strColor (j + 1)   strSwap

Figure 10.8   Color Array Swap Example

Substitute the correct numbers for the GetLowerBound and GetUpperBound methods. For this example it's 0 and 6. There's also a little math involved in the limit of the loop. It says to subtract 1 from the GetUpperBound so the loop runs from 0 to 5. That means it goes through this loop six times. That's one less than the total number of items in the array, just as it should be.

The If compares an item to the next item in the array. In this example, it compares strColor(j) to strColor(j + 1). The first time through the loop, j is 0 so it compares strColor(0) to strColor(1). If needed, the two items are swapped. The next time through the loop, j is 1 so it compares strColor(1) to strColor(2). If needed, the items are swapped and the loop continues. The last time through the loop, j is 5 so it compares strColor(5) to strColor(6) and swaps them if needed. At this point, Yellow is the last item in the strColor array.

Once you've completed this loop, the last array item will contain Yellow, which is the last color in the list alphabetically.

To get the next item to bubble through the list, you'll need to repeat the process. Once the entire loop has run again, the next item in the list will be in sorted order. You'll need to continue this until all items are sorted. There are seven items in the list, so you'll have to run through the entire loop process six times. To do that, you'll need another loop on the outside. The following is the bubble sort code for the strColor array:

```
Dim strColor() As String = {"Violet", "Indigo", "Blue",
   "Green", "Yellow", "Orange", "Red"}
Dim i, j As Integer
Dim strSwap As String

'Clear and display original content
rtbOut.Clear()
rtbOut.AppendText("Unsorted: " & vbNewLine)

For i = strColor.GetLowerBound(0) To strColor.GetUpperBound(0)
    rtbOut.AppendText(strColor(i) & vbNewLine)
Next i

For i = strColor.GetLowerBound(0)
  To strColor.GetUpperBound(0) - 1
    For j = strColor.GetLowerBound(0)
      To strColor.GetUpperBound(0) - 1
        If strColor(j) > strColor(j + 1) Then
            strSwap = strColor(j)
            strColor(j) = strColor(j + 1)
            strColor(j + 1) = strSwap
        End If
    Next j
Next i

'Display sorted content
rtbOut.AppendText(vbNewLine & "Sorted: " & vbNewLine)

For i = strColor.GetLowerBound(0)
  To strColor.GetUpperBound(0)
    rtbOut.AppendText(strColor(i) & vbNewLine)
Next i
```

Run a deskcheck on this to make sure the items get sorted.

VB Quiz 04

How many times does the i loop run?

How many times does the j loop run?

How many comparisons were made?

What is the correct order of the items in the array after it's been through the j loop once?

This program sorts a CD collection by artist. The file has a list of CDs along with the title and genre. Load the data from the file into arrays, one for the artist, one for the album, and one for the genre. Once they're in the arrays, sort them by artist and then display them on the screen.

The file is called CDSort.dat and has the following structure:
Artist, Album, Genre

```
"Moody Blues", "Days of Future Past", "Classic Rock"
"Newton-John, Olivia", "Have You Never Been Mellow", "Pop"
"Hill, Faith", "Fireflies", "Country"
"Coldplay", "X & Y", "Rock" "U2", "How to
   Dismantle an Atomic Bomb","Rock"
"Crow, Sheryl", "C'mon C'mon", "Rock"
"Clarkson, Kelly", "Breakaway", "Rock"
"Paisley, Brad", "Time Well Wasted", "Country"
"Beatles", "Help!", "Classic Rock"
"Ace of Base", "Cruel Summer", "Pop"
"Black Eyed Peas", "Monkey Business", "Rock"
"Gorillaz", "Demon Days", "Rap"
"Backyardigans", "The Backyardigans", "Childrens"
"Yearwood, Trisha", "Jasper County", "Country"
"311", "Don't Tread on Me", "Rock"
"Jones, Nora", "Come Away with Me", "Pop"
"Keith, Toby", "Honkytonk  University", "Country"
"Dylan, Bob", "No Direction Home", "Rock"
"Springsteen, Bruce", "Devils & Dust", "Rock"
"Rolling Stones", "Forty Licks", "Classic Rock"
"Queen", "A Night at the Opera", "Classic Rock"
"Abba", "Voulez-Vous", "Pop"
"Partridge Family", "Come on Get Happy!", "Pop"
"Cowsills", "The Rain, the Park & Other Things", "Pop"
```

Here's the code for it to load the arrays from the file:

```
'Open File
ofdCDSort.ShowDialog()
srdFile = New System.IO.StreamReader(ofdCDSort.FileName)

Do While srdFile.Peek <> -1

    'Parse
    ReDim Preserve strArtist(intCount)
    ReDim Preserve strAlbum(intCount)
    ReDim Preserve strGenre(intCount)
```

```
    'Read
    strLine = srdFile.ReadLine()
    strField = strLine.Split(",")
    strArtist(intCount) = strField(0)
    strAlbum(intCount) = strField(1)
    strGenre(intCount) = strField(2)
    intCount = intCount + 1
Loop

'Close
srdFile.Close()
```

Once the arrays are loaded, it's time to sort. Use two loops, just like in the example. There's an If statement inside the inner loop that compares one artist to the next. If needed, you'll swap them. That code is similar to the earlier example. When the artists are swapped, the album and the genre must be swapped as well. It takes three lines of code for each of them. Here's what the sort code looks like:

```
intCount = 1
For i = strArtist.GetLowerBound(0) To
  strArtist.GetUpperBound(0) - 1
    For j = strArtist.GetLowerBound(0) To
      strArtist.GetUpperBound(0) - 1
        If strArtist(j) > strArtist(j + 1) Then
            strSwap = strArtist(j)
            strArtist(j) = strArtist(j + 1)
            strArtist(j + 1) = strSwap
            strSwap = strAlbum(j)
            strAlbum(j) = strAlbum(j + 1)
            strAlbum(j + 1) = strSwap
            strSwap = strGenre(j)
            strGenre(j) = strGenre(j + 1)
            strGenre(j + 1) = strSwap
        End If
    Next j

    intCount += 1
    lblCount.Text = intCount.ToString
    lblCount.Refresh()

Next i
```

The variable intCount is used in the sort routine to count the number of records that have been sorted. The count gets displayed at the bottom of the outer loop. However, it sorts so quickly that the Label never gets a chance to update. That's where the *Refresh* method comes in handy. It forces the Label to refresh each time. If your computer is slow enough, you can see it increment. Refresh is very handy when working with loops that take a long time to process. It keeps the user informed.

Finally, a loop is needed to display the sorted records in a RichTextBox. Here's what that looks like:

```
'Output
For i = 0 To strArtist.GetUpperBound(0)
    strDetail = strArtist(i).PadRight(20) & _
    strAlbum(i).PadRight(33) & strGenre(i).PadRight(18)
    rtbOut.AppendText(strDetail & vbNewLine)
Next i
```

VB Tip:
ASCII Order

Computer sorts are done in ASCII order. See Appendix A for the ASCII chart. Greater than and less than comparisons are made according to that order. So, all the upper case letters come before any of the lower case letters. That might make a difference on a sort. In a sorted list of authors, e e cummings would end up near the end of the list, after all of the authors who use upper case letters to start their last name. Numbers come before any letters, so they show up first in an ascending sort.

One More Step

You can make the bubble sort faster and more efficient by tweaking the code. Once you've been through the array for the first time, you know the last item in the array contains what is alphabetically the last item in the list. The next time through the list, there's no reason to compare the last two items. Each successive trip through the array gets one more item to the end of the list. That means the inner loop can get shorter each time it's used. To do that, you need to change the limit for that loop. The first time it's used it runs through one time less than the total number of items in the array. The next time it runs through two times less than the total number of items in the array and so on. To get this to work, you need to subtract an ever-increasing number of iterations from the inner loop. The outer loop increases with each iteration, so it's easy to add a reference to the loop controller (i) to the limit for the inner loop. The first time through i is 0 and has no effect on the loop. The next time i is 1 so you subtract 1 from the limit for the inner loop. The next time it's 2 so you subtract 2 from the limit for the inner loop. Substitute this line in your code and your bubble sort will run even faster:

```
For j = strColor.GetLowerBound(0) To
  strColor.GetUpperBound(0) - i - 1
```

VB Tip

Open and run the CDSort program to see how it works.

Reverse Order

The code you have works well for alphabetical order, but what if you want reverse order? What if you're sorting numbers instead of strings and you want descending order? The solution is quite simple, you merely need to switch the sign in the If statement. Instead of the greater than sign (>) for alphabetical order, use the less than sign (<) for reverse order.

VB Tip: Sort Order

Use the greater than sign (>) for sorting in ascending and alphabetical order. Use the less than sign (<) for descending and reverse alphabetical order.

If you merely wanted to display the items in reverse order without changing the way they are arranged in the array, you could run the loop backward. Instead of starting with 0, start the loop at the upper limit and end it at 0:

```
For i = strColor.GetUpperBound(0) To 0 Step -1
```

This is the setup to display the strColor array in reverse order.

There's also a Reverse method built into arrays. When called, it simply reverses the order of the items in the array. For the strColor array, the code looks like this:

```
Array.Reverse(strColor)
```

The general form for the reverse method looks like this:

```
Array.Reverse(arrayName)
```

Array.Reverse is required and arrayName is the name of the array. So an array could be sorted in ascending order and quickly and easily reversed with this command. The elements in the array are reversed in memory.

```
Array.Sort(arrayName)
```

The Sort method for an array orders all the items in an array. It only works for a single-dimensional array. If there is another array with parallel data in it, then the two arrays can get out of sync. It sorts in alphabetical order. If you wanted your data in reverse order, then simply sort it using Array.Sort and then reverse the order using Array.Reverse.

Copying an Array

It's a simple matter to assign the value of a variable to another variable. You just use a simple line of code – something like this:

```
shoNewNum = shoNum
```

It takes the value of shoNum and assigns it to shoNewNum. The advantage is that you can manipulate shoNewNum as needed and not change the value of shoNum. The same thing can be done with an array, make a copy of it so you can manipulate the copy without changing the values in the original. The added advantage is that you can change the order of the values in the copied array without changing the original. There's just one line of code to copy an array. It looks like this:

```
Array.Copy(shoArray, shoNewArray, shoArray.Length)
```

The Copy method of the Array object (and arrays are objects, but don't worry about that for now) is used to take the existing array, shoArray, and create a new array, shoNewArray. shoArray.Length is the length of the array. You use that to copy all or part of an array. The syntax looks like this:

```
Array.Copy(array, newArray, length)
```

where array is the existing array, newArray is the new array, and length is the length of the new array. Arrays can eat up big chunks of memory so be careful when copying an array.

Potential Problems

There are many potential problems with sorting. Be sure all of the data are in arrays and that you understand the structure of the data. Bubble sorts used nested loops. The outer loop runs one time less than the total number of items in the array. The inner loop can be the same, but it can also be set up to make progressively shorter runs as it goes. Pay close attention to what is being swapped. Many times carelessness in the swap will corrupt the data and be sure to swap all related array items when needed.

VB Quiz 05

When you optimized the bubble sort, how many comparisons were made to sort the CDs?

What would you need to change to sort the CDs by album instead of artist?

What would happen if two CDs within the array had the same artist?

What would you need to do to sort them by title within the artist?

Selection Sort

The *selection sort* is a much faster sort than a bubble sort. Its logic is relatively easy to grasp as well. While the bubble sort makes comparisons and switches every time items are out of order, the selection sort makes comparisons, but only switches once per loop. That switch exchanges the item that's out of order with the item that belongs in that place in the list. Take a stack of DVDs. They are unordered and you want them in order by title. Figure 10.9 shows what they look like at the start.

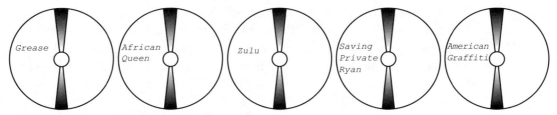

Figure 10.9   DVD Collection

In a selection sort, the first item is compared to the second item. If they are in order, move on to the next item. Then compare the first item to the third item. If they are in order, move on. This continues until you find an item that's not in order. When that happens, mark that item and remember its number. Continue through the list comparing the new item to the next item in the list. When you find one that's not in order, you mark that item and use it for comparison with the next item in the list. The process – compare the items, and when they're not in order, remember that item and use it for the next comparison – continues until you get to the end of the list. Once you've been through the whole list, you'd know what item should come first in the list and you'd swap the first item with that item.

You then start over, this time starting with the second item in the list. You'd continue to compare the items and mark them when they're not in order. At the end of the second pass, you'd know which item should be second in the list. At that point, you'd swap the items. You'd need to continue this looping process until all the items are in order. For a selection sort, that means repeating this process one time less than the number of items in your array.

Let's suppose you have a few DVDs that you want to place in order. Here's the list. Follow the algorithm to place them in order:

Grease African Queen Zulu   Saving Private Ryan   American Graffiti
First pass
Start with first item
Compare Grease to African Queen, remember African Queen
Compare African Queen to Zulu, do nothing
Compare African Queen to Saving Private Ryan, do nothing
Compare African Queen to American Graffiti, do nothing
Swap Grease with African Queen
New order after first pass
African Queen Grease Zulu   Saving Private Ryan   American Graffiti
Second pass
Start with second item
Compare Grease to Zulu, do nothing
Compare Grease to Saving Private Ryan, do nothing

Compare Grease to American Graffiti, remember American Graffiti
Swap Grease with American Graffiti
New order after second pass
African Queen American Graffiti   Grease Zulu   Saving Private Ryan
Third pass
Start with third item
Compare Grease to Zulu, do nothing
Compare Grease to Saving Private Ryan, do nothing
No swaps needed
Fourth pass
Start with fourth item
Compare Zulu to Saving Private Ryan, remember Saving Private Ryan
Swap Zulu with Saving Private Ryan
Sort complete

The following is the code for a selection sort. Do a deskcheck to make sure you understand the algorithm.

```
'Declarations
Dim strDVD() As String = {"Grease", "African Queen",
  "Zulu", "Saving Private Ryan", "American Graffiti"}
Dim i, j As Integer
Dim intMin As Integer
Dim strTemp As String

rtbOut.Clear()
rtbOut.AppendText("Unsorted: " & vbNewLine)

For i = 0 To 4
    rtbOut.AppendText(strDVD(i) & vbNewLine)
Next i

'Selection sort
For i = 0 To strDVD.GetUpperBound(0) - 1
    intMin = i
    For j = i + 1 To strDVD.GetUpperBound(0)
        If strDVD(intMin) > strDVD(j) Then
            intMin = j
        End If
    Next j

    strTemp = strDVD(i)
    strDVD(i) = strDVD(intMin)
    strDVD(intMin) = strTemp
Next i
```

```
'Output
rtbOut.AppendText(vbNewLine & "Sorted: " & vbNewLine)

For i = 0 To 4
    rtbOut.AppendText(strDVD(i) & vbNewLine)
Next i
```

The outer loop (i) runs one time less than the total number of items in the array. The inner loop (j) gets shorter with each pass. On the first pass it starts with the second item. That's i + 1. i is 0 on the first pass so i + 1 is 1. Then next time the inner loop (j) starts, i is 1 so the loop starts at i + 1, which is 2. This continues until the entire list has been sorted.

As the size of the list gets larger, a selection sort becomes even more efficient than a bubble sort. Instead of moving items one space at a time, the selection sort moves them many spaces. That makes the sort much faster for longer lists.

VB Tip   *Open and run the Selection program to see how it works.*

VB Quiz 06   *What variable stores the item currently being compared with the rest of the items in the list?*
Is the sorted list built from the beginning to the end or from the end to the beginning?
What is the biggest advantage of the selection sort over the bubble sort?

Potential Problems

Selection sorts have many of the pitfalls of a bubble sort. Check to make sure the arrays are properly filled. Make sure you swap all arrays when working with arrays of related data. Be sure to update the comparison variable when a swap is needed. Make sure you reset that variable when starting a new trip through the data.

Two-Dimensional Arrays

At times a simple array is too simple. That's because data are often interrelated. Take the points scored by a basketball team as an example. On a team, each player has a point total for each game. You could arrange the points for each game in its own array. That would certainly work, but it would be a little clumsy, just like individual variables are a little clumsy when compared to arrays. The solution is a *two-dimensional array*. One array could contain all the points scored for all the games. Think of all the points for an entire team for a season. Each game could be shown in its own column. Each player's points could be a row. Just like a one-dimensional array, all the data in a two-dimensional array must be of the same data type. In this example, the names would need to be stored separately. It might look something like the following table:

Player	Game 1	Game 2	Game 3	Game 4
Eric Kramer	22	14	18	24
Kenny Randolph	8	4	12	7
Matt Granger	12	11	7	8
Nick Lever	8	5	6	4
Jason Dover	12	15	8	9

To put these points into an array, follow the same process as a regular array. First declare the array and then populate it. If you know the dimensions of the array, include that in the declaration. If you don't, then you'd need to redimension the array as it's populated.

Creating a Two-Dimensional Array

Create a two-dimensional array:

```
Dim bytPoints(3, 4) As Byte
```

This creates an array named bytPoints. Remember these are zero-based. The array has four items in each row and can store columns with five items of data. The general form for declaring a two-dimensional array looks like this:

```
Dim varName(x, y) As Type = {{List1}, {List2}}
```

Dim creates the array, varName is the name of the array, and x and y represent the dimensions of the array. They are zero-based. Type is the data type. List1 and List2 are comma-separated lists of items for the array. List1 is for the first row and List2 is for the second row. Additional rows can be added as needed. The lists themselves are separated by a comma.

Here's a little example that will display the scoring as shown in the preceeding table:

```
Dim bytPoints(,) As Byte = {{22, 14, 18, 24}
{8, 4, 12, 7}, {12, 11, 7, 8},
{8, 5, 6, 4}, {12, 15, 8, 9}}

rtbOut.Clear()

rtbOut.AppendText(bytPoints(0, 0).ToString.PadLeft(3) & _
    bytPoints(0, 1).ToString.PadLeft(3) & _
    bytPoints(0, 2).ToString.PadLeft(3) & _
    bytPoints(0, 3).ToString.PadLeft(3) & vbNewLine)
rtbOut.AppendText(bytPoints(1, 0).ToString.PadLeft(3) & _
    bytPoints(1, 1).ToString.PadLeft(3) & _
    bytPoints(1, 2).ToString.PadLeft(3) & _
    bytPoints(1, 3).ToString.PadLeft(3) & vbNewLine)
```

```
rtbOut.AppendText(bytPoints(2, 0).ToString.PadLeft(3) & _
    bytPoints(2, 1).ToString.PadLeft(3) & _
    bytPoints(2, 2).ToString.PadLeft(3) & _
    bytPoints(2, 3).ToString.PadLeft(3) & vbNewLine)
rtbOut.AppendText(bytPoints(3, 0).ToString.PadLeft(3) & _
    bytPoints(3, 1).ToString.PadLeft(3) & _
    bytPoints(3, 2).ToString.PadLeft(3) & _
    bytPoints(3, 3).ToString.PadLeft(3) & vbNewLine)
rtbOut.AppendText(bytPoints(4, 0).ToString.PadLeft(3) & _
    bytPoints(4, 1).ToString.PadLeft(3) & _
    bytPoints(4, 2).ToString.PadLeft(3) & _
    bytPoints(4, 3).ToString.PadLeft(3) & vbNewLine)
```

Naturally, it would be easy to use a loop for this code. Rather than have multiple lines of output, just use a loop to get the code to repeat. It looks something like this:

```
Dim bytPoints(,) As Byte = {{22, 14, 18, 24},
    {8, 4, 12, 7}, {12, 11, 7, 8}, {8, 5, 6, 4},
    {12, 15, 8, 9}}
Dim i As Integer

rtbOut.Clear()

For i = 0 To 4
    rtbOut.AppendText(bytPoints(i, 0).ToString.PadLeft(3) & _
        bytPoints(i, 1).ToString.PadLeft(3) & _
        bytPoints(i, 2).ToString.PadLeft(3) & _
        bytPoints(i, 3).ToString.PadLeft(3) & vbNewLine)
Next i
```

Notice how i makes it possible to display each row in turn. Substitute the current value of i each time it runs through the loop and you'll cycle through all the items in the array.

You could take this yet another step and use another loop for the other dimension of the array. With a little modification of the output line, you'd get the same result. It looks something like this:

```
Dim bytPoints(,) As Byte = {{22, 14, 18, 24},
    {8, 4, 12, 7}, {12, 11, 7, 8}, {8, 5, 6, 4},
    {12, 15, 8, 9}}
Dim i, j As Integer

rtbOut.Clear()

For i = 0 To 4
    For j = 0 To 3
        rtbOut.AppendText(bytPoints(i, j).ToString
            .PadLeft(3))
```

```
        Next j
          rtbOut.AppendText(vbNewLine)
Next i
```

The code is much shorter, but it gets harder to read. The inner loop runs from 0 to 3. Each time through the loop, it displays the next item in the array. In this example, it displays a player's points. The inner loop displays all four games for a player. Once the inner loop has finished, it starts a new line. The outer loop runs from 0 to 4, once for each player. Step through the code one line at a time to be sure you understand how it works.

Using 4 and 3 for the upper bound of the loops is bad form. In this example, the limits of the array are known, so the faux pas is only minor. There is a better way to handle these. For the inner loop you use GetUpperBound(1), which gives you the upper end of that dimension of the array. Be sure to use 1 in the parentheses instead of 0. For the outer loop you could use GetLongLength - 1. GetLongLength is the number of rows in a two-dimensional array. It is similar to the Length method for a single-dimensional array. Both store the number of items. You must subtract 1 from this number because you're after the highest subscript in it, not the length. Of course, GetUpperBound(0) would work as well. Knowing this, you could change those two lines of code to

```
For i = 0 To bytPoints.GetLongLength(0) - 1
    For j = 0 To bytPoints.GetUpperBound(1)
```

or

```
For i = 0 To bytPoints. GetUpperBound(0)
    For j = 0 To bytPoints.GetUpperBound(1)
```

Loading a Two-Dimensional Array From a File

Two-dimensional arrays can be loaded from a file, it just takes a little more code than a one-dimensional array. If the same points, along with the player names, were stored in a file called BB.dat, it would look like this:

```
Eric,Kramer,22,14,18,24
Kenny,Randolph,8,4,12,7
Matt,Granger,12,11,7,8
Nick,Lever,8,5,6,4
Jason,Dover,12,15,8,9
```

You can see the data are arranged in the file in the same way as in previous examples. The real trick now is to read in a line from the file, parse it, and make sure the correct points get placed in the correct array variables. The code looks something like this:

```
'Declarations
Dim strFirstName(), strLastName() As String
Dim bytPoints(,) As Byte
Dim srdFile As IO.StreamReader
Dim chrDelimiter As Char = ","
Dim strFields() As String
Dim strLine As String
Dim intCount As Integer
Dim i As Integer

srdFile = IO.File.OpenText("BB.dat")
rtbOut.Clear()

Do Until srdFile.Peek = -1
    ReDim Preserve strFirstName(intCount)
    ReDim Preserve strLastName(intCount)
    ReDim Preserve bytPoints(3, intCount)

    'Read and Parse
    strLine = srdFile.ReadLine()
    strFields = strLine.Split(chrDelimiter)
    strFirstName(intCount) = strFields(0)
    strLastName(intCount) = strFields(1)

    For i = 0 To 3
        'i + 2 is used for the fields because the first
        'two are taken for the first and last names
        bytPoints(i, intCount) =
          System.Convert.ToInt16(strFields(i + 2))

        rtbOut.AppendText(bytPoints(i, intCount)
          .ToString.PadLeft(3))
    Next i

    rtbOut.AppendText(vbNewLine)
    intCount = intCount + 1

Loop

'Close
srdFile.Close()
```

The arrays are declared without any dimensions and the other variables needed for the program are declared. The RichTextBox is cleared so it always displays current information. The next lines open the BB.dat file. The file is read via the standard loop process and closed when the end of the file is reached. Each line from the file is read into strLine. At the top of the loop that reads the file, the array is redimensioned and the data in the arrays are preserved. The size of the row is set to 3 because there are 4 games, 0 through 3. The intCount variable is used to redimension the number of records. As always, you know how many items are in each record in a file, but you don't know the number of records. That's why the two-dimensional array is set to 3 and intCount.

As each record is read from the file, it's parsed. This time it is placed inside a loop. The For loop is controlled by i and runs from 0 to 3. Inside this loop it parses the next item from the line and then displays it in the RichTextBox. The loop runs four times, once for every game in the file. It parses all the items from each record and displays the results in the RichTextBox. After this loop has finished, a new line is added to the RichTextBox so it's ready for the next record. The next line is read from the file and intCount is incremented. intCount keeps track of the number of records in the file and the second dimension of the array. Once the file has been read, it's closed by the last line of code.

Currently, all this program does is read the file and display its contents. Of course, there's much more that can be done. As the file is read, you could determine the scoring average for each player, you could track the total points scored for each game, or you could find the high scorer for each game. There are many possibilities.

VB Tip   *Open and run the 2DArray program to see how it works.*

A Step Further

There are *multidimensional arrays* as well. The concept is the same as that for two-dimensional arrays. Related data are stored in variables that share the same name. However, instead of two subscripts, the three-dimensional array has three subscripts, a four-dimensional array has four, and so on. Two dimensions are easy enough to visualize. They are similar to a table or multiple rows of containers on the same shelf. Three dimensions are a little tougher. Think of them as having length, width, and height – a Rubik's Cube® is a good example. Arrays with even more dimensions are possible.

VB Quiz 07   *What data type was used for the two-dimensional array?*
                 Why do all the data in an array have to be of the same type?
                 How many loops are needed to navigate a two-dimensional array?
                 Describe a three-dimensional array for points for a team that plays together for multiple seasons.

Student Grade Program Case Study

Warren Peece needs you need to write a program to calculate grades for his Russian Literature class at Altered State. The program must read student test

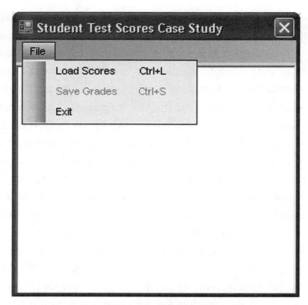

Figure 10.10   Student Test Scores Case Study Program

scores from a file. Each record in the file consists of a five-digit student ID number and four test scores. You do not know how many records are in the file. The file is called StudTestScores.dat. The data must go into arrays so they can be analyzed. Be as flexible as possible so the program can have features added to it as needed.

For each test the program should display on the screen:

the total number of scores;
the high score(s) and the corresponding student ID;
the mean, median, and mode; and
the standard deviation.

The program should then write the student ID, average, and grade to a file called StudGrades.dat. The file should be in order by ID to make it easy to enter final grades on the grade sheet. Grading is as follows: >=90%, A; >=80 to 90%, B; >=70 to 80%, C; >=60 to 70%, D; and < 60%, F. These data should also be displayed on the screen.

Use a RichTextBox to display the results on the screen. Use a menu for reporting items. The form should be similar to that in Figure 10.10.

As you plan, design, and code your program, you should keep in mind some development techniques. Don't work with the entire data file. Instead, take just a small sample of the data. That will shorten and simplify the process. In the real world you would never get to develop with live data, you would only work with a small sample file. Plan and develop for the future. It might mean more work, but it will make your program more flexible. Test as you go. As you get one part of the code completed, test it. Plan before you code. In the long run, it will save you time and trouble. Divide and conquer. Break the program into smaller steps and break those steps into small steps. Keep declarations, input, processing, and output in mind.

Open the StudTestScores.dat file, look at the structure of the data, then take some of the records and put them into a test file. Use that test file in development.

Next decide on the structure of your data so you can do your declarations. The student IDs should be in their own array. There are four test scores. You can determine that from looking at the data file. You could put the scores into separate arrays, one for each test, which would work just fine. The scores could also go into a two-dimensional array. It would be similar to the earlier example with basketball points. You could declare the arrays at the procedure level, but that severely limits the functionality of the program. A better idea would be to declare them at the module level. That way, they would work in any procedure.

Input comes from a file. You'll need to write code to load the data into the arrays. When should that be done? You could set it up to automatically load the file when the program runs. The disadvantage of that is that it ties your program to that one data file. To keep it flexible, you may want to set it up so the user can load any file with the correct structure. That way, test scores from other classes or other years could also be used. As long as the records in the other files have the same structure, they can be used, which makes your program that much more powerful. However, it will take planning on your part to get the processing requirements correct.

Processing involves many steps. You must produce several different outputs for this program. From the requirements, you can also see that you'll need to sort the data. It looks like the processing must be divided into multiple steps, numerous calculations must be performed, and searches must be done. Each of these steps should be planned and written separately.

The output goes to a RichTextBox on the screen and some of it must be written to a file. Again, it looks like you'll need multiple steps to handle this part of the project.

It might be a good idea at this point to fall back on a flowchart. Draw a general outline of what must be done, which will help. Your program will still follow the declarations, input, processing, and output format. As you look at the requirements, you can see that each test has the same requirements. For each one, you'll report the total number of scores, the high score, the mean, the median, the mode, and the standard deviation. Think of functions for these.

The number of scores can be determined by counting the records, which can be done when the data are loaded from the file. Use a module-level variable for that and it will be available throughout the program.

The high score for each test is determined by looking at each score. Keep track of the highest score and the student ID associated with it. Compare the high score to the next item in the list. Use an array for the score and another for the ID. Add to these arrays when there is a tie for the high score. When a higher score is found, clear the arrays and store the new high score and ID. Once the test scores array has been searched, display the high scores(s) and ID(s).

The mean is the average of all scores for that test. Add the scores for each test and divide by the number of tests. The median is the point where half of all the score lower and half are higher. To find the median, the scores must be sorted. It's then a matter of finding the midpoint and taking that score. The mode is the most frequent score. With a sorted list of scores, go through the list a record at a time. Compare the score to the next score on the list. If they are the same, add one to a counter. If it's different, reset the counter, update the compare score, and move on to the next item. Once the entire array has been processed, the most frequent score and the IDs associated with it should be known.

To calculate the standard deviation, you must first know the mean for that test. Next, the difference from the mean for each test score must be determined. Put these into an array. From there, square each of these differences. Again, these should be in an array. Add these squared differences together, then divide by the number of scores. The last step is to find the square root of this number. The result is the standard deviation. The formula for standard deviation is

```
SD = SqRt ((sum(x - mean)^2) / n)
```

where x is the score, mean is the mean of all the scores, and n is the number of scores.

In the real world, a programmer often runs into formulas or processes that they don't fully understand. The standard deviation might be a good example of this. If you understand the concept and the math behind it, that's great. If not, don't worry. In the real world, complicated processes and formulas would be handled by an expert. Your task as a developer would be to work with them to create the code, test it, and make sure it's correct.

To calculate the grade for each student, add the student's score for all the tests and divide by the number of tests. Then use a Case structure to determine the letter grade. The student ID, average, and letter grade must be displayed on the screen and written to a file. The records must be in order by student ID. It would be easiest to sort the records, both the IDs and the scores, before doing any calculations. Once the records are in order by ID, it's relatively easy to process them. Use a loop. Inside the loop, calculate the student's average, determine the letter grade based on that average, display the results on the screen, and then write the record to the file.

All or part of these requirements can be completed as directed by your instructor.

VB Tip   *Open and run the StudScoresCS program to see how it works.*

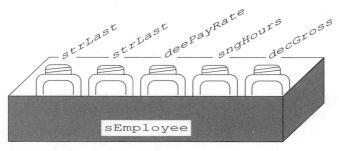

Figure 10.11   Employee Structure Example

Structures

Structures are another way to store data in the computer's memory. While an array can store only one data type, a structure can store multiple data types. While variables have been portrayed as containers, structures can be visualized as boxes that hold these containers. You could take many different data types and put them all together in a structure. Visually, you can see a structure as a boxful of containers (see Figure 10.11).

Employee Wages Program

Creating Structures

A structure looks like this:

```
'Create Employee Structure
Public Structure sEmployee
    Dim strLast As String
    Dim strFirst As String
    Dim decPayRate As Decimal
    Dim sngHours As Single
    Dim decGross As Single
End Structure
```

This example is the start of a structure for a payroll. It could store data for one employee. Of course the structure could be much more complicated and store all sorts of data for an employee, this is just a simple example. To store multiple items with the same structure, you'd need to create an array for the structure (more on that soon). Here is the general structure of, well, a structure:

```
Scope Structure sName
    Dim memberName As Type
    . . .
End Structure
```

Scope is the scope of the structure, Public or Private. s*Name* is the name of the structure and inside the structure are the declarations for the structure. Usually, this is where variables for the structure are declared. End Structure defines the end of the structure.

VB Tip
Use s as the prefix for a structure name. That makes it easy to recognize it as a structure.

The sEmployee structure above is the description for one container. There's not much room and it's certainly more hassle and more confusing than it's worth. However, the structure could be declared as an array. That way you have the advantage of multiple containers, each capable of storing an assortment of data types. To create an array of this structure, write the following:

```
'Create Array
Dim Employee(4) As sEmployee
```

This example creates five containers (0 to 4) that look exactly like the sEmployee container. It was declared in the Public Class. To assign a value to a *member* of a structure you need to refer to the name of the structure and its member. It could look like this:

```
Employee(0).strFirst = "Anne"
```

where Employee is the name of the structure. It's an array, so you need the reference to the subscript as well. Hit the dot and IntelliSense pops up with the members and methods for a structure. You can then use or assign it like any other variable. Picture this as assigning "Anne" to a container named strFirst inside a box called Employee. The Employee box is number 0 and there are several other boxes sitting next to it. The general form is

```
Structure.Member
```

where *Structure* is the name of the structure and *Member* is the name of typed variable.

VB Tip
The data type of a value must match the data type of that member in the structure.

Populating Structures

In this example, we'll simply assign the data to the structures. Normally, these would be loaded from a file:

```
'Populate Structure
Employee(0).strFirst = "Anne"
Employee(0).strLast = "Arkey"
Employee(0).decPayRate = 7.5
Employee(0).sngHours = 40
Employee(1).strFirst = "Kay"
Employee(1).strLast = "Oas"
Employee(1).decPayRate = 8
Employee(1).sngHours = 32
```

```
Employee(2).strFirst = "Sarah"
Employee(2).strLast = "Nade"
Employee(2).decPayRate = 7
Employee(2).sngHours = 30
Employee(3).strFirst = "Rane"
Employee(3).strLast = "Gage"
Employee(3).decPayRate = 7.25
Employee(3).sngHours = 40
Employee(4).strFirst = "Bob"
Employee(4).strLast = "Sledd"
Employee(4).decPayRate = 8
Employee(4).sngHours = 40
```

Once the data are assigned to the members of the Employee structure, they can be manipulated. This process is similar to processing data from an array. The real difference here is that you have to include the name of the structure, the subscript of the structure, and the member of the structure. Sticking with the analogy, you have to identify the data by the name of the box they're in, the number of the box, and the container in the box.

VB Tip   *When you type a period after the name of a structure, IntelliSense brings up a list that includes all the members of that structure.*

Manipulating Structures

The following code calculates the gross pay for each employee:

```
For i = 0 To 4
    Employee(i).decGross = Employee(i).sngHours *
        Employee(i).decPayRate
Next i
```

Employee(i) refers to the appropriate container. i controls the loop and runs from 0 to 4. Each trip through the loop grabs another Employee box. Notice that decGross is the variable for storing the gross pay for that employee. It's assigned the product of sngHours * decPayRate. All of these variables are in the same Employee box.

This simplified example gives you the basics for declaring a structure, creating an array with it, populating the members, and manipulating the data. Of course, the Employee structure could be much more complicated. It could contain dozens of members and the details of an employee's payroll record. The real advantage of a structure is that you can place all of these data into a single container and work with it as needed. If you had to change or update the structure, the changes could be made in one place and would be applied to all the containers in the structure. It's also another step down the road to objects.

VB Tip   *Open and run the Structures program to see how it works.*

Population Estimates Program

The data file, PopEst.dat, contains the state names, 2005 population, and the projected growth rate. From the population and the growth rate, the 2030 population can be estimated. In this example, the data are read from the file and placed in a structure. The structure is used to process those data and display the output in a RichTextBox. Of course, there are easier and better ways to do this than a structure, but it is a good of example of how to use a structure.

The structure is created as follows:

```
Public Structure sStates
    Dim strState As String
    Dim lngPop2005 As Long
    Dim lngPop2030 As Long
    Dim sngPercentChange As Single
End Structure
```

The name of the structure is sStates. Place it in the general declarations section at the top of the page. It contains variables for the name of the state, its population in 2005, and the growth rate. This is the description of the box, but it hasn't been created as yet. To create the boxes you need another line of code:

```
Dim States(49) As sStates
```

This line belongs in the Public class. It creates 50 identical boxes and each one holds variables for the state names, populations in 2005 and 2030, and the growth rate. Items in an array of structures are differentiated by their subscript, just like other arrays.

The process of loading the data from the file into the structure is similar to what you've been using. Once the file is opened and parsed, it is assigned to the members of the structure. Here is the relevant code from the processing loop:

```
Do While srdFile.Peek <> -1
    strLine = srdFile.ReadLine()
    'Parse
    strField = strLine.Split(chrDelimiter)
    States(intCount).strState = strField(0)
    States(intCount).lngPop2000 =
      System.Convert.ToInt32(strField(1))
    States(intCount).sngPercentChange =
      System.Convert.ToSingle(strField(2))
    ...
    intCount = intCount + 1
Loop
```

The loop reads data from the file one line at a time. Each line is parsed and then assigned to the appropriate variable. The intCount variable starts at zero and is incremented at the bottom of the loop. With each iteration, it increases by one. Each trip through the loop processes another line from the file and places the data into the next box of the array.

In this example, States(n) refers to the nth box of the array. To get to the individual variables inside that box, use the varName. So, States(4).strState contains California; States(16).lngPop2005 contains 4,041,769, the 2005 population of Kentucky; and States(36).sngPercentChange contains 0.147, the percentage change for Oregon.

The same loop can be used to calculate the population changes for each state. The code looks like this:

```
Do While srdFile.Peek <> -1
  . . .
  'Calculate
  States(intCount).lngPop2030 =
    States(intCount).lngPop2005 +
    (States(intCount).lngPop2005 *
    States(intCount).sngPercentChange)
  States(intCount).sngPercentChange =
    States(intCount).sngPercentChange * 100
  . . .
Loop
```

With each pass through the loop, the data are read from the file and stored in the variables for that structure. Once in the variables, the data can be processed. The first line calculates the increase and adds it to the 2005 population to arrive at the 2030 estimate. The second line multiplies the percentage increase by 100 so the output can be displayed as a percent. Take note of how the specific variables are referenced by the name of the structure (States), the subscript (intCount), and the variable name, lngPop2000, for example.

The output is handled by creating a detail line and then appending the detail line to the RichTextBox:

```
Do While srdFile.Peek <> -1
    . . .
    'Output
    strDetail = States(intCount).strState.PadRight(14) & _
      States(intCount).lngPop2000.ToString("n0")
        .PadLeft(12) & _
      States(intCount).sngPercentChange.ToString("n2")
        .PadLeft(8) & _
      States(intCount).lngPop2030.ToString("n0")
        .PadLeft(12)
```

```
      rtbOut.AppendText(strDetail & ControlChars.NewLine)
...
Loop
```

The first four physical lines form one logical line. The variables are converted to strings as needed, formatted, padded, and stored in strDetail. The last line takes strDetail and appends it to the RichTextBox.

Notice how these three blocks of code are all part of the same processing loop. Each segment represents a different computer operation. The first is input, the second is processing, and the last one is output. It is the same sequence that has been used in nearly all of your programs.

Here is the entire code for the program:

```
Public Structure sStates
    Dim strState As String
    Dim lngPop2000 As Long
    Dim lngPop2030 As Long
    Dim sngPercentChange As Single
End Structure
Public Class Form1
    Dim States(49) As sStates

    Private Sub btnEstimates_Click(ByVal sender As
      System.Object, ByVal e As System.EventArgs)
      Handles btnEstimates.Click
        Dim strField() As String
        Dim srdFile As System.IO.StreamReader
        Dim strLine As String
        Dim intCount As Integer
        Dim strDetail As String

        rtbOut.Clear()
        rtbOut.AppendText(" 2030 State Population
          Estimates")
        rtbOut.AppendText(vbNewLine & vbNewLine)
        rtbOut.AppendText("State 2000 Pop. %Change 2030
          Est.")
        rtbOut.AppendText(vbNewLine)

        'Open File
        ofdPop.ShowDialog()
        srdFile = New System.IO.StreamReader(ofdPop
          .FileName)

        Do While srdFile.Peek <> -1
            'Read
            strLine = srdFile.ReadLine()
```

```
        'Parse
        strField = strLine.Split(",")
        States(intCount).strState = strField(0)
        States(intCount).lngPop2000 =
        System.Convert.ToInt32(strField(1))
        States(intCount).sngPercentChange =
          System.Convert.ToSingle(strField(2))

        'Calculate
        States(intCount).lngPop2030 =
          States(intCount).lngPop2000 + _
          (States(intCount).lngPop2000 *
          States(intCount).sngPercentChange)
        States(intCount).sngPercentChange =
          States(intCount).sngPercentChange * 100

        'Output
        strDetail = States(intCount).strState
          .PadRight(14) & _
        States(intCount).lngPop2000.ToString("n0")
          .PadLeft(12) & _
        States(intCount).sngPercentChange
          .ToString("n2").PadLeft(8) & _
        States(intCount).lngPop2030.ToString("n0")
          .PadLeft(12)

        rtbOut.AppendText(strDetail & _
          ControlChars.NewLine)
        intCount = intCount + 1
      Loop

      'Close
      srdFile.Close()
    End Sub

    Private Sub btnExit_Click(ByVal sender As
      System.Object, ByVal e As System.EventArgs)
      Handles btnExit.Click
        End
    End Sub

End Class
```

Potential Problems

Structures have all the built-in problems of variables and arrays. The data type
of variables assigned to members of a structure must conform to that member.

An array created using a structure can be zero-based. IntelliSense is the best way to pick up on misnamed or misused members in a structure. Structures must be created outside of other procedures or functions. Structures are created with a Structure command, but must still be declared before they can be used.

VB Quiz 08   *Where are structures defined?*

How many members can be stored in a structure?

Where are structures declared?

Explain why all structures in an array must be identical while all members of a structure don't.

On Your Own

Write a program with an array that stores 10 items. Add the items to the array using an InputBox, display the list in a RichTextBox, and sort the array and display the list again.

Create a program with a structure suitable for your class schedule. The structure should have variables for the class number, name, location, date, time, and instructor. Use an array for the structure so each class can be included, and display the output.

Summary

This chapter introduced several ways of working with lists. An array is a list of similar variables that can be controlled with numbers. Arrays can be searched to find information. They can be sorted so the data can be organized, and they can have two or more dimensions. Structures are containers for related data. A structure is similar to a database record.

Review

An array is a series of related variables.

All variables in an array share a common name.

Array variables are distinguished by their index.

Arrays are zero-based.

All arrays must be declared before they can be used.

Arrays are easily manipulated with loops.

The unique number for each element in an array is called a subscript.

Arrays can be populated at the time they are declared.

Arrays can be loaded from a file or through user input.

An array can be resized at any time.

Use ReDim to resize an array.

Resizing an array can destroy the data in an array.

Use Preserve to resize an array without destroying the data already in the array.

Arrays are useful for searching through data.

A hit is when a search item returns a match.

A binary search is an efficient way to search through an ordered list.

A binary search eliminates half of the remaining items with each query.

When searching, sometimes a partial match is better than a exact match.

Many different algorithms exist for sorting data.

One of the easiest sorting algorithms is the bubble sort.

The selection sort is more efficient than the bubble sort.

GetLowerBound stores the smallest subscript in an array.

GetUpperBound stores the largest subscript in an array.

Length stores the number of items in an array.

Computer sorts are done in ASCII order.

Use the greater than symbol ($>$) for sorts in alphabetical order and the less than symbol ($<$) for reverse order sorts.

The order of items in an array can be reversed by using the Reverse method.

An array can be copied by using the Array.Copy command.

A selection sort is more efficient than a bubble sort.

A two-dimensional array works well for sets of related data.

GetLongLength contains the number of rows in a two-dimensional array.

Structures can store multiple types of related data in a single container.

Structures are similar to records in a database.

Use s as the prefix for a structure to make recognition easier.

An array structure can be used to work with multiple records.

A structure is declared outside of other procedures.

The data types in a structure are called members.

IntelliSense can display the members of a structure.

Terms

array	a set of related data; an object containing a list of similarly typed data; a group of related variables that has the same data type
binary search	a search algorithm that eliminates half the remaining items in a list with each successive search
bubble sort	a simple but slow algorithm for ordering items in an array
element	a variable in an array
hit	when a match is found in a search
index	a unique number starting at zero assigned to each element of an array

linear search	a search that starts at the beginning of a list and goes through each item in the list in order
member	a variable in a structure
multidimensional arrays	an array containing more than two dimensions of related data
populate	to assign data to the elements of an array
selection sort	a faster and more efficient algorithm than a bubble sort for ordering items in an array
structure	a user-defined data type; a collection of related items of differing data types
subscript	the element number of an array; in strState(39), 39 is the subscript of the array strState
two-dimensional array	an array of a single type that contains rows and columns of related data
zero-based	an array that numbers its elements starting at zero

Keywords

GetLongLength	the number of rows in a multidimensional array; the method that returns the number of rows in a multidimensional array
GetLowerBound	the lower limit of an array; the lower limit is 0
GetUpperBound	the upper limit of an array; the upper bound it the highest index in the array; it's one less than the length
Length	the number of items (elements) in an array
Preserve	the keyword used to preserve the data in an array when the array is resized
ReDim	the command to resize an array, short for ReDimension
Refresh	a method used to update the display of a control
Reverse	the method that reverses the order of the elements in an array
Structure	a user-defined data type; an object that contains related variables often of mixed data types

Self-check

1. An array can store many values, but they all must be of the same data type.
2. An array stores its values in memory.
3. The size of an array must be determined when the array is declared.
4. The index of an array is always an integer.
5. All data in an array are lost when the array is resized.

6. Array.Sort can be used to sort in ascending or descending order.
7. The Length method stores the total number of items in the array.
8. Generally, a bubble sort is faster than a selection sort.
9. In a two-dimensional array, one dimension of the array can be of one data type and the other dimension can be of another data type.
10. A structure can store multiple items with differing data types.
11. The command to resize an array is:
    A. Append
    B. Preserve
    C. ReDim
    D. Resize
12. An array index of 0 indicates:
    A. it's the first item in the array
    B. no matching item was found
    C. the array is empty
    D. the number 0 is stored in the array
13. GetLowerBound:
    A. finds the smallest item in an array
    B. finds the first item alphabetically in the array
    C. finds the lowest index number of the array
    D. finds the first unused element in the array
14. Which of the following would be best for declaring an array to store the chapter names of this text?
    A. Dim strTitle() As String
    B. Dim strTitle(15) As String
    C. Dim strTitle(14) As String
    D. Dim strTitle As String = 15
15. A linear search:
    A. starts searching with the first item in the array
    B. looks at each item in the array
    C. works with an unordered list
    D. all of the above
16. What does Array.Copy do?
    A. It makes a copy of an array using a different array name.
    B. It makes a copy of an array and places the items in ascending order.
    C. It checks the array for duplicate items.
    D. It compares two arrays to see if they are identical.
17. Which of the following would assign "Captain" to an array of sSoldier called Soldier containing a member called strRank?
    A. Soldier(0).strRank = "Captain"
    B. Soldier.strRank, 0 = "Captain"
    C. Soldier.strRank(0) = Captain
    D. Soldier(0).strRank = sSolider.Soldier.strRank.Captain

18. Which of the following would declare an array named strStudents that would contain 20 elements?

    A. Dim strStudents() As String

    B. Dim strStudents(20) As String

    C. Dim strStudents(0 To 20) As String

    D. Dim strStudents(19) As String

19. In the following line of code:

    ```
    EmpID.strSSN = strSSNInput
    ```

    A. EmpID is the variable name

    B. strSSN is a member of the EmpID structure

    C. strSSN is the structure

    D. EmpID is a variable in the strSSN structure

20. In an array declaration statement, items in an array list are separated by a:

    A. space

    B. comma

    C. semicolon

    D. tab

VB Quiz Answers

Quiz 01

```
Dim strState(49) As String
Dim shoScore(3) As Short
Dim decBalDue() As Decimal
Dim bytPoints(11) As Byte
```

Quiz 02

The array shoPlace(i) stores the number of homes a realtor has listed. There are five different values for i, 0 through 4. Each one stores the number of homes a realtor has listed.

9.80

1.20

It stores the subscript of the number of homes closest to the average.

The last item displayed is the number of homes closest to the average.

Quiz 03

Modular variables were used for the arrays so the data could be used in any procedure without passing it.

There are 200 students. 199 trips were made, one less than the number of elements in the array.

One thousand variables were needed – 200 for the IDs and 200 for each of the four test scores.

You would need to add all 800 scores and then divide by 800. One loop could be used. Add the current element from each score array as it's processed through the loop. After the loop has run, do the division.

Quiz 04

It runs six times, from 0 to 5.

It runs six times, from 0 to 5.

Thirty-six comparisons were made.

The correct order is Indigo, Blue, Green, Violet, Orange, Red, Yellow.

Quiz 05

Before it was optimized, 529 comparisons were made. 276 comparisons were made when it was optimized, a savings of nearly half.

Instead of comparing the artists (strArtist), you'd compare the album (strAlbum) in the If statement.

Two CDs with the same artist would stay in the same order. The comparison is equal so they wouldn't get swapped. Ideally, the code would be written so that CDs by the same artist would then be sorted by another field. In this example, you could use the album.

When the same artist had two CDs, the comparison was equal. You'd then compare the album title and sort accordingly. This would put two in order, but it wouldn't allow for more than two albums by the same artist. To sort by album within artist, you'd need a more sophisticated algorithm.

Quiz 06

The array strDVD(intMin) stores the current item.

It is built from beginning to end.

The selection sort is much faster than a bubble sort. It makes fewer swaps than a bubble sort.

Quiz 07

The data type for the two-dimensional array was Byte. All the elements of this array are of that type. The array stores points scored in a basketball game.

One of the limits of an array is that all the elements must store the same data type.

Two loops are needed. One loop controls the rows and the other controls the columns.

The first two dimensions would be similar to the existing two-dimensional array. The third dimension would be the season. Think of it as a box, perhaps a Rubik's Cube.

Quiz 08

Structure declarations go in the general declarations section of your code, which is at the top of the code page.

There is no real limit to the number of members in a structure. The real limitation is how it will be put to use.

Structures are declared in the form declarations. They can be declared individually or as an array.

A structure is defined by the different data types in it. Its purpose is to unite different data types into a single storage area. An array of structures is a related group of the same combination of differing data types.

Events and More Controls – Tips and Tricks for Programming

VB Quip   *The function of good software is to make the complex appear to be simple. – Grady Booch*

Good software does just that. It's easy to use, "intuitive" is the buzzword used in the industry. It does what it should and people actually like using it. Developers must keep two things in mind: getting the program to do what it should and making it useable – the two go hand-in-hand. A cool interface means nothing if the software doesn't perform. And, no matter how solid the code is, a clunky program is nearly worthless. Always think of both form and function. On the one hand, a developer must write code that works. On the other, a developer must always consider the end user. Never forget, you can't have one without the other!

New Events

You're familiar with several events such as Click, Load, and Scroll, but there are more, many more. In fact, there are far too many to cover in anything short of the dreaded user's manual. Every event can trigger code and every user action *raises* an event, that is, every time the user does something, from a click of the mouse to a peck of a key, a program can respond. How it responds and what it does are key to good software.

KeyPress

When a key is pressed, it generates a *KeyPress* event and also several other key events. These keystrokes can be *trapped* in various ways and the input can be used to determine what the user wants. If you press a key, you generally expect that character to appear on the screen – in a TextBox, for example. When you hold down the Shift key and press the same key, you get a different character, usually a capital letter. Hold down the Control key or the Alt key and then press the same key and other things happen. Hold down a different combination of these *modifier keys* and still more happens. The program is checking every keystroke and deciding what to do with it. That's how it knows you're using a shortcut to

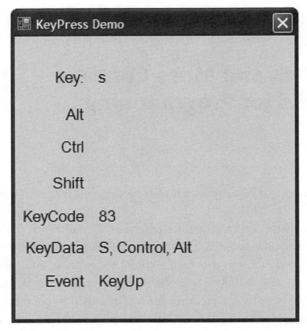

Figure 11.1   KeyPress Demo Program

save or print a file instead of typing in an "s" or a "p". Use a KeyPress event to determine which key was pressed. From there, the program can determine what should happen.

A KeyPress occurs when a key is pressed. The following example captures the *keystroke* and then displays it (see Figure 11.1):

```
Private Sub frmKeyPress_KeyPress(ByVal sender As Object,
    ByVal e As System.Windows.Forms.KeyPressEventArgs)
    Handles Me.KeyPress
    Dim chrKey As Char
    'Determine which key was pressed and display it
    chrKey = e.KeyChar
    lblKey.Text = chrKey
End Sub
```

Here *e.KeyChar* is the keystroke character. It's stored in chrKey and then displayed. The keystroke in e.KeyChar could be used as input and processed just like other input. That way, the simple press of a key could be used instead of a mouse click.

Modifier Keys

A *KeyDown* event determines if one or more of the modifier keys are used. The KeyDown event is triggered when any key is pressed down. *e.Control* is a Boolean that knows if a Control key was being held down during a KeyPress. *e.Alt* does the same for the Alt keys, and *e.Shift* handles the Shift keys. When True, that modifier key is down; it's False when it's not.

Here's an example:

```
Private Sub frmKeyPress_KeyDown(ByVal sender As Object,
  ByVal e As System.Windows.Forms.KeyEventArgs)
  Handles Me.KeyDown
    Dim intKeyCode As Integer
    Dim strAlt As String
    Dim strControl As String
    Dim strShift As String
    Dim strKeyData As String

    'Determines if Alt key is up or down
    If e.Alt Then
        strAlt = "Down"
    Else
        strAlt = "Up"
    End If

    'Determines if Control key is up or down
    If e.Control Then
        strControl = "Down"
    Else
        strControl = "Up"
    End If

    'Determines if Shift key is up or down
    If e.Shift Then
        strShift = "Down"
    Else
        strShift = "Up"
    End If

    'Returns all the information about a pressed key
    strKeyData = e.KeyData.ToString

    'Determines the keycode for the key that was pressed
    intKeyCode = e.KeyCode

    'Output
    lblAlt.Text = strAlt
    lblControl.Text = strControl
    lblShift.Text = strShift
End Sub
```

e.Alt is either True or False depending whether one of the Alt keys is down on the *KeyDown* event. It's True when it's down and False when it's up. e.Control does the same for the Control keys and e.Shift handles the Shift keys. The If statements turn the True or False status of the modifier key into "Down" or "Up" for display on the screen. Of course, there could be some significant processing based on whether the user wanted to use a modifier key in addition to a keystroke. It also works when more than one modifier key is held down at the same time.

The *KeyUp* event is triggered when a key is released. In this example, the Labels are cleared when the key is released:

```
Private Sub frmKeyPress_KeyUp(ByVal sender As Object,
   ByVal e As System.Windows.Forms.KeyEventArgs)
   Handles Me.KeyUp
      'Clears output
      lblAlt.Text = ""
      lblControl.Text = ""
      lblShift.Text = ""

      'Displays event
      lblEvent.Text = "KeyUp"
End Sub
```

Therefore, any keystroke generates a KeyDown, KeyPress, and KeyUp event and all of them can be used to trigger code in a program.

VB Tip　　　　　　*Open and run the KeyPressDemo program to see how it works.*

TextChanged

A *TextChanged* event is generated for every keystroke in a TextBox. It's also triggered whenever the text in a TextBox changes. Examples include deleting a character or copying or pasting text in a TextBox. TextChanged can be used to track the number of characters entered, to control the characters entered, or to edit the text.

This example uses the Length method to determine the number of characters in the TextBox. The TextChanged event for the TextBox is triggered with every keystroke and displays the number of characters in the TextBox.

```
Private Sub txtDemo_TextChanged(ByVal sender As
   System.Object, ByVal e As System.EventArgs) Handles
   txtDemo.TextChanged
      Dim shoLength As Short
```

```
'Gets and displays the number of characters entered
shoLength = txtDemo.TextLength

lblLength.Text = shoLength.ToString
```

```
End Sub
```

VB Tip   *Open and run the TextEvents program to see how it works. The program contains one*
other TextChanged event – one that prevents the entry of digits and capital letters.

The TextChanged event gives a developer the ability to examine every change to
a TextBox. In this example, the user cannot enter numbers in a TextBox. Code
in the TextChanged event checks every change to the text in the TextBox and
clears it whenever a digit is entered.

```
Private Sub txtLettersOnly_TextChanged(ByVal sender As
   System.Object, ByVal e As System.EventArgs) Handles
   txtLettersOnly.TextChanged
     'Clears the TextBox when a number is entered
     Dim strEntered As String
     Dim shoLength As Short
     Dim strLastEntered As String

     strEntered = txtLettersOnly.Text
     shoLength = txtLettersOnly.TextLength

     If shoLength > 0 Then
         strLastEntered = strEntered.Substring(shoLength
            - 1, 1)

         Select Case strLastEntered
             Case "0" To "9"
                   txtLettersOnly.Clear()
         End Select
     End If
End Sub
```

The contents of the TextBox are moved to strEntered. Its length is then stored
in shoLength. When the length is greater than zero, it gets the last character
entered and stores it in strLastEntered. The following line:

```
strLastEntered = strEntered.Substring(shoLength - 1, 1)
```

finds the last character. It subtracts 1 from the length of the string and uses that
value in the Substring method to get the last character. The Case structure then
checks to see if that character is a digit. If it is, it clears the TextBox. The Clear

method clears all the text from the TextBox and triggers another TextChanged event. That's why the If statement is needed.

The following code prevents the user from entering a digit in the TextBox. It employs some new methods as well, the *SelectionStart*, *SelectionLength*, *Copy*, *SelectAll*, and *Paste* methods.

```
Private Sub txtLettersAgain_TextChanged(ByVal sender
  As System.Object, ByVal e As System.EventArgs)
  Handles txtLettersAgain.TextChanged
    'Allows text but no numbers to be entered
    Dim strEntered As String
    Dim shoLength As Short
    Dim strLastEntered As String
    strEntered = txtLettersAgain.Text
    shoLength = txtLettersAgain.TextLength
        If shoLength > 0 Then
            strLastEntered = strEntered.Substring
              (shoLength - 1, 1)
            Select Case strLastEntered
              Case "0" To "9"
                txtLettersAgain.SelectionStart() = 0
                txtLettersAgain.SelectionLength =
                  shoLength - 1
                txtLettersAgain.Copy()
                txtLettersAgain.SelectAll()
                txtLettersAgain.Paste()
            End Select
        End If
End Sub
```

The user types a character for the TextBox, triggering a TextChanged event. It finds and checks the last character entered, just like the previous code. However, this code doesn't simply clear the TextBox. Instead, it copies the characters already in the TextBox, empties the TextBox, and pastes them back into it, without the offending digit at the end.

SelectionStart is a number and is used to mark the start of the selected text. In this case, it's 0, the beginning of the TextBox. SelectionLength is used to determine how many characters are selected. It's a number and it's set to one less than the number of characters in the TextBox. In other words, it selects everything except the last character. The Copy method copies the selected text. The SelectAll method selects all the text in the TextBox. That way, the Paste method replaces everything in the TextBox with the selected text– in this case, everything except the number at the end (see Figure 11.2).

VB Tip

The Copy, Cut, SelectAll, and Paste methods for a TextBox work the same way as their counterparts in other programs.

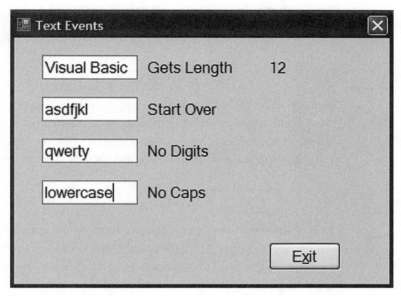

Figure 11.2   Text Events Program

Focus

The *Focus* method gives the focus to a control:

```
txtFirstName.Focus()
```

A user can make changes to a control when it has the focus. Use this command to set the focus to a specific control. That way, a user doesn't have to click on the control to activate it or tab through other controls to set the focus to one they need to use. For example, a user is entering data for new employees. When they click on the Save Button to save a record to a file, the Save Button clears the TextBoxes and sets the focus to txtFirstName so the user is ready to enter the next employee's data.

```
swrEmployees.WriteLine(strRecord)
txtFirstName.Clear()
txtLastName.Clear()
txtDept.Clear()
txtSecurityLevel.Clear()
txtFirstName.Focus()
```

GotFocus

The *GotFocus* event for a control is triggered when that control is given the focus. It can receive the focus either from the Focus method or from user interaction, say, a click or a tab. The code in a GotFocus event usually initializes variables or resets controls.

LostFocus

The *LostFocus* event for a control is triggered when that control loses the focus. It loses focus when a user sets the focus to another control by using the tab or clicking on another control. It's also triggered when the Focus method sets the focus to another control. LostFocus is usually used to clean up or validate entry.

Activated

The *Activated* event is triggered when a form becomes active and occurs when the Show method is used on a form or the user clicks on a form to make it active. It's similar to the Load event, however, the Load event only occurs when the form is first loaded. Use the Activated event to update the contents of a form or to set the focus to a particular control.

Mouse Events

There are a handful of mouse events, each one waiting to do the bidding of a developer.

MouseEnter

The *MouseEnter* event is triggered when the mouse moves over a control. MouseEnter is usually used to highlight or draw attention to the control that's selected.

MouseHover

The *MouseHover* event is triggered when the mouse pauses over a control.

MouseLeave

The *MouseLeave* enter is triggered when the mouse leaves a control. It can be used to reset the control to what it was before the mouse entered it.

MouseDown

MouseDown is the first part of what users usually think of a click. However, there are several events to a "click" event and the first is the MouseDown. It's triggered when the mouse button is pressed down. It's completed before the Click or MouseUp events.

MouseUp

MouseUp is the last part of the click. It's triggered when the mouse button is released. Of course the MouseUp and MouseDown events must occur over the same control for it to be a click. However, MouseUp occurs regardless of where the mouse is when the button is released.

MouseMove

MouseMove events occur when the mouse moves over a control. The location of the mouse is tracked using X,Y coordinates. The top left of the control is point 0,0 and is tracked for every control, even the form. You saw this in Chapter 7 when you moved PictureBoxes with loops. The values for X and Y for the mouse are stored in *e.X* and *e.Y*. As the mouse moves, these values are updated based on the mouse's location relative to the top left of the control:

```
Private Sub btnEvents_MouseMove(ByVal sender As Object,
  ByVal e As System.Windows.Forms.MouseEventArgs)
  Handles btnEvents.MouseMove
    'Finds and displays the x,y location of the mouse
    when it's inside the Button
    Dim strOut As String
    Dim X As Integer
    Dim Y As Integer
    'X is x location on the Button, Y is y locaton on
    the Button
    X = e.X
    Y = e.Y
    strOut = X.ToString & ", " & Y.ToString
    lblHover.Text = strOut
End Sub
```

Every time the mouse moves, it updates the X and Y values. These values are then displayed in the Label. MouseMove events are only triggered when the mouse moves over the control. A form has a MouseMove event, but it only updates when moving over the form. It doesn't work when the mouse moves over a control that's sitting on the form.

DoubleClick

In addition to the Click event, controls also have a *DoubleClick* event. The Click event is triggered when the first click is completed and the DoubleClick

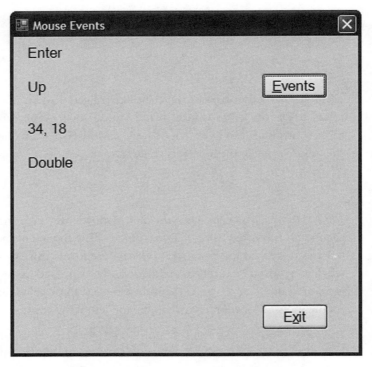

Figure 11.3   Mouse Events Program

is raised if two clicks on the same control happen in quick succession (see Figure 11.3).

VB Tip   *Open and run the MouseEvents program to see how it works.*

Potential Problems

Key events won't work when there are Buttons around. Don't use key events and Buttons on the same form. Always check to see which events will trigger the code. In your first programs, you probably put the wrong code in the wrong Buttons. Now you must make sure the correct events trigger your code. Code gets complicated quickly with events. In the past, a click triggered your code and it was probably well-behaved and you felt confident with what was happening and when it was happening. When code is added to other events, there's the potential for lots of things to happen. It might slow your program to a crawl and many unexpected things could happen. Be careful!

VB Quiz 01   *Describe how the Cut method works in a TextBox.*
                   What is the order of events when you click the mouse on a Button?
                   How does VB determine the mouse's location?

DragEnter

The *DragEnter* event is raised when the mouse moves onto a control. It differs from the MouseEnter event because the mouse button is down for the DragEnter event.

DragOver

The *DragOver* event is raised as the mouse moves over a control. It differs from the MouseHover event because the mouse button is down for a DragOver event.

DragLeave

The *DragLeave* event is raised as the mouse leaves a control. It differs from the MouseLeave event because the mouse button is down for a DragLeave event.

DragDrop

Several things must happen for a *DragDrop* event to happen. There must be a MouseDown on a control that's draggable, the mouse must move over another control that will allow an item to be dropped, and there must be a MouseUp on that control. It sounds complicated, but the program does most of the work. It simply means the user grabbed something and dropped it somewhere else.

VB Quip   *The trouble with programmers is that you can never tell what a programmer is doing until it's too late. – Seymour Cray*

Sample DragDrop Program

Drag and Drop is a powerful concept that lets users perform tasks by moving items around the screen. The code behind these moves does the real work (see Figure 11.4).

There are several requirements to drag and drop. There must be at least one control set up as the *source*. A ListBox or a TextBox works well, but others are fine, too. Generally, the text from these controls gets copied or moved to another location. There must be at least one control set up as a *target*. Set the AllowDrop property of this control to True. It's then capable of accepting content from another control.

The source material must be grabbed so it can be dragged to a new control. Use the MouseDown event for that.

```
Private Sub lstSource_MouseDown(ByVal sender As Object,
    ByVal e As System.Windows.Forms.MouseEventArgs)
    Handles lstSource.MouseDown
```

```
    'Grabs item so it can be moved
    lstSource.DoDragDrop(lstSource.SelectedItem,
      DragDropEffects.Move)
End Sub
```

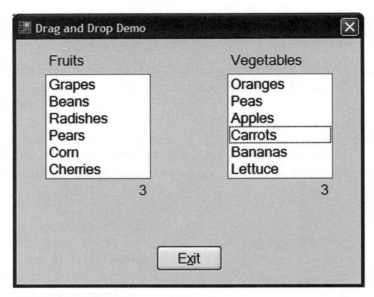

Figure 11.4   Drag and Drop Program

In this example the MouseDown event uses the *DoDragDrop* method to grab the selected item. The *DragDropEffects* is set to Move. It takes the selected item and makes it draggable to a new control.

There are two events for the target control: DragEnter and DragDrop. DragEnter checks to see if an item can be dropped into its target location. The format of the item must be something that the target control will accept. For example, the target must be able to handle a string if the user is dragging text. If it's expecting some other data type, it won't allow the transfer.

```
Private Sub lstTarget_DragEnter(ByVal sender As Object,
  ByVal e As System.Windows.Forms.DragEventArgs)
  Handles lstTarget.DragEnter
    'Checks to see if item can be dropped into this
    location
    If e.Data.GetDataPresent(DataFormats.Text) Then
        e.Effect = DragDropEffects.Move
    Else
        e.Effect = DragDropEffects.None
    End If
End Sub
```

In the preceding example, the target is a ListBox. e.Data.GetDataPresent (DataFormat.Text) has the text that's being moved. If the target accepts text then e.Effect is set to Move. In other words, it will allow the transfer. If not, then the item cannot be dropped.

VB Tip

When an item cannot be dropped, either because the control has AllowDrop set to False or because the item is the wrong data type, the cursor changes to the "no" symbol to indicate that drops aren't allowed.

The DragDrop event drops the item into its new location. If it's set to Copy, the original remains in place and a copy is dropped.

```
Private Sub lstTarget_DragDrop(ByVal sender As Object,
  ByVal e As System.Windows.Forms.DragEventArgs)
  Handles lstTarget.DragDrop
    'Drops object and removes original
    lstTarget.Items.Add(e.Data.GetData(DataFormats.Text))
    lstSource.Items.Remove(lstSource.SelectedItem)
    'Checks to see how many are in the right place
    CountNumRight()
End Sub
```

In this example, the *AllowDrop* property of the target is set to True. Text is being dragged from one control to another and the target, lstTarget, is capable of accepting text. The Add method for the ListBox adds e.Data.GetData (DataFormat.Text) to the ListBox. *e.Data.GetData*(DataFormat.Text) contains the data from the source control.

While this code moves items from one ListBox to another, there's very little processing that takes place. The real work is what happens when an item is dropped. Depending on the task, the possibilities are almost endless. For example, the user may want to transfer widgets from a warehouse to a retail store. The user might do a drag and drop in the program, but the code behind it actually handles all the work to put the process in motion. In another application, the drag and drop might transfer money from a user's savings account to a checking account. While they're dragging items on the screen, the program does the real work to check the account numbers, account balance, and security and then electronically transfers the amount from savings to checking.

```
Private Sub CountNumRight()
    'Counts the number of correct items in each ListBox
    and displays results
    Dim bytNumFruits As Byte
    Dim bytNumVeges As Byte
    Dim i As Integer
```

```
        'Counts number of correct vegetables
        For i = 0 To lstSource.Items.Count - 1
            Select Case lstSource.Items.Item(i)
                Case Is = "Beans", "Carrots", "Peas",
                "Radishes", "Lettuce",
"Corn"
                    bytNumVeges += 1
            End Select
        Next i
        'Counts number of correct fruits
        For i = 0 To lstTarget.Items.Count - 1
            Select Case lstTarget.Items.Item(i)
                Case Is = "Oranges", "Apples", "Bananas",
"Grapes", "Cherries", "Pears"
                    bytNumFruits += 1
            End Select
        Next i
        'If all items are in the right place, disables drag
        and drop
        If bytNumFruits = 6 And bytNumVeges = 6 Then
            lblDone.Text = "You Got It!"
            lstSource.AllowDrop = False
            lstTarget.AllowDrop = False
        End If
        'Displays the number of items in correct location
        lblFruit.Text = bytNumFruits.ToString
        lblVegetables.Text = bytNumVeges.ToString
End Sub
```

In the preceding example, the CountNumRight procedure gets called when an item is dropped. It checks to see how many vegetables are in the vegetables ListBox. Each time one of the items matches the vegetable list, it adds 1 to bytNumVeges. That value gets displayed at the end of the procedure. The same is true for the fruits ListBox. It uses the loop to check each item in the ListBox against the list of fruits. When there's a match, it adds 1 to bytNumFruits. The total number of correct items in each ListBox is displayed at the end of the procedure.

The last If statement checks to see if all the produce is in the correct place. When all six vegetables and all six fruits are in place, it displays feedback to the user and disables drag and drop by setting the AllowDrop property of the controls to False.

VB Tip	*Open and run the DragAndDropDemo program to see how it works.*
VB Quiz 02	*What does the AllowDrop property do?*
	How could the Fruits and Vegetables program be made flexible?

Potential Problems

Drag and drop makes a program cool. However, it complicates your code. Be sure to program the drop events because that's where the work takes place. Users are unpredictable so don't let them drag things they shouldn't and don't let them drop things where they shouldn't. Make sure all the controls get back to where they belong as well. Drag and drop takes practice, but it's well worth the effort!

VB Tip   *Open and run the DragAndDropGraphics program. It's a little dice game that demonstrates how to use drag and drop to control a program.*

New Controls

It's time to learn a few more controls from the Toolbox. Each one has its own strengths and weaknesses and each serves a useful purpose in the developer's repertoire.

VB Tip   *The ColorDialog and FontDialog are the same ones that are available in other Windows applications.*

ColorDialog

The *ColorDialog* lets a developer give the user the power to set the color of almost anything. Name the control dlgColor. The *ForeColor* property controls the font color for most controls. The *BackColor* property determines the background color. The ColorDialog works in much the same way as other dialogs. The control sits in the component tray when added to a form. Display and use the form with code like this:

```
dlgColor.ShowDialog()
lblDemo.ForeColor = dlgColor.Color
```

The first line opens the ColorDialog as a dialog box. The *Color* property contains the color the user sets. The second line sets that color as the ForeColor for the Label. Use the BackColor property to set the background color for a control (see Figure 11.5).

Set the ForeColor and BackColor manually by assigning the color in a line of code:

```
lblDemo.ForeColor = Color.Black
lblDemo.BackColor = Color.White
```

This line sets the ForeColor of lblDemo to Black and the BackColor to White. Just be careful not to set the ForeColor and BackColor to the same color. If you

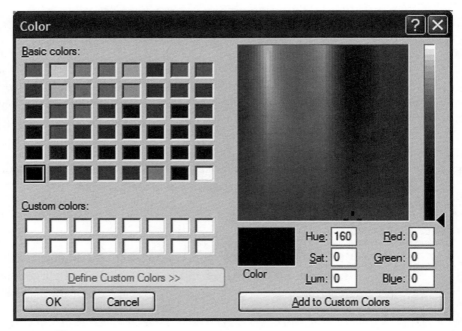

Figure 11.5   Color Dialog Screen

do, the text won't be visible. It's a good idea to use high-contrast colors to make the teasier to read, too.

FontDialog

The *FontDialog* lets a developer give the user the power to set the font properties of almost anything. Name the control dlgFont. The FontDialog controls the font, size, and style properties of text. The FontDialog works in much the same way as other dialogs. The control sits in the component tray when added to a form. Display and use the form with code like this:

```
Dim shoFontSize As Short
Dim strFont As String
Dim drwFontStyle As New System.Drawing.FontStyle

dlgFont.ShowDialog()
strFont = dlgFont.Font.Name
shoFontSize = dlgFont.Font.Size
drwFontStyle = dlgFont.Font.Style
lblDemo.Font = New System.Drawing.Font(strFont,
    shoFontSize, drwFontStyle)
```

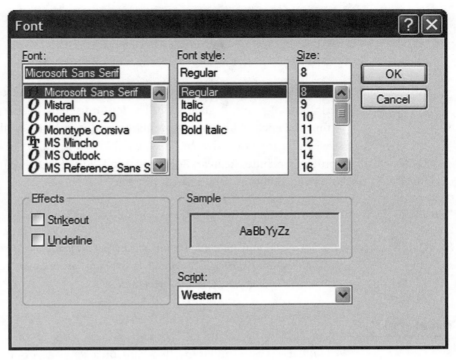

Figure 11.6   Font Dialog Screen

The Dim statements declare variables to hold the font, size, and style. Display the FontDialog with the ShowDialog method. The user settings are stored in several properties:

```
strFont = dlgFont.Font.Name
```

stores the *name* of the font in strFont.

```
shoFontSize = dlgFont.Font.Size
```

stores the font *size*, and the font style is controlled by

```
drwFontStyle = dlgFont.Font.Style
```

where drwFontStyle was declared as a FontStyle. *FontStyle* contains the styles from the FontDialog. Change the font for a control with a line similar to this:

```
lblDemo.Font = New System.Drawing.Font(strFont,
  shoFontSize, drwFontStyle)
```

which sets the font of lblDemo to a new instance of the font with the settings from the FontDialog. The strFont variable is the font, shoFontSize is the size of the font, and drwFontStyle is the style (see Figure 11.6).

Fonts can also be set manually in the code:

```
lblDemo.Font = New System.Drawing.Font("Microsoft Sans
    Serif", 10, FontStyle.Regular)
```

The preceding code sets the Font property of lblDemo to Microsoft Sans Serif font, 10-point, Regular style. The font must be available on the computer, it must be enclosed in quotation marks, and it must be spelled correctly. The size can be any point size, but it's a good idea to stick to the regular sizes. The FontStyle includes Regular, Bold, Italic, and Underline. Keep in mind that some fonts don't support some sizes and styles.

VB Tip   *Open and run the FontsAndColors program to see how it works.*

VB Quiz 03   *What are the pros and cons of letting the user set the font properties?*
What happens if the ForeColor and BackColor are the same color?
Why should font changes be used with caution?

LinkLabel

A *LinkLabel* is very similar to a hyperlink on a webpage, but it can do more than just link to a webpage. A LinkLabel can be used to send email or start another application. Use llb for its prefix. The *LinkClicked* event triggers a process that can start your browser, open your email, or start a program. Of course, regular VB commands work as well, which is handy if your application is designed to look and feel like a web application. The following code:

```
System.Diagnostics.Process.Start("http://www.cambridge
    .org")
```

uses the System class to start your browser. From there it opens the webpage specified. Be sure to enclose the URL in quotation marks.

The same System.Diagnostics.Process.Start command is used to open your default email application and address an email. For example:

```
System.Diagnostics.Process.Start("mailto:Mac@JimMcKeown
    .com")
```

starts an email message. And

```
System.Diagnostics.Process.Start("DiceDrag.exe")
```

runs a program – in this case, the sample drag-and-drop program. Be sure to specify the location of the application or include it in the same folder as your application. You computer must know where to find it.

ProgressBar

The *ProgressBar* is often used to indicate the status of a process. Sometimes the user has to wait for a file to load or for a series of calculations to complete. It's unfair to make the user wait without any feedback on the process. In a worst-case scenario, the user might think the computer has frozen and try to restart it in the middle of a process. Ouch!

Use prb for the prefix. There are three styles for a ProgressBar: Continuous, Block, and Marquee. Block is the default. Block and Continuous seem to work the best because they fill the ProgressBar and offer a rough indication of how far along the process is. Marquee indicates that there's a process running, but it doesn't provide an estimate for its completion. Marquee works well when you don't know how long a process will take.

Set the Minimum and Maximum values for the ProgressBar as needed. The ProgressBar uses this range. The Value property tracks the progress. As it changes, it indicates the progress of your process.

VB Tip

Use a For . . . Next loop to practice with a ProgressBar. Be sure to set the loop to run to a number with at least six digits. The Minimum and Maximum for the ProgressBar should be the same as the range for your loop.

MonthCalendar

The *MonthCalendar* is a quick and easy way to select a date. MonthCalendar displays the current month and can easily navigate to months in the past or future. Click on a date to select it – a fast and easy way for a user to select a date. Once selected, there are a number of methods to extract and work with the date. Use cal for the prefix.

The SelectionStart method determines the date selected by the user. From there, it's easy to select the Month, Day, Year, DayOfWeek, and other options. The current date is automatically set from the computer when the calendar loads. Use the *DateChanged* event to control the calendar. For example:

```
lblMonth.Text = calMonthly.SelectionStart.Month
lblDay.Text = calMonthly.SelectionStart.Day
lblYear.Text = calMonthly.SelectionStart.Year
```

The first line takes the month of the selected date and displays it. The second line displays the day and the last line displays the year (see Figure 11.7).

DateTimePicker

When space is limited, the *DateTimePicker* is handy. It's similar to the MonthCalendar, but it takes up less space. Use dtp for the prefix. The

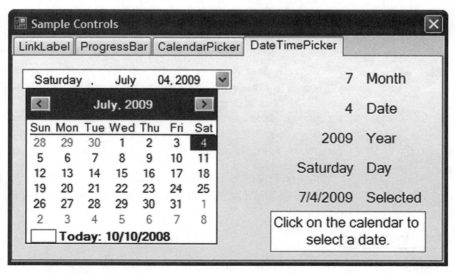

Figure 11.7   CalendarPicker Control

calendar starts as a dropdown box and expands when selected. From there, the user navigates through it like a MonthCalendar. There is one difference, however; the date is stored in the Value property and assigns values accordingly. Here's some code:

```
lblDTPMonth.Text = dtpCalendar.Value.Month
lblDTPDay.Text = dtpCalendar.Value.Day
lblDTPYear.Text = dtpCalendar.Value.Year
```

The first line gets the month and displays it in a Label. The next line gets the Day and displays it. The last line gets the year and displays it (see Figure 11.8).

VB Tip   *Open and run the Chap11SampleControls program to see how it works.*

Figure 11.8   DateTimePicker Screen

Predefined Forms

Visual Basic has several predefined forms. Until now you've ignored them and stuck to a Windows Form when adding a form to a project. No more! Visual Basic has numerous predefined forms and more are available online. The following are a few that come in handy.

Splash Screen

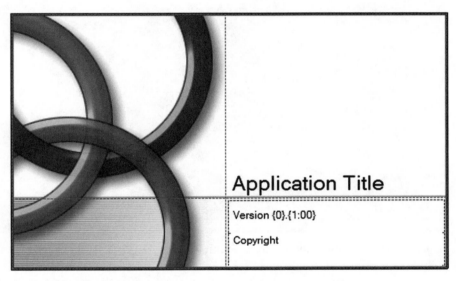

Figure 11.9   Startup Screen Example

A *splash screen* can also be called a startup screen. It's the first screen a user sees. It usually contains the name of the application and some other important information. This screen pops up as the rest of the application loads.

Add a form by selecting Add Windows Form . . . from the Project menu. In fact, almost any of the Add options in the Project menu will work. Select Splash Screen from the dialog box, name it, and a new splash screen opens. The Add New Item . . . button on the Toolbar works also (see Figure 11.9).

Application settings are available under Properties at the bottom of the Project menu. Use them to set your startup form. Otherwise, the startup screen is the default form that opens when you create your application. Use these settings to control your applications and your development environment.

The splash screen uses the name of your solution as the Application Title. If you don't want that, then set the Text of the ApplicationTitle Label to the name you want to use and delete the If statement under Application title in the splash screen code. Set the version and the Copyright the same way. Enter what

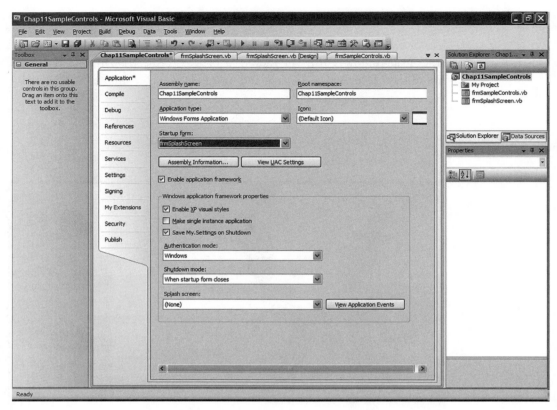

Figure 11.10   Applications Screen Example

you want in the Text property of these TextBoxes and remove the code from the splash screen. Custom graphics can be added as well (see Figure 11.10).

Of course, if you have an existing splash screen for your company or one your instructor wants, then use Add Existing Item... from the Project menu and select the file you want to use.

VB Tip   *The Title, Description, Company, Product, Version, and Copyright information can be set in the AssemblyInfo.vb file. The file is in the My Project folder of your solution. Be careful when making changes, though. You could damage your program!*

About Screen

Use an *About Screen* within an application so the user can see relevant information about the program. The About Screen should include the product name, version, copyright, company name, and a description or credits.

Create an About screen the same way you'd create a splash screen. Select About Box from the Add Windows Form... option of the Project menu. It creates a generic About form. Enter product information in the appropriate Labels of

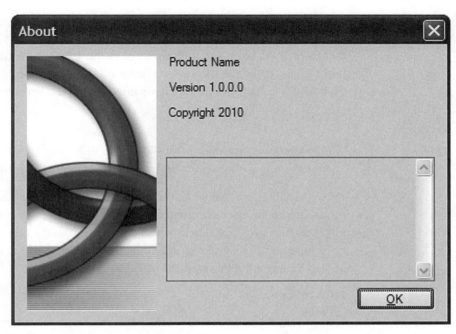

Figure 11.11   About Screen Example

the form. Delete the code associated with them; otherwise, it uses the default values of your application for them. Use your own graphic for it as well (see Figure 11.11).

VB Quiz 04   *When can you use a LinkLabel?*
                        When would a good developer use a ProgressBar?
                        What are the similarities and differences between a MonthCalendar and a DateTimePicker?
                        Why use a splash screen or an About screen?
                        What other useful templates are available?

Variable Scope

VB Quip   *Your most unhappy customers are your greatest source of learning. – Bill Gates*

Private, Public, and Static Visibility

Recall that the Dim keyword was used to declare local and module-level variables. These variables are visible where they are declared. In other words, a Dimmed variable is visible in the procedure or on the form where it's declared. They are not visible to other forms.

Private variables are visible only on the form where they're declared. They cannot be used across forms. If a variable has a Private scope, it works only on that form. That keeps variables confined to the areas where they'll be used, and it means you could use the same name for different variables on different forms. That comes in handy at times! Here's how to declare a Private variable:

```
Private mshoNum As Short
```

VB Tip   *Private variables are considered class-level variables because they will only work within the class where they are declared. Chapter 12 covers classes in more detail.*

Public variables are visible throughout your project. They are visible in any procedure on any form. Sometimes you just need access to a variable in many places in your program. That's where a Public variable is useful. Use them with caution, though. They take up space and too many of them get in the way. Here's how to declare a Public variable:

```
Public gshoNum As Short
```

Static variables are local variables that aren't destroyed in between uses. When a variable is Dimmed in a procedure, it's created, used, and discarded, all within that procedure. Usually it lasts for just a split second. It does its job and then disappears. Usually, that's a good thing, however, counters and accumulators are generally used in just one Button. Until now, their variables were declared at the module level so their values would persist in between uses. Static variables are declared in the procedure where they're used and they hold their value in between uses. They aren't discarded when the procedure ends, like Dimmed variables. Static variables aren't visible outside of a procedure. That makes them darn near perfect for most counters and accumulators. Here's how to declare a Static variable:

```
Static shoCount As Short
```

VB Tip   *Static variables are ideal for most counters and accumulators.*

By default, variables are Private and local. Only those with a Public scope are accessible by other forms. And even then, they must be referenced properly. For instance, gshoMainNum was declared as a Public variable on frmMain:

```
Public Class frmMain
    Public gshoNum As Short
End Class
```

To use it on another form, say frmSpecial, you must reference it like this:

```
frmMain.gshoNum += 1
lblNum.Text = gshoNum.ToString
```

where frmMain must be referenced to get to gshoNum. The explicit reference to frmMain makes the controls and public variables (and constants) visible to frmSpecial. It's handy, but it's a little messy until you're used to it. The following table describes the different access specifiers.

Access Specifier	Scope	Duration	Use
Dim	Procedure	Procedure	Any local-only variable
Private	Form	Form	Any form-level variable needed in more than one procedure on the form
Public	Global	Project	Any global variable needed in more than one form of a project
Static	Procedure	Form	Any local variable that must retain its value from one use to another (counters and accumulators)

Globals

Local variables work only in the procedure where they are declared. Module-level variables work anywhere on a form. But what do you do when you need the same data on multiple forms? That's where *global* variables come in handy. The same is true for procedures and functions that must be shared between forms. Create them as global variables and they'll work anywhere in a program.

Global variables are declared in their own *module* and are visible to any procedure on any form of a project. Use the Add Module . . . menu option in the Project menu to add a module to a project. Modules are added to the Solution Explorer just like other files in a project. The extension for a module is .vb. The name of the file should be the same as the module. The name should describe what the module does, so follow the same naming guidelines that you would use for a function.

Global variables are written with a g at the beginning to signify their scope. The other naming conventions and rules still apply. A Public variable in a module is visible throughout the project. Private variables are visible only within the module and Dim variables will only work within the scope of their declaration.

VB Tip   *A single global module can handle variables, procedures, and functions, so one module might be all that's needed for a project.*

Procedures

Procedures written into a module can be Public or Private depending on where they must be visible. Create them as a Public Sub to make them visible outside the module and use Private for those that won't be exposed to other parts of a project. In other words, a Public procedure in a module is visible to other parts of the project while Private procedures in a module can only be used by that module.

Functions

Functions created in a module can be Public or Private depending on where they must be visible. Create them as a Public Function to make them visible outside the module and use Private for those that won't be exposed to other parts of a project. In other words, a Public function in a module is visible to other parts of the project while Private functions in a module can only be used by that module.

The following code has two functions from a code module:

```
Module Module1
    'Only visible within this module
    Private Function CalcArea(ByVal sngLength As Single,
        ByVal sngWidth As Single) As Single
      Return sngLength * sngWidth

    End Function

    'Visible throughout the project
    'Calls private function CalcArea
    Public Function CalcVolume(ByVal sngLength As Single,
      ByVal sngWidth As Single, ByVal sngHeight As
      Single) As Single
      Return CalcArea(sngLength, sngWidth) * sngHeight
    End Function
End Module
```

CalcArea is a Private function and is only visible within the code module. CalcVolume is Public, so it's visible to other areas of the project. CalcVolume calculates the volume of a box. When called, it accepts the length, width, and height of the box. It then calls CalcArea and passes it the length and width. CalcArea returns the area, which is used by CalcVolume to find the volume.

The line

```
sngVolume = CalcVolume(sngLength, sngWidth, sngHeight)
```

calls the function from the form and gets the volume in return.

VB Tip   *Open and run the Globals program to see how it works.*

Overloading

Methods can be *overloaded*, which means a developer can write more than one function and use the same name for them as long as every function with that name has a different list of arguments. The argument list must be unique in number, type, or order. Here's an example:

```
Private Function CalcAverage(ByVal shoScore1 As Short,
    ByVal shoScore2 As Short, ByVal shoScore3 As Short,
    ByVal shoScore4 As Short) As Single
        Return (shoScore1 + shoScore2 + shoScore3 +
        shoScore4) / 4

End Function

Private Function CalcAverage(ByVal shoScore1 As Short,
    ByVal shoScore2 As Short, ByVal shoScore3 As Short)
    As Single
        Return (shoScore1 + shoScore2 + shoScore3) / 3

End Function

Private Function CalcAverage(ByVal shoScore1 As Short,
    ByVal shoScore2 As Short) As Single
        Return (shoScore1 + shoScore2) / 2
End Function
```

Each function is named CalcAverage. Until now that's been a no-no. However, now it's allowed because the function is overloaded. Each one has a different set of arguments. The first needs four numbers to work, the second needs three, and the last one expects two numbers. VB knows which one to use based on the number of arguments provided by the calling statement. When the developer codes the calling statement, IntelliSense automatically displays the number of overloads for that function and the arguments for it. A developer is free to select the one that fits best.

The example in Figure 11.12 has a varying number of arguments, but overloading works with different data types and with arguments in a different order.

Optional Parameters

Optional parameters are another way to make methods more flexible. The argument list for a function can contain one or more optional arguments. When optional parameters are used, the developer is free to supply any or all of the optional arguments or simply not use them. Here's the same average function written with optional parameters:

```
Private Function FindAverage(ByVal shoScore1 As Short,
    ByVal shoScore2 As Short, Optional ByVal shoScore3
    As Short = -1, Optional ByVal shoScore4 As Short =
    -1) As Single
```

```
If shoScore4 >= 0 Then
    Return (shoScore1 + shoScore2 + shoScore3 + shoScore4)/ 4
Else
    If shoScore3 >= 0 Then
        Return (shoScore1 + shoScore2 + shoScore3) / 3
    Else
        Return (shoScore1 + shoScore2) / 2
    End If
End If
End Function
```

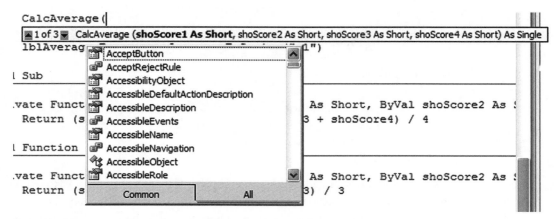

Figure 11.12　　Overloaded Averages CalcAverage Function

The first two scores are required. However, the third and fourth scores are optional, as indicated by the *Optional* keyword in the parameters list. Optional arguments in the list must have a default value. The default value is used if no value is passed to the function. The If statements check to see if an optional value was passed for shoScore3 and shoScore4. If nothing was passed, then the values are −1 and the average is calculated accordingly. The beauty of optional parameters is that a developer doesn't have to write multiple functions or select exactly the right one from a list when calling a function (see Figure 11.13).

Figure 11.13　　Overloaded Averages FindAverage Function

VB Tip　　　　*Open and run the OverloadedAverages program to see how it works.*

Event Handlers

Good programs typically have multiple ways to handle the same task. For example, the Copy command in a word processor can be handled with the Copy command from the Edit menu, Ctrl-C from the keyboard, the copy option from the popup menu of a right-click, or the Copy icon from the Toolbar. Having all of those options doesn't mean that you need to write separate code for all of them. An easier way is to put the *Handles* clause to work. When you create an event – a click event, for instance – VB generates a procedure for it and opens the procedure. At the end of the header line for the procedure is the Handles clause. It's this part of the command that actually determines the event that triggers your code. For example:

```
Private Sub btnExit_Click(ByVal sender As
   System.Object, ByVal e As System.EventArgs)
     Handles btnExit.Click
     End
End Sub
```

This is the typical procedure for an Exit Button. At the very end of the header is

```
Handles btnExit.Click
```

It's that part that actually makes the click on the Button run the code. So instead of writing separate procedures to do the same task, an easier way is to build a list of events that will trigger the procedure, like this:

```
Private Sub btnExit_Click(ByVal sender As System.Object,
   ByVal e As System.EventArgs Handles btnExit.Click,
   mnuFileExit.Click, tbxExit.Click
     End
End Sub
```

Each handler must include the name of the control and the event. Each handler is separated by a comma. When that event is triggered, it runs that procedure. When an event is triggered, it passes along some of its values in something called *Sender*. Sender contains the property values for that control. Use the Sender property to detect which control raised the event. You can customize your code from there.

Loan Calculator Program

The banking firm Dewey, Cheatam, and Howe needs a loan calculator program. The program must be able to calculate several types of loans: home loans and student loans with a term of years in addition to business, car, and consumer

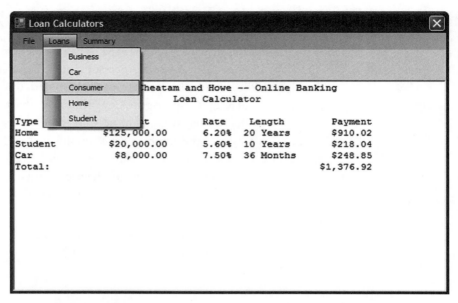

Figure 11.14   Loan Calculators Program

loans with a term of months. Users must be able to calculate the monthly payment for a loan, display the payment information, and calculate the total monthly payment on all their loans. The user selects the type of loan from the menu. This process opens a second form, where they select the terms of the loan. The Payment Button calculates the payment. The Cancel Button cancels the operation and returns them to the main form. The Accept Button adds the loan amount to the output. The main form is shown in Figure 11.14.

The calculator form is shown in Figure 11.15.

The program puts several new techniques to use, including a startup screen, a module, global variables, overloaded functions, and event handlers.

```
Private Sub LoanMenus_Click(ByVal sender As
   System.Object, ByVal e As System.EventArgs)
   Handles _mnuLoansHome.Click, mnuLoansCar.Click,
   mnuLoansConsumer.Click, mnuLoansStudent.Click,
   mnuLoansBusiness.Click
      'Determines which menu option was selected and
      'sends user to that form
      'Passes along the type of loan
      Select Case sender.Text
         Case Is = "Business"
            gstrLoanType = "Business"
            Dim frmMonths As New frmMonths
            frmMonths.ShowDialog()
         Case Is = "Car"
```

```
                        gstrLoanType = "Car"
                        Dim frmMonths As New frmMonths
                        frmMonths.ShowDialog()
                  Case Is = "Consumer"
                        gstrLoanType = "Consumer"
                        Dim frmMonths As New frmMonths
                        frmMonths.ShowDialog()
                  Case Is = "Home"
                        gstrLoanType = "Home"
                        Dim frmYears As New frmYears
                        frmYears.ShowDialog()
                  Case Is = "Student"
                        gstrLoanType = "Student"
                        Dim frmYears As New frmYears
                  frmYears.ShowDialog()
                  End Select
```

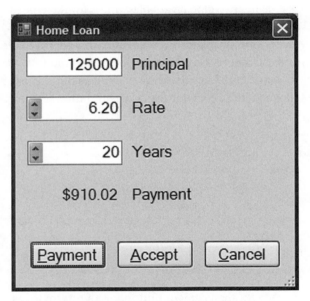

Figure 11.15   Loan Calculator Program – Home Loan Screen

The LoansMenu_Click procedure has events for all the loan options. Inside it is a Case structure that's controlled by Sender.Text. The correct form is created and loaded for the selected loan type. It also sets a global variable that displays the type of loan in the loan form.

```
Module Module1
    Public gstrLoanType As String
    Public gdecTotal As Decimal
    'Calculates monthly payment for a term in months
```

```
Public Function CalcPayment(ByVal decPrincipal As
   Decimal, ByVal sngRate As Single, ByVal
   bytMonthly As Byte) As Decimal
     Return Math.Abs(Pmt(sngRate / 1200, bytMonthly,
     decPrincipal))
   End Function

   'Calculates monthly payment for a term in years
   Public Function CalcPayment(ByVal decPrincipal As
      Decimal, ByVal bytYears As Byte, ByVal sngRate As
      Single) As Decimal
        Return Math.Abs(Pmt(sngRate / 1200, bytYears * 12,
decPrincipal))
   End Function
End Module
```

The module has two global variables: one is for the type of loan form and the other is the total of all loan payments. There are two overloaded functions called CalcPayment. One calculates payments for short-term loans over a matter of months and the other is for long-term loans with monthly payments extending over many years. Both have the same arguments but the order is different.

The following is the code for the Payment Button for short-term loans:

```
'Input
mdecPrincipal = Convert.ToDecimal(txtPrincipal.Text)
msngRate = nudRate.Value
mbytMonths = nudMonths.Value

'Processing
mdecPayment = CalcPayment(mdecPrincipal, msngRate,
  mbytMonths)
'Output
lblPayment.Text = mdecPayment.ToString("c")
```

This is the code for the Payment Button for long-term loans.

```
'Input
mdecPrincipal = Convert.ToDecimal(txtPrincipal.Text)
msngRate = nudRate.Value
mbytYears = nudYears.Value

'Processing
mdecPayment = CalcPayment(mdecPrincipal, mbytYears,
  msngRate)

'Output
lblPayment.Text = mdecPayment.ToString("c")
```

The code is similar except for the function calls. Note that the order of the arguments is different between them. That's how VB knows which function to use.

```
'Displays the loan type in the title bar
Me.Text = gstrLoanType ... " Loan"
```

The preceding code is in the Load event for the Months and Years forms. When the form loads, this code displays the type of loan in the Titlebar.

The code for the Accept Button looks like this:

```
Dim strOut As String
'Add to total payments
gdecTotal += mdecPayment

'Create output string for main form and display it
strOut = gstrLoanType.PadRight(12) & _
mdecPrincipal.ToString("c").PadLeft(14) & _
msngRate.ToString("n2").PadLeft(10) & ". ." & _
mbytYears.ToString.PadLeft(4) & " Years    " & _
mdecPayment.ToString("c").PadLeft(12) & vbNewLine
frmLoanCalculators.rtbOut.AppendText(strOut)

'Closes this form
Me.Close()
```

It adds the monthly payment to the total and creates and displays a detail line for the main form before closing the Payment form. Notice how it references the RichTextBox, rtbOut on frmLoanCalculator, and appends the text to this form.

VB Tip   *Open and run the LoanCalculators program to see how it works.*

VB Quiz 05   *How is variable scope similar to a set of keys for a building?*
                    Why use overloaded functions?
                    What are the risks and benefits of Public variables?
                    What is the purpose of an event handler?
                    How could the Loan Calculator program be improved?

Potential Problems

Use new controls with caution. It's a good idea to test them separately and get a feel for how they work and what they can do. Dialogs and predefined forms have many different properties and only a few were touched on here. Take some time to learn some of the others – it's worth it.

Scope is powerful and a little tricky. Public scope is wide open, so use it with caution. Private scope limits the scope to a form. Don't be afraid to start with

Public scope and then change it to Private later. That's a good way to keep control of your code. Use Static for counters and accumulators. Modules are great, but often overused. Take the time to plan before you code. That's the best way to get the upper hand with scope.

Overloading and optional variables are designed to make a function flexible. Use them to get the same outcome with varying input and parameters.

Fixing a Program

Joe Cuppa runs a 24-hour coffee shop and has tried unsuccessfully to write a small program to let his employees calculate their pay. He wants a program that lets the user enter hours, pay rate, and shift and outputs gross pay. He pays time-and-a-half for overtime and provides a shift differential −5% for swing shift and 10% for the graveyard shift. You hang out at his place, partly for the caffeine and partly for the free WiFi, and feel a little guilty about his problem, so you agree to help.

First, you look over the requirements of the program and make sure you understand the payscale. Next you take a little time to understand exactly what Joe wants the program to do, the inputs, processing, and output. Once you're comfortable with the requirements, you dive in.

You make a copy of the program files, just in case. If all else fails, at least Joe will still have a copy of his work.

VB Tip   *Open and run the ShiftDifferential program to see what's wrong with it.*

You try to run the program, but is has build errors. The Error List says:

Name 'CalcWages' is not declared.

You double-click on the first error and it takes you to the "blue line of death" for that error. The line says:

```
mdecPay = CalcWages(msngHours, mdecPayRate, msngShift)
```

You do some checking. There are two CalcWages functions in the Module1 file. The comments indicate that they should calculate the pay for first, swing, and graveyard shifts. Everything seems to be in place for them. There are no errors and it looks like the code should work. Then it dawns on you, the error said they weren't declared. You recall something similar with variables from Chapter 4. That problem wasn't a declaration problem so much as a scope problem. The CalcWages functions are Private instead of Public! No wonder. The functions are there, but with a Private scope, they're not visible to your form. You change both of them from Private to Public. That takes care of the problem.

You try again. This time the program runs, but Joe said the program has a splash screen. The file for it is there, frmStartup.vb. You check the project properties and the Startup form is frmShiftDifferential, not frmStartup. You make that change and try again. Now the splash screen works. You're feeling a little smug as Joe refills your cup for free.

Next, you check the About screen. It appears OK and you're thinking maybe you'll slip your name in as the developer. The Help screen is another matter. When you try it, the About screen shows up again. OK, not a problem. Joe probably pasted the code from the About menu into the Help menu and didn't change it. Right again. But, you get blue squigglies with your Dim statement. Hmmm. You point to it and it says it's not defined. You delete frmHelp from the Dim statement and try again. Maybe it's a spelling error. However, IntelliSense doesn't pick up on frmHelp. You check the Solution Explorer and there's no frmHelp file. Ah ha! You check the project folder and it's there. The problem is that it's not a part of the project. You add it to the project by selecting Add Existing Item . . . from the Project menu. You select frmHelp.vb and it gets added to the Solution Explorer. You try it again and it works. The smug smile creeps back to your face as you take another sip.

You run the program and the forms all work. But, nothing else does. You enter hours and pay rate, but get only $0.00 for output. Changing the shift doesn't help either. OK, you've seen this before. Output is 0, so you're thinking it's a logical error. A variable isn't getting assigned so it's multiplying by zero. Time for a deskcheck. You check your input and all seems in order there. The code calls CalcWages regardless of the shift selected. You concentrate on the day shift first. The variables msngHours, mdecPayRate, and msngShift are passed to the function. You jump over to the module to check that code. It's a little tough to move back and forth. However, a right-click of the Module1 tab lets you open a New Horizontal Tab Group. It's kinda neat because it splits the code window in two so you can see both at once. You don't remember how you picked that up, but you intend to remember it.

CalcWages is overloaded. One of them has two arguments, sngHours and decPayRate. The other has three arguments, sngHours, decPayRate, and sngShift. Both of them call another function called CalcRegularPay. That function is in the module as well and calculates regular and overtime pay. The first CalcWages function returns this value. The second calculates shift differential, 5% for swing shift and 10% for graveyard shift. That's the difference between the two. It takes a little checking but then you realize the main form calls the wrong overloaded functions. The first shift doesn't need the shift differential. Second and third shifts do need it, but don't have it. You change those lines of code, do a deskcheck, and fully expect the program to work.

It does, sort of. You enter hours and pay rate for regular pay and check the math. You test it with several numbers and combinations and everything seems OK. But when you try it for the swing shift and graveyard shift, nothing happens – so much for that smug smile. You keep testing and sometimes it works and sometimes not. Eventually, you notice it only updates your output when you change the hours or pay rate. You think, "It must be a problem with the output." You locate the one line of output:

```
lblPay.Text = mdecPay.ToString("c")
```

and it looks fine. So you decide to audit your code. You start with the output line and work backward through the code. No problems there; it all looks fine. That's when you notice the event handlers for the CalcPay procedure. The code is triggered by txtHours.TextChanged and txtPayRate.TextChanged events. So every time the hours or the pay rate changes, the code runs. But, it does nothing when the shift changes! You quickly add event handlers for the CheckChanged events for the three RadioButtons, like this:

```
Handles txtHours.TextChanged, txtPayRate.TextChanged, _
    rad1st.CheckedChanged, rad2nd.CheckedChanged,
    rad3rd.CheckedChanged
```

You try the program again and now the code runs every time a RadioButton changes. Good for you. Finally, you completely understand how event handlers work. Joe is completely impressed and the two of you ponder the meaning of life over another cup of coffee, Joe's treat.

VB Tip   *Open and run the ShiftDifferentialFixed program to see how it works.*

On Your Own

Write a program that determines what type of character has been entered into a TextBox. For every character entered, determine and display whether it's a consonant, vowel, number, or special character.

Write a simple drag-and-drop application to drop letters and numbers into their correct locations. Create three Labels with consonants and three with numbers. Set up "boxes" and drop them into their correct locations.

Write a program that lets the user select a date in the future using a Month-Calendar. Determine the number of days between now and that date.

Add a splash screen and an about screen to a program you've already written.

Write a program with overloaded functions. One function should determine the letter grade for a class when passed the midterm, final, and term paper scores. The other should determine pass/fail for a class when passed the term paper, midterm, and final scores. Test scores are Singles and the paper score is a Byte.

Summary

There are dozens of events for nearly every control and process in Visual Basic. Events are triggered by user actions and by processes within a program. An understanding of events and how, when, and where they happen is key to developing solid programs. Drag and drop provides a graphical method for user input. Controls are moved around the screen and dropped onto other controls, which trigger events that handle the work of a program. Several new controls were introduced. Several predefined forms were explained. The use of code modules was explained and new methods for controlling the scope of your code were covered. Overloaded functions and optional parameters were introduced.

Review

There is a series of events triggered when the user types from the keyboard.

A KeyDown event is generated when a key is pressed.

A KeyUp event is generated when a key is released.

A KeyPressed event is generated with every keystroke.

Modifier keys can be tracked with e.Control, e.Alt, and e.Shift.

The TextChanged event is raised with every change to the text of a control.

The SelectionStart method works with the first selected character in the text of a control.

The SelectionLength is the number of characters of a selection.

The Focus method sets the focus to the named control.

The GotFocus event is triggered when a control is given the focus and the LostFocus event is triggered when a control loses the focus.

An Activated event is triggered when a form becomes active.

There are several mouse events that are raised when the mouse is used.

MouseEnter is triggered when the mouse moves over a control, MouseDown happens when the mouse button is pressed, MouseUp occurs when the mouse button is released and MouseMove occurs when the mouse moves over a control.

The DoubleClick event works when the mouse is clicked twice on a control in rapid succession.

Drag and Drop is the term used to describe when controls are moved around the form and events are triggered by these movements.

DragEnter events occur when the mouse moves onto a control. DragOver occurs when the mouse moves over a control. DragLeave occurs when the mouse leaves a control.

DragDrop events occur when a draggable control moves over a control that allows drops and the draggable control is dropped.

The contents of a draggable control can be copied or moved from one control to another.

The ColorDialog is used to set the colors at runtime.

The FontDialog is used to set the font and font properties at runtime.

A LinkLabel is similar to a hyperlink and can be used to start applications or like a Button.

The ProgressBar is used to indicate the status of a process and to keep the user informed.

The MonthCalendar and the DateTimePicker display a monthly calendar and are used to set dates in a program.

Several predefined forms are built into Visual Basic. They simplify and standardize the development of applications.

The Splash screen is used when the program loads. The About screen is used to describe a program and its developers.

Use the Application screen to set your startup form and to control your development environment for a program.

The scope of a variable, procedure or function determines where a variable can be used.

Private scope is visible on the form where it's used. Public scope is visible throughout a program. Static scope is used in a procedure to preserve values from one use of the procedure to another.

Static scope is usually used for counters and accumulators.

Modules are separate files that are used to create variables, procedures, and functions that can be used in a program.

Overloading a function involves using the same function name more than once and varying the number, order, or type of arguments for it. Functions that share a name should accomplish the same task using different parameters.

Optional parameters are arguments that are included in a procedure or function call but are not required for the procedure or function to work.

Terms

About screen	a predefined form used to describe the program
Application settings	a window used to control the settings for an application
AssemblyInfo.vb	a file in an application that's used to set general information about a program
"blue line of death"	an underlined segment of code that will cause a runtime error; a sarcastic term for a runtime error
ColorDialog	a control that allows a user to select the color for a control at runtime
DateTimePicker	a control that's smaller than a MonthCalendar, but pops up to display a MonthCalendar with much of the same functionality
Drag and Drop	a programming concept that lets users perform tasks by moving a control on the screen
event handler	a method that responds to actions in a program, for example a click or a key press

FontDialog	a control that allows a user to select the font and its settings for a control at runtime
global	a variable, procedure, or function that's visible to any part of a program
keystroke	a character entered from the keyboard by the user
LinkLabel	a control similar to a hyperlink
modifier keys	usually the Shift, Control, or Alt keys; keys that modify or change another keystroke
module	a file that contains variables, procedures, or functions used in a program
MonthCalendar	a control that displays a monthly calendar and is used to select a date or dates
optional parameters	optional arguments for a function
overloading	the creation of a multiple functions with the same name, where each is unique in the number, order, or type of arguments
predefined forms	a set of forms the developer can add to an application
ProgressBar	a control used to indicate the progress or status of a process
raise	triggered or generated; the generation of an event
Source	a control that serves as the source for content used in a drag-and-drop event
Splash screen	a predefined form used as the initial screen when a program runs; the screen usually contains information about the application
Target	a control that serves as the destination for content in a drag-and-drop event
trapped	recorded; user actions such as a keystroke or a mouse movement are usually trapped by a program and then used to generate events

Keywords

Activated	an event that's triggered when a form becomes active; occurs when the Show method is used on a form or when the user makes a form that's already visible active
AllowDrop	a property that determines if a control will accept dropped items in a drag and drop
BackColor	a property of a control that determines the background color of a control
Color	a property for setting the color of a part of a control, for example, the foreground or background of a control

Copy	a method that copies the selected text of a TextBox to the clipboard
DateChanged	an event for a calendar that's triggered when the user changes the selected date
DoDragDrop	a method used to grab a selected item for a drag and drop
DoubleClick	an event that's triggered when two clicks occur on a control in quick succession
DragDrop	an event that's triggered when a control is dropped on another control
DragDropEffects	a property that makes a control draggable
DragEnter	an event that's triggered when the mouse button is down and the mouse moves over a control
DragLeave	an event that's triggered when the mouse button is down and the mouse leaves a control
DragOver	an event that's triggered when the mouse button is down and the mouse is dragged over a control
e.Alt	a Boolean that knows when the Alt key is being held down
e.Control	a Boolean that knows when the Control key is being held down
e.Data.GetData	a method that gets the data from the data source
e.KeyChar	the keystroke character entered by a user
e.Shift	a Boolean that knows when the Shift key is being held down
e.X	the X location of the mouse on a control
e.Y	the Y location of the mouse on a control
Focus	a method that gives the focus to a control; a control with the Focus accepts input from the user, usually in the form of typing or clicks
Font	a property that contains the font settings for a control
FontStyle	a property that contains the font styles from a FontDialog
ForeColor	a property of a control that determines the color of the text for that control
GotFocus	an event that's triggered when a control is given the focus
Handles	a keyword that determines the events that will trigger a procedure
KeyCode	returns the ASCII value of a keystroke
KeyData	contains all the information about a KeyPress event
KeyDown	an event that's triggered when a key is in the down position
KeyPress	an event that's generated when a key is pressed
KeyUp	an event that's triggered when a key is released

LinkClicked	an event that's triggered when there's a click on a LinkLabel
LostFocus	an event that's triggered when a control loses the focus
MouseDown	an event that's triggered when a mouse button is pressed down
MouseEnter	an event that's triggered when a mouse moves over a control
MouseHover	an event that's triggered when a mouse pauses over a control
MouseLeave	an event that's triggered when a mouse moves off a control
MouseMove	an event that's triggered when a mouse moves over a control
MouseUp	an event that's triggered when a mouse button is released
Name	a property that contains the font name
Optional	a keyword used to indicate that an argument in a parameter is optional
Paste	a method that pastes the contents of the clipboard into a TextBox
Private	a keyword used to describe the scope of a variable, function, or procedure; Private scope restricts its use to the form level
Public	a keyword used to describe the scope of a variable, function, or procedure; Public scope creates content available to all parts of a program
SelectAll	a method that selects all the text of a TextBox
SelectionLength	a method that determines the number of characters to select in a TextBox
SelectionStart	a method that determines the start of the selected text in a control; SelectionStart is the index of the first selected character
Sender	a property that contains values that are sent from the control that calls an event to the procedure that's triggered by the event raised by that control
Size	a property that contains the size of a font
Static	a keyword used to describe the scope of a variable; Static scope creates a variable that's available locally but it persists from one use to another; often used for local counters and accumulators
TextChanged	an event that's generated when the text of a TextBox changes

Self-check

1. Every keystroke generates a Click event.
2. All the information about a keystroke is contained in the KeyData for the keystroke.
3. A TextChanged event is raised every time a character is added to or removed from a TextBox.
4. The first mouse event triggered for a control is the MouseEnter event.
5. The correct order of events when clicking on a Button is MouseDown, Click, and MouseUp.
6. e.X and e.Y are updated with every move of the mouse.
7. DragDrop checks to see if a control can be dropped into a target location.
8. Changes in the Progress property of a ProgressBar are used to indicate the status of a process.
9. A program can have multiple startup screens.
10. Overloaded functions must have a unique list of arguments.
11. The term for the event started by moving the mouse, clicking, or entering text is:
    A. triggering an event
    B. raising an event
    C. generating an event
    D. activating an event
12. Each keystroke is trapped by:
    A. e.Keystroke
    B. e.Tap
    C. e.KeyChar
    D. e. KeyPress
13. e.X and e.Y are the:
    A. X, Y coordinates relative to the control the mouse is currently over
    B. X, Y coordinates of the screen
    C. current line of code and command being executed by the program
    D. top and left position on the form of the control the mouse is currently over
14. What is the correct order of events when the mouse moves over a control?
    A. MouseEnter, MouseHover, MouseLeave
    B. MouseHover, MouseEnter, MouseLeave
    C. MouseIn, MouseOver, MouseOut
    D. MouseEnter, MouseHover, MouseExit
15. GotFocus and LostFocus are:
    A. methods for enabling or disabling the AllowTab setting for a control
    B. events that occur when focus passes to a control and when a control loses focus

C. ways to change the Enabled property of a control

D. none of the above

16. All of the following must be true to drag and drop an item except:

A. the AllowDrop property of the target is set to True

B. the source contains data that can be dropped

C. the MouseHover event for the targer is raised

D. the data type of the source and target are the same

17. What does the following line of code do?

```
lblSample.ForeColor = Color.Green
```

A. sets the border color of the Label to green

B. sets the color of the text of the Label to green

C. checks to see if the color of the text for the Label is green

D. the command contains an error

18. A ProgressBar is used to:

A. indicate the progress of a process

B. display how much memory is being used

C. group Buttons into a line for easy use

D. indicate if a control can be dragged and dropped

19. Public variables:

A. work only in a module

B. work in any procedure on the form

C. work in any procedure for any form or module

D. work only in the procedure where they're declared

20. An overloaded function:

A. has too many processes and calculations that slow down a program

B. has more arguments passed to it than it can handle

C. shares its name with two or more functions, each with its own set of unique arguments

D. is a predefined function that uses optional arguments

VB Quiz Answers

Quiz 01

The Cut method works the same way as the Cut in other Windows programs. For example, it removes the selected text and places it in the Clipboard so it can be pasted somewhere else.

The order of events when a Button is clicked is MouseDown, Click, MouseClick, and MouseUp. Click and MouseClick are just a little different. MouseClick is just what it says, a mouse click. Click could include other things, such as hitting the Enter key when a Button has the focus or using a Button's shortcut key. It only becomes an issue when both the Click and MouseClick are programmed differently for the same control.

The mouse location on a form or any control on a form is determined by its X, Y location relative to the upper left corner of the control. The top left has coordinates 0, 0. X increases as the mouse moves right. Y increases as the mouse moves down. Areas above and to the left of a control have negative numbers. The numbers are pixel-based.

Quiz 02

The AllowDrop property must be set to True before items can be dropped into a control. Even when AllowDrop is True, there must be code in the control to handle the drop.

The fruits and vegetables are hard-coded into the ListBoxes and the code that checks them. These items could come from a file and get added when the program starts. They could be randomly added to each ListBox to provide variety for the user. If different files were used, the program could also be made more flexible. Then, instead of fruits and vegetables, almost any categories could be used.

Quiz 03

Flexibility is almost always a good thing. When the user can set their own font properties, the program is customized to suit the user's needs. Some people have trouble reading certain fonts and small font sizes. Some people are color blind and have trouble with certain colors. Control over the font settings would help these users. Sometimes users get carried away with font, style, and color changes. It might look good to them on the screen, but others might not like it. Of course, all this power and flexibility makes design and programming harder for a developer.

When both colors are the same, the user can't tell the difference between the text and its background. They won't be able to see anything!

Some changes won't improve the look of a program. Some make it more difficult to read and use. It may even make printing difficult if not impossible. Some fonts don't support certain sizes and styles.

Quiz 04

A LinkLabel can be used for external links to applications, email, and programs. In addition, it works just like a Button. Code the Click event for a LinkLabel and it works just like a Button. However, it takes less space, and, because it appears like a link on a webpage, it might be more familiar to users who use the web.

A good developer doesn't leave a user hanging. Whenever a process takes more than a few seconds to complete, the user should be notified. A ProgressBar is a rough indicator of how long a process is taking. It provides the user with an indicator. Otherwise, the user might think the program or their computer has problems and try to intervene.

Both display a calendar with which a user can navigate and select dates. The MonthCalendar takes up more space on a form. The DateTimePicker takes less space on the form, but requires room to open and may hide other controls on a form.

Use a Splash screen when a program starts as an indicator that the program is loading. It's a good opportunity to provide the user with basic information about a program. The About screen is available while the program runs and can provide quick information on the program at almost any time. They're a great place to provide credit to developers or to slip in a little plug for your company, too.

Many custom forms are available online. A Dialog and a Login form are available. Previously, these were created manually. You'll soon learn about Class and Module templates.

Quiz 05

Variable scope determines where a variable can be used. Building keys may be similar to this. Some keys work on any door. They're called master keys and custodians and security use them. Some keys might work for a particular floor or department. Secretaries might have these keys. Some keys work only on specific doors. These may be the keys for individual offices. A key that's meant for only one door is very similar to a local variable. It works only in a specific location. Some keys are like module-level variables. They'll work in several places, but won't work for everything. Master keys work everywhere, just like a global variable works in any procedure.

Overloaded functions add more flexibility to a program. For example, a developer might need a function that accepts Short data types and calculates the area of a circle and another that accepts Single data types to do the same thing. Rather than create two, each with a different name, the developer names both of them CalcArea. Each one accepts different arguments. The developer simply picks the one that works best for the current situation.

Public variables occupy more memory. Too many of them could slow performance, so use them with caution. They're useful because they can pass values from one part of a program to another and they can hang on to values between procedures.

An event handler takes a user event for a control and initiates the code associated with that event for that control. More than one event handler can be tied to the same code. The advantage is that sometimes the same code will work for more than one event.

The Loan Calculator program could be improved in several ways. There are no shortcut keys for the menu items. Some items should be disabled at times. For example, the Total options should be disabled once it's been used and then enabled once a new loan has been added. Right now there are five options in the Select Case when only two are needed. There's no Help or About screens. There's no exception handling to prevent a crash. The TextBox doesn't check for numeric input, which might cause a crash. The program should have loan limits and there should be a better way to set the interest rates.

Objects and Classes – Objects Are in a Class By Themselves

VB Quip

But what is it good for? – an engineer at the Advanced Computing Systems Division of IBM,
commenting on the microchip in 1968

Think of objects as tools. Better yet, think of them as building blocks. Imagine how hard a job would be if you had to create everything from scratch every time. Say you wanted to build a table. First, you'd need to make an axe to cut down the tree. Then you'd have to make a saw to cut the wood. You'd have to make your own nails to piece together the table, but that's only after you made your own hammer so you could pound the nails. Programming is like that sometimes – OK, usually. And it was certainly that way years ago. Everything was done from scratch and very little was reusable. However, there's been some progress since then. You saw reusable code when you learned procedures and functions. Objects and classes are that way, but on a grander scale. The controls in the Toolbox are objects, each specially created for a specific task. They're tools and, without them, development would be much tougher, and a whole lot less fun. Classes are code that defines an abstract data type – it's a thing, and the developer provides a description of it and determines how it can be used. This chapter shows you how to create objects with your code and how to define and use classes. This is the object-oriented concept of object-oriented, event-driven programming that was tossed around so blithely in Chapter 1.

Built-in Objects

The Toolbox is filled with built-in objects. An *object* is a programming element that contains data and methods. Until now, you've added them to a form by dropping them from the Toolbox. They can also be added in your code. The advantage to this method is that a developer can control when objects are created and removed. It makes programming more flexible and powerful. So, instead of creating all of your controls at design time, you can create and manipulate them at runtime instead. Here's how:

```
Dim lblDemo As New Label
Controls.Add(lblDemo)
```

```
With lblDemo
    .Visible = True
    .AutoSize = False
    .Font = New System.Drawing.Font("Arial", 18,
        FontStyle.Bold)
    .ForeColor = Color.Red
    .Top = 100
    .Left = 200
    .Text = "It Works!"
End With
```

The first line creates a new Label. You already saw this when you used multiple forms back in Chapter 8. The Dim statement creates a new instance – in this case, a Label – and it's named lblDemo. Place it in either the procedure or the declarations for a form.

Control is a class from the System.Windows.Forms class and it controls what you see on your form. It's perfect for adding and manipulating controls on your form. In the second line, it adds lblDemo to the collection of controls for the form.

The next block of code is new. The *With* block encloses a set of commands, all of them tied to the With statement. In this example all of the commands apply to lblDemo. Using the With statement is a shortcut to writing separate commands for each one. And the block makes it easy to see that every command applies to lblDemo. The block always starts with With and always ends with End With.

The code creates and displays the Label. It didn't exist until it was created in your code. Place the code in the Load event and the Label is created when the form loads. Put it in a Button, and the Label isn't created until the Button is clicked. It's powerful and gives a developer more control over a program.

It just makes sense that if you can create a control with code, you should be able to get rid of it with code as well. A *destructor* removes a control or an object. This line gets rid of the Label and removes it from memory:

```
lblDemo.Dispose()
```

It's a process called *garbage collection*. Languages use garbage collection to reclaim unused memory and free it for other uses. Many computer problems, from freezes and crashes to slow performance, can be traced back to poor memory management. Visual Basic does a better job of garbage collection and memory management than most languages. It is automatic and nearly painless. Just use the Dispose method and the object is gone forever. Forever, of course, meaning while the program is running.

VB TIP   *Once a control is disposed, it's gone and cannot be used again.*

Creating controls with your code is an important concept. By adding controls with code, a developer gains more control and flexibility over the size of a program. Disposing of them frees memory and makes a program more manageable.

The concept applies to other controls as well. And, with a little practice, it's easy to control when and where your controls appear.

So, how do you write code for these controls? As written, IntelliSense won't recognize the controls because they don't exist until runtime. And, as such, there are no events for them either, which severely limits their utility. However, events can be written for them, but it requires a little more knowledge. Here's how:

```
Friend WithEvents btnDispose As
    System.Windows.Forms.Button
```

Use the preceding code in the declaration section for a form or in a module. *Friend* is an access type. It's similar to Dim, Public, Private, and Static declarations. The last part creates an instance of the control – in this case, a Button – and gives it a name. *WithEvents* makes IntelliSense aware of the control and sets it up so events and procedures can be written for it.

VB Tip   *Run the BuiltInObjects program to see how it works.*

VB Quiz 01   *How would you bake a cake from scratch? How would you make a shirt from scratch?*
                    Why create controls in code when they can be added to a form at design time?
                    Why worry about memory management?
                    Explain garbage collection.

Creating Classes of Your Own

Developers have the ability to create their own classes in VB. They're useful because they're flexible. With a class, the developer decides what it contains, how it works, and where it's used. You are, in a very real sense, creating development tools for your projects. A *class* is an abstract data type that contains its own properties and methods. It's abstract because it only exists in code. As a developer, you define its properties and you use methods to decide how it handles data. Let's create a class called AccountBalance to keep track of the balance in a bank account to see how this works.

Anatomy of a Class

Create a class by adding a class file to your project (see Figure 12.1). Select Add Class... from the Project menu. A dialog appears. Select the Class icon and name the file. The name has a .vb extension and should describe the file, like AccountBalance.vb, EmployeeRecord.vb, or StudentGrade.vb.

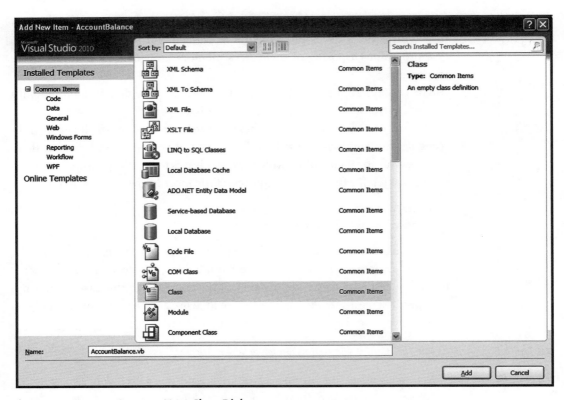

Figure 12.1 Create a New Class Dialog

The file gets added to the Solution Explorer. Double-click on it to open it the Code window. The code looks like this:

```
Public Class AccountBalance
    'Property Declarations
    'Get/Set statements
    'Methods
End Class
```

Public Class starts the class and End Class must be at the bottom. This is similar to the code for every form you've seen. The name of the class in this example, AccountBalance, is the name of the file. The code for your class is added inside these two lines. This code is considered a constructor. A *constructor* automatically creates a class and initializes the variables in a class every time it's called.

VB Tip *Follow the naming conventions for procedures and functions when creating classes.*

A Public class is open – or *exposed* – to all other classes in a project. Any project that references your project will also be able to use this class. It is the most open of the declarations. *Protected* declarations expose elements within the same class. *Friend* declarations can be used with a project but not outside of it.

Private declarations work only within a class. It's similar to the Dim statement. In general, Public lets others see your class. Friend works within your project and Private works only in your class.

Properties

The properties in a class are variables. Declare them in the same way you'd declare other variables. For example:

```
Public decBalance As Decimal
```

This example creates a Public property for the class. The property is called decBalance and is declared as a Decimal. Values for this property can be accessed through your code. Do this for all properties in a class. The advantage of this is that, as a developer, you decide what properties to expose. Do this through Get and Set functions.

The *Get* function is a special function that allows access to properties in a class. Use it to get the value of a property. The *Set* function is a special function that allows access to properties in a class. Use it to set the value of a property. Both are built into VB. Both appear when the property is created in a class. For example, when you enter this line:

```
Public Property Balance() As Decimal
```

VB automatically creates the Get and Set functions for it:

```
Public Property Balance() As Decimal
    Get

    End Get
    Set(ByVal value As Decimal)

    End Set
End Property
```

A developer always needs to write a little more code to make each one work properly. The Get function allows a developer to specify the value returned when the property is accessed. In other words, the developer determines the value returned by the property. The Set function allows a developer to specify the value assigned to the property:

```
Public Property Balance() As Decimal
    Get
      Balance = decBalance
    End Get
```

```
   Set(ByVal value As Decimal)
      decBalance = value
   End Set

End Property
```

In this example, the Balance property is a Decimal. When asked for the Balance property of the AccountBalance class, it gets the value in decBalance. The Set function sets decBalance to the value passed to it. The Set function executes every time the Balance property changes.

Methods

Class *methods* are similar to procedures and functions. They execute code and they can calculate and return values. For example,

```
Public Sub CalcBalance(ByVal decAmount As Decimal)
    decBalance = decBalance + decAmount
End Sub
```

This method accepts a value passed to it – in this case, decAmount. It then adds that value to decBalance. As used, it sets the Balance property to the new value. In effect, this method calculates the new account balance and sets the Balance property.

Using Classes

The class file creates and stores your class along with its properties and methods. To use them, there must be some code in your program. First, there must be an instance of the class:

```
Dim MyClassName As New ClassName
```

This code creates a new instance of ClassName and calls it MyClassName. ClassName is the name of the class you've already created and MyClassName is the name for the current instance of it. You now have something called MyClassName that has all the properties and methods of the original ClassName. This class is used the same way you've been using controls, properties, and methods all along. Simply type in MyClassName, then a period, and IntelliSense brings up the properties and methods for the class.

In this example (Figure 12.2), there's a little code for the form and some in the Update Button.

Figure 12.2   Account Balance Program

First, create an instance of the class. Do it with a declaration, like this:

```
Dim mAccountBalance As New AccountBalance
```

It creates a new instance of the AccountBalance class and names it mAccount-Balance. Place it in the declarations for the form so it creates it when the form is created. That way it remains in memory until the program ends.

The following code is from the Update Button:

```
Dim decDebitCredit As Decimal

'Display current account balance
lblBalance.Text = mAccountBalance.Balance.ToString("c")

'Calculate new balance
decDebitCredit = Convert.ToDecimal(txtDebitCredit.Text)

Call mAccountBalance.CalcBalance(decDebitCredit)

'Display new account balance
lblNewBalance.Text =
  mAccountBalance.Balance.ToString("c")
```

where decDebitCredit is a variable that stores the amount added or subtracted from the account. For now, use a minus sign to indicate a withdrawal.

The next line displays the current balance. It gets the Balance property of mAccountBalance, converts it to a string, and formats it as currency before displaying it in lblBalance.

The third line is input. It takes the value in the TextBox and assigns it to decDebitCredit. The next line is a procedure call. It finds the CalcBalance method in mAccountBalance and passes decDebitCredit to it. The method updates the current balance to reflect the latest transaction. The last line displays the new balance. It gets the Balance property of mAccountBalance, just like the first line of code. However, the balance was updated in between so it now has that new value. It displays it in lblNewBalance.

VB Tip   *Open and run the AccountBalance program to see how it works.*

ReadOnly and WriteOnly Properties

Properties in a class can be *ReadOnly* and *WriteOnly*. ReadOnly properties can be read but not changed. In other words, you can find out what they are, but you cannot modify them. WriteOnly properties can be changed, but they cannot be read. You can modify them, but you cannot find out what they are. In other words, you can get ReadOnly properties but you cannot change them and you can set WriteOnly properties but you cannot see them.

```
Public ReadOnly Property Grade() As String
    Get
        Grade = mGrade
    End Get
End Property
```

The preceding example is for a ReadOnly property. When declared, the keyword ReadOnly is inserted in the line. When it's created, it automatically has a Get function, but it cannot have a Set function. It's set up so a developer can find out what the property contains – in this case a grade – but its value cannot be changed. It may sound strange to have a property that can be seen and not changed, but the class is designed to set the grade elsewhere. That way, the class can be used, but the developer cannot change how it works.

```
Public WriteOnly Property Midterm() As Short
    Set(ByVal Value As Short)
        mMidterm = Value
    End Set
End Property
```

This example is for a WriteOnly property. When declared, the keyword WriteOnly is inserted in the line. When it's created, it automatically has a Set function, but it cannot have a Get function. It's designed so a developer can send

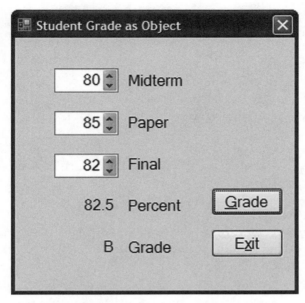

Figure 12.3   Student Grade Program

a value to it, in this case a score, but the developer cannot find out what is in it. It may sound strange to have a property that can be changed, but not seen, but the class is set up to use that value elsewhere. It's a good little security feature. Values can be sent to the class, but they cannot be seen or used anywhere else. And, if the developer passes a value to the class, the developer already knows it and so there's no benefit to returning it and a great deal of comfort knowing it cannot be seen or used anywhere else.

Student Grade Class

Let's try another example to reinforce and expand your understanding of classes. This example is for student grades. There are just three inputs for the program: the scores for a midterm, a term paper, and a final. The midterm is 20% of the grade, the term paper is 30%, and the final is 50%. Grades are calculated on a 90–80–70–60 scale. The user enters the scores and the program returns the letter grade. The program uses a StudentGrade class that does the work for the program. The form is shown in Figure 12.3.

Its code looks like this:

```
Dim mGrades As New StudentGrade
Private Sub btnGrade_Click(ByVal sender As ...
     'Declarations
     Dim mGrades As New StudentGrade
     Dim bytMidterm As Byte
```

```
        Dim bytPaper As Byte
        Dim bytFinal As Byte

        'Input
        bytMidterm = nudMidterm.Value
        bytPaper = nudPaper.Value
        bytFinal = nudFinal.Value

        'Processing
        Call mGrades.CalcGrade(bytMidterm, bytPaper,
          bytFinal)

        'Output
        lblPercent.Text = mGrades.Percent.ToString
        lblGrade.Text = mGrades.Grade
    End Sub
```

The user enters their scores in the NUDs and clicks the Grade Button. The first line of the Button creates a new instance of StudentGrade called mGrades. That is, it *instantiates* it. It means to create a new instance of the object.

The input is dropped into variables, which are used in the call statement in processing. It calls the CalcGrade method in the mGrades class that was just created. The values are passed along and used to determine the student's percentage and grade. The last two lines display Percent and Grade properties of the mGrades object.

The code for the StudentGrade class looks like this:

```
Friend Class StudentGrade
    Private mMidterm As Short
    Private mFinal As Short
    Private mPaper As Short
    Private mPercent As Single
    Private mGrade As String = "NA"
    Public WriteOnly Property Midterm() As Short
        Set(ByVal Value As Short)
            mMidterm = Value
        End Set
    End Property
    Public WriteOnly Property Final() As Short
        Set(ByVal Value As Short)
            mFinal = Value
        End Set
    End Property
```

```
Public WriteOnly Property Paper() As Short
    Set(ByVal Value As Short)
        mPaper = Value
    End Set
End Property
Public ReadOnly Property Percent() As Single
    Get
        Percent = mPercent
    End Get
End Property
Public ReadOnly Property Grade() As String
    Get
        Grade = mGrade
    End Get
End Property
Public Sub CalcGrade(ByVal midterm As Short, ByVal
  paper As Short, ByVal final As Short)
    If midterm >= 0 And paper >= 0 And final >=
      0 Then
        mMidterm = midterm
        mPaper = paper
        mFinal = final
        mPercent = (midterm * 0.2) + (paper * 0.3) + _
            (final * 0.5)
    End If
    Call CalcLetterGrade()
End Sub
Private Sub CalcLetterGrade()
    Select Case Percent
        Case 90 To 100
            mGrade = "A"
        Case 80 To 90
            mGrade = "B"
        Case 70 To 80
            mGrade = "C"
        Case 60 To 70
            mGrade = "D"
        Case 0 To 60
            mGrade = "F"
        Case Else
            mGrade = "NA"
    End Select
End Sub
End Class
```

The class is declared as a Friend in the declaration in the first line, which means it can only be used in this project. There are several Private variables declared. Because they are declared as Private, these variables aren't visible outside of the class. In this example they're used to help calculate and assign values to the properties in the class.

The CalcGrade procedure is at the bottom. It accepts the three values passed when it's called. These values are used to assign values to the Midterm, Paper, and Final properties and are used to calculate the percent. That value is assigned to the Percent property. The CalcLetterGrade procedure uses a Case to assign the letter grade to the Grade property. As a Private procedure, CalcLetterGrade isn't visible outside of the class. That prevents tampering.

Midterm, Paper, and Final properties are WriteOnly. They can be assigned a value, but they cannot be read outside of the class.

Percent and Grade are ReadOnly. They cannot be assigned values from outside the class, but it is possible to see their values from the outside.

This example introduces an important concept, encapsulation. *Encapsulation* hides the data and features of a class. Others are protected from the complexity of the class and are given access to only the features permitted by its author. In this example, outsiders are permitted access to the CalcGrade method and can set the Midterm, Paper, and Final properties. They cannot control the way the Percent and Grade are determined even though they can see them.

This same class is used later in the Array of Objects section.

VB Tip   *Open and run the ClassGrade program to see how it works.*

Object Browser

Once a class is created, it's visible in the Object Browser. Open the ClassGrade program and then open the Object Browser to see it (see Figure 12.4). Select Object Browser from the View menu or press Ctrl-Alt-J. ClassGrade is right at the top of the list. Navigate through it to see the properties and methods for it. That's always a good way to learn about a class.

Potential Problems

It may seem like a great deal of work to use classes, and at the start, it is. You probably looked at other parts of programming in the same way when you were first introduced to them. Classes make code reusable and they make it easier to use. Classes limit what can be seen and used and who can see it and use it. Classes are building blocks and as such pave the way for bigger and better programs. You'll see that shortly.

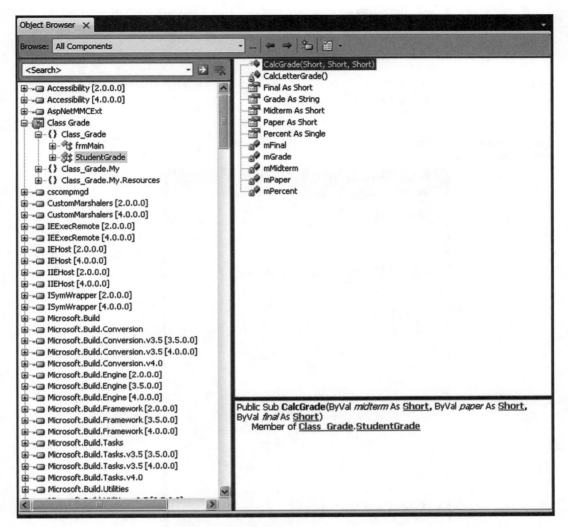

Figure 12.4   Grade Class in the Object Browser

Once an object is destroyed, it's gone. It cannot be retrieved. Be careful when disposing an object.

Be careful when creating classes. If you cannot see the class, it's declared at the wrong level. Although granting too much access to a class is a bad thing, if there's too little, it won't work.

Use IntelliSense to work with your classes. Create the classes before writing the code that uses the classes, that way, IntelliSense can help you. In that respect, it's very similar to writing a procedure or function before calling it.

Use ReadOnly when you don't want a developer to change your values. Use WriteOnly when you need them to pass values to your class.

VB Quiz 02   *Describe how a class is similar to a blueprint.*

Why is it a procedure in the class and a method when it's called?

When should you use ReadOnly and WriteOnly properties?

VB Quip   *Measuring programming progress by lines of code is like measuring aircraft building progress by weight. – Bill Gates*

Employee Pay Class

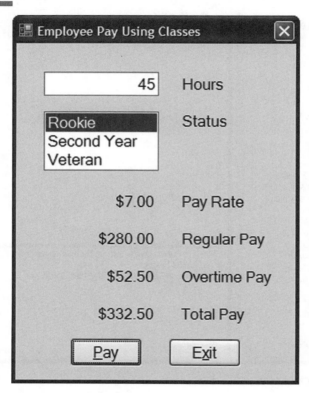

Figure 12.5   Employee Pay Program

Tara Dactil is a paleontology professor and runs an archeology site during the summer. She employs numerous students and pays them based on their work experience. First-year students get $7.00 per hour, second-year students get $8.50 per hour, and the rest get $10.00 per hour. She needs a little application to calculate their wages based on their hours and experience. Input is the number of hours and their experience (see Figure 12.5).

Here's the code for the Pay Button:

```
Public Class frmEmployeePay
    Dim mEmployeePay As New CalcEmployeePay
```

```
Private Sub btnPay_Click(ByVal sender As
  System.Object...
    'Declarations
    Dim sngHours As Single
    Dim intStatus As Integer

    'Input
    sngHours = Convert.ToSingle(txtHours.Text)
    intStatus = lstStatus.SelectedIndex

    'Processing
    mEmployeePay.CalcPay(sngHours, intStatus)

    'Output
    lblPayRate.Text = mEmployeePay.PayRate
      .ToString("c")
    lblRegPay.Text = mEmployeePay.RegPay
      .ToString("c")
    lblOTPay.Text = mEmployeePay.OTPay.ToString("c")
    lblTotalPay.Text = mEmployeePay.TotalPay
      .ToString("c")
  End Sub
End Class
```

CalcEmployeePay is the name of the class. It's declared as mEmployeePay in the program.

```
Dim mEmployeePay As New CalcEmployeePay
```

The program gets the hours from the TextBox and uses the SelectedIndex of the ListBox to help determine the payrate. These values are passed to the CalcPay method of the class:

```
'Input
sngHours = Convert.ToSingle(txtHours.Text)
intStatus = lstStatus.SelectedIndex

'Processing
mEmployeePay.CalcPay(sngHours, intStatus)
```

The properties of the class are used for the output. Note how the PayRate, RegPay, OTPay, and TotalPay properties of the class are assigned to output:

```
'Output
lblPayRate.Text = mEmployeePay.PayRate.ToString("c")
lblRegPay.Text = mEmployeePay.RegPay.ToString("c")
```

```
lblOTPay.Text = mEmployeePay.OTPay.ToString("c")
lblTotalPay.Text = mEmployeePay.TotalPay.ToString("c")
```

The CalcEmployeePay class needs to get hours and status and then calculate and return payrate, regular pay, overtime pay, and total pay. Exactly how it does this is hidden from the user. As long as the developer of the class documents their work, a programmer can make use of the class.

```
Friend Class CalcEmployeePay
    Private mRegHours As Single
    Private mOTHours As Single
    Private mPayRate As Decimal
    Private mRegPay As Decimal
    Private mOTPay As Decimal
    Private mTotalPay As Decimal
    Const OTRate As Single = 1.5

    Public ReadOnly Property PayRate() As Decimal
        Get
            PayRate = mPayRate
        End Get
    End Property
    Public ReadOnly Property RegHours() As Single
        Get
            RegHours = mRegHours
        End Get
    End Property
    Public ReadOnly Property OTHours() As Single
        Get
            OTHours = mOTHours
        End Get
    End Property
    Public ReadOnly Property RegPay() As Decimal
        Get
            RegPay = mRegPay
        End Get
    End Property
    Public ReadOnly Property OTPay() As Decimal
        Get
            OTPay = mOTPay
        End Get
    End Property
    Public ReadOnly Property TotalPay() As Decimal
        Get
            TotalPay = mTotalPay
        End Get
```

```
        End Property
        Public Sub CalcPay(ByVal sngHours As Single,
          ByVal intStatus As Integer)
            Select Case intStatus
                Case Is < 0
                    mPayRate = 0
                Case Is = 0
                    mPayRate = 7
                Case Is = 1
                    mPayRate = 8.5
                Case Is = 2
                    mPayRate = 10
            End Select
            If sngHours > 40 Then
                mRegHours = 40
                mOTHours = sngHours - 40
            Else
                mRegHours = sngHours
                mOTHours = 0
            End If
            mRegPay = mRegHours * PayRate
            mOTPay = mOTHours * PayRate * OTRate
            mTotalPay = RegPay + OTPay
        End Sub
End Class
```

The class has the scope of Friend so it can only be used with this project. There are several Private variables used to get values and make calculations. There are six ReadOnly properties. These values can be viewed, but they cannot be modified outside of the class.

The CalcPay procedure accepts two values, the number of hours worked and the employee status. Employee status is passed as an integer. Recall that it's the SelectedIndex of a ListBox. The Case structure uses that value to determine the pay rate and set the PayRate property. It then determines the regular hours and overtime hours and sets the RegHours and OTHours properties. Finally, it calculates and sets the RegPay, OTPay, and TotalPay.

How it calculates these values is hidden in the class, encapsulated. A programmer that uses this class can pass hours and employee status to it and then get a handful of property values in return. The programmer doesn't have control over how it calculates. That way, a developer can create a class and write the algorithm for it so other programmers can use it. Developers take the time to get the calculations correct and programmers can use them, knowing they're correct. This strategy provides for greater consistency and accuracy. For example, a credit card company might have a long, complicated formula for determining the credit limit for a customer. They wouldn't allow multiple formulas, written by any number of programmers, to float around in their code – that's just asking for trouble. Instead, they'd create a class that contains the formula and allow programmers access to the class. That way it's consistent. And, if they ever changed the rules, one change to the class would automatically handle the change in every place it's used. Without it, every program that calculates a credit limit would have to be updated. And, they'd have to hope that all the updates were made and that they were made correctly. That's a tall order.

In a business setting, developers write classes and document them. Programmers then use them in their programs. This process has two great advantages. One, it saves time because programmers don't have to reinvent the wheel every time they write a program, and two, it provides consistency between programs. Below is the sample documentation for this class. The following table contains properties of the CalcEmployeePay class.

CalcEmployeePay Class
Name: CalcEmployeePay.vb
Location: Corporate Library – Payroll Folder
Author: Jim McKeown
Date: 03/16/2009
Scope: Friend

Properties	Data Type	Status	Use
PayRate	Decimal	ReadOnly	Employee pay rate
RegHours	Single	ReadOnly	Regular hours in a week up to 40
OTHours	Single	ReadOnly	Hours greater than 40 in a week
RegPay	Decimal	ReadOnly	PayRate * RegHours in a week
OTPay	Decimal	ReadOnly	OTHours * PayRate * OTRate (1.5)
TotalPay	Decimal	ReadOnly	RegPay + OTPay
Methods	Values passed	Data Type	Use
CalcPay	Hours worked	Single	Number of hours worked in a week
	Status	Integer	Employee status from 1 to 3

Array of Objects

A single instance of an object is useful, but it has its limits. Once it goes out of scope, it's gone. That's great for some uses, but it has its drawbacks. Just like a single variable, a single instance of an object has its place and its limits. So, just like you can create an array of variables, you can create an array of objects.

In general, it's a two-step process. First create an array and declare it with the object type of your choice. Then loop through the array and create a new instance of the object for each element of the array. The general form is

```
Dim MyObject(n) As Object
For i = 0 to n
    MyObject(i) = New Object
Next i
```

where Object is the name of the object and MyObject is the name of the array of those objects. The loop creates a new instance for each item in the array, where i controls the loop and n is the number of items in the array. From there, the array can be manipulated with a loop and the individual objects can be controlled with the subscript. Each object in the array has the same characteristics as the original and can be manipulated like any other object.

Student Grade Class Array

The following example expands on the student grades class you saw earlier. In this example (see Figure 12.6), an array of five objects is created. Each object calculates the percentage and grade for a student. It then calculates the class average from the array.

Here are the general declarations:

```
Const mintMax As Integer = 4
Dim mGrades(mintMax) As StudentGrade
Dim mshoNum As Short
```

The constant sets the size of the array. In this case, it handles five items. The second line creates an array called mGrades of StudentGrade type. All five items in the array will look like the StudentGrade class. The last variable is a counter used for processing and output.

The Load event looks like this:

```
'Instantiate each element in the array
Dim i As Integer
For i = 0 To mintMax
    mGrades(i) = New StudentGrade
Next i

'Display header
rtbOut.AppendText(" Grades and Averages" & _
  vbNewLine & vbNewLine)
```

```
rtbOut.AppendText("Student Midterm Paper Final Percent
    Grade" & vbNewLine)
```

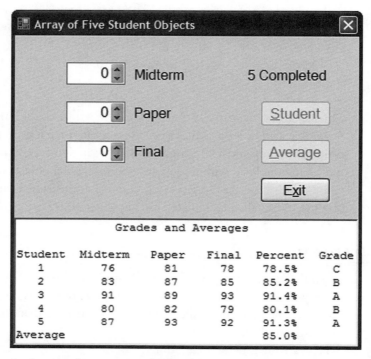

Figure 12.6   Student Grade Program – An Array of Objects

It does two things. First, it instantiates each element in the array. The loop takes one element at a time and creates a new instance of StudentGrade. The last lines display the header in the RichTextBox.

Enter the scores for a student and then click the Student Button to calculate and display the score. The code for the Button looks like this:

```
'Declarations
Dim bytMidterm As Byte
Dim bytPaper As Byte
Dim bytFinal As Byte
Dim strOut As String
Dim shoStudentNum As Short

'Input
bytMidterm = nudMidterm.Value
bytPaper = nudPaper.Value
bytFinal = nudFinal.Value
```

```
'Processing
Call mGrades(mshoNum).CalcGrade(bytMidterm,
    bytPaper, bytFinal)
shoStudentNum = mshoNum + 1

'Output
strOut = shoStudentNum.ToString.PadLeft(4)
strOut += bytMidterm.ToString("n0").PadLeft(10)
strOut += bytPaper.ToString("n0").PadLeft(9)
strOut += bytFinal.ToString("n0").PadLeft(8)
strOut += mGrades(mshoNum).Percent.ToString.PadLeft(8)
    & "%"
strOut += mGrades(mshoNum).Grade.PadLeft(6)
rtbOut.AppendText(strOut & vbNewLine)

'Increment array
mshoNum += 1

lblNum.Text = mshoNum.ToString & " Completed"

'Clear NUDs
nudMidterm.Value = 0
nudPaper.Value = 0
nudFinal.Value = 0

'Check to see if completed
If mshoNum > mintMax Then
    btnStudent.Enabled = False
    btnAverage.Enabled = True
End If
```

The scores come from the NumericUpDowns. These values are passed to the CalcGrade method of the mGrades class in the processing part of the code. The other line in processing is an offset to manage the difference between the array number and the student number.

The output section builds an output string and displays it in the RichTextBox. It uses the assignment scores as posted on the form. The Percent and Grade properties of mGrades are used to display the student's average and final grade. These are ReadOnly properties from the class.

The next lines increment mshoNum, the variable that controls the array. It then displays the number of grades completed. This line makes it easier for the user to track progress. Next, the NUDs are cleared just to make the interface a little cleaner.

The If statement checks to see if the end of the array has been reached. When it is, the Student Button is disabled and the Average Button is enabled. That way, the user can only enter scores for five students.

The Average Button calculates the average for the class and displays it. The code looks like this:

```
Dim i As Integer
Dim intPercentTotal As Integer
Dim sngPercentAverage As Single

For i = 0 To mintMax
    intPercentTotal += mGrades(i).Percent
Next i

sngPercentAverage = intPercentTotal / i

rtbOut.AppendText("Average".PadRight(35) & _
    sngPercentAverage.ToString("n1") & "%")
btnAverage.Enabled = False
```

The loop runs through the array. On each pass it adds the value in the Percent property of mGrades. Below the loop, it calculates the average and displays it in the RichTextBox. The last line disables the Average Button.

The class is the same as the one used earlier in the chapter. Code reuse and consistency – two important points to remember!

VB Tip   *Open and run the ClassGradeArray program to see how it works.*

Adding an Existing Class to a Program

It's relatively simple to add a class to a program (see Figure 12.7). Find the class file you want to add to your project. It has a .vb extension. In a corporate setting, the file and its documentation are maintained in a library. Copy the file to your project folder. Select Add Existing Item . . . from the Project menu. Add the class file to your project and it will appear in the Solution Explorer, ready for use. However, in the real world, you'd probably just link to the file in the library.

VB Quiz 03   *In the EmployeePay program, which properties aren't used in the output?*
How would you modify the array program to handle a class with 20 students?
Why are bug fixes and updates easier with classes?
What should happen when a class gets modified?

Inheritance

VB Quip   *It always takes longer than you expect, even when you take into account Hofstadter's Law.*
– Hofstadter's Law

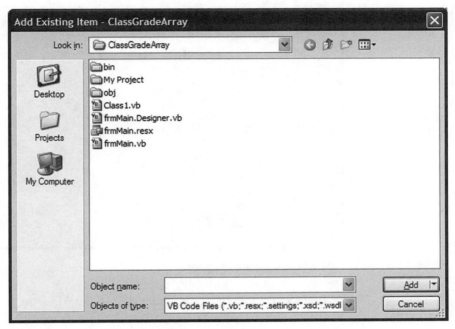

Figure 12.7   Add an Existing Class Dialog

Classes can be used to create other classes. This concept is called *inheritance*. Inheritance is the ability to create a class that's based on another class. In short, the properties and methods of an object can be incorporated into new objects. The original class is called a *base class*. A class created and extended from a base class is called a *derived class*. For example, there are many departments on a campus that need student information. Nearly all of them need the first name, last name, and student ID. These could be the properties for a base class called Student. The Student class could be extended for other uses. The bookstore could use the Student class and extend it with a Balance property to track the account balance for a student. The Registrar's office could extend the Student class with properties and methods for the student's major, credits, grades, and GPA. Other offices might need the Student class along with email and phone number. You get the idea. Simply dumping all your student data into one large class is unworkable. The library shouldn't know how much is left on your meal plan account and the bookstore shouldn't have access to your overdue books. None of them should have access to financial aid or registration.

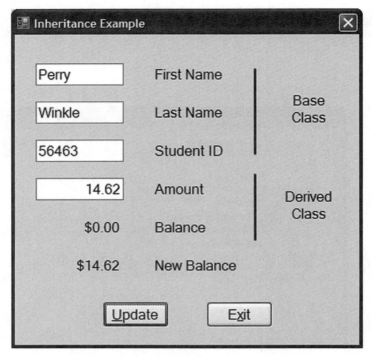

Figure 12.8   Inheritance Example Program

That's where inheritance becomes so valuable. Place the important data and processes in your Student class – in this example, your name and ID. Then extend as needed with other classes. The library class inherits the Student class and extends it with properties for overdue books and fines and a method to calculate the fine. The bookstore creates a class, inherits the Student class, and adds a property for the account balance. All of them can use the base class, but they cannot see or use properties from the other classes.

Student Inheritance Example

An example of inheritance is shown in Figure 12.8. The base class is called Student and is shown below. Other classes can inherit from it. The class has three properties: FirstName, LastName, and StudID.

```
Public Class Student
    Private mstrFirst As String
    Private mstrLast As String
    Private mstrStudID As String
    Public Property FirstName() As String
        Get
```

```
                FirstName = mstrFirst
            End Get
            Set(ByVal value As String)
                mstrFirst = value
            End Set

        End Property

        Public Property LastName() As String
            Get
                LastName = mstrLast
            End Get
            Set(ByVal value As String)
                mstrLast = value
            End Set

        End Property

        Public Property StudID() As String
            Get
                StudID = mstrStudID
            End Get
            Set(ByVal value As String)
                mstrStudID = value
            End Set

        End Property

    End Class
```

The Bookstore class is shown below:

```
Public Class Bookstore
    Inherits Student
    Private mdecBalance As Decimal

    Public Property Balance() As Decimal
        Get
            Balance = mdecBalance
        End Get
        Set(ByVal value As Decimal)
            mdecBalance = value
        End Set
    End Property
```

```
        Public Sub CalcBalance(ByVal decAmount As Decimal)
            mdecBalance = mdecBalance + decAmount
        End Sub
End Class
```

The name of the class is Bookstore. The first line inside the class sets up the inheritance. In essence, the contents of the Student class become part of the Bookstore class. In addition, the Bookstore class has a Balance property and a CalcBalance method. So, the Bookstore class extends the Student class. Use it like any other class.

Here's most of the code from the form showing how it's used in a program:

```
Public Class frmInheritance
    Dim mBookstore As New Bookstore

    Private Sub btnUpdate_Click(ByVal...
        Dim decDebitCredit As Decimal

        'Display current account balance
        lblBalance.Text = mBookstore.Balance.ToString("c")

        'Calculate new balance
        decDebitCredit = Convert.ToDecimal(txtAmount.Text)
        Call mBookstore.CalcBalance(decDebitCredit)

        'Display new account balance
        lblNewBalance.Text = mBookstore.Balance
           .ToString("c")
    End Sub
```

The general declarations create a new instance of the Bookstore class and names it mBookstore. The Update Button displays the old balance on the account. The new balance is calculated by adding the user input to the old balance. It then displays the new balance.

VB Tip   *Open and run the StudentInheritance program to see how it works.*

VB Quiz 04   *What other properties should be added to the Student base class?*
                  Compare the AccountBalance class used earlier in the chapter with the Bookstore class.
                  Between the Student class and the Bookstore class, what properties and methods are
                  in the mBookstore object?

Employee Inheritance Example

Another good example of inheritance is employees. A business may have a base class called Employee that contains basic properties such as last name, first

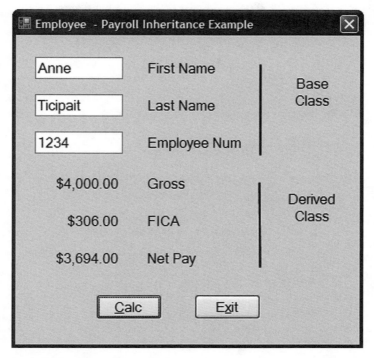

Figure 12.9   Payroll Inheritance Example Program

name, ID, and department. Of course, there could be others, but this is more than enough for a good example. Other classes could inherit from this base class. The Payroll department needs these properties and a long list of others, including Social Security number, classification, salary, gross pay, net pay, and all the various deductions. Most of these shouldn't be shared outside of the Payroll department. (Just think of the problems a shared SSN could present!) The Personnel department needs the base information and others such as years, hire date, supervisor, and security clearance. The IT department needs the base class and things like computer information and workgroup. This example puts together a simple base class called Employee that's inherited by the Payroll class (see Figure 12.9).

Here's the Employee class:

```
Public Class Employee
    Private mstrFirst As String
    Private mstrLast As String
    Private mstrID As String

    Public Property FirstName() As String
        Get
```

```
              FirstName = mstrFirst
         End Get
         Set(ByVal value As String)
              mstrFirst = value
         End Set

    End Property

    Public Property LastName() As String
         Get
              LastName = mstrLast
         End Get
         Set(ByVal value As String)
              mstrLast = value
         End Set

    End Property

    Public Property ID() As String
         Get
              ID = mstrID
         End Get
         Set(ByVal value As String)
              mstrID = value
         End Set

    End Property

End Class
```

The Employee class is a separate file called Employee.vb. It's in the solution folder, but could be stored elsewhere. This example has three properties: FirstName, LastName, and ID. All can be inherited in other classes.

The Payroll class looks like this:

```
Public Class Payroll
    Inherits Employee
    Private mdecSalary As Decimal = 48000
    Private mdecGross As Decimal
    Private mdecFICA As Decimal
    Private mdecNetPay As Decimal
    Const sngFICARate As Single = 0.0765

    Public WriteOnly Property Salary() As Decimal
```

```
        Set(ByVal value As Decimal)
            mdecSalary = value
        End Set
    End Property

    Public ReadOnly Property Gross() As Decimal
        Get
            Gross = mdecGross
        End Get
    End Property

    Public ReadOnly Property FICA() As Decimal
        Get
            FICA = mdecFICA
        End Get
    End Property

    Public ReadOnly Property NetPay() As Decimal
        Get
            NetPay = mdecNetPay
        End Get
    End Property

    Public Sub CalcSalary(ByVal strEmployeeNumber
      As String)
        Select Case strEmployeeNumber
            Case Is = "1234"
                Salary = mdecSalary
                mdecGross = mdecSalary / 12
                mdecFICA = mdecGross * sngFICARate
                mdecNetPay = mdecGross - mdecFICA
        End Select
    End Sub
End Class
```

It inherits the properties from Employee because of the Inherits Employee command in the first line. Payroll has the WriteOnly property Salary. In this example, it's coded with 48000. In the real world, this value would probably come from a file or database. Gross, FICA, and NetPay are all properties. The class has one method called CalcSalary. It checks the employee ID, and if it's "1234" then it calculates the gross pay for the month, the withholding, and the net pay. In practice, there would be more security, but it's enough for this example. Gross, FICA, and NetPay properties are ReadOnly. They can be changed inside the class, but they cannot be changed from the outside.

Following is some of the code from the EmployeePayroll form:

```
Private Sub btnCalc_Click(ByVal sender As System.Object,
    ByVal e As System.EventArgs) Handles btnCalc.Click
        'Declarations
        Dim Payroll As New Payroll
        Dim strFirst As String
        Dim strLast As String
        Dim strEmpNum As String

        'Input
        strFirst = txtFirst.Text
        strLast = txtLast.Text
        strEmpNum = txtEmpNum.Text

        'Processing
        Call Payroll.CalcSalary(strEmpNum)

        'Output
        lblGross.Text = Payroll.Gross.ToString("c")
        lblFICA.Text = Payroll.FICA.ToString("c")
        lblNetPay.Text = Payroll.NetPay.ToString("c")
    End Sub
```

A new instance of Payroll is created in the Button. Its name is Payroll. The input section gets the ID, which is passed to the CalcSalary method in processing. The output section gets the Gross, FICA, and NetPay values from the Payroll class and displays them. The value gets displayed only when the correct ID is provided.

VB Tip

Open and run the EmployeeInheritance program to see how it works. Use 1234 for the ID.

VB Quiz 05

What's needed to complete the Payroll class?

How many properties and methods does the Payroll class have?

Where should the base class be stored?

Potential Problems

Ah, where to start? First, always check the names, properties, and methods of a class. Be sure these are correct. IntelliSense is a great help with this. Make sure the classes and properties have the right scope. Public is wide open, which makes development easier but creates security problems. Private is restricted, but it creates visibility problems when used. Friend limits access to a class from the outside. ReadOnly and WriteOnly properties can create problems. ReadOnly properties have a Get but no Set. WriteOnly properties have a Set but no Get. Use ReadOnly when you want to know the value but don't need to change it. Use WriteOnly when you want to change a value but don't want others to see it. Variables declared in a class should stay in a class. When the values need to go outside of it, use a Get. Classes are similar to variables in scope. When created in a Button, they're only visible in the Button and are destroyed when the Click event is over. Classes created in the general declarations are visible on the whole form. Unless a destructor is used, they'll remain in memory until the form is closed.

Why Use Classes?

Classes are easier to use with a little practice. Large projects almost always use classes. They offer distinct advantages to developers. They allow the segmentation of development. A team of developers can work on their own and easily assemble the parts into a whole. Changes, modifications, and updates are all easier with classes, because each is a building block. One change or update almost automatically gets incorporated into all the places where it's used. It places a premium on planning, but those dividends pay off with a better product in the end. But, perhaps the greatest advantage is that classes make code reusable. Once created, it's easy to copy, modify, or extend a class. With it, a project becomes an extension of previous work. Without it, every project must start from scratch.

Fixing a Program

Knuckle Head Lighthouse is a popular tourist attraction in the area. Sue Veneer has taken advantage of this by setting up a little curio shop nearby. Business is good, but she wants to be prepared for the future. Part of her plan is to track customers. Right now her software doesn't work and although she knows a little programming, objects are lost on her. She needs your help to fix her Customer program (see Figure 12.10), and she wants some suggestions on how to improve it. Sue explains that the program should get the basic info on the customer and their purchase. She wants to be able to calculate the amount of the sale and add the transaction to a file for later reference. She also has a little "Round Up" promotion. Customers are free to round their purchase up to the next dollar. That money goes to the Knuckle Head Lighthouse Preservation Fund.

You open the program and do a little inspection to get familiar with the form and the code. There's a Customer class and Sue says it's supposed to be the building block for all other classes. "Base class" you think to yourself, but you're

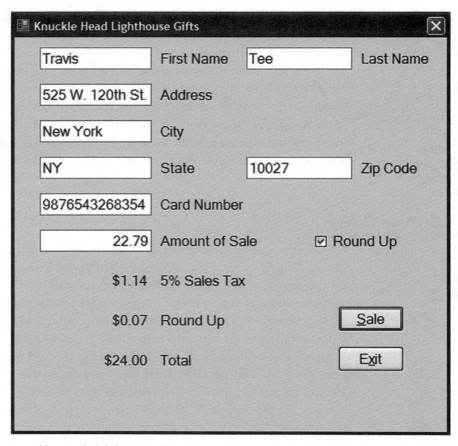

Figure 12.10   Knuckle Head Lighthouse Gifts Program

too polite to correct her. There's a Purchases class as well. You check and there's no Inherits command. Without it, it can't use the Customer class. You add:

```
Inherits Customer
```

You scroll through the code and see some "blue lines of death" and decide to check them out. One line says

```
strDetail = FirstName
```

and the error message on it says it's "not accessible in this context because it is 'Private.'" You're not quite sure what that means, but you realize that a Private declaration limits where it can be used and the "not accessible" probably means it can't see the FirstName property. You tab back to the Customer class. All of the properties are set to Private. Ah ha! Private properties won't work outside of their class. You set about changing the properties to Public, but then you change your mind. Why not change just the FirstName property to see if that helps?

You do and it removes the error from that line of code. Now it's OK to change the other properties in the Customer class to Public and that seems to help.

Next, you check the code for the form. The first error is on this line:

```
mPurchase.AmountSale = Convert.ToDecimal
  (txtAmountSale.Text)
```

It says AmountSale is ReadOnly. The line tries to assign the value from the TextBox to the AmountSale property of mPurchase. As ReadOnly, it can only read the value in AmountSale, it cannot change it. AmountSale is a property of the Purchase class so you jump to that code. You change ReadOnly to WriteOnly, but that seems to make it worse. As WriteOnly, it doesn't like the Get command. It must be changed to a Set so you can set the value of the property. You change it to read as follows:

```
Public WriteOnly Property AmountSale() As Decimal
    Set(ByVal value As Decimal)
        mdecAmountSale = value
    End Set
End Property
```

Now the amount of the sale can be set in the object. That makes sense, the change enables the program to add the amount of the sale to the object.

The next error is in this line:

```
Call CalcPurchase()
```

There's no CalcPurchase procedure in the code for the form. You type in class names one at a time and let IntelliSense display the properties and methods. Eventually, you locate one in the Purchase class. The little voice inside you says, "Next time use the Object Browser." You agree, but rationalize that it's a small program and you probably found it faster without it. The only way to get to it to call the CalcPurchases procedure is to call it literally. You change the line to

```
Call mPurchase.CalcPurchase()
```

Now, it goes looking for it in the mPurchase object. One more bug squashed! You glance up at the lighthouse in the distance and decide to get a picture of it for the background of your desktop.

There's still one error that shows up (although you know from experience, there might be several lurking in the code). The RoundUp property looks like this:

```
Public Property RoundUp() As Boolean
    Get
        mblnRoundUp = value
    End Get
```

```
    Set(ByVal value As Boolean)
        RoundUp = mblnRoundUp
    End Set

End Property
```

It doesn't like the value variable. You point to it and it says it's not declared. The line looks OK, so you're not quite sure what the problem is. You check around a little and compare it to other commands in the code and then the metaphorical fog of confusion lifts and you understand the problem. The command is wrong. A Get is used to retrieve the value in the property and a Set used to assign a value to the property. The commands are turned around! It's a common mistake. You move the line in the Get to the Set and then move the line in the Set to the Get so it looks like this:

```
Public Property RoundUp() As Boolean
    Get
        RoundUp = mblnRoundUp
    End Get

    Set(ByVal value As Boolean)
        mblnRoundUp = value
    End Set

End Property
```

The program runs! It works! The crowd goes wild! And then the foghorn goes off and snaps you back to reality. You clean up a little bit, add some comments to the code, and take note of that little Round Up idea. That's not a bad way to give back a little extra.

Sue also wants some ideas on how to improve and upgrade the program. Here's what to do:

1. Get the email address of the customers. That way you can target ads based on their purchases and you can keep them informed on the lighthouse restoration.
2. Update the program to track what was purchased. You explain that it's a way to track both the purchases and inventory.
3. Track other aspects of the sale. Keep track of the date and time so you can see when you do the most business.
4. Make the program more user friendly. Add a ListBox for the state to make that a little easier. Add a mask to the TextBox for the Card Number to prevent errors.
5. Write other programs to work with the data files. One could handle the total sales, taxes, and Round Up. Write another to analyze the sales.

6. Add exception handling to the program.

7. Sue is so grateful for your help that she arranges a lighthouse tour for you – not just the regular tour, but a special one to the very top of the lighthouse. You've heard the view is great from there!

VB Tip   *Open and run the CustomerClassFixed program to see how it works.*

On Your Own

Add one of the extras to the Knuckle Head Lighthouse Gifts program.

Use the Object Browser to explore the CustomerClassFixed program.

Write the code to add a header to a form. Use code to declare and create a Label. Center your name in the Label and place it at the top of the form.

Write a class called Library for the StudentInheritance program that lists the title, author, publisher, and copyright for an overdue book as well as the date it is due.

Summary

Objects are essential to modern programming. This chapter introduced the fundamentals of object creation and use. Controls can be created in code. Developers can create their own classes complete with their own properties and methods. These objects can inherit from other objects, extending their function and capabilities.

Review

Objects are programming elements that contain data and methods.

Toolbox controls can be created from scratch with code.

The Controls.Add method is used to add a control to a form.

The With command is used to control a block of commands for a specific object.

Use a destructor to remove an object.

Garbage collection reclaims unused memory, freeing it for other uses.

Declaring a control WithEvents allows events to be written for the control.

Classes are created with a constructor.

Classes can be exposed in several ways, using Public, Private, Friend, and Protected.

Classes have properties that are used to store data.

Property values are stored with a Set command and accessed with a Get command.

Class methods are similar to procedures and functions.

Properties in a class can be limited by making them ReadOnly or WriteOnly.

ReadOnly properties can be viewed but not changed.

WriteOnly properties can be changed, but not seen.

Instantiation creates a new instance of an object.

The Object Browser lists all classes and objects and the properties and methods associated with them.

Classes are generally stored in a library so others can use them.

All classes should be documented so a programmer can figure out how to use them.

An array of objects can be created by declaring an array of the object and then instantiating each element of the array.

Classes can be shared with other classes.

A base class can be inherited by other classes. The derived class then has the properties and methods of the base class.

Terms

base class	a class that's used as the basis for other classes
constructor	code that automatically creates a class and initializes its variables
derived class	a class that's an extension of a base class; a class that inherits properties and methods from a base class
destructor	code the destroys a control or class; used to eliminate unused objects and return memory to the system
encapsulation	hiding the data and features of class so that others cannot see its complexity
exposed	term used to describe where an object is visible and can be used in a program
garbage collection	the process of removing objects and from memory to free resources for other use
inheritance	the ability to create a class that's based on another class
instantiate	to create a new instance of an object
methods	blocks of code in a class that execute code and calculate and return values
object	a programming element that contains data and methods

Keywords

Friend	an access type used to declare the scope of a variable or control; keyword used to expose elements within a project but not outside of it
Get	function of a class that allows a value to be retrieved
Inherits	used to add a base class to another class
Private	keyword used to expose an element within a class only

Protected	keyword used to expose elements within the same class
ReadOnly	used to set the property of a class so it can be read, but not modified
Set	function of a class that allows a value to be set
With	a block of code that applies commands to a specified control
WithEvents	a command used to allow events for objects created at runtime
WriteOnly	used to set the property of a class so it can be written, but not viewed

Self-check

1. A control is an object.
2. The With command works with multiple properties for the same control.
3. Controls are removed from a form using a disposal.
4. Controls added at runtime can only have events if they're added using the Handles Events command.
5. The properties of a class are read with a Get statement and assigned with a Set statement.
6. Classes without a Set statement are classified as WriteOnly.
7. Encapsulation is the process of hiding data and features in a class.
8. The Toolbox contains a list of all classes and their properties and methods.
9. A derived class gets properties and methods from a base class.
10. Use the Inherits command to include one class in another class.
11. A programming element that contains data and methods is a(n):
    A. data type
    B. object
    C. property
    D. method
12. Classes have all of the following advantages except:
    A. portability
    B. reuse
    C. permanence
    D. segmentation
13. The removal of items from memory is known as:
    A. dumping
    B. garbage collection
    C. cleansing
    D. encapsulation
14. The WithEvents command:
    A. lets a developer add events to controls created at runtime
    B. lets a developer add properties to a class
    C. makes a class transportable to other programs
    D. all of the above

15. Instantiate means to:
    A. include an object in a program
    B. assign values to the properties of a class
    C. create a new instance of an object
    D. use one class as the basis for another class

16. Inheritance is:
    A. the ability to set the properties for multiple controls with one line of code
    B. the ability to add properties and methods to a class
    C. the ability to create a class based on another class
    D. why you're nice to your creepy uncle with the bad toupee

17. If you saw the following command,

    ```
    Inherits AFortune
    ```

    A. you'd know AFortune is a base class
    B. you'd know AFortune is a derived class
    C. you'd know the properties and methods of the base class become part of AFortune
    D. you'd know AFortune is encapsulated in your class

18. Which of the following is not an advantage of classes?
    A. portability
    B. segmentation
    C. reuse
    D. standardization

19. Friend declarations are available:
    A. anywhere
    B. only in the procedure where they're declared
    C. only on the form where they're declared
    D. only in the project where they're declared

20. When it's inside a class, it's called a procedure, but when it's outside the class, it's referenced as a(n):
    A. method
    B. function
    C. variable
    D. object

VB Quiz Answers

Quiz 01

A cake needs flour. So, you'd need to grow the wheat, harvest it, and grind it into flour. A cake needs eggs. So, you'd need chickens to lay the eggs (or you'd need eggs to hatch so you'd have chickens, but that's a philosophical debate for another time). The same applies for the other ingredients. Mix the ingredients and bake them.

For a shirt, you'd need cloth. Cut it according to the pattern and sew the individual pieces together according to the directions. Then add the collar and buttons. Now, if you had to grow the cotton for the shirt, that would complicate the process.

Everything happens in the memory of the computer. Its management determines how fast an application is, how well it performs, and, when it crashes, it's as likely as not because of memory mismanagement. Poor memory management means a bloated application that's slow and unresponsive.

Garbage collection handles and releases unused memory. When a variable, procedure, class, or form is no longer needed, it's released from memory. This frees that memory for other uses. Without it, an application would grab more memory as it runs and eventually overwhelm the computer.

Quiz 02

A class provides an outline – a detailed structure for the properties and methods needed to complete a task. They can be used over and over again, just like blueprints. The class doesn't contain the actual data, but it does define what the object will look like.

Inside a class, it's called a procedure because it follows the definition of a procedure. It's self-contained, it's invoked with a Call statement, and it accomplishes a task. It's a method because it's called externally and it works with data in that class.

Use ReadOnly when you need to know the value for the property but you don't need to change the value. Use WriteOnly when the value needs to be updated, but you don't need to access that value.

Quiz 03

RegHours and OTHours aren't in the output. RegHours contains the regular hours and OTHours are for overtime hours.

The two lines in the code for the form

```
Const mintMax As Integer = 4
Dim mGrades(mintMax) As StudentGrade
```

determine the size of the array and create the array. Change the 4 to 19 and make the array size 20. The array is instantiated in the Load event with a loop that runs from 0 to mintMax.

A change to a class filters down to all the places that use that class. Without classes, each change would have to be located and updated individually. There's a substantial risk that some changes could be missed and that incorrect changes may be made. Changes to a class are much faster, safer, easier, and more flexible than manual changes.

Changes to a class should be documented, both in the class itself and in the library where it's stored. Class changes should be posted so those affected by the change can test their code to see if it's affected.

Quiz 04

What gets added varies depending on need, and any property that's added is available to all the classes that inherit the Student class. Personally identifiable data such as an address or phone shouldn't be added. However, there are some properties that could be added. Advisor, Major, and Class would probably be acceptable.

The major difference between the two is the

```
Inherits Student
```

command used in the Bookstore class.

FirstName, LastName, and StudID are in the Student class. The Bookstore class inherits these three and has a Balance property and a CalcBalance procedure. Code that uses the Bookstore class has access to FirstName, LastName, StudID, and Balance properties and a CalcBalance method.

Quiz 05

As such, it calculates gross pay. In addition, it could split the FICA deduction to include Social Security and Medicare deductions. Other deductions could be calculated as well, including medical and dental coverage, withholding, and other taxes. There might also be deductions for 401(k) and other allowances.

It has four properties (Salary, Gross, FICA, and NetPay) and one method (CalcSalary).

A base class gets stored in a library where it's accessible to developers. When a base class changes, the programs that use it must be updated and compiled before they're used. In these examples, the base class is simply copied to the folder for a solution and then added to the program.

Graphics – The Visual (and Audio) Side of Visual Basic

VB Quip   *Computer science education cannot make anybody an expert programmer any more than*
studying brushes and pigment can make somebody an expert painter. –Eric Raymond

"A picture is worth a thousand words," or so said Frederick R. Barnard nearly ninety years ago. He was selling advertising for streetcars and couldn't have had computer graphics in mind. In fact, the first computer was still a generation away. But, he was pretty accurate because it just might take a thousand words of computer code to generate a good picture. Remember that the computer takes baby steps and every step has to be clearly described. The same is true with graphics. You can place pictures on your form and you can create graphics – beautiful graphics if you take the time – but you have to write some code to do it. Visual Basic can draw lines and shapes, it can work with text, and it's great with colors. It just takes a little work to create them and a little code to do it right. This chapter introduces the basics for graphics, sound, and multimedia. When it's over, you'll be able to play sound and video, create simple shapes, and draw and paint with the computer.

Graphic Basics

There are several ways to add graphics to a program. You've already worked with the PictureBox to add graphics. But there's so much more. Visual Basic can draw lines, simple shapes, filled shapes, patterns, text, pictures, and even paint!

There are a couple of commands needed to add graphics to a program. First, you have to create a graphics object. Then you need to instantiate it. It goes like this:

```
Dim grfImage As Graphics
grfImage = Me.CreateGraphics
```

The first command creates a new *Graphics* object. The second line creates the graphics for the control. After that, graphics can be added to the control in several ways.

The general form for these commands is

```
Dim grfName As Graphics
grfName = Me.ControlName.CreateGraphics
```

Use grf for the prefix for graphics objects. Graphics can be placed on almost any control, but they usually appear on a Form or a Tab. Graphic controls are created in the general declarations or in a control. Then use the *Create-Graphics* function for the control. CreateGraphics is a function in the System.Drawing.Graphics Namespace and is responsible for drawing graphics on a control. It is a set of classes and methods for drawing two-dimensional shapes such as lines, rectangles, ellipses, arcs, and pies. Text is also a snap. And remember, squares are rectangles with even sides, and ovals and circles are ellipses. Graphics is a part of the GDI+, *Graphics Device Interface*, which is responsible for drawing graphics and images.

From there, all you need is a command or set of commands to do the actual drawing. The command used depends largely on what's being drawn.

Color

Table 13.1   RGB Color Table

Red	Green	Blue	Result
0	0	0	Black
255	255	255	White
255	0	0	Red
0	255	0	Green
0	0	255	Blue
255	255	0	Yellow
255	0	255	Fuchsia
0	255	255	Cyan
128	128	128	Gray

Visual Basic can draw in almost any color. It does millions of colors, more than the human eye can distinguish. These colors are all shades of red, green, and blue, generally referred to as *RGB*. Each color is specified as a mixture of red, green, and blue in a range from 0 to 255 (see Table 13.1). The amount of each of these determines the color and each color is represented by a set of these three numbers. 0, 0, 0 represents black. Think of each as the amount of light in that color. With 0 for each part of an RGB color, there's no color – in this case, it's black. On the opposite end, 255, 255, 255, you get white, the mixture of light for all three of these colors. Vary the amount from 0 to 255 and you'll get any color or shade.

VB Tip   *Run the ColorChanger program to see an example of RGB color (see Figure 13.1).*

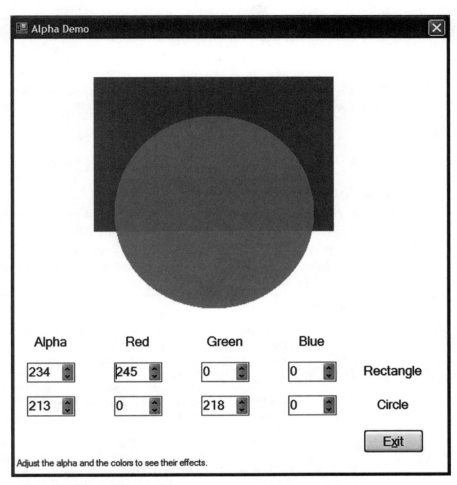

Figure 13.1   Alpha Test Program

Color is a structure in Visual Basic and is represented either as a named color or by its RGB components. Create a color object with a declaration:

```
Dim clrExample As Color = Color.Black
```

where clrExample becomes the color and it must be assigned a color when declared. Type in "Color." and IntelliSense displays a list of dozens of named colors. From there, clrExample can be used to set the color in a drawing command.

Color can be assigned from its RGB components as well. For example:

```
Dim clrGreen As Color = Color.Black
clrGreen = Color.FromArgb(0, 255, 0)
```

The first line creates clrGreen as a color and makes it black. The next line assigns a new color to it. *FromArgb* is a function with three or four arguments.

The first is optional and, when used, represents alpha. The others are red, green, and blue and must always be used. *Alpha* is the *opacity* of the color and opacity is the transparency of the color: 0 is transparent and 255 is opaque. Think of 0 as a window and 255 as a wall and the numbers in between as translucent. The last three numbers are the amounts of red, green, and blue, in that order. For this example, it creates green.

VB Tip   *Open and run the AlphaTest program to see how it works.*

Shapes

Visual Basic draws in many *shapes*. Shapes fall into two categories, draws and fills. Drawing a shape produces an outline. Filling produces a solid color or pattern for the shape. Specify the shape, color, location, and size when creating a shape. The following table lists possible shapes and their drawing methods.

Shape	Command	Result
Line	DrawLine	a line of varying width from one point to another
Rectangle	DrawRectangle	an outline in the shape of a rectangle
Square	DrawRectangle	an outline in the shape of a rectangle with all sides of equal length
Oval	DrawEllipse	an outline in the shape of an oval of a specified color and size
Circle	DrawEllipse	an outline of a circle with a specified color and width
Arc	DrawArc	a curved line
Pie	DrawPie	the outline of a pie-shaped wedge
Polygon	DrawPolygon	an outline with straight edges of a non-uniform length
Rectangle	FillRectangle	a solid rectangle of a specified size and color
Square	FillRectangle	a solid shape with all sides of equal length
Oval	FillEllipse	a solid oval of a specified color and size
Circle	FillEllipse	a solid shape with the edges a uniform distance from the center
Pie	FillPie	a solid wedge representing part of an oval or a circle
Polygon	FillPolygon	a solid shape with straight edges of a non-uniform length
Text	DrawString	a line of text with the font, color, size and style selected
Image	DrawImage	an image from a file

Coordinates

The location of a graphic is determined by its relative location to the upper left corner of a control. Recall that the top left corner of a form has x,y coordinates 0,0. These increase as you move left and down from that spot. Negative numbers are to the left and above the corner of the control. The same applies to other controls. You've seen this before when sizing and placing controls and with mouse movements. The x,y coordinates are measured in pixels and a typical computer screen has about a million pixels.

VB Quiz01   *What color do you get when red, green, and blue are all nearly equal?*
                     Explain opacity.
                     What is an ellipse?
                     What's the difference between a draw and a fill?

Drawing

VB Quip   *Programming is an art form that fights back. – Anonymous*

Once a graphics object has been defined and instantiated on a control, like this,

```
Dim grfImage As Graphics
grfImage = Me.CreateGraphics
```

you're ready to draw on it.

Color

You already know how to change the color of a control by changing the BackColor property. You can do the same thing with a color command, like this:

```
grfImage.BackColor = Color.FromArgb(255, 0, 0)
```

which sets the color of the form to red. This is handy for changing the background color or for redrawing your "canvas" when you're done drawing.

Use Color to set the color of lines and shapes as needed. It can be set using the ColorDialog as well. For example,

```
clrDialog.ShowDialog()
clrMyWorld = clrDialog.Color
```

opens the ColorDialog control and allows the user to select a color. When the ColorDialog is closed, it sets clrMyWorld to the color selected. From there, the clrMyWorld object can be used to set the drawing color.

Pens and Brushes

A *Pen* consists of a color and a line width and is typically used to draw lines and outlines (see Figure 13.2). *Brushes* are used to fill the interior of a shape with a standard color.

A Pen must be declared and assigned a color and width, like this:

```
Dim penPal as New Pen(Color.Black, 4)
```

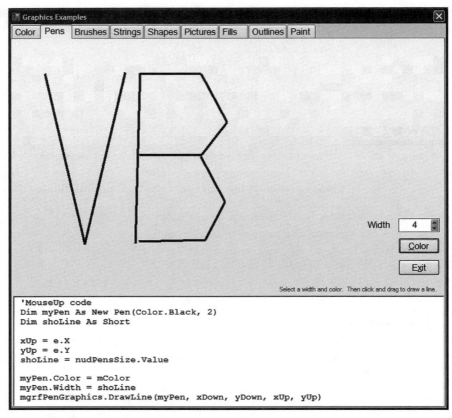

Figure 13.2   Graphics Examples – Pens

where penPal is the name of the Pen, the color is set to black, and the drawing width is four pixels. From there, the Pen can be used to draw lines or shapes. It can also be assigned with variables, like this:

```
Dim penPal as Pen
Dim clrSelected As Color = Color.Black

clrDialog.ShowDialog()
clrSelected = clrDialog.Color
intPenSize = nudPenSize.Value
penPal.Color = clrSelected
penPal.Width = intPenSize
```

where penPal is declared as a Pen. The ColorDialog is used to select a color and the width comes from a NumericUpDown. The last two lines set the Color and Width properties for the Pen. It's then ready to use to draw a line or a shape.

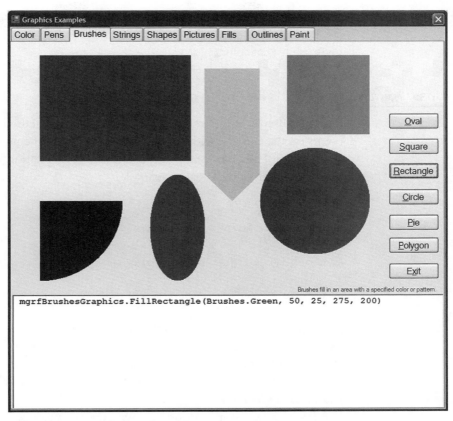

Figure 13.3   Graphics Examples – Brushes

Brushes determine the fill color for a shape (see Figure 13.3). Brushes use a standard set of named colors and look like this:

```
Brushes.NamedColor
```

where NamedColor is color called by name. IntelliSense brings up the list when you type Brushes and the period. Use it as part of a command to fill a shape.

Custom Brushes colors are set by declaring a *SolidBrush* color. It's easy:

```
Dim myBrush As SolidBrush
Dim clrSelected As Color = Color.Black

clrDialog.ShowDialog()
clrSelected = clrDialog.Color

myBrush = New SolidBrush(clrSelected)
```

where myBrush is declared as a SolidBrush, and crlSelected is declared as a color. Use the ColorDialog to select a color for clrSelected. Then use clrSelected to set myBrush to that color.

Lines, Points, Shapes, and Fills

Lines are drawn on a Graphic using the *DrawLine* method. It connects two points on the Graphic with a straight line. Designate the points with their x,y coordinates. The DrawLine method includes a Pen setting that contains the color and width of the Pen. For example:

```
Dim grfImage As Graphics
grfImage = Me.CreateGraphics

Dim penPal as New Pen(Color.Black, 4)

grfImage.DrawLine(penPal, xStart, yStart, xEnd, yEnd)
```

grfImage is the Graphic. It uses the DrawLine method to draw a straight line between two points. penPal is the Pen. It's set to black with a width of 4 pixels. xStart, yStart indicates the starting position of the line and xEnd, yEnd is the ending point of the line. Adjust those values to change the color of the line, its width, and its location.

A *Point* is an x,y coordinate on a Graphic. Declare a Point with a Dim statement and assign a coordinate in a single statement like this:

```
Dim pntStart As New Point(50, 25)
```

where pntStart is the name of the location with an x value of 50 and a y value of 25. Or, use two statements like this:

```
Dim pntCorner As Point
pntCorner = New Point(100, 100)
```

The x and y in the second statement could be variables as well.

It's time to put it all together. You can draw shapes using one of several Fills (see Figure 13.4). For example, *FillRectangle* creates a solid rectangle of the size and color specified and draws it in a specific location. It does squares as well. Just remember to make the sides of equal length. *FillEllipse* creates oval and circles of any color and size and places them where you want them. Just keep in mind that the width and height must be the same for a circle. In addition you can create pies, polygons, and patterns. Perfect!

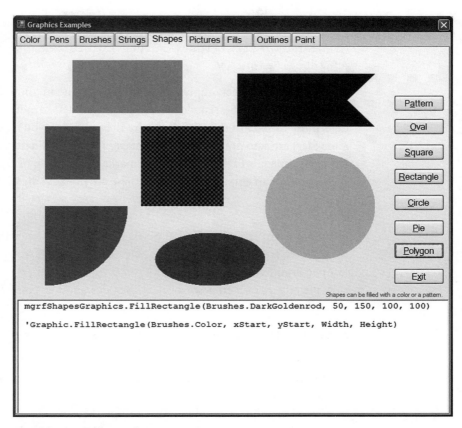

Figure 13.4   Graphics Examples – Shapes

Rectangles and squares are coded like this:

```
grfImage.FillRectangle(Brushes.Color, xStart, yStart,
   Width, Height)
```

where grfImage is the Graphic and FillRectangle is the method. Brushes.Color is the specified color. xStart and yStart create the top left corner of the rectangle. Width and height determine the size of the rectangle. If they're the same size, you'll get a square.

```
grfImage.FillRectangle(Brushes.Chartreuse, 100, 25,
   200, 100)
```

creates a light green rectangle wider than it is long near the top left corner of the form.

VB Tip   *All circles are ovals, but not all ovals are circles. Use an ellipse to create them.*

Oval and circles are coded like this:

```
grfGraphic.FillEllipse(Brushes.Color, xStart, yStart,
    Width, Height)
```

where grfImage is the Graphic and FillEllipse is the method. Brushes.Color is the specified color. xStart and yStart create the top left corner. Width and Height determine the size of the oval. If they're the same size, you'll get a circle. xStart and yStart are actually outside of the image. The x coordinate marks the extreme left of the image and the y coordinate marks the very top of the image. Because the corners of an ellipse are rounded, these are not actually on the image!

```
grfImage.FillEllipse(Brushes.Crimson, 250, 350, 200, 100)
```

creates a bright red oval. It's 250 pixels from the left side of the form and 350 pixels down from the top. It is twice as wide as it is tall. It would be a circle if the last two arguments were the same.

A pie is part of a circle or oval. It includes another pair of arguments. For example:

```
grfImage.FillPie(Brushes.Color, xStart, yStart, Width,
    Height, startAngle, sweepAngle)
```

where grfImage is the Graphic and FillPie is the method. Brushes.Color is the specified color. xStart and yStart create the top left corner of the completed oval or circle. Keep this in mind because it might be some distance from the actual wedge. Width and height determine the size of the oval or circle, but you're only creating one part of it. That's where startAngle and sweepAngle come in. The angle is an integer that represents the starting angle for the pie. An angle of 0 is at three o'clock, a horizontal line from the center to the right. 90 is a vertical line pointing down from the center, 180 points to the left, and 270 points up. Integers from 360 and up work as well. It just keeps circling like a snowboarder on a half-pipe. Dude! The sweepAngle determines the width of the slice in degrees. 90 gets you a quarter of the pie, 180 gets you half of it. You get the idea, it's junior high geometry.

```
grfGraphics.FillPie(Brushes.DeepPink, -100, 150, 300,
    300, 0, 90)
```

creates a pink wedge. The top left of the circle is actually off the left side of the form. It's a circle because the width and height are the same. The start angle is 0 and it's 90 degrees wide. So the image is the lower right portion of a pink circle.

A polygon has straight sides, usually four or more, and it doesn't have to be a rectangle or a square. A polygon is outlined by its corners. Each point is determined and the outline eventually leads back to its origin. Declare the points for it and then create a polygon as *PointF* with those points. From there, use the FillPolygon method to create the image, like this:

```
Dim pnt1 As New Point(400, 50)
Dim pnt2 As New Point(650, 50)
Dim pnt3 As New Point(600, 100)
Dim pnt4 As New Point(650, 150)
Dim pnt5 As New Point(400, 150)
Dim myPolygon As PointF() = {pnt1, pnt2, pnt3, pnt4, pnt5}

grfGraphic.FillPolygon(Brushes.MidnightBlue, myPolygon)
```

The first lines create five different points. Draw a line from one Point to the next to create an outline. The last Point connects back to the first to complete the shape. The next line takes these five points and creates a PointF, a polygon. A shape with more sides, like a hexagon or an octagon, has more points. Use the FillPolygon method to create the image. There are two arguments for it, the Brushes color and the PointF.

Patterns take a little more work. There are many built-in patterns (or you can use your own images as well) that create a pattern instead of a solid color. These require the *Drawing2D* class and you must create a style and a pattern. Try this:

```
Dim myStyle As New System.Drawing.Drawing2D.HatchStyle

myStyle = Drawing2D.HatchStyle.LargeCheckerBoard

Dim myHatch As New System.Drawing.Drawing2D
   .HatchBrush(myStyle, Color.Black, Color.Red)

mgrfShapesGraphics.FillRectangle(myHatch, 225, 150,
   150, 150)
```

The first line creates a Drawing2D class with HatchStyle, a two-color checked pattern. The next assigns the LargeCheckerBoard HatchStyle to myStyle. The next line creates the pattern myHatch as a black and red checkerboard pattern. This pattern fits into the arguments for a rectangle (or any other shape). In this example, it creates a square with the classic red and black checked pattern. Try some other patterns as well. You can even do gradients with them!

Text

Use the *DrawString* method to add text to a Graphic (see Figure 13.5). The text can be any font, size, style, or color and can be placed anywhere on a graphic.

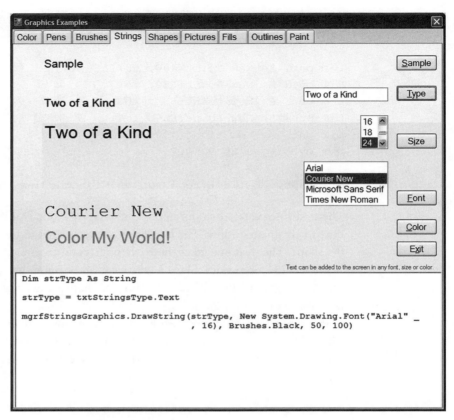

Figure 13.5   Graphics Examples – Strings

The text doesn't wrap to a new line like word-processed text, though. It works like this:

```
grfGraphic.DrawString("Sample", New System
    .Drawing.Font("Arial", 16), Brushes.Black, 50, 25)
```

The text inside the quotation marks gets displayed. The next argument determines the font and its size. Brushes.Black sets the color to black, but it could be any Brushes color. The last two numbers are the x and y coordinates where the text appears. You can substitute variables for any of the arguments.

Images

A PictureBox works well for some images, but images can be added to a Graphic as well (see Figure 13.6). Try this:

```
Dim imgCUP As Image
imgCUP = Image.FromFile("CUP.bmp")
grfGraphic.DrawImage(imgCUP, 100, 100)
```

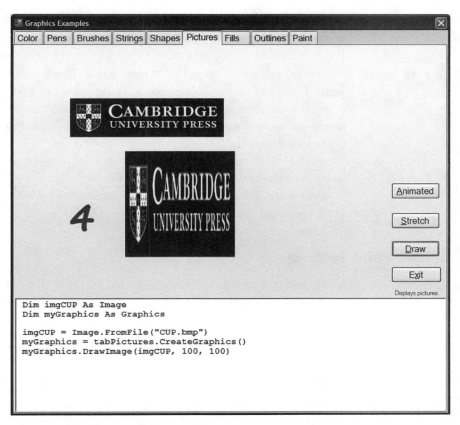

Figure 13.6   Graphics Examples – Pictures

The first line creates an *Image*, which is simply a graphic. The second line loads the "CUP.bmp" image from the file. Be sure to put the file in the Debug folder or include the correct path to find it. The last line draws the image at the x,y location specified. As written, it automatically makes the image its correct size. Add a Width and Height to the command and it stretches or compresses the image to fit. For example,

```
grfGraphic.DrawImage(imgCUP, 100, 100, 200, 150)
```

resizes the image so it's 200 pixels wide and 150 pixels tall.

VB Tip   *Open and run the MousingAround program to see more.*

Potential Problems

Almost any control can become a surface for drawing graphics. Don't pick the wrong surface. Pay attention to the colors. Graphics drawn in the same color as the BackColor won't be visible. Each drawing type has different arguments so care must be taken to select the correct location and size. Fills create a solid shape and Draws create an outline. Graphics must be declared and instantiated before they're used. It's easy to add images to a Graphic, but be sure to put the image file in the correct location so your program can find it. Finally, the VB drawing tools are neat and fun to use, but they don't always render correctly or redraw when needed. They work best when you limit the number of other applications running at the same time.

VB Quiz 02

What are the differences between Pens and Brushes?

How would you change the checkerboard to a checked tablecloth?

How many possible RGB colors are there?

Simple Paint Tutorial

VB Quip

The first 90% of the code accounts for the first 90% of the development time. The remaining 10% of the code accounts for the other 90% of the development time. –Tom Cargill

There's a good reason it's called "Visual" Basic. Let's put some of these graphics tools to work by creating a simple little paint program. When completed, you'll be able to draw freehand in any color or size, draw shapes, and add text.

The form looks like the one shown in Figure 13.7. The painting surface is the white area. It's a drawing surface called a *Rectangle* that will be covered in due course. There are several Buttons and a TextBox that's used to enter text. At the bottom is a *ToolStrip*. Use it to group a set of related Buttons.

Here are the general declarations:

```
Dim mgrfPainter As Graphics                        'Creates Graphic
Dim xDown As Integer                               'Starting X position
Dim yDown As Integer                               'Starting Y position
Dim xUp As Integer                                 'Ending X position
Dim yUp As Integer                                 'Ending Y position
Dim mblnCanPaint As Boolean = False                'Used to paint when set to True
Dim mblnDrawShape As Boolean = False               'Used to draw shapes when set to True
Dim mblnDrawRectangle As Boolean = False           'Used to draw rectangles when set to True
Dim mblnDrawSquare As Boolean = False              'Used to draw squares when set to True
Dim mblnDrawOval As Boolean = False                'Used to draw ovals when set to True
Dim mblnDrawCircle As Boolean = False              'Used to draw circles when set to True
Dim mblnDrawLine As Boolean = False                'Used to draw lines when set to True
Dim mblnWriteText As Boolean = False               'Used to draw text when set to True
Dim mrecPainter As System.Drawing.Rectangle        'Drawing surface
Dim mclrSelected As Color = Color.Black            'Sets painting color
Dim mstrText As String                             'String for adding text
```

```
Dim mstrFont As String = "Arial"          'Sets intial font
Dim mintBrushSize As Integer = 12         'Sets initial Brush size
```

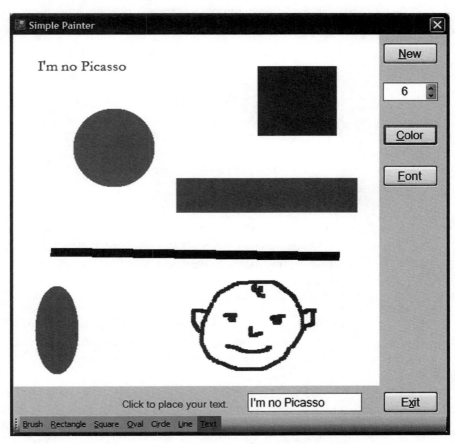

Figure 13.7　　　Simple Painter Program

And here's the code for the Load event:

```
Private Sub frmPaintTutorial_Load(ByVal sender As
    System.Object, ByVal e As System.EventArgs)
    Handles MyBase.Load
    'Instantiates Graphic and sets its size
    mgrfPainter = Me.CreateGraphics
    mrecPainter.Height = 500
    mrecPainter.Width = 500
End Sub
```

The mrecPainter object is declared as a Rectangle. It defines an area of the screen. The Load event sets its Width and Height at 500 pixels and creates the Graphic. Eight different Boolean variables handle the settings to control which tool is in use. xDown, yDown, xUp, and yUp track the starting and ending location of the mouse and are used to determine the bounds for drawing. Other variables control the graphic settings.

Click the New Button to create a new drawing surface. It activates other Buttons as well. Here's the code:

```
Private Sub btnNew_Click(ByVal sender As
    System.Object, ByVal e As System.EventArgs)
    Handles btnNew.Click
        'Creates a new paint area and displays Buttons
        mgrfPainter.FillRectangle(Brushes.White, mrecPainter)
        tlsShapes.Visible = True
        btnColor.Visible = True
        btnFont.Visible = True
        nudBrushSize.Visible = True
End Sub
```

The location of each image is controlled by the x,y location of the mouse. Use the MouseDown event to get the starting location and the MouseUp event to get the ending location. Freehand painting is handled a little differently and is discussed later.

The MouseDown code,

```
Private Sub frmPaintTutorial_MouseDown(ByVal sender
    As Object, ByVal e As System.Windows.Forms
    .MouseEventArgs) Handles Me.MouseDown
        'Determines the mouse location
        'Sets the xy starting point for drawing graphics
        'Starting point cannot be outside the drawing area
        'Sets mblnCanPaint to true so painting can be done
        xDown = e.X
        yDown = e.Y

        If xDown > 500 Then xDown = 500
        If yDown > 500 Then yDown = 500

        mblnCanPaint = True
End Sub
```

gets the x,y location when the mouse button is pressed. If it's pressed outside of the bounds of the rectangle, the values are set to 500. This prevents drawing outside the boundaries of the image. The mblnCanPaint variable gets set to True. It's used in the MouseMove event to control freehand painting.

The MouseUp event does most of the work for the program. It has several blocks of code, each controlling a specific drawing tool:

```
Private Sub frmPaintTutorial_MouseUp(ByVal sender As
    Object, ByVal e As System.Windows.Forms.MouseEventArgs)
```

```
Handles Me.MouseUp
    Dim xStart As Integer
    Dim yStart As Integer
    Dim xEnd As Integer
    Dim yEnd As Integer
    Dim xDistance As Integer
    Dim yDistance As Integer
    Dim bshFill As SolidBrush
    Dim penLine As New Pen(Color.Black, 2)

    'Sets Brush to selected color
    bshFill = New System.Drawing.SolidBrush(mclrSelected)

    'Turns off painting when the mouse is up
    mblnCanPaint = False

    'Gets the XY position when the mouse button is released
    xUp = e.X
    yUp = e.Y

    'Resets mouse position if it's outside drawing area
    If xUp > 500 Then xUp = 500
    If yUp > 500 Then yUp = 500

    'Draws selected shape when True
    If mblnDrawShape Then
        'Sets Brush size
        mintBrushSize = nudBrushSize.Value
        'Compares X start and end positions
        'Sets low value to XStart and high value to XEnd
        'Does the same for Y start and end positions
        'Enables user to create shapes from any direction
        If xUp < xDown Then
            xStart = xUp
            xEnd = xDown
        Else
            xStart = xDown
            xEnd = xUp
        End If
        If yUp < yDown Then
            yStart = yUp
            yEnd = yDown
        Else
            yStart = yDown
```

```vb
            yEnd = yUp
        End If

        'Calculates length of X and Y
        xDistance = xEnd - xStart
        yDistance = yEnd - yStart

        If mblnDrawRectangle Then
            'Draws Rectangle
            mgrfPainter.FillRectangle(bshFill, xStart, _
                yStart, xDistance, yDistance)
        End If

        If mblnDrawOval Then
            'Draws Oval
            mgrfPainter.FillEllipse(bshFill, xStart, _
                yStart, xDistance, yDistance)
        End If

        If mblnDrawCircle Then
            'Draws Circle
            mgrfPainter.FillEllipse(bshFill, xStart, _
                yStart, xDistance, xDistance)
        End If

        If mblnDrawSquare Then
            'Draws Square
            mgrfPainter.FillRectangle(bshFill, xStart, _
                yStart, xDistance, xDistance)
        End If

    End If

    If mblnDrawLine Then
        'Draws straight line
        penLine.Color = mclrSelected
        penLine.Width = mintBrushSize
        mgrfPainter.DrawLine(penLine, xDown, yDown, xUp, yUp)
    End If

    If mblnWriteText Then
        'Draws text
        mstrText = txtText.Text
        mgrfPainter.DrawString(mstrText, New _
            System.Drawing.Font(mstrFont, mintBrushSize), _
            bshFill, xUp, yUp)
```

```
        End If

End Sub
```

These lines

```
'Turns off painting when the mouse is up
mblnCanPaint = False

'Gets the XY position when the mouse button
   is released
xUp = e.X
yUp = e.Y

'Resets mouse position if it's outside drawing area
If xUp > 500 Then xUp = 500
If yUp > 500 Then yUp = 500
```

determine the mouse location when the mouse button is released. If the mouse button is released outside of the drawing area, the X and Y locations are set to 500, and mblnCanPaint is set to False to stop the painting. When it's True, the brush is down, and when it's False, the brush isn't painting.

Shapes are drawn with their respective Fill command as shown:

```
'Draws selected shape when True
If mblnDrawShape Then
    'Sets Brush size
    mintBrushSize = nudBrushSize.Value
    'Compares X start and end positions
    'Sets low value to XStart and high value to XEnd
    'Does the same for Y start and end positions
    'Enables user to create shapes from any direction
    If xUp < xDown Then
        xStart = xUp
        xEnd = xDown
    Else
        xStart = xDown
        xEnd = xUp
    End If
    If yUp < yDown Then
        yStart = yUp
        yEnd = yDown
    Else
        yStart = yDown
        yEnd = yUp
    End If
```

```vb
                    'Calculates length of X and Y
                    xDistance = xEnd - xStart
                    yDistance = yEnd - yStart

                    If mblnDrawRectangle Then
                        'Draws Rectangle
                        mgrfPainter.FillRectangle(bshFill, xStart, yStart, _
                            xDistance, yDistance)
                    End If

                    If mblnDrawOval Then
                        'Draws Oval
                        mgrfPainter.FillEllipse(bshFill, xStart, yStart, _
                            xDistance, yDistance)
                    End If

                    If mblnDrawCircle Then
                        'Draws Circle
                        mgrfPainter.FillEllipse(bshFill, xStart, yStart, _
                            xDistance, xDistance)
                    End If

                    If mblnDrawSquare Then
                        'Draws Square
                        mgrfPainter.FillRectangle(bshFill, xStart, yStart, _
                            xDistance, xDistance)
                    End If

                End If

            If mblnDrawLine Then
                'Draws straight line
                penLine.Color = mclrSelected
                penLine.Width = mintBrushSize
                mgrfPainter.DrawLine(penLine, xDown, yDown, xUp, yUp)
            End If

            If mblnWriteText Then
                'Draws text
                mstrText = txtText.Text
                mgrfPainter.DrawString(mstrText, New System. _
                    Drawing.Font(mstrFont, mintBrushSize), _
                    bshFill, xUp, yUp)
            End If
```

A Boolean called mblnDrawShape turns on the drawing tools. Each shape is controlled by its own Boolean that's set to True when its tool is selected.

```
'Sets Brush size
mintBrushSize = nudBrushSize.Value
```

sets the Brush size from the NumericUpDown control.

The following lines determine the starting and ending location for shapes:

```
'Compares X start and end positions
'Sets low value to XStart and high value to XEnd
'Does the same for Y start and end positions
'Enables user to create shapes from any direction
If xUp < xDown Then
    xStart = xUp
    xEnd = xDown
Else
    xStart = xDown
    xEnd = xUp
End If

If yUp < yDown Then
    yStart = yUp
    yEnd = yDown
Else
    yStart = yDown
    yEnd = yUp
End If

'Calculates length of X and Y
xDistance = xEnd - xStart
yDistance = yEnd - yStart
```

Recall that shapes have a starting and an ending position and use the distance between them to determine the size of the graphic. This is all well and good if the user always draws from the top left to the lower right. But that's seldom the case, so the code determines the starting and ending points for X and Y based on their values. The code checks the values for xDown and xUp. The lower value becomes xStart and the higher value becomes xEnd. yStart and yEnd are determined in the same way. The xDistance is the difference between these two locations. The yDistance is determined in the same way. That way the user can draw from any direction and it will still create an image!

Shapes are drawn by the following code:

```
If mblnDrawRectangle Then
    'Draws Rectangle
    mgrfPainter.FillRectangle(bshFill, xStart, yStart,
      xDistance, yDistance)
End If
If mblnDrawOval Then
    'Draws Oval
    mgrfPainter.FillEllipse(bshFill, xStart, yStart,
      xDistance, yDistance)
End If

If mblnDrawCircle Then
    'Draws Circle
    mgrfPainter.FillEllipse(bshFill, xStart, yStart,
      xDistance, xDistance)
End If

If mblnDrawSquare Then
    'Draws Square
    mgrfPainter.FillRectangle(bshFill, xStart, yStart,
      xDistance, xDistance)
End If
```

Depending on the tool selected, the appropriate shape is drawn. Note that squares and circles are drawn using the xDistance value. The width and height values are both set to xDistance.

Placing text on the screen is a little more complicated. The user must enter their text in the TextBox, they must select the Text tool from the ToolStrip, and they must click on a location to place the text.

```
If mblnWriteText Then
    'Draws text
    mstrText = txtText.Text
    mgrfPainter.DrawString(mstrText, New
      System.Drawing.Font(mstrFont, mintBrushSize),
      bshFill, xUp, yUp)
End If
```

The code uses the x,y location from the MouseUp event as the location to place the text. mblnWriteText is only True when the Text tool is selected.

The MouseMove event controls freehand painting. The code is

```
'Handles mouse moves
'Sets the Brush size
```

```
'Paints on the screen only when mblnCanPaint is
  true and others are false
'Checks mouse location and keeps mouse within paint
  area
'Adjusts for mouse location and Brush size
Dim intBrushSize As Integer

intBrushSize = nudBrushSize.Value
If mblnCanPaint And Not mblnDrawShape And Not
  mblnDrawLine And Not mblnWriteText Then
    xDown = e.X
    yDown = e.Y

  If xDown > 500 Then xDown = 500 - intBrushSize
  If yDown > 500 Then yDown = 500 - intBrushSize

  mgrfPainter.FillEllipse(New SolidBrush(mclrSelected),
    xDown, yDown, intBrushSize, intBrushSize)
End If
```

The BrushSize, from 2 to 24, is determined by the NumericUpDown and is stored in intBrushSize. The mouse location is updated every time the mouse moves and the new x,y location becomes the location for a new ellipse in that location. It draws when mblnCanPaint is True and when the shape, line, and text Booleans are set to False. It checks to see if the x,y locations are outside of the drawing area and sets them back to 500 if needed. It draws a new circle every time the mouse moves!

The Color Button displays the ColorDialog. Its code simply displays the dialog and stores the selected color in mclrSelected where it can be used as needed in any tool:

```
Private Sub btnColor_Click(ByVal sender As System.Object,
  ByVal e As System.EventArgs) Handles btnColor.Click
    'Displays ColorDialog
    clrDialog.ShowDialog()
    mclrSelected = clrDialog.Color
End Sub
```

The Font Button displays the FontDialog. Its code simply displays the dialog and stores the font and size in variables where they can be used as needed to display text:

```
Private Sub btnFont_Click(ByVal sender As System.Object,
  ByVal e As System.EventArgs) Handles btnFont.Click
    'Display font dialog to set font and size
    fntDialog.ShowDialog()
```

```
      mstrFont = fntDialog.Font.Name
      mintBrushSize = fntDialog.Font.Size
End Sub
```

The ToolStrip is a handy little control. With it, you can add other controls and group them together. It's small and easy to create and use. ToolStrips are added to the component tray and can be docked to the edge of a form. Use tls for its prefix.

The ToolStrip buttons work together and only one at a time is used. The ChangeButtons procedure controls the "look and feel" for the buttons:

```
Private Sub ChangeButtons()
      'Changes BackColor for ToolStrip buttons
      'Turns off all the painting settings
      tlsShapesRectangle.BackColor = Color.LightBlue
      tlsShapesOval.BackColor = Color.LightBlue
      tlsShapesCircle.BackColor = Color.LightBlue
      tlsShapesSquare.BackColor = Color.LightBlue
      tlsShapesBrush.BackColor = Color.LightBlue
      tlsShapesLine.BackColor = Color.LightBlue
      tlsShapesText.BackColor = Color.LightBlue

      lblTextDirections.Visible = False

      mblnDrawShape = False
      mblnDrawRectangle = False
      mblnDrawOval = False
      mblnDrawCircle = False
      mblnDrawSquare = False
      mblnDrawLine = False
      mblnWriteText = False
End Sub
```

The procedure changes the BackColor of all the buttons to LightBlue. To the user, they'll appear "off." The Boolean for drawing shapes is set to False, as are the separate Booleans that control the individual shapes. All the buttons in the ToolStrip call this procedure. Each button in the ToolStrip then adjusts its BackColor and sets its variables as needed to draw. The code for each is below:

```
Private Sub tlsShapesRectangle_Click(ByVal sender As
   System.Object, ByVal e As System.EventArgs) Handles
   tlsShapesRectangle.Click
      'Settings for drawing rectangles
```

```
        ChangeButtons()
        If mblnDrawRectangle Then
            tlsShapesRectangle.BackColor = Color.LightBlue
            mblnDrawShape = False
            mblnDrawRectangle = False
        Else
            tlsShapesRectangle.BackColor = Color.DarkGray
            mblnDrawShape = True
            mblnDrawRectangle = True
        End If
    End Sub


    Private Sub tlsShapesOval_Click(ByVal sender As
      System.Object, ByVal e As System.EventArgs) Handles
      tlsShapesOval.Click
        'Settings for drawing ovals
        ChangeButtons()
        If mblnDrawOval Then
            tlsShapesOval.BackColor = Color.LightBlue
            mblnDrawShape = False
            mblnDrawOval = False
        Else
            tlsShapesOval.BackColor = Color.DarkGray
            mblnDrawShape = True
            mblnDrawOval = True
        End If
    End Sub


    Private Sub tlsShapesCircle_Click(ByVal sender As
      System.Object, ByVal e As System.EventArgs) Handles
      tlsShapesCircle.Click
        'Settings for drawing a circle
        ChangeButtons()
        If mblnDrawCircle Then
            tlsShapesCircle.BackColor = Color.LightBlue
            mblnDrawShape = False
            mblnDrawCircle = False
        Else
            tlsShapesCircle.BackColor = Color.DarkGray
            mblnDrawShape = True
            mblnDrawCircle = True
        End If
    End Sub
```

```vbnet
Private Sub tlsShapesSquare_Click(ByVal sender As
   System.Object, ByVal e As System.EventArgs) Handles
   tlsShapesSquare.Click
     'Setting for drawing a square
     ChangeButtons()
     If mblnDrawSquare Then
         tlsShapesSquare.BackColor = Color.LightBlue
         mblnDrawShape = False
         mblnDrawSquare = False
     Else
         tlsShapesSquare.BackColor = Color.DarkGray
         mblnDrawShape = True
         mblnDrawSquare = True
     End If
End Sub

Private Sub tlsShapesBrush_Click(ByVal sender As
   System.Object, ByVal e As System.EventArgs) Handles
   tlsShapesBrush.Click
     'Settings for paintbrush
     ChangeButtons()
     If mblnDrawShape Then
         tlsShapesBrush.BackColor = Color.LightBlue
         mblnCanPaint = False
     Else
         tlsShapesBrush.BackColor = Color.DarkGray
     End If
End Sub

Private Sub tlsShapesLine_Click(ByVal sender As
   System.Object, ByVal e As System.EventArgs) Handles
   tlsShapesLine.Click
     'Settings for adding lines
     ChangeButtons()
     If mblnDrawLine Then
         tlsShapesLine.BackColor = Color.LightBlue
         mblnDrawLine = False
         mblnDrawShape = False
     Else
         tlsShapesLine.BackColor = Color.DarkGray
         mblnDrawLine = True
         mblnCanPaint = False
     End If
End Sub
```

```
Private Sub tlsShapesText_Click(ByVal sender As
   System.Object, ByVal e As System.EventArgs) Handles
   tlsShapesText.Click
     'Settings for adding text
     ChangeButtons()
     If mblnWriteText Then
         tlsShapesText.BackColor = Color.LightBlue
         mblnWriteText = False
         mblnDrawShape = False
     Else
         tlsShapesText.BackColor = Color.DarkGray
         mblnWriteText = True
         mblnCanPaint = False
     End If

     'Displays prompt for TextBox
     lblTextDirections.Visible = True
End Sub
```

VB Tip   *Open and run the PaintTutorial to see how it works.*

Sound

VB Tip   *Make sure your sound is at a reasonable level and the mute is unchecked. Think of others and use headphones if you have them.*

There are three ways for Visual Basic to play sound. One way is to play a sound file. Another way is to play a built-in sound that comes with your system. The third way is to generate your own sound.

Playing Sounds

The first method takes only one line of code:

```
Sound.PlayWaveFile("gameover.wav")
```

It plays a short wav file. You might recognize it as the Bill Paxton line from Fox's 1986 film, *Aliens*. The syntax is pretty simple:

```
Sound.PlayWaveFile(filename.wav)
```

where filename.wav is the name of the wav file. Be sure to put it in quotation marks. Just like data files, it's a good idea to put the file in the Debug folder. That way your program can find it. Of course, you could include the drive and path for the file so your program can find it.

Your computer comes with several built-in sounds. They're the ones you hear when performing common tasks. Play them like this:

```
Sound.PlayWaveSystem("SystemExit")
```

It plays a simple chord. The syntax for playing system sounds is

```
Sound.PlayWaveSystem(systemSound)
```

where systemSound is the name of the sound in quotation marks. Here's a short list of sounds:

```
"AppGPFault"
"Close"
"MailBeep"
"Maximize"
"MenuCommand"
"MenuPopup"
"Minimize"
"Open"
"RestoreDown"
"RestoreUp"
"SystemAsterisk"
"SystemExclamation"
"SystemExit"
"SystemHand"
"SystemQuestion"
"SystemStart"
".Default"
```

Simply place it inside the parentheses of the Sound.PlayWaveSystem command. Yes, the last one says .Default. Try it if you don't believe me!

Generating Sounds

Sounds are generated with a *Beep*. The general command is

```
System.Console.Beep(frequency, duration)
```

where frequency is the pitch from 37 to 32767 and duration is the length of the sound in milliseconds. The following table gives approximate keyboard values for some notes:

Pitch	Keyboard Value
264	low C
280	C# or D-
297	D
313	D# or E-
330	E
352	F
374	F# or G-
396	G
418	G# or A-
440	A
467	A# or B-
495	B
528	middle C

VB Tip   *If you double the value, you'll get the same pitch but one octave higher.*

To play a sound, simply plug in the frequency and duration. To play music, string together several sounds. Try this:

```
System.Console.Beep(264, 400)    'C
System.Console.Beep(264, 400)    'C
System.Console.Beep(396, 400)    'G
System.Console.Beep(396, 400)    'G
System.Console.Beep(440, 400)    'A
System.Console.Beep(440, 400)    'A
System.Console.Beep(396, 800)    'G
System.Console.Beep(352, 400)    'F
System.Console.Beep(352, 400)    'F
System.Console.Beep(330, 400)    'E
System.Console.Beep(330, 400)    'E
System.Console.Beep(297, 400)    'D
System.Console.Beep(297, 400)    'D
System.Console.Beep(264, 800)    'C
```

It plays the children's song *Twinkle, Twinkle, Little Star*.

Put the Beep command inside a loop to vary the pitch. For example:

```
For j = 250 To 1200 Step 20
    System.Console.Beep(j, 30)
Next j
```

The pitch increases with every pass through the loop. Decrease the pitch this way:

```
For j = 1200 To 250 Step -20
    System.Console.Beep(j, 30)
Next j
```

Now, combine the two loops inside another loop, like this:

```
For i = 1 To 4
    For j = 250 To 1200 Step 20
        System.Console.Beep(j, 30)
    Next j
    For j = 1200 To 250 Step -20
        System.Console.Beep(j, 30)
    Next j
Next i
```

to produce a siren sound. While computer-generated sounds are tacky, they are useful and usually fun. If you combine a list of notes and use loops, there's almost no limit to the sounds you can create!

Windows Media Player

Use *Windows Media Player* to play sound files and movies (see Figure 13.8). It's capable of playing many types of files, from MP3 files to MPEG movies.

Figure 13.8   Choose Toolbox Items – Windows Media Player

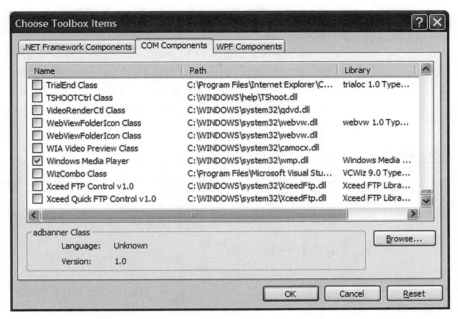

Figure 13.9   Adding Windows Media Player to the Toolbox

However, it does take a little work to set it up because the Windows Media Player control isn't in the Toolbox.

To use it, right-click in the Toolbox and select Choose Items... That opens the Choose Toolbox Items dialog. There are three tabs at the top of it. Select the COM Components tab. Scroll through the list to find Windows Media Player. The list is alphabetized so it's near the bottom. Click on the CheckBox and click the OK button, which adds it to the Toolbox. Double-click on it to add the control to a form. Resize the control as needed. Sounds don't need the top of the screen, but movies do, so adjust it as needed. Name it with wmp as the prefix (see Figure 13.9).

There's only one command needed to make it work. Double-click on the control to create an Enter event. The code is

```
wmpBirthday.URL = "birthday.avi"
```

The control's name is wmpBirthday, and URL is the property containing the name of the file to play. In this case, it's a short movie file.

Change the URL property to view different movies or sounds. It's a good idea to put the files in the Debug folder. Of course, they can be anywhere if you supply the drive and path for them. And the OpenFile dialog works well to select files. There's nothing to it!

VB Quiz 03   *What is the ItemClicked event for a ToolStrip? How can it be used?*

How would you create a calligraphy brush for painting?

What would it take to create a Karaoke player?

Creating Charts

Data usually have a greater impact when presented visually. So, why not create simple charts with your data? You can even animate them. You already know how to create rectangles. Those are great for bar charts. You can draw lines for line charts and you can create circles and arcs for pie charts.

Bar Charts

Clara Fie want to see how many hours she spends studying for each of her classes. Here's her data:

```
Botany    6
Visual Basic    12
History    7
PE    1
Rhetoric    8
```

A simple bar chart showing the class and the number of hours should do the trick and the longer the bar, the more time spent studying. The data are in a small data file that must be read. That might seem a bit much, but it really makes it easier. All you must do is update the data file and the chart changes. The code and the chart are shown below and in Figure 13.10.

```vb
Public Class frmBarChart
    Dim mgrfChart As Graphics

    Private Sub frmBarChart_Load...
        mgrfChart = Me.CreateGraphics
    End Sub

    Private Sub btnExit_Click...
        End
    End Sub

    Private Sub btnPlot_Click...
        Dim srdStudyTimes As System.IO.StreamReader
        Dim strClass As String
        Dim shoHours As Short
        Dim strRecord() As String
        Dim strLine As String
        Dim intNameLocation As Integer
        Dim intHoursLocation As Integer = 25
        Dim intBarLength As Integer
```

```
        'Set filename
        srdStudyTimes = New
          System.IO.StreamReader("StudyTimes.dat")

        'Heading
        mgrfChart.DrawString("Clara Fie Study Times",
          New System.Drawing.Font("Arial", 24) _ ,
          Brushes.Black, 50, 25)
        Do Until srdStudyTimes.Peek = -1
            'Input
            strLine = srdStudyTimes.ReadLine
            strRecord = strLine.Split(",")
            strClass = strRecord(0)
            shoHours = Convert.ToInt16(strRecord(1))

            'Processing
            'Increments variables so each item displays in
            'its own area
            intNameLocation += 75
            intHoursLocation += 75
            intBarLength = shoHours * 25

            'Output
            'Draws class, hours and horizontal bars to
            'indicate study times
            mgrfChart.DrawString(strClass, New
              System.Drawing.Font("Arial", 16) _
              , Brushes.Black, 50, intNameLocation)
            mgrfChart.DrawString(shoHours.ToString, New
              System.Drawing.Font("Arial", 16) _
              , Brushes.Black, 50, intHoursLocation)
            mgrfChart.FillRectangle(Brushes.Green, 85,
              intHoursLocation, intBarLength, 25)
        Loop

        'Close File
        srdStudyTimes.Close()

        'Draws legend at the bottom
        mgrfChart.DrawString("Times in hours per week",
          New System.Drawing.Font("Arial", 12) _
          , Brushes.Black, 50, 525)
    End Sub
End Class
```

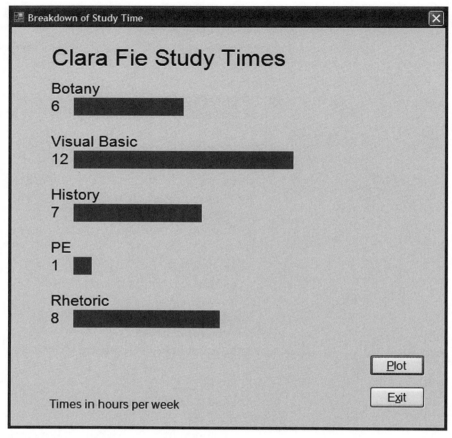

Figure 13.10   Bar Chart Program

The Graphic object is declared in the Declarations,

```
Dim mgrfChart As Graphics
```

and instantiated in the Load event:

```
mgrfChart = Me.CreateGraphics
```

Several lines are needed to handle the file input:

```
Dim srdStudyTimes As System.IO.StreamReader
srdStudyTimes = New
    System.IO.StreamReader("StudyTimes.dat")

Dim strRecord() As String

Do Until srdStudyTimes.Peek = -1
    'Input
    strLine = srdStudyTimes.ReadLine
```

```
        strRecord = strLine.Split(",")
        strClass = strRecord(0)
        shoHours = Convert.ToInt16(strRecord(1))
Loop

srdStudyTimes.Close()
```

The file contains the class name and the hours of study. These are used for calculating the length of the bar and for display.

Three variables are needed to help with the chart:

```
Dim intNameLocation As Integer
Dim intHoursLocation As Integer = 25
Dim intBarLength As Integer
```

They're updated inside the loop and are used to change the Y locations of the graphics:

```
intNameLocation += 75
intHoursLocation += 75
intBarLength = shoHours * 25
```

Three lines are needed to draw each data point for the graph:

```
mgrfChart.DrawString(strClass, New
    System.Drawing.Font("Arial", 16), Brushes.Black,
    50, intNameLocation)
mgrfChart.DrawString(shoHours.ToString, New
    System.Drawing.Font("Arial", 16), Brushes.Black,
    50, intHoursLocation)
mgrfChart.FillRectangle(Brushes.Green, 85,
    intHoursLocation, intBarLength, 25)
```

The first line displays the name of the class, the second line displays the study hours for the class, and the third line draws a rectangle to represent the study time. The variables control the screen locations and are incremented with each pass through the loop:

```
mgrfChart.DrawString("Times in hours per week", New
    System.Drawing.Font("Arial", 12) , Brushes.Black,
    50, 525)
```

The last line displays the legend for the chart.

Line Charts

Luke Ruttive needs to display stock prices for Global Reserve Electronic Enterprises of Delaware. The data are in a file and a line chart is just the thing for displaying trends. Quarterly stock prices for three years are stored in a file where they must be read and displayed.

```
1,2009,28.38,1.50
2,2009,32.13,3.75
3,2009,33.50,1.37
4,2009,28.75,-4.75
1,2010,31.25,2.50
2,2010,35.63,4.38
3,2010,36.13,.5
4,2010,34.13,-2
1,2011,32.25,-1.88
2,2011,33.88,1.63
3,2011,33.88,0
4,2011,34.13,.25
```

The data file shows the fiscal quarter, the year, the closing stock price for the last day of the quarter, and the stock's change in price from the last quarter. Each record in the file becomes a line on the chart (see Figure 13.11).

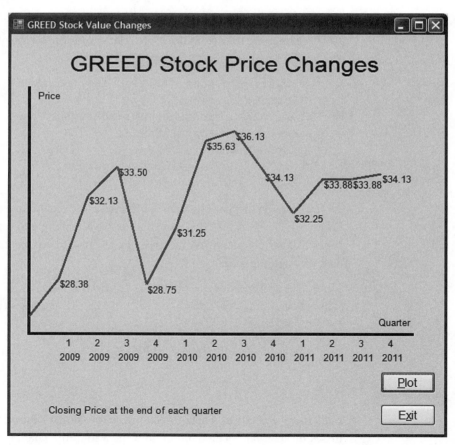

Figure 13.11   Line Chart Program

```vb
Public Class frmLineChart
    Dim mgrfChart As Graphics

    Private Sub frmLineChart_Load...
        mgrfChart = Me.CreateGraphics
    End Sub

    Private Sub btnExit_Click...
        End
    End Sub

    Private Sub btnPlot_Click...
        Dim srdStockPrices As System.IO.StreamReader
        Dim strQuarter As String
        Dim strYear As String
        Dim decPrice As Decimal
        Dim decChange As Decimal
        Dim strRecord() As String
        Dim decOldPrice As Decimal = 30
        Dim strLine As String
        Dim sngSpacing As Single = 40
        Dim penChartLines As New Pen(Color.Black, 4)
        Dim penPlotLines As New Pen(Color.Black, 3)
        Dim sngX As Single
        Dim sngXOld As Single = 25
        Dim sngY As Single
        Dim sngYOld As Single = 400
        Dim sngChange As Single
        'Set filename
        srdStockPrices = New _
            System.IO.StreamReader("GREEDPrices.dat")

        'Heading
        mgrfChart.DrawString("GREED Stock Price Changes", New _
        System.Drawing.Font("Arial", 24) , Brushes.Black, _
            75, 25)
        'Chart lines
        'Draws boundaries for chart and labels them
        mgrfChart.DrawLine(penChartLines, 25, 75, 25, 425)
        mgrfChart.DrawLine(penChartLines, 23, 425, 550, _
            425)
        mgrfChart.DrawString("Quarter", New System.Drawing _
            .Font("Arial", 10), Brushes.Black, 500, 400)
        mgrfChart.DrawString("Price", New System.Drawing _
            .Font("Arial", 10), Brushes.Black, 35, 80)
```

```vb
'Draws legend at the bottom
mgrfChart.DrawString("Closing Price at the end of each
    quarter", New System.Drawing.Font("Arial", 10),
    Brushes.Black, 50, 525)

Do Until srdStockPrices.Peek = -1
    'Input
    strLine = srdStockPrices.ReadLine
    strRecord = strLine.Split(",")
    strQuarter = strRecord(0)
    strYear = strRecord(1)
    decPrice = Convert.ToDecimal(strRecord(2))
    decChange = Convert.ToDecimal(strRecord(3))

    'Processing
    'Location change is calculated from old
    'price and new price
    sngChange = ((decChange / decPrice) * 100) * 10
    sngX = sngXOld + sngSpacing
    sngY = sngYOld - sngChange
    'Change color Green for price increase, Red
    'for price decrease
    If decChange >= 0 Then
        penPlotLines = New Pen(Color.Green, 3)
    Else
        penPlotLines = New Pen(Color.Red, 3)
    End If

    mgrfChart.DrawLine(penPlotLines, sngXOld,
        sngYOld, sngX, sngY)

    'Output
    'Draws labels
    mgrfChart.DrawString(decPrice.ToString("c"),
        New System.Drawing.Font("Arial", 10)
        Brushes.Black, sngX, sngY)
    mgrfChart.DrawString("  " & strQuarter, New
        System.Drawing.Font("Arial", 10) ,
        Brushes.Black, sngX, 430)
    mgrfChart.DrawString(strYear, New System.Drawing
        .Font("Arial", 10) , Brushes.Black, sngX, 450)
    'Updates X and Y location for starting point of
    'next line
    sngXOld = sngX
    sngYOld = sngY
Loop
```

```
        'Close File
        srdStockPrices.Close()
    End Sub

End Class
```

The Graphic object is declared in the Declarations,

```
Dim mgrfChart As Graphics
```

and instantiated in the Load event:

```
mgrfChart = Me.CreateGraphics
```

Several lines manage file input:

```
Dim srdStockPrices As System.IO.StreamReader
srdStockPrices = New System.IO
  .StreamReader("GREEDPrices.dat")
Dim strRecord() As String

Do Until srdStockPrices.Peek = -1
    'Input
    strLine = srdStockPrices.ReadLine
    strRecord = strLine.Split(",")
    strQuarter = strRecord(0)
    strYear = strRecord(1)

    decPrice = Convert.ToDecimal(strRecord(2))
    decChange = Convert.ToDecimal(strRecord(3))
Loop
srdStockPrices.Close()
```

The file contains the quarter, year, closing price, and the price change from the previous quarter.

These variables manage the chart. They control the line colors and data points:

```
Dim decOldPrice As Decimal = 30
Dim strLine As String
Dim sngSpacing As Single = 40
Dim penChartLines As New Pen(Color.Black, 4)
Dim penPlotLines As New Pen(Color.Black, 3)
Dim sngX As Single
Dim sngXOld As Single = 25
Dim sngY As Single
Dim sngYOld As Single = 400
Dim sngChange As Single
```

The lines on the chart move up when the stock price increases. This is a little tricky because the Y location decreases as it moves up. That means Y decreases as price increases. There's some math needed for that. These lines do that nicely:

```
sngChange = ((decChange / decPrice) * 100) * 10
sngX = sngXOld + sngSpacing
sngY = sngYOld - sngChange
```

The first line calculates the percentage change in price and it multiplies the change by 10. This increases the magnitude of change for the chart and makes the changes easier to see. The last two lines update the X and Y locations. Remember, the starting point for the next line is the ending point of the last line.

The next lines determine the color of the line, green lines when the stock value increases and red lines when it decreases.

The line itself is drawn with this code:

```
mgrfChart.DrawLine(penPlotLines, sngXOld, sngYOld,
   sngX, sngY)
```

It draws a line from the previous x,y location (sngXOld, sngYOld) to the next x,y locations (sngX, sngY).

Once the line has been drawn, the current x,y values (sngX and sngY) get moved to sngXOld and sngYOld. When the next record is read, it calculates new values for sngX and sngY so the next line can be drawn. The following code handles that task:

```
'Updates X and Y location for starting point of next line
sngXOld = sngX
sngYOld = sngY
```

These lines draw the chart heading, boundaries, and labels:

```
'Heading
mgrfChart.DrawString("GREED Stock Price Changes", New
   System.Drawing.Font("Arial", 24) , Brushes.Black,
   75, 25)

'Chart lines
'Draws boundaries for chart and labels them
mgrfChart.DrawLine(penChartLines, 25, 75, 25, 425)
mgrfChart.DrawLine(penChartLines, 23, 425, 550, 425)
mgrfChart.DrawString("Quarter", New
   System.Drawing.Font("Arial", 10), Brushes.Black,
   500, 400)
mgrfChart.DrawString("Price", New
   System.Drawing.Font("Arial", 10), Brushes.Black,
   35, 80)

'Draws legend at the bottom
mgrfChart.DrawString("Closing Price at the end of
   each quarter", New System.Drawing.Font("Arial", 10),
   Brushes.Black, 50, 525)
```

Although the chart is custom made, it does provide a starting point for charts with some real power and flexibility.

Pie Charts

Rhoda Dendron runs a nursery. Her sales are in four general categories: flowers, plants, trees, and shrubs. A simple pie chart should be able to depict her sales. Here's the data from the file:

```
Flowers,448378
Plants,301218
Trees,148377
Shrubs,102027
```

A pie chart depicts parts of a whole. To do this, the data must be read and the total sales calculated before the chart is drawn. Use an array to load the data and then draw the chart. The code and chart are shown below and in Figure 13.12.

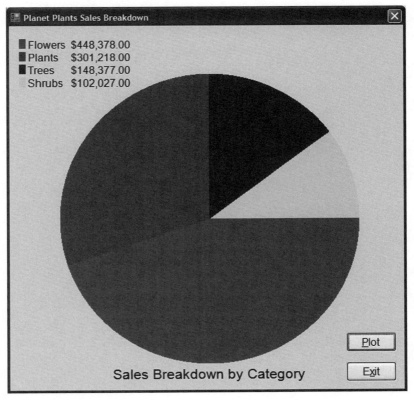

Figure 13.12   Pie Chart Program

```
Public Class frmPieChart
    Dim mgrfChart As Graphics
    Private Sub frmPieChart_Load...
        mgrfChart = Me.CreateGraphics
    End Sub

    Private Sub btnExit_Click...
        End
    End Sub

    Private Sub btnPlot_Click...
        Dim srdSales As System.IO.StreamReader
        Dim strCategory() As String
        Dim decSales() As Decimal
        Dim strRecord() As String
        Dim strLine As String
        Dim decTotalSales As Decimal
        Dim i As Integer
        Dim sngOldArc As Single
        Dim sngArc As Single
        Dim shoYChange As Short = 20

        'Set filename
        srdSales = New
          System.IO.StreamReader("PlanetPlants.dat")

        'Load data from file into an array
        Do Until srdSales.Peek = -1
            'Resize arrays
            ReDim Preserve strCategory(i)
            ReDim Preserve decSales(i)

            'Input
            strLine = srdSales.ReadLine
            strRecord = strLine.Split(",")
            strCategory(i) = strRecord(0)
            decSales(i) = Convert.ToDecimal(strRecord(1))

            'Find total sales
            decTotalSales += decSales(i)

            i += 1

        Loop

        'Close File
        srdSales.Close()
```

```vb
For i = 0 To strCategory.GetUpperBound(0)
    'Calculate size of pie slice and draw chart
    'Percentage of total sales is calculated as
    'percentage of total pie
    sngArc = (decSales(i) / decTotalSales) * 360

    'Select color and draw slice based on item
    'First line draws slice
    'Second line draws color in legend
    'Third line is category
    'Fourth line is sales
    Select Case i
        Case Is = 0
            mgrfChart.FillPie(Brushes.Red, 75, 75, 450, 450,
                sngOldArc, sngArc)
            mgrfChart.FillRectangle(Brushes.Red, 15,
                shoYChange, 10, 15)
            mgrfChart.DrawString(strCategory(i), New
                System.Drawing.Font("Arial", 12),
                Brushes.Black, 25, shoYChange)
            mgrfChart.DrawString(decSales(i).ToString("c"),
                New System.Drawing.Font("Arial", 12),
                Brushes.Black, 90, shoYChange)
        Case Is = 1
            mgrfChart.FillPie(Brushes.Green, 75, 75, 450,
                450, sngOldArc, sngArc)
            mgrfChart.FillRectangle(Brushes.Green, 15,
                shoYChange, 10, 15)
            mgrfChart.DrawString(strCategory(i), New
                System.Drawing.Font("Arial", 12),
                Brushes.Black, 25, shoYChange)
            mgrfChart.DrawString(decSales(i).ToString("c"),
                New System.Drawing.Font("Arial", 12),
                Brushes.Black, 90, shoYChange)
        Case Is = 2
            mgrfChart.FillPie(Brushes.Blue, 75, 75, 450,
                450, sngOldArc, sngArc)
            mgrfChart.FillRectangle(Brushes.Blue, 15,
                shoYChange, 10, 15)
            mgrfChart.DrawString(strCategory(i), New
                System.Drawing.Font("Arial", 12),
                Brushes.Black, 25, shoYChange)
            mgrfChart.DrawString(decSales(i).ToString("c"),
                New System.Drawing.Font("Arial", 12),
                Brushes.Black, 90, shoYChange)
```

```
                    Case Is = 3
                        mgrfChart.FillPie(Brushes.Yellow, 75, 75, 450,
                            450, sngOldArc, sngArc)
                        mgrfChart.FillRectangle(Brushes.Yellow, 15,
                            shoYChange, 10, 15)
                        mgrfChart.DrawString(strCategory(i), New
                            System.Drawing.Font("Arial", 12),
                            Brushes.Black, 25, shoYChange)
                        mgrfChart.DrawString(decSales(i).ToString("c"),
                            New System.Drawing.Font("Arial", 12),
                            Brushes.Black, 90, shoYChange)
                    Case Is = 4
                        mgrfChart.FillPie(Brushes.Purple, 75, 75, 450,
                            450, sngOldArc, sngArc)
                        mgrfChart.FillRectangle(Brushes.Purple, 15,
                            shoYChange, 10, 15)
                        mgrfChart.DrawString(strCategory(i), New
                            System.Drawing.Font("Arial", 12),
                            Brushes.Black, 25, shoYChange)
                        mgrfChart.DrawString(decSales(i).ToString("c"),
                            New System.Drawing.Font("Arial", 12),
                            Brushes.Black, 90, shoYChange)
                End Select

                'Stop point of arc becomes start point for
                'next arc
                sngOldArc += sngArc

                'Changes Y location on legend
                shoYChange += 20
            Next i

            'Draw labels
            mgrfChart.DrawString("Sales Breakdown by
                Category", New System.Drawing.Font("Arial", 16),
                Brushes.Black, 150, 530)
        End Sub
End Class
```

The Graphic object is declared in the Declarations,

```
Dim mgrfChart As Graphics
```

and instantiated in the Load event:

```
mgrfChart = Me.CreateGraphics
```

Several lines manage file input and place the data into arrays:

```
Dim srdSales As System.IO.StreamReader
Dim strCategory() As String
Dim decSales() As Decimal
Dim strRecord() As String
Dim strLine As String

srdSales = New System.IO.StreamReader("PlanetPlants.dat")

Do Until srdSales.Peek = -1
    'Resize arrays
    ReDim Preserve strCategory(i)
    ReDim Preserve decSales(i)

    'Input
    strLine = srdSales.ReadLine
    strRecord = strLine.Split(",")
    strCategory(i) = strRecord(0)
    decSales(i) = Convert.ToDecimal(strRecord(1))
    i += 1
Loop

'Close File

srdSales.Close()
```

The file contains the categories and the monthly sales figures. The categories go into the strCategory array and the sales belong in decSales. The total sales are accumulated in decTotalSales. You need this to calculate the size of each individual slice of the pie.

The second loop handles each category. Here's the loop:

```
For i = 0 To strCategory.GetUpperBound(0)
    sngArc = (decSales(i) / decTotalSales) * 360
    Select Case i
        'Case statements for each category
    End Select

    'Stop point of arc becomes start point for next arc
    sngOldArc += sngArc

    'Changes Y location on legend
    shoYChange += 20
Next i
```

It starts at 0 and runs to the UpperBound of the array.

Just inside the loop is a line that calculates the size of the slice. The starting point for the next slice is the ending point of the previous slice. The sngArc variable gets added to sngOldArc to become the next starting point.

The shoYChange variable is for the legend. It moves the starting point for each line down 20 pixels:

```
'Calculate size of pie slice and draw chart
'Percentage of total sales is calculated as percentage
  of total pie
sngArc = (decSales(i) / decTotalSales) * 360
```

The sales for a category are divided by the total sales to get the percentage. Multiply that to get the size of the slice in degrees.

Each slice is handled by its own part of a Case structure:

```
Case Is = 0
    mgrfChart.FillPie(Brushes.Red, 75, 75, 450,
      450, sngOldArc, sngArc)
    mgrfChart.FillRectangle(Brushes.Red, 15,
      shoYChange, 10, 15)
    mgrfChart.DrawString(strCategory(i), New _
      System.Drawing.Font("Arial", 12), _ Brushes.Black,
      25, shoYChange)
    mgrfChart.DrawString(decSales(i).ToString("c"), _
      New System.Drawing.Font("Arial", 12), _
      Brushes.Black, 90, shoYChange)
```

The Case is based on the array item. Each Case statement selects a different color and draws its slice of the pie. The second line draws a small rectangle in that color for the legend at the top left of the chart. The third line draws the category name and the last line displays the sales for that category. Each gets drawn in turn until the chart is completed.

The last lines draw a title at the bottom of the chart:

```
'Draw labels
mgrfChart.DrawString("Sales Breakdown by Category", New _
  System.Drawing.Font("Arial", 16) , _ Brushes.Black,
  150, 530)
```

Of course, charts are far more complicated than that, but this is a start. In the real world, the points are calculated so the charts can be resized. Arrays are used because charts have a varying number of points. The finer points such as color, font, size, and style are all variables set by the user. Still, it's a good start.

VB Quiz 04　　*How would you draw gridlines on the bar chart?*

How would you "explode" the first item in a pie chart?

The code for the pie chart has an extra Case statement. What would it take to add a Miscellaneous category?

VB Quip　　　　　　　　　*There is no programming language – no matter how structured – that will prevent programmers from making bad programs. –Larry Flon*

Potential Problems

Graphics don't always draw correctly and sometimes they don't redraw. The alpha setting for a layer adds transparency to graphics, so watch out for graphics that bleed. It's a great feature, but it can be frustrating, too. There are ways to save your graphic creations, but they're a little beyond the scope of a beginner. If you create a graphic that you really want to save, then take a screenshot of it and save it or print it to a file. Multimedia files are great, but be sure to put them in the correct folder or provide the path to them. Another way to handle them is to use the OpenFile dialog. Be careful with sounds. While you're having fun, you're annoying others nearby. Sound falls under the category of "bells and whistles." Sounds seem impressive, but add little to the functionality of a program, so be judicious when using them.

Fixing a Program

Art Galurry tried to create a simple program called DrawStuff for his kids (see Figure 13.13). His goal was to be able to draw simple shapes on the screen, just a little something for his children to enjoy. However, it doesn't work and he needs your help. You gently remind him that you can't even draw stickmen, but he insists it's your programming skills he needs.

You run the program, but it crashes when you try to draw a triangle. The same thing happens when you try to draw a diamond. The error says "Object reference not set to an instance of an object" and both times it crashed trying to draw a shape in the MouseUp event. The lines look OK, but it's the error message that troubles you. The error says you have an object declared, but not instantiated. So, you start checking for references for mgrfCanvas. It's declared in the Declarations and has to be or you'd get a build error when you try to run it. This is a tough one so you check references and examples of programs. The program crashed on different lines but had the same error both times. That's a

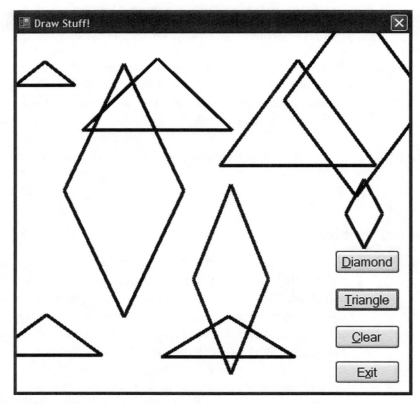

Figure 13.13   Draw Stuff! Program

good indication that the problem lies elsewhere. You finally locate it in the Load event. mgrfCanvas was never instantiated. You add

```
mgrfCanvas = Me.CreateGraphic
```

to the Load event and the error disappears. Wahoo!

You run the program again and hope for the best. You try to draw a triangle, but it nearly fills in the screen. You try to clear the screen to try again and it turns black. You start over and try the diamond, but get big, black X instead. You try to clear the screen and it turns black. Clearly the program still has issues because you've seen at least a couple more errors. You run the program again and simply try to clear the screen. Again, it goes black so you decide that's a good place to start. The Clear Button says:

```
mgrfCanvas.FillRectangle(Brushes.Black, 0, 0, 500, 500)
```

The size seems right. It starts in the upper left corner (0,0) and goes to 500,500, the lower right corner. However, it fills with Black and that's the problem. Art wants the screen to be white when it's cleared. You make a quick change and test it again. Good for you.

Now, back to the strange shapes. You try a diamond and still get that big, black X. It's drawing a shape, but it's not the right shape and it seems way too big. Again, this one is tough. All the arguments for DrawLine commands are variables so it's time for a little programmer's trick. You add some code just above the DrawLine commands. Using paper and pencil, find the points to draw a diamond. Then, hardcode these values. Try

```
xStart = 100
yStart = 25
intXLCorner = 25
intYLCorner = 125
intXRCorner = 175
intYRCorner = 125
intYBottom = 225
```

It still draws an X and tinkering with the values doesn't seem to help. So, you remove them and try something else. Add comment marks (apostrophes) to the last three DrawLine commands. That leaves the code in place, but they won't execute when you run the program. It's another programmer's trick. If you like, use the Comment button in the Toolbar.

When you run the program, it draws a big box. That's strange because the command is DrawLine. You hardcode 0, 0, 200, 200 into the command and try again. You know this should give you a line from the top left to the middle of the screen, but you still get a box. Then it dawns on you. It is drawing a line – a big, fat, black line. You check the line that declares your pen object and, sure enough, the line is 255 pixels wide:

```
Dim penBlack As New Pen(Color.Black, 255)
```

Just the hint of a smile creeps into the corners of your mouth, "a Mona Lisa smile" says your inner voice. You change it to 4 and try again. Big smile! You now get a line. Quickly you uncomment the other lines and try again. It works! You've got diamonds.

Your smug smile quickly disappears when you try the triangle. It's drawing a crazy shape that looks a little like an envelope with the flap open or maybe simple house. It's a strange shape to say the least, and abstract art isn't your forte.

These lines draw the triangle:

```
mgrfCanvas.DrawLine(penBlack, xStart, yStart,
    intXRCorner, intYRCorner)
```

```
mgrfCanvas.DrawLine(penBlack, xStart, yStart,
   intXLCorner, intYLCorner)
mgrfCanvas.DrawRectangle(penBlack, intXLCorner,
   intYLCorner, intXRCorner, intYRCorner)
```

Well, a triangle is just three lines, so you put comments in front of the last two lines and give it a try. It draws a diagonal line. That seems OK. You remove the comment from the next line and try again. Even better. The shape is either a mountain, an inverted 'V', or that envelope flap you just saw. At any rate, the other line must be for the base of the triangle. You remove the comment for the last line and try again, but the box is back. A closer inspection of the line reveals that it says DrawRectangle instead of DrawLine. You slip in the change. That did it! It draws a triangle. Your inner voice interrupts, saying, "This triangle could be created using the DrawPolygon command." Art is impressed and, with a few more additions, his budding Picassos will have a program.

He asks about adding sound to the program, but you talk him out of it.

VB Tip   *Open and run the DrawStuffFixed program to see how it works.*

On Your Own

Write a program to randomly draw shapes on the screen. Vary the shape, size, color, and location.

Find the notes for a children's song and write a program to play it.

Add the words to it to create a sing-along.

Write a program with various sound effects such as buzzers, sirens, beeps, and tones.

Use Window Media Player to create a slideshow of your favorite pictures or movies.

Write a program to create a pie chart of your monthly budget. Limit it to five categories and use the PieChart program to display the results.

Write a program to create a bar chart with vertical bars.

Write a program to create a scatter chart. Points on the chart are generated by their relative location on X and Y axes.

Summary

This chapter introduced the multimedia capabilities of Visual Basic. Graphics in almost any size, shape, and color can be created and displayed on the screen. You learned how to create a simple paint and drawing program. The basics of sound were introduced as well as the Windows Media Player. You also learned how to create simple types of charts and graphs.

Review

Use a Graphics object to create screen graphics.

Graphics objects must be instantiated with the CreateGraphics command.

Graphics are part of the GDI+, Graphics Device Interface.

Colors are a combination of red, green, and blue.

RGB colors each fall in a range from 0 to 255.

There are over 16 million different color combinations.

Colors can be represented by name or by their RGB combination.

Color commands can include the alpha for the color. Alpha represents the opacity of the color and ranges from 0 to 255.

Shapes consist of various draw and fill commands.

Shapes are placed on the screen by their x,y coordinates.

Use a Pen to draw lines and outlines. It contains a color property and a width property.

Use a Brush to fill in shapes. Custom Brush colors are set by declaring a SolidBrush color.

Lines are drawn with the DrawLine command.

Squares and rectangles are draw with the DrawRectangle command.

Circles and ovals are drawn with the DrawEllipse command.

Pie slices are drawn with the FillPie command.

A Point defines a single point on the screen.

A Polygon is a series of points that draws a shape. It uses the FillPolygon command.

Patterns are drawn using the Drawing 2D class.

Text is added to the screen using the DrawString command.

Images are added to the screen using the DrawImage command.

Fill commands create a shape and Draw commands create an outline.

A Rectangle is a defined drawing surface.

The ToolStrip is a container to manage a group of related controls. Usually, it controls buttons, but others work as well.

Shapes are drawn with a starting point and an ending point and use the distance between them to determine the size of the shape.

Visual Basic plays sound files using the Sound command.

Visual Basic plays system sounds with the Sound.PlayWaveSystem command.

Sounds are generated using the Beep command.

The Beep command has two arguments, the frequency and the duration.

Sound frequency is a value from 37 to 32767. The duration is measured in milliseconds.

Specific pitches represent the notes on a keyboard.

Windows Media Player plays sound files and movie files.

Simple charts can be created from data files and a series of Graphic commands.

Terms

alpha	the opacity part of a color
frequency	the pitch of a sound in the range from 37 to 32767
graphics	shapes or pictures on the computer
Graphics Device Interface (GDI+)	responsible for drawing shapes and images in a program
opacity	the transparency of a color represented by a range from 0 to 255; 0 is transparent and 255 is opaque
RGB	red, green, blue; the typical set of computer colors; by mixing these colors, almost any color can be created
shapes	geometric patterns drawn on the screen; lines, rectangles, and ellipses drawn with the Graphic commands
system sound	a series of sounds built into the operating system
ToolStrip	a container used to group related controls, usually buttons
Windows Media Player	a program that plays multimedia files; a control that can be added to a VB program

Keywords

Beep	the command to generate a sound of a specific frequency and duration
Brushes	used to fill the interior of a shape with a color
Color	a structure with a list of named colors; color controls can be created from RGB as well
CreateGraphics	a function that instantiates a graphic object
DrawLine	method used to connect two points with a straight line
Drawing2D	a class used to create and draw patterns and fills for graphics
DrawString	command used to draw text on the screen
FillEllipse	graphic command used to create ovals and circles
FillPie	graphic command used to create a "slice" of a pie
FillPolygon	graphic command used to create shapes
FillRectangle	graphic command used to create a rectangle
FromArgB	a function with four arguments: alpha, red, green, blue; used to assign a color
Graphics	a two-dimensional drawing surface on a control
Image	a graphic; a class used to define a graphic
Pen	used to draw lines and outlines; consists of a color and a width

Point	an x,y coordinate on a graphic
PointF	a command used to create a polygon; a series of points that creates a polygon
Rectangle	a defined drawing surface on the screen
SolidBrush	used to create a Brush in a custom color
Sound	a class used to play sound files
Sound.PlayWaveFile	the command used to play a wav file
Sound.PlayWaveSystem	the command used to play a system sound

Self-check

1. In VB, color consists of a mixture of red, green, and blue.
2. Opacity is the number of colors that can be displayed by a graphic.
3. The Draw command produces outlines while the Fill command produces solid objects.
4. Lines are generally drawn with the Brush object.
5. A single X,Y location on a Graphic is called a Point.
6. Graphic objects cannot display text.
7. Images can be stored anywhere and will still display on a form.
8. A ToolStrip must appear at the top of a form.
9. The greater the frequency, the higher the sound.
10. The Windows Media Player is a special control that's not found in the standard ToolBox.
11. Graphics are a part of the:
    A. System.Drawing namespace
    B. System.Graphics namespace
    C. System.Images namespace
    D. System.Pictures namespace
12. Colors in VB are a mixture of:
    A. black, white, and shades of gray
    B. red, yellow, and blue
    C. red, green, and blue
    D. lines and patterns
13. The transparency of a Graphic is controlled by the:
    A. Opacity property
    B. Beta property
    C. Delta property
    D. Zeta property
14. Pens draw ___ while Brushes are used for ___.
    A. shapes, colors
    B. text, shapes
    C. straight lines, curves
    D. lines, fills

15. A Point is:
    A. a single pixel on the screen
    B. a single X,Y coordinate on a Graphic
    C. the top left location for any Graphic
    D. the named center point for an ellipse

16. The DrawEllipse command:
    A. draws circles
    B. draws ovals
    C. draws ellipsis
    D. all of the above

17. A polygon is a:
    A. filled rectangle
    B. series of concentric circles
    C. series of connected points
    D. container for text

18. In the FillPie command, three o'clock represents the:
    A. 45 angle
    B. 90 angle
    C. 120 angle
    D. 0 angle

19. The DrawImage command:
    A. allows the user to freehand draw on the screen
    B. saves a graphic image from the screen to a file
    C. adds a file image to the screen
    D. all of the above

20. Keyboard sounds can be simulated using the:
    A. Play command
    B. Beep command
    C. Sound command
    D. Pitch command

VB Quiz Answers

Quiz 01

Equal parts of red, green, and blue result in gray. When the numbers are small, the gray is darker, closer to black. Recall that 0, 0, 0 is black and 255, 255, 255 is white. So, larger numbers make the shades of gray lighter.

Opacity is the amount of light that's visible through a surface. Glass lets all the light pass through it. It has an opacity of 0. A wall has an opacity of 255 because no light gets through it. Objects that let some light through, like a pair of sunglasses, have an opacity somewhere in between. In Visual Basic, when the opacity is less than 255, some of the background shows through. The lower the alpha number (opacity), the more shows through.

An ellipse is a circle when the edges are a uniform distance from the center. It's an oval when it's "squashed" or flattened.

Draws complete a line or an outline. A Fill creates a solid shape or a pattern.

Quiz 02

Pens are for drawing lines of a specific width. Brushes are used to fill solid shapes. Pens have a color and a width. Brushes only have a color.

The colors were set to Black and Red. Simply change Black to White and you'd get the classic tablecloth pattern.

There are 256 shades of red, 256 shades of green, and 256 shades of blue. Use any combination of them. So, 256 * 256 * 256 = 16,777,216 possible colors.

Quiz 03

The ItemClicked event is triggered every time a control in a ToolStrip is clicked. Move the code in the ChangeButtons procedure to tlsShapes ItemClicked event. Then remove the ChangeButtons call from the seven buttons in the ToolStrip. The program still works just fine because the ItemClicked event is triggered every time a button is clicked in the ToolStrip.

A calligraphy brush is taller than it is wide. Currently the width and height of the Brush are the same size. Change this line of code:

```
mgrfPainter.FillEllipse(New SolidBrush(mclrSelected),
    xDown, yDown, intBrushSize, intBrushSize)
```

so the height is now five times greater than the width. Use this line of code instead.

```
mgrfPainter.FillEllipse(New SolidBrush(mclrSelected),
    xDown, yDown, intBrushSize, intBrushSize * 5)
```

You can make the change by simply placing a comment mark in front of one line and removing it from the other.

Karaoke players provide the lyrics and the sound for a song. Simply mix the lines with lyrics in with the lines for the sound. The program won't execute a new line until the previous line is finished. Just display a lyric and then play the sound. Force it to update the screen with the Refresh command. You'll be the hit of the party!

Quiz 04

The grid is a set of evenly spaced lines. One set is horizontal and the other is vertical. Each set could be drawn individually or a pair of loops could be used to draw each set.

Circles and pie slices are drawn from the top left corner of the circle. For a circle, it's the intersection of the far left side of the circle and the very top of the circle. That point is usually easy enough to visualize. For a pie slice, think of the whole circle and find the point in the top, left corner. That x,y location is the basis for the chart. Now, simply move this location down and to the right, by increasing both X and Y values. It effectively moves the slice off the pie, "exploding" it!

Just add the Miscellaneous category and the sales figure to the data file and it should work. Try it!

LINQ to SQL – The World Runs on Databases

VB Quip

I have traveled the length and breadth of this country and talked with the best people, and I can assure you that data processing is a fad that won't last out the year. – editor in charge of business books for Prentice-Hall, 1957

The world runs on databases. The modern world relies on them and would be lost without them. Business depends on them, from storing employee and payroll data, to customer data, supplies, manufacturing, transportation, and inventory – you name it. It seems like everything these days is on the computer. In fact, if it's not on the computer, it's probably old and outdated. The key then, is being able to access these data, manipulate them, update them, search them, sort them, and make them work for you. That's where LINQ to SQL comes in. It's the connection between your VB program and a database. In this case, it's an Access file, but the same principles hold true for access to almost any type of database. You'll get the basics to connect to a database, view it, update it, and use it. It takes several programming classes and a couple of database classes to get good at it, but here you'll get a taste of it and some general principles to get you started.

Background

Databases come in several forms, but by far the most popular *database management system* (DBMS) is a *relational database*. You're familiar with flat-file databases with data in a table that's organized into neat rows and columns. They're simple and easy to use and understand. Relational databases can have many tables that are tied together by *key fields*, fields that share a common name and have the same data. They are more complicated but far more powerful. Access databases are this way. In the corporate world, relational databases drive business. They provide the data and figures needed to make business decisions and carry out business plans. Companies invest huge amounts of money in equipment and people to create, maintain, and manage these data. *Database managers* spend their days working with the data, maintaining data, and making data available for business processes.

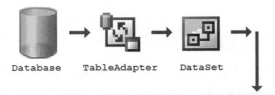

Database   TableAdapter   DataSet

ID	LastName	FirstName	CustNum	Address	City	State	Zip	Since	Last	Preferred	AcctBalance	Interests
1	Knottanother	Penny	NZ49554	1 Penny Lane	Cheap Hill	TN	37035	9/15/2003	2/4/2009	☐	0.0000	Finance
2	Withoutta	Trace	GH42390	237 Hwy 176	Lost Cabin	WY	82642	2/23/2004	5/7/2009	☐	27.45	Mystery
3	Helmut	Cam	TY22050	314 Linden Ave.	Germantown	IA	51046	7/16/2005	11/19/2008	☑	52.08	Electronics
4	Lumber	Jack	RB29045	23 Benner Pike	Axemann	PA	16823	10/12/2007	4/23/2009	☑	0.0000	Outdoors
5	Dommi	Nate	WN5002	204 Rose Lane	Overlook	KY	42038	5/26/2007	4/2/2009	☑	17.23	Outdoors
6	Purga	Tory	PB60544	201 County Road 4050	Styx	TX	75143	8/20/2006	1/15/2009	☑	28.27	Self-Help
7	Twist	Ty	MQ65432	1218 College Inn Road	Bread Loaf	VT	05766	9/10/2008	9/2/2008	☐	23.94	Cooking
8	Reelis	Tate	AP95483	305 Modoc St.	Bonanza	OR	97623	6/9/2006	1/10/2009	☑	51.26	Business
9	Elder	Barry	JS10039	903 Ward Line Road	Elder	LA	70655	12/18/2008	12/18/2008	☐	0.0000	Outdoors

Display

Figure 14.1   Database Access Diagram

In Visual Basic, this data manipulation is handled with *Language-Integrated Query* (LINQ) and *Structured Query Language* (SQL) in what's commonly called *LINQ to SQL*. SQL is the language of most databases. It handles requests for data – *queries* in the vernacular. These requests determine what tables to use, the records to request, the fields in the records to retrieve, and the conditions used to search through the data. There are whole books on SQL, but you need only a handful of commands to understand the basics. While SQL handles the requests on the database side, LINQ manages things on the Visual Basic end. Together, they make a powerful combination. The database stores data and your Visual Basic program provides an interface for the user to see the data. LINQ to SQL is the way to get the data from the database to the screen.

VB Tip   *To learn more about SQL, check out the SQL Primer in Appendix G.*

Connecting to a Database Tutorial

Connecting to a database is a matter of a few clicks and some practice. In general, a developer selects the database – in this case, an Access file – and determines where to display the data, in this example a DataGridView (see Figure 14.1). A wizard does the heavy lifting.

1. You'll need the NEC.mdb database for this tutorial. Place a copy of it on your computer. The Desktop works well, but any location is fine as long as

Figure 14.2   Add Data Source Screen

you can locate it when needed. Open it and look at it if you like, but make sure you close it before you begin the tutorial.

VB Tip   *When an Access file is in use, it creates another file. For NEC, it's NEC.ldb. This file locks the database so others cannot change it. Just don't try to have a database open in more than one application at a time.*

2. Create a new solution and name it DatabaseTutorial. Name the form frmDatabaseTutorial. Resize the form to 800, 600. Add a *DataGridView* control to your form and name it dgvNEC. A DataGridView is the control that displays the database records. This one is for the NorthEast Central High teachers' database. It's an Access file named NEC.mdb and contains data on the staff for the school.

3. Save your solution. If you wait until later, it won't be able to establish a connection to the database.

4. The next step is to add a *DataSource* to the DataGridView (see Figure 14.2). Select the DataSource property for the dgvNEC control. The DataSource property lets the developer select the database file. The DataSource starts out as none, so click on the link that says Add Project Data Source.... This starts the wizard that guides a developer through the steps to connect to a database.

5. The Data Source Configuration Wizard asks for a data source type, and you want to connect to a database (see Figure 14.3). Select the Database icon and click Next. Note the symbol for a database at the top of the window. It's called a *canister* and is the standard characterization for a database. It looks

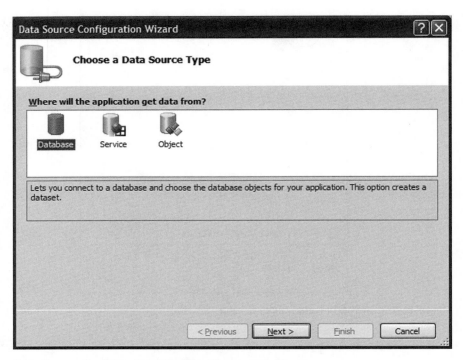

Figure 14.3   Data Source Configuration Wizard – Choose Data Source

a little like a tin can. This option creates a *DataSet*. A DataSet holds the database records in memory for quick and easy access. It's similar to the way an array stores data from a file in memory for faster and easier processing.

6. The next step is to create a connection to a database. Click on the New Connection . . . button (see Figure 14.4).

7. When the Add Connection dialog appears, select Change . . . to change the Data source to Microsoft Access Database File and click OK (see Figure 14.5). This establishes Access as the type of database for use in this program.

8. The Add Connection dialog is now set up to work with Access files and it looks a little different (see Figure 14.6). Select Browse . . . and locate the NEC.mdb file. Click on it to select it and click the Open button. It adds the file and path to the Database file name. Click on the Test Connection button at the bottom to check the connection. It should work. Don't worry about the User name or Password settings. It works fine without them. Click OK.

9. A dialog pops up asking if you want to copy this file into your project folder. This happens when local files (files on your computer instead of those from a source on the network) are used (see Figure 14.7). Click Yes and it copies the file automatically every time the application runs.

10. Click Next to save the connection string (Figure 14.8).

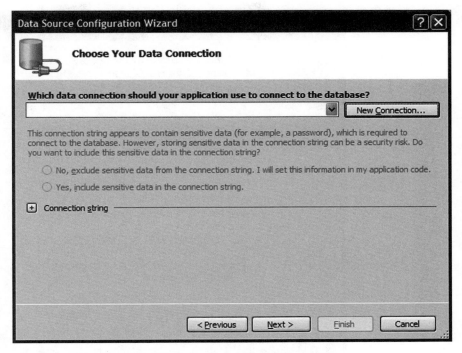

Figure 14.4   Data Source Configuration Wizard – Choose Data Connection

11. The last step is to select the database objects for the DataSet (see Figure 14.9). This determines the tables and fields available when your program runs. Expand the Tables CheckBox and click on NEC. That selects the NEC table. Expand it to see a list of fields. Leave them selected. Click Finish and you've created a connection between your program and a database!

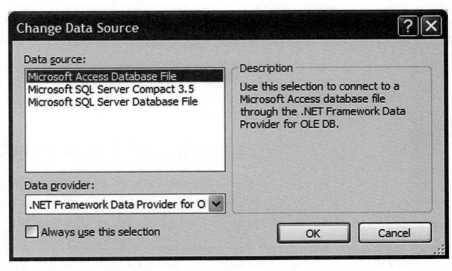

Figure 14.5   Data Source Configuration Wizard – Change Data Source

Figure 14.6   Data Source Configuration Wizard – Add Connection

12. It takes a few seconds, but the DataGridView adds and displays the field names. The NEC.mdb file gets added to the Solution Explorer. Several controls were added to the component tray as well – more on those shortly. Run your application and you'll see the data from NEC.mdb neatly displayed on the form. Now, isn't that the best thing you've seen since this morning's sunrise?

VB Tip   *The connection between your program and a database is temporary. It lasts only long enough to transfer the data to and from the DataSet. In that sense, it's very similar to file I/O.*

Figure 14.7   Data Source Configuration Wizard – Local Connection Warning

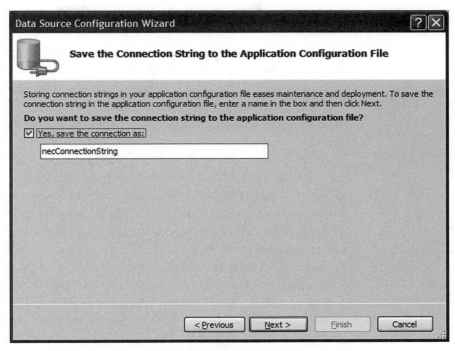

Figure 14.8　　Data Source Configuration Wizard – Save Connection String

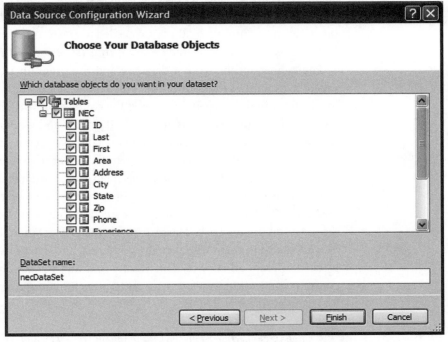

Figure 14.9　　Data Source Configuration Wizard – Choose Your Database Objects

What Just Happened?

The wizard just set up a connection between the program and the database. It's only a temporary connection that's established long enough to pass data back and forth when needed, but it handles most of the tricky stuff. The Solution Explorer has an icon for the NEC.mdb database in it. A double-click on it opens the file in Access. There's a DataSet file in the Solution Explorer as well, but just ignore it. Its content is beyond our scope right now.

Select Database Explorer from the View menu to open it in the Toolbox area. Tabs at the bottom let you switch between the Toolbox and the Database Explorer. The *Database Explorer* lists the data connections in your project. Click on the plus icons to expand the view of the database. It lists the Tables and other contents of the NEC database. Expand the Tables folder to view the NEC table and expand that to see the list of fields in the table. It's a handy reference for the tables and fields in the database.

The component tray has three items in it: the NecDataSet, the NECBinding-Source, and the NECTableAdaper. The DataSet stores the data from a database in the computer's memory. The *BindingSource* stores connection information and provides navigation, filtering, sorting, and updating capabilities. The *TableAdapter* takes data from the tables in a database and passes them to your program. The BindingSource pulls together the data from various tables in a database. The TableAdapter gets the data and passes it back and forth between the program and the database. The DataSet is the data stored in memory while the program is running. All three are needed to create a connection, get the data, and manage the data while the program runs (see Figure 14.10).

The connection between a database and the program is temporary. When called, it establishes the connection, grabs the data it needs, and places the data in a DataSet in memory. It then severs the connection with the database. There are several advantages to this approach. It's quick and clean and doesn't tie up resources. Databases are usually stored on a database server that's accessed over the network. Maintaining a connection to the server ties up resources and slows down systems. Once the request has been handled, the database is free to handle transactions from other systems. Response times from a server over a network are relatively slow, so even a simple correction to a record might take several seconds over the network. The process is much faster when the data are loaded into a DataSet in memory. Changes, additions, and deletions to the data in the DataSet are sent all at once. This is safer and more secure than maintaining a constant connection. While it's not without its limitations, it is a good solution for many business problems.

VB Tip   *A database connection can be created manually as well by adding the controls to the component tray and setting their properties as needed.*

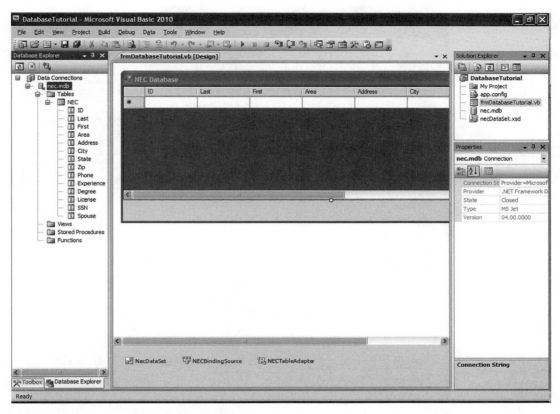

Figure 14.10   NEC Database Program Screen

A Closer Look

The wizard created a connection with the NEC file, grabbed all the data from the table, and dropped it into the DataSet. The DataSource of the DataGridView is the NecDataSet, which displays at runtime. As is, it took all the fields from all the records in the table and added them to the DataSet. Most of the time only some of the data are needed.

Click on the DataGridView control. At the bottom of the Properties window is a link called Edit Columns... (see Figure 14.11). Click on it to change the columns in the DataGridView and their order. It opens a dialog that allows the developer to add or remove columns in the DataGridView. Each column is a field from the table. Select a column on the left and click the Remove button to remove it from the DataGridView. Click on a column and use the up and down arrow buttons in the middle to change its location in the list, which also changes the column order in the DataGridView. The column properties are on the right side. The *HeaderText* property contains the column heading for selected column in the DataGridView. Use this to rename the column headings in a report.

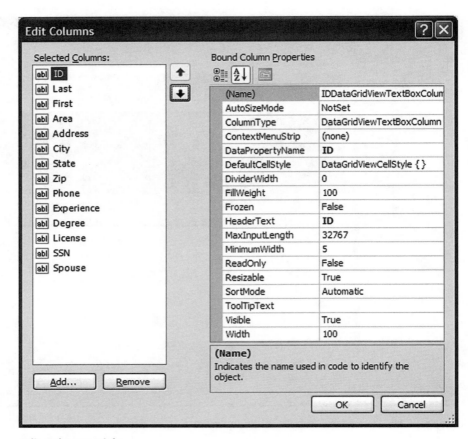

Figure 14.11   Edit Columns Dialog

VB Tip   *If there's no link to Edit Columns in the Properties window, then right-click on the DataGridView itself and select Edit Columns. . . .*

Click on the TableAdapter to display its properties. There are several links for it at the bottom of the Properties window. Click on the Preview Data . . . link to view it. Once opened, click the Preview button to view all the columns and rows from the DataSet. This is handy when a developer needs a quick glance at the data.

VB Tip   *Open and run the DatabaseTutorial program to see the finished version.*

VB Quiz 01   *What is the name of the database used in this example?*
How many fields (columns) are in the database?
Does the number of records (rows) in the database in this example matter?
What is the name of the DataSet?
Why is the connection to the database a temporary one?
Think about how changes to the records would end up in the database.

VB Quip   *For now, we assume that self-evolving robots will learn to mimic human traits, including, eventually, humor. And so, I can't wait to hear the first joke that one robot tells to
another robot. – Lance Morrow*

Wages Tutorial

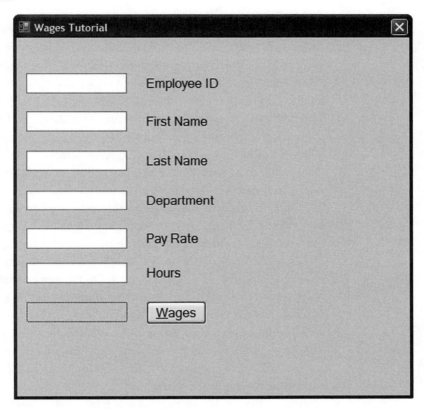

Figure 14.12   Wages Tutorial Program

Individual controls accept data from databases as well. A TextBox, a Label,
or almost any control will hold data when bound to a DataSet. This tutorial
provides the basics for connecting controls to a database. When completed, it
should be able to get employee data, calculate wages, and update records.

VB Tip   *Open the Wages database file in Access to see what it looks like. Be sure to close it before
you start the tutorial.*

1. Create a form that looks like Figure 14.12 and name the controls.
2. Create a new BindingSource and name it bdsWages. The BindingSource
   appears in the component tray.

Figure 14.13   Wages Tutorial Component Tray

3. Select the DataSource property for the bdsWages BindingSource. In the dropdown, select Add Project Data Source.... This opens a wizard where you can select the database and determine the settings for the connection.

4. Select Database as the source type and click Next. This step and the next five are the same as the earlier tutorial.

5. The next step is to create a connection to a database. Click on the New Connection... button.

6. When the Add Connection dialog appears, select Change... to change the Data source to Microsoft Access Database File and click OK. This establishes Access as the type of database for use in this program.

7. The Add Connection dialog is now set up to work with Access files and it looks a little different. Select Browse... and locate the Wages.mdb file. Click on it to select it and click the Open button. It adds the file and path to the Database file name. Click on the Test Connection button at the bottom to check the connection. It should work. Don't worry about the User name or Password settings. It works fine without them. Click OK. The Wages database file is now your connection.

8. A dialog pops up asking if you want to copy this file into your project folder. This happens when local files (files on your computer instead of those from a source on the network) are used. Click Yes and it copies the file automatically every time the application runs.

9. Click Next to save the connection string.

10. The next step is to select the database objects for the DataSet. This determines the tables and fields available when your program runs. Expand the Tables CheckBox and click on tblWages. That selects the tblWages table. Expand it to see a list of fields. Leave them selected. Click Finish.

11. The component tray now has a WagesDataSet in it and a check of the DataSource property of the BindingSource bdsWages shows it's linked to the WagesDataSet. Now select the *DataMember* property and set it to tblWages. This adds the TblWagesTableAdapter to the component tray (see Figure 14.13).

12. The next step is to bind the controls to the data. Select the txtID TextBox. Expand the DataBindings property. Select the Text property under DataBindings. Then select the bdsWages, expand it, and select the ID property. Be sure to select the Text property in DataBindings and not the regular

Figure 14.14   Wages ID Field Selection Dialog

Text property. Once selected, it says bdsWages – ID. The regular Text property has a canister in it, indicating the property is bound to a data field (see Figure 14.14).

13. Repeat this for the other TextBoxes and bind them to the appropriate data fields.
14. Save your project.

At this point, the database connection has been established and the controls have been bound to the DataSet. As yet, it won't work. If you run it, it "works," but it only displays the first record. The problem is that there's no way to navigate through the records. It's time to add a *BindingNavigator*. A BindingNavigator provides a user interface for navigation and manipulation of data bound to controls on a form.

15. Add a BindingNavigator to the top of the form by dragging it from the ToolBox. Name it bdnWages (see Figure 14.15).
16. Set the BindingSource property for the BindingNavigator to bdsWages. This links it to your data.

Run the program again and you'll see that the navigation buttons on it allow you to move through the data. Each record shows up in the TextBoxes.

Figure 14.15   Wages Tutorial Toolbar

Look at the code and notice there is one line in the Load event:

```
Me.TblWagesTableAdapter.Fill(Me.WagesDataSet.tblWages)
```

This code fills the TableAdapter when the program starts. The next steps add functionality to the BindingNavigator and its buttons.

17. The BindingNavigator has several buttons but not all the ones that are needed. Right-click on the bdnWages BindingNavigator and select Insert Standard Items. It adds many of the standard buttons including Cut, Copy, Paste, New, Open, Save, Print, and Help. Remove all of these except the Save button. Right-click on each button and select Delete to remove it.

18. Now insert a new button on the bdnWages BindingNavigator. Click on it to select it and a dropdown appears. Click on the down arrow and select button from the list. It adds a button to bdnWages. You'll use the button as an Exit button shortly.

19. The icon for the button is – plain. Add a little life to it by changing the Image property. Right-click on it and select Set Image . . . (or select Image from the Properties). Browse until you find the Exit.gif file. That replaces the ho-hum image with one that's a little more exciting.

20. Double-click on your new Exit button and code it to end the program. Type in the following:

```
End
```

21. Next, code the Save button. Type in

```
'Update records in file
Try
    bdsWages.EndEdit()
    TblWagesTableAdapter.Update(WagesDataSet.tblWages)
Catch ex As Exception
    MessageBox.Show("An error has occurred.", "Save",
      MessageBoxButtons.OK, MessageBoxIcon.Error)
End Try
```

The Try-Catch prevents a crash in case of an error. That's good because databases are finicky. The Try has two lines. The first line says to EndEdit for the data. The second line updates the DataSet and the file. Until then, changes to a record are not sent to the file.

22. Next, code the Delete button. Type in the following:

```
Try
    WagesDataSet.tblWages.Rows(bdsWages.Position).Delete()
    TblWagesTableAdapter.Update(WagesDataSet.tblWages)
```

```
Catch ex As Exception
    MessageBox.Show("An error has occurred.", "Save",
      MessageBoxButtons.OK, MessageBoxIcon.Error)
End Try
```

The first line deletes the current row in the DataSet. The row is determined by the Position in the BindingSource. The second line updates the DataSet and the file. It's the same line used in the Save button.

23. Add the following line to the Add button:

```
lblWages.Text = ""
```

It clears the text from the Label so there's no confusion when a new record is added.

24. Add the following code to the Wages button:

```
'Calculate and display wages
Dim decWages As Decimal
Dim sngHours As Single
Dim decPayRate As Decimal

sngHours = WagesDataSet.tblWages
    .Item(bdsWages.Position)(5)
decPayRate = WagesDataSet.tblWages
    .Item(bdsWages.Position)(4)
decWages = sngHours * decPayRate

lblWages.Text = decWages.ToString("c")
```

The first two lines get the values from the DataSet. It finds the Position in the DataSet. *Position* is the current record in the DataSet. The last number is the field number. It's similar to the way individual fields were split and assigned to variables in file I/O. Field 4 is the PayRate field and Field 5 is the number of Hours. The next line calculates wages and the last line displays it in the Label (see Figure 14.16).

Wrap-up

Connecting a control to a field from a database is a quick and easy way to display and manipulate data. The BindingNavigator makes navigation easier, and a little code makes it easy to add, delete, and update records. A VB interface makes it easier to work with the data. In fact, the interface for most databases is, well, less than adequate. As a developer, it's easy for you to customize the interface and make it appealing to a user. And that's the whole idea, isn't it?

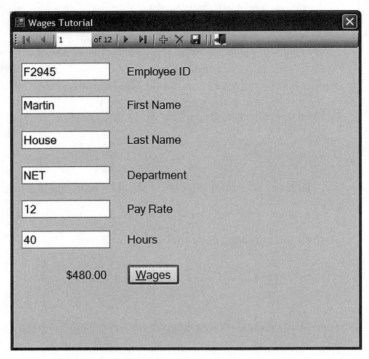

Figure 14.16   Finished Wages Tutorial Program

Potential Problems

There are dozens of potential pitfalls. Be sure to select the correct connection type. Check the DataSet to make sure it includes the correct data. Be sure to associate the proper field with the correct control. And make sure to use the Text property under DataBindings for your connection. Be sure to fill your DataSet when the form loads. Use Try-Catch to catch any connection problems. Never try to open a database in two applications at once. And always keep a backup of your data, just in case.

VB Tip   *Open and run the WagesTutorial program to see the finished version.*

VB Quiz 02   *What would happen if the wrong field was associated with a control?*
What would happen if changes were made to the records, but never updated?
Why is it easier to calculate the wages on the form than it is to get the data from the file?

VB Quip   *If all you ever learn are bells and whistles, the only thing you'll be able to do is make noise. – Jim McKeown*

Customer Queries

Databases are useful, but sometimes all the data just get in the way. A *query* looks through a database and retrieves data that match the search criteria. A query can do several things. It finds records that match the search, displays the selected fields in the result, and orders the records for easy reference. We'll use a DataGridView and learn the basics for finding and ordering all fields in a query.

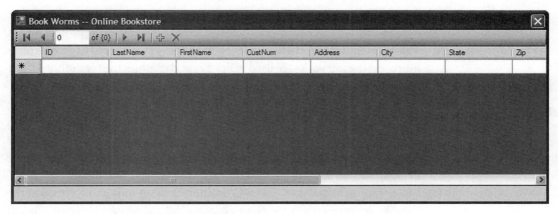

Figure 14.17   Customers Queries Screen

VB Tip   *Open the Customers database file in Access to see what it looks like. Be sure to close it before you start the tutorial.*

1. First, create a new form that looks like Figure 14.17, name the controls, and add a DataGridView to it.
2. Add a BindingSource and name it bdsCustomer. The BindingSource appears in the component tray.
3. Select the DataSource property for the bdsCustomers BindingSource. In the dropdown, select Add Project Data Source . . . This opens a wizard where you can select the database and determine the settings for the connection.
4. Select Database as the source type and click Next. This step and the next five are the same as the earlier tutorials.
5. The next step is to create a connection to a database. Click on the New Connection . . . button.
6. When the Add Connection dialog appears, select Change . . . to change the Data source to Microsoft Access Database File and click OK. This establishes Access as the type of database for use in this program.
7. The Add Connection dialog is now set up to work with Access files and it looks a little different. Select Browse . . . and locate the Wages.mdb file. Click on it to select it and click the Open button. It adds the file and path to the Database file name. Click on the Test Connection button at the bottom to

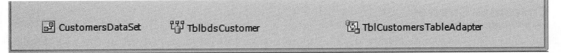

CustomersDataSet   TblbdsCustomer   TblCustomersTableAdapter

Figure 14.18   Customers Tutorial Component Tray

check the connection. It should work. Don't worry about the User name or Password settings. It works fine without them. Click OK. The Customers database file is now your connection.

8. A dialog pops up asking if you want to copy this file into your project folder. This happens when local files (files on your computer instead of those from a source on the network) are used. Click Yes and it copies the file automatically every time the application runs.

9. Click Next to save the connection string.

10. The next step is to select the database objects for the DataSet. This determines the tables and fields available when your program runs. Expand the Tables CheckBox and click on tblCustomers. That selects the tblCustomers table. Expand it to see a list of fields. Leave them selected. Click Finish.

11. The component tray now has a CustomersDataSet in it and a check of the DataSource property of the BindingSource bdsCustomers shows it's linked to the CustomersDataSet (see Figure 14.18). Now select the DataMember property and set it to tblCustomers. This adds the TblCustomersTable-Adapter to the component tray.

12. Save your project.

13. Add a BindingNavigator to the top of the form by dragging it from the Toolbox. Notice how it's visible above the DataGridView. Name it bdnCustomers.

14. Set the BindingSource property for the BindingNavigator to bdsCustomers. This links it to your data.

Run the program again and you'll see the navigation buttons on it that allow you to move through the data.

Look at the code and there is one line in the Load event:

```
Me.TblCustomersTableAdapter.Fill(Me.CustomersDataSet
    .tblCustomers)
```

This code fills the TableAdapter when the program starts. You could program the buttons for it. The steps are similar to those used in the Wages Tutorial. However, the purpose of this tutorial is to introduce queries, so we'll skip those steps for simplicity's sake.

15. Click on the TblCustomersTableAdapter TableAdapter in the component tray and select Add Query... at the bottom of the Properties window. It

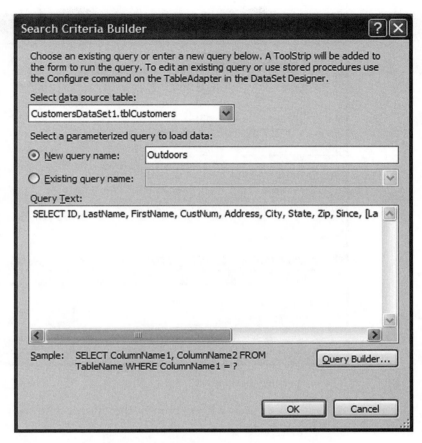

Figure 14.19   Customers Search Criteria Builder Screen

displays the Search Criteria Builder wizard. The data source table is already set. Select a New query name and enter Outdoors to build a query of customers interested in the outdoors (see Figure 14.19).

16. Click on the Query Builder... button to open the Query Builder dialog. The top section has the fields listed for tblCustomers and all the fields are selected. Because we're using a DataGridView, leave all the fields selected.

VB Tip   *All the fields must be selected when using the DataGridView.*

17. The second section has a list of the fields and the search criteria for it. Use this section to build your query. Scroll down to the Interests field. It's the last field in the list. Move over to the field column and type in Outdoors. This creates a query that looks through all the records and returns those with Outdoors listed as an Interest. When you click away from it, it changes the Filter to

```
= 'Outdoors'
```

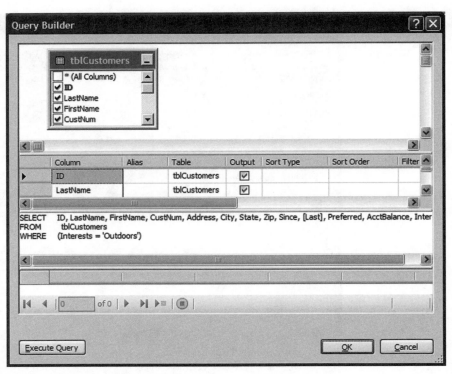

Figure 14.20   Customers Query Builder

and adds to the query being built in the third section. Notice that the third section now reads:

```
SELECT     ID, LastName, FirstName, CustNum, Address,
  City, State, Zip, Since, [Last], Preferred,
  AcctBalance, Interests
FROM       tblCustomers
WHERE    (Interests = 'Outdoors')
```

That is a simple SQL statement. The WHERE clause was added to the SQL statement being built. The statement says to select all the fields (it lists them) from tblCustomers. Further, it says to select only the records that have "Outdoors" in the Interests field (see Figure 14.20).

18. Click OK to close the Query Builder.
19. Click OK to close the Search Criteria Builder and create your query. It adds a ToolStrip named Outdoors to the component tray and displays the ToolStrip between the BindingNavigator and the DataGridView on the form.
20. Run the program and all the records are loaded and displayed in the Data-GridView. Click on Outdoors to run the query. The DataGridView updates and displays only those records with Outdoors listed in the Interests field.
21. Check the code and you'll see it's added the necessary code to the click event for the Outdoors button on the ToolStrip.

```
Try

  Me.TblCustomersTableAdapter.Outdoors
    (Me.CustomersDataSet.tblCustomers)
Catch ex As System.Exception
     System.Windows.Forms.MessageBox.Show(ex.Message)
End Try
```

22. Let's add another query to display all the records again. That way we can move back and forth between all the customers and a select list of them. Click on the TblCustomersTableAdapter TableAdapter in the component tray and select Add Query... at the bottom of the Properties window. It displays the Search Criteria Builder wizard. The data source table is already set. Select a New query name: and enter All to build a query of all customers.

23. Click on the Query Builder... button to open the Query Builder dialog. Again, because we're using a DataGridView, leave all the fields selected. And, because there's no search criteria to exclude records, all of them are displayed. The query looks like this:

```
SELECT      ID, LastName, FirstName, CustNum, Address,
  City, State, Zip, Since, [Last], Preferred,
  AcctBalance, Interests
FROM        tblCustomers
```

24. Click OK to close the Query Builder.

25. Click OK to close the Search Criteria Builder and create your query. It adds a ToolStrip named All to the component tray and displays the ToolStrip on the form.

26. Run the program and all the records are loaded and displayed in the Data-GridView. Click on Outdoors to run the query. The DataGridView updates and displays only those records with Outdoors listed in the Interests field. Now, click on All and all the records get displayed.

27. Check the code and you'll see it's added the necessary code to the click event for the All button on the new ToolStrip.

```
Try

    Me.TblCustomersTableAdapter.All(Me.CustomersDataSet
       .tblCustomers)
Catch ex As System.Exception
    System.Windows.Forms.MessageBox.Show(ex.Message)
End Try
```

28. Two ToolStrips are a little much, so let's do a little cleanup. Add a button to the original ToolStrip. Click on it and a dropdown appears. Click on it and

select a button. Right-click on the button and select DisplayStyle. Change it to Text.

29. Double-click on the All button to open a click event in the code window. Find the following code:

```
Try

    Me.TblCustomersTableAdapter.All(Me.CustomersDataSet
        .tblCustomers)
Catch ex As System.Exception
    System.Windows.Forms.MessageBox.Show(ex.Message)
End Try
```

It's in the ToolStrip you just created. Move this code to the click event for the All button.

30. Run the program and test it. The queries should both work. Delete the second ToolStrip and you're set!

VB Tip   *Open and run the CustomerQueries program to see the finished version. Additional queries have been added.*

When you create a DataSet, VB generates an .xsd file (see Figure 14.21). You can view it by selecting the TableAdapter and clicking on Edit Queries in DataSet Designer at the bottom of the Properties window. It contains the XML schema. Don't worry about the details of *XML* (Extensible Markup Language) or the *schema*. Just be happy to know these are documents that define and validate the content and structure of your data. They're used to exchange data between applications.

VB Tip   *You can edit a query by selecting it in the TableAdapter. Click on the CommandText property and open the dialog. It opens the Query Builder.*

VB Quiz 03   *What happens if you don't select all the fields for a query?*
                    What makes the Query Builder useful?
                    How were the records sorted in the Payable query? What SQL code was needed to do it?

Potential Problems

Database access isn't for the faint of heart. If the database is corrupt, your program won't work. Your database file cannot be in use by another program. If it is, you won't be able to open it in your VB program. Don't delete or change the code that's automatically generated. Unless you know what you're doing, it could cause problems. You must bind your DataSet to a DataGridView or to individual

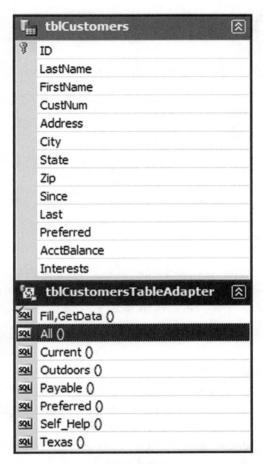

Figure 14.21   Customers DataSet1.xsd

controls such as TextBoxes and Labels. Be sure to include a BindingNavigator so you can move between records. It's risky to delete the controls from the component tray or remove the files from the Solution Explorer. It could make your program unstable.

On Your Own

Take a look at Appendix G, Structured Query Language (SQL) Basics, for a brief introduction to SQL.

Add the following queries to the Customer program:

Customers from your state
Customers without Preferred status
Customers named Ecks, Ray
Customers since 2008

Use the Customers database to create a program that displays the data in TextBoxes and CheckBoxes. Add the controls and code to allow the user to update the database.

Create a program that uses the KidsFirst database. Use a DataGridView and add the following queries:

All students in Miss Brooks class
All students without a pet (look for 'none')
All seven-year-old students
All seven-year-old students in Mr. Moore's class
All students in order by LastName
All students in descending order by Locker

Summary

Visual Basic has controls that can link it to a database. This chapter contains tutorials to demonstrate how to connect to an Access file and manipulate records in the file. Database controls were introduced and simple SQL examples were provided.

Review

Databases are essential to the modern world.

A database management system controls the data in a database, access to the data, and the relationships among the data.

A relational database has multiple tables related by key fields. The most powerful databases are relational databases.

Database managers are responsible for working with and maintaining databases. They control access to the data and work with developers to create business solutions.

Database management in Visual Basic is handled by LINQ to SQL.

LINQ stands for Language-Integrated Query and SQL stands for Structured Query Language.

SQL is the language used to access and manage the data in a relational database.

A query is a request for data in a database.

A DataGridView is a control used to display data from a database.

A DataSource property in a DataGridView determines the database associated with a control on a form.

A DataSet holds database records in memory rather than maintaining a connection to a database.

A wizard runs through the steps needed to establish the connection between a database and your program.

The Database Explorer lists the data connections for a project. It is located on a tab along with the Toolbox.

A BindingSource stores connection information and provides navigation, filtering, sorting, and updating capabilities.

The TableAdapter takes data from the tables in a database and passes it back and forth to the DataSet.

The HeaderText property has the column heading for the fields in the DataGridView.

The DataMember property of a DataSet creates a TableAdapter.

A BindingNavigator control provides the user interface of data bound to controls on a form.

Buttons on a BindingNavigator are used to navigate through the records in a DataSet.

The Position is the current record in a DataSet.

The Query Builder is used to create SQL queries. Its interface is designed to build the SQL statements rather than having the user type in the commands.

The Filter command in the Query Builder is used to create WHERE statements in an SQL command.

SQL queries are stored in buttons on a ToolStrip.

.xsd files contain the XML schema for a DataSet. They're used to validate the content and structure of your data.

XML stands for Extensible Markup Language.

Terms

BindingNavigator	provides a user interface for navigation and manipulation of data bound to controls on a form
BindingSource	a control that stores connection information and provides navigation, filtering, sorting, and updating capabilities for a DataSet
canister	a symbol that represents a database; it looks something like a soup can
Database Explorer	a window that lists the database connections for a project; the Database Explorer is adjacent to the Toolbox
database management system	a database and the software to manage it

database manager	a person who manages and maintains databases; not as cool as a programmer, but almost
DataGridView	a control used to display data from a DataSet
DataMember	a property of a DataSet that sets the table used in a DataSet
DataSet	a place in memory that holds database records for quick and easy access in a program; a DataSet stores changes, additions, and deletions until they are sent back to update the database
DataSource	a property of a DataGridView or other control that allows a developer to select a database file
HeaderText	a property that contains the column heading for the selected column in a DataGridView; used to rename column headings in a report from the database field name to a more descriptive name
key field	a field shared by two or more tables in a database; key fields are the link between tables in a relational database
Language-Integrated Query (LINQ)	programming implementation that allows SQL statements to be integrated into a program
LINQ to SQL	the implementation of SQL statements into a program using the tools available in .NET; a seamless way to connect to a database
query, queries	a search or searches in a database; queries return specified fields from selected records and display them in a specific order
relational database	a database with multiple tables and relationships between tables
schema	a diagram or plan detailing the structure of your content; for VB, it

	contains the structure for your DataSet
SQL (Structured Query Language)	a database development language that allows for the searching, filtering, organizing, and reports of records from a database
Structured Query Language (SQL)	a database development language that allows for the searching, filtering, organizing, and reports of records from a database
TableAdapter	a control that takes data from tables in a database, molds it, and passes to a program
XML (Extensible Markup Language)	a specification for creating content and structure for data; XML is an open standard specification widely used as a specification language for data and the web

Keywords

Position   the current record in a DataSet

Self-check

1. Relational databases are the most popular database management systems.
2. Data in a key field must be unique for each record.
3. Each database has a key field.
4. A successful query should return just one record.
5. The Access file must be open before Visual Basic can view any of its records.
6. A DataSet holds database records in memory for fast and easy access.
7. Only TextBoxes can be bound to a field in a DataSet.
8. Changes to a DataSet are automatically and immediately written back to the database.
9. The Position property maintains the current row in the DataSet.
10. All SQL commands must be written manually.
11. A key field:
    A. must contain unique data in each record of the table
    B. ties tables in a database together
    C. is a key component of a relational database
    D. all of the above

12. A query is:
   A. a request for data
   B. a check to see if a database exists
   C. an attempt to update records in a database
   D. a command to copy all the data from a database into the computer's memory
13. The person responsible for maintaining and managing data in a database is a:
   A. developer
   B. network administrator
   C. database manager
   D. data entry employee
14. LINQ to SQL handles:
   A. database connections
   B. queries
   C. data manipulation
   D. all of the above
15. In a DataGridView, the connection to the database is handled by a:
   A. DataSource
   B. DataManager
   C. FieldShaper
   D. Database Explorer
16. While in use, records are held in memory because:
   A. databases are only updated once a day
   B. it's faster and easier to access them
   C. each query to a database requires a login and password
   D. all of the above
17. A list of all the databases connected to your project is maintained by the:
   A. Solution Explorer
   B. TableAdapter
   C. Database Explorer
   D. DataGridView
18. The TableAdapter:
   A. automatically resizes columns and text so it all displays in a DataGridView
   B. displays fields in alphabetical order by field name
   C. takes data from the database and passes them to the DataSet
   D. all of the above
19. A BindingNavigator:
   A. controls the movement forward and backward through the records
   B. controls the connection between tables in a database
   C. ties controls on a form to the correct fields in a database
   D. none of the above

20. The number of the current record in a DataSet is maintained by the:
    A. Index property
    B. Position property
    C. RecNum property
    D. key field

VB Quiz Answers

Quiz 01

The database name is NEC.

There are 13 fields in the file.

The number of records doesn't matter. In this respect it's similar to the number of records in a file use for I/O.

The DataSet is named NecDataSet.

The program establishes a connection only long enough to gather the data needed and transfer it to the DataSet. If needed, it reestablishes the connection to update the database file. That way, the program isn't dependent on a connection to a file or a network connection. It's much faster to have the data in a DataSet than it is to rely on access to the database each time the data are needed.

Changes to records, additions or deletions, must be saved back to the database. It takes a user action and some code to reestablish the connection and update the database.

Quiz 02

The data would display but would be in the wrong place. Something similar to this may have already happened with records in file I/O. Even worse, however, would be if the wrong data were saved to the database because the wrong field was associated with a control.

This could happen if the data in the database weren't updated. That might happen if changes were made but not sent back to the database file. Mistakes wouldn't get corrected, old records wouldn't be removed, and new records couldn't be added.

The general rule is to store the data and calculate the answers as needed. This saves space in the database and makes it faster and easier to access the data. Remember, data access is considered slow.

Quiz 03

A DataGridView needs all the fields to work properly. If the query selects only some of the fields, the program will generate an exception. Be sure to select all the fields for the DataGridView.

Query Builder simplifies database queries. Without it, a developer would need to know at least some SQL to do even a simple query. With Query Builder, the hard work is done for you. Query Builder is useful because it eliminates most of the mistakes that might occur in writing code. Besides, it's way more fun to use.

The records were sorted in ascending order by LastName. The SQL code for it is ORDER BY LastName.

Crystal Reports – Tying Databases to Output

Man is still the most extraordinary computer of all. – John F. Kennedy

The world runs on databases. Data of all kinds are tracked and stored, managed, massaged, manipulated, and, sometimes mangled. You got of taste of that in the last chapter. You even saw a little of it with control breaks back in Chapter 9. A report is the key tool for managing data. With a report, data become information, a list of numbers becomes a total or an average, and meaningless figures become a report, complete with a colored chart. Crystal Reports is a full-featured database reporting tool from Business Objects®. It crunches the numbers and produces printable reports. It's one of literally hundreds of third-party add-ons for Visual Studio. It handles data from almost any database and integrates it into reports.

VB Tip   *Crystal Reports works with the Professional version of Visual Studio. It will not work with the Express Edition. A thirty-day free trial of Crystal Reports is available from SAP at http://www.sap.com/solutions/sapbusinessobjects/index.epx*

Crystal Reports Tutorial

VB Tip   *Place the database files in a folder on your hard drive called C:\CRFiles. That makes your reports easily portable.*

Be sure to use the Professional version of Visual Studio and have either the trial version or the full version of Crystal Reports installed on your system. Make sure the TouristStops.mdb database is in the C:\CRFiles folder on your system. TouristStops is an Access database that contains information on vacation spots throughout the United States. Open it in Access, browse through it to get a feel for the data, but don't make any changes, and exit before you try to use it in Visual Studio. If needed, replace it with a backup copy from your files.

We'll create a report with it for a summer trip through the New England states. When it's done, the report will have the stops in those states, in order by state, along with the location, the cost, and the estimated time for each stop. It will be grouped by state with costs and time for each state.

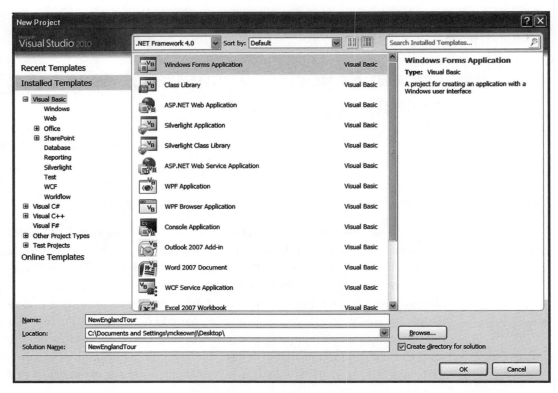

Figure 15.1   Create the New England Tour Project

Creating a Simple Report

VB Tip   *Open and run the NewEnglandTourFinal to see the completed report.*

There's no code to write when generating a report. In fact, most of the heavy lifting is managed by the *Report Wizard*. You'll quickly see how easy it is to create and manage reports. Create a new Visual Studio solution and name it NewEnglandTour (see Figure 15.1). Name the form frmNewEnglandTour. Change the WindowState to Maximized. Set the MinimizeBox and MaximizeBox to False. Set the Text property of your form to New England Summer Tour.

Save your project.

Next add a *CrystalReportViewer* control to your form (see Figure 15.2). The CrystalReportViewer should be in the Reporting section of your Toolbox. Name it crvNewEnglandTour. Use crv as the prefix for a CrystalReportViewer.

Save your project.

Right-click on the crvNewEnglandTour control and select Create a New Crystal Report. Name it NewEnglandTour.rpt and click OK. The extension used for report files in Crystal Reports is rpt. This creates a new report file and it shows up in your Solution Explorer.

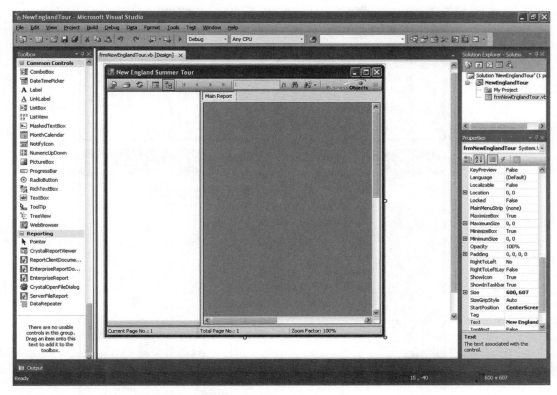

Figure 15.2   Crystal Reports Viewer Added

Once saved, it automatically opens a Create a New Crystal Report Document. Select Using the Report Wizard. Select Standard. Click OK. This starts the report generation process and lets you select the fields and records for a report, orders them, groups them, and displays them (see Figure 15.3).

Now it's time to connect your Access file to the CrystalReportViewer. Expand the Create New Connection tab. Expand the Access/Excel (DAO) tab. Navigate to the C:\CRFiles folder and select the TouristStops.mdb file. If the file is located somewhere else, then locate it and select it.

Click Finish. This creates a connection between your database file and your report (see Figure 15.4).

Next, select "Sites" on the Available Data Sources on the left side and click on the > or just double-click on "Sites" to move it to the Selected Tables on the right side of the screen. Click Next, which adds the Sites table to your report. You'll see it appear in the Selected Tables window on the right side (see Figure 15.5).

The last step is to add the fields from the Sites table. For your first report, simply add the Name, Location, City, State, Cost, and Time fields. Add them one at a time by double-clicking on them. Alternatively, you can add them by clicking on them and then clicking on the > button. Either way, they'll show up in the Fields to Display window on the right side (see Figure 15.6). The order

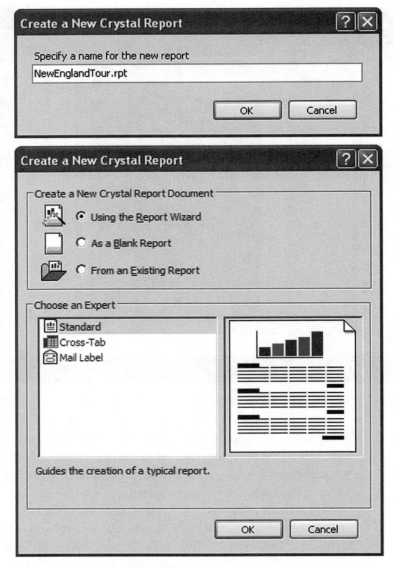

Figure 15.3   Create a New Crystal Report Screen

they appear in the window is the order they'll display in the report. That order isn't critical on this first try, but remember it for future reports. Click Finish. You've just created a report. Well done!

Save your project. It's now ready to run.

VB Tip   *From time to time, Visual Studio adds an extra reference to the code. For example:*

```
NewEnglandTour.NewEnglandTour
```

might show up. It appears in two places and gets highlighted when you try to run your program. Simply remove the last instance of it in those places and you'll be good to go.

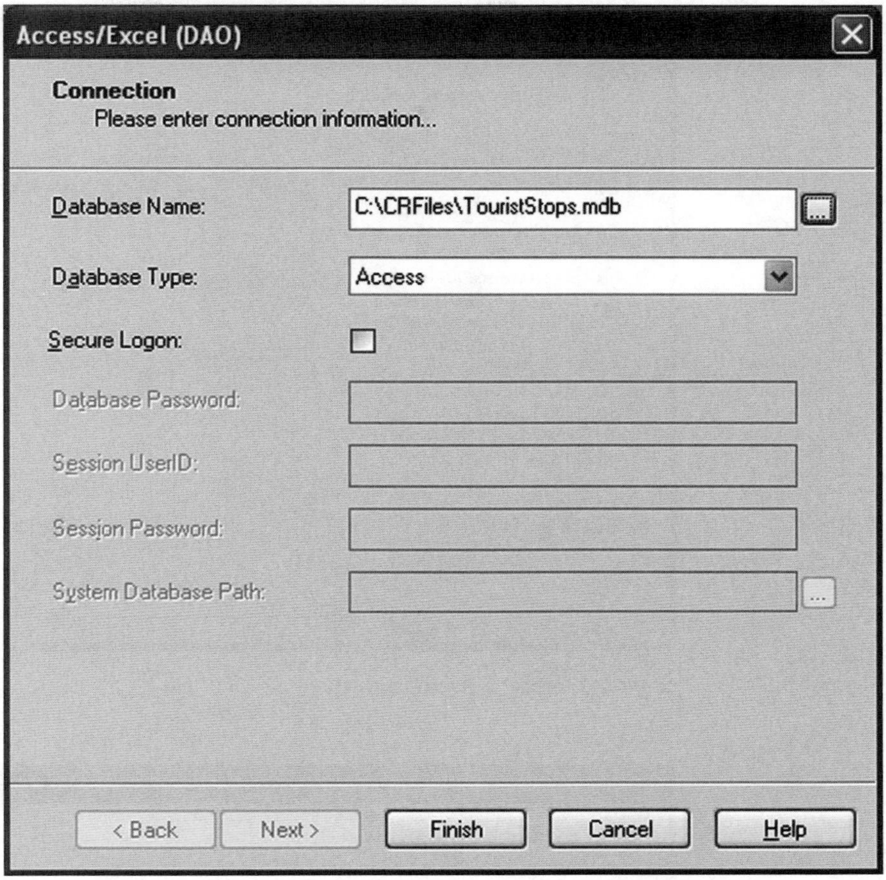

Figure 15.4   Access Database Connection Screen

Modifying a Report

Your report is a good first step, but it's a little messy. OK, it looks like the aftermath of a four-year-old's birthday party. Let's do something about it.

The *Main Report Preview* shows what your report should look like when printed. That's great, but the columns aren't the right width. Some are too wide and others are too narrow and the rest of the report is a little plain. There are two parts to display the fields. The first part displays the column heading and the second part controls the detail lines. Both need a little work.

Section2 (Page Header) shows up in white and displays the column headings. The objects in this section can be edited just like the object in the title.

Section3 (Details) is where the field data gets displayed and it controls the look of the detail line. Changes to this section change the way the records display in the report.

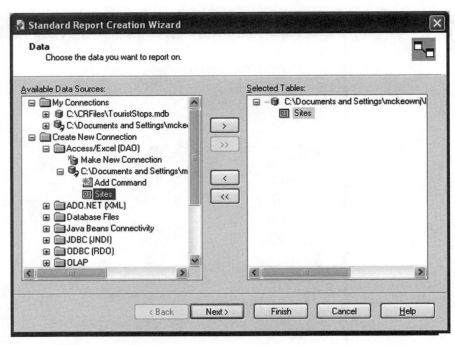

Figure 15.5   Standard Report Selected Tables

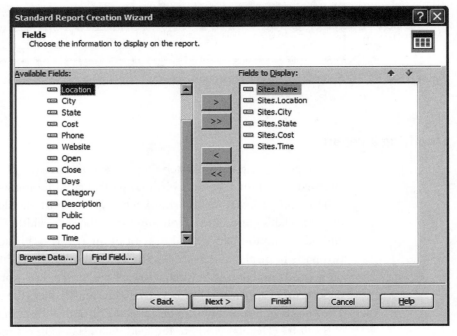

Figure 15.6   Standard Report Selected Fields

Right-click on the Name in the Page Header section and choose Edit Text Object. A *Text Object* is custom text added to a report. It can be a column heading or a title – just about anything you want. Change the name to Points of Interest. The name of the field is the same, but now the column heading is a bit more descriptive. Now, shift-click on each column heading until all are selected, which lets you edit all of them at once. Right-click on one of them and select Format Multiple Objects. Click the Font tab and select 12 point and Bold and then click OK. It changes all the column headings. You'll notice it cuts off the bottom of the text, so you should resize the objects to make them a little taller.

Click on Main Report Preview to see the changes. Then save your report.

Now, let's make changes to the Details section. The State column is too wide. Click on the State object in the Details line (not the Page Header) to select it. Click and drag on the handle to make it smaller. Then click and drag it to the right to move it closer to the Cost column. The first action makes the column narrower. The second one reduces the clear space between the two columns. It's very similar to moving and resizing a TextBox.

Save the report and preview it to see the changes. It looks better, but the heading is off. Resize and move the column header (use the Page Header this time) to place it above the report column and preview it again. Much better.

The City column is too wide and there's a gap between it and the State column. Click and drag to select both the City object in the Page Header and the City object in the Details. Resize both and move them to the right. Be careful not to let them overlap with the State column.

Save and preview the report.

This time select both Location objects. Make them a little wider and move them to the right until they almost touch the City column. Now, instead of using the Main Report Preview button at the bottom, select the Preview Report option from the Crystal Reports menu at the top. It does the same thing, but you probably didn't even notice that menu until now.

The name field must be much wider. Select the Name objects (remember, the column heading now says Points of Interest). Nothing to it.

Resize and move them as needed. Save and preview the report. It's not perfect, but you like what you've done.

Take note of the last two sections. Section4 (Report Footer) shows up at the end of the report. It's used for totals and such – more on that shortly. Section5 (Page Footer) shows up at the bottom of every page. Right now it contains the page number, but you could add almost anything you wanted or needed and it would get displayed on the bottom of every page.

Save the report and run it. You can navigate through the pages and see the entire report (see Figure 15.7). It's not perfect, but it's pretty nice, didn't require any code, and was quick and easy to create. Boy, Howdy!

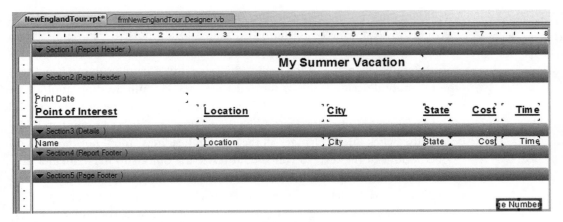

Figure 15.7   New England Tour Report Design Screen

Adding Groups and Totals to a Report

There are two ways to add groups and totals to a report. The first is to include them when creating the report by using the Report Wizard. That's quick and easy and you'll see that later. The other way is to add them from the Field Explorer. The *Field Explorer* is on the left side of the screen, in the same location as the Toolbox (see Figure 15.8). It displays the tools and controls for Crystal Reports.

First insert a new *Group*. A Group orders and separates a report by a chosen field. It's very similar to control break processing and uses the ORDER command from SQL. However, unlike control breaks, the data don't have to be ordered in the file before the report is generated. Right-click on Group Name Fields in the Field Explorer, select Insert Group . . . , and a popup appears. Select Sites.State, which orders the report by the State field. Select in ascending order . . . and the report is alphabetized by state name. Click OK and two things happen: a group item gets added to the Group Name Fields in the Field Explorer and the group gets added to a new section called the GroupHeaderSection1 in the report. Preview the report and you'll discover the report is now ordered alphabetically by state and each group contains the records for that state. Nothing to it!

The report wizard has a *Running Totals* option for use when creating new reports. Because this report has already been generated, we'll have to add it through the Field Explorer. Right-click on the Running Total Fields item in the Field Explorer and select the New . . . option. It opens the Create Running Total Field screen. For this, we want totals for each state for both Cost and Time fields. It's easy. First, fill in the Field to summarize. Select the Sites.Cost field from the Available Tables and Fields on the left. Click the > button to add it. Select sum for the Type of summary. This creates a running total for the Cost field. In the Evaluate section, select the "For each record" option and the "On change

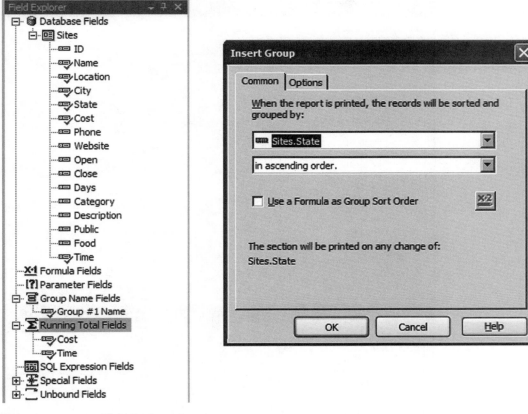

Figure 15.8   Field Explorer Screen

of group" option. This includes every record in the running total and creates a total for each state. Click OK and it creates an item under the Running Total Fields in the Field Explorer. Click and drag this item to the report to include it in the report. Drop in the GroupFooterSection1 and place it directly under the Cost column. It's now in the report and will show up in the preview.

The process is similar for adding running totals for the Time. Add it and try it.

Grand totals are easy to do as well. Create a new Running Total Field for the Sites.Cost column. Under Evaluate, select "For each record". These are the same as before. However, this time, select "Never" and click OK. That way the total never gets reset. It adds a new item to the Running Totals Fields in the Field Explorer. Click and drag this item to the report and place it under the Cost column in the Report Footer. Preview it and you'll see a grand total for all the records. This is exactly like the minor control break program you wrote back in Chapter 9. However, this time there wasn't any code involved!

Repeat this process to add a running total for the Time. Now add some text in the Report Footer that says "Total". Right-click in the Report Footer space, select Insert, and add a new Text Object. Type in "Total" and format it to Bold. It shows

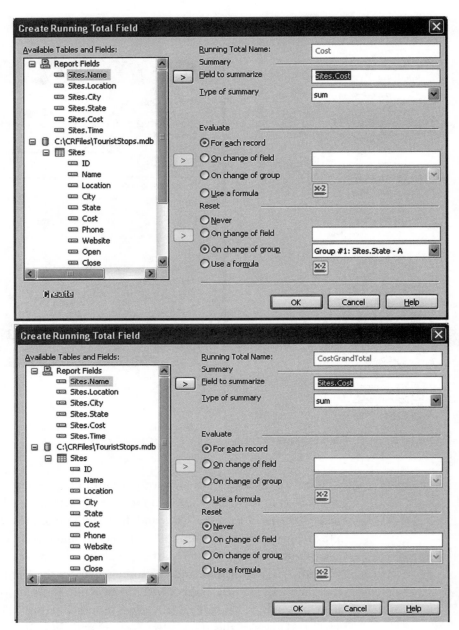

Figure 15.9   Create a Running Total Screens for Fields and Groups

up at the bottom of the last page and displays the grand total (see Figure 15.9). Save it and run it. Excellent!

Crystal Report Queries

VB Tip   *Crystal Reports follows the Table.Field naming convention. Table refers to the name of the table and Field is a field from that table.*

The last thing is to create a query to limit the report to just the New England states. From the Crystal Reports menu, select Report. Then choose the Select Expert option and click on Record. . . .

Use the Choose Field dialog to select the table and the field to query. For this example, select Sites.State and click OK.

The Select Expert creates the query for the report. From the Sites.State dropdown, select the "is one of" option. Then add the New England states one at time. Either type them in or select them from the dropdown list. Be sure to include "ME", "NH", "VT", "MA", "RI", and "CT". Then click OK. It creates a query that selects the record when the state field contains one of these values.

Save your report. Preview it and you'll see it has selected records from just these states, grouped them by state, and included the costs and time totals for each group (see Figure 15.10).

The following is the SQL statement for this query:

```
SELECT 'Sites'.'Name', 'Sites'.'Location', 'Sites'.'City',
   'Sites'.'State', 'Sites'.'Cost', 'Sites'.'Time'
FROM    'Sites' 'Sites'
WHERE   ('Sites'.'State'='CT' OR 'Sites'.'State'='MA'
   OR 'Sites'.'State'='ME' OR 'Sites'.'State'='NH' OR
   'Sites'.'State'='RI' OR 'Sites'.'State'='VT')
ORDER BY 'Sites'.'State'
```

It selects the appropriate fields from the Sites table, where the state is one of the six New England states, and then orders them by state. Brilliant!

VB Tip   *Open the MySummerVacation.pdf file to see the printed report.*

VB Quiz 01   *Explain the process for copying your database files to C:\CRFiles.*
          Why generate reports?
          Why use a specific application like Crystal Reports *to generate reports?*

Creating a Report Using the Report Wizard

VB Quip   *That's the thing about people who think they hate computers. What they really hate are lousy programmers. – Larry Niven*

Now let's try to create another report, but let's do it using just the Report Wizard. You already have an idea of what a report looks like and what it can do, so the Report Wizard should make it quick and easy.

VB Tip   *Most wizard commands have a Previous button so you can go back and make changes. It's easier than starting a report over from scratch!*

This report is similar to the NewEnglandTour. This time we'll generate a similar report for a tour of the Southwest. Here goes!

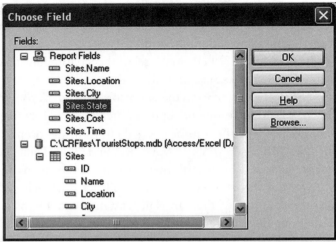

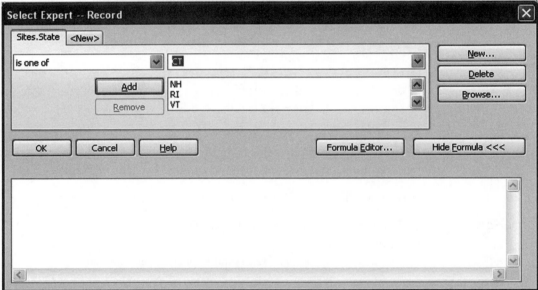

Figure 15.10   Choose Fields Screens

Create a new Visual Studio solution and name it SouthwestTour. Name the form frmSouthwestTour. Change the WindowState to Maximized. Set the MinimizeBox and MaximizeBox to False. Set the Text property of your form to Southwest Summer Tour.

Next add a CrystalReportViewer control to your form. The CrystalReportViewer should be in the Reporting section of your Toolbox. Name it crvSouthwestTour. Use crv as the prefix for a CrystalReportViewer.

Save your project.

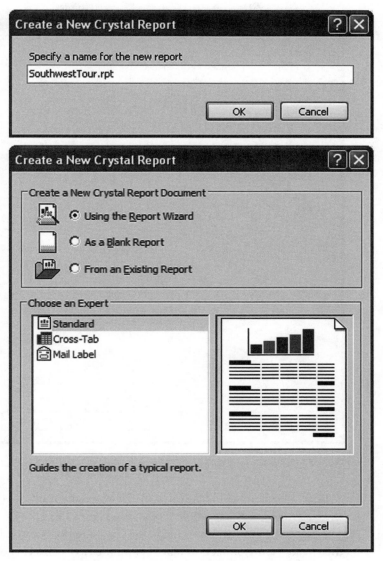

Figure 15.11   Create the Southwest Tour Report Screen

Right-click on the crvSouthwestTour control and select Create a New Crystal Report. Name it Southwest.rpt and click OK. rpt is the extension used for report files in Crystal Reports. This creates a new report file and it shows up in your Solution Explorer.

Once saved, it automatically opens a Create a New Crystal Report Document. Select Using the Report Wizard. Select Standard. Click OK. This starts the report generation process and lets you select the fields and records for a report, orders them, groups them, and displays them.

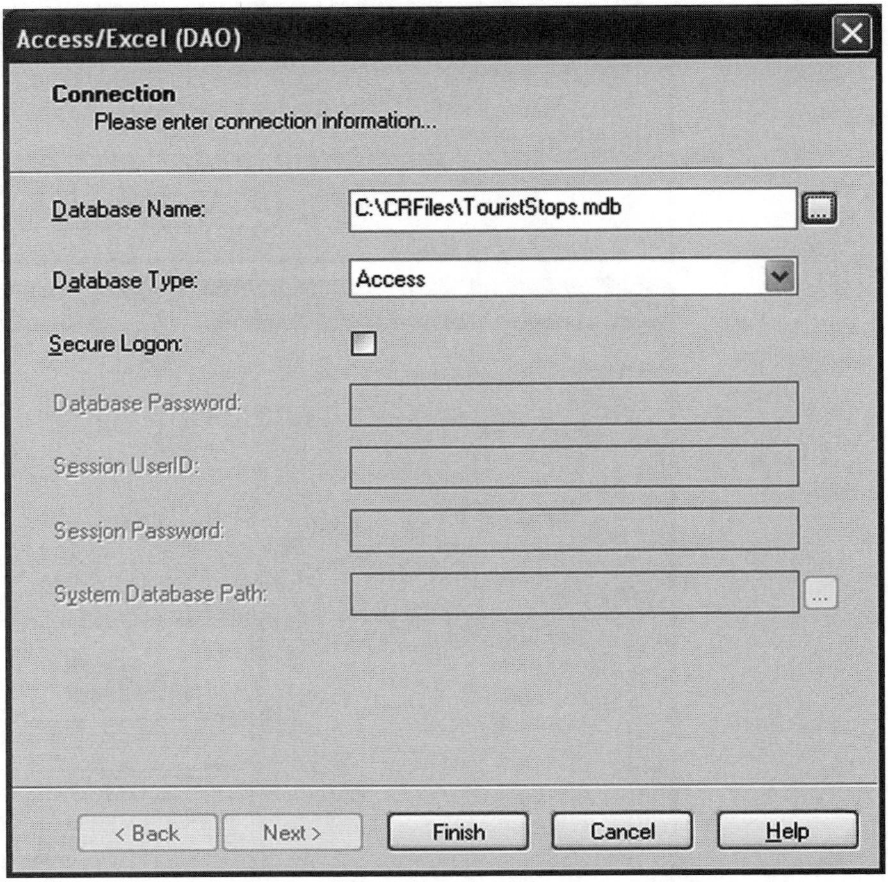

Figure 15.12   Access Database Connection Screen

So far, this is almost identical to the NewEnglandTour. But this time, we'll use the wizard to create the whole report (see Figure 15.11).

Next, connect your Access file to the CrystalReportViewer. If needed, expand the Create New Connection tab. Expand the Access/Excel (DAO) tab. Navigate to the C:\CRFiles folder and select the TouristStops.mdb file. If the file is located somewhere else, then locate it and select it.

Click Finish. This creates a connection between your database file and your report (see Figure 15.12).

Double-click on "Sites" to move it to the Selected Tables on the right side of the screen. Click Next. This adds the Sites table to your report. You'll see it appear in the Selected Tables window on the right side (see Figure 15.13).

Now add the fields from the Sites table. Add Name, Location, City, State, Cost, and Time fields. Add them one at a time by double-clicking on them. Alternatively, you can add them by clicking on them and then clicking on the > button. Either way, they'll show up in the Fields to Display window on the

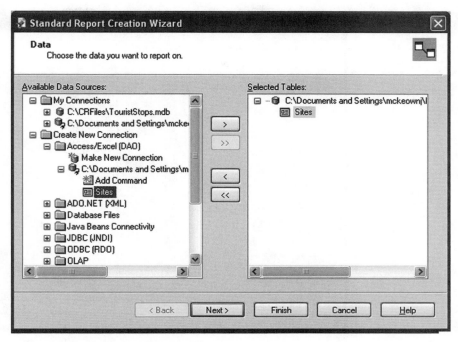

Figure 15.13   Standard Report Selected Tables

right side (see Figure 15.14). The order in which they appear in the window is the order they'll display in the report. Click Next.

This is where this report differs from the first. This time, we'll continue to work through the wizard to complete the report. On the Grouping screen, select Sites.State and click Next. This groups your report by the State field (see Figure 15.15). The states will be in ascending order because that's the default order. It could easily be changed by selecting "in descending order" from the dropdown.

Click Next on the Summaries screen. This creates summary fields for both the Cost and Time fields. These fields are numeric (see Figure 15.16).

The next screen is the Group Sorting screen (see Figure 15.17). Simply ignore it and click Next. It sorts the groups based on summarized totals.

The next screen is for a chart. We don't need a chart, so simply click Next.

The next screen is for the Record Selection screen (see Figure 15.18). It determines the records that end up in the report. We'll filter this report by State and select states in the southwestern United States. Click on Sites.State in the Available Fields window on the left. Then select "is one of" from the dropdown on the right. Add "TX", "NM", "AZ", "UT", and "NV" by typing them in or by selecting them from the dropdown list on the right.

The last screen is for the Template. Select "Gray Scale" from the list of Available Styles and click Finish. That's it! You now have a report (see Figure 15.19).

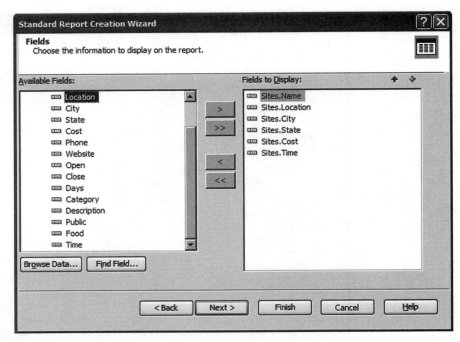

Figure 15.14   Standard Report Selected Fields

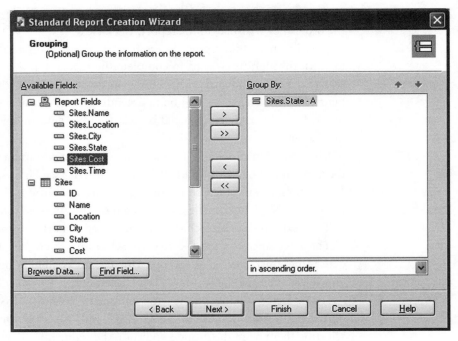

Figure 15.15   Standard Report Grouping Screen

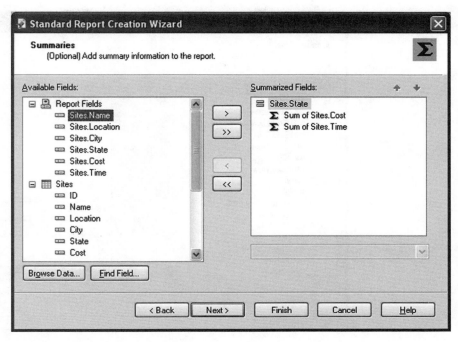

Figure 15.16   Standard Report Summaries Screen

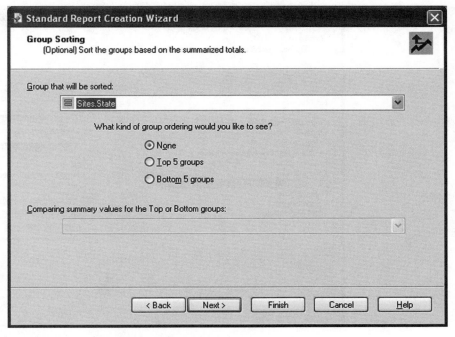

Figure 15.17   Standard Report Group Sorting Screen

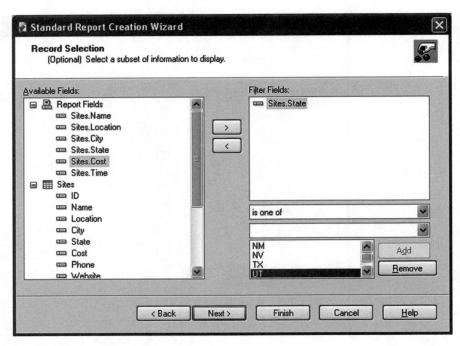

Figure 15.18　　Standard Report Record Selection Screen

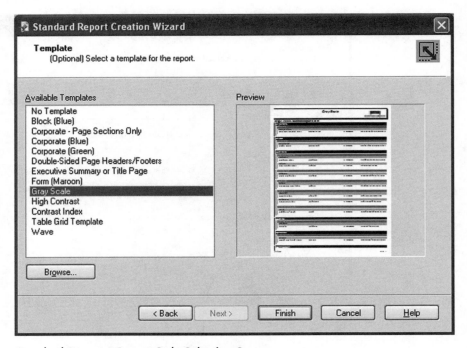

Figure 15.19　　Standard Report – Report Style Selection Screen

Save the report and then preview it. It's rough, but it has what you're looking for. What's more, it was quick and easy. Now use the Main Report screen to modify the report format and you'll be ready for the road.

VB Tip	*Open the SouthwestTour.pdf file to see the printed report.*
VB Tip	*Open and run the SouthwestTour program to see the finished report.*
VB Quiz 02	*Add some Special Fields to your report. Add the time to page header. Replace the page number field in the page footer section with the Page N of M field. And, add a report header.*
	What would it take to update the report when there are changes? For example, what would you do if the prices changed or you decided to visit another site?
	How is a report similar to the control break reports in Chapter 9?

Mailing Labels

VB Quip	*The person who knows "how" will always have a job. The person knows "why" will always be his boss. – Diane Ravitch*

The last tutorial is to create mailing labels. They're inherently useful and easy to create. Let's go.

This example uses the Customers.mdb Access file. It's in the CRFiles folder, so open the database and take a look at it before you start. Close the database before you move on.

Create a new Visual Studio solution and name it CustomerLabels. Change the WindowState to Maximized. Set the MinimizeBox and MaximizeBox to False. Set the Text property of your form to Customer Labels.

Next add a CrystalReportViewer control to your form. The CrystalReportViewer should be in the Reporting section of your Toolbox. Name it crvCustomerLabels. Use crv as the prefix for a CrystalReportViewer.

Save your project.

Right-click on the crvCustomerLabels control and select Create a New Crystal Report. Name it CustomerLabels.rpt and click OK. rpt is the extension used for report files in Crystal Reports. This creates a new report file and it shows up in your Solution Explorer.

Once saved, it automatically opens a Create a New Crystal Report Document. Select Using the Report Wizard. Under Choose an Expert, select Mail Label and click OK. This starts the report generation process and lets you select the label style, fields, and records for your report (see Figure 15.20).

Now the wizard takes over to guide you through the process. When the Data screen opens, select the Customers database from the CRFiles folder. Use the tblCustomers table as the Selected Table and click Next. This links the report to the database file and uses the Customers table in the report (see Figure 15.21).

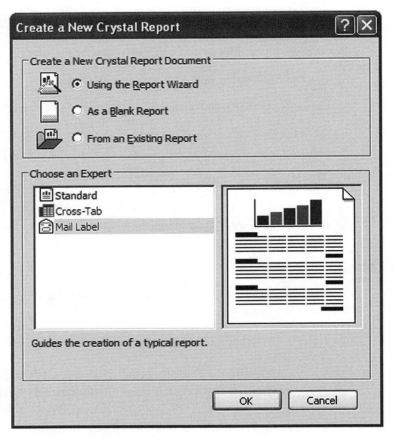

Figure 15.20   Create a New Mailing Labels Report

In the Fields screen, select the fields for the report. Be careful because the order in which they're selected is the order used to display them in the report. We're creating mailing labels for envelopes so select LastName, FirstName, Address, City, State, and Zip from the Available Fields window on the left (see Figure 15.22). Add them one at a time by double-clicking on them or by clicking on them and then clicking the > button. Each is added to the Fields to Display window on the right. Once all have been added, click Next.

Use the next screen to select the type of mailing label (see Figure 15.23). The Mailing Label Type dropdown has a long list of label types and most manufacturers of printing labels include a number and label dimensions for their product. It's easy to match your labels with the correct listing. If the correct type isn't available, simply choose your own settings. For this example, select Address (Avery 5160) to use Avery® address labels. Click Next.

The next screen is the report filter. No filter is needed for this example. Normally, this screen is used to determine the records for the report and it

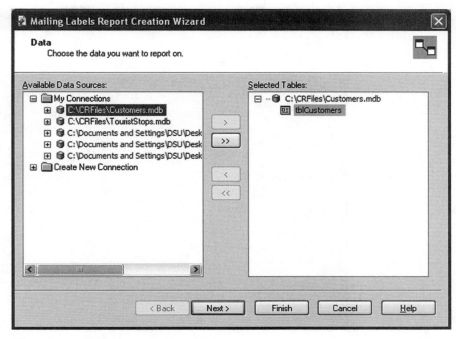

Figure 15.21   Mailing Labels Report Creation Wizard

Figure 15.22   Mailing Labels Field Selection Screen

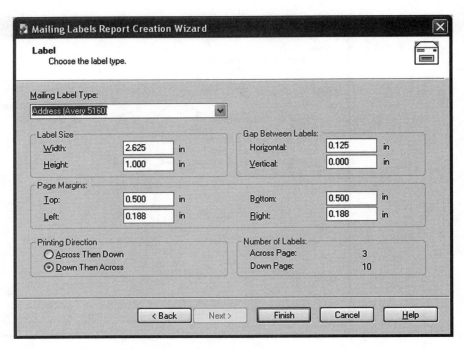

Figure 15.23   Mailing Labels – Label Type Selection Screen

would be used to select the mailing labels to be printed. We want all of them, so leave the filter empty. You're ready to generate a report so just click Finish (see Figure 15.24).

Crystal Reports sets up the Main Report. We're not quite satisfied with it, though. Each field is on its own line, which doesn't look quite right for mailing labels. Time for some changes. Put the LastName and FirstName fields on the Details a line. Resize them as needed so they don't overlap. The Details b line is empty and that just doesn't look right. Move the Address field up to Details b. Then move the City field up to Details c and move the State field up to that line as well. Finally, move the Zip field up to Details d. That should do it.

Save your report. Then preview it to see what it looks like (see Figure 15.25). You just created a set of mailing labels! Bravo!

VB Tip   *The MailingLabels.pdf file has the printed report.*

The report can be modified by using the Field Explorer options or the Crystal Reports menu.

VB Tip   *Open and run the CustomerLabels program to see the finished report.*

VB Quiz 03   *In addition to envelope labels, what else could it be used for?*
          Should the CustNum field be used for the mailing labels?

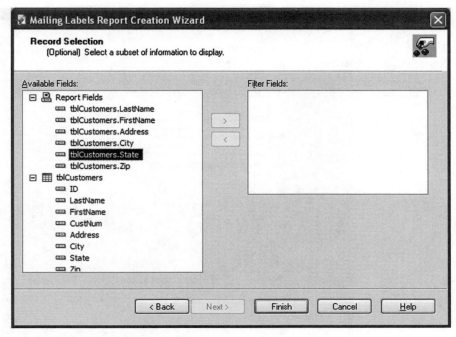

Figure 15.24   Mailing Labels Record Selection Screen

Potential Problems

Placement of the database file is critical. If the database gets moved or the connection to the server is lost, there may be problems. Crystal Reports has an option to keep the data with the report, which is good and bad. The data stay with the report so you'll be able to look at or print those data. That's good. However, it also means the data may become outdated. If you need a daily report that's updated every day, you need access to the data.

It takes practice to get good at generating reports. You have to know where the data are, what they mean, what data you want, and how to present those data. All of that takes practice.

Report wizards are great for going through the basic steps for creating a report, but many times a good report requires some tweaking to get it just right.

Pay attention to report headers and footers and page headers and footers. They can be confusing. Report headers show up at the start of a report and report footers appear at the end. Page headers and footers appear on every page. And, don't confuse the fields with the column headings. Column headings show up at the top of the page in a report. Fields display the data for a record.

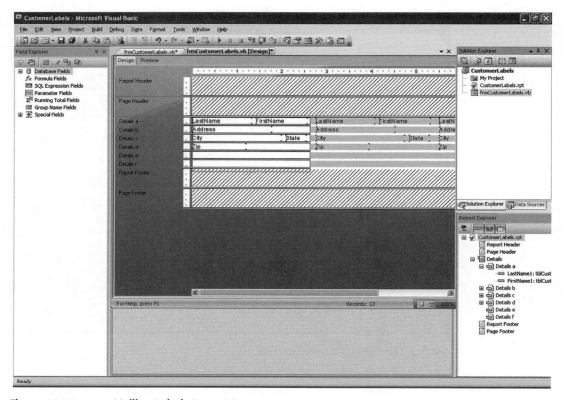

Figure 15.25   Mailing Labels Report Screen

On Your Own

Create your own vacation plans. Select a region to visit or some surrounding states and plan a trip.

Generate a report that includes all the national parks from the TouristStops database.

Create name badges. Use the Customers database and generate labels that have the first and last names only on them. Be sure to make them large enough to read.

Use the KidsFirst database to generate a report. Include only Miss McGee's students in the report.

Generate a set of mailing labels using the Northwind database.

Summary

This chapter is an introduction to database reporting using Crystal Reports. Reports are how managers sift through data to find useful information. Reports organize data and display it in useful ways. In short, they make sense out of the data. Crystal Reports is a full-featured report generation tool for use with Visual Studio. It can access almost any database and create almost any type of report. It includes report wizards to make report generation quick and easy.

Review

Crystal Reports is a report generation tool available from Business Objects. A free, thirty-day trial is available from their website.

Crystal Reports works with the Professional version of Visual Studio. It will not work with the Express Edition.

The Report Wizard breaks report generation into a series of steps.

The CrystalReportViewer is a control in the ToolBox.

Use crv as the prefix for a CrystalReportViewer.

Every report generates a report file. The report file appears in the Solution Explorer.

Use the Excel/Access DAO option to create connections to Excel and Access files.

Records in a database become detail lines in a report.

The Main Report Preview shows a preview of the report. It's a quick and easy way to see changes made in a report.

A Report Header shows up at the top of a report. The Report Footer shows up at the end of the report.

The Page Header appears at the top of every page. The Page Footer appears at the bottom of every page.

The Details section displays the detail line, one for every record in the report.

A report has multiple sections, each with its own display area.

Changes to the Details section are reflected in the detail lines of a report.

Display options such as font, size, and style can be changed in a report.

Reports can include special fields such as the page number, date, and time. Others are available as well.

Reports can grouped and include group totals. These are similar to control breaks.

Use the Field Explorer to make changes to a report.

Reports can be ordered by a field or grouped by criteria.

Crystal Reports can be used to create charts.

Crystal Reports has special fields that are used to display date and time, page numbers, filename, and more.

Crystal Reports can produce mailing labels and many other types of labels.

Avery labels are packaged printer labels that are available in many shapes and sizes. They are designed to work easily with Crystal Reports.

Terms

CrystalReportViewer	a control in the Toolbox that adds a report viewer to a solution; the standard viewer for database reports when using Crystal Reports with a Visual Basic project
Field Explorer	a window in the same place as the Toolbox that stores the tools and controls for Crystal Reports
Main Report Preview	a button used to create the preview of a report in Crystal Reports
Report Wizard	a series of screens that manages the report generation process in Crystal Reports
Running Totals	an option in Crystal Reports for producing control totals for a group of records
Text Object	custom text added to a Crystal Report; column headings, titles, and other text added to improve the appearance of a report

Keywords

ORDER BY	a SQL command used to group related records in a report

Self-check

1. Crystal Reports requires the Professional version of Visual Basic.
2. Crystal Reports works with almost all relational databases.
3. A Crystal Report must be created using a wizard.
4. The user must select the fields to include in a report.
5. Grouped records are based on a field that contains an equal value for all records.
6. The order of the records in a report is the same as the order of the records in the database.
7. A query limits the number of records in a report.
8. The order of the fields in a report must be the same as the order in the database.
9. Use the Running Totals option to generate totals for a group of records.
10. The current date and time can be included in a report.
11. Crystal Reports:
    A. can access files anywhere as long as there's a connection between the program and the database
    B. cannot access files on a network drive

    C. can only access files in the bin\Debug folder

    D. can only access files in the C:\CRFiles folder

12. The fastest and easiest way to create a Crystal Report is to:

    A. use a template

    B. create it manually

    C. use the report wizard

    D. create it at the command line

13. A page header:

    A. generally displays the column headings

    B. can be used to display the date and time

    C. can be used to display the page number

    D. all of the above

14. In a report, detail lines are created using:

    A. Details

    B. LiveView

    C. Text Objects

    D. none of the above

15. A Text Object can be used to display:

    A. a department's name

    B. a supervisor's name

    C. special text or information on the report

    D. all of the above

16. The Field Explorer:

    A. contains the tables and fields available in a report

    B. is typically located on the left side of the screen in the same area as the Toolbox

    C. lists Special Fields in a report

    D. all of the above

17. If you saw Employee.Dept, you'd know:

    A. Dept is the table and Employee is the field

    B. Employee is the table and Dept is the field

    C. the field name is Employee.Dept

    D. the report is named Employee.Dept

18. Report files show up in the:

    A. Data Sources

    B. Solution Explorer

    C. Report Folder

    D. Database Explorer

19. Every detail line in a report:

    A. comes from a record in the database

    B. is the result of a separate query

C. is a separate field in the database

D. appears on its own page in a report

20. The Report Header:

A. shows up on the top of every page

B. displays the title of the report

C. contains the headings for each column

D. cannot be modified

VB Quiz Answers

Quiz 01

Locate the CRFiles folder using Windows Explorer. Right-click on it and select Copy. Navigate to the root of drive C:\. Right-click and select Paste.

Another way is to open the C:\ folder. Then open the folder containing the CRFiles folder. Hold down the control key and drag the CRFiles folder into the C:\ folder. With the control key down, it copies the folder instead of moving it.

Reports provide a snapshot of the data. A report shows what the data looked like at a particular point in time. This is handy for archiving data. Usually, it's inconvenient to carry a database with you. However, it's usually very easy to produce a report. When printed, it becomes very portable. Furthermore, reports provide details, totals, and insights that are usually not available with just the data. Often, there's so much data that, as a whole, it won't provide a clear picture. With a report, the data become organized and a clearer picture often emerges.

Specific applications, like *Crystal Reports*, are very good at what they do. They're designed to complete specific tasks and offer many features that standard applications don't. This makes them ideal for enhancing the capabilities of Visual Studio.

Quiz 02

Data Time is under Special Fields in the Field Explorer. Select it and drag it to the report. Place it in a page header across from the Data Date object. Then go to the page footer section and delete the Page Number object. Replace it with the Page N of M object. It automatically puts in the numbers when the report is generated. Finally, insert a text object in the report header, add the text, and format it.

Reports filter, order, and display records. They don't modify the data. To make changes to the database, you'd need to open it and modify the records. In this case, you must open Access and make the changes there. These changes would be reflected in the next report you generate.

Both reports organize and display data. Both display report totals for groups of records and for the entire database. Crystal Reports is more flexible and requires less work to create reports.

Quiz 03

There are many ways to use labels, some of which are very creative. Use them for folders, or as labels for tapes, boxes, and other containers. Use them for name tags and property tags. Create some with your name on them and use them to label your books.

CustNum is the customer number. For security reasons, it's a bad idea to use it on a mailing label. These days, you must be careful using any identifiable information. It still must be secure, even in printed form.

American Standard Code for Information Interchange (ASCII) Table

Decimal	ASCII	Binary
0	null	00000000
1	Start Of of Heading (SOH)	00000001
2	Start Of of Text (STX)	00000010
3	End Of of Text (ETX)	00000011
4	End Of of Transmission (EOT)	00000100
5	End Of of Query (ENQ)	00000101
6	Acknowledge (ACK)	00000110
7	Beep (BEL)	00000111
8	Backspace (BS)	00001000
9	Horizontal Tab (HT)	00001001
10	Line Feed (LF)	00001010
11	Vertical Tab (VT)	00001011
12	Form Feed (FF)	00001100
13	Carriage Return (CR)	00001101
14	Shift Out (SO)	00001110
15	Shift In (SI)	00001111
16	Data Link Escape (DLE)	00010000
17	Device Control 1 (DC1)	00010001
18	Device Control 2 (DC2)	00010010
19	Device Control 3 (DC3)	00010011
20	Device Control 4 (DC4)	00010100
21	Negative Acknowledgement (NAK)	00010101
22	Synchronize (SYN)	00010110
23	End of Transmission Block (ETB)	00010111
24	Cancel (CAN)	00011000
25	End of Medium (EM)	00011001
26	Substitute (SUB)	00011010

(*continued*)

Decimal	ASCII	Binary
27	Escape (ESC)	00011011
28	File Separator (FS) Right Arrow	00011100
29	Group Separator (GS) Left Arrow	00011101
30	Record Separator (RS) Up Arrow	00011110
31	Unit Separator (US) Down Arrow	00011111
32	blank	00100000
33	!	00100001
34	"	00100010
35	#	00100011
36	$	00100100
37	%	00100101
38	&	00100110
39	'	00100111
40	(	00101000
41	)	00101001
42	*	00101010
43	,	00101111
44	-	00101100
45	.	00101101
46	.	00101110
47	/	00110111
48	0	00110000
49	1	00110001
50	2	00110010
51	3	00110111
52	4	00110100
53	5	00110101
54	6	00110110
55	7	00111011
56	8	00111000
57	9	00111001
58	:	00111010
59	;	00111111
60	<	00111100
61	=	00111101
62	>	00111110
63	?	00111111
64	@	01000000

Decimal	ASCII	Binary
65	A	01000001
66	B	01000010
67	C	01000011
68	D	01000100
69	E	01000101
70	F	01000110
71	G	01000111
72	H	01001000
73	I	01001001
74	J	01001010
75	K	01001011
76	L	01001100
77	M	01001101
78	N	01001110
79	O	01001111
80	P	01010000
81	Q	01010001
82	R	01010010
83	S	01010011
84	T	01010100
85	U	01010101
86	V	01010110
87	W	01010111
88	X	01011000
89	Y	01011001
90	Z	01011010
91	[	01011011
92	/	01011100
93	]	01011101
94	∧	01011110
95	–	01011111
96	'	01100000
97	a	01100001
98	b	01100010
99	c	01100011
100	d	01100100
101	e	01100101

(*continued*)

Decimal	ASCII	Binary
102	f	01100110
103	g	01100111
104	h	01101000
105	i	01101001
106	j	01101010
107	k	01101011
108	l	01101100
109	m	01101101
110	n	01101110
111	o	01101111
112	p	01110000
113	q	01110001
114	r	01110010
115	s	01110011
116	t	01110100
117	u	01110101
118	v	01110110
119	w	01110111
120	x	01111000
121	y	01111001
122	z	01111010
123	{	01111011
124	|	01111100
125	}	01111101
126	~	01111110
127	<del>	01111111
128	€	10000000
129	•	10000001
130	‚	10000010
131	*f*	10000011
132	„	10000100
133	…	10000101
134	†	10000110
135	‡	10000111
136	^	10001000
137	‰	10001001
138	Š	10001010
139	‹	10001011
140	Œ	10001100

Decimal	ASCII	Binary
141	•	10001101
142	Ž	10001110
143	•	10001111
144	•	10010000
145	'	10010001
146	'	10010010
147	"	10010011
148	"	10010100
149	•	10010101
150	–	10010110
151	—	10010111
152	~	10011000
153	TM	10011001
154	š	10011010
155	›	10011011
156	œ	10011100
157	•	10011101
158	ž	10011110
159	Ÿ	10011111
160	non-breaking space	10100000
161	¡	10100001
162	¢	10100010
163	£	10100011
164	¤	10100100
165	¥	10100101
166	¦	10100110
167	§	10100111
168	¨	10101000
169	©	10101001
170	a	10101010
171	«	10101111
172	¬	10101100
173	soft hyphen	10101101
174	®	10101110
175	–	10110111
176	°	10110000
177	±	10110001
178	2	10110010

(*continued*)

Decimal	ASCII	Binary
179	³	10110111
180	´	10110100
181	µ	10110101
182	¶	10110110
183	·	10111011
184	¸	10111000
185	¹	10111001
186	°	10111010
187	»	10111111
188	¼	10111100
189	½	10111101
190	¾	10111110
191	¿	10111111
192	À	11000000
193	Á	11000001
194	Â	11000010
195	Ã	11000011
196	Ä	11000100
197	Å	11000101
198	Æ	11000110
199	Ç	11000111
200	È	11001000
201	É	11001001
202	Ê	11001010
203	Ë	11001011
204	Ì	11001100
205	Í	11001101
206	Î	11001110
207	Ï	11001111
208	Ð	11010000
209	Ñ	11010001
210	Ò	11010010
211	Ó	11010011
212	Ô	11010100
213	Õ	11010101
214	Ö	11010110
215	×	11010111
216	Ø	11011000
217	Ù	11011001

Decimal	ASCII	Binary
218	Ú	11011010
219	Û	11011011
220	Ü	11011100
221	Ý	11011101
222	Þ	11011110
223	ß	11011111
224	à	11100000
225	á	11100001
226	â	11100010
227	ã	11100011
228	ä	11100100
229	å	11100101
230	æ	11100110
231	ç	11100111
232	è	11101000
233	é	11101001
234	ê	11101010
235	ë	11101011
236	ì	11101100
237	í	11101101
238	î	11101110
239	ï	11101111
240	ð	11110000
241	ñ	11110001
242	ò	11110010
243	ó	11110011
244	ô	11110100
245	õ	11110101
246	ö	11110110
247	÷	11110111
248	ø	11111000
249	ù	11111001
250	ú	11111010
251	û	11111011
252	ü	11111100
253	ý	11111101
254	þ	11111110
255	ÿ	11111111

Flowchart Table

Flowcharts are used in several ways. Sometimes they're used to define a problem. At other times they're used to present the flow of a program. They can be used as a deskcheck for the logic in a program. For beginning programmers, they represent the visual flow of program code. In general, they are the symbolic representation of code – a graphical way to depict the events of a program or segment of code.

Several standard symbols are used and there are numerous other ones that are familiar to those in the trade. The basic symbols are provided in this Appendix.

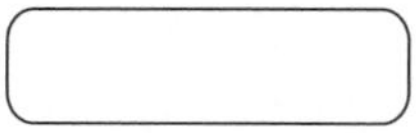

Figure B.1   Start/Stop Symbol

Every program or procedure should have one of these at the beginning and another at the end (see Figure B.1). They indicate the starting and ending point of the code.

Figure B.2   Input/Output Symbol

Every input to a program should have an input symbol (Figure B.2). Use one for every TextBox, NumericUpDown, and for other types of input as well.

Every output from a program should have an output symbol. Use one for every Label and one to indicate a line of output to a RichTextBox. Use them for other types of output as well.

Figure B.3   Processing Symbol

Processing generally means a calculation. Use a processing symbol when assigning or changing the value of a variable (see Figure B.3). Usually, processing is a mathematical formula, but it can also indicate changes to a string variable.

Figure B.4   Decision Symbol

Decision symbols indicate a split in the path of a program (Figure B.4), where the code separates into two or more possible routes. A decision structure indicates the available paths and the condition needed for each path. If statements use them to direct the flow in one direction when the condition is True and the other way when the condition is False. Loops use them to indicate when to continue or terminate a loop.

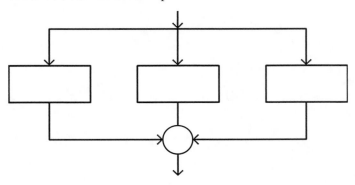

Figure B.5   Case Symbol

Case symbols indicate multiple splits in the path of a program to handle each condition of a Case (Figure B.5). One variable controls the Case, and each possible output has its own processing path and symbol. Indicate the control variable at the top and the condition for each path.

Figure B.6   Procedure Symbol

A procedure indicates a section of the code separate from the main line of a program (Figure B.6). The procedure symbol calls the procedure or function and control of the program passes to it. When the procedure is complete, control returns to the place where it was called. The name of the procedure should be indicated inside the procedure symbol.

Figure B.7   Flowline Symbol

The flowline indicates the direction of flow in a program (Figure B.7). The arrows can point in any direction, depending on the needs of a program.

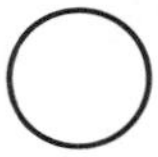

Figure B.8   Connector Symbol

A connector indicates where two or more paths in a program converge (Figure B.8). They can be used with decision structures, loops, or when there's a break in the flow because of page or space limitations.

My Application

VB Tip

Open and run the MyTest program to see how it works.

Visual Basic has a feature called My Objects. It's a set of objects that are implicitly available to your programs. It provides easy access to some of the settings and tasks you need for building killer apps. The My namespace is divided into seven objects, which are listed in Table C.1. We'll take a look at some of them, but you're free to explore all of them.

Type My. into your code and a list of properties appears. Use this list to check or set property values. Drill down into them and you'll be able to control the forms and controls of a project.

My.Computer controls computer resources including the time, operating system, computer name, network settings, and more.

My.Application accesses properties and procedures directly related to your application. With it, you can access and control the settings for your program. These include the name, versions, and path of the program.

My.User allows access to the user name on the computer and operating system authentication.

Table C.1 Visual Basic My Namespace

Namespace	Use
My.Computer	Provides information about your computer such as its name, clock, network detail, etc.
My.Application	Provides information about the current application such as path, assembly name, version, and environmental variables
My.User	Provides information about the current user, such as user name and authentication
My.Resources	Reads resources used by the application
My.Forms	Provides access to all the forms and controls in a project
My.WebServices	Provides access to the web services being used
My.Settings	Provides a method to read and store application configuration settings

My.Resources provides access to resources in a program. The Resource-Manager controls some settings, Culture controls local (country) settings, and developers can access assigned resources such as graphics from here.

My.Forms provides access to all forms in a project and to the controls on a form. With this object, nearly every control is available.

My.WebServices controls the available web services in a project. (Web services were not covered in this text.)

My.Settings controls program settings. These can be changed, saved, and loaded when needed. This is a way to manage settings, make changes, and then undo them. It can also be used to set user settings and customizations.

Customizing Your VB Environment

Your best bet for controlling the development environment is not to make changes to it until you're comfortable with the basic controls. Stick with the default settings early on and it will be much less confusing. When you're ready to move on, then you can try some of these things.

Possibly the best advice is to use the Reset Window Layout menu option in the Window menu. It resets all the group tabs to their default settings, which comes in handy when one of them disappears or won't dock properly.

The pushpin in the taskbar locks a group in place. The down arrow next to it controls the settings for that tab. If you close one of the windows, it's easy to reopen it from the View menu (see Figure D.1).

Use Shift-Alt-Enter to toggle between full screen mode and normal mode. It's handy when working with a large form or with a particularly large block of code.

The Output and Task List windows seldom need to be open. They're pesky and seem to get in the way between program runs. Simply close them to free up space in your screen. Usually they're not needed, and they're easy enough to open up when they are needed.

The View menu is a quick and handy way to open a window when needed. Just select the appropriate item from the menu.

The Choose Toolbox Items option in the Tools menu determines which controls appear in the Toolbox. Generally, it's not a good idea to remove items

Figure D.1   Toolbox Controls

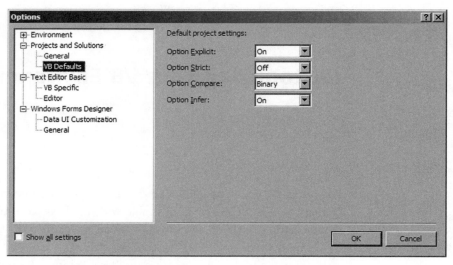

Figure D.2   Tools and Options Settings

from the Toolbox, but there are some that just seem to take up space. The best use of this option is to add items to the Toolbox, and there are several that are useful in a project.

The Customize option in the Tools menu gives you control over your Toolbars and Commands. Some projects might call for a custom set of menus and controls. The Customize option is where you set them and it will make development easier because you can place the controls at your fingertips.

Options in the Tools menu is perhaps the most useful of the custom settings. With it, you can change the development environment. The Fonts and Colors option under Environment lets you change the font, size, and color of your code. The default is 10-point Courier New, but others work also. VB Specific in the Text Editor Basic has several useful settings. However, the Editor settings are the most useful. Use them to change the tab size of code and to set the indentation. If long lines of code are a problem, click the Word wrap option; long lines of code will wrap like a word processor. Line numbers places line numbers on the left side of your code, which are a helpful reference and make finding your code much easier. They're also useful for instructors (see Figure D.2).

Use the General option under Projects and Solutions to set the default location for saving your projects. The Save New Projects When Created option automatically saves a project when it's created, which is a helpful option for beginners who tend to forget to save their projects.

VB Defaults under Projects and Solutions contain several useful items. Option Explicit controls variable declaration. The default is "on" and it forces the explicit naming and typing of variables in a program. Option Strict forces explicit conversion of data types. The default is "off." When on, it forces a developer

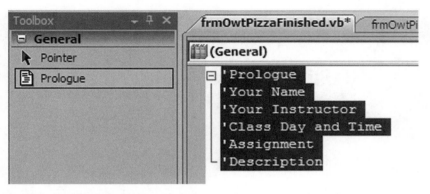

Figure D.3   Prologue Code Snippet Sample

to convert all input and variables to the correct type, which is important in a development environment, and it prevents many potential problems, but it's more of a hassle in a learning environment.

You can add snippets of code to the Toolbox with a simple drag and drop. Just select the text you want, then drag and drop it into the Toolbox. You'll get an icon with Text in the label. Point to it and you'll see the code you just copied. Drag it back to the code window to paste it. It's like having a large clipboard with multiple copy and paste functions. Point to the control in the Toolbox to see the code in a popup. Right-click on it and select Cut or Delete to get rid of it. Right-click and select Rename to rename it. It's available in any project and a great way to copy and paste code (see Figure D.3).

VB Tip   *Drag your prologue into the Toolbar to create a clipping. Right-click and rename it Prologue. It's now available in any project!*

Using Help

The Start page offers help and information on the latest topics. There are several good lessons for beginners in the Getting Started section. Browse through those when you have a chance (see Figure E.1).

The first place to go for help is the Help menu (Figure E.2). It offers several choices. The "How Do I" menu opens a page on the MSDN site with a place to ask questions. This site provides a great forum for getting help from the worldwide community of programmers. Just be careful to do some research before you ask your question. Some of the answers are already posted.

The Search feature is easy to use and a great resource. Selecting Visual Basic in the Filtered by section limits a search to Visual Basic content. Next, type in a keyword or two in the Look for section. It brings up an alphabetical list of help topics as it narrows your search. Then select the best topic from the list and read the explanation in the main window. Often there are examples and other content that's hyperlinked to the explanation (see Figure E.3).

Figure E.1   Help Getting Started Screen

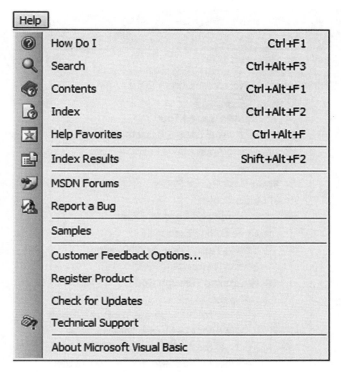

Figure E.2   Help Screen

Figure E.3   Help Index Screen

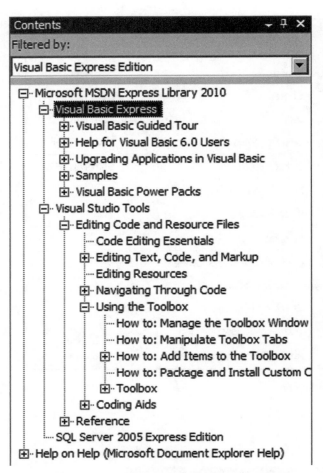

Figure E.4   Help Contents

The Contents option provides a tree structure of Help topics (see Figure E.4). Expand and collapse the entries as needed to find a search topic. Click on the entry to open an explanation in the main window.

The Index option brings up an alphabetical list of topics (see Figure E.5). Start typing in a topic or a term and it moves through the alphabetized list to find the term. Click on a term to display that topic's help in the main window.

Help Favorites is a list of saved Help topics. Use it to save searches for later reference. Add a topic to Help Favorites by clicking on the Add to Help Favorites button on the Toolbar. It looks like a sheet of paper with a plus sign on it. Then use the Help Favorites menu to return to the topic whenever it's needed.

Some Help items are on your computer. These include general help as well as many sample files. There's also a wealth of online help available. In addition,

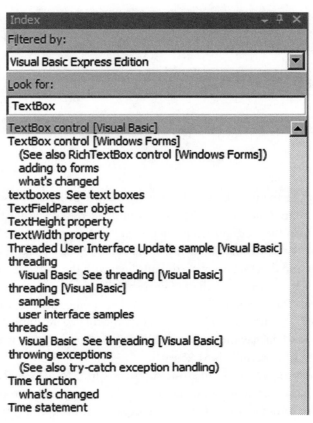

Figure E.5   Help Index Topics

there's a wealth of websites with help, tutorials, information, samples, and forums. Most of them are updated and there are usually enough viewers to answer your questions. If you have a question, there's probably someone out there that has already answered it or someone who will.

Using Debug

Note: Use the First Eats – Debugging Practice program to practice debugging. The program has bugs in it. It is recommended that you try this once you have a grasp of the concepts from Chapter 4.

First Eats is a small breakfast stand run by Sonny Daze. It serves a variety of bagels and drinks. Sonny needs your help with the software for the stand. Right now it won't calculate the bill correctly. The program should get the number of items for each item on the menu, calculate the subtotal, calculate 7.5% sales tax, add the subtotal and the tax to find the total, determine the total number of items, and display the output. Bagels are $1.25 each, coffee is $2.95 each, juice is $1.50 each, and milk is $1.25 each.

The program has numerous comments in it to help explain what the code does. Consider these comments as you figure out how the program should work. If these comments aren't enough to explain the program, you should add more. Then consider these comments as you write comments for your own programs. Very often the comments written with the code are insufficient to explain what should happen. This is especially true when looking at someone else's code or when returning to your own code after weeks, months, or years.

A good debugging technique is to set breakpoints and then watch to see what happens to the code. Set a breakpoint by clicking on the gray strip to the left of that line of code. A red ball appears in the strip next to that line of code and the code is highlighted in red. Remove a breakpoint by clicking on the ball. The program stops at a breakpoint, allowing a developer to examine the code while the program is running. Breakpoints are great for stopping a program in the middle of a run so you can check on it.

Once the breakpoints are set, run the program by pressing F5. Enter values and click on the controls as needed. When the code hits a breakpoint, it pauses. A developer can then go to the code window to examine the code. Simply point to a control or a variable in the code and a little popup appears, showing its current value. Press F11 to run the next line of code. (You can also use the Step Into command in the Debug menu.)

Visual Basic also has Watch windows, which automatically track values. A Watch window can be opened only while the program is running. From the

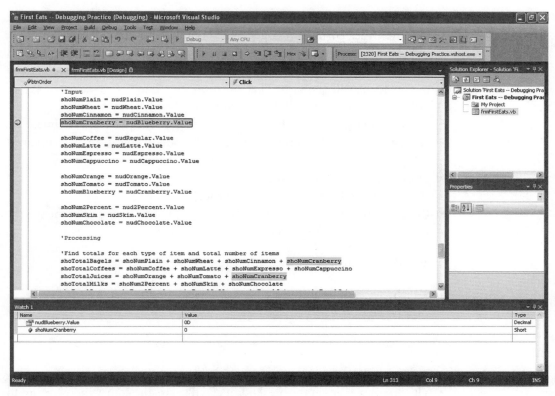

Figure F.1   First Eats Debugging Screen

Debug menu, select Windows, then select Watch and then select Watch 1. It opens a window where you can add variables and control properties. These will automatically update as you run the program. It's as if the program is doing the deskcheck for you! Type (or copy and paste) the name of the variable or the control property that you want to track in the Name column. The Value column displays its current value and updates automatically. The type column displays the data type. The screen below provides an example. The nudBlueberry.Value property and the shoNumCranberry variable are being watched. Both currently have a value of 0. The 0D for nudBlueBerry.Value represents 0 for a Decimal variable. Watches come in handy for finding and squashing bugs (see Figure F.1).

- Open and run the program to see what happens. Take note of what you see. Then look at the code until you have a feel for it.
- Set a breakpoint on the line:
  `shoNumCranberry = nudBlueberry.Value.`
- The line is in the input section of the code near the bottom of the code window.
- Run the program and set values for each type of bagel. Use a different value for each one to make it easier to track them. Click the Order Button.

- The code window automatically opens up and displays the breakpoint. Notice that the Order Form is still open and running. Point to nudBlueberry.Value in the line with the breakpoint. A popup appears displaying its current value, the value you just entered. Point to shoNumCranberry in the same line. The popup for it still shows 0. That's because this line hasn't executed yet. A breakpoint always stops without running the line.
- Press F11 to run this line. F11 steps through the code one line at a time.
- Now, point to shoNumCranberry again. The popup now displays its updated value.
- Press F5 to run the rest of the code.
- What is the problem with this line of code?
- Check the other input lines. There's one other bug to be found in them.
- Remove the breakpoint by clicking on the red ball.

Now, let's try a breakpoint with a Watch.

- Set a breakpoint on this line:
  ```
  decTotal = decSubtotal + sngSalesTax.
  ```

This is a good place to look for bugs because the total sale was $.08.

- Run the program, enter values for the items, and click the Order Button.
- The program stops at the breakpoint and displays the code window. Point to the variables to check their values. Obviously, something is wrong.
- Select Watch 1 from the Watch submenu of the Windows menu in the Debug menu. This opens a Watch window on the screen.
- Enter decTotal, decSubtotal, and sngSalesTax on separate lines in the Name column of the Watch window. It automatically displays their values and will update them as you move through the code.
- Press F11 to step through the line of code. In the Watch window, decTotal updates to 0.075D. Why does decTotal have that value? What's the bug?
- Fix the bug by changing sngSalesTax to decSalesTax. You want the amount of the tax, not the tax rate.
- The decSubtotal variable has a 0 in it. The subtotal is the pretax value of the sale. It shouldn't be 0.
- Break the program by pressing the Stop button in the Toolbar (or by pressing Ctrl-Alt-Break or by selecting Stop Debugging in the Debug menu).
- Add a breakpoint at the start of the processing section. Just add it at the `'Processing` comment line.
- Run the program, enter values, and click the Order Button.
- The program stops at the first breakpoint. Now press F11 to run one line at a time. Pay attention to the Watch window and the decSubtotal variable as you use F11 to step through the code. The value of decSubtotal never changes! As

you look at the processing code, you'll see there's no line that adds the value of the items to decSubtotal. No wonder it's 0!

- Fix this problem by adding the total for each item to decSubtotal.

Add this code:

```
decSubtotal = decCostBagels + decCostCoffees +
    decCostJuices + decCostMilks
```

just below the comment that says 'Calculate subtotal, sales tax and total.

- Run the program again, enter values, and click the Order Button.
- Press F11 to step through the code. Pay attention to the value for decSubtotal. Now it works!
- Continue to press F11 through the rest of the code. Once all the code has run, the order form reappears. Lo and behold, it now displays a total for the order.
- Remove the breakpoints.

Breakpoints are useful, but good code requires testing, too. Sometimes it's just a matter of trial and error and paying attention to detail.

- Run the program, enter 1 for the number of plain bagels, and click the Order Button.
- Check to make sure the values are correct. Sometimes a calculator or a spreadsheet really helps.
- Continue to check the program. Order 1 wheat bagel and click the Order Button. Order 1 cinnamon bagel and click the Order Button. These seem to work as well.
- Things fall apart when you try to order a blueberry bagel. It doesn't add 1 to the Total Items and it doesn't calculate the correct prices.
- The shoNumBlueberry variable contains the number of blueberry bagels ordered. Do a search to find all instances of shoNumBlueberry in your code. Use Quick Find in the Edit menu.
- Enter shoNumBlueberry in the Find and Replace window and click Find Next.
- It shows one instance in the declarations and another in the input section. It's not used after that, so the number of Blueberry bagels isn't added to the total.
- Find the line that adds the number of bagels together. Check the code and you'll find it adds the number of cranberry juices to the bagels, but not the number of blueberry bagels.
- Change the line to fix the bug.
- Now, check to see if the juice orders are correct.
- Enter 1 for orange juice and click the Order Button.
- There's a problem. The amount of the sale is correct, but the total number of items is off.

- Set a breakpoint at the start of the Processing code. Run the program, enter 1 for orange juice, and click the Order Button.
- Step through the code line by line using F11 until you spot the error.
- If you don't see the error, stop the program and try again. This time add watches for shoNumOrange, shoTotalJuices, and shoTotalItems.
- Run the program again and step through the code until you find the bug.
- The problem is that shoTotalItems contains two shoTotalJuices and no shoTotalMilks.
- Fix the bug and test the program again. The juices should be correct.

Continue your testing with the coffee orders.

- Enter 1 for regular coffee, and click the Order Button. It works.
- Enter 1 for a latte and click the Order Button. It works.
- Enter 1 for an espresso and click the Order Button. Oops! Espresso doesn't show up in the Total Items or in the sales figures.
- Check the declarations for the name of the variable for espresso. Then do a Quick Find to see where it's used.
- You'll discover there appears to be two names for the espresso order, shoNumEspresso and shoNumExpresso. That can happen.
- Change shoNumExpresso to shoNumEspresso. That's quick and easy with the Quick Replace command in the Edit menu.
- Test the program again. The coffees should be correct.

Test the milk orders to see if they are correct.

- Enter 1 for 2% milk, and click the Order Button. It displays $1.50. However, the GroupBox shows the price as $1.25. The two don't jibe, but which one is wrong?
- Check the requirements to make sure the price is correct. Sonny says the price is $1.25.
- Check the constants in the declarations for the price of the milk.
- Change the price to 1.25.
- Test the program again. The milks should be correct.

Obviously, you can't test every possible combination and every possible order. So there's no way to be sure you've found all the bugs. However, you can be confident that the program works correctly even if some possible combinations weren't checked. Here are some tips:

✓ Check the items using 1 for a value. That makes the math easy. However, there are some mistakes that you can't catch using 1. So,
✓ Check the items using 0 for a value. That might catch some problems, but 0 can mask some problems as well. So,

✓ Check the items using various other numbers: 2, 5, and 10 work well and the math stays fairly simple.

✓ Check the items with the largest possible value. That might catch some problems such as a data type that's too small for the work it needs to do.

✓ Check one item at a time. It isolates a problem and lets you see little things that might be off.

Bug List

```
shoNumCranberry = nudBlueberry.Value
```

should be

```
shoNumBlueberry = nudBlueberry.Value
shoNumBlueberry = nudCranberry.Value
```

should be

```
shoNumCranberry = nudCranberry.Value
decTotal = decSubtotal + sngSalesTax
```

should be

```
decTotal = decSubtotal + decSalesTax
decSubtotal = decCostBagels + decCostCoffees +
   decCostJuices + decCostMilks
```

is missing from the code. Add it to the Calculate subtotal, sales tax, and total section.

```
shoTotalBagels = shoNumPlain + shoNumWheat +
   shoNumCinnamon + shoNumCranberry
```

should read

```
shoTotalBagels = shoNumPlain + shoNumWheat +
   shoNumCinnamon + shoNumBlueberry
shoTotalItems = shoTotalBagels + shoTotalCoffees +
   shoTotalJuices + shoTotalJuices
```

should read

```
shoTotalItems = shoTotalBagels + shoTotalCoffees +
   shoTotalJuices + shoTotalMilks
shoTotalCoffees = shoNumCoffee + shoNumLatte +
   shoNumExpresso + shoNumCappuccino
```

should read

```
shoTotalCoffees = shoNumCoffee + shoNumLatte +
   shoNumEspresso + shoNumCappuccino
Const decPriceMilk As Decimal = 1.5
```

should read

```
Const decPriceMilk As Decimal = 1.25
```

Structured Query Language (SQL) Basics

Structured Query Language (SQL) is the language of databases. It's designed to manage and retrieve data in a relational database management system. SQL has dozens of commands and can handle almost any data-related task thrown at it. It started out as an IBM product in the 1970s designed to handle IBM's original relational database management system. SQL spread and adapted and was standardized in the 1980s. In addition to standard commands to handle queries, it can insert, delete, and update records. Over the years, other features such as procedures, control-of-flow statements, and user-defined data types were added. While not without its critics, SQL remains a powerful and flexible tool for database management.

SQL has many commands, but a mere handful will suffice for now. They include the following:

SELECT	Used to select the fields to include in a query
FROM	Used to select the table to use in a query
WHERE	Used to set search conditions for a query
ORDER BY	Used to determine the order in which records are displayed
GROUP BY	Used to group records based on a specified field

The following examples use the KidsFirst Access database. It contains data on several first grade classes at an elementary school. Always include a SELECT command and a FROM command in your query. You must give the database the table and the fields to include in the output. The WHERE and ORDER BY commands provide additional control. The GROUP BY command organizes records by a chosen field.

SELECT

The SELECT command gets a list of fields from the table. Make sure the field names are spelled correctly and separate them with a comma. If you want all the fields from a particular table, just use SELECT *. The asterisk is a wildcard that selects all the fields.

```
SELECT LastName, FirstName, Teacher
SELECT *
SELECT tblFirst[LastName], tblFirst.[FirstName],
  tblFirst.[Teacher]
```

The first example selects the LastName, FirstName, and Teacher fields.

The second example selects all the fields.

The third example selects the LastName, FirstName, and Teacher fields. It explicitly uses the fields from the tblFirst table. This one is handy when selecting fields from multiple tables.

FROM

```
FROM tblFirst
```

This example specifies the tblFirst table from the database. If more than one table is to be included in the query, separate them with a comma.

WHERE

The where command determines the records included in the query, similar to the comparisons in an If statement. The general form is

```
WHERE field (= < > <= >= <>) 'value'
```

It's not as bad as it looks. Always include the WHERE keyword. Then tell it the name of the field used in the comparison. Use a relational operator for the comparison. The 'value' argument must have apostrophes for strings. Simply use the value when it's a number.

```
WHERE Teacher = 'Kotter'
WHERE Age = 6
WHERE Teacher = 'McGee' AND Age = 7
WHERE Pet = 'cat' OR Game = 'soccer'
```

The first example looks at the Teacher field. When the teacher is Kotter, that record is included in the query. Note the apostrophes surrounding Kotter. SQL uses these instead of quotation marks to mark the beginning and the end of a string.

The second example looks at the Age field and returns all records where the age is 6. Age is a numeric field, so the value doesn't need to be inside apostrophes.

The third example uses an AND. Both requirements must be met before the record is included in the query. In other words, the query selects only the 7-year-olds in Miss McGee's class.

The last example finds those records where the Pet is a cat or the Game is soccer. Both fields are strings, so apostrophes are needed.

ORDER BY

ORDER BY sorts the records in ascending or descending order by field. Multiple fields can be included by including them in the list and separating them with a comma. Records are sorted by the first field in the list. If needed, they are then ordered by the next field. Use DESC to place records in descending order. ASC is for ascending order and its use is optional.

```
ORDER BY Locker
ORDER BY Test DESC
ORDER BY LastName, FirstName
```

The first command orders the records by the Locker field. By default, they're sorted in ascending order.

The second command orders the records by the Test field. They are listed in descending order.

The third command orders the records in ascending order by LastName. When two or more records have the same LastName, these records are ordered by FirstName.

GROUP BY

GROUP BY groups records based on a common characteristic. A group may be the same value in a field, such as the same teacher or the same age or favorite game. It might be a specified range such as all lockers less than 100 or lockers from 100 to 150. Once grouped, subtotals and report totals can be generated.

```
GROUP BY Teacher
GROUP BY Game
```

Example

Here is a SQL statement based on the KidsFirst file (see Table G.1).

```
SELECT FirstName, LastName, Teacher, Age, Locker
FROM tblFirst
WHERE Teacher = 'Johnson' AND Age = 6
ORDER BY Locker DESC
```

Table G.1   SQL Query Results

FirstName	LastName	Teacher	Age	Locker
George	Martin	Johnson	6	192
Jessica	Price	Johnson	6	171
James	Smith	Johnson	6	104
Christopher	Anderson	Johnson	6	93
Andrew	Green	Johnson	6	90
Joyce	Diaz	Johnson	6	81
Walter	Mitchell	Johnson	6	73
Douglas	Phillips	Johnson	6	28

It returns the four fields, in order, from the SELECT command. The records are FROM the tblFirst table. It returns only WHERE the Teacher is 'Johnson' and the Age is 6. And, the records are in ORDER BY Locker.

Answers to Self-Check Questions

Chapter 1

1. F

Most computer errors are programming errors, but sometimes there are problems with the computer itself.

2. T
3. T
4. F

The project folder for a program contains several folders and numerous files. Be careful not to move or rename them.

5. T
6. F

Input comes from the user. The program uses it to solve a problem and returns the output to the user.

7. F

The Toolbox stores the controls. Properties are displayed in the Properties window.

8. T
9. F

Control names cannot contain spaces, however, some special characters are allowed.

10. T
11. D

A program takes input, processes it, and returns the answer(s) as output.

12. A

Typically, the assembly requires completion of a set of directions. Usually, it means following a set of directions.

13. A

Generally, an algorithm is a series of steps designed to solve a problem.

14. C

A developer designs a program, develops the algorithm, writes the code, and tests a program.

15.   D

All of the above are examples of events. They are all user interactions with a program.

16.   A

A variable keeps track of a value while a program is running. The settings for a control are its properties. An algorithm explains the steps in a process. A bug is a mistake in a program.

17.   D

The Solution Explorer has a list of the forms and files used in a program.

18.   B

Variables store the values that are used in making calculations. The results are stored in variables, too.

19.   C

Labels should start with the lbl prefix. They cannot start with a number and spaces aren't allowed in the name.

20.   A

IntelliSense tracks every control in a program and manages the properties for these controls.

Chapter 2

1.   T

2.   T

3.   F

Numeric variables are initialized to 0, however, string variables are initialized to null.

4.   F

The value of a variable can be initialized by the developer. It can be assigned at runtime from input from the user. It can be assigned a value from a calculation.

5.   T

6.   F

A Short stores only whole numbers from -32768 to 32767. A Decimal stores positive and negative real numbers.

7.   F

Division using the slash (/) may result in a number with decimals. Division using the backslash (\) finds only the integer part of the quotient. It finds only the whole-number part of the answer.

8.   T

9.   T

10.   T

11.   C

A bit is a single 0 or 1. Combine eight of them to create a byte. Four bits, half a byte, is a nibble.

12.   B

The Dim statement names a variable, determines its data type, and initializes it.

13.   B

The rules for writing a programming statement is its syntax.

14.   A

Variable names cannot contain spaces. Names are strings and should have a prefix of str. The correct syntax is Dim strVariableName As String.

15.   B

num is not a valid prefix for a variable. strLocation could be a name or address, decSalary could be the annual pay for an employee, and shoWeight could be the weight of an object.

16.   D

Declare the variable as a String. It contains letters and numbers so numeric data types won't work.

17.   D

The variable must be capable of storing numbers with decimals. It won't store negative numbers. Single, Double, and Decimal data types will work.

18.   C

Solve what's in parentheses first, the do exponentiation, multiplication and division, and addition and subtraction from left to right.

19.   A

The processing symbol for a flowchart is the rectangle. Use one for each assignment statement.

20.   C

Use a rectangle to indicate processing.

Chapter 3

1.   T
2.   F

Controls have properties, but variables don't.

3.   F

Comments have no effect on the speed of a program.

4.   T
5.   F

A program with a logical error still runs, but it produces erroneous output. A program with a syntax error will not run.

6.   F

Strings store their values differently than numeric data types. As a result, the values are not equal.

7.   T
8.   T

9.   T

10.   F

Numbers should never be Strings. Numbers with decimals should be declared as Single, Double or Decimal. All of these can store numbers with decimal places.

11.   C

Labels, TextBoxes, and Buttons are all controls found in the Toolbox. Properties describe controls.

12.   D

An event is something done by the user, usually with the mouse or the keyboard.

13.   A

An event is an action, a property describes a control, and a control is an object that can be seen on a form.

14.   C

Green text is a comment. All comments start with an apostrophe. Blue text indicates a keyword – a word that has special meaning in VB.

15.   A

A syntax error is a command that the computer doesn't understand. It is an error in the way a command is written.

16.   B

Working backward through the code to see where and how values were assigned is an audit.

17.   A

Data type conversion takes a value and converts it from one data type to another.

18.   B

The TabIndex is a number. Pressing the tab key activates the controls in order by their TabIndex number.

19.   C

Convert.ToInt16 converts a String to a 16-bit integer. Short variables are 16 bits long.

20.   C

Shorts are larger than Bytes – a Short can store larger numbers than a Byte. Longs are larger than Shorts and Integers are larger than Longs.

Chapter 4

1.   F

Module-level variables can be declared using the Dim statement.

2.   F

Counters can increment by 1 or any other value. Counters can decrement by any value as well.

3.   T

4.   T

5.   T
6.   F

The Load event is triggered when the form is loaded and just prior to it being displayed.

7.   F

Add text to a RichTextBox using AppendText.

8.   T
9.   T
10.   F

Strings cannot contain a quotation mark.

11.   C

Accumulators keep a running total. They keep track of the total of values added to it.

12.   C

It multiplies by 2 instead of adding (or subtracting) a set amount to a value.

13.   B

Use Now() to get the current date and time from the computer.

14.   C

Excel functions are called methods in Visual Basic. Most of them make the same calculations.

15.   A

The Max method finds the larger of two numbers while the Min method finds the smaller of two numbers.

16.   D

An event handler handles the code and the event that triggers that code.

17.   C

When the value of a NumericUpDown is changed, either by typing in a number or by clicking on the navigation arrows, it generates a ValueChanged event.

18.   A

A detail line is one line of output in a report. Detail lines in a report are similar to one another.

19.   A

Use the ampersand (&) to join two strings.

20.   B

Use the Length method to determine the number of characters in a string.

Chapter 5

1.   T
2.   F

The Then part can be empty. Be sure there's code in the Else part. Sometimes the Then is left empty to improve the logic or readability of a program.

    3.   F

If statements can evaluate any data type. Just be sure to compare apples to apples.

    4.   F

String comparisons must match exactly, so this statement is False.

    5.   T

    6.   F

Use a diamond to depict an If structure in a flowchart.

    7.   F

Use an End If for every If statement in a nested If structure.

    8.   T

    9.   T

    10.   T

    11.   B

The comparison in an If structure will always be either True or False.

    12.   A

An If structure completely inside another If structure is a nested If.

    13.   B

IsNumeric tests a value to see if it's a number. When it is, it returns True.

    14.   D

When one value can produce several possible outcomes, use a Case structure.

    15.   C

When faced with one option or the other but not both, use XOr.

    16.   A

Data validation involves checking user input to see if it is acceptable prior to an attempt to process the input.

    17.   D

In ASCII, numbers come before letters and upper-case letters come before lower-case letters.

    18.   C

And, Or, Not, and XOr are logical operators.

    19.   D

A is incorrect because no value can be $<= 10$ and > 20. B is incorrect because shoMyNum $= 4$ but the Not reverses it. C is incorrect because numeric values cannot be compared to string values without first converting them to the same data type.

    20.   D

All of the above are aids to programming. Comments help explain the code. Flowcharts provide a graphical depiction of program flow. Pseudocode is a textual description of a program.

Chapter 6

1. T
2. F

While loops run as long as the condition is True, but Until loops run as long as the condition is False.

3. F

Although the number of iterations is predetermined for some loops, others cannot be known beforehand.

4. F

For loops are controlled by a numeric value. While loops and Until loops can be controlled by a numeric value, but they can also be controlled in other ways.

5. T
6. T
7. T
8. F

Each trip through a loop is called an iteration.

9. F

An infinite loop is a logical error. A flaw in the developer's logic is its root cause.

10. T
11. A

A For . . . Next loop works best when the number of iterations is known in advance.

12. D

The Step command isn't needed when a For . . . Next loop increments by 1. It is needed when a For . . . Next loop increments or decrements by a value, including decimals, other than 1.

13. B

Each trip through a loop is called an iteration.

14. C

The loop runs 11 times: 10, 9, 8, 7, 6, 5, 4, 3, 2, 1, 0.

15. D

The final value of i is 8. It goes through the loop 8 times.

16. B

A nested loop is when one loop is completely inside another loop.

17. C

i starts at 1 and the loop ends when it reaches 5.

18. A

A user login is a great place for a bottom-driven loop. It takes at least one attempt to enter the correct login.

19.   B

Exit For is used to get out of a For . . . Next loop before it's completed all of its iterations.

20.   B

When inside the loop, the detail line repeats with every trip through the loop.

Chapter 7

1.   T
2.   T
3.   F

A procedure can call another procedure.

4.   F

The symbol for a procedure is a rectangle with extra lines on the sides.

5.   T
6.   T
7.   F

A function returns one value.

8.   F

A function can accept any data type and these data types can be mixed. However, the arguments passed to a function must be in order.

9.   T
10.   T
11.   B

Complicated processes are often broken into smaller, simpler steps, a process called modularization.

12.   A

Values passed are called arguments.

13.   A

Arguments passed ByRef can modify the value in the original variable.

14.   D

All of the above. A function call must have the same number of arguments, they must be of the same data type, and they must be passed in the same order.

15.   B

Functions return a value while procedures do n't. There's virtually no limit to the number of arguments they can have.

16.   B

The first menu should be the File menu and the last one should be the Help menu. While shortcuts are nice, they're not required.

17.   C

Arguments passed ByVal cannot be changed. Arguments passed ByRef can modify the value of the original variable.

18.   D

It might be better to have an expert write a complicated formula. Functions are best when they're used in more than one place or there's a chance the formula might be changed or updated from time to time.

19.   B

A Tick is 1/1,000th of a second. In other words, there are 1,000 Ticks in a second.

20.   C

Controls that don't appear on the form, such as Timers, are stored in the component tray. It appears just below the form at design time.

Chapter 8

1.   T
2.   T
3.   F

Any combination of the CheckBoxes in a group can be selected at any time.

4.   F

Items in a ListBox are numbered starting at 0.

5.   F

Items can be added or removed from a ListBox at runtime. Use the Items.Add method to add items and the Items.Remove method to remove items.

6.   F

The default event for a TrackBar is the Scroll event.

7.   T
8.   T
9.   T
10.   F

A MaskedTextBox forces the user to input characters in a pattern specified by the developer.

11.   A

A GroupBox organizes and separates a series of RadioButtons or CheckBoxes.

12.   B

Change the Checked property to True to select a RadioButton or a CheckBox.

13.   D

They're input. Normally, a user selects them as an indication of their preference.

14.   B

Only one RadioButton in a group can be selected. Use a nested If to find out which one it is. Once that's known, there's no need to keep checking the other RadioButtons. Stacked If statements must be used for CheckBoxes. Any combination from none of them to all of them could be selected, so each CheckBox must be examined.

15.   C

The items in a ListBox are stored in a collection.

16.   A

The CheckedChanged event is the default for RadioButtons and CheckBoxes. Selecting an item in a ListBox generates a SelectedIndexChanged event. Moving the pointer on a TrackBar generates a Scroll event.

17.   C

A Load event is generated when a Form is first loaded. When the Form is closed, it triggers a FormClosing event.

18.   D

The default character is a space, but other characters can be used as well. The minimum length of the output is set by the developer. If the output string is longer than the length set by the developer, it still displays all the characters in the string.

19.   B

The Trim method removes spaces from a string.

20.   D

The pattern requires the first character to be a 'b'. The second character can be any letter. The third and fourth characters must be 'bb'. Any number of characters can follow.

Chapter 9

1.   F

Items in a file are generally separated by commas, however, tabs work as well. In fact, almost any character can be used.

2.   T

3.   F

The bin\Debug folder is the default location, but data files can be stored anywhere. Just make sure the program knows where to find the file.

4.   F

Records are read one line at a time. While one command can read all the records, the command must be repeated once for each record in the file.

5.   T

6.   F

The OpenFileDialog is used to open files, however, files can be opened without it.

7.   T

8.   F

Exception handling helps with programming errors. It won't help with logical errors.

9.   T

10.   F

Records must be in order by the key field, but the field can be in ascending or descending order.

11.   D

All of the above are true.

12.   B

A comma is generally used. A tab works well, too.

13.   A

StreamReader is used to read data from a file. It's used for input.

14.   C

When a record is parsed, each field is separated into its individual parts.

15.   C

Use the AppendText method to add records to an existing file. If the file doesn't exist, it is created.

16.   D

A program automatically looks in the bin\Debug folder unless it's told to look elsewhere. A data file can be stored anywhere. It can be found by coding its exact location or by using a file dialog box. No name needs to be coded when a file dialog box is used. A file cannot be used for input and output at the same time. However, it might be opened for input for one use and opened for output at another time for a different use.

17.   C

Syntax errors are usually caught in development. Logical errors are usually caught through a deskcheck or audit. Exception handling catches errors at runtime.

18.   A

The Try block is the code that normally runs. When there's a problem – an exception – the Catch block runs.

19.   C

The Object Browser is a hierarchy that lists the namespaces in Visual Basic.

20.   B

In a control break program, the key field is ordered. A change in the value of the key field triggers the control processing.

Chapter 10

1.   T

2.   T

3.   F

An array can be declared without any items in it. It can be declared with a specific number of items in it. The size of the array can be changed dynamically while the program is running.

4.   T

5.   F

When an array is resized with the ReDim command, only the data in the array are lost. To resize the array and maintain the data already in it, use ReDim Preserve.

6.   F

Array.Sort sorts in ascending order only. Use Array.Sort and then Array.Reverse to put records in descending order.

7.   T

8.   F

A bubble sort is a relatively slow sorting algorithm.

9.   F

All the items in an array must be of the same data type. That's true for multidimensional arrays as well.

10.   T

11.   C

ReDim resizes an array. It can make an array larger or smaller. Use ReDim Preserve to preserve the data already in the array.

12.   A

Arrays are zero-based so an index of 0 indicates it's the first item in the array.

13.   C

GetLowerBound returns the lowest index number of the array.

14.   C

The first one would work, but the third one correctly sized the array at the start.

15.   D

A linear search looks at each item. Typically, the search starts at the beginning of the array, but it could start at the end as well. It works with an unordered list or a list that's sorted by another field.

16.   A

Array.Copy takes an array and creates a duplicate array with a new name. The arrays are identical except for the names and the items in the arrays are identical and in the same order.

17.   A

It assigns the string "Captain" to the strRank member in the 0th element of the Soldier structure.

18.   D

It creates an array named strStudents with 20 items, 0–19, in it. The array stores string items.

19.   B

EmpID is the structure and strSSN is a member of that structure. Think of EmpID as the box and strSSN as a container in the box.

20.   B

In the Dim statement for an array, the items can be added to the array using a list with the items separated by commas.

Chapter 11

1.   F

A mouse click generates a Click event. A keystroke generates a KeyPress event. It also generates KeyDown and KeyUp events.

2.   T

3.   T

4.   T

5.   F

The correct order is MouseDown, MouseUp, and Click.

6.   T

7.   F

DragEnter checks to see if a control can be dropped into its target location.

8.   F

Changes in the Value property of a ProgressBar are used to indicate the status of a process.

9.   F

A program can have only one startup screen.

10.   T

11.   B

The correct term is raising an event.

12.   C

e.KeyChar catches each keystroke when entered so it can be handled by a program.

13.   A

e.X and e.Y contain the location of the mouse relative to the control the mouse is over.

14.   A

The correct order of events is MouseEnter, MouseHover, and then MouseLeave.

15.   B

GotFocus and LostFocus are events. When a control gets the focus, it raises a GotFocus event. When the focus passes to another control, the LostFocus event is triggered.

16.   C

The MouseUp event, not the MouseHover event, triggers the drop.

17.   B

It sets the ForeColor property of lblSample to green. The text of the Label shows up in green.

18.   A

Use a ProgressBar to indicate the progress of a process. For example, it can be used to indicate the iterations left for a loop or the progress of record processing.

19.   C

A Public variable works anywhere in a program. It's visible on any form or module.

20.   C

An overloaded function has two or more functions with the same name. Each function has its own set of unique arguments.

Chapter 12

1.   T
2.   T
3.   F

Controls are removed using a destructor.

4.   F

Controls added at runtime can only have events if they're added using the WithEvents command.

5.   T
6.   F

Classes without a Set statement are ReadOnly. Their values cannot be changed.

7.   T
8.   F

The Object Browser contains a list of all classes and their properties and methods.

9.   T
10.   T
11.   B

Objects contain data and methods.

12.   C

Classes can be created and removed with ease. They are not permanent.

13.   B

The general term for removing items from a program to free memory is garbage collection.

14.   A

When created WithEvents, a developer can add event procedures in the code that can be used by the class.

15.   C

Instantiate means to create a new instance of an object.

16.   C

Inheritance is when one class is used as the basis for other classes. The abilities of the base class are inherited by the derived class.

17.   A

AFortune is a base class and its properties and methods become part of your new class.

18.   D

Standardization is not an advantage. In fact, one of the biggest advantages of classes is customization – the ability to change and adapt a class to any situation or need.

19.   D

The Friend declaration makes variables and methods available only within a project. They are not exposed outside of the project.

20.   A

Inside a class, it's written and used as a procedure. When used outside of the class, it's known as a method.

Chapter 13

1.   T

2.   F

Opacity is the transparency of a graphic. Its range is 0 to 255, where 0 is transparent and 255 is opaque.

3.   T

4.   F

Brushes are used for fills. Use the Pen object to draw lines.

5.   T

6.   F

Graphic objects can display text using the DrawString method.

7.   T

8.   F

A ToolStrip can appear anywhere on a form.

9.   T

10.   T

11.   A

The System.Drawing namespace contains the classes for drawing objects.

12.   C

Colors are a mixture of red, green, and blue (RGB).

13.   A

Opacity is the transparency of a graphic.

    14.   D

Pens draw lines of various widths. Brushes are used to fill shapes.

    15.   B

A Point is a single X,Y location on a Graphic. It consists of two integers.

    16.   D

DrawEllipse draws ellipses. The width and height determine the size and shape. When they're the same, you get a circle.

    17.   C

A polygon is a series of Points. Connect the points to create the polygon. It automatically takes the last point and links it to the first point.

    18.   D

For FillPie, three o'clock is the 0 angle. Pie slices can start at this point.

    19.   C

DrawImage is the command used to add an image from a file to the screen.

    20.   B

The Beep sound can be used to simulate keyboard sounds. The pitch determines the note.

Chapter 14

    1.   T
    2.   T
    3.   F

Every table should have a key field. A database may have many key fields.

    4.   F

A successful query might return many records or just one.

    5.   F

An Access file cannot be open. If it is, Visual Basic won't be able to read it.

    6.   T
    7.   F

There are many controls that can be bound to a field in a DataSet.

    8.   F

Changes to a DataSet are only written to the database with an Update command.

    9.   T
    10.   F

The Query Builder is a fast and easy way to build SQL commands.

    11.   D

All of the above are significant components of key fields.

    12.   A

A query is a request for specific data. The data must match certain criteria before being retrieved.

13.   C

A database manager is responsible for managing and maintaining data in a database.

14.   D

LINQ to SQL handles all of these duties.

15.   A

The DataSource handles the connection between a database and a DataGridView.

16.   B

Access to the records is much faster when the data are loaded to a DataSet.

17.   C

The Database Explorer (on the left side in a separate tab from the Toolbox) has a list of all the databases in a project.

18.   C

The TableAdapter takes data from the tables in a database and passes them to a DataSet.

19.   A

The BindingNavigator allows the user to move forward and backward from one record to another.

20.   B

The Position property keeps track of the current record in a DataSet.

Chapter 15

1.   T
2.   T
3.   F

A report can be generated with a wizard or it can be created manually.

4.   T
5.   F

Records grouped by a field can be equal or they can be grouped because they are in a range of values.

6.   F

The records in a report can be in any order.

7.   T
8.   F

The fields in a report can be in any order.

9.   T
10.   T
11.   A

Crystal Reports can access files regardless of where they're stored.

12.   C

The report wizard is a quick and easy way to generate a report.

13.   D

All of the above can be displayed in a page header, but the column headings are the most common.

14.   A

Use Details to place fields when creating a detail line in a report.

15.   D

Almost any text can be displayed in a Text Object.

16.   D

The Field Explorer lists almost everything related to a report.

17.   B

Standard notation in Crystal Reports is Table.Field, where Table is the table name, followed by a period, and Field is the field name.

18.   B

The Solution Explorer contains a list of the reports generated in a project.

19.   A

A detail line is generated from a specific record in a database.

20.   A

The Report Header shows up at the top of the first page and usually contains the report title.

Control and Variable Naming Conventions

This appendix contains Tables I.1 through I.3, which list control and variable naming conventions.

Table I.1   Data Type Prefixes and Ranges

Data Type	Prefix	Range	Bytes
Byte	byt	0 to 255	1
Short	sho	−32,768 to 32,767	2
Integer	int	−2,147,483,648 to 2,147,483,647	4
Long	lng	−9,223,372,036,854,775,808 to 9,223,372,036,854,775,807	8
String	str	0 to ~2 billion	1 per character
Decimal	dec	1.0e−28 to 7.9E+28	16
Single	sng	1.5E−45 to 3.4E+38	4
Double	dbl	5.0E−324 to 1.7E+308	8
Date	dat	January 1, 0001 to December 31, 9999 0:00:00 to 23:59:59	8
Boolean	bln	True or False	2
Char	chr	one Unicode character	2
Object	obj	data of any type	—

Table I.2   Variable Prefixes

Variable	Prefix
Local	None
Module	m
Global	g
Structure	s

Table I.3   Control Prefixes

Control	Prefix
Binding Navigator	bdn
Binding Source	bds
Button	btn
CheckBox	chk
CheckedListBox	clb
ColorDialog	dlg
ComboBox	cbo
CrystalReportViewer	crv
CrystalReportDocument	crd
DataGridView	dgv
DateTimePicker	dtp
FontDialog	dlg
Form	frm
GroupBox	grp
HScrollBar	hsb
Label	lbl
LinkLabel	llb
ListBox	lst
MaskedTextBox	mtb
MenuStrip	mnu
MonthCalendar	cal
NumericUpDown	nud
OpenFileDialog	ofd
Panel	pnl
PictureBox	pic
ProgressBar	prb
RadioButton	rad
RichTextBox	rtb
SaveFileDialog	sfd
TabControl	tab
TableAdapter	tbl
TextBox	txt
Timer	tmr
ToolTip	ttp
TrackBar	trb
VScrollBar	vsb
WebBrowser	web

Index